KU-723-891

THE DEATH OF A PRESIDENT

Also by William Manchester

PORTRAIT OF A PRESIDENT
THE LONG GAINER
A ROCKEFELLER FAMILY PORTRAIT
BEARD THE LION
SHADOW OF THE MONSOON
THE CITY OF ANGER
DISTURBER OF THE PEACE

THE DEATH OF A PRESIDENT

NOVEMBER 20 – NOVEMBER 25
1963

BY

WILLIAM MANCHESTER

WORLD BOOKS : LONDON

First published in Great Britain
by Michael Joseph Ltd. 1967
This edition published by World Books 1968
by arrangement with Michael Joseph Ltd.

Printed in Great Britain by Richard Clay (The Chaucer Press), Ltd., Bungay, Suffolk

For all
in whose hearts
he still lives—
a watchman of honour
who never sleeps

CONTENTS

FOREWORD

On February 5, 1964, Mrs John F. Kennedy suggested that I write an account of the tragic and historic events in Texas and Washington ten weeks earlier. That is the first breath. The second, which must quickly follow, is that neither Mrs Kennedy nor anyone else is in any way answerable for my subsequent research or this narrative based upon it. My relationships with all the principal figures were entirely professional. I received no financial assistance from the Kennedy family. I was on no government payroll. No one tried to lead me, and I believe every reader, including those who were closest to the late President, will find much here that is new and some, perhaps, that is disturbing. That is my responsibility. Mrs Kennedy asked me but one question. Before our first taping session she said, 'Are you just going to put down all the facts, who ate what for breakfast and all that, or are you going to put yourself in the book, too?' I replied that I didn't see how I could very well keep myself out of it. '*Good*,' she said emphatically. And so I am here, weighing evidence and forming judgments. At times you may find my presence exasperating. You may decide in the end that I have been a poor judge. But you may not conclude that I have served as anyone's amanuensis. If you doubt me you may as well stop at the end of this paragraph.

Actually, I discovered, the Kennedy family had not been eager to have any book written about the President's death. Understandably they needed time to heal. But shortly after the burial in Arlington various writers solicited their co-operation in such a project. It soon became apparent that volumes would appear in spite of their wishes. Under these circumstances Jacqueline Kennedy resolved that there should be one complete, accurate account. I had not been among those who had approached her. (I had been living in the Ruhr, and was writing German history.) At that time I had not even met her. However, her husband had told her about me, and she had read a magazine profile I published about him the year before his death. Robert Kennedy also remembered my acquaintance with his brother. After consultation other members of the family agreed with Mrs Kennedy that, in light of the fact that apocryphal versions of those days were already in press, it would be wise to have a book written by an author whom the President had known. It was further decided that the work should be based upon material gathered while memories were still fresh. Hence the invitation to me.

My first two calls were upon Bill Moyers at the White House and Chief Justice Earl Warren. It was essential that the new President, whose confidence Moyers deservedly enjoyed, know what I proposed to do. It was equally imperative that the Presidential Commission which the Chief Justice headed understand the exact nature of my inquiry. The Chief Justice was unfailingly polite to me, and he recognized that while the lines of the two investigations might occasionally intersect, they certainly did not run parallel to one another. The Commission was conducting a criminal probe. I was exploring the full sweep of events during what were, in some respects, the most extraordinary hours in the history of our country. They were focusing upon the assassin of a President, I upon the Presidency itself.

During the next six months we exchanged some confidences, and inevitably we ran across each other's tracks. Sometimes I had been there first; I saw John McCone a month before the Commission did, and I interviewed Mrs Johnson three weeks before she sent her statement to Earl Warren. On the other hand, I did not begin my Texas trips until the last member of the Commission had left Dallas, and its report to President Johnson was on the bookstore counters long before I scheduled the first of my formal interviews with Secret Service agents. By then I was alone in the field. I was to remain there until early 1966, when the trail began to grow cold. It therefore seems fair to assume that should any new studies of this subject appear in the near future, they must be largely based upon the Commission's work, mine, or both. Had any other major investigator been around, I certainly would have heard the echo of his footsteps.

Because I have been at this task longer than anyone else I have not only felt entitled to record my opinions; I believe that I have an inescapable obligation to do so. Withholding them would be shirking a grave duty, and among other judgments you will find a partial assessment of the Warren Report. An audit of my chief sources of information appears at the end of this volume. Unlike the Commission, however, I shall not publish my files. For one thing, it would be a formidable undertaking. (Mrs Kennedy's answers to the Commission's questions occupy two and a half pages; my tapes with her run ten hours.) But that is not the chief reason. Throughout this work I was obliged to weigh questions of taste. Indeed, the final manuscript was so sensitive that the author's judgment seemed an inadequate safeguard against possible lapses in taste. Therefore the advice of five men with special qualifications was solicited—two close friends of the Kennedy family, two Special Assistants to the President who served under both John Kennedy and Lyndon Johnson, and the editor of *Profiles in Courage*, who also edited this book. The suggestions of each were carefully weighed. This is not to suggest that I am suppressing anything. I am merely retaining, for the time being, material of a personal nature which serves no legitimate purpose. Should there be any who think this means that I intend to dodge prickly issues, they have obvious recourse. To paraphrase President Kennedy's Berlin challenge, *Lass' sie nach dem Buche kommen.*

The moment I began to write I went to the mat with the issue of annotation. I arose with a painful verdict: no page-by-page footnotes, other than those necessary to the immediate sense of a passage. It hurt because I knew that every statement, every fact, every quotation in my manuscript could be followed by a citation. Throughout the text you will, of course, find the names of individuals to whom data are clearly attributed. Chapter notes, however, would require a tag for everything. The protection of sources prohibits such procedure here. Arthur M. Schlesinger, Jr., who faced the same problem, reached the same conclusion. He will place a fully annotated manuscript under seal in the Kennedy Library. Similarly, I am considering the deposit there of eighteen volumes of transcribed interviews, which I have indexed as appendices to this book, and twenty-seven portfolios of documents, with the understanding that all these would be made available to qualified scholars after the death of all direct descendants of John F. Kennedy who were living at the time of his assassination.

A word about method. In the course of the inquiry I approached every person who might shed light upon this complex of events. I retraced President Kennedy's last journey from Andrews Field to San Antonio, Kelly Field, Houston, Carswell, Fort Worth, Love Field, Dealey Plaza, Parkland Hospital, back to Love and back to Andrews, over the ambulance route to Bethesda Naval Hospital and then to the White House, the great rotunda, St Matthew's, and Arlington. I went over every motorcade route, searching for men and women who had been spectators, and in Dallas I walked from Love Field to the overpass, looking for potential sniper's nests as well. Every scene described in the book was visited: the rooms in the executive mansion, Hickory Hill, Brooks Medical Centre, the Presidential hotel suites in Houston and Fort Worth, the Houston Coliseum, the Fort Worth parking lot and ballroom, the Paine garage and bedrooms, Marguerite Oswald's house, Oswald's tiny room in Dallas, Parkland's Major Surgery and Minor Medicine areas, Bethesda's seventeenth-floor suite and basement morgue, the pavements of Washington, the pews of St Matthew's.

Colonel Swindal and his crew patiently led me back and forth through the compartments of the Presidential aircraft. I crawled over the roof of the Texas School Book Depository and sat in Oswald's sixth-floor perch. I rode his Dallas bus, watch in hand. Before taxi driver Bill Whaley died in Dallas he picked me up at the spot where he had picked up Oswald, drove me over the same route in the same taxi at the same speed, and dropped me off at the same kerb. I stood where Officer J. D. Tippit died. I darted over the last lap of Oswald's flight to the Texas Theatre. In Dallas police headquarters I sat where the assassin had sat, rode down in the same elevator accompanied by Dallas patrolmen, and took notes on the underground garage while standing where Oswald was shot. With a Secret Service agent and Dallas eyewitnesses to the assassination as my guides, I went over the stretch of Elm Street where the President laid down his life. In Washington, Hyannis Port, and elsewhere I studied each pertinent office, embassy, and home—over a hundred of them—right down to the attic mentioned on the last page of the epilogue of this volume. I even had the damaged Dallas-to-Bethesda coffin uncrated for inspection, and I have visited the hillside below Custis-Lee Mansion in every season.

Research, of course, is no substitute for wisdom. The sum of a million facts is not the truth. Nevertheless all these trips were necessary. I had to immerse myself in this subject until I knew more about it than anyone else. Only then could I move on to the critical stage: the comparison of witnesses' statements. Fortunately for history, virtually every incident was observed by several pairs of eyes and ears. This was even true of telephone conversations between two men; there were usually technicians on the wire or eavesdroppers on either end. By evaluating all recollections and matching them against my own knowledge and circumstantial material I could reconstruct the past with some confidence. Where this proved impossible—where I was faced with two irreconcilable versions from equally reliable sources—I have set down both, indicating possible reasons for the conflict.

We have not recovered from the catastrophe of late November 1963. I cannot pretend to be aloof, though I have certainly tried to be objective. Nor do I offer this study as a definitive work. In time I myself shall merely become a source for future historians as yet unborn. Yet it was imperative that this chronicle be laid before the generation of Americans who suffered through those days. I believe President Kennedy would have wanted them to know precisely what happened. That is why I wrote this. Nearly everyone agreed with me, and I should like to pay tribute to the host of people who relived the most dreadful hours of their lives with me. Of all I approached only one, the assassin's widow, failed to respond to my request for co-operation. None of the interviews was easy. No one had expected that they would be. I could not dilute my questions and still be faithful to my task, and over half the subjects experienced moments of emotional difficulty. Sometimes it was necessary to knock on the same door again and again. Often I found that after the state funeral of November 25, 1963, a principal figure had thrust his memories of that weekend into a remote corner of his mind. Unless summoned by the Commission, he had not discussed them with anyone until I called. Bringing them out was agonizing, almost unendurable. Lyndon Johnson is a supreme example of this. Twice, in May of 1964 and April of 1965, the President agreed to receive me and go through everything. In the end he found he could not bear to do it. I explained that he was a vital witness, he agreed, and we ultimately solved the dilemma by written questions and written answers. Some of the replies were detailed; to other inquiries he had no comment. It should be added that he has not seen the book in any form.

While no author can share responsibility for his work, I am greatly indebted to an extraordinary number of individuals for their co-operation, time, and advice. Indeed, there are so many of them that there simply is not room to list them here, and rather than omit some I shall name none, trusting they will understand. However, I must make one exception to this rule—an expression of deepest gratitude to my wife, who alone knows the cost.

W.M.

Wesleyan University
Middletown, Connecticut

but the generation of Americans who survived him and the widow. Because President Kennedy would have wanted them to know precisely what happened. Thanks to his widow, nearly everyone [illegible] with him and I should like to [illegible] to the [illegible] people who [illegible] the most [illegible] hours of their lives with me. Of all I approached only one, the assassin's widow, refused to [illegible] my request for cooperation. None of the interviews was easy. No one had expected that they would be. I could not disguise my questions and be faithful to my task, and even the subjects' apparent moments of calm, [illegible] seemed [illegible] to knock on the same door again and again. Often I found that after the state funeral of November 25, 1963, [illegible] that [illegible] and thrust the memory of that weekend into a remote corner of his mind. Others, [illegible] by the [illegible] had not discussed them with anyone [illegible] I [illegible] thinking about [illegible] was [illegible] almost unendurable. Lyndon Johnson is a [illegible] example of this. [illegible] in May of 1964 and April of 1965 [illegible] to receive me and [illegible] In the end he found he could not bear to do it. I explained that it was a [illegible] and we ultimately solved the dilemma by written questions and written answers. Some of the replies were [illegible] to other chapters. He had no comment. It should be added that he has not seen the book in any form.

With one exception [illegible] responsibility for his work. I am greatly indebted to an extraordinary number of [illegible] for their [illegible] time, and [illegible] Index, there are so many of them that their [illegible] is not meant to [illegible] them, and [illegible] them [illegible] I shall [illegible] will understand. However, I must make one exception in this [illegible] expression of [illegible] to my wife, who alone knows the cost.

W. M.

[illegible]

GLOSSARY

The First Family

Lancer	The President
Lace	The First Lady
Lyric	Caroline Kennedy
Lark	John F. Kennedy, Jr.

Vice Presidential Group

Volunteer	The Vice President
Victoria	Mrs Johnson
Velvet	Lynda Bird Johnson
Venus	Lucy Baines Johnson
Vigilant	Walter Jenkins

Places

Castle	The White House—Executive Mansion plus the two office wings (WHCA)
Crown	The Executive Mansion (WHCA)
Angel	Aircraft 26000 (Air Force One)
Charcoal	Temporary Residence of President (sometimes 'Base')
SS 100 X	Presidential automobile
Halfback	Presidential follow-up car (SS)
Varsity	Vice Presidential follow-up car (SS)
Cabin	Hyannis Port, Massachusetts
Hamlet	Auchincloss home on O Street
Château	Glen Ora, Presidential retreat
Crossroads	Middleburg, Virginia
Acrobat	Andrews Field
Calico	Pentagon
Carpet	White House garage
Cork	FBI headquarters, Washington
Central	Executive Office Building (EOB)
Volcano	LBJ Ranch, Texas

Official Family

Wand	Kenneth O'Donnell
Willow	Evelyn Lincoln
Wayside	Pierre Salinger
Market	Dr George Burkley

Watchman	General Chester Clifton
Warrior	Malcolm Kilduff
Wing	General Godfrey McHugh
Witness	Captain Tazewell Shepard
Tiger	Colonel James Swindal
Freedom	Secretary Dean Rusk
Secret Service Agents	
Domino	James Rowley
Duplex	Gerald Behn
Deacon	Floyd Boring
Dazzle	Clint Hill
Dandy	Lem Johns
Digest	Roy Kellerman
Daylight	Jerry Kivet
Debut	Paul Landis
Dusty	Emory Roberts
Dagger	Rufus Youngblood
Dasher	Tom Wells
Dresser	Bob Foster
Drummer	Lynn Meredith
White House Communications Agency	
Star	Colonel George McNally
Satchel	The Bagman
Sturdy	Art Bales
Shadow	Ira Gearhart

O powerful, western, fallen star!
O shades of night! O moody, tearful night!
O great star disappear'd! O the black murk that hides the star!
O cruel hands that hold me powerless!
  O helpless soul of me!
O harsh surrounding cloud, that will not free my soul!

WALT WHITMAN
When Lilacs Last in the Door-Yard Bloom'd

'Ω ξεῖν', ἄγγειλον Λακεδαιμονίοισ, οτι τῆδε
κείμεθα τοῖς κείνων ρήμαοι πειθόμενοι

Go, stranger, and in Lakëdaimôn tell
That here, obedient to their laws, we fell.

Simonides at Thermopylae

Prologue
LANCER

Despite obvious differences in temperament and style John Kennedy and Lyndon Johnson shared one grand passion—politics—and in the tranquil autumn of 1963 a political issue was about to take the President and his Vice President a thousand miles from Washington, into deepest Texas. They had to go, because the state's Democratic party was riven by factionalism. Governor John Connally and Senator Ralph Yarborough were stalking one another with shivs. In 1960 the Kennedy–Johnson team had carried Texas by just 46,233 votes, an eyelash. If the Governor and the Senator didn't agree to a truce soon, the national ticket wouldn't stand a chance there next fall. No party writes off twenty-five electoral votes, so both Kennedy and Johnson were going down to patch things up. They had to make a major production of the trip, with Connally and Yarborough, apparently reconciled, appearing by their sides in the state's five major cities. As a climax there would be a call at the LBJ Ranch, where the Vice President would invite the President to feast upon the culinary specialties of his house.

Long afterwards Johnson would guardedly recall that there had been 'some discussion of the Texas political situation' between the Chief Executive and himself. There was more to it than that. Although Kennedy enjoyed campaigning, this came at an awkward time, and at first the necessity for political intervention had eluded him. The Lone Star State was, after all, the Vice President's fief. In 1960 he had stumped it brilliantly. As a professional Kennedy coolly assessed the present crisis and concluded that he must go after all. But he reached the decision grudgingly. It appeared to him that Johnson ought to be able to resolve this petty dispute himself; the trip seemed to be an imposition.

How do you explain to a President, who has all the power, that his Vice President has become virtually impotent in his home state? You don't explain it. He wouldn't understand; he would suspect you of evasion. Johnson had been running a broken field since birth, but his current problems were authentic. They arose in part from his stance as a public figure. Like Kennedy in New England he had burst upon the national scene as a maverick, a vote-getter who made no secret of his lack of sympathy for the advocates of doctrinaire solutions to complex issues. That moderation was the secret of his strength at the polls. Yet he paid a price for it in the councils of his party. Because he clung to the middle of the road he had failed to inspire any deep loyalty from either the Democrats' liberal or conservative wings—and was therefore regarded by both as an outsider.

In larger part, however, his dilemma that week before what would be the third Thanksgiving of the Kennedy administration was an ironic consequence of the party's national victory over Richard Nixon and Henry Cabot Lodge. Kennedy, who had been the junior Senator from Massachusetts, had stepped up to the Presidency. Johnson, formerly the mighty Majority Leader of the Senate, had become Vice President—which was also a step, but not up. The office he had inherited was but poorly understood. In the 174 years since the first inaugural the American people had displayed a monumental lack of interest in the Chief Executive's backup; perhaps one in a million, for example, knew that between 1845 and 1849 the Vice President of the United States had been named Dallas. Everyone agreed that the second greatest gift the electorate could bestow was an empty honour, yet only those who had held it knew how hollow it really was. 'A pitcher of warm spit,' John Nance Garner had called it, and an earlier wit had written, 'Being Vice President isn't exactly a crime, but it's kind of a disgrace, like writing anonymous letters.'

Anonymity was uncomfortably close to the truth. Johnson had found that he was a stand-by without a script. Politically he was nearly a cipher because he lacked a power base. Some Congressmen had more influence. Men with sole claim to constituencies have a few plums to distribute, but the only fruits a Vice President can grant are those the President grants *him*. The right to reward loyalty with jobs is an office-holder's lifeblood. Johnson, formerly red-blooded, was now anaemic. To pry loose a federal judgeship for one of his most faithful Texas supporters, Sarah T. Hughes, he had been obliged to wage a major battle against objections inside and outside the government—Sarah, having passed the age for judicial appointments, had been listed as unqualified by the American Bar Association. The Vice President had filed a claim for half of Ralph Yarborough's Senatorial patronage, advancing the argument that his former constituents in Texas continued to regard Lyndon Johnson as their senior Senator. Kennedy had been understanding. Johnson had been told that he could pick up half the state's patronage, naming

Texas' judges, customs officers, and border guards—subject to Yarborough's veto. But Connally, his former protégé, was unimpressed. And Yarborough, of course, was furious.

Thus the Vice President's problems were not of his making. They were institutional; as any of his thirty-six predecessors in the office could have told him, they came with the territory. Unrealistically, Kennedy looked to him to take a strong hand on the Hill. This meant more than liaison. Larry O'Brien, the President's Special Assistant in charge of legislative liaison, provided enough of it for the entire Afro-Asian bloc. What the Chief Executive really wanted was a Vice President who could act as though he were still a majority leader, and that was impossible; it couldn't work. In the early Kennedy days Washington's press corps had briefly assumed that the performance might be a success. It was a failure, though not of will, as the President came to conclude.

Correspondents also swallowed the fable of an upgraded Vice Presidency, a carry-over from the previous administration, in which it had been equally bogus. The distance between the President's lovely oval office in the West Wing of the White House and the Vice President's across the street in Room 274 of the Executive Office Building could be covered in a few minutes' brisk walk. Yet in a sense it was an unbridgeable chasm. Newspapermen were aware of every move the First Family made. The second family was largely disregarded. In the Dallas suburb of Irving a young Russian immigrant named Marina Oswald had never even heard the name of Lyndon Johnson, and in Washington his celebrity value was so small that his home telephone—he was entitled to only one White House extension—was listed in the public directory. Mrs Johnson had never seen the inside of the famous Presidential plane, the Boeing 707 with the tail number 26000, the Secret Service code name 'Angel', and the popular designation of 'Air Force One'. On Johnson's own official flights newspapermen christened his plane 'Air Force Two', and the Secret Service encoded it as 'Angel Two'. But there really was no such aircraft. Indeed, the Vice President lacked jurisdiction over any government plane. Aircraft 26000 was merely the flagship of a fleet, all of which belonged to the Chief Executive. Three additional 707's bearing the tail numbers 86970, 86971, and 86972 were at his disposal for flights he deemed important. Should Johnson need one of them for official purposes, it would be assigned to him by the President's Air Force Aide, Brigadier General Godfrey McHugh, and sometimes the request was denied.

Lyndon Johnson was, in short, a prisoner of his office, and John Kennedy, never having occupied that barren cell, had no concept of its barrenness. Yet, while unfamiliar with the details, he knew that the Vice Presidency was, as he privately described it, 'a miserable job', and he went out of his way to honour Johnson and invent missions for him. He even revised White House protocol in his behalf. Convention, for example, required that when the two men attended ceremonial occasions together the President should slowly descend the executive mansion's Grand Staircase alone while his Vice President sneaked down in an elevator. Kennedy ordered that Johnson accompany him, be photographed with him, greet guests with him. The Vice President, in other words, was to act as though he lived in the house. But the blunt truth was that he didn't live there. Nothing could alter the fact that his real address was 4040 Fifty-second Street, NW. The chasm remained intractable.

Johnson certainly wasn't bitter. As he put it in a Texas idiom, he was resigned to 'hunkering down', playing second fiddle. He admired the President. Determined to give satisfaction, he never made a move or scheduled a speech without first checking with a Kennedy aide, and at meetings of the National Security Council he refrained from expressing himself on questions of policy unless the Chief Executive specifically requested him to do so. His real difficulty was that there was so little for him to do. Apart from presiding over the Senate his official tasks were busy work, and three years of relative inactivity seemed to have sapped his vitality. Prior to the Texas trip his chief duty was to prepare for it. Clearly he did not enjoy the desperate need for this fence-mending tour on his own home ground. He had nothing to gain from it and, should it fail, much to lose. If the President was a reluctant Texas tourist, his Vice President wasn't far behind him.

Early in the month Johnson spoke in Welsh, West Virginia, and dedicated a California aircraft factory. Then he flew down to the ranch and spent most of his time selling tickets to political dinners over the telephone. On Tuesday, November 19, he took a Braniff flight to Dallas and spoke to the American Bottlers of Carbonated Beverages, praising the efficacy of soft drinks and denouncing 'people who bellyache about everything America does'. It is a measure of Vice Presidential status that the motorcade route which Kennedy and Johnson were to follow in that same city on Friday had received final approval the previous afternoon at a meeting in a private Dallas club. The participants—Secret Service agents and local businessmen—saw no need to consult the Vice President, and copies of the Dallas *Times-Herald* describing the route appeared on the streets while he was addressing the bottlers.

Two hours after he had landed at Love Field he was winging home on another Braniff flight. There, at least, was a challenge. The President would be spending Friday night and Saturday morning at the ranch. Johnson was still a thoughtful host, and lately his friends had become anxious over persistent reports that he might be dumped from the ticket next year. Lady Bird, who had come down a week early to supervise preparations, marshalled the staff. Bess Abell, her personal secretary, was dispatched to Austin, over sixty miles away, for fresh lettuce. Liz Carpenter, executive assistant to the Vice President, joined the servants in scrubbing windows. A list of Presidential tastes was drawn up. Poland water and Ballantine's Scotch were acquired for the Chief Executive, champagne and Salem cigarettes—Jacqueline Kennedy switched back and forth between Newports and Salems—for the First Lady. There was considerable fuss about where the White House phones should go. They had to be available, but inconspicuous; this part of the trip was supposed to be a *rest.* Terry-cloth hand towels were laid out in Mrs Kennedy's room (she disliked smooth linen ones); note was made of the fact that the President wished a thermos in his room with tepid water (not iced). Lady Bird personally prepared a double bed for the President's plywood board and horsehair mattress. Outside, a Tennessee walking horse was groomed, should the President or the First Lady decide to ride. After several conferences entertainers were hired for a forty-five-minute whip-cracking and sheep-herding show, to give the Kennedys some idea of what the West was really like.

Johnson made the final inspection. The performers rehearsed to his satisfaction. The phones were properly placed by Signal Corps technicians from the White House Communications Agency. Furniture was rearranged (the President's special bed made this necessary), cooks were engaged to bake a hundred pies, and there were flowers and fruit in every room. The Vice President had done everything a Vice President can do—unless, of course, the President dies. All that remained was to greet the Presidential party at San Antonio International Airport. Aircraft 26000 would reach the terminal there at 1.30 p.m., November 21, 1963. Since Johnson would be accompanying the President on the tour, government transportation had been authorized for him; the Presidential party's backup plane, Aircraft 86970, would arrive at the same time and then serve as 'Air Force Two' during the trip. Weather predictions were good; therefore the Johnsons arranged to fly the seventy miles to San Antonio in their private Queenaire Beechcraft. Johnson wanted to be sure they were early. He felt that it would be inexcusable for him to be elsewhere when the President of the United States came down the ramp, and he instructed his pilot to have them at the terminal well before 12.30. There would be time on his hands, but he had grown accustomed to that. The future promised a quick return to light duty: a synagogue dedication in Austin, Sunday, a B'nai B'rith speech in

New York, Monday. The notes for both were ready, so he made other plans. At the San Antonio terminal Thursday he would have lunch with Lady Bird and spend the rest of the hour getting a leisurely haircut.

'Oh, God,' read a tiny plaque on the President's desk, 'thy sea is so great and my boat is so small.' And now he would be obliged to spend three precious days on a tricky detour among the rocks and shoals of Texas politics. For Kennedy the excursion brought but one consolation: his wife was going to accompany him. Her decision had come as a surprise, for she had never been much of a company wife. 'I really do not think of myself as First Lady,' she had said, 'but of Jack as President.' Winning votes was his job, the home and children hers. His closest advisers had usually agreed, although their motives had been quite different. As Irish Yankees they tended to see the entire country as a macrocosm of the wards they had heeled. Jacqueline Kennedy spoke with a finishing-school accent and wore an aura of what they called the *haut monde*. That sort of background produced hardly any mileage in South Boston. It was John Connally who had pointed out that Kennedy's ascension to the Presidency had changed everything. Elegance might be a liability for the wife of a minor politician, but it was an enormous asset to a First Lady. Voters, and especially women voters, admired beauty and style in the executive mansion. One of a President's duties is to *preside*. It was exciting to know that a queenly figure stood by his side, and it would be even more exciting—and headier political medicine—if Texas could see her there.

As late as October 4, 1963, when Connally had made his request, the possibility seemed remote. Undeniably Mrs Kennedy had enjoyed her role in the White House. It had, in fact, come as an agreeable surprise to her. She had heard so much about the responsibilities of the Presidency that she had expected it would keep her husband from her. As it had turned out, she and the children had seen more of him than ever before. Previously he had been absent from them for weeks on end, arriving home groggy with fatigue. In the mansion he led a relatively normal family life, and later she would remember strolling rapturously through the south grounds that first spring, thinking, *let me stay as happy as this forever with Jack*. But the summer of 1963 had dealt them a staggering blow. In August they had lost an infant son forty hours after birth, and only those who were close to the First Family knew how profoundly that loss had affected them.

Patrick Bouvier Kennedy had died in the oxygen chamber of a Boston hospital. When the doctors announced that it was all over,

Pierre Salinger had seen the stricken father weeping in an adjacent boiler-room. Kennedy wept again when he told his wife and once more after the Mass of the Angels in Richard Cardinal Cushing's residence on Commonwealth Avenue. Only the President and the prelate remained in the chapel; the others had left for the Brookline graveside. In his grief the father had put his arm around the little coffin. He could do it—it was that small—but he couldn't carry it, and the old Cardinal had rasped, 'Jack, you better go along. Death isn't the end of all, but the beginning.' At the Brookline grave Kennedy had lingered again until nearly everyone had gone; Dave Powers had watched him lean over and touch the ground and say softly, to himself, 'It's awful lonely here.' Then he returned to his wife, to comfort her after what had been the penultimate misfortune which can come to a woman. All fall her convalescence had been the chief concern of his private life. And afterwards, after the total eclipse in Dallas, she would remember how she had told him, 'There's just one thing I couldn't stand—if I ever lost you . . .' Her voice had drifted off, leaving the unthinkable unspoken, and he had murmured reassuringly, 'I know, I know.'

She had wanted to stay with him and the children. Normality, routine—it seemed the best way to cure her depression. He had a different plan: she should forget herself in other lands. Politically, she suggested, this was unwise. With the election a year away, a cruise on a Greek millionaire's yacht was no prescription for votes, but his mind was made up. So she went, and the separation became a strange hiatus between tragedy and tragedy. It was a greater separation than either had expected. Despite modern communications, despite the highest priority in the world, they were almost as far apart as a Victorian couple. The telephone, she had thought, would bridge the distance. But the difference in time zones proved insuperable. She would wait three hours and then learn from the little local switchboard that they had 'lost the connection'. Eventually she decided that calls might be indiscreet anyhow, since every word would be overheard, so she wrote him ten-page letters, punctuated with dashes like everything she wrote. She told him how much she missed him, of her sorrow that he could not, at the moment, share with her the tension-free atmosphere of the Mediterranean.

To her astonishment, he had been right about the trip. The thing actually worked. Everywhere she was fêted—her sister Lee, who accompanied her, wrote Kennedy in a feigned sulk, complaining that Jackie had been laden with presents, while Lee herself got only '3 dinky little bracelets that Caroline wouldn't wear to her own birthday party'. For the First Lady those weeks were a diversion, which was precisely what the President had intended. Greece and Morocco had been so unreal, such a complete cut-off, that she returned on October 17 in far better spirits than she had thought possible. In the past she had been against magazine publicity for the children. Now *Look* prepared a spread of pictures of young John. After two golden weekends at Atoka, their country home in Middleburg, Virginia, she resolved to look to the year ahead. At the time of Patrick's death it had been announced that she would rest until January 1. Now Dr John Walsh, her obstetrician, felt her recovery was already complete, so she decided to reappear sooner. Moreover, her activity wouldn't be restricted to affairs which interested her; although she found football boring, for example, she was thinking of attending the Army-Navy game with the President after Thanksgiving. 'We'll just campaign,' she told him. 'I'll campaign with you anywhere you want.' And when he asked her whether that included the expedition with Lyndon, she flipped open her red leather appointment book and scrawled 'Texas' across November 21, November 22, and November 23.

The next day he informed Ken O'Donnell and Larry O'Brien, has two chief political advisers. Congressman Albert Thomas of Houston, who was present, recalled later that the three of them 'fell over backward'. She had never been to Texas or the Southwest; hadn't, indeed, been west of Middleburg since the election. When Salinger told the press on November 7, it was news everywhere. Lady Bird wrote her from the ranch, 'The President's on page five, Lyndon's on the back page, but you're on the *front* page,' and Charlie Bartlett, a newspaperman and family friend, phoned Kennedy that a St Louis news dealer had informed him, 'That girl's got *brains*.' The President commented dryly, 'As opposed to the rest of us, I suppose.' But to her he said, 'It really shows, doesn't it? When you aren't around all the time, you're so much more valuable when you *do* come.' Clearly he was delighted.

It was equally clear—and struck her as odd—that he was nervous. He was afraid that later she would regret having gone. He wanted her to enjoy this trip so she would make others. And because of that fierce competitive spirit which was rooted in his childhood he was determined that his wife should look her best in Texas. Kennedy determination could be an awesome force, and in this case it carried him into an exotic land usually closed to husbands. For the first time in their marriage he asked his wife what she intended to wear. Dallas especially interested him. 'There are going to be all these rich Republican women at that lunch, wearing mink coats and diamond bracelets,' he said, 'and you've got to look as marvellous as any of them. Be simple—show these Texans what good taste really is.' So she tramped in and out of his room, holding dresses in front of her.

The outfits finally chosen—weather permitting—were all veterans of her wardrobe: beige and white dresses, blue and yellow suits, and, for Dallas, a pink suit with a navy blue collar and a matching pink pillbox hat.

Observing that he was still concerned, she asked him, 'If it's so important that I look all right in Dallas, why do I have to be blown around in a motorcade first?' He knew why. Exposure, like patronage, was a source of political strength. You had to move through crowds. And you had to move slowly. He remembered a sardonic El Paso letter after his trip there last June: 'We enjoyed you going by in your jet.' Nevertheless he had always been a bear for detail, and he tried to do something about this one; twice on the day before their departure for Texas he telephoned Pamela Turnure, his wife's press secretary, to discuss the First Lady's hair. Pam suggested putting up the bubbletop on the Presidential car. No, he replied; that was out of the question. Barring rain, they had to be where the people would see them. Pam recommended a shorter route. Another veto; the motorcade had to last forty-five minutes. They discussed women's hats until the President, out of his element and painfully aware of it, reduced it to a joke. 'Take a forty-five-minute drive around Washington in an open car with Dave Powers,' he ordered. 'See what you look like when you come back.'

That was on Wednesday, November 20, 1963, the second of his last two full days in Washington, and anyone under the impression that the President of the United States was devoting his full energy to wardrobes and coiffures is invited to examine his activity during those final White House hours. Monday had been a day of formal speeches and informal politicking in Florida (another ten electoral votes that couldn't be written off), and Tuesday he had reached the office early. His telephone log for the next forty-eight hours records a barrage of official calls to the Cabinet, the sub-Cabinet, Presidential aides, the Supreme Court, and the Congress. There were seven phone conversations with Robert Kennedy, who later remembered that his brother's manner then—as, indeed, for the past ten days—was rather gloomy.

Certainly he had been saturnine that Tuesday morning. The children were in the country with their mother, cutting school, so he had missed his French lesson after breakfast. This was a closely guarded secret. Charles de Gaulle was becoming increasingly difficult to deal with, and the President had concluded that the most effective way to tackle Gaullian *amour propre* would be to learn his language—*really* learn it—and then negotiate in it. It was pure Kennedy, a decision undertaken with zest and pursued with improvisation. His teacher was Madame Jacqueline Hirsch, Caroline's French teacher. Since September she had been tutoring the President and his daughter mornings in the mansion. 'How long do you think it will take me?' he had asked Madame Hirsch at the outset. 'A year,' she had replied. He couldn't resist the challenge: 'I bet I do it in six months.' Undeniably he was making amazing progress. Unable to suppress the temptation, he tried a few sentences on visitors from a former French colony, and while no one had guessed what he was up to, Madame Nicole Alphand, the bird-eyed wife of the French Ambassador to Washington, had heard vague rumours and had relayed them to her husband.

No lesson today, however, so he stalked dourly over to the office and asked Mrs Evelyn Lincoln, his dark, frail secretary, who looked far more like a schoolmarm than Jacqueline Hirsch, 'Where are those clowns?' Clowns, unless otherwise specified, meant O'Donnell, O'Brien, and Powers. 'They're home, worn out from Florida,' she said. He snorted. Instead of the distraction Powers would have provided, his office was invaded by a delegation from the Poultry and Egg National Board, lugging the President's annual Thanksgiving turkey and shepherded by that master carver, Senator Everett N. Dirksen of Illinois. They were followed by other appointments: the U.S. Ambassador of Ghana, a conference of ninety state educators, Secretary of State Rusk, the U.S. Ambassador to Indonesia, and—another secret project—Pierre Salinger.

At midnight Pierre would fly to Honolulu with Dean Rusk and McGeorge Bundy for a Vietnam council of war; then he, Rusk, and five other Cabinet members would proceed to Japan. You couldn't conceal all Pierre's movements, and the press knew he would be in Tokyo. They had been told, and they believed, that it was a junket, a joy ride. It wasn't. Kennedy hadn't forgotten his predecessor's Japanese fiasco, when leftist riots had forced Eisenhower to cancel a call there. He meant to restore American prestige with a February visit. Pierre's job was to set things up.

The President was seated behind his desk, signing letters. Perched on the end of his nose was a pair of spectacles. During the past three months his farsightedness had grown more marked, an inevitable sign of age, and except in public he relied entirely upon his glasses.

'I'm off tonight,' Salinger said. 'I just wanted to say good-bye.' Kennedy looked up and smiled. Pierre told him that Mac Kilduff would act as his press secretary in Texas. Normally the No. 2 man in the press office was Andy Hatcher, but Hatcher, a Negro, would stay in Washington.

'Who's going to handle Chancellor Erhard's visit here?' Kennedy inquired. The West German Chancellor was to arrive Monday, and Salinger wouldn't return until Wednesday.

'Andy will be here.'

'OK, that'll be fine.' The President paused and removed his glasses. Then he said, 'I wish I weren't going to Texas.'

'Don't worry about it,' Salinger said. 'It's going to be a great trip, and you're going to draw the biggest crowds ever.'

Kennedy smiled again. 'Hurry back.'

Dusk gathered in the Rose Garden, night fell, and the appointments continued: the Hon. Roger Hilsman, the Hon. James Bell, Mr Richard Helms, Mr Hershel Peake. Special Assistant Fred Holborn came over from the East Wing for talks about Germany and the new Presidential Medal of Freedom, and at this point the solemnity, the deep voices, and measured discussions of issues were interrupted by a familiar intrusion. Mrs Kennedy was still at Atoka, but the children were back. Young John burst in weeping with a cut nose, consoled by Caroline. The nose was quickly bandaged, and they stayed in Mrs Lincoln's office, Caroline quietly drawing pictures and John playing with a child's tea set. Mac Bundy, dropping by for his farewell, was given a mock serving of John's 'cherry vanilla pie'. He stood gravely, pretending to munch; then, having pronounced it delicious, he was allowed to depart for Hawaii.

Walter Heller, Chairman of the President's Council of Economic Advisers and the last visitor of the day, was doggedly scooping up invisible portions with a toy spoon when Kennedy beckoned him in. 'I'll be back in a minute,' the economist promised the boy, 'but I have to talk to your daddy first.' 'Daddy' sounded awkward to Heller, but 'the President', he knew, would seem even stranger to the boy. In the office he reported on unemployment and Kennedy's new anti-poverty programme. 'I'm still very much in favour of doing something on the poverty theme if we can get a good programme,' the President told him, 'but I also think it's important to make clear that we're doing something for the middle-income man in the suburbs. But the two aren't at all inconsistent with each other. So go right ahead with your work on it.' With that, he took the children for a swim in his pool and then retired after dinner, to an evening of paperwork in the yellow-walled oval study on the second floor of the mansion.

It was incredible how much he could cover between their bedtime and his own. There were the drafts of the Texas speeches. There was a personal matter—he planned to surprise the First Lady Christmas morning with a fur rug. There were new items of political significance, for 1964 pressures were building up month by month. He had a strong hunch that the GOP would follow its death wish and nominate Barry Goldwater, but he couldn't count on such fantastic luck, so he was planning a maximum effort. Since Labour Day, for example, Johnson's trusted aide, Cliff Carter, had been setting up Texas headquarters in Austin. The President's brother-in-law, Steve Smith, was now spending four days a week in Washington on National Committee business. Pat Lucey was already at work in Wisconsin, and Helen Keyes in Cleveland. If Goldwater became the sacrificial lamb, so much the better; he would vanish in an historic landslide, carrying a handful of states. The size of the Democratic majority was a matter of conjecture, but the President was confident of a smashing re-election. Before he left office, he felt, he would be the senior statesman of the West, perhaps of the world, and he was already planning the second Kennedy administration. The Cabinet would have to change. His brother wanted to bow out as Attorney General; he had already begun to speak of his Justice Department years in the past tense. The second most powerful man in the government couldn't retire in his thirties. But where would he be most useful? Then there was Dillon, who wanted to leave the Treasury and return to his banking firm. And there was also the matter of Rusk. Aware that the President intended to be his own foreign minister, Rusk had leaned on him increasingly in other ways. After the second inaugural, the Cabinet would almost certainly be headed by Secretary of State Robert S. McNamara. Who would then lead the military establishment? Secretary of Defence Robert F. Kennedy? Probably not; the younger Kennedy, eager to do something about the deteriorating situation in Latin America, had tentatively decided that once Rusk had left he would ask to be Assistant Secretary for Inter-American Affairs. But the Cabinet reshuffle could wait. Meantime there was the everlasting, exasperating problem of Congress.

Ordinarily the legislative leadership breakfasted with the Chief Executive Tuesday. Because of his Florida trip the breakfast had been postponed and was, at 8.45 a.m., his first meeting on Wednesday. To the guests in the executive mansion—Senators Mansfield, Humphrey, and Smathers and Congressmen Albert and Boggs—the President seemed buoyant that morning. That didn't prevent him from goading them. Here it was November, practically Thanksgiving, nearly the end of the year, and they hadn't even passed the regular appropriation bills. What were they *doing* up there? They exhorted him to be patient. Unhooking his spectacles, he worried the bridge of his nose with his restless right hand—that busy, fisting hand which at times seemed to have a life of its own—and murmured in an aside, 'Things always look so much better away from Washington.' Senator Hubert Humphrey of Minnesota and House Whip

Hale Boggs of Louisiana, who had heard the murmur, strolled over to the West Wing with him afterwards. Some Congressmen, they said, were disturbed over reports that there might be trouble in Dallas. Kennedy shrugged. He and Boggs had held this conversation before, when he had been threatened with a New Orleans demonstration in 1962. His reply now was the same: the notion that an American President could not go into any American city was simply unacceptable. Boggs then mentioned the strife among Texas Democrats. 'Mr President,' he said half-jokingly, 'you're going into quite a hornet's nest.' Kennedy replied absently, 'Well, that always creates interesting crowds.'

In his office, bright now with the promise of a crisp autumn day, he plunged afresh into administrivia. At 9.15 Under Secretary of the Treasury Henry Fowler reported new developments on the tax bill. Fowler, a courtly Virginian and a favourite of the President's, was given a pep talk and a glimpse of Kennedy's latest ship model. At 9.30 three Berlin high school students tiptoed in shyly and were greeted. At 9.42 a delegation of tank officers honoured the President with the Eighth Armoured Division Citation. At 9.31 there had been a telephone report from Douglas Dillon: the Secretary was on the Hill, testifying about the wheat sale to Russia. That was a *real* hornet's nest, and at 9.48 Smathers returned with Larry O'Brien for pointers on the Senate strategy. After them, in order, Angie Duke of the State Department pranced in, squiring the U.S. Ambassador to Sierra Leone; Jerry Wiesner, the President's science adviser, introduced a delegation of American scientists just back from the Geneva Conference on Space Communications; Democratic National Committeeman John Bailey beamed as Lena Horne and five fellow entertainers received Presidential handshakes; Secretary Orville Freeman and Charlie Murphy reviewed agricultural problems before Freeman made his own departure for the Cabinet trip; and then Dick Goodwin entered escorting seven Latin-American intellectuals. Kennedy detained the escort a moment. On Friday Goodwin was to be named his Special Assistant for Cultural Affairs, but first the President wanted his thoughts about U.S. personnel posted in Latin America. By the time Goodwin had given them it was nearly lunch time. There were a few minutes for private business. Jim Reed, Assistant Secretary of the Navy and a close Kennedy friend since their days together in PT boats, had been moonlighting as real estate agent for the President, negotiating a July lease for a summer home on Hyannis Port's Squaw Island. Actually Kennedy wanted to buy the house, but the owner, a Pennsylvania textile manufacturer, was being difficult. He wouldn't sell, and at first he had insisted on $3,000 rent. Too much for a month, Kennedy had protested. Reed had just settled for $2,300, and now the President signed the lease with a flourish and went off for a swim with Dave Powers, jester in residence.

The day ended with a minor crisis. After a nap he had returned for more ambassadorial appointments. Carl Rowan (Finland) followed Douglas Henderson (Bolivia). Then there was a brief lull. Feeling at a loose end, Kennedy wandered into Mrs Lincoln's office and found her chatting with her aunt, Mrs Nettie Carlson of Polk, Nebraska. Mrs Carlson, meeting her first President, flushed. 'Why not take a picture?' Kennedy suggested. Flustered feminine protests: she'd spoil the picture. 'Call Captain Stoughton,' he commanded, and Cecil Stoughton, the chubby, genial White House photographer, appeared to snap the three of them. The crisis ended Mrs Carlson's embarrassment. A State Department limousine disgorged Under Secretary U. Alexis Johnson—with both Rusk and George Ball away he was running Foggy Bottom—and two frowning aides. The Cambodians were being impossible again. Prince Norodom Sihanouk seemed determined to wind up inside the Chinese tiger. He had just asked the United States to terminate economic assistance to his country. Q.: Should our ambassador in Pnompenh reason with him? A.: He should not. Kennedy was blunt. All aid was to end immediately, this very afternoon. Since it was already 5.50 p.m., the three diplomats hurried off. Kennedy peered out and waved at Mrs Carlson, who tittered, and Evelyn Lincoln's phone rang.

'It's Mrs Kennedy,' she told the President. 'The judges are waiting upstairs.'

Jacqueline Kennedy had again moved up the date for her reemergence into public life. Plans for the executive mansion's annual judicial reception had specified that Mrs Earl Warren would act as the President's hostess. Mrs Kennedy had decided to remain in Virginia, saving her strength for Texas. She expected to resume her official duties in the mansion on Monday, November 25, at the state dinner for Chancellor Erhard. A phone conversation with her husband at 7.45 the evening before the reception had changed her mind, however, and after a five-mile gallop on her Arabian gelding that Wednesday morning she had returned. At noon a helicopter had deposited her in Anacostia—Kennedy, sensitive to Congressional criticism, reserved the mansion helipad for official business—and one of the black Mercurys from the White House garage on Twenty-second Street had whisked her through the Southwest Gate at 1.19 p.m. Upstairs a pyramid of unanswered correspondence awaited her, but Nancy Tuckerman, her social secretary, had sent over a thoughtful note: 'Forget the Treaty Room until you come back. I thought you might like to see the list of people invited tonight. . . . Good luck!' Pam Turnure had relayed word of the President's calls to her, and the First Lady had summoned Kenneth of Lilly Daché, the hairdresser. Then she had slipped into a gown of mulberry-coloured velvet. While Kennedy had been instructing the State Department to tell off the Cambodians she had entered the yellow study, ready for the first guests.

The reception, which was destined to be John Kennedy's last public appearance in the capital, was divided into two acts. In Washington the name of the game is protocol, and no one enjoys playing it more than judges. Nobody, on the other hand, was readier to set it aside than the Kennedys. Obviously the President had to receive the Supreme Court. But that was only eleven couples, counting the retired justices. Even after the minor jurists had been included it was still the mansion's smallest formal affair. Everyone wanted to meet the President, and the Attorney General felt that some of the clerks and secretaries who worked unsparingly for the administration should have a chance to see him. This being a Justice Department function, the guest list was therefore expanded. The first act, upstairs, featured the Court and the Attorney General. Downstairs the cast for the second act waited—565 Justice functionaries and White House spear carriers. These included some of the most devoted New Frontiersmen: the volunteers who had come to Washington three Januarys ago to line snowbound Pennsylvania Avenue, fan ablaze the spark he had ignited, and acquire themselves the celebrated *élan* which the nation had come to know as the Kennedy style.

That style had an almost magical quality. There was an air of high drama about the man; as Eisenhower put it privately, Kennedy had become 'the darling of the population'. Something was always happening to him—something always lay just ahead. And beneath the public crescendos his life was vibrant with countless personal anticipations. Everything interested this man. The dullest detail office, financed by the sales of Jacqueline Kennedy's dollar guide-could excite him. There was, for example, the redecoration of his book to the White House. The decorators had been ready for weeks, waiting for him to be absent from his desk for a day and a half. The Texas trip would give them ample time. This afternoon the new draperies had been hung in the Cabinet Room, and on Friday the bright rug would be put down in the office itself. Interior decorators are a nuisance to most executives. The Chief Executive was fascinated, and eager to see their work.

And then there were the private celebrations. The season, as pencilled notations in the First Lady's appointments book testified, was a time of anniversaries. In September she and the President had been married exactly a decade. Today was Bob Kennedy's birthday. Friday, Ted and Joan Kennedy were to celebrate their fifth anniversary—too bad to be away in Texas—and next week John would be three years old and Caroline six. Caroline was now old enough to visit friends overnight. In a room across the corridor she had put aside her pink bear and Raggedy Ann, anticipating Friday noon, when she would leave to spend her first weekend away from relatives with little Agatha Pozen, whose mother had taken the two girls through Arlington's Custis-Lee Mansion last March. Caroline, enchanted, had told her father of it, and the following weekend he had crossed the river with Charlie Bartlett to see for himself. The view *was* spectacular; 'I could,' he had told Bartlett, 'stay here for ever.'

Awaiting the Chief Executive, the party upstairs sipped cocktails and exchanged light banter. Ethel Kennedy, startling in a pink chenille suit, was at her tart best. She and her husband had just left a surprise birthday party at Justice—he had been given a Monopoly Game, the spaces on which had been altered to read 'Lyceum Avenue', 'Land on White House and get Camp David free', etc.—and she was baiting William O. Douglas, the Richard Halliburton of the bench. 'Why *do* you take such nutty trips?' she demanded. 'Why not try something different? Like a cruise or a resort?' The First Lady raised a point of order about *Tropic of Cancer*; the Court politely deliberated. The wives of Byron White and Arthur Goldberg, Kennedy's two Supreme Court appointees, acted as associate hostesses while Jacqueline Kennedy detached herself, moved over to Douglas' blonde, twenty-four-year-old bride of three months and asked (as though it hadn't been settled) what sort of clothes would be appropriate for her to wear in the Southwest.

Joanie Douglas was grateful for the attention. This was her first judicial reception, her first evening in the White House, and although she had been raised as a Republican she regarded John Kennedy, in her words, 'as a noble figure moving through the pages of history'. Nina Warren had noticed her nervousness. On the way over she had coached her, and now the eminent hostess was doing her best. Still Joanie was wretched. Why on earth, she wondered miserably, had she worn black? So *drab*. None of the other women were in it. And why was Bob Kennedy so stern? Could it have been something she had done? (It wasn't. The Attorney General had just remembered that this reception was supposed to have *three* acts. The lesser judges, hurt because they had been swallowed up in the downstairs mêlées of 1961 and 1962, had objected, and he had directed that a special room be set aside for them. Apparently his order had miscarried. He pictured them down below, crimson with rage, and frowned.) The new Mrs Douglas, watching him, bit her lip. And then the door opened, and she forgot him, her gown, everything. It was the President.

Gliding across the thick rug, burnished black shoes glistening, broad shoulders slightly hunched, glowing with hospitality, he circled the room ceremoniously, starting with the Chief Justice. Justice Douglas introduced his bride: 'I want you to meet the management.' Kennedy had anticipated this moment; he had read of her youth and had predicted that the older Court wives would be jealous of it. 'Management has my sympathies,' he murmured, smiling broadly. 'I appreciate the grave responsibilities of your office.' The Attorney General stepped over to talk to her, and his brother alighted on a sofa, conferring with three justices. Next week, he told Goldberg, he wanted to speak to him about a personal matter. Goldberg assumed this meant engaging union labour for Kennedy's country house; as a former labour lawyer Goldberg had made such arrangements for him in the past. He nodded, and the President, waving away a daiquiri, transferred to the upholstered Northern Porch rocker under the gold mantel clock. Byron White—the perennial All-American, built like an oak, a Kennedy friend for twenty-four years and a fellow officer during the war—sat on his left. Then the ladies moved in, the wife of retired Justice Stanley Reed leading the pack.

You couldn't blame them. This chance came only once a year. On various pretexts they broke off conversations and advanced in little rushes, fussing merrily among themselves, edging chairs closer to the rocker. Potter Stewart's wife had never talked to the President, and thanks to White she won the coveted spot in front. 'You surely know Mrs Stewart,' he said as he left; 'she would like to chat with you for a few minutes, Mr President.' The chat lasted nearly fifteen minutes. Nursing a ginger ale and feeling rather guilty because her husband was a junior justice, she thawed as the President spoke. It was a trick he had. He remembered amazing details about other people in the government. She confessed a crime: she had just stolen a matchbox labelled 'The President's House'. He pointed out that the back of it bore an AFL-CIO label. Yes, she remembered, such labels had to be on campaign literature when Mr Stewart ran for the city councilman years ago. He closed his eyes, opened them. Hadn't that been in Cincinnati? he inquired. And hadn't Stewart gone on to become Vice Mayor? Suddenly she found they were discussing the tangle of Ohio politics, city by city.

A silent witness was Joanie Douglas. Normally loquacious, she was speechless here. Because Kennedy's newspaper photographs were black-and-white, she had unconsciously (and, she realized, idiotically) expected him to be black-and-white here. Instead, he was tanned, vibrant; an outdoorsman like her husband. Peering up as he drew out 'Andy' Stewart, Joanie reflected that he was rather like her own father: an aloof aristocrat viewing the company with a sardonic, perceptive eye.

A third wife watched from across the room. Ethel Kennedy had been the President's sister-in-law since 1950. Next to the First Lady she knew him better than any of the women present, and chatter about matchboxes and obscure Buckeye candidates didn't deceive her. That was social instinct; it was no clue to what he was really thinking. And presently she realized that something very grave must be on his mind. He had leaned back in the rocker, his hand cupped under his chin, and was gazing out with hooded grey eyes. The Chief Justice called over jocularly that Texas would be rough. There was no reply; Kennedy had withdrawn into a private sanctuary of thought. *Why*, Ethel wondered, *is Jack so preoccupied?* Just before the group prepared to drift towards the stairs, she crossed over and greeted him herself. In the past, no matter how complex his problems, the President had always responded. Not now. For the first time in thirteen years he was looking right through her.

Texas *would* be rough. In his heyday Earl Warren had been a great politician, the champion of California. But he had never encountered anything as cabalistic as the Democratic party in the Lone Star State. Here, as elsewhere, the national leadership did what it could to keep the peace. Politics was the art of the possible. But Texas scorned peace. Each county was an autonomous duchy, each was faction-ridden. The jinn lived in a state of constant anarchy, raiding one another's castles and swatting innocent vassals. They were political cannibals, and a naïve outsider venturing among them could be eaten alive.

John Kennedy was not naïve. Massachusetts politics was scarcely orderly, and he knew Texas just as he knew Ohio. At the Los Angeles convention of 1960, where Johnson had attempted to wrest the Presidential nomination from him, Kennedy himself had been smitten by partisans, who had spread rumours that he would not live out his first term because he was 'diseased'. (After Los Angeles they blandly explained that they had been referring to Addison's disease.) On several occasions since then he had recrossed the state, most recently on June 5. Connally had consented to the coming trip at the Cortez Hotel in El Paso, and for the past two weeks guides from the Democratic National Committee had been scouting the most treacherous marshes. The President, however, hadn't read their reports. His task was to govern. Advance planning was left to others, principally to O'Donnell, who had duties of his own. Thus the White House was only vaguely aware of details about the blazing feud between two of the major Texans.

Actually it was an old feud, older than the feuders themselves. Its origins were ideological, and it had first come to a head in the volatile 1930's. The rightists hegemony, then known as Jeffersonian Democrats and Texas Regulars, had bolted Roosevelt. As early as 1944 the rightists had sent a rival delegation to the national convention. Later, as Shivercrats and States' Righters, they had deserted Adlai E. Stevenson; in 1952 both the Democratic Governor and the Democratic National Committeeman in Texas campaigned for the Republican national ticket. Four years later the moderates revolted. Encouraged by Sam Rayburn, Byron Skelton, a moderate Texas attorney, had accepted the post of National Committeeman. But the muddle had only grown worse. The Populist heirs had staged an uprising of their own, forming a liberal faction called the Democrats of Texas (DOT).

DOT's hero was Ralph Yarborough, who ran three unsuccessful campaigns before becoming a U.S. Senator in 1957. Yarborough had the manner of a river-boat confidence man. Voluble, flowery, with an accent stickier than red-eye gravy, he was for ever squabbling with other Democrats. Nevertheless he was the only Texas liberal to hold state-wide office. Lacking powerful backers, lacking money—his campaign debts were huge—he refused to abandon his fidelity to what the Dallas *Morning News* defined as the 'liberal-leftist axis'. Even the dissolution of DOT left him unshaken. In Los Angeles, when the rest of the state party rallied to Johnson's favourite-son candidacy, he supported John Kennedy. They punished him by refusing him a seat in the Texas delegation; the Senator had to sit in the gallery as a spectator. Reprisals would have gone farther, but Rayburn intervened. Then a year later, the Speaker died. His calming influence vanished with him. The rightists were free to gang up on the Populist maverick. Mister Sam, as they put it in a quaint phrase, had 'pissed on his last campfire'.

Furthermore, they now had a leader cut from whipcord. Johnson had never won their complete trust. In John B. Connally, Jr., however, he had presented them with a priceless gift. Connally had been Johnson's administrative assistant and Kennedy's Secretary of the Navy, and now he was his own governor. Outsiders still thought of him as a Kennedy–Johnson man. They were mistaken. If he had any fugleman it was Sid Richardson, the Fort Worth oil millionaire for whom he had worked in the late 1950's. Connally had become one of the most reliable links in the Texas gas-and-oil ring; in the dated rhetoric of the earlier Populists he might have been described as a

Tool of the Interests. He looked the part—tall, heavily handsome, with grey curly hair and a ripe, almost feminine mouth—but there was nothing bogus about his convictions. He had sold out to no one. His conservatism, like Yarborough's liberalism, was genuine.

The Governor was a classic example of the poor boy who has risen above his origins and despises them. Those who have never endured poverty might judge him harshly for this. They would be unjust, for a man who has known squalor in childhood can only remember it with contempt. (How he uses his contempt is, of course, another matter; Lyndon Johnson's background was much the same, but his politics were very different.) All that can be said for the Governor's youth is that he had seen a lot of Texas. John B. Connally, Sr. had been a tenant farmer, a barber, a grocer, a bus driver on the San Antonio–Corpus Christi route—the family moved to San Antonio so they could see him between trips—and then he had returned to the soil, doubling as a freelance butcher to stave off disaster. When ranchers wanted steers slaughtered, old John did the dirty work. One of the son's most graphic recollections was of helping with this carnage. The elder Connally would drive his scarred black Model T Ford; Carlos Estrada, his Mexican helper, sat alongside with the knives and saws; eight-year-old John, Jr. perched in the back, cradling in his arms a battered bucket. It was his task to carry water while the two men carved and chopped, and because 'brains and eggs' were a rancher's delicacy, he would always remember how carefully they had handled the brains, the precious light blue brains.

From such a youth the boy could go nowhere but up. After the Alamo, San Jacinto; after John B. Connally, Sr., John B. Connally, Jr. Life *had* to be better than this, he *must* get a hand-hold on that bottom rung and climb the golden gangway. And he did. At the University of Texas he became the biggest man on campus. He married the most popular co-ed, he acquired suavity and guile, he became a friend of wealthy men and then their staunch ally. Studying the hardship of the Texas poor had made Ralph Yarborough an adversary of those whom he regarded as responsible for it. Indigence itself was John Connally's enemy. As Johnson said privately, Connally only felt comfortable in $300 suits and custom-made shoes and in the company of other men wearing them. The wall between him and his boyhood could never be thick enough. As Governor he had strengthened his alliances, carefully disassociating himself from the liberalism in Washington. Once more labour groups and 'libs', as liberals were locally known, had trouble getting seated at state conventions. Connally came out against federal spending, oil imports, and Medicare, and he appeared on statewide television to oppose Kennedy's civil rights bill. Like the President, he had his eye on the coming election. There was a strong possibility that he might be opposed in the Texas primary. This was the time to shore up defences. Barring primary upsets, Connally and Yarborough would be campaigning with Kennedy—and Johnson, if the President again picked Lyndon as his running mate—next fall. All would face reelection on November 3, 1964. The Governor candidly admitted that he wanted to run ahead of the ticket. In private he was greedier than that. He wanted Yarborough to lose, and with that in mind he planned to make political capital out of the forthcoming Presidential tour.

His position was strong. As chief executive of the state, he would be host to the national Chief Executive, and the White House was taking a tolerant view of his independence. Larry O'Brien called Congressman Albert Thomas; when the caravan from Washington reached Houston for the Thomas testimonial dinner, Larry said, it would be nice if the Governor played a key role. The Congressman took the hint. He phoned Austin and asked Connally to introduce him. Word was passed to the rest of the state's Congressional delegation that all local details were to be handled by Austin.

In a show of scrupulosity the trip, at Connally's request, was divided into 'political' and 'non-political' phases. San Antonio, Forth Worth, and Dallas were non-political; Houston and Austin were political. To avoid offending him, John Bailey, Chairman of the Democratic National Committee, would not join the group until it reached Austin. He would fly there on a Delta Air Lines flight during the Dallas motorcade. The committee was even going to pay for the fuel consumed by the Presidential aircraft, and Bailey engaged in complicated arithmetic based on the Air Force's estimate that the plane cost $2,300 an hour while airborne.

The Governor, as O'Brien and O'Donnell put it, was being 'dealt a big hand'. The first inkling of how he intended to play that hand came early in October. Before flying east to discuss details of the trip he conferred in Dallas' Adolphus Hotel with the city's power elite—J. Eric Jonsson, chairman of the powerful Citizens Council; Robert Cullum, president of the Chamber of Commerce; R. L. Thornton, Sr., chairman of the Mercantile National Bank; Joe Dealey, son of Ted Dealey, publisher of the Dallas *Morning News* (Ted himself was absent in Washington); and Albert Jackson of the Dallas *Times-Herald*. In effect, the Governor apologized for the President's forthcoming visit. He himself was in a bind, he said. He compared his role to that of a captain; the admiral had asked permission to board his ship. He couldn't tell the Chief Executive *not* to come. But he wanted them to know that he had no intention of becoming 'Kennedy's errand boy'. Indeed, if he used the occasion to humiliate Yarborough, there was a good possibility that Texas liberalism might be crushed. This was a superb opportunity to crowd the libs off stage. 'I don't intend to default to the liberals,' he explained. 'I've got to have a non-political body to represent Dallas, and you gentlemen are it by your associations.'

In the capital on October 3, he called a meeting of Texans on the Hill—Yarborough was not asked—and told them that the President wanted to visit the state's four major cities: San Antonio, Houston, Fort Worth, and Dallas. Kennedy's strength in Texas, as Connally saw it, was among 'Negroes and brass-collar Democrats'. Unfortunately they were poor, and the national leadership wanted the journey to be a fund-raising drive. 'I think it is a mistake,' he said. 'You know that the people who are for Kennedy are people without money. I've checked with businessmen and they aren't about to contribute to his campaign.' At this point there was a brief flare-up. Henry B. Gonzalez, the San Antonio liberal, broke in. 'What businessmen did you talk to?' he asked angrily. 'If they're the ones you've been appointing, I wouldn't expect them to be for Kennedy, because they are a bunch of Republicans. I'll get you businessmen. You may not like them, though, because they won't support you.' Agitated, the Governor chain-lit one cigarette from the stub of another, but he stuck to his theme: the trip should be non-partisan. The following day he took much the same line with Kennedy, adding a few choice words about Yarborough. Ultimately a compromise was reached. In San Antonio the President would dedicate six new buildings at an Air Force base (non-political). In Houston he would attend the dinner for Albert Thomas (political, though of no advantage to anyone except Thomas). Civic leaders would greet the Chief Executive in Fort Worth and Dallas (non-political), and the only fund-raising would be in Austin, the state capital and the Governor's home. Connally assigned each Congressman a quota of tickets to the Austin dinner; Yarborough's quota was sent to him.

Keep the Presidency above politics—that was the Governor's plea. Of course, it was absurd. He wasn't dealing with children. Both the Hill and the White House knew that the Presidency *is* politics. Kennedy's difficulty was that he couldn't alienate Connally; if a ceremonial tour would give the appearance of a united Democratic front in Texas, he would settle for that. The only man who could persuade the Governor to go farther was his old mentor, the Vice President, who was keeping mum. According to Johnson, he had not been consulted about the desirability of the expedition. His 'first word from President Kennedy was that he was planning to make the trip. From this point, there was fairly intensive discussion of the details'. At first the Vice President was an enthusiastic advocate of fund-raising. Recently a Massachusetts banquet had raised $680,000 for the party. His pride in Texas had been challenged, and despite emphatic denials from the White House the rumour persisted that Kennedy would cut him from the '64 ticket, Johnson's own radar had picked up a few alarming blips. Determined to prove that his popularity was still strong, he had proposed four Texas banquets where the faithful would demonstrate their loyalty to Kennedy *and* Johnson by emptying their pockets into next year's war chest.

Like Johnson, Yarborough had sensitive antennae. He had guessed at his plight. He had to maintain a discreet silence until October 19, for on that date (as Connally well knew) he had scheduled a testimonial dinner of his own in Austin to clear up campaign obligations. Once it was over he began sending out ominous signals. He reminded the White House that he had a record of unwavering devotion to Kennedy. Was he to be snubbed in his home state? If so, he preferred to brood in Washington. He was reassured. On three separate occasions Larry O'Brien phoned him, promising, in his slow resonant voice, that there would be no Presidential slurs. It was the President's most earnest wish that the Senator be a member of his party, O'Brien said, and he meant it. For Kennedy a trip without Yarborough would be worse than no trip at all. There would be indignation among the Texas liberals, and retribution in the campaign to come.

However, no one in the White House—and no one in Washington, except the now silent Vice President—could speak for the Governor, and since leaving the capital Connally had been busy spinning his intricate webs. The first silken threads were encountered by Jerry Bruno, the chunky, saddle-nosed advance man for the Democratic National Committee. Bruno landed at the Austin airport late in the evening of October 28 and was instantly greeted by rival delegations, one of them representing Connally and the other Yarborough. Acting on instructions from O'Donnell he made excuses to the Senator's men. Next day he had lunch with the Governor in Austin's Forty Acres Club and then flew on to survey the entire route of the forthcoming trip. In six years as a politicians' politician Bruno had been tempered by several Presidential primaries and one general election. Never before had he encountered so many different contact men. The National Committee had a foil in each county, and that should have been enough. But the Governor had fielded a second team, the Senator a third, the Vice President a fourth, and labour—which had its own problems in Texas—a fifth. In his Dallas visits of October 30 and November 1, Bruno learned of one Connally scheme to put Senator Yarborough in his place, the details of which are important because they involve the choice of the site at which the President would speak and, as a consequence, the motorcade route he would follow from the airport to the site.

Bruno himself preferred the large ballroom in the Sheraton-Dallas Hotel. He was disappointed. A women's organization had reserved it, and the management declined to suggest that the ladies move. The President, Bruno was bluntly told, would have to hire a hall elsewhere. No one had signed up Dallas' Memorial Auditorium. It had a seating capacity of eleven thousand, but the local hosts argued against it for that very reason; the larger the crowd, they felt, the more cranks there would be. This being Dallas, they weren't admirers of the President; they were, however, worried about the reputation of their city. That left three choices: the Women's Building, in the shadow of the Cotton Bowl, and, over on Industrial Boulevard, Market Hall and the Trade Mart. The bottlers' association would be convening in Market Hall. They could have been persuaded to move, but Bruno saw no point in annoying them. He preferred the Women's Building. It was rather drab, but for that very reason, he pointed out, it would attract working people. The hosts were disconsolate. They urged he pick the showy Trade Mart. As Republicans they could be ignored. The Democratic Governor could not be treated so lightly, however, and it developed that the low-ceilinged Women's Building was unsuitable for one of his schemes. In Dallas and in Austin he wanted two-tiered head tables. The President, the Vice President, and the Governor would sit at the top table. Lesser officials—such as the state's senior Senator—would be relegated to the lesser table. Yarborough would be low man on the totem pole.

It was within Bruno's power to make a final decision on the spot, and later he had to live with the fact that had he insisted on the Women's Building then the Dallas motorcade would not have passed beneath the Texas School Book Depository. Because he hesitated on November 1, the matter remained unsettled a week later, when the Secret Service advance man, Winston G. Lawson, was ordered to Dallas. The Secret Service regarded the Women's Building as safer—there were sixteen hidden catwalks in the Trade Mart—but either site was acceptable. The issue was bucked up to the White House, where the policy was still to appease Connally. On November 14 O'Donnell opted for the Trade Mart, though the two-tiered head table was rejected.[1] The Governor was content. The ploy would be

[1] The Warren Commission reported that the luncheon site was selected by the Secret Service with O'Donnell's approval. This is incorrect. The decision was a political decision, made by politicians. Bruno was among the witnesses whom the Commission did not summon.

just as effective in Austin, and there he held an ace in the hole. He planned a reception for the President in the executive mansion. There would be no invitation for Senator Yarborough.

Thus calculated discourtesies threatened the entire expedition before it had even left Washington. Connally was playing a deep game. It should be added that he was playing it shrewdly. His model, ironically, was John F. Kennedy, who had been pre-empting the nation's political centre for the past three years. The difference was that Kennedy had never attempted to purge anyone, and that the Texas centre, as interpreted by the Governor, excluded the very people who had worked for Kennedy in 1960. Echoes of their discontent had begun to reach the President; even as the judicial reception moved towards its lively climax, the White House communications centre received a telegram from three San Antonio liberals expressing disappointment over the brevity of his scheduled stop in Bexar County, which had given him his largest Texas majority against Nixon.

The only city where everything was going smoothly was Houston. At the outset Houston had seemed impossible. The Democratic county chairman was treated as an outcast by all factions. But Bruno's local advance man from Washington, Marty Underwood, had been toiling like a drudge. For ten days he had been holed up in the historic Rice Hotel, presiding over peace councils, and he had even persuaded the two Spanish-American groups, the LULACS and the Pesos, to rally together under the LULACS banner. Underwood was receiving deft assistance from a zealous local public relations man named Jack J. Valenti, the representative of Congressman Thomas—Thomas, the survivor of four cancer operations, who yearned for retirement but remained on the Hill at the express wish of the President and the Vice President. Elsewhere in the state discontent was pandemic. Some unhappiness was inevitable. A Chief Executive's time is limited, and Brownsville, San Benito, Corpus Christi, and Freeport would never understand why he couldn't spare a few hours for them. Most of the clamour, however, came from Kennedy supporters who had been stung by Connally tactics. They were unaware of Yarborough's predicament. They merely knew that the President was coming, and that the Texans who would be meeting and fêting him were largely Republicans and apostate Democrats. But one fact loomed above all others: half the population of the state was concentrated in six of the state's 254 counties. In two days of strenuous motorcading Kennedy might greet a million Americans before returning to Sunday's conference with Henry Cabot Lodge, Monday's state dinner for Erhard, Tuesday's legislative breakfast—back, in short, to his splendid captivity.

It was time to move the judges' party downstairs. Rocking forward, the President sprang to his feet and crooked a finger; a Marine Corps captain who had entered unobtrusively quietly ordered two men in dress uniforms to carry the Stars and Stripes and the blue and gold Presidential flag to the stairhead. The President moved off in that direction; behind him his three military aides guided everyone to his proper place, Warren first, Goldberg and the Attorney General last. The wives joked about rank, yet when Joanie Douglas tried to hang back, invisible hands thrust her forwards; though she herself was conspicuously new, her husband's appointment to the Court dated from Roosevelt's second administration.

That was the only confusion. The aides made everything easy. For ten minutes they had been mingling among the guests, sizing things up, and they blended so gracefully into the social tableau that it was difficult to believe that their campaign ribbons were authentic. Was it true that Ted Clifton (Maj. Gen., USA) had commanded a battalion at Anzio? He was something out of D'Oyly Carte. Had Taz Shepard (Capt., USN) really won a Navy Cross for extraordinary heroism in the Solomons? His face was as seamless as a midshipman's. And Godfrey McHugh was the unlikeliest of all. He didn't even sound like an American. Raised in Paris by a Dun & Bradstreet father, Brigadier General Godfrey McHugh (USAF), better known as God, spoke English with a pronounced French accent.

Down the Grand Staircase the military aides marched in a glittering rank behind the Commander in Chief, Ted on the right, God front and centre, Taz on the left. Approaching the bottom, valour suddenly vanished; they fled like fugitives. It was time for photographs, and douzepers mustn't appear to be publicity hogs. While they sneaked away, Mr Justice Burton, too infirm for stairs, got off a hidden elevator and edged into the picture. Simultaneously the first flash bulb exploded. For precisely two minutes Captain Stoughton perspired heavily, holding a super-wide Hasselblad single-reflex 38-mm. lens with a 90-degree angle over the bobbing heads of lobby guests, trying to get the entire Court in one frame. A feminine command ended the blaze of light—Pam Turnure whispered, 'Finished!' Half blind, Evelyn Lincoln and her aunt emerged from behind a white marble pillar and stumbled towards the scarlet tunics of the Marine Band as the President turned ceremoniously towards the East Room. In the next instant they were half-deafened. The band struck a martial chord. There were ruffles and flourishes and then, in lively cadence, the crashing strains of an old Scottish air:

Hail to the Chief who in triumph advances!
Honour'd and bless'd be the evergreen pine!
Long may the tree, in his banner that glances,
Flourish, the shelter and grace of our line!

Godfrey McHugh, rigidly at attention, glanced covertly at the President and suppressed a Gallic gesture of impatience. He did wish the Chief would remember to stand still while he was being hailed. God himself was something of a sport; years ago he had water-skied on the Chesapeake Bay with young Jacqueline Bouvier, and she had once called him 'gay and impetuous'. Nevertheless he could contain himself for *politesse*. Kennedy couldn't. Of all the Presidents Godfrey had served, only this one refused to pause and salute the flag.

Dum-de-dum. It was over. Already the released chieftain was plunging towards the dense mass in the East Room, where, it developed, the Attorney General's earlier concern had been unjustified. His instructions had been followed to the letter. The crowd under the gigantic ballroom chandeliers consisted entirely of minor judiciary. They were welcomed, their wives were solicited about this and that, they were left; the President and the First Lady were gently shouldering their way through eager, babbling crowds in the Green Room, the Blue Room, the Red Room. The guests included Sandy Fox, the White House calligrapher, who inscribed invitations; J. Bernard West, the mansion's chief usher; and Jerry Behn, Head of the White House Secret Service Detail—though Jerry wouldn't be making the Texas trip; Roy Kellerman, an assistant, was taking his place. Others were even more familiar: Barney Ross, who as an ensign had been shipwrecked behind Japanese lines with Lieutenant Jack Kennedy in 1943; Chief Marshal Jim McShane, the hero of Oxford, Mississippi; and, to quote Sandy's list, the Honourable David F. Powers.

The Honourable Mr Powers called bringing your wife to the mansion 'making points'. All the men present had been permitted to make points, and the girls downstairs were as ebullient as the Court ladies upstairs. If your back was turned towards a door, you could still tell when the President crossed the threshold. The whole room would light up. 'He's *beautiful*!' cried a Justice Department bride in the Green Room. 'They *both* are,' her husband whispered. They actually were. No one could remember when the First Family had been so radiant. Anxiety arising from Mrs Kennedy's long absence disappeared entirely as she swept along in her husband's wake. Her camellia beauty was exquisite as Dresden, her lovely brown eyes like vast pools. Dean Markham, confronting her, forgot that this was a formal occasion and blurted out, 'Hi, Jackie!' Dr Walsh eyed her professionally and decided she had never looked more fit. Then he leaned towards the President and mentioned seeing young John's pictures in the new issue of *Look*. Kennedy, delighted, laughed aloud. The doctor turned to his own wife. 'You see?' he murmured. 'His whole life is wrapped up in the boy.'

The President himself had few points to make here. These were the faithful. However, they were his friends; he wanted them to enjoy themselves in his home. Political habit, moreover, was strong. He knew people liked to be noticed and were flattered when their names were remembered. Before Markham, one of the huskiest New Frontiersmen, could present his wife, Kennedy quickly interrupted, 'Of course I know Sue,' and he urged Mrs Kennedy, 'Be sure to say hello to Jack McNally's wife Irene.' She needed little urging. Social skills and political arts weren't so very different. 'She's so jolly!' she said of Mrs West when West, using the dexterity of a chief usher, managed to thrust her ahead. It was only a word, yet West knew it meant there would be fewer complaints at home when he toiled late at the mansion. Working the opposite side of the crowd, the President had singled out the new Postmaster General, John A. Gronouski, whose first White House reception this was, and the Secretary of the Treasury. Phyllis and Douglas Dillon told him he was in wonderful form. Dillon added, 'This is hello and good-bye. We're leaving for Japan.' '*I* know,' Kennedy replied, making a face. '*You're* off to Japan—and *I've* got to go to Texas.' He smiled, but added with obvious feeling, 'God, how I wish we could change places!'

A buffet and a punch bowl awaited him in the State Dining Room. He brushed past it, returned to his office, slipped on his spectacles, and pored over foreign cables for an hour. The First Lady lingered a little longer, then went upstairs with her brother-in-law. To him she repeated that she was looking forward to Texas, and to more campaigning later. Presently his wife bounced in. The Attorney General had guests of his own at home, she reminded him, although, of course, she didn't put it that way. This was the family. There was no protocol here, no titles. It was Jackie, Bobby, and Ethel, and when the President stepped off the Otis elevator after Bobby's and Ethel's departure he was simply Jack, starved for dinner. Everything was quiet. Caroline and John, having spent the afternoon with their grandmother in Georgetown, were back in their twin bedrooms off the north corridor with Maude Shaw, the Kennedys' British nurse. Jack and Jackie could dine alone, and their few telephone calls were largely restricted to relatives and friends—his sister, Eunice Shriver; his sister Pat's husband, Peter Lawford; Charlie Bartlett.

There were no cables here, either. The correspondence was equally familial. A note from Jackie's mother urged her to enjoy herself. Another letter, from Jackie's mother-in-law, was in much the same vein. Rose Kennedy had been to New York City and had discussed the President's most recent visit with a variety of people. She noted that the President had dispensed with the usual police escort, and that the public enthusiastically approved this move.

The sole interruption that evening was a phone call from Under Secretary of State George Ball. Ball had just returned from a series of European conferences. He had automatically become Acting Secretary the moment he set foot on U.S. soil, and at 9.20 p.m. he reported for duty. Momentarily Jack had to be President again. He ticked off a few matters which might be elusive. Ball promised to keep his eye on them. 'Good,' said the President. 'I'll be back from Texas Sunday. Come out to Camp David. Cabot Lodge will be there, and we can go over these things.' Then he hung up and returned to the privacy and peace of the mansion's second floor.

Elsewhere the White House was less quiet. Godfrey McHugh had forwarded the Air Force's weather forecast for Texas, predicting maximum temperatures in the fifties over the next two days. That would be perfect, and on the third floor packing could proceed at full speed. Mrs Kennedy's dark little Dominican maid, Provi Parades, was busily folding the blouses and skirts the President had chosen. Provi was being especially attentive, for this would be her mistress' first trip without her. Starting now, and throughout the campaign, Mrs Kennedy's personal secretary would double as maid on the road. Down the corridor, George Thomas, Kennedy's portly Negro valet, was filling two suitcases and a black, brassbound Navy foot locker. George's last chore was to make sure the shirts in the foot locker would not wrinkle. Afterwards there was the inevitable banging of luggage.

And two floors below, the reception for the judges was continuing. It had turned into a party. After the First Family had left, the Marine Band had moved into the East Room, the Air Force's Strolling Strings into the lobby; both were playing selections from *My Fair Lady* and *Camelot*:

Don't let it be forgot
That once there was a spot
For one brief shining moment
That was known as Camelot. . . .

The guests were dancing. On the whole they were a nimble lot, and several leaders exhibited dash and verve. The servants beamed on the swirling skirts, the spinning tailored backs, and, at each deep turning dip, the lithe nyloned legs. This, after all, was what the East Room had been designed for. Its proper name was the East Ballroom, and the Kennedy couples, the young mesomorphs and their elegant ladies, seemed right for it. To them there was nothing unusual about this dance. For them life was at flood tide; the future promised a thousand such evenings. Only after the great darkness had enveloped the mansion would it evoke Byron's description of another party:

There was a sound of revelry by night,
And Belgium's capital had gathered then
Her Beauty and her Chivalry, and bright
The lamps shone o'er fair women and brave men;
A thousand hearts beat happily; and when
Music arose with its voluptuous swell,
Soft eyes looked love to eyes that spake again,
And all went merry as a marriage bell. . . .

The Brussels ball of June 14, 1915, had ended in a peal of Napoleonic cannon, the roll of drums, the hot clatter of mustering squadrons, and terror-stricken whispers of an approaching enemy. The judicial reception of November 20, 1963, continued undisturbed. Secret Service agents gaily two-stepped across the waxed boards unaware that within three days the corpse of the President they had sworn to protect would lie in a wooden box on the very floor where they now pirouetted. Had they but known, they would have given their lives for his. There was no inkling. Officers also whirled, while their constitutional Commander in Chief slept above them. The mightiest military force in history was powerless to avert the disaster. Its sentinels reported nothing; they had nothing to report. Cannon were mute, steeds stabled, drums hushed. Every frontier was as silent as fate.

And yet . . .

Warp and woof, the pattern of fate, cast invisible shadows. In the White House that Wednesday Commander Oliver S. Hallett, USN, was toiling over late dispatches from the President's Situation Room. The messages were unimportant, but the assistant naval aide's presence in the mansion was an extraordinary irony. Too new to be invited to the reception, Commander and Mrs Hallett were nevertheless linked by an uncanny destiny to the event that now lay less than forty hours away. Hallett had been posted here nine months ago. Previously he had been on submarine duty, and before that both he and his wife had worked in the ten-storey Moscow apartment building which served as the U.S. Embassy to the U.S.S.R. He was the naval attaché; she was the embassy's receptionist. On the last day of October 1959, a spindly youth with eyes oddly set, as though they belonged to two different faces, strode into the front hallway and slammed his green passport on Joan Hallett's desk. In a Southwestern accent he informed her that he had come to renounce his American citizenship.

Receptionists don't handle such matters. Neither do attachés. The legation was a small world, however, and the Halletts saw the embittered young man repeatedly as he returned for interviews with Ambassador Llewellyn E. Thompson and members of the U.S. consulate. The consuls gave him a lot of argument; it was their policy to woo would-be defectors, on the ground that American misfits were less dangerous back in the United States. In time the Commander and his wife lost track of the case. Their orders were cut and recut; like Llewellyn Thompson, who became Ambassador at Large in October 1962, they were brought home. Hallett joined the President's official family at 1600 Pennsylvania Avenue, and the young Halletts were enrolled in Stone Ridge parochial school with the children of the Robert F. Kennedy's and the Sargent Shrivers. The Soviet apartment house, with its bugging devices and its exasperating intrigue, lay in the past. They were glad to be free of it. Yet they still talked of Moscow, and sometimes the Commander, his wife, and their sixteen-year-old daughter Caroline wondered what had become of the weedy malcontent. They recalled him vividly: his arrogance, the peculiar density in his eyes, the way he would snatch the New York *Herald Tribune* from Joan's desk and then—for he had been a great reader—devour every word. He had been obnoxious, but he had made a distinct impression. All three Halletts remembered the face and the name of Lee Harvey Oswald, though they had no recent information about him. In their fireside discussions they assumed he was still in the Soviet Union.

And yet . . .

Oswald wasn't in Russia. He had notified the consulate that he had seen the light, and in June of 1962, with the help of a State Department loan, he had returned to Texas, bringing with him a lynx-eyed young Russian wife and an infant girl. His subsequent movements became a matter of intense interest after his death, but after the chaff had been sifted only two significant facts remained: he had stumbled from failure to failure, and he had finally returned to Dallas, Texas.

Much of the later confusion was to arise from his political pretensions. Oswald liked to characterize himself as a Marxist. Really he hadn't the ideals of a cat, and in his lucid moments he knew it. He was against democracy, Communism, the world. In an autobiographical sketch written before his return to America he acknowledged 'a mean streak of independence brought on by neglect', and during his voyage home he wondered what would happen if somebody—obviously himself—would

> stand up and say he was utterly opposed not only to the governments, but to the people, too the entire land and complete foundations of his socially. I have heard and read of the resugent Americanism in the U.S., not the ultra-right type, but rather the polite, seemingly pointless Americanism expressed by such as the 'American fore group' and the freedom foundation, and yet even in these vieled, formless, patriotic gestures, their is the obvious axe being underground by the invested interests of the sponseres of there expensive undertaking. To where can I turn? to factional mutants of both systems, to odd-ball Hegelian idealists out of touch with reality religious groups, to revisinist or too abserd anarchism. No!

His ravings stamp him as an incoherent hater, nothing more. Looking for doctrine in them is like looking for bone in a polyp. Yet he had tried to defect, and both his conduct in Russia and his bizarre behaviour after his return brought him under the active surveillance of the Federal Bureau of Investigation. Inasmuch as the Bureau's handbook charged agents to be on the alert for information 'indicating the possibility of an attempt against the person or safety of the President', one might have assumed that the seventy-five-man FBI office in Dallas would have relayed word of his presence to the five-man Secret Service office there. Nothing of the sort happened. His file was in the hands of FBI Agent James P. Hosty, Jr., a husky, thirty-five-year-old Notre Dame graduate and an outspoken admirer of John F. Kennedy. Since November 4, 1963, Hosty had known that Oswald was employed as a labourer in the Texas School Book Depository at the corner of Houston and Elm streets. This warehouse provided the deadliest sniper's roost on the Presidential motorcade route, because the motorcade was scheduled to first zig and then zag directly beneath its windows. A gunman could size up the President's car as it approached the building from the front, wait while it pivoted sharply at his feet, and fire as it crept slowly out of the turn to his right. Hosty, however, didn't make the connection. He had received no official notification of the route, and when local newspapers published a map of it, his sole concern was whether or not Jim Hosty would catch a glimpse of Kennedy. 'I noticed that it was coming up Main Street,' he said five months later. 'That was the only thing I was interested in, where maybe I could watch it if I had a chance.'

But the Secret Service should have inspected the building anyway.[2]

But it didn't.

On November 18 Lawson, the Service's advance man, rode over the motorcade route with Dallas Police Chief Jesse Curry and Forrest V. Sorrels, the agent in charge of the local Secret Service office. Sorrels was the most impressive of the three. He was a native of Red River, Texas, and looked it—lean, stooped, and craggy, with the piercing eye of an old cop. Once in Tucson he had counted the cash taken from a thief named John Dillinger. In 1935 he had joined the SS, as younger agents now called it, and when Franklin D. Roosevelt had dedicated the Robert E. Lee statue on Dallas' Turtle Creek Boulevard, Sorrels had led him over these same streets. He didn't have to be reminded of the danger from snipers. As Curry, who was driving, swung from Cedar Springs Road into Harwood Street, Sorrels glanced up at the Dallas skyline, saw his own dentist's office and said aloud, 'Hell, we'd be sitting ducks.' The other two concurred and shrugged. There were over twenty thousand windows overlooking the route; obviously they couldn't have a man in every one. It would take an army, and would defeat the very purpose of the motorcade. Therefore no windows were inspected, and when the police car turned from Main into Houston, and Lawson asked, 'Say, what's the Texas School Book Depository?' Curry and Sorrels explained that it was just a warehouse for textbooks.

Conceivably the FBI and the Secret Service did do all that could have been done. Possibly Curry's department met its responsibilities by deciding to end supervision of Friday's crowd at Houston and Main, a block short of the ambush, on the ground that traffic would begin to thin out there. Maybe it too was too much to ask those Dallas patrolmen who were in the vicinity of the warehouse to follow the example of New York policemen by turning their backs on the President to scan overlooking windows—in which event they, like the pedestrians around them, would have seen the waiting rifleman in the window. Perhaps every man did his duty. Perhaps the blow could not have been averted. Perhaps it is hindsight to suggest otherwise.

And yet, and yet . . .

Even hindsight, if it be that, has its uses. In time all fate's

[2] In 1961 Michael W. Tortina, Chief Inspector of the Secret Service, told this writer that wherever a Presidential motorcade must slow down for a turn, the entire intersection is checked in advance.

shadows emerge and become visible. One lurked in Hosty's FBI file, a second in Sorrels' instincts. Because Commander Hallett worked in his East Wing office, a third shade of memory lay in the White House itself that Wednesday evening in 1963. And a fourth appeared briefly, unseen, in the Attorney General's home at 4700 Chain Bridge Road, McLean, Virginia, later that same night.

Like the judicial reception it was a strange occasion for portents. The old mansion behind the oversized mailbox marked 'R. F. Kennedy' was ablaze with cheer. Nearly sixty close friends had gathered to salute the owner's thirty-eighth birthday. During the dinner Acting Secretary of the Navy Paul B. 'Red' Fay, Jr., another genial veteran of the President's PT career, acted as toastmaster. At ten o'clock the party moved into the next room and danced to the subdued strains of an accordion. The outstanding event of the evening, it then seemed, was the limping cakewalk of Barney Ross, who was showing off. The dancers went home a half-hour after midnight. After staying up two hours longer talking to Gene Kelly in the library, Bob Kennedy retired, and Ethel arose with a start. It had just come to her: her birthday present to him, a Finnish bath, lay unopened in the basement. In the excitement she had completely forgotten it. There was just too much going on, life was too full; as she had told Byron White before he had left, 'It's all going too perfectly.'

But another guest, Ken O'Donnell, had departed with two fragmentary memories which would lie dormant and then arise phantom-like over the weekend. David Brinkley's wife had inquired about the unrest in Dallas. O'Donnell, taciturn as always, said little.

Later Bob Kennedy had asked him, 'Did you see that letter from Byron Skelton?'

O'Donnell had nodded. He had seen it.

All month the Democratic National Committeeman from Texas had been troubled by a premonition. This in itself was unusual, for no one had ever accused Byron Skelton of being skittish. Now in his late fifties, he was senior partner of the law firm of Skelton, Bowmer, and Courtney; director of the First National Bank of Temple, Texas; and past president of Temple's Chamber of Commerce. With his neat black suits, soft voice, and abundant grey hair he was a poster of Southern respectability, and three years earlier he had played a leading role in staging the historic confrontation between the Roman Catholic Kennedy and sceptical Protestant preachers of the Greater Houston Ministerial Association. Skelton's performance in Houston had earned the respect and gratitude of the President. Now Kennedy was returning for a grand tour of the state's urban centres. The National Committeeman should have been proud, even elated.

He wasn't. He was disturbed. The Presidential schedule included a stop in Dallas, and lately Skelton had been eyeing that city with growing uneasiness. The atmosphere there had become so highly charged by inflammatory statements that he was genuinely concerned. An unstable, suggestible individual—'a nut', as he put it to his friends—might easily be incited. And so, on November 4, he had decided to act. 'Frankly,' he had written the Attorney General that morning, 'I am worried about President Kennedy's proposed trip to Dallas.' Quoting a famous Dallas resident who had recently declared that 'Kennedy is a liability to the free world', Skelton commented that 'A man who would make this kind of statement is capable of doing harm to the President', and concluded that he would 'feel better if the President's itinerary did not include Dallas'. He asked that cancellation of the stop receive 'earnest consideration'.

Nor did he stop there. Two days later he wrote Walter Jenkins, Lyndon Johnson's right-hand man, expressing further misgivings about the city. He would, he told Jenkins, prefer that the President and the Vice President omit it from their itinerary, and to make certain he had touched all bases he flew to Washington the following week and talked to John Bailey and Jerry Bruno at the National Committee. In a long session with Bruno he carefully reviewed the political climate in Dallas and his own apprehensions about it. It wasn't safe, he repeated; regardless of previous commitments it should be avoided.

The upshot of all Skelton's efforts was an enormous zero. On November 8 the Attorney General, who knew him and took him seriously, forwarded his letter to O'Donnell, who decided it was an unsupported hunch. Both Jenkins and Bruno concluded that Skelton was merely annoyed because he and Mrs H. H. Weinert, Democratic National Committeewoman for Texas, were not included in the Presidential party. In fact they were entitled to feel slighted. The failure to consult either of them about the trip (they had learned about it from newspapers) was a singular breach of political etiquette, arising from Connally's insistence that the White House deal with no one but him. Bruno conceded as much to Skelton, and Jenkins took the matter up with the Governor. Yet the snub was comparatively trivial. Presidential security was, or should have been, the overriding consideration. Skelton had felt so, and he had tried very hard to make his point.

Had the President known of Skelton's anxiety, he would doubtless have gone to Dallas anyhow. The visit had been announced. The city expected him. Backing out at this late date would have been extremely awkward. He was not a man to hide. Like Churchill, he believed that courage was the one quality which guaranteed all the rest. And as he had reminded Hale Boggs, a President of the United States is President of all the states. He cannot permit himself to be intimidated in any one of them. Threats are like 'Hail to the Chief'; they are part of the office. Even before Kennedy could be inaugurated a deranged man named Richard Paul Pavlick had wired seven sticks of dynamite on his own body in an attempt to blow up both himself and the President-elect, and during the first year of the new administration the White House had received nearly a thousand menacing letters. Some were quite frightening. Yet there was an air of unreality about all of them, for the confrontations with cheering crowds were so very different. It was true here, it was true abroad; everywhere Jacqueline Kennedy had gone with her husband he had been bathed in bright waves of affection. She couldn't even imagine anyone throwing a tomato at him.

Kennedy, of course, knew that the Presidency was a vulnerable position. Every chief of state is aware of the special hazards he faces. As the King of Italy remarked in 1897, after dodging the dagger thrust of a would-be assassin, '*Sono gli incerti del mestiere*'—'These are the risks of the job.' Later the King was, in fact, shot to death; it was a newspaper clipping about the deed which inspired the murderer of William McKinley. Franklin Roosevelt told his wife, 'If a man doesn't mind getting caught, he can make an attempt on the President's life,' and Eisenhower believed anyone could kill him, provided the killer was willing to forfeit his own life. Kennedy joked about it. In California an admirer of John F. Kennedy had tossed a tiny life jacket into the Chief Executive's car. There had been no advance notice. *Thump*—there it was on the seat between the President and Dave Powers. 'If anyone wanted to kill you, you wouldn't be around,' he told Dave. And shortly before the Texas trip, when a speeding motorist passed the car in Virginia, he remarked to Bartlett, 'They shouldn't allow that. He could have shot you, Charlie.' Powers and Bartlett had dutifully laughed. The subject really wasn't funny. Yet what else could you do?

Security, it seemed, rested in the strong, competent hands of the Secret Service. In the sixty-two years since the assassination of McKinley the Service had become a legend. No one suspected that it might be living on that legend, that some of its procedures had become stagnant or obsolescent. Yet they had. On any trip outside Washington, for example, Secret Service agents were obliged to rely heavily on co-operation from local law enforcement officers. Frank Wilson, Franklin D. Roosevelt's Secret Service Chief, had carefully evaluated the efficiency of police departments in every major American city. (Dallas, he had found, was one of the least efficient.) That practice had been discontinued. The Service now kept itself posted on only one municipal police force, New York's. In Chief Wilson's day, as in 1963, fear of snipers had been a constant headache. But in Roosevelt's motorcades agents standing on running boards had provided the President with a human shield. Fixed running boards were no longer practical. The Secret Service retained a follow-up car with them; on modern, low slung automobiles, however, they looked absurd. The last Presidential car to have them, a 1949 Lincoln Cosmopolitan, had been retired on July 1, 1953. Kennedy's car, a custom-built Lincoln which had been delivered to the White House on June 14, 1961, was equipped with hydraulic side steps which could be swung out from a dashboard control. They were supposed to serve as running boards. Unfortunately, the Secret Service design of them was faulty. Jutting out, they became lethal; they would have turned bystanders into casualties, so they were never used. In their absence the key agent in the car was the man behind the wheel. If the driver in Dallas had been provided with an emergency drill—cut the wheel and stand on the accelerator at the first sign of trouble—a gunman might have been limited to one shot. There was no such drill. Indeed, in a city like Dallas the Presidential chauffeur had to keep a sharp eye on the car immediately in front of him. He didn't know the route himself; he had never driven it before.

The final line of defence, which was to become crucial on November 22, 1963, was the individual agent's reflexive speed—his capacity to respond swiftly to an emergency. There were standardized tests to measure this ability. A red light flashed, the subject hit a brake pedal, the result was clocked on a dial calibrated in tenths of a second. Periodic examinations were required of jet pilots, among others.[3] Unfortunately the others did not include Presidential bodyguards. Agent Clint Hill, for example, had never heard of the tests, and at this writing, they remain a mystery at Secret Service headquarters. Even to experts physiological reaction is mysterious, but there are certain constants; a man's reflexes slow down as he ages, and the pace at which he lives may slow them still further. The Secret Service pace was furious. Congress encouraged an agent to

[3] Airline pilots provide an excellent illustration. Each six months they must demonstrate their proficiency in all the physical and mental skills required by their profession. This testing is done both in the aeroplane in which they fly and in special electronic flight simulators where performance in situations which would be hazardous in an actual aeroplane can be evaluated. Both normal and emergency manoeuvres are included. Second, the Federation Aviation Agency requires them to submit to strenuous physical examinations—also at six-month intervals—by designated aeromedical specialists. Finally, the airlines themselves give aircraft captains annual checkups.

drive himself. Under Public Law 763 he received no overtime pay whatever unless he had exceeded his shift schedule by seventy-eight hours during a three-month period. In 1963 there was no need to invoke the law. Men assigned to the White House Detail were married to their jobs; they were averaging between fifty and eighty hours of overtime *every* month. They didn't complain. Indeed, they had come to depend upon the additional pay to support their families. It increased agents' incomes by over $1,000 a year; they were earning as much as FBI men. There was one serious drawback. The strain was taking its toll and they knew it. 'At forty,' they said among themselves, 'a man on his detail is *old*.' The calibrated test dial would probably have agreed. Yet Service tradition dictated that the posts closest to Kennedy should be reserved for senior men. Bill Greer, who was to be the President's driver in Dallas, was fifty-four; Roy Kellerman, who would sit beside Greer, was forty-eight. Younger, more agile agents were relegated to advance assignments or, at best, to the follow-up car.

Legally, Douglas Dillon was answerable for any threat to John Kennedy's life. Congress had assigned the responsibility to the Secretary of the Treasury after McKinley's death. The Secret Service had continued to be part of the Treasury Department, but over the years agents had become indistinguishable from the President's personal staff. O'Donnell used them as messengers, and at airport stops they distributed PT-shaped tie clips among spectators. Campaigning was stimulating, they enjoyed it. As bodyguards, on the other hand, they sometimes felt frustrated. Kennedy, like Lincoln, refused to live in a cage. 'How do you protect this man?' an exasperated agent had asked Cardinal Cushing at Patrick's funeral. The young President was more active than Eisenhower, more anxious to be among the people, and, as O'Donnell once told Agent Jerry Behn, 'Politics and protection don't mix.' Yet one way *not* to protect him was to harry him with so many needless precautions that he bridled. Both Kennedys felt that the Service was overzealous at the wrong times—sitting on a placid stretch of beach, Mrs Kennedy had been dismayed to see agents in a Coast Guard cutter roaring down on a fisherman's rowboat. A consequence of such churlishness was that the President was inclined to overrule the Service, which meant that good advice was apt to be tossed out with the bad. It was a good idea, for example, to have agents perched on the broad trunk of the Presidential Lincoln when crowds threatened to grow disorderly. The trouble was that they were always there. Kennedy grew weary of seeing bodyguards roosting behind him every time he turned around, and in Tampa on November 18, just four days before his death, he dryly asked Agent Floyd Boring to 'keep those Ivy League charlatans off the back of the car'.

Boring wasn't offended. There had been no animosity in the remark. The President liked the men on the detail, and they knew it. They were, in fact, an extremely attractive group. 'Ivy League charlatans' may have been a trifle sharp, but it was descriptive. They were bright, lithe, virile, outgoing. Unfortunately, they were inclined to be tactless, and when President Kennedy had visited Venezuela the Attorney General had personally supervised his protection. Security on that trip had been airtight, with no unpleasant aftertaste. Venezuela had been a special situation. There had been real concern about the Chief Executive's safety there. Caracas had been, and continued to be, a notorious trouble spot. President Betancourt could be shot any day, President Kennedy told Hubert Humphrey the week before he took off for Texas.

No one, including Byron Skelton, dreamed that Kennedy's own plight was far graver than Betancourt's, though there were many who feared that he might be embarrassed in Dallas. Skelton's persistence set him apart, but his anxiety doesn't. Even as he was calling at National Committee headquarters in Washington, Evangelist Billy Graham was attempting to relay his own foreboding to Kennedy through Senator Smathers, a mutual friend. The Dallas mood was no secret. That same week Presidential assistant Fred Holborn called Henry Brandon of the London *Sunday Times* twice, advising him to make the Texas trip on the ground that there might be trouble; because of this tip from the White House Brandon was to be the only foreign correspondent in Dallas on November 22. In the United States the announcement that the President would visit there had provoked a widespread reaction. The most casual newspaper readers—even those who couldn't place the city on a map—knew that it had a history of ugly incidents. In the 1960 campaign a mob of Dallas housewives had sprayed the Lyndon Johnsons with saliva, and now, when Lady Bird thought of returning there, her hands made nervous fists. More recently, UN Ambassador Adlai E. Stevenson had been assaulted on UN Day, October 24. The following day Presidential Assistant Arthur M. Schlesinger, Jr. telephoned the Ambassador in Los Angeles, forwarding Kennedy's congratulations for calm behaviour under stress. Stevenson remarked that he had been shocked by the current of hatred in Dallas. He seriously wondered whether the President should go there and asked that his doubts be passed along. Schlesinger hung up, then hesitated. Would it do any good? He doubted it. The trip would proceed as planned; O'Donnell would merely believe that his view of Stevenson as a fussy old man had been sustained. Relations between the President and his Ambassador would have been damaged, to no purpose. Schlesinger was still undecided when Stevenson called back to withdraw his objections. Since leaving Dallas, Schlesinger concluded, Stevenson had regained his perspective.

Perhaps it was just the other way round. Adlai's judgment may have been more acute when he was on the scene. Evaluation now is difficult, for the recollections of all who had sounded the tocsin were soon to be coloured by events. Yet one thread binds every one of them. The closer an observer was to Dallas, the graver was his concern. Bill Greer, the Chief Executive's chauffeur, was tranquil. A native of Ireland, Greer regarded inland motorcades as safe; seaports, with their large foreign populations, seemed riskier to him. The Secret Service generally regarded Dallas as a tough town, and the Vice Presidential detail thought their man might be the target of a demonstration, but it was the experience of veteran agents that local communities feel honoured when a President visits them, and partisan feelings are put aside. Presidential advisers who knew Dallas by reputation—Douglas Dillon, Special Counsel Theodore C. Sorensen, Assistant Press Secretary Malcolm Kilduff—thought that there might be a few boos. To Texas Democrats living in Washington—Congressmen Gonzalez, Olin Teague, Jim Wright—the prospects were more ominous. They looked for placards or eggs. The state's small GOP delegation on the Hill scurried for cover. Senator John Tower declined an invitation to appear in Dallas on November 22, and Congressman Bruce Alger cancelled a banquet which was to have been held in the Marriott Hotel that evening in his honour. Texans in Texas were still more nervous. Connally told Kennedy he thought people in Dallas were 'too emotional', and that the stop there should be reconsidered. An Austin editor, contemplating Dallas, predicted that 'He will not get through this without something happening to him.'

Perhaps the most clear-cut warning to the President himself came from Senator J. William Fulbright of Arkansas, a liberal from a state which borders Texas. During his re-election campaign the year before Fulbright had been the target of violent attacks by the Dallas *News*. Because of the city's history of political violence he deeply distrusted it. Although he had friends there he had declined several invitations to visit them. He was afraid—physically afraid—and he readily admitted it. On October 3, the day before Kennedy's final planning conference with Connally, Fulbright pleaded with the President to by-pass Dallas. The Chief Executive and the Senator spent the better part of that Thursday together, flying to Little Rock in the Presidential aircraft and then by helicopter to Heber Springs for the dedication of Greers Ferry Dam. Both during the trip down and the luncheon which followed, Fulbright repeatedly declared, with all the emphasis he could command, that 'Dallas is a very dangerous place', that '*I* wouldn't go there', and 'Don't *you* go'.

In Dallas itself there was genuine alarm. Ralph Yarborough's two brothers, both Dallas lawyers, sent him almost identical accounts of widespread local hatred for the President. A Dallas woman wrote Salinger: 'Don't let the President come down here. I'm worried about him. I think something terrible will happen to him.' U.S. Attorney H. Barefoot Sanders, the ranking Justice Department official in that part of the state and the Vice President's contact man in Dallas, told Johnson's Cliff Carter that the city's political climate made the trip 'inadvisable'. Civic leadership had been jittery from the outset. The tide of local animosity towards the federal government had crossed the breakwater, and they knew it. They were openly concerned that crowds might become uncontrollable. 'I think we ought to see whether or not we can persuade President Kennedy to change his mind about visiting Dallas,' Stanley Marcus told his top executives. 'Frankly, I don't think this city is safe for it.'

Steps were taken to keep the turnout minimal. Ordinarily a Presidential visit is the occasion for a school holiday. If elections aren't imminent, and especially if a Chief Executive hasn't passed through a city recently, the proclamation of such a holiday can almost be assumed. Dallas decided to make an exception. Superintendent W. T. White stated that no pupil would be allowed to welcome the President unless his parents appeared and escorted him from the classroom. Indeed, members of the host committee didn't want many adults to see him either. They had opposed the motorcade. Inasmuch as they had packed the hall in which he was to speak with conservatives, this would have meant that the twelve hundred Dallas Democrats who had worked for Kennedy's election in 1960 wouldn't even have seen him, so they were overruled there. They had succeeded in preventing any formal stops (the small but hardy band of Dallas liberals wanted him to pause and dedicate something, *anything*), and their choice of the hall itself had been accepted. The possibility of any intruder crashing the luncheon seemed remote. It was to be a small, polite, catered affair in the arboreal Trade Mart, with the President surrounded by the architectural pride of Dallas: balconies, an indoor pond, live trees, a fountain that could shoot clear up to the ceiling, and parakeets flying around wild. In what passed for wit in Dallas those days one entrepreneur told another entrepreneur that he would try to arrange a few parakeet droppings in Kennedy's soup.

This, however, was a very private remark. The public thrust was towards the creation of a favourable atmosphere on short notice. The

Mayor asked Dallas to redeem itself and shed its reputation as the 'Southwest hate capital of Dixie'. The president of the Chamber of Commerce and the chairman of the Citizens Council requested citizens to refrain from demonstrating. Both newspapers ran editorials calling for restraint; the *Times-Herald* hoped 'both the world and John F. Kennedy will like what is seen here', and even the *News*, the bonfire of the right, conceded that 'another incident similar to the one involving Stevenson could deal Dallas a deadly blow on the national level, particularly from a political standpoint'. On November 18 the City Council rushed through an ordinance outlawing attacks on visiting speakers. Two days later Jesse Curry took action. Almost any step was a giant step for Curry. The police chief in the city which was to become the scene of the crime of the century was bland and ineffective. Still, the more incisive leaders of the business community had impressed upon him that these were exceptional circumstances. Accordingly, he publicly put Dallas on notice that his department would take 'immediate action to block any improper conduct' Friday. He went further. If uniformed officers were inadequate to protect this guest, he declared, private individuals were entitled to make citizen's arrests. A police chief who reminds the public of the right of citizen's arrest is fingering the panic button. He is, in effect, designating each individual a deputy. Yet Curry's forces were hardly understrength. He had drawn on every available reserve, cancelling all departmental leave and marshalling seven hundred policemen, firemen, sheriffs, state police, Texas Rangers, and agents of the Texas Department of Public Safety, the Governor's FBI. The city glittered with badges. Dallas had never seen such rigid security.

The occasion for these unprecedented precautions was a visit by the President of the United States.

There was a chorus of warnings: And then there was a catastrophe. Between the two lies an abyss which can never be adequately explored——

Between the idea
And the reality . . .
Falls the Shadow.[4]

Ten months after the tragedy the Warren Commission found 'no evidence' of any connection between the crime of Lee Harvey Oswald and the city's 'general atmosphere of hate'. It should be noted that the finding was a consensus. Individual commissioners had strong reservations. The verdict was influenced by expediency. The

[4] T. S. Eliot, *The Hollow Men*.

Commission's members hoped their report would receive the widest possible acceptance. A majority believed that conjecture about Dallas might tend to discredit their other findings. Therefore they hedged. They acknowledged that the assassin had known of Dallas' political tension, but they concluded that there was 'no way to judge what the effect of the general political ferment present in that city might have been, even though Oswald was aware of it'.

The key word here is 'judge'. Obviously, it is impossible to define the exact relationship between an individual and his environment. One might as well try to photograph nostalgia or submit passion as an exhibit. Honour, integrity, and love—and hate—cannot be pierced with thumbtacks and displayed on bulletin boards. Yet all exist. Some motives lie beyond the rules of evidence. Like the shadow

Between the emotion
And the response . . .
Between the desire
And the spasm[5]

they are elusive. If we discuss them, we are speculating. But legitimate speculation is one of the duties of historians. Their sources cannot be confined to fingerprints, ballistics tests, and spectrographic examinations. The Dallas assassin did not belong to a conventional criminal conspiracy. This is conceded. It may also be beside the point. Lee Oswald was called 'a loner'. Nearly everyone seized upon the word to describe him, and also to explain him. They were all wrong. It is true that he had a one-track mind. The mind of every assassin runs on a narrow-gauge track. But there are no loners. No man lives in a void. His every act is conditioned by his time and his society. John Wilkes Booth was not an agent of the Confederacy. Despite early assumptions, he had acted on his own. But his victim was murdered at a critical hour in our history, in a city swarming with Southern sympathizers and hardened by seditious talk. Establishing the precise link between deed, era, and locale is a hopeless task, yet to suggest that there was no relationship—that the crime in Ford's Theatre could have been committed in a serene community, untroubled by crisis—is absurd.

Like Booth, Oswald was to be slain by a vigilante who thwarted interrogation. Nevertheless the stage he had chosen survived him, and a great deal is known about the community which worried Byron Skelton, Senator Fulbright, and so many others. On November 15 the Department of Justice had sent O'Donnell a confidential, comprehensive report on Dallas. Most of the 747,000 residents, it noted,

[5] *Ibid.*

were native Americans of 'Anglo-Saxon, Scotch–Irish stock', and lately the population had been growing rapidly, the largest group of newcomers arriving from rural Texas, Louisiana, and Arkansas. In the metropolis these transplanted Southerners remained 'conservative politically and socially', for their new community shared their outlook: 'Dallas's political conservatism stems from a fundamentalist religious training and years of conditioning.' Recently this viewpoint had sharpened. Attitudes had become 'overtly active' and 'politically militant' with 'the maturity of independent oil wealth, and the recent industrialization'.

Dallas money was new money, and there was a lot of it. In the South Dallas outranked all other cities in manufacturing, wholesaling, insurance, and banking, and each October it was the site of the largest state fair in the nation. The older families, whose wealth had come from cotton, were overshadowed; power had passed to the new men. In many ways they used it admirably. Wherever racial integration threatened to become a problem, they yielded quietly. Status-conscious and civic-minded, they presided over a clean city, free of corruption and relatively free of commercial vice (heavy fines had driven professional prostitutes thirty-two miles away, into neighbouring Fort Worth), and the city fathers displayed a resolute interest in the Dallas Symphony Orchestra, the Dallas Civic Opera, the Museum of Fine Arts. They were frankly image-conscious. Culture and learning contributed to a pleasing civic façade; O'Donnell had a surfeit of facts about Dallas Baptist College, Bishop College, Southern Methodist University, and the University of Texas Southwestern Medical School and its many clinics in an institution named—a knell—Parkland Memorial Hospital.

Images are greasepaint. The truth about a city cannot be gleaned from its advertisements about itself. Other indices are more reliable, among them local voting patterns. In 1963 Dallas was a Republican stronghold. Its occupational profile alone would have cinched that. A phenomenal 53.5 per cent of its wage earners were professional men, managers, salesmen, or clerks. White-collar, 97 per cent Protestant, and swollen by thousands of smalltown former rustics who had been freed from traditional Democratic allegiances, the city had been acclaimed in a local editorial as 'a centre of resurgent Republicanism'. Actually, it was more of an enclave. The surrounding countryside remained unconverted. Thirty miles north of 'Big D', as the city liked to be called, lay the Fourth Congressional District, 220,000 voters strong. The district, which had been Sam Rayburn's domain, was still solidly Democratic. In 1960 Kennedy and Nixon ran neck and neck in seventy-one of north-east Texas' seventy-two counties. Big D, the spectacular exception, rejected Kennedy overwhelmingly (by 62.5 per cent), while re-electing a Republican Congressman and eight Republican legislators. Dallas had become the despair of Byron Skelton. He had long ago conceded the lion's share of its 1964 vote to the opposition.

His warnings to Washington hadn't been inspired by partisanship, however. A National Committeeman doesn't court votes by hiding his candidate. If Skelton had been determined to improve Kennedy's showing, he would have wanted the people of Dallas to see the President. That wasn't the problem. There was something else in the city, something unrelated to conventional politics—a stridency, a disease of the spirit, a shrill, hysterical note suggestive of a deeply troubled society. In Dallas this was particularly dismaying because for some time the city's cherished image had been blemished by a dark streak of violence. The harlots and the grafters had gone, but the killers were multiplying. Texas led the United States in homicide, and Big D led Texas. There were more murders in Dallas each month than in all England, and none of them could be traced to the underworld or to outsiders; they were the work of Dallas citizens. In the past year the figure had grown by 10 per cent. Furthermore, nearly three out of every four slayings (72 per cent) were by gunfire, for Big D had no requirement for firearms registration, no firearms control of any sort; the one attempt at such legislation had been struck down by a local court. Before November 22 there had been 110 Dallas murders in 1963. Brutal death had become part of the way of life; it was discussed almost casually. The day the Presidential visit was announced Abraham Zapruder, a dress manufacturer who had moved down from New York, engaged a stranger in an informal civil rights debate. The man conceded that Washington had the power to back racial equality. 'God made big people,' he said of Kennedy. Pointing to himself he added, 'And God made little people.' Then he drawled, 'But Colt made the .45 to even things out.' Zapruder was taken aback. He had never heard such talk in Manhattan's garment district. He snapped, 'People like you we don't need.'

Nevertheless they were there. In that third year of the Kennedy Presidency a kind of fever lay over Dallas County. Mad things happened. Huge billboards screamed 'Impeach Earl Warren'. Jewish stores were smeared with crude swastikas. Fanatical young matrons swayed in public to the chant, 'Stevenson's going to die—his heart will stop, stop, stop, and he will burn, burn, burn!' Radical Right polemics were distributed in public schools; Kennedy's name was booed in class-rooms; junior executives were required to attend radical seminars. Dallas had become the mecca for medicine-show evangelists of the National Indignation Convention, the Christian

Crusaders, the Minutemen, the John Birch and Patrick Henry societies, and the headquarters of H. L. Hunt and his peculiar activities. In Dallas a retired major general flew the American flag upside down in front of his house, and when, on Labour Day of 1963, the Stars and Stripes were hoisted right side up outside his own home by County Treasurer Warren G. Harding—named by Democratic parents for a Republican President in an era when all Texas children were taught to respect the Presidency, regardless of party—Harding was accosted by a physician's son, who remarked bitterly, 'That's the Democrat flag. Why not just run up the hammer and sickle while you're at it?'

This was more than partisan zeal. It was a chiaroscuro that existed outside the two parties, a virulence which had infected members of both. Undoubtedly many of the noisiest radicals were Republicans, and one of their popular local heroes in the city was Congressman Alger, best remembered for his presence during Mrs Johnson's spit shower three years earlier. But in Dallas County the other party wasn't much different. Most Democratic candidates offered the voters, not a choice, but a radical echo. The Congressman at Large from Big D, a son of a bedding manufacturer, was technically a Democrat. It didn't matter. In Washington Joe Pool was scarcely distinguishable from Alger. Heavily backed by Dallas' big money, he fought civil rights, called for an end to all foreign aid, described the Defence Department as an insult to the Dallas Federation of Women's Clubs (and demanded that it apologize), and told his constituents that the Kennedy administration had 'turned my stomach'. Pool denied that he never did anything constructive; he was extremely proud of his perfect attendance record at sessions of the House Un-American Activities Committee. On the Hill he was regarded as a curiosity; at home he was just another typical Dallas Democrat. After all, it had been thirty-one years since the Dallas County Executive Committee had supported the national ticket. General Edwin Walker was a Dallas Democrat; so, for that matter, was H. L. Hunt. Mayor Earle Cabell had been elected on the Democratic ticket, which, in the Alice-in-Wonderland of local Republican oratory, made him 'the Socialist Mayor of Dallas'. But that was just political pyrotechnics. Even Birchers knew Earle Cabell wasn't really a dedicated conscious agent of the Communist conspiracy. Five years earlier he had backed Alger; he was a past president of the ultra-conservative Texas Manufacturers Association, and he had been present when the local chapter of the Birch Society was founded in a Dallas hotel suite. After November 22, 1963, when political fashions suddenly changed, the Mayor's memory of his past associations became extremely hazy. He had been converted; he was now a Johnsonian Democrat on most issues. And he hadn't actually joined the Society that evening. He and Elizabeth 'Dearie' Cabell—the pet names of Texas politicians' wives become part of the public domain—listened to the tape-recorded indoctrination lecture and left. But their friends were members, and he was as cognizant of, and as respectful of, the prevailing political winds as any German functionary of the early 1930's. Cabell had attended the meeting because he had been told that the subject was to be anti-Communism. He and Dearie had to be concerned about that. Rightist enthusiasm was a civic responsibility, like the Dallas Council of Churches and the Dallas Cowboys, and thirty of the Mayor's cronies, all businessmen, joined in a tribute to Robert Welch, the eminent candy manufacturer, at the Dallas Statler Hilton.

Two Congressmen, a mayor, a retired general, and a resident billionaire would form an impressive phalanx in any city. There were other spokesmen of Dallas' rebellious mood: the stocky, cowboy-booted executives who affixed 'KO the Kennedys' stickers to their chrome bumpers; the bleached-blonde dowagers with the fun game, 'Which Kennedy do you hate the most?' (correct answers: [1] Bobby, [2] Jack, [3] Teddy, [4] Jackie); and the prosperous, well-educated young marrieds who gathered over jumbo highballs in the suburbs of Highland Park and University Park to swap jokes about assassination, gags about the hot line to the Vatican that ended in a Rome sewer, stories about Jack walking on water while Jackie water-skied, and lewd gossip—best told by wags who could imitate a Boston accent—about the First Family.

Dallas had no corner on hate. Blaming the President is an American custom almost as old as bundling. He is, after all, the biggest target in the land, and the formation of every Presidential cult is followed by the congealment of an anti-cult. 'Remember,' Woodrow Wilson warned his daughter when his first administration was sailing along smoothly, 'the pack is always waiting to tear one to pieces.' Andrew Jackson was portrayed as an adulterer, Lincoln as a baboon, Harry Truman as an incompetent haberdasher. Thomas Jefferson was 'Mad Tom', and even Washington was scarred. 'I am accused of being the enemy of America, and subject to the influence of a foreign country,' he wrote Mad Tom, '. . . and every act of my Administration is tortured, in such exaggerated and indecent terms as could scarcely be applied to Nero, to a notorious defaulter, or even to a common pickpocket.'

Some of the Lone Star faithful looked forward to the induction into the Presidency of a lanky, two-gunned non-fictional John Wayne. That spring Cuban exiles living in Miami received a broadside declaring: 'Only through one development will you Cuban patriots ever live again in your homeland as freemen, responsible as must be the most capable, for the guidance and welfare of the Cuban people.' This blessing would come to pass

> if an inspired Act of God should place in the White House within weeks a Texan known to be a friend of all Latin Americans . . . though he must under present conditions bow to the Zionists who since 1905 came into control of the United States, and for whom Jack Kennedy and Nelson Rockefeller and other members of the Council of Foreign Relations and allied agencies are only stooges and pawns. Though Johnson must now bow to these crafty and cunning Communist-hatching Jews, yet, did an Act of God suddenly elevate him into the top position (he) would revert to what his beloved father and grandfather were, and to their values and principles and loyalties.

The dodger, decorated with cowpokes and a profile of the Alamo, was dated April 18, 1963, and signed, 'A Texan who resents the Oriental influence that has come to control, to degrade, to pollute and enslave his own people.'

A strong President must expect abuse. Kennedy had established a vigorous Presidency, and the pullulation of radicals (who had been relatively quiet under his less assertive predecessor) had followed. In some small communities they dominated local society. But they were nearly always a conspicuous minority. When the *Delaware State News* of October 18, 1963, declared, 'Yes, Virginia, there is a Santa Claus. His name right now happens to be Kennedy—let's shoot him, literally, before Christmas,' the editor's colleagues were shocked, and he was denounced. What set Dallas apart was its size and the lack of any effective opposition. There was no debate, because there was no rebuttal. Dallas was the one American metropolis in which incitement to violence had become respectable. Welch had been regaled by the local establishment. Stevenson's visit was boycotted by them, and admirers of the President—indeed, of the Presidency, for the cancer had grown that malignant—had been few, dispirited, and mute. It is a remarkable fact that when President Kennedy had arrived in Dallas on October 10, 1961, to visit Sam Rayburn's deathbed, he had been greeted by just one public official: the chief of police.

The apparent unanimity baffled outsiders, including fellow Texans. Congressman Gonzalez, whose Bexar County was as heavily Democratic as Dallas was Republican, came to Dallas to receive an NAACP award. He departed bewildered. The ceremony was held in a little Baptist church, and it was like a meeting of the underground. The hosts seemed terrified; they glanced nervously over their shoulders, spoke quickly, thrust the plaque in his hands, and disbanded. After returning to Washington Gonzalez had the impression that the whole experience had been a bad dream. He joked about it; he said he wouldn't campaign there without a safe-conduct, and he told the President, 'Dallas is like the Congo. It isn't ready for self-government.' Actually he had things backwards. Self-government was precisely what Dallas lacked. In its absence the community was ruled by a committee of powerful merchants. As the Justice Department report to O'Donnell put it, 'Dallas leadership is now centred in a Citizens Council composed of its chief business executives.' Since 1937 key decisions had been made by the thirty members of this group and its political arm, the Citizens Charter Association. In the selection of local officials they functioned much like a Hanseatic oligarchy picking medieval burgomasters. Most of the lieges weren't radicals themselves. They were merely distrustful of democratic disorder, confident that their benevolent despotism provided a more efficient substitute. Because they displayed an astonishing indifference towards radical excesses, however, they bore a heavy responsibility for the city's political atmosphere. In that climate—in the vacuum which should have been filled by a healthy diversity of opinion—the strange ideology of the Right had sprouted and flourished. It was malevolent and nihilistic, and on American soil it had an alien look.

Its roots weren't alien—that was what gave it such an enormous appeal for men bewildered by the complex challenges of the 1960's. The origins of Dallas' implacable hostility to the New Frontier lay in a profound longing for the values, real and imagined, of the old frontier. No one could successfully depict John Kennedy as a plainsman. Even the Moscow cartoonists, who liked to draw every American leader as a sinister cowhand, had to give it up. Chaps didn't look right on him, tooled boots wouldn't fit, and a five-gallon hat was preposterous. His legs weren't bowed. He never loped or spat. His accent evoked no memories of the golden West—it was almost another language—and his *Weltansicht* was entirely lacking in yippee.

This, for knee-jerk absolutists, was the sticking point. Kennedy's private wealth and starchy New England vowels were bad enough. The ultimate outrage, however, was his challenge to their tribal instincts. The President, for example, was a thoughtful man. That sounds harmless, even estimable. But on yesterday's frontier the man who paused to think didn't survive; he had to rely on ginger and instinct and attack his problems, not with reason, but with his bare fists. Kennedy refused to give the world a kick in the old kazzazza. Instead, he called for diversity, tolerance, non-conformity. For the man who kept faith with yesterday, this was a desecration. Pioneer society had demanded total conformity. Everyone had to stick together, wear the same label, and circle the wagons against disaster. It had to be that way; otherwise the Indians would have wiped out the lot.

So the Eastern stranger was a threat. In some cases 'religion' had taught the sons of yesterday how to deal with such threats. On the evening of November 20, when the President was receiving the Supreme Court in the executive mansion, a snowy-haired man who described his occupation as 'itinerant preaching' told the five thousand delegates to the Baptist General Convention of Texas that the American electorate had made 'one of the greatest blunders in its history when it put a Roman Catholic President in the White House'. Religious convictions, said the Rev. J. Sidlow Baxter, must outweigh political loyalties. In 1964 he urged them 'to vote not Democrat or Republican, but Protestant'. His audience rose in acclamation, cheering 'Amen'.

That was the choice. It was as simple as that. Stevenson had told his Dallas hecklers, 'I believe in the forgiveness of sin and the redemption of ignorance'; they believed in neither. Of course, they had no intention of killing the President. They didn't even discuss it seriously. Dallas' assassination jokes were meant as diversions. The germ of piety, however, was very real. The fundamentalist attacks on Kennedy carried strong overtones of Isaiah and Jeremiah, and the thunder of moral indignation is clearly evident in the editorials of the Dallas *Morning News,* whose anti-administration crusade was the key to Big D's absolutism.

The *News* was the oldest business institution in the state, dating back to 1842, when Texas was a republic. Nearly everyone read it—Lee Harvey Oswald pored over its columns, and even Byron Skelton subscribed so his wife could keep abreast of the Neiman-Marcus ads. The publisher and chairman of the board was E. M. 'Ted' Dealey, a heavy man with green-tinted spectacles, a voice like a file, and an unflinching devotion to what he called 'the spirit of Kit Carson and Daniel Boone'. As the most venerable voice in Dallas, the *News,* under Dealey's leadership, had made radical extremism reputable in the early 1960's. In the fall of 1961 he was one of a group of Texas publishers who had been invited to a White House lunch. To the astonishment of his fellow guests he had produced and read aloud a savage indictment of his host. He wanted everyone to know that Ted Dealey was no moron 'to be led around by the nose' or lured 'to your side by soft soap'. He had reached the conclusion that 'We can annihilate Russia and should make that clear to the Soviet government.' Unfortunately for America, he said, 'You and your Administration are weak sisters.' What was needed was 'a man on horseback to lead this nation, and many people in Texas and the Southwest think that you are riding Caroline's tricycle'.

The President had flushed. He could ignore incivility, but—and this was what Dealey would never understand—he resented the allusion to his three-year-old daughter. She had nothing to do with this, and introducing her name was the act of a clod. Frostily Kennedy replied, 'Wars are easier to talk about than they are to fight. I'm just as tough as you are, and I didn't get elected President by arriving at soft judgments.' That answer was omitted from the *News* account of the incident ('GRASSROOTS SENTIMENT TOLD'). Instead, the editors ran readers' reactions ('COMMENT HEAVILY ENDORSES DEALEY STATEMENT TO JFK'), including tributes from Bruce Alger and H. L. Hunt. 'Thank the Lord for a man with the guts to say what you said,' wrote one admirer, and another asked, 'Why the kid gloves?' The *News* reported that it had received over two thousand phone calls, telegrams, and letters, and that over 84 per cent of them had expressed approval.

There is no reason to doubt that report. To staunch subscribers—and to viewers of television station WFAA, which was owned by the A. H. Belco Corporation, which was owned by Dealey—the publisher's stand had been unexceptionable. Roy S. Truly, superintendent of the Book Depository, disapproved strongly of Kennedy's policies abroad and believed he was a 'race mixer' at home. Ron Fischer, a young clerk in the nearby county auditor's office, regarded the President as 'a real leftist' who had 'let those men get murdered' in Cuba. To Howard L. Brennan, a forty-four-year-old pipefitter working in the same neighbourhood, Kennedy had been 'too soft in the Cuban missile crisis'. Lee Oswald's brother Robert had voted the Democratic ticket in 1960. Now, concerned about 'socialism and big government', he had become a Goldwater backer.

In the two months before John Kennedy's last trip to Texas there was something almost Orwellian about the *News*. To understand some passages, you had to know the code—there were references to Franklin D. Roosevelt's 'Queer Deal', the 'American Swivel Liberties Union', and 'the Judicial Kremlin' (the United States Supreme Court). The national capital was a bizarre city inhabited by 'an unknown number of subversives, perverts, and miscellaneous security risks' and ruled by a dangerous faker. Occasionally members of the *News* staff disagreed about what sort of faker he was. Sometimes he was dismissed as an idiot—when the Nuclear Test Ban Treaty was signed, he was branded '50 times a fool'. Other times he appeared to be a cunning thief—'although definite proof' had 'not yet been established', it seemed that he had accepted a

'$22,000 bribe from a swindler' to stop certain deportation proceedings. More often he was portrayed as a Judas who followed 'the communist line, which is an atheistic, godless line'; who supported forces of disorder with 'communist-front affiliations'; who championed unwed motherhood, welfare chisellers, and 'compulsory unionism'; and who was eager to take 'a man's income tax and, without his permission, spend it abroad as "foreign aid" in countries which deny the existence of a Supreme Creator'.

But it is idle to look for subtle delineations in the *News*'s concept of the President. The paper was mounting an all-out assault on the President. On October 10 readers learned that 'Mr Kennedy's State Department' had 'loudly objected to seizure of power by anti-communist forces' in the Dominican Republic and Honduras. Earlier in the month an editorial had hailed publication of a bitterly anti-Kennedy book, written by a captious writer, who, according to one of the closest confidants of Kennedy, had never met the President. Now the paper began serialization of the text, with an editor's note assuring subscribers that since 'all the facts are documented', the author could and would 'introduce you to the real John F. Kennedy'.

Given time, the heaviest ironies pass unnoticed. No one thought it singular that the façade of the *News* building should carry the credo, sculpted in gigantic letters:

BUILD THE NEWS UPON THE ROCK OF TRUTH AND RIGHTEOUSNESS CONDUCTED ALWAYS UPON THE LINES OF FAIRNESS AND INTEGRITY ACKNOWLEDGE THE RIGHT OF THE PEOPLE TO GET FROM THE NEWSPAPER BOTH SIDES OF EVERY IMPORTANT QUESTION

—G. B. DEALEY.

George B. Dealey (1859–1946) was Ted's father. His statue, visible from the building, dominates a little park three blocks down Houston Street. There stands George, sturdily facing downtown Dallas in a bronze business suit, his broad bronze back turned to four bas-relief panels acclaiming Dealey contributions to local journalism, history, philanthropy, and civic leadership. Beyond the panels lies a railroad overpass (underpass if you are a motorist) spanning traffic from Commerce, Main, and Elm streets. In New England the green area would be designated a common. Readers of the *News* have long known it as Dealey Plaza, and as such it has become at least as famous as Ford's Theatre. This is as sardonic as the credo. For the memorial was an afterthought. The park itself was built between 1938 and 1940 by the WPA, which, as every old *News* subscriber knows, was the most notorious boondoggle of FDR's Queer Deal.

In some respects the plaza itself is queer. It rather resembles a crude baseball diamond built on a slope. The green is fan-shaped and flanked by curious little white concrete bleachers whose real function is obscure. They can only be meant to be ornamental. On most days the spectacle is quite boring—all you can see is the statuary, stagnant pools on either side, and three noisy streams of automobiles—and anyone anxious for a good view would ignore them and ascend to an upper floor of one of the adjacent buildings. The most prominent of these is the sore-eyed, tan brick structure at the corner of Houston and Elm which began as railroad offices, became a branch of the John Deere Plow Company, served later as the headquarters of a wholesaler for fancy groceries, and was converted, early in the 1960's, to a warehouse for the Texas School Depository. The interior is grimy, the two freight elevators are temperamental. But if you really want a proper perspective of the Dealey Memorial, the north-east window on the sixth floor of the warehouse is incomparable.

Book One
CHARCOAL

1

WAND

Before breakfast on Thursday, November 1, the President of the United States drew on his back brace, laced his shoes, the left one of which had a quarter-inch medical lift, slipped into the clothes his valet had selected, anchored his conservative tie with a bright PT boat clip, and pocketed a black leather wallet containing $26 in bills, a gold St Christopher medal which was clipped to it, and Massachusetts driving permit 053332D. As usual, his signature was as legible as a doctor's prescription, but the text identified the licensee as John F. Kennedy of 122 Bowdoin Street, Boston. It warned that unless this licence was renewed, his right to drive in the Commonwealth would expire on May 29, 1965, making him subject to arrest by Massachusetts State Police, and it gave a terse description of the potential offender: height 6/00, hair code 4 (brown), eye code 6 (grey), date of birth 05/29/17. The small card was the only identification he carried.

He inspected the reflection in his bedroom mirror before setting out. The dresser glass was cluttered. Thrust into the frame at odd angles were a picture postcard of the Kennedy 'ancestral home' in Ireland; another postcard from Amalfi, Italy ('I like Italy better than Hyannis but I like Hyannis a little bit more because there's fairs. I miss you daddy very much X Caroline'); a scribbled schedule of Washington Masses ('St Stephen's 8, 9, 10, 11 high, 12 noon; Holy Trinity 8, 9, 10 high, 11.15, 12.05; St Matthew's 10 high, 11.30, 12.30'); a snapshot of Caroline standing in her mother's shoes; a Polaroid shot of Jackie; and an old photograph of Jack, Jackie, Bob, and Ethel. In the group picture Jackie seemed thoughtful, Ethel and Bob were beaming, and the President himself was conspicuously youthful. He lacked that look this morning. Nearly three years in the White House had taken their toll. His code 4 hair was flecked with grey, his face was lined, especially around the mouth. Eisenhower continued to call him 'the boy', but at forty-six he obviously had his full growth and then some. Yesterday at the pool he had weighed in at exactly 172½. He was in fighting trim and in the prime of life. The reflection in the looking glass was that of what physicians call a ruddy, well-nourished, Caucasian male. His Lindbergh profile was still lean and handsome, his code 6 eyes were clear, his complexion glowed, with just a faint touch of crimson at the temples. The swing into Florida had given him a light tan. He looked like a successful, confident American father about to embark on a crucial business trip, which is precisely what he was.

'Caroline!' he called. 'John!'

He clapped his hands, and they came running—John in plaid short pants, Caroline in a blue leotard and a dark blue velvet dress. Maude Shaw had told the children that their parents were going to Texas. That meant nothing to John, but his sister had learned a lot of geography from her father's trips. She liked to make the partings which preceded them memorable. Last night she had chosen her clothes with special care and laid them out by her bed—to Miss Shaw's exasperation, she had changed her mind in the morning—and she had been primping just outside, awaiting the deep, familiar voice of command. The President knew it was unwise to disregard her sprucing; you ignored now and paid later. He murmured a gallant compliment and swept on to the table, trailing them in his wake.

Their mother was having her hair combed, so they had him pretty much to themselves at breakfast, babbling excitedly as he riffled through the newspapers and telephoned an instruction to Under Secretary of Defence Ross Gilpatric. At 9.15 the President's daughter had to go to school. She embraced him and whispered ''Bye, Daddy' (''*Bye, Caroline*') and was gone in a twinkle of thin, blue-clad legs. The President left for the West Wing a half-hour later, but there was no farewell for John. Kennedy liked to spend as much time as possible with his son; he intended to take him to the airport. The little boy bided his time, playing with toy planes and watching the cloudy sky outside. A fine, smoke-coloured rain had begun to fall.

The President spent a crowded hour in his office. Two more U.S. ambassadors received their marching orders (to Upper Volta and Gabon). He then signed Air Force promotion lists for God McHugh, telephoned Bob Kennedy and Arthur Goldberg, inscribed a book for Professor Clinton Rossiter, autographed a picture for a Worcester, Massachusetts, school superintendent, phoned Bob again, and sent his personal condolences to the survivors of five American servicemen who had made the supreme sacrifice abroad. 'I want you to know,' he wrote two Texas children, that your father was an outstanding soldier who repeatedly demonstrated his loyalty and devotion to duty. These fine qualities won for him the respect and admiration of those with whom he served. As you grow older you will realize the full importance of the service your father rendered his country and will take pride and comfort in the knowledge that his countrymen are deeply grateful for his contribution to the security of the Nation. Mrs Kennedy joins me in extending our heartfelt sympathy to you in the loss of your father.[1]

He strolled into the Cabinet Room and admired the draperies which had been hung yesterday. Fingering the red border of one, he called to Evelyn, 'When do we get ours?' 'While we're in Texas,' she called back. 'Rugs, too?' he asked. 'Rugs, too,' she assured him. 'Good,' he said. 'When we get back we'll have new offices.' Then he told her to get Ted Sorensen, and Ted entered with his Texas speeches. They had been bouncing drafts back and forth for a week. It was an old routine, and although the result was joint authorship it bore the unmistakable JFK stamp, for Ted had adopted the literary style which could be discerned in Kennedy's first book, published thirteen years before the two men met. The President was concerned now about his Trade Mart speech. He wanted to be sure Dallas got the message, so they sat across from the old nautical desk Mrs Kennedy had resurrected from a White House storeroom, donned their glasses, and sat in intent silence while the President pored over the original and Ted fingered a carbon.

'It's good,' the President finally said. But the Dallas *News* wouldn't think it good. Sorensen had preserved his toughest passages, and Kennedy could be as rough as a Pier 6 brawl in Boston's old Ward 8. 'There will always be dissident voices heard in the land,' Big D's tycoons and their wives were to be told, 'expressing opposition without alternatives, finding fault but never favour, perceiving gloom on every side and seeking influence without responsibility. These voices are inevitable. But today other voices are heard in the land—voices preaching doctrines wholly unrelated to reality, wholly unsuited to the Sixties, doctrines which apparently assume that words will suffice without weapons, that vituperation is as good as victory and that peace is a sign of weakness.' The right-wing notion 'that this nation is headed for defeat through deficit, or that strength is but a matter of slogans', he would say, 'is nothing

[1] Kennedy personally wrote the family of every American who died in uniform during his Presidency. The lines to Box 813, Kirbyville, Texas, are particularly eloquent, but there were between forty and fifty such letters each month. Whenever one of them produced a reply, he invited the widow and children to Washington for a talk in the Rose Garden.

but just plain nonsense'. Strength, he would conclude acidly, is meaningless without righteousness—'For as was written long ago: "Except the Lord keep the city, the watchman waketh but in vain." '

The President worried his ear lobe. Maybe he should leaven the text with a little wit. Weren't there some good stories about Texas? Ted said he'd consult his joke file. He departed in pursuit of mirth, and the President rang for Evelyn. 'How about this weather report?' he asked. He waved Godfrey McHugh's forecast. 'I want that checked.' At 10.42 a.m. she tiptoed back with bad news. There was a new prediction from Texas. The next two days would be hot. 'Hot?' Kennedy cried in dismay. He lunged for his telephone console and dialled his wife's maid's extension. 'Pack some cool dresses,' he said urgently. Fresh dismay on the other end, a stream of excited Spanish (Provi had never really mastered English), and then the stammer: 'Too late, Meester President. They are all packed. Muggsy'—Muggsy O'Leary, Kennedy's Jack-of-all-trades—'peeked them up at nine o'clock. They are already in thee chopper.' Kennedy hung up and swore mightily under his breath. All his careful planning, all his precautions to make certain that his wife would have a good time, and now debacle. He pictured her riding in the Dallas motorcade, perspiring in that pink suit, and made a grim face at Evelyn Lincoln.

God had blundered badly. It wasn't the first time, either. Before the Caracas trip McHugh had confidently promised blue skies, and when they landed the airport was being lashed by a driving rainstorm; the President and the First Lady had been obliged to stand at attention, drenched and frozen, through both the Venezuelan and American national anthems. There had been plenty of rockets over that. McHugh's alibi had been that his forecast had been passed on sea-level temperatures and Caracas was in the mountains. It wouldn't happen again, he had vowed, and to make certain that it didn't he had mobilized every veteran meteorologist in the government. Before a trip McHugh would assemble reports from the U.S. Weather Bureau, from Andrews Field, and from the weather bureau at the Chief Executive's destination. Data would be accumulated on the present and on the predictable future. Godfrey hadn't stopped there; he had purchased three expensive thermometers in Washington. One would be assigned to an advance man who would stand on a ramp at the very spot where the President would disembark from Aircraft 26000. A second reading would be taken inside the downtown hall where he was to speak, and a third at the next stop on his schedule. All these statistics were incorporated in a formal procès-verbal to the Commander in Chief from Brigadier General Godfrey

McHugh, USAF. It was very military, and it was infuriating, because for reasons unknown to its inventor the system didn't work. The result was this Thursday-morning dilemma.

Kennedy's blood was up. He dialled McHugh's extension, chewed him out, and summoned O'Donnell. 'Damn it, Kenny, let's check with local airports from now on,' he stormed. 'Or let Mrs Lincoln do it. The whole United States Air Force mounts a high-level mission against a not-so-very-difficult target and misses it completely, and then my secretary gets on the horn and scores a bull's-eye. From now on, clear it with Mrs Lincoln. She's accurate. She's also cheaper.' He swore again. 'Hot. *Hot.* Jackie's clothes are all packed and they're the *wrong* clothes.' Another oath. He rose, wrathful. 'Yes, Ted. What is it?'

The unlucky intruder was Ted Reardon, the oldest member of the Irish-Harvard mafia, who had been with the President since Kennedy's freshman term in Congress. Reardon had an administrative problem. Christmas and New Year's Day were going to come in the middle of the week this year. The last time that had happened Eisenhower had been President, and Ike had given all government employees a half-day off on the eve of each holiday. Reardon thought that was a good precedent.

Still mad, the President gave him a baleful look. 'They get twenty-six days a year as it is. Why should they be given any time at all?'

'It's Christmas, boss!' Reardon protested.

The boss grunted, like Scrooge. O'Donnell said quietly, 'Political year coming up.'

But that merely reminded Kennedy of something else. He jabbed a finger at Reardon. 'You brought Bud Wilkinson here as my physical fitness adviser. Is he going to run for the Senate?'

A political colloquy followed. Reardon hedged. So did O'Donnell. The President told Reardon to review Wilkinson's chances with Bob Kennedy—and suddenly it was 10.45, departure time. 'I've got to pick up John,' he said, heading out, 'but I want to discuss this Oklahoma thing as soon as I get back.'[2]

'What about the troops?' Reardon asked hopefully. 'Do they get any time off?'

'Oh—do what you two want,' the President called over his shoulder. 'Give them the half-day. Draw it up and I'll sign it later.'

On the mansion's second floor he almost collided with his wife's maid. 'Where's John?' he demanded.

[2] In 1964 Wilkinson did run on the Republican ticket in Oklahoma. His slogan was 'Put the best man in the game'. His opponent, a Kennedy Democrat, replied that the future of the world is no game, and Wilkinson vanished in the anti-Goldwater landslide.

'Well, I don't know,' Provi remonstrated timidly. 'It's raining, and Miss Shaw doesn't want heem to go.'

'She's scared of getting him wet.' He laughed. 'Go down the hall and make sure he's dressed now. I want to take him with me.'

In moments the delighted little boy was snug in his London Fog raincoat and sou'wester, which actually resembled a miniature Army fatigue hat. Nanny appeared, fidgeting. 'Bye-bye,' Miss Shaw said anxiously, and then the Otis elevator door closed on them. At the bottom, at Secret Service Post F-5, Agent Bob Foster of the kiddie detail joined them. The President snatched up a hat, and they ran out to the helipad, where most of the Texas party had gathered, together with a handful of hardy well-wishers who had strolled out from West Wing offices to see them off. Evelyn Lincoln, Ted Clifton, and three agents were already aboard helicopter No. 1. Young John joined them. Dr George Burkley was on No. 2; Mac Kilduff was in No. 3 with reporters of the White House press pool. A humble God stood off to one side while Kennedy, bareheaded in the drizzle, pocketed Sorenson jokes, listened absently to Andy Hatcher, and glanced through some last-minute papers for Fred Holborn, notably a velvet-gloved jab at the State Department. Foggy Bottom was being difficult about a commission which the White House wanted to establish contacts with youth abroad. The President had dictated one of his 'I-Mean-What-I-Say' memorandums, and now he initialled it.

Ken O'Donnell stood off to one side, the squire awaiting orders. Larry O'Brien trotted up, wheezing. 'Hello, Charlie,' he greeted Ken. 'Hello, Harry,' Ken replied, responding to a private joke. O'Brien heard the President muttering furiously, 'Her *winter* clothes!' and asked *sotto voce*, 'What's the story on the weather?' 'McHugh must have averaged it out,' O'Donnell whispered. 'I'll tell you later.' But Kennedy's spirits were returning. Holborn handed him a witty memo from McGeorge Bundy, requesting a two-week vacation at the end of January. He grinned and scrawled across the bottom of it, 'Fine—I think it's time I left myself. JFK.'

It really was time, so he vaulted into No. 1. But they couldn't leave just yet. Mrs Kennedy hadn't appeared, and after fingering a shaving scar, pulling up a sock, and drumming his fingers on his right knee, the President made a fist.

'See if she's waiting over there,' he ordered.

General Clinton and Agent Clint Hall ran in by the Rose Garden, found her and fetched her, and presently she scrambled aboard in a two-piece white wool *bouclé* dress and a coat—just the thing for a chilly day. Her husband took a sharp breath and glared at McHugh.

Now the rotors began to spin. Like great brown wasps the three choppers trembled on their pad, rose, and dipped towards Andrews AFB, a twelve-minute ride to the south-east. The President's departure was always a memorable spectacle, and passers-by paused to observe the take-off. Sorensen and Holborn looked up from the soggy lawn. Charles Fincklin, the White House's Negro maître d'hôtel, peered out through the trembling, naked branches of Andrew Jackson's magnolias. House Whip Boggs, who happened to be driving past on South Executive Avenue, stopped his car, leaped out to wave farewell, and abruptly stopped, feeling ridiculous when he realized that no one could possibly see him from above. Across East Executive Avenue Henry Fowler had been scowling at columns of tax figures in the Treasury Building office. He turned in his massive leather chair as the whirring choppers fled past the Washington Monument. And on the opposite side of the mansion, on West Executive Avenue, Dean Markham had been watching the boarding and the flight with Don Ellinger, a visitor from Texas. 'I didn't know O'Brien and O'Donnell were going,' Markham said absently. 'Of course,' said the Texan. 'It's a political trip.' He described the Connally–Yarborough feud and added, as the gigantic wasps disappeared into the overcast, 'This is a trip the President can't win, no matter what happens.'

In the autumn of 1963 the White House telephone number was still NAtional 8-1414,[3] and when the man of the house was home communications were relatively simple. Of course, the President himself didn't answer the phone. A light would flash on a forty-bulb switchboard on the fourth floor of the Executive Office Building, and if you knew the name of a Presidential aide one of the women operators would instantly connect you with the proper extension, from which you could be transferred to the oval office or the mansion. But the moment the Chief Executive left his heli-pad all that changed. The Presidency shifted gears. Elaborate security precautions went into effect.

Even names were changed. Code replaced them.[4] The White House was no longer the White House. It was Castle, and during a trip the President's precise location at any given moment was Charcoal. He himself was no longer John Kennedy. He was Lancer, who was married to Lace, whose children were a daughter named Lyric and a son named Lark. The First Family was all in the L's—though Lyric's and Lark's grandmother lived in a Georgetown house which was referred to as Hamlet. Secret Service men were in

[3] That winter the digits took over, and it was changed to 456–1414.

[4] From time to time names and groupings were changed. One man, who was Porter (P) in November 1963, later became Super (S), and then River (R). He has retired.

the D's Chief James J. Rowley was Domino; Roy Kellerman, Digest; Clint Hill, Dazzle; Floyd Boring, Deacon; Paul Landis, Debut. Lynn Meredith, Bob Foster, and Tom Wells of the kiddie detail were, respectively, Drummer, Dresser, and Dasher. W's were for staff. Ken O'Donnell, Lancer's chief vassal, was Wand. Evelyn Lincoln was Willow; Pierre Salinger, Wayside. Mac Kilduff, who was to do Wayside's press chores on the Texas trip—and who, ironically, had been told to start looking for another job because Wand had decided he was expendable—had been christened Warrior. Generals Clifton and McHugh were Watchman and Wing. Taz Shepard, who would be minding the store at Castle during the Texas trip, was Witness. V's were reserved for the Vice President and his family. Lyndon Johnson was Volunteer. Lady Bird, who had never had much luck with names, became Victoria.

Tourists thought of the President's home as stationary, at 1600 Pennsylvania Avenue. They were wrong. The White House was capable of multiple division. It could be in several cities simultaneously. The girls on the fourth floor of the EOB remained on duty, but the real White House was wherever Lancer happened to be, and once he hit the road the key switchboard was a jungle of colour-coded wires in the executive mansion's east basement, manned by élite Signal Corps technicians of the White House Communications Agency. It was a national security precaution that Lancer always be within five minutes of a telephone. Colonel George McNally, alias Star—this was the S group—saw to it that he was much closer than that. There were phones in the President's helicopter, phones aboard Aircraft 26000, portable phones spotted fifty feet away from every airfield space where 26000 would park, and radiophones in his motorcade cars, operating on two frequencies. Like the Secret Service and the Democratic National Committee, Colonel McNally had a corps of advance men. By dawn of that Thursday morning temporary switchboards had been installed in trailers and hotel rooms in San Antonio, Houston, Fort Worth, Dallas, Austin, and at the LBJ Ranch. Each had its own unlisted phone numbers. The Dallas White House, for example, was in the Sheraton-Dallas Hotel. It could be reached through RIverside 1-3421, RIverside 1-3422, and RIverside 1-3423, though anyone who dialled one of them and lacked a code name of his own would find the conversation awkward.

S's advance man for the Texas trip was Warrant Officer Art Bales (Sturdy), a gaunt thirty-year veteran who knew every executive in the Southwest Bell Telephone Company, could bug any line from the nearest manhole or conduit, and had the facilities to scramble almost any conversation or to disconnect it without notice. When out of town the President needed one clear circuit to Washington at all times, which meant that Bales had to be prepared to pull the plug on a Cabinet member, if necessary. (Once the Secretary of State had found himself talking to a dial tone.) In motorcades Bales would ride in the Signal control car. By tradition this was the last vehicle in the caravan, and his companion there, and his room-mate at hotel stops, was a swarthy S man, Warrant Officer Ira D. Gearhart.

Gearhart, or Shadow, had been assigned the most sinister task in the Presidential party. No one called him by his Christian name, his surname, or even by his code name. He was 'the man with the satchel', or, more starkly, 'the bagman'. The bag (also known as 'the black bag' and 'the football') was a thirty-pound metal suitcase with an intricate combination lock. Within were various bulky Strangelove packets, each bearing wax seals and the signatures of the Joint Chiefs. Inside one were cryptic numbers which would permit the President to set up a crude hot line to the Prime Minister of the United Kingdom and the President of France on four minutes' notice. A second provided the codes that would launch a nuclear attack. The rest contained pages of close text enlivened by gaudy colour cartoons. They looked like comic books—horror comics, really, because they had been carefully designed so that any one of Kennedy's three military aides could quickly tell him how many million casualties would result from Retaliation Able, Retaliation Baker, Retaliation Charlie, etc. Taz Shepard had prepared these Doomsday Books. No one liked to think about them, much less talk about them, and on trips the man with the football was treated as a pariah. He needed Art Bales's company. His only job was to stick around, lug the satchel, and remember that vital combination in case the duty aide forgot it. Yet both he and his ghastly burden were necessary. At the outset of the nuclear age Harry Truman would have had four hours to think things through if Soviet bombers had appeared over Canada in force. In the Kennedy administration that time had been cut to fifteen minutes, and it was shrinking.

In Dallas both warrant officers were destined to play crucial roles—Bales, because a hospital emergency room is the worst possible place to establish secure communications; Gearhart, because the bagman was a stranger to agents of the Vice President's Secret Service detail. In Washington, however, they were merely two names to be checked off a long manifest. A President's entourage is enormous. There were S teams, D teams, W teams, secretarial pools, political advisers, medical men, the military, the luggage crew—it seemed endless. Each group had a standard trip drill and a bible. The luggage bible, for example, began with a pre-trip trip to a closet beside the carpenter's shop in the White House basement. There, on the night before each take-off, an Army master sergeant extricated two portable three-inch plywood bed boards and a five-inch horse-hair mattress and sent them via truck to the MATS (Military Air Transport Service) terminal at Andrews Field for loading. Two men were responsible for the American and Presidential flags and the Presidential seals, one of which had to be correctly mounted before every Kennedy speech. Whenever Volunteer accompanied Lancer it was necessary to rent an electric podium which would be exactly seventy-six inches away from the Vice President's bifocals. Every member of the party was issued a 3 × 5 card telling him his position in the caravan ('Miss Turnure: you will ride in AF # 1 during the Texas trip. You will ride in the VIP bus on all stops in Texas'), and everyone had been issued an identification pin. The background colour for these changed from trip to trip, but the patterns were constant. Those for staff members were elliptical, with a dot in the middle. Signals pins were crossed by a diagonal line. Secret Service agents had lapel bars with a break in the middle, and since the colours for Texas were to be white on red, each agent looked as though he were wearing an Army good conduct medal.

Agent Bob Foster wore no bar on the short hop to Andrews. He and his ward weren't going anywhere, though John, Jr., being young and very much a Kennedy—already he had his father's eyes and jaw—wasn't reconciled. As the chopper settled down beside the immaculate splendour of Air Force One his mother and father hugged him. 'I want to come,' he told his father, his voice beginning to break. 'You can't,' the President said gently. The little boy began to cry. Since photographers had assembled on the airstrip, the Kennedys decided to leave him in the helicopter; otherwise there would be unfortunate halftones on tomorrow's front pages. The President kissed his sobbing son for the last time and patted the trembling shoulders in the small London Fog coat. Then he looked at the agent who would be staying behind. He said, 'You take care of John, Mr Foster.'

'Yes, sir,' said Foster, who thought this odd, because although there had been tearful farewells before, he had never been given such an instruction. The travellers descended, and Foster settled into the Presidential chair, holding the child in his lap. He diverted him with a story about Bertram the Beaver, another about Jaggy the Jaguar, a third about Jasper the Jet. His repertoire exhausted, they waited and squinted until, as the graceful white fuselage of Aircraft 26000 rose in the murky sky, its blue flashings vanishing in scudding clouds, John sighed. He always loved to watch that plane.

Earlier in the morning five thousand cheap handbills had appeared on the streets of Dallas. At the top were two offset photographs of the President, one full face and one in profile. The effect was that of a Bertillon police poster, and it was deliberate, because the headline read:

WANTED
FOR
TREASON

'THIS MAN,' the dodger declared, 'is wanted for treasonous activities against the United States', and it offered a seven-point bill of particulars. The Chief Executive was accused, among other things, of betraying the Constitution, 'turning the sovereignty of the U.S. over to the communist controlled United Nations', betraying such friends as Cuba, having 'been WRONG on innumerable issues', including Cuba and the Test Ban Treaty, encouraging racial riots, invading 'a sovereign State with federal troops', upholding the Supreme Court 'in its Anti-Christian rulings', and appointing 'Anti-Christians to Federal offices'. The last count charged that 'He has been caught in fantastic LIES to the American people (including personal ones like his previous marriage [*sic*] and divorce).' In sum, the broadside was an incendiary amalgam of all the invective being spread by Kennedy's enemies. Any hater, left or right, could find fuel in it.

Its significance may be exaggerated, however. There was no connection between the President's assassin and its printers. And Kennedy's Dallas enemies were already aflame anyhow. A few more faggots weren't going to raise their temperature much. That same morning, the loudspeaker at W. E. Greiner Junior High School, just across the Trinity River from the Texas School Book Depository, announced that students could go to tomorrow's motorcade provided their parents came for them. It was the opening period; Warren Harding's fourteen-year-old son was attending his first class of the day. Just before the bell sounded the teacher told her pupils to put their books aside. 'Nobody here will be let out for that parade,' she told them. 'I don't care if your whole family shows up. You still have to be in this class. He's not a good President, and I don't say that because I'm a Republican. It don't make no matter whether it's him or his brother Bobby. One's as bad as the other. You're not going, I'm not going, period.' She smiled faintly, a smartly dressed young woman in her mid-twenties. 'If I did see him,' she said, 'I'd just spit in his face.'

An hour later, at 10.30 a.m., the first edition of the afternoon *Times-Herald* hit the streets. One of the clerks at the Book Depository bought a copy at Elm and Houston and ran inside, waving the newspaper map of the motorcade route. He created a hubbub in the grimy warehouse; his fellow workers were plainly excited. Tuesday's report was confirmed. The President's car was going to pass beneath their windows, cruising slowly towards the triple underpass.

Aircraft 26000 departed Andrews at 11.05 EST. For a fleeting instant the great rotunda of the Capitol lay under the swept-back left wing like a squat chess piece; then they were up and away, zooming towards the South-west at 550 mph. Colonel Jim Swindal was a story-book pilot, a rakish Alabaman with a Terry-and-the-Pirates profile, and he had a dream plane to fly—a hundred tons of gleaming machinery, exquisite appointments, and air-conditioned, soundproof cabins. Boeing called it a 707; the Air Force, a VC-137; but under any of its various names it had become known to the world as the personal flagship of the American President.

Essentially it differed little from its sister ships. All were equipped with identical Pratt-Whitney jets, and when they weren't flying the same guards watched over them. But 26000 was John Kennedy's plane, a projection of himself. He had supervised Raymond Loewy's design of it, had ordered its blue motif (the engine pods of 86970, 86971, and 86972 were painted red), and since its commissioning on October 21 of the previous year he had flown 75,000 miles aboard it. On the wall of its stateroom amidships, on its pillowcases and crockery, and in the centre of each of its telephone dials were reproductions of the gold Presidential seal. They alone made it unique. But the plane also had a personality of its own—it subscribed to fifteen magazines and five daily newspapers—and all other flights, military and civilian, deferred to it. Its progress was monitored on radar screens, and a chain of Secret Service checkpoints was established on the ground beneath its airborne route. Should it make a forced landing, an agent in a souped-up car could be on the spot very quickly. Indeed, the failure of the ranking agent aboard to report that he was passing checkpoint Able or Baker would have been sufficient to start the sirens screaming. Before Swindal landed or took off from any airport, the field was unavailable to other aircraft for fifteen minutes. Although he could fly with any two of his four jets, his crew inspected each of them at each stop. In flight, 26000 was assigned air-lane priority. Only after it was aloft were its backup and press planes allowed to leave, and they had to pass it in the air so their passengers could disembark at the Chief Executive's destination and arrange themselves before he descended his ramp to the strains of 'Hail to the Chief'.

The press, forty Washington reporters and the one foreign correspondent—Brandon of the London *Sunday Times*—flew on a chartered airliner; they were represented aboard 26000 by the reporters of the White House press pool, a quartet of veterans from the wire services, television networks, news magazines, and metropolitan dailies. The pool would change at each stop, with Bob Baskin of the Dallas *News* joining it in Dallas. The thirteen Texas Congressmen making the trip were also to be rotated. Space had been reserved on 26000 for four of them. Each would be allowed to ride in and out of his own district on the prestigious flagship; otherwise, unless Kennedy wished to talk to them, they would languish in the luxurious boredom of the backup plane. This rule even applied to Albert Thomas, their dean, and on the leg to San Antonio Thomas' companions were Woody Taylor, Victoria's Secret Service agent, and, unexpectedly, Godfrey McHugh. Normally, McHugh would have ridden on 26000. He was, after all, the Air Force Aide. He had had a hand in Loewy's design, and had chosen the painting of a French farmhouse which hung over the President's Air Force One bed. But God was temporarily in exile, and the number of his airborne doghouse was 86970. He peered out, brooding, as they doglegged past Colonel Swindal's cockpit.

Aloft, the two doors on 26000's port side could not be discerned. The forty-five windows beneath the huge blue-and-white legend 'United States of America' resembled those of a conventional airliner. They were deceptive. The interior was divided into compartments. Swindal, his smashed-down cap at a jaunty angle, sat in the nose with the four officers of his staff, surrounded by black leather-padded knobs and luminous dials. Behind them was the communications shack: two million dollars' worth of electronic gear, including teletype machines, the hooded cryptographic device, and a flying switchboard linking the plane to the White House Signals board and the Secret Service network on the ground. Then came the forward galley and crew's quarters, and then the staff area—thirty seats and two desks with electric typewriters. After that, a closed door; the stateroom, or office, lay beyond. There, five miles up in the sky, his polished shoes resting on a blue rug adorned with a golden eagle and thirteen gold stars, President Kennedy could hold conferences and telephone subordinates as easily as though he were in his Castle's West Wing.

Behind the office was a corridor leading past Kennedy's private quarters, a bath and a bedroom. (There was no mistaking his bed for the First Lady's; the inboard mattress was thin and rock-hard.) Aft of these quarters lay the final cabin, a galley and six chairs reserved for military aides and senior Secret Service men, and that Thursday noon Agents Roy Kellerman and Clint Hill were leafing through magazines in this tail compartment. The rear of the plane was quiet. The President had unbuckled his worn black alligator briefcase and spread the contents on the stateroom desk. His spectacles mounted on his nose, he was studying diplomatic cables marked 'EYES ONLY, PRESIDENT', a black briefing book on the Erhard visit, and intelligence reports from the CIA and the Defense Intelligence Agency. Across the aisle, his wife and Pam Turnure were working on a speech. It was to be the only one she would deliver in Texas, and would be quite brief. Since she was going to appear before the LULACS—the League of United Latin-American Citizens—she had decided to speak in Spanish. Some of the phrases were difficult. In the stillness of the stateroom her soft Castilian could be heard clearly: '*Estoy muy contenta de estar en el gran estado de Texas. . . . La noble tradición española que tanto contribuyo a Texas. Esta tradición comenzó cien años antes de que se colonizara Massachusetts, el estado de mi marido. . . .*' If she was trying to tease the grandee at the desk, he wasn't taking the bait. He didn't understand Spanish. He turned pages rapidly, speed-reading at twelve hundred words a minute, ignoring the familiar voice and its incomprehensible accents.

In the staff area that would have been difficult. The aisle forward of the big door was in an uproar. Ralph Yarborough was embattled. In the last few days he had learned the details of the trap Governor Connally had laid for him, and they were harrowing. It looked as though Austin would be an Alamo for him. The senior Senator was going to be stripped of his dignity. He would be marched across the stage and curtly introduced like a visiting fireman, and that was all. No toasts. No words about his years of service, no place of honour. He had sold $11,300 in tickets to tomorrow night's Austin dinner, and there wouldn't even be a place for his wife. As the crowning insult, the Connallys were going to cut him publicly. They would entertain the Kennedys at a formal reception, and every little Panhandle legislator would be on hand, but the Senator wouldn't be allowed to crash the gate.

The more he thought about it, the more wrathful he became. He turned up his great organ of a voice, and his Texas drawl thickened marvellously. 'Everywhere' came out '*ahverwhare*', 'thing' '*thang*', 'right' '*raht*', 'something' '*sawmthin*', 'your' '*youah*', 'you' '*yew*'. Rustic vernacular crept into his speech until it became almost as alien as Jacqueline Kennedy's Spanish. Connally and Johnson—for he had held the Vice President guilty as a co-conspirator—were as black as a Republican heart. Well, the fear-makers had chosen parlous times to mobilize a political *Wehrmacht*. He was no longer a starry-eyed country boy from a kindly Texas hearth. He'd been a judge in the Lone Star's Third Judicial District; he'd been a United States Senator for six and a half years, and he was going to rear back and come out fighting. In the end ahverthang would be fine.

In other words, he was alarmed. Yet every poll taken that fall had shown that his popularity margin with state voters was five or ten points wider than those of Connally or Kennedy–Johnson. He was a bread-and-butter man, and bluebonnet Texas appreciated bread-and-butter issues. He could be fairly confident of surviving the long knives of Austin. His real concern was the President, to whose star he had hitched his wagon. In his present mood the Senator was highly sceptical of the Governor's party loyalty. During a national campaign, he suspected, Connally's support of Kennedy would be token support. Even if they all went all out, Yarborough told Mac Kilduff and Congressmen Joe Kilgore, John Young, Tiger Teague, and Henry Gonzalez, the outlook was bound to be cloudy. He invited them to take a look at the Mexican vote. Mexicans were volatile—Gonzalez nodded in agreement—and with himself and Connally on the same ticket, they would be asked to buy a very mixed bag. Some would shy away. A lot of others would split their tickets.

Jim Matthias, a pool reporter, brought him back to the Austin reception. 'What's your reaction to that?'

'I've had many telephone calls and letters from friends because Mrs Yarborough and I were not invited to the mansion,' the Senator said.

Matthias sharpened the question: 'How does it feel to be slapped in the face?'

Stung, Yarborough snapped, 'Well, I'm not surprised. Governor Connally is so terribly uneducated governmentally, how could you expect anything else?'

The reporter wrote it down. Now the vendetta was on the record. Once 26000 landed the quote would be relayed to the press plane.

Thus, with the party less than an hour out of Washington, rifts had already begun. Gonzalez, though less outspoken than Yarborough, was clearly unhappy. He told Teague his troubles. Here they were flying into San Antonio, his home town, and Connally had manoeuvred affairs so that the entire visit would be non-political. Even ceremonial opportunities weren't going to be properly exploited. The motorcade would pass within a block of the Alamo, but no arrangements had been made for the President to lay a wreath there. Then there was the matter of the John F. Kennedy High School. At Gonzalez' urging, a new school in San Antonio's Edgewood District had been named for the Chief Executive. It was only two blocks north of Kelly Field. Dedicating it wouldn't take more than five minutes. But O'Donnell and O'Brien had told Gonzalez that there weren't five minutes to spare. The Congressmen had just been checking the schedule. They were to spend two hours in San Antonio—and three hours in Dallas, the enemy camp. Whose side were they on, anyhow?

Teague murmured sympathetically. And at that point the big door opened and the President himself strode into the staff compartment, puffing on a long, thin cigar.

Henry Gonzalez smiled. He had never seen him smoke. He started to ask slyly whether the cheroot came from Castro and then, as the other Congressmen converged on them, he thought better of it. Henry's instincts were sound. Unwittingly he would have touched on a sore point. The cigar actually *was* Cuban, though pre-boycott. The firm of H. Uppman had been using Havana tobacco since Edward VII became its client, and Kennedy was a confirmed Uppman customer.

'Congratulations on that press conference, Mr President,' Kilgore said. 'The way you handled Goldwater—saying he was real busy selling TVA—that was something.'

Kennedy sprawled in a seat across the aisle and swung his leg over the arm. 'The damnedest thing,' he said, 'is that Barry really means it.'

Gonzalez turned the most recent issue of *Newsweek* to the last page and handed it to him. 'Seen this?'

The pruneface of Raymond Moley stared up at Kennedy. Under the head 'TAMPER WITH AN IMAGE?' Moley exhorted the Arizonan to stand fast and offer 'a real alternative to what the Kennedy Administration is giving us now'.

The President laughed aloud. 'Barry can do no wrong in Moley's eyes,' he chuckled. In fact, the Barry boom was becoming the biggest joke in politics. The right-wing columnists were urging Goldwater to stick to his eighteenth-century guns, which was what Goldwater wanted to do—which was what Kennedy wanted him to do. If the Senator won the GOP nomination next summer, the President would clearly win the mandate he had missed in 1960. He read Moley again, rolled the magazine into a bat, and slapped his knee. 'That's terrific!'

Observing his change in mood, Gonzalez said, 'Mr President, I don't think it's right to let Bruce Alger have equal time with me.'

Kennedy looked baffled, and Larry O'Brien moved in. Since legislative liaison was Larry's job, if a Congressman was making a pitch, he wanted to hear it.

Gonzalez explained that their itinerary gave Alger's city an hour more than San Antonio. 'Mr President, we have the only school in the country named for you. Even Boston hasn't done that. You should drop in.'

'We're pressed for time,' Kennedy said uneasily. 'We've had to cut some things out.'

'Later then,' Henry pleaded. 'It's a political problem for me——' He saw O'Brien signalling him to stop, and he stopped.

The President batted his knee. 'OK, Henry,' he said toughtfully. 'I'll come back later.'

'Is that a promise?' Gonzalez asked quickly.

'It's a promise,' Kennedy said, rising and shrugging as Larry's lips silently formed an anguished *When?* The President glanced at his watch. They were on Central Standard Time now, and he moved the hands an hour back, to 1.15 p.m. 'We'll be in your district in fifteen minutes, Henry.'

'*Viva* country,' Gonzalez smiled.

'Bexar County,' Kennedy said professionally.

With that, he vanished through the door and returned to his homework. It was several minutes later, and his cigar was a stub, when he became aware of a tightly corseted feminine figure tiptoeing back towards the bedroom. Mary Gallagher, his wife's personal secretary, was starting her duties as maid. While he had been with the Congressmen the First Lady had finished her speech and changed to a fresh white dress and black leather belt. Mary had snapped up the back while Mrs Kennedy critically inspected the black beret which went with it. The comb that attached it to her hair was on the back of the beret. She wanted it switched to the side, and had been waiting in the private quarters while Mary went into the staff area to change the stitching.

'That's fine,' said Jackie, fastening it in place.

There was a light tap on the door. Her husband looked in.

'You all right?' he asked her.

'Fine,' she repeated, beaming at his reflection in her mirror.

'I just wanted to be sure,' he murmured, turning away. Apparently he was still apprehensive that she might not enjoy the trip.

Sergeant Joe Ayres, 26000's husky chief steward, appeared in the corridor outside.

'We've entered our glide pattern, Mr President.'

They squinted out. The light blue wings were skimming over low, thinly grassed *pichachos* and sandy tracts of barren ground. Under an aluminium sky the city ahead shimmered brightly, a skyline on a plain. There had been no reprieve for Godfrey McHugh: San Antonio was going to be hot.

Below, Lyndon Johnson had just emerged from the terminal

barbershop and was lining up greeters. Usually Lady Bird was at his elbow on such occasions, but she had glimpsed her college roommate in the waiting crowd, and the two women were embracing enthusiastically, leaving him to cope. There was a lot to cope with. Because the ostensible reason for the Presidential call here was a visit to nearby Brooks Aerospace Medical Centre, Air Force Secretary Eugene Zuckert had appeared, and he wanted to know where he should stand. Other slots had to be found for Mrs John Connally, Waggoner Carr, Attorney General of Texas, and an Air Force lieutenant general. Then there were the members of the Vice President's own entourage: Cliff Carter, Liz Carpenter, and Marie Fehmer, Lyndon's young secretary. Behind them, perspiring and craning their necks, stood the twenty-six members of the Chamber of Commerce's red-carpet delegation, and from behind *them* came sounds of an awkward row. Mayor W. W. McAllister of San Antonio, it developed, had run afoul of the Secret Service. He had brought his camera and had been sneaking pictures of the President's blue Lincoln convertible and the Secret Service's armoured Cadillac, which had been flown down from Washington the night before, when an agent demanded to see his press pass. McAllister hadn't one, and he let it be known that he had no intention of being pushed around. He was the *Mayor,* this was *his* town. Lyndon was at his best in such situations. The two men were urged to reason with one another, and everyone was assigned a small place to stand. The press and backup planes were parking. The reception committee was almost ready. Only one man was missing.

Unfortunately, he was the host.

And now, with 26000's landing imminent, the field was closed to other traffic.

At the last minute the control tower received a frantic signal from a private plane hovering over the eastern horizon. 'DV arriving,' it was warned—Distinguished Visitor meant the President—and the plane's passenger radioed back that as Governor of Texas he was fairly distinguished himself. Connally had been in Houston, addressing a luncheon of the Texas Manufacturers Association in the Sheraton-Lincoln Hotel. Aware that he was perilously late, he had borrowed a white Jetstar from a friendly oil millionaire. The San Antonio tower immediately granted him an exception to the 26000 rule; he skidded in, jumped out, pumped the clammy hands of the twenty-six businessmen, spotted Nellie's white dress, and slipped into the reception line beside her.

'I've been holding my breath for you,' she whispered, fingering her pearl necklace.

'There it is!' shouted a man, and there it was—the Stars and

Stripes on Air Force One's tail taxiing gracefully across a distant airstrip. 'Jackie!' cried a woman, and the crowd took it up: 'Jackieee! Jackieee!' The Governor relaxed and grinned. He had prophesied that she would be popular. He'd have to remind the President.

A ramp was wheeled up, the rear door opened, and the First Lady emerged first, smiling her shy, hesitant smile. The mob roared. Lady Bird waved affectionately. Then the lithe, familiar figure appeared in the doorway, fingering a button of his jacket. Another roar. Ralph Yarborough should have been third, but Ralph, aware that Henry Gonzalez was the city's favourite Texan, gently shoved Henry ahead of him. Everyone was baying now, and even the jaded officials burst into applause when the President wrung the Mayor's hand, cut to one side, and waded into the Congressmen's huge family.

'Happy birthday!' he greeted Bertha Gonzalez. Her eyes glistened. How had he known? Ted Clifton's father-in-law, a retired colonel living in San Antonio, also started violently when the President paused to compliment him on his daughter. Hard of hearing, the Colonel asked those around him, 'Did he say Anne's name?' He had remembered her; his flypaper memory was his trademark, and as he moved along the line he had a personal word for every other greeter. Children were Jacqueline Kennedy's speciality. Cradling a bouquet of yellow roses—the card, from Al Meyer, North Towne Florist, expressed 'respect and gratitude for your contributions to the cultural advancement of our country and to the image of the American Woman which you have carried abroad'—she scanned the sea of eager faces for small spectators and saved her brightest smiles for them.

Meanwhile the motorcade was forming. It was a set piece for the Secret Service, with variations to allow for the unaccustomed presence of the Vice President. The luggage truck and a pilot car, manned by local police, cruised a quarter-mile ahead, sizing up the route. The motorcade proper was led by a police car whose passengers included the Secret Service man stationed in San Antonio and the Washington agent who had advanced the city. Then came the feature attraction: the four-ton Lincoln, with Greer at the wheel, Kellerman beside him, the Connallys on the jump seats, and the Kennedys in the rear. The others might switch places, but the President always occupied the right rear seat unless he chose to surrender it to another chief of state. The Governor of Texas was not so regarded, and Kennedy would be staying put on this trip. The Secret Service liked that. Agents would know exactly where he was on all the Texas motorcades and could keep a watchful eye on him.

Immediately behind the Lincoln, Agent Emory Roberts would be in charge of the eight-passenger '55 Cadillac, a moving arsenal which White House correspondents called the Queen Mary. Two agents would stand on each of the Queen's running boards, and Powers and O'Donnell would occupy the jump seats. Next came the Vice President's rented convertible, with Agent Rufe Youngblood sitting beside the driver, and then, in order, the Vice Presidential follow-up car, Agent Lem Johns commanding; the Gonzalez limousine; Mac Kilduff's pool car; two convertibles for still photographers and newsreel men; and a long caravan of exuberant Congressmen shepherded by Larry O'Brien. Towards the end, in front of the communications car, every motorcade had a bus labelled 'VIP'. The VIP's were not really very important. They were staff who lacked priority: Mary Gallagher, Pam Turnure, Johnson's people, and, for the present, God. In Texas, O'Donnell had decided, Evelyn Lincoln and Dr Burkley would also ride in the bus. The decision was not appreciated by them. When crowds grew heavy, VIP buses were sometimes cut off—in Rome one had been lost for two hours. Evelyn felt that a secretary should be near her boss, and Burkley protested that there was always a chance that the President might be hurt. They had been marooned earlier in the year in Frankfurt. It had been disquieting. The likelihood that either would be needed here seemed remote, however, so they had been overruled.

Among the staff O'Donnell's word was law. He had personally approved each appointment, including Colonel Swindal's, and he could transfer them if they grew unruly. But he was powerless in Congress, as Ralph Yarborough was about to demonstrate. The Senator was stalking towards the north side of the terminal on his short, powerful legs when a flock of local liberals surged up and told him they had heard about the Austin plot. Rather than face humiliation there, they suggested, he should leave the party in Dallas. He nodded vigorously; he had reached the same conclusion. 'And don't get in the same car with Johnson,' said a friend of their ideological leader, Maury Maverick, Jr. who, though he was a state Democratic committee man, had been barred from the airport by Connally men. The man went on, 'Every liberal here and in Houston knows what Connally and Johnson are trying to do to you, and they're waiting to see if you'll knuckle under to it.'

Yarborough was perplexed. 'Did you say Johnson's car?'

The motorcade was about to depart, yet he still didn't know where he was supposed to sit. To a man with his trembling ego this was important, and he had tried very hard to find out. His instructions from the White House had been conflicting. Last June in El Paso he had ridden with the President. Early in the planning of the current trip he had been told that would be out this time. Then he had been assured that he would be with the President and the Governor. Three days ago the signals had been changed again; Larry O'Brien had suavely informed him that in each city he would share a car with the most popular local figure—usually the mayor. According to the Senator's subsequent memory, however, at no point had the Vice President's convertible been mentioned.

'They're fixing to put you there,' Maverick's friend insisted, and he was right, for as Yarborough approached the crocodile of automobiles he was confronted by Agent Youngblood, a slender, balding, aggressive Georgian.

'Senator, you're scheduled to ride in the Vice President's car here,' Youngblood said, relaying another O'Donnell decree.

Yarborough looked right through him, spun on his heel, and walked up to Gonzalez. 'Henry,' he said, 'can I hitch a ride with you?'

The Congressman was delighted. So was the White House press corps. All forty correspondents had the Senator's Air Force One quote now, and local reporters had given them the San Antonio motorcade assignments. When they saw him avoiding the Vice President, they drew the inevitable conclusion. They decided to call it a snub.

Youngblood slid into the front seat of the rented convertible, turned, and spread his hands. 'Well,' he said, 'I told him.'

The situation was awkward for the Johnsons. Every other car was packed. Their back seat would easily accommodate three people, and no matter how they spread themselves, they were obviously missing a passenger. As Lady Bird put it later, 'We'd been told Ralph was going to be with us, but every time we looked for him, he wasn't there.' Lyndon stared straight ahead. Connally was to blame, but Connally was safe and snug in the big Lincoln; it was Johnson who was losing face. Life, President Kennedy had once observed, is unfair.

It was also being unfair to Kennedy, whose day this should have been. When a reporter asked Gonzalez what he thought the day's lead story should be, Henry replied, 'San Antonio gives President a boisterous reception.' The newspaperman shook his head. 'Yarborough refuses to ride with Lyndon Johnson,' he said. Gonzalez, indignant, said, 'Boy, you're really giving it to him, aren't you?' 'That's news,' the man said defensively, and by traditional standards it was. Correspondents had to take note of it, just as they were obliged to dwell on the scattered Goldwater banners in the crowd, the obscure placard 'WE WELCOME PRESIDENT KENNITTY', and the way Kennedy raised his eyebrows at the NAACP sign outside the airport—'MR PRESIDENT, YOU ARE IN A SEGREGATED CITY'—and leaned forward to question Connally about it, raising his voice to be heard above the whirring of a police helicopter three hundred feet overhead.[5]

Yet the Congressman, though biased, had a point. The real excitement that afternoon had nothing to do with political blood-letting. It had been captured, oddly, by an afternoon newspaper which had gone to press while the President was still in the air, and which hit the streets as his motorcade nosed between the palm trees at the terminal entrance and turned east on Loop 410, headed downtown. Under the headline 'CHEERS FOR JFK, JACKIE', the San Antonio *Light* had written: 'President John F. Kennedy, visiting the Alamo City for the first time, flew into San Antonio Thursday to a wildly enthusiastic greeting.' The editors of the *Light* hadn't been guessing. They had known the greeting would be enthusiastic, because they knew their *Viva* subscribers. A school holiday had been proclaimed, stores had put up their Christmas decorations a week early, labour was out in force, the Democratic organization was marshalling the party faithful. The parade couldn't miss, even if the Kennedys' drawing power had been myth. As it happened, that power had been underrated. The turnout was fantastic. Over 125,000 people were jammed along the route, and they had transformed their city.

On an ordinary day it is a drab community, an oleograph of the Southwest. Palms are attractive but rare. In the overpopulated neighbourhoods, greenery has been replaced by ugly Laundraterias, El Rancho bars, Bar-B-Q night-spots. Homes are roofed with campy terra cotta, new construction is bogus Old World housing, and several petrol stations are dingy replicas of the Alamo. The number of filling stations is staggering. Like most cities in the Southwestern United States, San Antonio sometimes gives the curious impression that it is inhabited by automobiles. Entire blocks are devoted to the care and feeding of motor vehicles. Signs advertise paint body shops, tyre stores, wheel alignment establishments, greaseries, transmission specialists, tune-up bargains, seat covers, hydraulic services. 'Chevvy Land', 'A-1 Auto Parts', and 'Free Valves and Rings'. Motels and trailer parks outnumber hotels; car graveyards are more

[5] 'Not', the San Antonio *News* reported of the helicopter, 'that there was any danger.' *News* coverage of that Thursday's events was rather captious. One writer described Jacqueline Kennedy as 'taciturn' and complained that she was aloof from the people. Another called security agents 'nit-pickers', adding that 'taxpayers foot the bill while the Secret Service heroes gumshoe around thinking up different kinds of new—and ruinously expensive—duties for themselves'. These comments appeared the following afternoon, November 22, 1963.

conspicuous than cemeteries. There are U-Drive-Its and U-Haul-Its, drive-in stores and drive-inn restaurants, and drive-in theatres littered with souvenirs of last night's love.

This anarchy was invisible to the distinguished visitor because it had been masked by a mantle of humanity. The kerbs were dense with shining Latin faces. They hadn't come to stare, or even just to cheer; thousands of individuals had given considerable thought to an original reception, and the President became as much spectator as spectacle. At Howard School each pupil was waving an American flag. At Alamo Heights High School parents stood with their children, and on St Mary's Street an entire student body had gathered behind an enormous purple-and-white 'BRECKINRIDGE HIGH SCHOOL WELCOMES YOU'. Lady Bird, who shrewdly discounted mass-produced placards, saw hand-lettered signs on every side: 'WELCOME, JGK', 'BIENVENIDO, MR PRESIDENT', and 'JACKIE, COME WATERSKI IN TEXAS!'

Two cars ahead, the Kennedys started counting jumpers and screamers and gave up. Everybody was one or the other except a cripple in a wheel chair, and when the President got out to shake the cripple's hand he was nearly swept away. They stopped again outside Incarnate Word College—Mrs Kennedy wanted to change seats with Connally; the wind was blowing her hair—and a nun narrowly missed the President with a lunging movement that looked much like a flying tackle. In the business district they encountered delirium: a blizzard of confetti floated down on them at the intersection of Travis and Broadway, the mob was screaming with a single voice, and conversation within the Lincoln had become impossible. Meanwhile the motorcade had begun to come unstuck. The battery in the pool car had gone dead, marooning the press in a chaos of yelling Spanish Americans and blocking the cars behind it. Kellerman signalled Greer to hit the gas; the lead cars sped out to Brooks Medical Centre.

But the Centre was no sanctuary. The Air Force had set up nine thousand folding chairs for people who wanted to hear the President's brief speech of dedication. There were twenty thousand waiting to occupy them. The public relations officer, a quiet lieutenant colonel, was stunned. Nobody had briefed him on the problems that come with such a multitude, and he was momentarily overwhelmed. Six high school superintendents arrived posing as correspondents for their school papers and were seated in the press section. A man dressed as a priest and carrying a black bag was ushered to the front before a horrified acquaintance recognized him as a mental patient. An elderly woman had just finished a painting of blue-bonnets; she wanted to give it to the President. An elderly man wanted to give him two ears of Texas hard corn. In the confusion none of the officers noticed the arrival of the White House flag detail. When the last crackpot had been whisked away, they found the President's flags and seal miraculously in place on the podium; the base band was playing 'The Man I Love', and the man himself was emerging from his Lincoln. Simultaneously a woman with a glassy stare detached herself from the crowd and lurched at his wife. She sobbed, 'Mrs Kennedy, Mrs Kennedy, please touch my hand!' Their fingers brushed. 'Oh, my God!' the woman wept. 'She really did touch me! She really did!' The First Lady shrank back, her face frozen in a fixed smile.

Suddenly everything was under control. Agents, policemen, and Air Force MP's moved in. The tail of the motorcade arrived—the pool car had been left at one of the nine San Antonio garages specializing in battery repairs—and even the VIP bus was there. Evelyn Lincoln and Mary Gallagher were peering out, waving at the platform, and Godfrey McHugh was clowning in pantomime. The President laughed. The General had been forgiven, which was a good thing; in two hours he would take over as Kennedy's officer of the day.

The brisk wind had grown brisker. Over half the audience couldn't hear the speech, a ringing reaffirmation of the New Frontier.

'. . . we . . . stand on the edge of a great new era filled with both crises and opportunity, an era to be characterized by achievements and challenge. It's an era which calls for action, and for the best efforts of all those who would test the unknown and the uncertain in every phase of human endeavour. It is a time for pathfinders and pioneers. . . .'

Mrs Kennedy could hear. She sat directly behind him, listening as intently as any young wife who had never heard a President speak.

'. . . the wartime development of radar gave us the transistor and all that it made possible. . . .'

I never knew that, she thought, surprised.

'This nation has tossed its cap over the wall of space—and we have no choice but to follow it,' he said, turning to his last 5×7 card. '. . . with the help of all those who labour in the space endeavour, with the help and support of all Americans, we will climb this wall with safety and with speed—and we shall then explore the wonders on the other side.'

During the applause Major General T. C. Bedwell, Jr., commander of the base, asked Kennedy if he would like to see four youths in an experimental tank, breathing pure oxygen at a simulated altitude of nearly thirty thousand feet. The oxygen chamber wasn't on the schedule; Bedwell was merely making a hospitable gesture. To his surprise, Kennedy said he would like it very much. They trooped over to Building T-100, where Dr B. E. Welch, a phlegmatic young scientist, shook hands with the Kennedys and escorted them to the tank's circular window. From inside, the youths, popeyed, beheld the President of the United States. He was in an inquisitive mood. Donning a headset, he subjected them to one of his typical grillings. How long had they been up in there? Exactly how high were they supposed to be? What did they eat? How did they feel? Why had they volunteered? 'Thank you very much. Jackie?' He was offering her the earphones. But her hair was already dishevelled from the wind, and the beret was in the way. She laughed and shook her head.

He drew Dr Welch aside. He had one more inquiry: 'Apart from space research, there must be other medical implications here. Do you think your work might improve oxygen chambers for, say, premature babies?'

The scientist rather thought it might. Nevertheless the question puzzled him. He had been busy in his laboratory this past year and had rarely glanced at a newspaper. He wondered why the President should be concerned with infant mortality and why, as Kennedy turned for a final glance into the steel tank, his tanned face should seem so pensive.

Immediately after the departure of the Presidential party from San Antonio International Airport Colonel Swindal had moved his three-plane fleet to nearby Kelly Field, and there, at 3.48 p.m., the Kennedys reboarded Aircraft 26000. They were drenched and limp. The attrition of vitality, the ineluctable toll of such a journey, had begun. At Brooks Kennedy had tried to rest briefly in the Lincoln while the First Lady made her farewells. Harassed by a band of housewives who kept hissing. '*Psst! Your wife,* Mr President!'—they were unaware that etiquette dictates that a President, alone among American husbands, may precede his wife—he had given up and gone to fetch her. The motorcade was resumed. During the half-hour drive which followed, the automotive nature of the landscape signs became depressingly evident ('Need gas, Mr President? We give out stamps'), and someone had neglected to tell the railroads about the parade; a freight train had to be halted at a grade crossing. At Kelly itself five thousand government workers gave them a thunderous cheer. It was exhilarating but depleting. After two Cokes the President and Mrs Kennedy retired to their bedroom.

Their life together now had nearly a full day to run. Yet this was to be their last hour of serenity. The tyranny of events and exhaustion would begin to close in when they finished the two-hundred-mile lap to Houston. Actually, they hadn't even an hour. In this plane the hop took only forty-five minutes. Privacy was that limited, confined to a tiny blue cabin racing thirty thousand feet above the tessellated green and brown plains of central Texas, the long straight roads which led from farm to market, the tidiness of lonely farms, the vast stretches of mouse-coloured desert, of outcrop and barren land and dry river beds, and then: a complex of irrigation canals; a sinuous river crowded with thick shoulders of live oak; the geometric patterns of suburbia; Houston. Their time was up.

The President emerged in a fresh shirt and summoned Albert Thomas.

'How did it go?' he inquired.

At Kelly he had requested Thomas, who had come aboard with the shift of Congressmen, to step into the Yarborough–Connally brawl and 'get them sweetened up'. For the past half-hour Houston's senior Congressman had been trying. First he had taken the Senator to the front of the staff area and told him things had gone far enough. Yarborough had tentatively agreed. In the interests of harmony he would speak at the Thomas testimonial dinner this evening. He had made just one condition. His wife was going to meet him at the Houston airport, and he wanted the Yarboroughs to ride into town with the Thomases. This, of course, was a blind. He wanted a pretext to avoid the Johnson car. Since the decoy was named Opal Yarborough, however, courtly Albert Thomas couldn't object.

'OK,' Kennedy said tightly. 'And the Governor?'

'John's dragging his feet,' said the Congressman.

After escorting the Senator to his seat, Thomas had led Connally forward. The fight had to end, he repeated; it was time everyone shook hands. The Governor was evasive. When Thomas suggested that Connally introduce the President at the dinner, and Yarborough the Vice President, he got an argument. During introductions, he was told, the Senator should be benched. Reluctantly Thomas agreed. He sought other concessions and got none. It was all very unsatisfactory. 'You're a grown boy,' he snapped at the Governor, who replied frostily that he wanted to talk to Larry or Ken.

'I got to them first,' Thomas said. 'I told them to sit tight.'

There was a grinding sound: 26000's slowing brakes went out, then its landing flaps. The President looked reflective. He asked, 'How do you feel about Houston?'

'Nervous,' Thomas said nervously. San Antonio had impressed him. He wanted his district to put on as big a show, and he promised the President that it would. 'My people have been busy as a cranberry merchant,' he said. 'They'll deliver.'

'We'll see,' said the President.

They saw a repetition of San Antonio's airport welcome. There was Lyndon, waiting at the foot of the ramp like Grover Whalen; there was the Mayor, all effusion; there were three dozen yellow roses for the First Lady and a white orchid from Albert Miller, Florist; and eight thousand Texans packed around the terminal's cargo entrance, sweating in the ferocious afternoon heat and yelling hoarsely for 'Jackieee'. Thomas needn't have worried. During the past week Jack Valenti had virtually taken a leave of absence from the public relations firm of Weekley and Valenti. As general chairman for tonight's dinner he had sold 3,450 tickets, and he had pulled all the promotion stops in an effort to meet his commitment to O'Donnell. If Air Force One landed before dark, he had written Ken on November 1, he guaranteed 'the enormous downtown working crowd', from '200,000 to 300,000'.

Houston lacked the ardour of San Antonio. The turnout was really about 175,000. It was no Dallas, but liberals were a minority here; Houston's Harris County had gone to Nixon in 1960 by a handsome margin. Today the local right wing had erected several noisome posters along the Presidential route: 'WATCH KENNEDY STAMP OUT YOUR BUSINESS', 'BAN THE BROTHERS', 'KENNEDY, KHRUSHCHEV, AND KING', and a biplane over the field tugged a warlike streamer reading 'COEXISTENCE IS SURRENDER'. Yet despite Kennedy's tardy arrival —his visit to the oxygen chamber had thrown everything off—the dominant mood was enthusiastic. Thomas waved at his applauding constituents and bowed to the President. 'Well?' he asked proudly. 'OK,' Kennedy laughed. 'You win.'

At the gate fence both Kennedys gave themselves to the mob. This kind of campaigning was unfamiliar to Jackie, but she had taken the bit, and her husband was appreciative; from time to time he glanced back at her, smiling encouragement. Once she nearly vanished. Both her wrists were grasped by several talon-like hands, and in near panic she felt herself being dragged over the railing. The talons slackened and she staggered back, juggling yellow roses. 'Don't leave me,' she panted at Albert Thomas. 'Don't get too far away.' 'That's enough,' he called, and he and two of his friends, both septuagenarians, ran interference for her until she reached the car.

The blue Lincoln had been flown on to Dallas in a cargo plane for tomorrow's motorcade there. Here the President would ride in a smaller white convertible. Otherwise the caravan was the same, and Ralph Yarborough remained its most prickly figure. Marty Underwood, the Houston advance man, approached Yarborough and Johnson separately, pointing out to each that they were supposed to be together. Johnson was agreeable, the Senator wasn't. 'We have you scheduled for that car,' Underwood insisted. Yarborough just shook his head. Agent Youngblood made a second attempt to tame him. 'You were supposed to be with the Vice President in San Antonio, Senator,' he said reproachfully, 'and you're supposed to be there here, too.' 'I'm riding with my wife if that's all right with you,' Yarborough said thickly. 'Well, you're scheduled to ride in the Vice President's car for the rest of the trip,' the agent said, and reported back to Johnson. 'I've bugged him enough,' he said, exasperated. Lyndon said nothing. He nodded stonily.

After a hundred yards all the cars slowed to a crawl. The alternative was mayhem: people had swarmed out on the concrete ribbon of the Gulf Freeway, where people never are. Even Valenti hadn't expected this, and John Connally was dumbfounded. Lady Bird, using her homely yardstick, took note of a wizened old man holding a hand-lettered 'WELCOME KENNEDY'; a dozen uniformed Girl Scouts from 'Troop 1381'; a little boy with a faded American flag, standing rigidly to attention. Mrs Kennedy pointed excitedly—on Travis Street the spectators were packed ten and twelve deep, and behind them the traffic was backed up for miles. The President said wryly, 'That's why I've started going into New York without a police escort. For every vote we're winning here, there's some poor guy who can't get to his home over there'—he gestured towards the blocked bridges crossing Buffalo Bayou, on their right—'and who'll be two hours late to his dinner. *He* won't love us. He'll just be furious.'

Mrs Kennedy thought Houston a curious city, two blocks of Manhattan in the middle of a prairie. Houston in turn ogled her. When the column of celebrities drew up outside the Rice Hotel forty minutes later, Hugh Sidey of *Time* scurried up and down kerbs, asking people why they had come. 'To see the President and Jackie,' they said or, often just 'For Jackie.' Kennedy asked Dave Powers to estimate the crowd. 'For you? About as many as turned out the last time you were here,' said Dave, 'but a hundred thousand more have come to look at Jackie.' Women naturally wanted to know what she was wearing. The effect on men was more unsettling. Max Peck, who ran the Rice, was a man of the world. Once, while managing a Washington hotel, he had been stuck in an elevator for twenty minutes with President Truman and Agent Jerry Behn and had preserved his aplomb, but now, as his bellboys unfurled a red carpet, he himself turned brick-red. Swinging open the First Lady's door with a flourish, he babbled idiotically, 'Good evening, Mrs President'.

Main Street was bedlam. Lyndon was on the loose. He had once taught school two blocks from here; he saw a covey of old friends and bore down on them emitting affable cries as pint-sized Valenti bobbed in his wake. The President strolled to the corner of Main and Travis, and he wanted to go farther. The Houston Police Department, anticipating this, had fashioned an ingenious barricade to discourage him. Directly across from the hotel entrance a hundred motorcycles were parked hubcap to hubcap, facing outwards. Trembling hands waggled frantically behind the bikes, but Kennedy couldn't reach them without vaulting the handlebars. He gave it up. His wife took his hand, and they followed Max Peck across the jammed lobby, into an elevator, up to the $150-a-day International Suite on the fifth floor.

Max had had it redecorated with Mrs President in mind. The walls were blue, blue-green, and cream; the carpeting was an arabesque of blue flowers. Except for the tiny bathroom it was exquisite. There was a duplicate of the oval office rocking chair, a basket of fruit in the living-room, and Dom Pérignon, *pâté de foie gras,* and fine caviar. A table supported Jack Daniels, Cutty Sark, and a dozen bottles of Heineken's, Kennedy's favourite beer. In the background a maître d'hôtel was lighting little fires under chafing-dishes. The entrée, it seemed, was to be quail. *Aren't they nice in Texas?* the First Lady thought, and she said aloud, 'It's grand.' 'You're the first to occupy it,' Max murmured, retreating.

The President removed his coat and soggy shirt and sat in the rocker, leafing through a pile of newspapers. Jackie retired. Towards the end of the flight from San Antonio she had read a magazine while her husband napped, and now she dozed in her room while he, stripping to his shorts, reworked tonight's speech. Aides ducked in and out. Mac Kilduff brought Texas anecdotes which Sorensen and Bill Moyers had telephoned him. The President considered them and rejected them; he could do better himself. Powers had touched base with the local politicians; for once they were happy. O'Donnell had agreed to bring in a group photograph of schoolchildren for a Presidential autograph. And the usual nuts were abroad. At 6.34 p.m. an eccentric telegram of support arrived from a man who described himself as a former Catholic altar boy who had become a Protestant minister and chairman of his Masonic lodge. He asked that his wire be read 'on the air tonight'.

Awake, Mrs Kennedy put on a black cut-velvet suit, a double strand of pearls, and diamond earrings. Then the President dressed while Pam Turnure appeared in the suite entrance with a minor emergency. Reporters wanted copies of the First Lady's address, now imminent. The hotel had put four typists at Pam's disposal, and she needed to check the original. She did and darted off. The Kennedys then dined alone. They had to eat before any public banquet; once they arrived at the head table there would be too many distractions.

The rest of the Presidential party was scattered throughout the hotel and city. In the lobby Larry O'Brien was meeting Jack Valenti for the first time. Larry checked the final plans for the dinner and watched Valenti bound off with a dispatch case under his arm, never dreaming that he would ever see him again; then he strolled into the hotel's Flag Room restaurant with O'Donnell and Powers. Others were resting upstairs, and the room assignment of each offered a clue to his status. Lowly Congressmen were huddled around a communal bar in 301. Albert Thomas, a distinguished exception, had an apartment on the thirteenth floor; the Attorney General of Texas had been given another on the tenth. Ralph Yarborough and John Connally, through an appalling oversight, were sharing the seventeenth floor. (Lookouts were posted, like Hatfields and McCoys. Luckily the two never met in the passage.) Because the testimonial banquet would be routine, most of the press, like the mafia, had decided to skip it, and Henry Brandon of the London *Sunday Times* was dining with an Englishman who lived in Houston. The host painted a dark picture of anti-Kennedy sentiment among Texas rightists. To Brandon his countryman seemed obsessed with the subject. The radicals couldn't be more vicious, the man said over and over; the situation couldn't possibly be exaggerated.

The Rice's fifth floor, the President's, was reserved for those closest to him: Larry, Ken, Dave, Evelyn, Dr Burkley, Generals Clifton and McHugh. The Secret Service arsenal was in 528, the Houston White House switchboard in 514–516. Directly overhead, the Vice President was eating in his sixth-floor Gold Suite ($100 a day) with Lady Bird. His smaller staff was clustered around him. Immediately across the hall, in 625, Liz Carpenter was changing her clothes and reflecting with some despair that she hadn't had much luck making friends among the President's staff. They didn't exactly cut her. They just maintained their distance. Maybe blood is thinner and cooler in Massachusetts, she thought, straightening seams. Liz was at the mirror, inspecting herself, when the Gold Suite door swung open on the other side of the passage and its occupant hurried towards the stairs. Lyndon B. Johnson had an appointment with John F. Kennedy.

The substance of the meeting—their final conference together—is unclear. According to Johnson's recollection nineteen months later, 'There definitely was not a disagreement. . . . There was an active discussion' in which the two 'were in substantial agreement'. He did not define the nature of the discussion, but if the memories of others are to be credited, the President and his successor had words over the state's political feud. Precisely what was said is unknown, for one President is dead, and a whirlwind was about to descend upon the other, blurring the sequence of events leading up to it. They were alone. Mrs Kennedy had withdrawn into the next room to rehearse. Although aware of raised voices in the background, she was concentrating on her speech. The caterer and the hotel servants, who were in and out, heard Yarborough's name mentioned several times. All had the impression that Kennedy felt the Senator was not being treated fairly, and that he was expressing himself with exceptional force. Johnson controlled his celebrated temper in his chief's presence, but in the words of one man on duty outside, 'he left that suite like a pistol'. Max Peck, watching him shoot into the corridor, long legs pumping, thought he looked furious.

'What was that all about?' Jacqueline Kennedy asked, coming in after the Vice President had left. 'He sounded mad.' The President looked amused. 'That's just Lyndon,' he said. 'But he's in trouble.'

On a sudden impulse she blurted out that she disliked Governor Connally.

He asked, 'Why do you say that?'

'I can't stand him all day. He's just one of those men—oh, I don't know. I just can't bear him sitting there saying all these great things about himself. And he seems to be needing *you* all day.'

'You mustn't say you dislike him, Jackie. If you say it, you'll begin thinking it, and it will prejudice how you act towards him the next day. He's been cozying up to a lot of these Texas businessmen who weren't for him before. What he was really saying in the car was that he's going to run ahead of me in Texas. Well, that's all right. Let him. But for heaven's sakes don't get a thing on him, because that's what I came down here to heal. I'm trying to start by getting two people in the same car. If they start hating, nobody will ride with anybody.'

So she shook it off. It was nearly time for her appearance, anyhow. The LULACS were waiting downstairs in the Grand Ballroom, and committing her remarks to memory had been unexpectedly difficult. 'Oh, Jack, it's *awful*,' she moaned as they went to the door. 'Something's happened to me. I used to be able to memorize *any*thing in ten minutes. All through South America I'd just memorize those things five minutes before. I must be cracking up.'

'No, no, no,' he said soothingly. 'You'll be great.'

But she wasn't so sure. She speculated on whether something could have happened to her memory. Fleetingly she wondered whether last August's tragedy could be responsible.

Jay Watson, the Rice Hotel auditor, had a clever scheme. The Grand Ballroom was on the mezzanine. Walking there from the elevator, the Kennedys would pass the San Jacinto Room, so Watson had reserved it for a cocktail party. At the proper moment, he thought, he and a group of fellow Houston accountants could step into the mustard-coloured corridor for a private viewing of the President. The ruse seemed foolproof, but there was a fatal flaw in it. He had failed to take the Secret Service into account, and the Service's drill for buildings covered everything. Over the past nine days, for example, agents had interrogated every employee of the Houston Coliseum, where the Thomas dinner was to be held. Each air-conditioning unit in the Rice had been checked for poison gas. Armed sentinels had mounted guard on a low roof just outside the windows of the International Suite, and in the Grand Ballroom itself a Presidential appearance at the LULACS' head table had been vetoed on the ground that Kennedy would be too exposed there; instead, a temporary podium had been erected on the south side of the hall. The San Jacinto Room plot never had a chance of surviving this kind of vigilance. While the accountants merely drained martinis, an agent quietly secured all rooms leading to the mezzanine, and when the time came for Watson to move his party he discovered that they were locked in. Kennedy passed within a few feet of the San Jacinto Room, unaware that thirty enraged auditors were pounding on the door.

He couldn't hear them because there was so much other noise. The seven hundred LULACS were in full voice, surging forward, jostling one another, hoping for a handshake. The scrimmage became fierce. The President leaned over two muscular-dystrophy patients from Liberty, Texas; Captain Stoughton took a photograph for their campaign; and Max Peck, recovering his balance in the background, was astounded to find that every button on his coat *and* his shirt had been ripped off. 'You're busy, Mr President,' a member of Max's staff said. Kennedy winced. 'It's rough,' he said feelingly. In the ballroom, after his Vice President had spoken, he talked briefly about the *Alianza*. 'In order that my words will be even clearer to you,' he concluded, 'I am going to ask my wife to say a few words to you also.' That was her cue. She suppressed her stage fright, and her classical accent fell quaintly on ears accustomed to Mexican diction:

'... *pero es una tradición que se mantiene viva y vigorosa. Ustedes estaban trabajando por Texas y por los Estados Unidos. Muchas gracias y viva la LULACS!*'

'*Olé!*' they roared. It really hadn't been that great. He had told them more. But she had given it to them in their own tongue. 'Jackie spoke in Spanish,' wrote Dave Powers. 'They all loved and cheered here.' Leaving the ballroom, Dave noted, the Kennedys 'exchanged eyes'—Lady Bird thought the First Lady's husband 'looked beguiled'—and on their way to the car the President collared a bilingual spectator, questioned him closely, and relayed word to her that she had been wonderful. She wasn't impressed by his witness. What else could the poor man say? But she was pleased by the gesture, touched that he was still waging an all-out Kennedy campaign to sell Texas to her.

The motorcade in the dark was their fourth of the day, and there were to be two more before they could sleep. Even ovations can become a bore. She asked wearily, 'Who organized this testimonial for Albert Thomas, anyway?'

'Albert Thomas,' the President said quizzically. In detail he gravely explained how Thomas had made the plans, written speeches praising himself, run all over the state selling tickets, cooked the——

'*Jack!*'

At the Coliseum Valenti, the real mastermind, was having almost as much trouble with the Secret Service as an auditor. Agent Emory Roberts demanded to see his White House pass. He didn't have one, had never seen one. If two Houston patrolmen hadn't stepped forward to identify Valenti, he would have been escorted out. Once inside, however, he was entirely at home among the labyrinth of concrete passages. Indeed, he contrived to be the only outsider in the backstage lounge that had been set aside for the President and the Vice President—a trick both Yarborough and Connally would have given a lot to know. He lurked there while the Kennedys and Johnsons chatted pleasantly, waiting for the paying customers to finish their Chicken Virginia, and when they took their seats at the head table he crept along in their wake. There was no seat there for him, so he crouched beneath the President's legs like a Metropolitan Opera prompter. He heard little that was inspiring. It was a typical testimonial. A gigantic sign overhead read, 'HARRIS COUNTY SAYS, "THANK YOU, CONGRESSMAN THOMAS."' One by one eminent speakers rose, cleared their throats, were reminded of threadbare anecdotes, and paid fulsome tributes to the Congressman. A committee presented him with a Cadillac. The dilemma over introductions might have provided some spice, but Thomas skilfully avoided that by handling them himself, buying time for the peacemakers. The President himself didn't contribute much eloquence. The finest passages in his speech (and the only ones Mrs Kennedy would remember later) were Biblical: '"Your old men shall dream dreams, your young men shall see visions,"' and '"Where there is no vision, the people perish."' Most of his address was statistical—Texas ranked fifth among the states in prime military contract spending—and the text was a rather crass reminder that a lot of Houston bread was buttered in the Pentagon. But Kennedy had a way of delivering pedestrian prose as though it were classical Latin. And he enlivened the address with a deliberate slip. Next month, he declared, the United States was going to launch the space programme's biggest booster, firing 'the largest payroll—payload—into space, giving us the lead'. He added swiftly: 'It will be the biggest payroll, too!'

The President laughed, apparently relaxing. But he wasn't relaxed. In press conferences he could be at ease, despite the size of the television audience. Question-and-answer sessions were a challenge, a test of intellect. He had never learned to enjoy formal speeches, however, and his casual appearance was a triumph of the will. Unlike Lyndon, he was not an extrovert. To his audiences his easy air seemed unstudied. Very few knew how hard he had toiled to achieve it. On a rostrum the illusion of spontaneity was almost perfect; only his hands would have betrayed him, and he was careful to keep them out of sight. They weren't out of Valenti's sight, though. They were just above him, vibrating so violently at times that they seemed palsied. Now and then the right hand would shoot up and out, the index finger stabbing the limelit air to make a point. The moment it dropped the trembling would begin again. Several times he nearly dropped his 5 x 7 cards. *Why, the President's nervous*, thought Valenti, dumbfounded, and he felt like an eavesdropper, which in a way he was.

It was after 9.30 when the travellers left the head table, and they couldn't rest until they had reached another hotel in another city. There was some confusion outside the Coliseum. On the spur of the moment the Vice President decided that he wanted more company on the rest of the trip. Valenti, who was still hanging around, was drafted. He thrust his car keys at his wife and left her frowning on the sidewalk; Mary Margaret Valenti had been Senator Lyndon Johnson's secretary before she became Jack's wife, and she wasn't cowed by the Vice President's title. She was anxious that Jack not be away overnight because she had just had a baby. Attorney General Carr and his wife were temporarily separated, and she protested tearfully that she wouldn't fly without him. Congressman Teague was darting to and fro, looking frantically for an empty car, when he heard a heckling voice call, 'Hey, Tiger! Why don't you get Yarborough to ride with you?' It was the President. He was peering out of a closed Cadillac limousine and chuckling.

Inside were Mrs Kennedy; John Jones, publisher of the Houston *Chronicle*; and his wife, Freddie. Thomas had been responsible for their presence, which turned out to be another piece of hard luck for

Johnson. Jones told Kennedy that tomorrow's *Chronicle* would indicate 57 per cent of Texas voters were for Yarborough and 50 per cent for Kennedy–Johnson. With that kind of backing, the Senator was no man to cross. Freddie Jones was not an admirer of the Vice President. Freddie also held strong views about various Texas cities. She was fond of Fort Worth. It was small, poor, and proud of being known as Cowtown, Where the West Begins. 'But *Dallas*!' She didn't think much of Dallas. 'It's a merchant's town—really, a terrible town.' Jackie liked Freddie, and she wondered vaguely what Dallas would be like.

At the airport Marty Underwood had lined up Houston's Presidential police detail; before leaving a community it was a Kennedy custom to shake hands with each officer who had served in his escort. There was another throng here, and though they held back, Underwood was to recall next day how vulnerable the President had been on that dark airstrip. Then the advance man was called away; Pam Turnure, it developed, had become lost in the bowels of the Coliseum. Air Force One's take-off was delayed ten minutes while a car fetched her. Aloft the President came forward to call, 'Ralph, I've just heard about the *Chronicle* poll—congratulations on how well you're doing,' and check some reports with Godfrey McHugh.

At 11.07 p.m. the three planes landed among the hulking grey steel sheds and preposterous Strategic Air Command billboards ('PEACE IS OUR PROFESSION') of Carswell Air Force Base on the outskirts of Fort Worth. Thursday's final motorcade formed in a light rain. Yarborough, assuming that there wouldn't be much of a turnout at this hour and in this weather, asked Agent Youngblood if there would be room for him in the Vice President's car here. The Senator had guessed wrong. All along the city's East–West Freeway drenched ranks hailed the Kennedys, and for the first time there were clear shouts of 'Lyndon! There's LBJ!' The Johnsons and Connallys were delighted. Lady Bird recalled that Fort Worth's Hotel Texas had been the scene of some of the most dramatic moments in her husband's career. To Nellie Connally, remembering the days when her husband worked for Sid Richardson here, Fort Worth was 'like coming home'.

Outlanders took a different view. A marquee outside the hotel read 'WELCOME, MR PRESIDENT', but this wasn't like the suave Rice. The quarters set aside for the President were actually smaller and cheaper than the Vice President's. The lobby was solid with jostling, hooting men in cream-coloured five-gallon hats. Agent Lem Johns lost his shaving gear in the confusion; in Room 660 two other members of the party were so crowded that they had to take turns unpacking; Captain Stoughton, who was bunking with the bagman here, had difficulty unlocking his door. One member of the hotel staff, who might have been helpful, ran around mugging for photographers. 'The hotel arrangements,' as O'Donnell said later, 'were all screwed up.'

Kennedy conferred with O'Donnell for ten minutes. The political feud was discussed but briefly. There hadn't been much about it in the evening papers; the stories filed by correspondents covering the trip had reached newsrooms too late. Dick Goodwin had called twice from Washington with a minor problem. The *New York Times* had learned of his new job and had decided to make him tomorrow's 'Man in the News'. So far he had declined comment; what should he do? The President instructed him to prepare an announcement of his own appointment, dating it for release tomorrow. The First Lady was also being badgered by the press, and through Pam she sent reporters word that Thursday had been 'a wonderful day. Texas friendliness was everything I'd heard it to be.' Then she and the President went up to their three-room suite on the eighth floor and found it to be anything but warm. Something was wrong with the air conditioner; it was going full blast. Kennedy ordered it turned off.

Mrs Kennedy had been given a drab green room overlooking a neoned parking lot bordered by two loan companies, two bus stations, a garage, a theatre. On a table was a medley of messages: a card from the Italian Vice Consul; a telegram from the second vice president of the National Association of Coloured Women's Clubs; several religious cards from Catholic well-wishers; the score of a song written by a local composer; a gaudy certificate citing 'Jacqueline B. Kennedy' for 'Outstanding Community Service' and embellished by a gold foil seal and a broad red, white, and blue ribbon; fresh flowers from the Chamber of Commerce (Gordon Boswell, Florist); and—a stirring from the enemy camp—a file card from a Republican college student bearing a sardonic greeting and the signature 'AuH_2O'. Beside the table was her luggage. Where was Mary Gallagher? She had been sidetracked. Dead tired, yet aware that the morning would be hectic, Mrs Kennedy crouched over her bags and started pulling out clothes.

Before retiring she joined the President.

'You were great today,' he said.

'How do you feel?'

'Oh, gosh, I'm exhausted.'

His vitality was illusory, like his debonair manner. Half asleep, he was planning ahead. 'Don't get up with me,' he called. 'I've got to speak in that square downstairs before breakfast, but stay in bed. Just be at the breakfast at nine-fifteen.' She said good night.

Before turning out the light she carefully laid out tomorrow's navy blue blouse, navy handbag, low-heeled shoes, pink suit, and pillbox hat.

While the Kennedys slept in 850, most of the rest of their entourage were still up, and some were really jumping. Five floors above them, in the more spacious Will Rogers Suite, Lyndon jovially entertained members of his tong. Off the lobby John Connally held court hour after hour in the hotel's coffee shop, which never closes. Bob Baskin of the Dallas *News* told him of Yarborough's snappishness, and Connally issued a ringing call for harmony. Duty kept some Secret Service men awake. The twelve-to-eight shift mounted guard outside 850. Clint Hill instructed Congressman Jim Wright of Fort Worth to join the President promptly at quarter-to-eight in the morning. Muggsy O'Leary, posted at the hotel entrance, saw a figure lying on a roof diagonally across from Kennedy's window, and a policeman scurried off to chase him away. As agent in charge Roy Kellerman had special responsibilities. With Hill and Bill Duncan, who had advanced this leg of the trip, he inspected the parking lot; he examined the entrances and exits the President would use and ordered Kennedy's Fort Worth car secured for the night. Then, after a cup of coffee, he went to bed.

Others were already asleep: Greer, Emory Roberts, the Vice Presidential Detail. The crews of 26000 and 86970, after leaving guards at the planes—this was routine, even at a SAC base—checked into a nearby motel. But nine agents of the White House Detail, unknown to Kellerman, were out on the town. They started with beer and mixed drinks at the Fort Worth Press Club with Mac Kilduff; then seven of them continued at a colourful establishment called 'The Cellar', ordering 'Salty Dicks', a nonalcoholic speciality of the house. One stayed until 5 a.m.[6] Fellow drinkers during those early-morning hours included four agents who were to ride in the President's follow-up car in Dallas, and whose alertness was vital to his safety. At various times they were joined by three agents of the twelve-to-eight shift—who were officially on duty, assigned to guard the President's bedroom door—and who chose to break the boredom of sentry duty in this fashion.

Godfrey McHugh was duty officer. Had unidentified bombers arrived over Canada, the General would normally have been summoned instantly from his room, 831. The General wasn't in 831, however. Fort Worth happened to be God's home of record. At

[6] In fairness it should be noted that films of the following morning's activities suggest that this man was—with Clint Hill—one of the most agile members of the detail. Therefore his name is not given here.

midnight he had looked in on General Clifton in 829 and told him he was passing him the baton—'Hold the satchel' was his expression. Clifton then went out for a half-hour, though he was within reach of the local White House operator. McHugh meanwhile had driven a Secret Service car five miles away to the chic suburb of Westover Hills and was visiting his former employers, two oilmen named Robert N. and E. J. McCurdy. The call wasn't much fun for Godfrey. He was devoted to his Commander in Chief, and the McCurdy brothers were vehemently anti-Kennedy. Each time he tried to talk about petroleum they launched a new lecture, the gist of which was that the President was wrecking the country, using American wheat to feed Red soldiers, and generally selling out to Russia. After two hours McHugh concluded that his trip to Westover Hills had been a mistake and drove back.

No strange blips had appeared on Canadian radar screens. It was an exceptionally quiet night, here and abroad. The only foreign news of note was a Labour victory in a British by-election and a Soviet note complaining about American convoys to Berlin. At home the Birdman of Alcatraz had died at seventy-three, Jimmy Hoffa's most recent trial had proceeded smoothly in Nashville. the Dow-Jones industrial average had closed at 732.65, and the American Legion post in Abilene, Texas, had removed a portrait of the President of the United States from its walls on the ground that he was controversial. Change a name here, a figure there, and the same stories could have been published a year earlier.

In Dallas, thirty miles east of Fort Worth, earlier alarms appeared to have been unfounded. On the surface, at least, everything was serene. Richard M. Nixon, now a Pepsi-Cola attorney, slept soundly after a busy day on the floor of the bottlers convention, across from the Trade Mart. Final preparations for the big parade had been completed that afternoon when Forrest Sorrels of the Secret Service supervised the unloading of the blue Presidential Lincoln and the armoured follow-up car—both were now stored in Love Field's underground garage—and ordered a fleet of Lincolns and Mercurys from a Dallas Ford agency and buses, for the press and the VIP's, from the Continental Trailways system. At 11 p.m. U.S. Attorney Barefoot Sanders came home to receive a welcome message: his baby sitter informed him that Sam Bloom of the Citizens Council had left word that several tickets for tomorrow's Trade Mart lunch were being set aside for admirers of the President. Sanders began parcelling them out.

Half a continent away, the nation's capital was placid. That wasn't unusual. Few taxpayers realized it, but the District of Columbia was among the most staid metropolises in the country.

Most households retired early. An exception that evening was a dinner party on Highland Place attended by Goodwin and Senator Edward M. Kennedy, but that was because the guests of honour were Goodwin's Latin Americans, who were accustomed to late hours. There were few other official functions of any consequence. Aircraft 86972 was now in Hawaii—Secretaries Rusk and Dillon and their wives were staying in the guest house of Admiral Harry D. Felt, CINCPAC—and the only Cabinet members left in Washington were Robert Kennedy, McNamara, Celebrezze, and the new man, Postmaster General Gronouski. Apart from the Latin-American fiesta, the liveliest event in official Washington that evening was a movie. Arthur Schlesinger, a film fan, was showing a preview of *From Russia with Love* in the White House theatre. Afterwards Ted Sorensen predicted that the President would enjoy it.

One of the dullest events was a meeting of the National Association for Mental Health in the Shoreham Hotel. The speaker of the evening was Senator Hubert H. Humphrey of Minnesota; his topic was 'Mental Health and World Peace'. Reporters understandably avoided it. They had no way of anticipating how topical his speech was to be. Humphrey had been giving Dallas considerable thought and had concluded that communities as well as individuals 'can be afflicted with emotional instability, frustrations, and irrational behaviour'. He cited 'that emotional instability that afflicts a significant but small minority in our midst that some call the extreme right, some the Birchers, some the wild men of reaction. . . . They still see the world in total black and white. They are looking for immediate and final answers. They are still substituting dogma for creative thought. They are still angry, fearful, deeply and fundamentally disturbed by the world around them.' And on this evening of November 21, 1963, Humphrey warned the behavioural scientists that 'the act of an emotionally unstable person or irresponsible citizen can strike down a great leader'.[7]

Two floors above the White House theatre, in her quarters between the bedrooms of the First Family's children, Maude Shaw was knitting alone. All day the children had been too busy to miss their parents. Caroline had attended a classmate's seventh-birthday party in Chevy Chase, and Agent Tom Wells had taken John to a toy shop on Wisconsin Avenue. After dinner John and his sister played with what the agents of the kiddie detail called 'blocks' and their English nanny stoutly insisted were 'bricks'. Then came their daily baths and their story hour. Caroline brushed her teeth and John

[7] In the Shoreham audience was Senator Dan Inouye of Hawaii. Next time they met he told Humphrey in awe, 'You told us—you were telling us!' Humphrey replied, 'But I didn't know it.'

pored over picture books until bedtime. Until recently he had slept with a stuffed grey bear. Conscious of being a boy, he now took toy trucks and helicopters into his crib. But Caroline still doted on her soft animals. As Miss Shaw turned out the light she had heard the President's daughter whispering to them that tomorrow they were going to have an adventure. For the first time in their lives, Caroline had promised, they would sleep away from relatives, and they must be on their best behaviour.

Among the thousands of Fort Worth motorists who crossed the President's motorcade route Thursday evening was a heavy-jowled practical nurse named Marguerite Claverie Oswald. She had just finished a 3-to-11 p.m. shift at the Hargrove Convalescent Centre, turning her sleeping patient over for the last time and leaving a clean bedpan, and she was en route to her own home on the other side of Trinity Park when she saw two policemen barring her usual exit from the East–West Freeway. With characteristic vim she ignored them. Stepping on the accelerator of her blue-grey 1954 Buick, she vanished in the darkness and the rain, and their startled expressions, illumined for a flickering instant in her headlights, provided her, as she later recalled, with a brief sense of satisfaction. It was a smaller triumph than she imagined. She was under the impression that the motorcade had already begun. Had the President been in the vicinity, she would have been diverted. Actually, she parked the Buick outside her two-room frame duplex in the 2200 block of Thomas Place at 11.15 p.m., five minutes before Kennedy left Carswell Air Force Base. But she liked to think she had held things up a bit.

Marguerite Oswald often saw herself as the target of nameless forces; she was a woman of many resentments and felt them all keenly. Aged fifty-six, she had a reedy, scolding voice, and in conversation she was highly vocal on status and money, each of which she coveted and lacked. Although she had been married three times, she had nothing to show for it. One man had died and the other two had quit her, the last one after accusing her of crippling physical assaults upon him. Physically she was capable of it. She was a powerfully built women; muscles knotted in her thick neck; she had the complexion of mottled pewter. A jury had agreed with the plaintiff, finding that Marguerite had been 'guilty of excesses, cruel treatment, or outrages'. Now she lived on her $9-a-day income as a shifter of bodies and bedpans, husbanding an $80 bank account and hoping her car and her elderly female patient would survive for another year or two.

She didn't mind poverty, provided strangers were quite clear about the difference between what she called 'poor people' and 'poor trash'. The daughter of a New Orleans streetcar conductor (who, she liked to point out, had received 'a citation' on retirement), she was proud of her talent for frugality and had passed it along to her youngest son, who had just turned twenty-four. Marguerite and Lee Harvey Oswald were alike in other ways, too. Various acquaintances were subsequently to describe him as tense, withdrawn, maladjusted, waspish, insolent, secretive, and 'kind of drawn up', with a 'fixed-focus mind'. In Moscow he had given Commander Hallett the impression that he was 'fleeing from a skeleton in the family closet'. Everyone thought him cold and arrogant, and certainly Marguerite was those. Even as a young woman she liked to be known as 'the boss'. By her own account she had been fired from 'about five' jobs. Of herself and Lee she would later say, 'I've been persecuted and he's been persecuted. They've all turned their backs on me before and they'll do it again.'

Lee's father was the husband who had died. His fatal heart attack had come two months before the boy's birth, leaving Marguerite as the sole parent. Under the circumstances mother and son might have formed a tender bond. They didn't. Lee slept with her until he was nearly eleven years old, but propinquity is not affection. Neither is refusal to discipline a child; when little Lee tangled with adults, Marguerite snapped that the charges were 'trumped up'. In reality she was in a poor position to evalute such accusations. She was away during the day, and she had forbidden Lee to call her at work. Because she disapproved of playmates, he spent a remarkable amount of time alone. Very early he became a flagrant truant. He preferred to lounge around the house, watching television and reading comic books. At the age of thirteen his truancy brought mother and son to the attention of a school psychiatrist, who concluded that Marguerite did not grasp that Lee's withdrawal was a form of 'protest against his neglect by her and represents his reaction to a complete absence of any real family life'. To his probation officer Lee said, 'Well, I've got to live with her. I guess I love her.'

He wasn't pressed for a definition of love. It is quite possible that he had no real concept of it. Already he had acquired a violent, brutal personality. Once he chased his half-brother with a knife. (She passed this off as a 'little scuffle'.) Another time, brandishing another blade, he threatened his half-brother's wife. This scuffle was larger, and Marguerite tried to intervene. But it was too late. She had lost control of him. He had grown too big for discipline, and instead of obeying he turned on her and struck her. Already irrevocable patterns of behaviour had formed in him; already he had become truculent with men and inadequate with women—and quick to rage at both.

Although his IQ was high (118), his report cards didn't show it. On the record he was a dunce, and after completing the ninth grade he dropped out of school. Emulating his brother Robert, he enlisted in the Marine Corps, an unfortunate choice for a youth who resented authority. He baited officers, and they gave him the back of their hand. Fellow enlisted men scorned him as 'Ozzie Rabbit'. His three years in uniform became a miserable string of petty infractions and two courts-martial, culminating, after his attempt to defect to Russia, in an undesirable discharge. Yet Marine training leaves marks on the most stubborn recruit. The Corps' courses in marksmanship are the best in the world, and Private Oswald had qualified as a sharpshooter with the M-1 rifle on the San Diego range. It was his first skill, and his last.

He had also picked up the habit of sirring older men, a trait that favourably impressed Roy S. Truly, the conservative superintendent of the Texas School Book Depository. Most young men were disrespectful these days, Truly thought. Here was a refreshing exception, and Oswald was hired on October 15, 1963, at $1.25 an hour. Although filling book orders in the dingy warehouse was menial work, he was lucky to get it. His wife was expecting her second baby—five days after the superintendent took him on she was delivered of another daughter at Parkland Hospital—and since his return from Russia he had passed through one cycle of frustration after another. His Soviet adventure wasn't responsible. He had kept that a secret. The bleak truth was that he couldn't do anything right. He hadn't even been able to hold a job as a greaser of coffee machinery. Bit by bit the sickening truth was emerging: no one wanted him, no one had ever wanted him. He had sailed to the U.S.S.R. to escape his disappointments in his own country. Thwarted there, too, he had sailed back. The month before Truly employed him he had tried to run to Havana, which was on bad terms with both Moscow and Washington, but in Mexico City the Cubans wouldn't even grant him a visa. By then Lee Harvey Oswald had become the most rejected man of his time. It is not too much to say that he was the diametric opposite of John Fitzgerald Kennedy.

Oswald was aware of this. Significantly, he attributed the President's success to family wealth; as he saw it, Kennedy had had all the breaks. Like many delusions this one had a kernel of truth. The President was ten times a millionaire. But that was only one of a thousand differences between them. One man had almost everything and the other almost nothing. Kennedy, for example, was spectacularly handsome. Although Oswald's voice hadn't yet lost its adolescent tone, he was already balding, and he had the physique of a ferret. The President had been a brave officer during the war, and while strapped to a bed of convalescence he had written a book which won a Pulitzer Prize. Oswald's record in the peacetime service had been disgraceful, and he was barely literate. As Chief Executive and Commander in Chief, Kennedy was all powerful. Oswald was impotent. Kennedy was cheered, Oswald ignored. Kennedy was noble, Oswald ignoble. Kennedy was beloved, Oswald despised. Kennedy was a hero; Oswald was a victim.

Since childhood Oswald had been threatened by a specific mental disease, paranoia. In the end the paranoiac loses all sense of reality. He is overpowered by a monstrous feeling of personal resentment and a blind craving for revenge. No one can predict what will trigger the catastrophe in any given case. It may never come; men and women with paranoid minds often live out their miserable lives without breaking once. Oswald, however, was not fated to be one of them. There came a time when the terrible spark flared through the fragmented dust of his ego, when the sheet of flame began its fatal advance across the layers of firedamp.

Whatever the complex nature of that combustible, we now know beyond reasonable doubt what kindled the firestorm in Lee Oswald. It was the disintegration of his marriage. We also know when the wave overwhelmed him. It fell on the evening of Thursday, November 21, 1963.

His mother did not know it. Marguerite wasn't even aware that her son lay in a bed less than ten miles from her. She had seen neither him nor her daughter-in-law for over a year, and had made no attempt to find out what had become of them. The truth is that she didn't seem to care. She had her own lonely life to live, and after laying out tomorrow's white uniform she sank heavily into bed. She wanted to be asleep before midnight. She liked to rise early and watch daytime television.

At 4.40 p.m. Thursday, while the Kennedys were deplaning in Houston after their peaceful forty-five-minute flight from Kelly Field, Lee Oswald had ended his day's work in Dallas and begged a lift to suburban Irving, in the battered black nine-year-old Chevrolet of Wesley Frazier, a scrawny Alabaman and fellow employee. To the best of Frazier's recollection, Oswald had approached him a few minutes after both had learned, from the map on the front page of the afternoon *Times-Herald*, that tomorrow's parade would pass the warehouse.

'Could I ride home with you this afternoon?' Oswald inquired.

'Sure,' said Frazier. 'Like I told you, you can go home with me any time you want to. Any time you want to see your wife, that's all right with me.'

Then it struck him that there was something odd about today's request. In the past Oswald had gone to see his wife on Fridays, for the weekend, and this was a Thursday. Ordinarily he spent the week in a Dallas rooming house at 1026 North Beckley Avenue.

'Why are you going home today?' Frazier asked.

'To get some curtain rods,' Oswald explained. 'You know—to put in an apartment.' Frazier, unaware that Oswald's furnished room on North Beckley was already equipped with jalousies, nodded understandingly.

The trip from the warehouse to Irving was a toboggan ride over a rolling, ten-lane concrete highway which passes through a singularly barren tract of land bordered by heavy industry, fiilling stations, and night clubs. Oswald said nothing, but Frazier didn't think that peculiar; he was often moody. Today, however, his thoughts must have been remarkable. Some time, probably during the afternoon, he had slipped into the Book Depository's shipping department and fashioned a brown paper bag to conceal a bolt-action, clip-fed, 6.5 millimetre Mannlicher-Carcano rifle. Oswald owned such a weapon. Last winter, under the assumed name of 'A. Hidell', he had sent a coupon from the *American Rifleman* and a money order for $21.45 to Klein's Sporting Goods, Inc. in Chicago. In return a gun bearing serial number C2766 and a four-power telescopic sight had been shipped to Dallas Post Office Box 2915 on March 20. Using the same alias, Oswald had ordered a .38 Smith & Wesson revolver, but the smoke screen was clumsy, even for him. Both order slips had been in his handwriting. Box 2915 was rented in his name, and in his wallet he carried a crude counterfeit Marine Corps certificate of service identifying the bearer as 'Alek J. Hidell'.

The revolver was in his furnished room. The rifle was hidden in a brown and green blanket which, together with several sea bags containing his personal belongings, was stored in the cluttered garage of Michael R. Paine at 2515 West Fifth Street in Irving, a few steps from Frazier's home. Oswald was going home to get it now. His earlier conversation with Frazier, coming directly after the news that the President would be within easy range of the warehouse tomorrow noon, leaves very little doubt that the two events were connected.[8]

[8] A subsequent controversy developed over whether or not the shots fired from the warehouse on November 22 had been difficult ones, and echoes of the dispute are heard today. Here the author must appear briefly as an expert witness. This writer has carefully examined the site in Dallas and once qualified as an Expert Rifleman on the U.S. Marine Corps range at Parris Island, S.C., firing the M-1 rifle, as Oswald did, from 500, 300, and 200 yards. From the sixth floor in the Book Depository Oswald would look down on a slowly drifting target less than ninety yards away, and his scope brought it within twenty-two yards. At that distance, with his training, he could scarcely have missed.

Yet there is every reason to believe that his decision at this point was tentative. He had not quite reached the point of no return, and his behaviour after he reached Irving suggests that it would have taken very little to dissuade him. Despite Oswald's envy of the President, John Kennedy was not the central figure in his life. That person was Marina Oswald. Like his rifle, his wife was at 2515 West Fifth Street, and he went to her first. Only after she had turned him away, only after she had made it emphatically clear that she did not want him—only then did he reach for the gun.

The Paine home was deceptive. From the outside it was a modest, one-storey, four-room frame house like hundreds of thousands of others in the Southwest. The built-in garage was used for storage, which is not uncommon. Although the interior showed little taste and was almost barren of feminine charm, it was practical and comfortable. The living-room, facing the street, was equipped with a sofa, a high-fidelity set, and a new Zenith television set. The kitchen in the rear was dominated by a large, sturdy table. The garage was off the kitchen, to the left; on the right there were a bathroom and two small, rather sparsely furnished bedrooms shielded by white Venetian blinds. The building was an ordinary suburban home. It was people who made it extraordinary.

Michael Paine, the head of the household, was not in residence. He was a slight, fair, rather wispy design engineer at the Bell Helicopter plant in Fort Worth. His father was an ardent Communist, and as a boy Michael had tagged along to party meetings and had tried to wrestle with *Das Kapital* and the *Communist Manifesto*. He found the people at the rallies too intense, the books too steep. He had a hazy conviction that the world needed changing, but he felt that the change needn't be so drastic. It was a girl who provided him with the prescription for milder tonic. Michael was introduced to his future wife, Ruth Hyde, at a folk dance meeting, and after their marriage on December 28, 1957, he became a minor participant in the sociopolitical movements of which she was the driving force, notably the East–West Contacts Committee. The committee encouraged pen pals in the Soviet Union; Ruth was the chairman. Unfortunately, interest in reform wasn't enough to keep the Paines together. In September of 1962, just before their fifth wedding anniversary, they separated. He moved into an apartment. She remained in the house with their two children.

Ruth was the stronger parent, and by far the more interesting. The daughter of a physician and an ordained female Unitarian minister, she was a graduate of Antioch and a Quaker convert. Her appearance was equally striking; in the autumn of 1963 she was a slender, dark-eyed brunette of thirty-one, with a soft, musical contralto voice and handsome, if slightly equine, features. She impressed everyone as a pious, highly intelligent young matron. There were almost no lengths to which Ruth Paine would not go as a Samaritan. She was charitable, she was a regular blood donor at Parkland Hospital, and when, five months after she and her husband parted, she encountered a fair-haired twenty-one-year-old Slavic girl badly in need of comfort, the consequences were predictable. They met at a party on February 22, 1963. Lonely, Ruth needed a crony. She sought the girl's address on the spot and then wrote to her. Her new acquaintance had something to offer in return for friendship. Ruth's work in the East–West Contacts Committee had stimulated her interest in the Russian language, and now Marina was about to seek Ruth's help and protection.

Thus Marina Nikolaevna Oswald became the link between her husband and the Paines. Ruth, at the same time, became her chief benefactor. To be sure, other people—members of the Fort Worth–Dallas Russian community—took a benevolent interest in the girl. But Ruth's bonhomie eclipsed theirs. Indeed, since Michael was absent, the relationship was largely confined to three people. Henceforth the lives of Ruth, Marina, and Lee would be tightly bound together. The husband and the older woman became rivals for the friendship of the blonde wife, while she apparently toyed with first one and then the other. It was a new situation for Marina. She had been born the unwanted, illegitimate daughter of an Archangel *dyevushka*; she had never learned her father's identity. In some respects her background resembled Lee's. As a child she had been a disciplinary problem, and on at least one occasion she had seriously contemplated suicide. But Marina had one enormous advantage which he lacked. Physically she was far more attractive. She aroused protective instincts and invited rescue. Her husband had spirited her away from the U.S.S.R., and now Ruth, more resourceful than Lee, was about to spirit her away from him.

Even before Ruth's appearance the Oswalds' marriage had become a cruel farce. In Minsk Lee had thought he had found a beautiful dedicated Communist who would for ever be his *Marinenka*, his submissive darling. Only the beauty had been real. On every other count she had proved a disappointment. He had expected her to scorn the world that scorned him and reject the materialism of a capitalist society which was bourgeois and which he couldn't afford anyhow. Instead, she herself had become a parody of a bourgeois housewife, hounding him for new gadgets and movie money, jeering at him because he was such a poor competitor in the capitalistic wage market, and ridiculing him because he failed to gratify her sexual appetite—because, as she told him in front of others, he was 'not a man' in bed.

At first he snapped '*Malachi!*'—'Shut up!' Then, being Lee, he literally struck back. Shortly after his return to America his mother, before bowing out of the picture, had noticed that her lovely daughter-in-law's face was marred by a black eye. To Marguerite it was clear that, as she later put it, 'Everything was not according to Hoyle, as we say in our American way of life.' But to depict the husband as a brute and his wife as a cowering innocent would be incorrect. It was much more complex than that. In the spring of 1963, when Ruth was seeing a great deal of the Oswalds, she observed that they were always 'arguing and bitching at each other, and neither seemed to know what to do about it'. Actually, Marina was the better fighter. She knew his weaknesses, and she was a quick girl with a knee. Eventually it was Lee who capitulated, Lee who allowed her to shut him in a bathroom as punishment, Lee who sank to his knees in the dark and wept bitterly as the greater darkness of his private nightmare enveloped him.

Once Ruth and the Oswalds had become well acquainted, Marina behaved like a minx with Lee. Openly flattering Ruth in front of him, she would undercut him, telling him that Ruth's Russian had become better than his. This was no trifle, and it showed the sureness of her feline instinct. Lee's attainments were limited enough as it was. His marksmanship might convince his wife of his masculinity, but the prospects for demonstrating it in urban Texas were few. (He was already plotting to create opportunities, though; on April 10, 1963, when the friendship between the two women was beginning to blossom, he tried to impress Marina by killing Major General Edwin A. Walker with his new mail-order rifle. As he squeezed the trigger the General moved, and the shot missed.) In mocking his one linguistic achievement Marina was going for the jugular. Ruth knew it; she was well aware of the game; she realized that her Russian really wasn't as proficient as Lee's.

Two weeks after his attempt on the General's life, Lee left Texas to look for a job in New Orleans, and Marina moved in with Ruth. This first such arrangement was brief; it ended in May, when the Oswalds were reunited. Despite her misgivings, Ruth reluctantly drove Marina and the baby to Louisiana. Almost at once the quarrelling began again, and Ruth, feeling, as she recalled afterwards, 'very uncomfortable in that situation', left them. On May 25 Marina sent her a strange letter. She was simultaneously playing both the ill-used wife and the separated friend: 'I'm ashamed to confess that I am a person of moods. And my mood currently is such that I don't feel much like anything! As soon as you left all "love" stopped, and I am very hurt that Lee's attitude towards me is such that I feel each minute that I bind him,' she wrote. Her husband wanted her to leave America, 'which I don't want to do at all'. Lee had told her 'that he doesn't love me, so you see we came to mistaken conclusions. It is hard for you and me to live without a return of our love—interesting, how will it all end?' In any event, she wanted Ruth to know that 'My feelings towards you are sincere and I like you. . . . I kiss and hug you and the children.'

Ruth Paine acted swiftly, and, perhaps, imprudently. Perhaps to her Lee seemed like Michael—a man who couldn't decide whether or not he wanted his wife. In any event she had a plan to settle everything. On June 1 she informed Marina that she was preparing to divorce Michael, and on July 11 she made a suggestion: 'If Lee doesn't wish to live with you any more, and prefers that you go to the Soviet Union, think about the possibility of living with me. . . . I would be happy to be as an aunt to you and the children.' She had money from her parents, she explained, and there would be other money coming in from Michael. The following day, in a letter written at 2 a.m., she declared: 'I love you, Marina, and want to live with you. I hope that you and Lee will agree.'

The die was cast. Ruth was anxious to come south again, to bring Marina back and have a civilized discussion—'to talk with Lee about everything'. She wrote again two days later, adding details and begging for a reply. The answer was effusive. 'Dear, dear Ruth!' Marina responded. '. . . Sweet Ruth, I am so grateful for your good and sympathetic heart.' Nevertheless she had not made a final break with her husband. 'Lee sends greetings,' she wrote, 'but he doesn't know about the content of your letters.' Once before, she revealed, she had threatened to leave him for Ruth, and he had been stung. 'Many times he has recalled this matter to me and said that I am just waiting for an opportunity to hurt him. It has been the cause of many of our arguments.' Ruth refused to be discouraged. She plunged ahead, planning their new life together and asking Marina to address her by the familiar Russian 'thou' ('*ty*'). In a letter postmarked August 11 Marina complied, adding a 'kiss and embrace'.

Late in September Ruth drove down to fetch Marina, Marina's young daughter June, and a carload of miscellaneous Oswald belongings back to Texas. Lee Oswald's last real home had been broken up. He had never had much; now he was left with nothing. It was a critical moment for him, and Ruth noticed that he 'looked very bleak' when he kissed his wife and daughter good-bye. His attempted flight to Cuba followed two days later, and when that failed he rejoined the two women in Texas on October 4. But neither of them wanted him. By now Ruth had established a more stable relationship than anything he had ever offered Marina. She was a better companion, a more successful breadwinner, and a more efficient householder. To be sure, he was a male. But his wife had found his virility wanting.

In Irving she provided a stable environment that the unwanted Archangel bantling had never known. Emotionally secure, Ruth trained the girl to correct her own Russian. Lee, who felt threatened every minute, hated to be corrected, and he had gone so far as to forbid it. Ruth owned a Chevrolet station wagon and could take the whole family on outings; Lee didn't even have a licence. Shabby apartments had been the best shelter he could afford. Ruth had a comfortable house complete with shiny appliances, a deep-freeze, a sunny yard, a sandbox, and swings. Her $80 weekly cheque from Michael and her other resources provided them with a steady, adequate income. On October 14, in a letter to her mother, she frankly admitted that her own marriage was on the rocks and disclosed that she was setting aside 'mad-money'—'money to move east on'. Marina's husband was no match for that; he continued to be impecunious. Nor did Ruth's advantages over him end there. As a college graduate she was both authoritative and informative. She could casually discuss what she called 'parent–child relationships' and 'in-person dialogues', and she could refer to her own ambition for 'some expression of myself that is larger than the duties of being a wife and a housekeeper'. Knowledgeable about the world, she was a source of practical advice about matters which perplexed Lee. As a veteran deadbeat he should have known where to get free medical advice for his pregnant wife, but it was Ruth who steered her to Parkland's free clinics. Lee himself became Ruth's almsman. It was she who gave him Sunday driving lessons, she who set up his job interview with Roy Truly, she who resolutely took charge when he was her guest. On his visits she was a generous hostess, offering him unlimited access to the TV set for football games and movies of violence, which enthralled him. Her typewriter was available for his pretentious appeals to the Soviet Embassy in Washington, and she loaned him her copies of the Dallas *News*.

Ruth's chief efforts, of course, were devoted to Marina. Here her ingenuity developed unexpected veins of richness. For example, she was even helpful with the vexing problem of sexual frustration. She was among those to whom Marina had complained that Lee was inadequate. Ruth explained that they were both separated from their husbands, and she proposed that in the first week of December (six weeks after the birth of Marina's second child) they should go to a Planned Parenthood clinic for 'consultation on this matter of satisfaction.' But the greatest rewards were not in the conferring of blessings by Ruth, a have, upon Marina, a have-not. They lay in the normal friendship of two women who were genuinely fond of one another, enjoyed one another's company and shared an abiding affection for their babies. Their unusual communal unit, in fine, was happy and prosperous. Although the future remained hidden, two adults and four children had made a sensible adjustment to a new way of life. The thing worked.

It worked, that is, for those who were included. Lee Oswald had been pointedly excluded. Since Michael Paine was absent by preference, Lee was the only individual frozen out by the arrangement, and for him it was a grim exile. Not only was he shut off from his wife; he was also isolated from his children. The children were important to him. In the fugue of Lee's psychosis there was one sane streak, his performance as a father. As Ruth had observed, he had loved to come home with an armload of groceries and shout ahead in Russian, '*Devochki!*'—'Girls!' Now that had been denied him. He had been cozened, or had cozened himself, of his manliness, and his chances of getting it back appeared exceedingly dim. If at times Ruth seemed to be a Lady Bountiful cradling a cornucopia that disgorged an endless stream of marvels, it must be remembered that with every gesture she was asserting her role as head of the new household. Lee's occasional presence was by her grace and on her terms. And they were very harsh terms. He had to accept his status as an outsider in what had been his own family.[9]

That is an extremely long string to attach to any gift, but she had been firm. His fists didn't intimidate her. To Ruth, Lee looked like a weakling. She knew enough Marxism to recognize his babblings about it as a sham. On this she agreed with Michael, who as the son of a Communist was even more qualified to pass judgment upon Lee's authenticity. During one of their random encounters he had watched Oswald gawking at the Paine television screen with glazed eyes. 'For a revolutionary,' he had murmured with amusement, 'this guy sure does a lot of sitting.' Poking around the crowded garage, Michael had moved Lee's blanket roll twice. He assumed it contained camping equipment. As an engineer he knew from the moment of inertia that the tube within the blanket was iron or steel. The thought flickered across his mind that tent poles were made of metal these days, but that wasn't his business; indeed, as he recalled

[9] Everyone who has questioned Ruth Paine, this writer included, has been impressed by her exceptional forthrightness. After the assassination she talked to Jessamyn West, a fellow Quaker. Miss West noted that when she spoke of Ruth's 'kindness to the Oswalds' Ruth corrected her, 'reminding me that she had gained as much in her association with Marina Oswald as she had given'.

later, he felt 'a little embarrassed' to be handling another man's belongings, and he never dreamed of untying it to peer within. The contents would have stupefied him. He had already weighed the possibility of Lee's becoming a source of violence and ruled it out. Although something of a stranger in his own household, Michael was aware of a new relationship in it, and he had concluded that Lee wasn't going to make trouble—that 'he wouldn't be a danger to Ruth'. Like his wife he dismissed Oswald as a pretentious, self-pitying lout. Ruth went even further. She was so unimpressed by the counterfeit ideologue that she didn't hesitate to lay down the law to him. She didn't want him in her house, she said, and Marina didn't either. He would be allowed to see his children occasionally, but otherwise he wasn't welcome. He must learn to accept the fact that he had made a new home. And outwardly, at least, he did accept it. His appearances on Fifth Street were so uncommon that he never even kept a razor there. His real home became his furnished room on North Beckley Avenue. On his trips to Irving he was, in effect, an estranged husband who has been granted weekend visitation privileges.

To Ruth it seemed that Lee was as obvious as a parchisi board. Marina, on the other hand, was more of an enigma. That was part of her charm. You never knew what would turn up next. Ruth was not entirely hoodwinked. She was conscious of what she called 'a wall' in her companion. As she put it later, 'You go so far with her and then she draws a shade.' Yet she had no inkling of the horror behind the shade. She never guessed the extent of Marina's duplicity. Apparently the girl had told her everything about Lee. Since her confidences had included the most delicate secrets of the marriage bed, it was reasonable to assume that she had omitted nothing of consequence. In fact she had left out a good deal. She knew all about her husband's aliases. He had told her about his shot in the dark at Walker, and using a box camera she had photographed him holding the 6.5 Mannlicher-Carcano carbine and the .38 Smith & Wesson revolver. At the very moment that she was leaving him for Ruth, during that long drive back to Texas, she knew that he was trying to get to Havana. But she had divulged none of this to her new companion.

In view of their rapport, Marina's reticence on these subjects is unfathomable. At the express wish of Chief Justice Warren, who found her appealing, the President's Commission treated her with exceptional consideration. In retrospect her own lack of consideration for the woman who had become her benefactress appears inexcusable. Most unforgivable, she kept her trusting friend ignorant of the significance of the brown-green blanket roll in the Paine garage. She was keenly aware of the rifle inside, and of the fact that as long as it lay there it would be available to Lee, whom she knew to be a thwarted assassin. Ruth was a devout friend. She said a Quaker grace at meals. As a matter of religious conviction she rejected all forms of violence; Marina knew that. Yet in defiance of conventions which are as highly honoured in Russia as in the United States she had deliberately withheld from Ruth the astounding information that they slept each night beneath a roof that sheltered a high-powered weapon armed with full-jacketed military cartridges and a muzzle velocity of 2,165 feet per second.

It was approximately 5.25 p.m. when Wesley Frazier dropped Lee off and drove on to his own house, a half-block away. Because Marina was alone with the children—Ruth had gone to the grocery store—only Marina's account of the ensuing scene at 2515 West Fifth Street survives, but it scarcely reflects credit on her and there is no reason to doubt it. Certainly it has the ring of truth.

She was first startled to see her husband, and then she was indignant. His arrival was entirely unexpected. Before coming out he was supposed to telephone and ask Ruth's permission. He knew the women didn't want him there during the week, which probably explains why he hadn't called. There was another reason for his wife's choler, however. Last weekend, at her request, he had remained in Dallas. Lee had been on his best behaviour lately. He was carefully avoiding rows; he saw little enough of his wife and children as it was. Therefore when she had told him to stay away—this was on Friday, November 15—he had replied that since he wasn't wanted he would quietly accede to her wishes, and that afternoon Frazier had driven to Irving alone. The following Monday, November 18, while watching young Junie play with Ruth's telephone dial, Marina had a whim. She wanted to call Lee at his rooming house. Neither of the women had ever called him there before, but Ruth had the phone number, WHitney 8–8998. He had scribbled it down for her before Marina's recent confinement, with the thought that she might let him know when his wife's labour pains began. It was typical of Lee's ineptness that he neglected to explain that he was living in Dallas under an assumed name. The baby had been born on a Sunday, when he was in Irving, thus averting a crisis then. On November 18, however, when Ruth dialled the number at Marina's request, the voice on the other end told her that no person named Oswald lived at 1026 North Beckley. Next day Lee called Marina, and she learned from him that his housekeeper and his fellow roomers knew him as O. H. Lee. Irrationally, he was furious with her for having phoned. She was even more furious—it was impossible to keep *this* from

Ruth—and although he called back several times that day she refused to talk to him.

Now it was Thursday, and although Lee told her he had come to make peace, she continued to sulk. Sallow, dismal, and penitent, he repeatedly tried to start a conversation with her. He told her of his loneliness, of how much he missed the children. To him Ruth was 'a tall and stupid woman'; he said that he detested her. Marina refused to listen to him, and he grew increasingly disturbed. But he wouldn't quit. In her words, 'He tried very hard to please me.' He put away diapers for her and lavished attention on Junie and the infant. When she remained implacable, he pleaded with her not to be angry with him; it upset him so. Then he made his proposal. He wanted her to leave Ruth. He was tired of living by himself. He suggested that the reason for their present row was that although they were husband and wife they were 'not living together'. Again and again he repeated that her preference for Ruth was unbearable for him. He didn't want Marina 'to remain with Ruth any longer'. He wanted her and the children with him, and if she would only nod her head he would 'rent an apartment in Dallas tomorrow'.

At this point the station wagon drove up. Ruth had finished shopping. She saw Lee as she drew over to the kerb; he was playing on the lawn with Junie while Marina sat apart, pouting. Like Marina, Ruth was surprised to find him there, but she didn't reproach him. Instead, she decided to divert him by mentioning the imminent arrival of John Kennedy. Kennedy had, in fact, been very much on her mind. In the supermarket she had wondered whether there were any way she and Marina could take the children into Dallas tomorrow morning and find a suitable observation point along the parade route. She had even thought of Lee in this context, wishing that he was working in the Book Depository building on Elm Street, which would command such an excellent view of the motorcade. She knew the building well. A thousand times, driving into the city through the triple underpass, she had consulted the red, white, and blue neon Hertz sign on its roof, which provided passing motorists the latest time and temperature readings. But the Book Depository had two warehouses in Dallas, and Ruth was under the impression that he was employed in the other one, several blocks north of the plaza; it was the older of the two and, on November 21, the better known. So her suggestion remained unmade. Striding up with an armful of groceries, as he himself had done when he was head of this family, she merely said to him in Russian, 'Our President is coming to town'—'*Nahsh President Preyehdid y gorodoo*'. Oswald made no reply. He brushed past her and went out to the car to help her carry in the grocery bags.

Embarrassed, Marina drew Ruth aside and apologized for Lee's presence. She hadn't known that he was coming, she whispered; it wasn't her fault. Ruth murmured that she understood, and together the two mothers prepared supper. Marina, however, was unable to concentrate on her domestic duties. Lee persisted in begging her to quit Ruth. Whenever they were out of the other woman's hearing he resumed his wheedling, and although she maintained her arctic silence it was impossible to ignore him completely.

At 6.30 he joined them at the table. He said little during the meal. He could scarcely woo Marina in Ruth's presence. Toying with his food, he sat at the end of the long table, aloof, tense, brooding. He was preparing a new line of argument, and once the dishes had been cleared away he renewed his entreaties with his wife until, at last, she spoke to him. His appeals, she coldly informed him, had left her unmoved; she intended to stay here with Ruth. It was much more sensible that way. After all, while she was here and he was in Dallas, he was spending less money. But money didn't mean much to Oswald any more. At the prospect of further loneliness, he became more agitated. To this, Marina made what at first seemed to be an encouraging response. His niggardliness had always been a bone between them. She pointed out that with two young daughters it was difficult for her to wash everything by hand, and asked him to buy her a washing machine.

Really crawling now, he capitulated. He wanted her back on any terms, and he promised her the machine.

Then he discovered that she had been only trifling with him. Sarcastically she told him to go and spend the money on himself. She didn't need his largesse. She had found an asylum here with Ruth. She could manage without him.

That was the breaking point for Oswald. He had nothing left, not even pride. Taking advantage of his obvious desperation, his wife had trapped him into committing himself, and then she had let him have it. He had been a miserable husband to her. But he was the man she had married. He had brought her to the United States. He deserved better than that.

After her snub he quit. In Marina's words, 'He then stopped talking and sat down and watched television and then went to bed.' The interval between their final rupture and his early retirement was nearly two hours. Darkness came down upon Irving; the President of the United States spoke sharply to the Vice President in a Houston hotel room 240 miles to the south-east; and Oswald remained hunched in the shadowy living-room. The mothers, busy with their children, had no time for him. Marina glanced in once and saw him staring at an old film of a World War II battle. Apparently he was intent upon the flickering Zenith screen. In fact, he was going mad.

Madness is not a virus. It does not strike all at once. Lee Oswald's disease had been in process all his life. Unquestionably his mother had been a far greater influence in his life than either Marina or Ruth. They were dealing with an abnormal man whose snarl of problems had existed long before either of them met him, and while the situation may have contributed to his breakdown, it would be both unjust and inaccurate to hold either accountable for it. They had grave problems of their own, and Lee himself had contributed greatly to Marina's.

Nevertheless, the impact of his confrontation with his wife on November 21 may have been decisive, and it seems clear that the total eclipse of his reason occurred shortly before 9 p.m. that evening, a few minutes after Jacqueline Kennedy had finished her brief Spanish speech in Houston, and while she and the President were making their way across the crowded lobby en route to the Thomas dinner. The time is established by two observations made by the women in the Fifth Street house. At nine o'clock Marina noticed that her husband had gone into her bedroom and closed the door. Simultaneously Ruth, who had just finished settling her children, crossed the kitchen, entered the garage to lacquer toy blocks, and found that the garage light was on. Immediately she knew that Lee had been in there. Marina had been with her, and Marina was always careful about lights anyhow. Leaving the switch on was characteristic of Lee's carelessness, and Ruth didn't give it a second thought. Yet there can have been only one reason for his trip to the garage. He went for the rifle. Whether he slipped the weapon into the brown paper bag and took both to the bedroom or left them in the garage is a matter of conjecture. The second course seems far likelier. In the bedroom he would have risked discovery by Marina, the only person in the world who would have guessed the full implications of the concealed rifle and who might have tripped over it if the baby, whose bassinet was a few feet from the bed, awoke her before dawn. Leaving it where it was, he could pick it up just as easily, and more safely, at daybreak.

Ruth finished the blocks and then talked to Marina, who bathed and retired at 11.30 p.m. Undressing in the dark, she tiptoed across the linoleum floor, turned down the embroidered white counterpane, and slid into the double bed beside her husband. In the moments before slumber she had the distinct impression that he was lying there awake. Since he slept until the alarm next morning—usually he rose early and turned the alarm off—it seems probable that sleep did, indeed, come to him very late. But Marina was in no mood for a truce. She was still angry. Wordlessly she turned on her side, drew up the bedspread, and dropped off.

Outside the bedroom's small windows a light rain continued to fall. Overhead, invisible stars turned in the clouded sky. A wind had risen, tugging damply at mailboxes and wires and loose sashes, making furry little sounds in unswept gutters and storm drains. Thursday became Friday. The night sped on.

2

SS 100 X

Two hours before dawn on Friday morning, the faithful began to gather on the fringes of the parking lot across from Fort Worth's Hotel Texas. Drifting up Commerce Street in small groups, they lit cigarettes and leaned against the shabby store fronts, smoking and yawning. It was a marvel that they were there at all. The rain had continued to fall, and they had no assurance that the speech here would not be called off. But this speech had been scheduled as a concession to the working class supporters of Yarborough, and Kennedy's reputation for hardiness was part of his charisma, so they came in increasing numbers, until the lot had begun to fill up like a parade ground before roll call. There were only a few feminine umbrellas, only a scattering of pretty secretaries; it was largely a masculine crowd: union men in waterproofs and stout shoes who swapped friendly shoves, called jovially to the mounted policemen in yellow rain gear who were watching over them, and craned their necks for some sign of the legendary Secret Service. By daybreak over five thousand spectators were staring up at the banal brown-brick façade of the hotel. Occasionally you heard a hoarse, lusty cheer.

Inside, early risers whose accommodations faced the lot became aware of the teeming below. At six o'clock, with an hour of darkness left, Bob Baskin of the Dallas *News* staggered sleepily to the window of Room 326 and glanced down at the rain-slick streets. Baskin decided to stay put; he could hear the speech from here over the public address system. Five floors above him and a half-hour later, Rear Admiral Dr George Burkley heaved himself out of the bed in 836 and dialled room service, ordering breakfast. Like all members of Kennedy's staff, the chunky, shy physician had learned to function on the road with a few hours' sleep. It was important to be up before the President; you never knew when to expect an urgent call from him, and several men had routine tasks which must be finished before he awakened.

Master Sergeant Joe Giordano, who had been dressed fifteen minutes before the doctor, rolled out and was now supervising the affixing of the Chief Executive's seals to the flatbed truck in the lot and the podium of the hotel's Grand Ballroom. Ted Clifton tapped on the door of 804 and asked the bagman if he had packed. Gearhart had, and his room-mate, Cecil Stoughton, was loading his camera with fast film and cleaning lenses. Bill Greer and Henry Rybka, the Presidential chauffeurs, had already left the hotel. They were in the Fort Worth police garage, fetching the President's temporary car and his Secret Service follow-up car. On the floor below Kennedy, the communications centre had begun to stir. Colonel Swindal was reporting from Carswell. His crews had checked out of the motel, his aircraft was ready to go. A teletype machine in the centre came to life with a sprinkle of bells. The keys chattered out the CIA's daily intelligence précis for the President. A Signalman sealed them in twin envelopes and handed them to Godfrey McHugh, who signed for them, trotted up a flight of stairs, and stood respectfully outside Suite 850, awaiting the familiar voice of command. He would have to sign again, noting the precise time the Commander in Chief received the secret reports, and Godfrey liked a tidy record.

These were the technicians. In theory they would have followed identical routines if the President had been named Bert Lahr. In practice, as several of them were to discover that day, their loyalty to the man in Suite 850 had become surprisingly personal, and could not be transferred to anyone else. Officially, however, they owed their allegiance to an institution, the office of the Presidency. The politicians, with whom they coexisted, were a different breed. Political fealty was completely individual. As a group they were more colourful, more convivial, and less efficient than the technical staff. On principle they distrusted clockwork procedure, but they, too, were obliged to operate on tight schedules, and the baying from the parking lot gave them a special incentive. They had to rouse themselves and find out what was happening, and once they saw all those voters, yesterday's exhaustion was forgotten; they were ready to go.

They were going to need a lot of inspiration. Charcoal would be highly mobile today. In 835 Ken O'Donnell, the man most likely to receive an early Presidential summons, ran his eye over today's itinerary as he shaved. It would be another backbreaker; two speeches here; the hop to Dallas; the long ride to the Trade Mart; another speech; a flight to Bergstrom Air Force Base outside Austin, where the head coach of the University of Texas Longhorns would present the President with an autographed football; a motorcade through the city; a series of receptions; a valedictory speech at the

Austin fund-raising banquet; a final motorcade; and a helicopter ride to the LBJ Ranch. There was enough for any appointments secretary to worry about. But O'Donnell's cup hadn't quite passed. He now had to cope with a politician's most exasperating problem, inclement weather.

Not all Texans were as rugged as the workmen in the square below. If the skies really opened, today's crowds would dwindle, raining out the President. Furthermore, at any moment Ken would be expected to make a decision about the Lincoln in Dallas. Buckling the unwieldy plastic bubbletop on the convertible took time. It would be absolutely necessary in a thunderstorm. Suppose the clouds vanished, however. In a closed car Kennedy would be almost invisible to the waiting multitudes. O'Donnell squinted out at the grey drizzle. It was exasperating, and there was no way of telling which way it would turn; yesterday McHugh had shown how unreliable forecasts could be.

Jacqueline Kennedy presented another complication. Alone, the President would shrug his way through a storm, but his solicitude yesterday suggested that he would object strenuously to a wet wife. Neither a technician nor a politician, she was an unfamiliar member of the team, a new cog in the apparatus, and they were all adjusting to her. Obviously she was worth it; San Antonio and Houston had convinced everyone with political awareness that she would add tremendous zest to the coming campaign. From their windows six storeys above the lot the Connallys were discussing her as they studied the swarming square below. Nellie argued that she had seemed stiff on arrival; John countered that she had been enjoying herself by evening; both agreed that she was a priceless ornament.

Her presence had other implications. Under peripatetic circumstances a First Lady inevitably creates plights for other ladies. None of them, for example, had been told what she was going to wear or which public appearances, if any, she would be making here this morning. Clint Hill, her own bodyguard, didn't know until he reached the hall outside Suite 850. Learning that she would not be going to the lot, Clint settled down with a mug of coffee and a roll. Nellie and Lady Bird lacked even that information, and they were in a quandary. As the Governor's wife Nellie felt that she must make an appearance. (At the breakfast, to her dismay, she would presently find herself wearing a pink wool suit, a twin of Mrs Kennedy's.) If Nellie was going, Bird decided she should, too. It was a matter of duty. She wasn't in the mood for public appearances. The Second Lady felt out of sorts this morning. Dallas was very near now, and the thought of it oppressed her. She was a loyal wife and a staunch trouper, but this was one stop she didn't relish. Dressing in the Vice-

Presidential suite, she noticed that her hands were trembling with anxiety.

Others remained preoccupied with Big D. Down the hall from the Johnsons, Tiger Teague was calling colleagues from 1302, taking soundings and expressing his misgivings about the city. Roy Kellerman phoned Agent Lawson at Love Field and asked, 'Are we going to be all right in Dallas?' 'Oh, yes,' Lawson assured him. 'It is a good programme.' With Dallas in mind, Rufe Youngblood inquired of another agent, 'Anything new from PRS?' The Service's Protective Research Section, which, in response to a request from Lawson on November 8, had spent ten minutes checking the city in which Adlai Stevenson had been assaulted less than a month before, had nothing to report, but the agent wordlessly handed Youngblood a copy of Friday morning's Dallas *Morning News,* turned to page 14.

The entire page was devoted to an advertisement, ominously bordered in black like an announcement of mourning. Under the sardonic heading, 'WELCOME MR KENNEDY TO DALLAS', an organization styling itself as 'The American Fact-Finding Committee'—a local co-ordinator of the John Birch Society and Nelson Bunker Hunt, the son of H. L. Hunt, it later developed, were the committee's most prominent members—asked the President twelve rhetorical questions. He was accused of responsibility for the imprisonment, starvation, and persecution of 'thousands of Cubans'. The ad declared that he was selling food to Communist soldiers who were killing Americans in Vietnam, hinted strongly that he had reached a secret agreement with the U.S. Communist party, and asked, among other things, 'Why have you ordered or permitted your brother Bobby, the Attorney General, to go soft on Communists, fellow-travellers, and ultra-leftists in America, while permitting him to persecute loyal Americans who criticize you, your administration, and your leadership?'

It was another 'Wanted for Treason' broadside. But there were two differences. This denunciation was reaching a vast audience through the pages of a respected newspaper. And it was appearing within hours of the President's arrival.

'Mr Kennedy,' the ad concluded, 'WE DEMAND answers to these questions, and we want them NOW.'

In her drab quarters at 2220 Thomas Place Marguerite Oswald settled down for her daily six-hour television bout. She began, as usual, with NBC's 'Today' show, and at 7.08 a.m., as the first olive light of day brightened her damp windows, she saw Dallas Police Chief Jesse Curry appear on her tiny screen, describe the elaborate precautions he had taken, and warn that immediate action would be taken against anyone who attempted to spoil the President's visit.

In Dallas Father Oscar Huber, CM, a gentle, bespectacled priest, had risen as usual at 5 a.m. in his modest room at the rectory of Holy Trinity church, three miles from Parkland Hospital. After morning prayers and meditation he had begun his regular routine of parish activities, but he was keenly aware that the motorcade of America's first Roman Catholic Chief Executive was going to pass within three blocks of the church. He tried in vain to interest his fellow priests in making the stroll. They intended to stay here and watch it on television. 'Well, I'm going,' he told them. 'I'm seventy years old and I've never seen a President. I'll be hanged if I'm going to miss this chance.'

U.S. Attorney Barefoot Sanders had also been up early, distributing the last twenty-five luncheon tickets allotted to Dallas Democrats. At this late hour they would have to be delivered by messenger, and some wouldn't arrive until noon. Their elated recipients would be on the streets, fighting their way through the traffic around the Trade Mart as the motorcade reached its climax.

Democratic National Committeeman Byron Skelton, lacking an invitation, was still feeling rather left out. As a loyal member of the party, however, he had bought two gold-coloured, $100 tickets to tonight's testimonial in Austin, and after lunch he planned to drive down with his wife Ruth, wearing a black tie in the hope that he would be seated at the head table. To make certain that his desk would be clear, he was making an unusually prompt start for his panelled law offices in Temple's First National Bank Building. As he strolled down the city's main street he saw a young Republican storekeeper motioning to him through his plate-glass window. The man was holding up a copy of the Dallas *News* ad and grinning.

Joe Dealey, the son of the publisher of the *News*, was far from delighted. Joe had returned home from Miami late the day before. He opened his copy of the newspaper to page 14 and felt stricken. Normally the copy would have been submitted to him or to the paper's advertising director. But the director had been out of town, too, so it had gone all the way to the top and had been approved there by Ted Dealey. Joe immediately called his father and reproached him. It was, he said, 'like inviting someone to dinner and then throwing tapioca in his face'. Ted was unmoved. He had read the ad meticulously, and he argued that it merely 'represented what we have been saying editorially'. That wasn't the point, Joe countered. 'The timing is bad,' he said. He thought of the time he and other conservative young businessmen had spent in their eleventh-hour attempt to polish up the blemished image of Big D and hung up, bitterly discouraged. It was too late now. The thing was in print.

At the indoor birdhouse of the Trade Mart the last spoon had been laid at the President's place, and outside workmen were erecting two flagpoles, for the Stars and Stripes and the flag of Texas. It was slow going. They had to vie with a group of youthful anti-Kennedy pickets carrying placards reading 'YANKEE, GO HOME' and (in red letters) 'HAIL CAESAR'. Appropriately they looked indignant; they were members of the Dallas Indignant White Citizens Council. They also looked out of breath. They had plastered their mouths with adhesive tape, 'to show', one scribbled on copy paper for a *Times-Herald* reporter, 'that we are being muzzled'. A policeman watched them narrowly. Backstage in the Mart a White House phone had been plugged in; beside it stood a rocking chair with a hand-quilted cover. Everything in the main hall had gone smoothly, with one trivial exception. Flowers had been a problem. Because of Texas pride in yellow roses, the hosts in the four other cities Kennedy was visiting had exhausted the supply of state florists. The Trade Mart had imported five hundred yellow blossoms from California, and two dozen of these now graced the head tables. None had been left over for the welcoming ceremonies at Love Field, however, so substitute bouquets were being prepared—white roses for Lady Bird, red roses for Jacqueline Kennedy. Mrs Earle Cabell was to hand Mrs Kennedy the red bouquet. Dearie hoped the First Lady wouldn't notice the difference.

Marina Oswald awoke before the bedside alarm rang at 6.30. She had been up twice with the baby, and her temper of yesterday evening had not improved. She nursed the child while her husband stood at the foot of the bed, dressing in a work shirt and grey trousers. He spoke; she looked up drowsily. His slender shoulders framed against the solid blue-green walls, he told her to stay where she was. He would fix his own breakfast. This could only have been an attempt to open a conversation, for she never rose for him anyway. Then he declared that he really wanted her to buy everything she wanted—clothes for herself, and especially shoes for little Junie. Marina made no response. Returning the baby to the crib, she closed her eyes and instantly fell into a deep sleep. He knew that they were through, and apparently he wanted her to know it, too. Before departing he slipped off his wedding ring and left it in the little china cup that had belonged to her grandmother. Yet he was as good as his word, or as good as his meagre hoard of cash would permit. This was the day the chronic failure was going to demonstrate that he could succeed at something, that he was a man, and did not deserve contempt. In the bedroom he left $187 in bills. He kept $15.10. That wouldn't take him very far. But he knew he wasn't going far.

In the kitchen he made a cup of instant coffee. Leaving the cup for Ruth to clean, he walked a half-block eastward on Fifth Street, carrying the rifle and telescopic sight in the brown paper wrapping he had brought from Dallas the previous afternoon, and thrust his thin balding head in the kitchen window of the corner house where Wesley Frazier, who lived with his sister's family, was having breakfast. The young Alabaman's mother had never met Oswald. Startled, she asked, 'Who's that?' 'That's Lee,' her son said. 'Well, I guess it's time to go.' After hurriedly brushing his teeth he donned his coat and joined Oswald outside. Frazier had a habit of glancing over his shoulder as he slid behind the wheel, and this morning he noticed the strange bundle on the back seat. 'What's in the package, Lee?' he inquired. 'Curtain rods,' Oswald replied curtly. 'Oh, yeah,' said Frazier. 'You told me you were going to bring some today. Where's your lunch?' 'I'm going to buy it,' Oswald said. Frazier nodded, turned the ignition on, and shifted gears. There was grime on the windows of his old Chevrolet, and the drizzle was making it worse. 'I wish it would rain or just quit altogether,' Frazier muttered irritably. 'I wish it would do something to clear off the windshield.' The drops were growing larger. Forgetting about the buff-coloured parcel behind him he hunched forward and concentrated on the road ahead. He hoped they wouldn't be late. They were supposed to be in the Book Depository at 8 a.m. It was now 7.25.

Five minutes later in Fort Worth, the Chief Executive's leisurely valet entered the Hotel Texas' Suite 850 and tapped on the door of the master bedroom. 'Mr President,' George called gently. He heard a stirring of covers and crossed the threshold. 'It's raining out,' he murmured. 'That's too bad,' Kennedy said groggily. He thought about it a moment and then groaned.

While he showered and shaved, George laid out his clothes: a blue-grey, two-button suit, a dark blue tie, and a white shirt with narrow grey stripes. The shirt was striking, the gem of George's foot locker. During a conference with Ambassador Alphand the President had noticed that the French diplomat was wearing one like it. 'Nice,' he had remarked with a puckish grin. 'From London?' Alphand, springing to the honour of Paris tailors, replied that it was from Cardin's, and the White House had placed an order with Cardin's the next day. Kennedy counted on his wife to show Dallas what real style was, but he intended to prove that he knew something about good taste himself.

While dressing he decided to have a look at the parking lot. It couldn't be seen from where he was, so he impulsively crossed into Mrs Kennedy's room.

'Gosh, look at the crowd!' the President cried, peering down. 'Just look! Isn't that terrific?'

Excitedly telling his wife he would see her later, he darted back to George. A waiter had brought him a light breakfast. He hurriedly sipped coffee, chewed half a bun, and was knotting his tie when Dave Powers came in. The President greeted him with relish. 'Have you seen the square? And weren't the crowds great in San Antonio and Houston?' Dave acknowledged it. 'Listen, they were terrific!' said Kennedy. 'And you were right—they loved Jackie.'

He had already discounted the rain and was eager to head downstairs. A President, however, can rarely move from A to B. The several hats he wears—the toppers of Chief Executive and Head of State, the shako of Commander in Chief, the bowler of political leader—are for ever piled on his head in a giddy pyramid. Already Godfrey had entered the suite; it was time Kennedy turned aside for the CIA report. Spectacles in place, he swiftly read the situation estimates on Saigon, Cyprus, and Korea. At his direction, casualty reports from Vietnam were included each day, and there were precise accounts of formal and informal statements by Charles de Gaulle and Nikita Khrushchev. These were always a matter of intense interest. A Chief Executive's major problem, George Washington had said, is 'seclusion from information'. Reliance on the press was inadequate; heads of state, Kennedy had learned, are occasionally misquoted.

Nevertheless the press was vital. It reached a somewhat larger audience than CIA summaries, and a President should know what his people are reading. Unlike Eisenhower, who had ignored newspapers, Kennedy scanned the leading metropolitan dailies every morning. Since he was on a political swing, he was naturally alert to reactions to the tour's first day. He found them, and he found them dismaying. The Chicago *Sun-Times* was comforting: 'Some Texans, in taking account of the tangled Texas political situation, have begun to think that Mrs Jacqueline Kennedy may turn the balance and win her husband this state's electoral vote.' But that was exceptional. Overnight the strife between Connally and Yarborough had become the biggest political story in the nation. Texas papers were giving it special prominence, and the Dallas *News* led the pack with two abrasive stories on the front page: 'STORM OF POLITICAL

CONTROVERSY SWIRLS AROUND KENNEDY ON VISIT' and 'YARBOROUGH SNUBS LBJ'. A third, inside, was headed: 'PRESIDENT'S VISIT SEEN WIDENING STATE DEMOCRATIC SPLIT'.

Kennedy angrily thrust the paper aside, missing, for the moment, the inflammatory ad on the next page. (He also overlooked a dispatch from the local soft-drink conclave: 'NIXON PREDICTS JFK MAY DROP JOHNSON', and a story on today's Dallas schedule reporting that 'the motorcade will move slowly so that crowds can "get a good view" of President Kennedy and his wife'.) The blood-letting had become serious. Seizing the phone, Kennedy told O'Donnell that he wanted Senator Yarborough in the Vice Presidential car, and no excuse would be accepted. Maybe the Senator had been more sinned against than sinning, but enough was enough; the whole expedition was in danger of coming a cropper. Ken and Larry O'Brien must spell out the alternatives for Yarborough: either he rode with Lyndon today or he walked.

Stepping into the hotel corridor to join Congressman Wright's party, the President was still frowning. He spotted Clint Hill and Muggsy O'Leary in the Secret Service post and stepped over to them. 'Mary Gallagher wasn't here last night to help Jackie,' he said tartly. 'Mary hasn't any business in motorcades. She's supposed to reach hotels before we do, and so far she's batting zero. Get her on the ball.'

His flash of temper was over. He saw an elderly woman in a wheelchair, a resident of the hotel, and paused to speak gently to her. A few doors beyond, he paused again outside Evelyn Lincoln's room. Evelyn, after breakfasting with three Texas friends, had lined them up outside in a stiff self-conscious, Sunday-best rank. 'More of your relatives?' he asked with a twinkle, gracefully giving her an opening for introductions.

In the lobby his entourage swelled until, as he crossed the red-brick paving of Eighth Street outside, it included Lyndon Johnson, John Connally, Ralph Yarborough, several Congressmen, and Raymond Buck, president of the Fort Worth Chamber of Commerce. The President waded happily into the crowd, disregarding the drizzle, which had now become a fine mist. Bill Greer had brought a raincoat for him and held it aloft on his arm. Kennedy shook his head. Laughing exultantly, he mounted the flatbed truck. Yet not everyone there felt so enthusiastic. Hugh Sidey of *Time* was struck by the difference between the President's mood and the Vice President's. Sidey wished Johnson a good morning, Johnson's answering greeting, he noted, was 'dour, mechanical, perfunctory'.

'There are no faint hearts in Fort Worth!' Kennedy cried into the microphone. The union men cheered, and there were scattered shouts of 'Where's Jackie?' He pointed to her eighth-floor window. 'Mrs Kennedy is organizing herself,' he said, smiling. 'It takes her a little longer, but, of course, she looks better than we do when she does it.'

Larry and Ken had moved into Dr Burkley's room to watch the speech. Both looked grave. They had already made their first pitch to Yarborough, and they had struck out. The Senator had argued that his behaviour wouldn't affect the Presidential party—that the desire of so many thousands of people to be near the President was solid proof of his popularity. The two veteran pols knew their boss wouldn't buy that. Then they looked up. As he paid tribute to Fort Worth's work on the TFX fighter plane, they studied the ragged, scudding clouds on the far horizon and prayed that they would go away.

Organizing herself at her dressing table and listening to her husband's voice booming over the PA system below, Jacqueline Kennedy was pleased that it was raining; she hoped the top would be on that car. She was concerned about her hair becoming dishevelled. She knew she looked tired. She glanced into the mirror. To Mary she moaned, 'Oh, gosh. One day's campaigning can age a person thirty years.'

The rain lifted as Wesley Frazier entered the outskirts of greater Dallas, and before parking two blocks north of the Book Depository he switched off his windshield wiper. The Hertz sign overhead revealed that he had arrived in good time, so he let his engine idle for several minutes, on the theory that he was charging the battery. Then Oswald impatiently got out, carrying his package. Frazier followed, but in the manner of youth he became diverted by the switching of locomotives on the railroad tracks which lay between his parking place and the back of the warehouse, and by the morning traffic whizzing past on Stemmons Freeway, to the west. He straggled farther and farther behind. By the time he reached the building Oswald had climbed the loading platform and vanished inside.

Oswald's movements in the next few minutes are a matter of conjecture, based solely on circumstantial evidence. Superintendent Truly later recalled meeting him by a book bin, saying, 'Good morning, Lee,' and receiving the customary reply, 'Good morning, sir.' But Truly was vague, and he had no recollection of the package. It is quite possible that he was thinking of another morning—that Lee had already ascended to the sixth floor, using either one of the two freight elevators or the enclosed stairway in the north-west corner of the Book Depository, to conceal his weapon near the site he had already selected.

There, as in so many ways, blind chance had played into his hands. The old flooring had become oily. Truly, observing that books which had been stored there frequently became stained, had ordered it replaced with battleship-grey plywood. Half the floor was to be redone at a time. In preparation for the work, the rear, or northern, area had been largely cleared of cartons by doubling up in front. Thus the southern side, which would face the passing motorcade, was a crowded jungle of cartons and wheeled book trucks. Concealment was easy, and it was there, some time during the morning, that Oswald built his sniper's perch of boxes in the south-east corner, from which the President would be seen approaching dead ahead and then departing to the right front. One pile of boxes hid him from snoopers in the Dal-Tex Building on the opposite side of Houston Street, which would be to his left as he fired. Others would serve as props when he aimed; still others would be used to provide a backstop against which ejected shells would bounce as he worked the bolt for each fresh shot.

It was a squalid roost. The old floor was especially filthy here. The white-brick walls were chipped and scarred and covered with a patina of thick dust. Even after the window had been opened the interior was gloomy, and the naked 60-watt bulbs overhead merely washed the cramped scene with a sickly glow. But that was of no consequence to Oswald. He would be firing outside, not in. His bead would be drawn on a figure moving down Elm Street, to his right front. And by noon the daylight there would be broad as broad.

Across Houston Street, Abraham Zapruder strode into the office of his garment business on the fourth floor of the Dal-Tex building.

'Sunshiny!' he chirped to his secretary in his stage Yiddish.

'Where's your camera?' she demanded severely.

'At home,' he said timidly. They were good friends and often played this private game, pretending that she henpecked her boss.

'Mr Z., you march right back there. How many times will you have a crack at colour movies of the President?'

Zapruder fingered his bow tie and protested weakly. 'I'm too short. Probably I wouldn't even get close.'

'The crowd'll be light downstairs,' she shot back, and when he hesitated she said firmly, 'Hurry up! You can make it in twenty minutes.'

It wasn't a bad idea, he reflected. He turned back to the elevator on his short legs, grumbling. 'Chased home by my own girl. It looks bad.'

She feigned impatience, and he said, 'OK, Lillian, OK! So I'm going!'

'We are going forward!' the President cried vibrantly, concluding his speech in the lot. As the union men whistled and stamped he descended from the truck, shook hands with the mounted policemen, murmured to Henry Brandon, 'We're doing better than we thought,' and re-entered the hotel. The formal breakfast was next on the schedule. In the elevator, however, Mac Kilduff persuaded him to make an unscheduled stop. Kilduff had read the papers and shared Kennedy's concern. He had persuaded Connally to hold a press conference, and he thought the President should discuss it with the Governor first.

In the Longhorn Room, down the mezzanine corridor from the ballroom, Kennedy reviewed Connally's prepared statement. It was bland and rather meaningless. The Governor had always stood four-square for harmony in public. His own jarring notes were sounded backstage, and Ralph Yarborough's present stonewalling was a result of them. Nevertheless the statement was something. Kennedy endorsed it and returned to the hall, where he ran into Yarborough himself and bluntly told him to ride in the Vice Presidential car. 'For Christ's sake cut it out, Ralph,' he snapped. The Senator, taken aback and upset by Yankee forthrightness, remonstrated that he had ridden to this very hotel with Johnson. Kennedy shook his head. It wasn't good enough. That had been in the dark. If the Senator valued the President's friendship, he would stick to Johnson like Duco. Nothing less would do; the President had no intention of being fobbed off with evasive action. Leaving the dismayed Senator, who had been searching for new evasions, Kennedy stepped into the kitchen of the Grand Ballroom, from which he would make his entrance. He glanced over his shoulder, the commander checking his troops. Behind him his entourage was wedged in a solid phalanx between stainless steel sinks and gigantic kettles. One member was missing. To Agent Bill Duncan he murmured, 'Where's Mrs Kennedy? Call Mr Hill. I want her to come down to the breakfast.' In a louder voice he inquired, 'Everybody set?' There was a murmur of assent, and at 9.05 a.m.—the precise moment that American Airlines Flight 82, bearing Richard M. Nixon, departed Love Field for what was then called Idlewild Airport—he said, 'All right, let's go.'

Jacqueline Kennedy did not appear for another twenty minutes. The opening formalities droned on. The Texas Choir sang 'The Eyes of Texas'. Toastmaster Raymond Buck presented all the other guests, and in the back of the block-long hall there was a minor disturbance when a local panjandrum challenged General McHugh's credentials. ('Do you know who I am?' God asked indignantly.) Now and then an agent glanced furtively at his wristwatch. Liz Carpenter, shifting impatiently, concluded that the President must be annoyed. Mrs Kennedy knew what she was doing. Her husband wanted her to be elegant in Dallas, and she meant to be. But it *did* take time. Ultimately she came to the choice of gloves. She wavered over two pairs, long white and short white; she decided the short gloves were more restrained, and held up her wrists while Mary Gallagher buttoned them. Now she was ready for the Belle Starrs. In fact, she had become so preoccupied with Dallas that she had completely forgotten the ceremony downstairs. When the elevator stopped at the mezzanine floor, she was confused. 'Aren't we leaving?' she asked Clint Hill. 'No, you're going to a breakfast,' he said.

In the kitchen the chief chef, Otto Druhe, ogled her while Clint awaited a signal from the head table. Raymond Buck provided it. Like a ringmaster he called, 'And now—an event I know you have all been waiting for!' Buck swept his arm towards the kitchen door. The introduction lacked only a stentorian roll of snare drums. She appeared smiling tentatively, and was greeted by pandemonium. Two thousand cheering Texans were standing on their chairs. The klieg lights and the fake candles in the ballroom's huge candelabra were blinding, and for a moment she was really frightened; she had never been through anything like this alone; she felt sure she would stumble. Then she saw her husband smiling at her. He seemed far away, but he was beckoning reassuringly, standing steadfast as she moved towards him through the strange valley of clamour, her hand outstretched, her eyes on his. Their hands touched. The tumult subsided.

It was time for presents. Their hosts had boots for her, a five-gallon hat for him. In O'Donnell's suite, where Ken and Larry were watching the ceremonies on television, this was a moment of high mirth. They knew how the President always avoided queer costumes, how he had never forgotten the pitiful photograph of Calvin Coolidge in an Indian headdress; and they wondered how he would get out of this one. He side-stepped it deftly by announcing that he would put it on in Washington on Monday. But his wife was hoping he would wear it sooner. As he began his address—'Two years ago I introduced myself in Paris by saying that I was the man who had accompanied Mrs Kennedy to Paris. I am getting somewhat the same sensation as I travel around Texas. Nobody wonders what Lyndon and I wear'—she thought ahead to tomorrow at the LBJ Ranch. Lady Bird had asked her to ask the President if there was anything special he would like there. 'I'd like to ride,' he had replied. She remembered now what a good rider he was, and how, during the summer of their engagement, he had galloped bareback through the fields of Newport on a work horse. That Stetson would be decidedly becoming when he mounted an LBJ horse, she reflected. She thought he looked silly in ordinary hats, but anything picturesque—his naval officer's cap, the silk hat at his inaugural—was splendid on him.

Although she had not seen the ranch, she vividly recalled her husband's account of his visit there eight days after his election to the Presidency. It had been a singular experience, and in one respect a distressing one. The afternoon they arrived the Vice President proposed a dawn hunt the next day. To Kennnedy shooting tame game was not sport, and he had tried to bow out gracefully. To him all killing was senseless. But how do you explain such scruples to a gracious host? You don't. He would never understand. He might even think you squeamish, and that was the crux of Kennedy's problem. As a national leader he was obliged to resolve any doubts about his mettle.

Besides, Lyndon had been dogged. He was determined to be cordial, and this was the finest treat his ranch could offer. All that day he had gone to great lengths to assure Kennedy of his fidelity. Johnson's lieutenants had been called in and told firmly that their personal allegiance to him must be forgotten. The Austin–Boston axis was about to be replaced by the capital in Washington. Starting now, they all had but one leader. They must obey his commands, anticipate his needs, please him in every way. He thought he himself was doing precisely that. Had he dreamed that his hunting invitation might give offence, he would never have mentioned it. To Johnson, Kennedy's reluctance seemed a polite gesture, like demurring at a second drink or a second helping. It needed cajoling. This was a local custom, he explained, taking the new chief's arm in his tactile way. This was something you just *did*. An eminent guest was expected to join in the ritual. And besides, he'd enjoy it—it'd be right-smart, by-God, hog-heaven *fun*.

So at 7 a.m. on November 17, 1960, they had turned out, yawning, by the ranch's field-stone façade. Johnson wore the uniform of the occasion: a stained, shapeless cowboy hat and a weather-beaten leather jacket. Kennedy had donned a checkered sport coat and slacks—a fellow guest, peering at him sleepily, thought he looked like a football fan. As the dawn shadows withered away they piled into a white Cadillac and tooled along under a flawless sky to a sight of breath-taking natural beauty, and there the guest of honour did what was expected of him. The mechanics were relatively simple. Hitting a bull's-eye isn't much of an accomplishment. You kiss the stock with your cheek, line up the sights, take a deep breath and let a little out, then hold the breath to keep an even strain, and gently squeeze. Changing a tyre requires more skill.

Only in hunting animals that isn't all. There is one other matter, one fraction of a moment which to this hunter was anguish. It is the confrontation, when the killer faces his prey. In that instant, in the season before his inaugural, John Fitzgerald Kennedy had squinted down the barrel of a high-powered rifle and looked into the face of the life he was about to take. He had committed himself; he couldn't flinch. He fired and quickly turned back to the car. Yet he couldn't rid himself of the recollection. The memory of the creature's death had been haunting, and afterwards he had relived it with his wife, *pour vider l'abcès*, to heal the inner scar.

Nor had that been the end of it. Early in the new administration Lyndon had had the trophy mounted—not just the antlers, but the head, too—and one morning after a legislative leadership breakfast he came loping across the South Lawn of the White House, lugging it under his arm. The President of the United States had felled this quarry on his ranch. That made him proud, and he assumed that the President was proud, too. After all, it had been a magnificent shot. Why not display it on the wall of the Presidential office? he suggested. Kennedy, feigning interest, was inwardly appalled. After the Vice President had departed he ordered the head put away and forgotten. It wasn't forgotten, though. Lyndon telephoned a jovial inquiry from his suite in the Executive Office Building, just across West Executive Avenue from the White House. Where was that deer? When was it going up? Later he mentioned it again, and then again. Eventually the trophy, like any other gift that has been repeatedly declined, became an issue between them, and once more Kennedy acceded. A great man must walk softly. Presidents must yield little points to win big ones, and really, this point was very small, a half-forgotten fico. The specimen was hung, not in the oval office, but in the nearby Fish Room. The President had granted a favour—how great a favour only the First Lady knew—and his Vice President had been genuinely pleased. Give and take; win a few, lose a few; that was the strategy of public office. In one version of his pet joke, the last line of which could be adapted to the occasion, he used to tell his friends that 'The three most overrated things in the world are the state of Texas, the FBI, and hunting trophies.' Nevertheless the memory of the incident was distasteful.

Gesticulating emphatically at the audience in the Hotel Texas' ballroom Kennedy finished his breakfast remarks. 'A ripsnorting political speech,' a reporter commented to Ted Clifton, who was sitting with the bagman in an improvised lobby behind the last line of tables. Three New York newspapermen accosted Powers there. 'Wasn't Jackie sensational?' he asked them. 'Did you ever see a greater ovation?' Doug Kiker of the *Herald Tribune* asked back, 'Are you going to use her much in the campaign?' Dave was vague. He couldn't be sure. Anything could happen. He wasn't going to commit himself. But Al Otten of the *Wall Street Journal* pressed the matter. Like several other White House correspondents, Otten's feelings towards Kennedy were ambivalent. He liked him as a man, yet resented him as President, and a Kennedy triumph disturbed him. He asked sourly, 'When are you going to have her come out of a cake?' Powers looked him up and down. Sounding every vowel in his Boston accent, he snapped back, 'She's not that kind of bunny.'

Dave's vagueness had been unnecessary. The First Lady, whose nerve was stronger than anyone in the Irish mafia then suspected, was quite recovered. She felt buoyant, and back in the suite she decided to reassert her determination to make every political trip between now and next November. The President was on the phone, summoning O'Donnell. Hanging up, he told her they wouldn't have to leave here until 10.40. 'Do you mean we have a whole hour to just sit around?' she asked incredulously. 'Oh, Jack, campaigning is so easy when you're President. Listen, I can go anywhere with you this year.' As Ken came into the drawing-room Kennedy said, 'How about California in the next two weeks?' 'Fine. I'll be there,' she promised, and was rewarded with one of Ken's rare smiles. She had always been in awe of this Celtic Calvinist, with his taut face, sardonic manner, and quiet, almost fanatical devotion to her husband. She really didn't know him very well. The President lived his life in compartments and kept walls between compartments virtually airtight. Ted Sorensen, for example, was even closer to him than O'Donnell, yet Sorensen was remote to both his wife and O'Donnell. The only man who spanned all aspects of the President's life was the Attorney General. Sorensen had been called the President's alter ego. John Kennedy's true second self was Robert Kennedy. But even his brother, who had been O'Donnell's team-mate on the Harvard football team, sometimes found Ken silent and forbidding. O'Donnell was ascetic, tough, and inscrutable. He had only one passion, President Kennedy, and his devotion was inflexible. Unlike O'Brien, he wasn't one of the merry Irish. This was the first time the First Lady had seen him beam. Startled, she burst into laughter. The President chuckled, and O'Donnell grinned openly.

Today was the ninety-fifth birthday of John Nance Garner, and at 10.14 a.m., while her husband called Uvalde, Texas, to wish the former Vice President a pleasant anniversary, she strolled through their rooms. She returned with an astounding discovery. In the fatigue of last night and the haste of this morning neither Kennedy had noticed that they were surrounded by a priceless art exhibition. On the walls and tables were a Monet, a Picasso, a Van Gogh, a Prendergast, and twelve other celebrated oil paintings, water colours, and bronzes. A catalogue, which had also been overlooked, disclosed that the exhibit was in their honour. 'Isn't this sweet, Jack?' she said as he hung up on Uvalde. 'They've just stripped their whole museum of all their treasures to brighten this dingy hotel suite.' He knew it had been for her, and taking the catalogue he said, 'Let's see who did it.' There were several names at the end. The first was Mrs J. Lee Johnson III. 'Why don't we call her?' he suggested. 'She must be in the phone book.' Thus Ruth Carter Johnson, the wife of a Fort Worth newspaper executive, became the surprised recipient of John Kennedy's last telephone call. She was home nursing a sick daughter. She had watched the ballroom breakfast on WBAP-TV, and when she heard the President's voice she was speechless. He apologized for not phoning earlier, explaining that they hadn't reached the hotel until midnight. Then Mrs Kennedy came on. To Mrs Johnson she sounded thrilled and vivacious. 'They're going to have a dreadful time getting me out of here with all these wonderful works of art,' she said. 'We're both touched—thank you so much.'

O'Donnell had a far less agreeable surprise for the President. While Kennedy was speaking in the ballroom Kilduff had leafed through the Dallas *News*, found the ugly advertisement, and brought it directly to O'Donnell's rooms. Now Kennedy saw it for the first time. He read each word, his face grim, and handed it to Jackie. Her vivacity disappeared; she felt sick. The President shook his head. In a low voice he asked Ken, 'Can you imagine a paper doing a thing like that?' Then, slowly, he said to her, 'Oh, you know, we're heading into nut country today.' O'Donnell took that paper to a window and reread it. The President prowled the floor. Abruptly he paused in front of his wife. 'You know, last night would have been a hell of a night to assassinate a President,' he murmured. He said it casually, and she took it lightly; it was his way of shaking off the ad. He had what she called 'a Walter Mitty streak'. Like a little boy he would watch a passing jet from the fantail of the *Honey Fitz*, wondering aloud if he could fly it, picturing himself wrestling with the controls. 'I mean it,' he said now, building the daydream. 'There was the rain, and the night, and we were all getting jostled. Suppose a man had a pistol in a briefcase.' He gestured vividly, pointing his rigid index finger at the wall and jerking his thumb twice to show the action of the hammer. 'Then he could have dropped the gun and the briefcase'—in pantomime he dropped them and whirled in a tense crouch—'and melted away in the crowd.'

Lyndon Johnson came in immediately after this 007 caper. His sister and brother-in-law, Mr and Mrs Birge Alexander, were with him; they wanted to shake hands with a President. Lyndon introduced them, and then, respectful as always, he quietly withdrew, motioning them to accompany him. But his visit had reminded Kennedy of the party's fratricidal tendencies; the President ordered Ken to call Larry immediately and tell him Yarborough must ride with the Vice President even if the Senator had to be picked up and thrown into the back seat. At the end of the call he snatched the phone from O'Donnell and said deliberately to O'Brien, stressing each word, '*Get him in the car.*' Ken left to join Larry, and Jacqueline Kennedy examined the still uncertain sky. She hoped it would darken. It would be ridiculous to spend all that time getting ready and then ruin everything in a forty-five-minute ride in an open car. 'Oh, I want the bubbletop,' she said wistfully.

The issue was being resolved against her at that very moment. The President, anticipating the result, was changing to a lightweight suit in his bedroom. He had a hunch they were heading into more hot weather. Down the hall O'Donnell was on the phone with Roy Kellerman. On another line Kellerman was holding Agents Sorrels and Lawson, who were standing by in Dallas. They were at Love Field with the top. Should it go up? Ken asked how things looked over there, and Roy relayed the question. The weather bureau had hedged and the Dallas *News* had predicted rain, but Sorrels felt positive the wind would blow the storm eastward.

'If the weather is clear and it's not raining, have that bubbletop off,' O'Donnell said. Then they all crossed their fingers.

But not for long. Awaiting Yarborough in front of the hotel, O'Donnell and O'Brien anxiously scrutinized the clouds, and as they watched their spirits lifted. In the distance a thin ribbon of lemon-coloured light appeared. The phenomenon had become familiar when they were barnstorming the country in 1960. Repeatedly the *Caroline*, the candidate's private plane, had battled through a thunderstorm which had turned to bright sunshine as they touched down, and once in Louisville a *Caroline* landing had ended three weeks of steady rain. O'Donnell took a deep breath. It was going to be a day with a halo around it, a glittering lacuna of a day. There would be no bubbletop. O'Brien winked at him and said, 'Kennedy weather, Charlie.'

The motorcade to Carswell was ready. There were three lines of cars in the street outside—Congressional convertibles on the far side, staff Mercurys in the middle, and Lincolns, for the most eminent, at the kerb. Some vehicles were already occupied. The press buses had filled early, because none of the reporters wanted to miss Ralph Yarborough's exit, and in one of the Mercurys young Marie Fehmer was reading the *News* ad. Dallas was Marie's home town. She felt suffused with a sense of shame. Like most members of Johnson's staff, she had never met the President. A University of Texas coed until June of 1962, she had watched John Kennedy from afar, and this morning she had braved the rain to see him in the parking lot. The vicious slanders in the *News* had nothing to do with politics, she thought. The paper was entitled to dislike Kennedy and criticize him, yet decent Americans respected the office of the Presidency. *Uncivilized*, she kept thinking; this attack was *uncivilized*. As a Dallasite she understood the incivility. Dallas Democrats had learned to live with such outrages. The outsiders around her wouldn't make allowances, however. They would be just furious, and she couldn't blame them. Marie huddled behind the newspaper, wishing she could hide and wishing she had a nobler shield.

Governor Connally had just held his press conference in the Longhorn Room. He was standing on the sidewalk, waiting for the Kennedys and talking to Bob Baskin. Baskin was looking forward to a ride on Air Force One with the press pool. He hadn't read his own paper yet; the blow would fall after he had boarded the plane. They were just finishing their chat when Yarborough trudged out, deep in thought. O'Brien darted to his side. 'We wish you'd reconsider, Senator,' he began. 'The President will be very pleased if you ride with the Vice President.' Yarborough, dogged, was about to shake his head. O'Brien scanned the press buses. He said swiftly, 'They're watching us, you know. This is their big story.' The Senator planted his legs and intoned, 'I'll be proud to talk to them about proof of the President's popularity, Larry. The multitudes who have thronged the streets of Texas' greatest cities in an unprecedented outpouring of affection offer far more ample proof than anything I can do.' He glanced up. It wasn't taking. Larry was just standing there stolidly. 'Look,' Yarborough said. 'I'll issue a statement.' Impassively Larry replied, 'You can issue a statement of ten thousand words, but nothing will be as effective as you getting in that car.' Out of the corner of his eye he observed the Johnsons emerging from the hotel. It was 10.40. They were ready to go. Unexpectedly, Yarborough then capitulated. 'Well, if it means that much——' he began resignedly. 'It does,' said O'Brien, cutting him off. Turning to Johnson he muttered, 'The Senator is riding with you and Mrs Johnson.' In an undertone the Vice President replied, 'Fine.'

An incident of *opéra bouffe* followed. O'Brien escorted them to the car. Yarborough was behind the driver, Lady Bird in the middle, Lyndon on the right. Just as Larry was about to close the Senator's door in muted triumph, a National Committee advance man appeared on the other side with Nellie Connally. The five-passenger Lincoln assigned to the President for the drive to the airfield would accommodate only the Kennedys, the Governor, and Kellerman and Greer of the Secret Service. The Governor's lady had to go elsewhere. To the advance man this seemed the logical place, and he started to put her in the back beside Johnson. But this was a five-passenger car, too. There was room for just three people in the rear. As the Vice President and Mrs Johnson slid over to make room for the new arrival, Yarborough, on the far side from Nellie, was being inexorably squeezed out.

Recognizing a blessing in disguise, he began edging off the seat and back towards the sidewalk. Larry was aghast. He thought bitterly, *There goes the old ball game*. In desperation he resorted to physical force. Blocking the Senator's broad shoulders with his own stocky hips, he flapped his hand frantically at the advance man, who got the message. Without explanation—there was really nothing he could have said—he plucked Nellie out and escorted her to the front seat. Puzzled, the Governor's wife found herself riding between the police driver and Rufus Youngblood. What made it all doubly awkward was that the Johnsons would be flying to Dallas on the backup plane, which meant that she must board Air Force One with Yarborough. As they drew away there were cheers outside the car and a deathly silence inside. Lady Bird, however, was the essence of tact. Like a charming guide, she commented gaily on the passing scenery, the highlights of which were the Allright Auto Parts emporium, a wasteland of parking lots, the Greenwood Cemetery and Mausoleum, and, after they had re-entered Carswell, a row of stark sheds housing nuclear weapons.

O'Brien, in another car, dried his forehead. The temperature was creeping towards the eighties, and the humidity remained high. But so far everything was in control. It was 11.08. Unless a crowd had gathered inside Carswell they should be able to hold to the schedule. Another throng here was unlikely. This was a maximum-security area. Nevertheless the instant they stopped they were mobbed. Every mechanic and grease monkey had turned out to see the President off. For fifteen minutes they milled around, shouting lustily and holding out rough hands while Colonel Jim Swindal, in his cockpit high above them, studied his watch. The other official aircraft, 86970, was fully loaded. The Johnsons, Marie Fehmer, Liz Carpenter, Cliff Carter, Colonel George McNally of the White House Communications Agency, and the Congressmen there had fastened their seat belts and were squirming restlessly, for they couldn't take off until 26000 did. From the Presidential plane's staff area John Connally stared down at the turmoil. Nothing in Texas newspapers had prepared him for these tumultuous receptions. Kennedy was a controversial Easterner. Why should Air Force enlisted men go into such a frenzy over him? They couldn't *all* be from Massachusetts.

The President and Mrs Kennedy mounted the ramp at 11.23. Evelyn Lincoln photographed them with a new Polaroid and followed, brushing past Mac Kilduff. Kilduff was lost in thought, 'I'll be glad when this next stop is over,' he said under his breath. 'It's the only one that worries me.' Sitting beside Mary Gallagher, Evelyn suggested to her, 'Why don't you come along on the Dallas motorcade?' Mary shook her head. 'Can't! I've already missed two hotels.' Evelyn persisted: 'Remember Adlai Stevenson? We may run into some demonstrations.' 'Demonstrations?' Mary asked skittishly. Yet it sounded exciting, and she decided to take a chance and go. After all, she had worked for the Kennedys for nearly eleven years. She was entitled to a little fun. She just hoped the President didn't find out.

Aboard the backup plane Henry Gonzalez opened a copy of the Dallas *News* to page 14. ' "Welcome, Mr Kennedy," ' he read aloud. His round face brightened. 'Say, somebody must've got the word! Dallas is joining the union!' He read a few lines and gave a little leap, bucking against his seat belt. Beside him Congressman Mighty John Young of Corpus Christi said dryly, 'That's right, Henry. Read it. Read *all* of it.' Tiger Teague, on the other hand, was enjoying a false dawn. Teague had been the chief Cassandra of the Congressional delegation, but outside Carswell's operations office Connally had told him that they were going to go to the Trade Mart directly upon arrival. Misunderstanding, Teague thought that meant no motorcade, no exposure to cranks, and he had written off most of his anxieties.

O'Brien watched the President's embarkation. 'Flying to Dallas?' asked the driver. Larry looked over his shoulder and nodded. With Fort Worth chauvinism the man called, 'That's the hell hole of the world.'

Ted Clifton wondered why they were flying at all. On so short a hop Aircraft 26000 would rise no higher than five thousand feet. The moment Swindal finished climbing he would enter his glide pattern. The flight itself would last only thirteen minutes, but counting the rides out to Carswell and in from Love the Fort Worth-to-Dallas trip was going to take nearly two hours. Even with liberal allowances for parades on both ends, a city-to-city motorcade on the toll road could easily beat that. Presidential time was precious, and the General raised the point with O'Donnell. 'I've been over that with the Secret Service,' Ken said. 'It's good logistics but poor politics. With two fields we have two landings, and for a politician nothing except weather is more important than a good airport arrival.'

He gave the clouds a final reading. There weren't many left to read. Each passing minute vindicated Agent Sorrels' forecast. There were still a few rain showers on the horizon, and the cloying, muggy air here was giving them a bumpy ride. But it was the storm's dying spasm. When Pamela Turnure leaned over and peered down at the dull, flat plain below, she saw the last of the overcast rise 'like an awning', revealing a translucent sky. Shafts of sunlight traced cheerful patterns on the deep blue carpeting, and in the communications shack Ralph Yarborough jubilantly clapped O'Brien on the back. 'That's all we need,' he chortled. 'By the time the President leaves Austin a million people will have seen him. That's one Texan in every ten. Why, Larry, he's going to sweep this state next fall!' O'Brien made a fast calculation. The Senator was right, it *was* impressive. He said, 'I believe you.'

Then he awaited Yarborough's pitch. He knew one was coming. In politics no one sacrifices a rook for a pawn. Outside the hotel the Senator had yielded to Presidential pressure (and a little Irish muscle). Now he was entitled to lay an arm on Larry. O'Brien had written the textbook of Kennedy politics; he knew. Since Yarborough himself would be running for re-election next November, he was bound to exercise his option. He did. 'I'm in the dangedest pickle,' he confided. 'Anything I can do?' O'Brien asked solicitously. 'It's about tonight,' said Yarborough. He signalled to birdlike Albert Thomas in the aisle, inviting him to join the huddle, and poured out his Austin problems to both of them. Texas voters had a way of scorning men who turned the other cheek. And Austin would make the wounds crueller because it was Yarborough's home. If anyone could solve this one for him, the Senator vowed, he'd be everlastingly grateful.

'Let me have a crack at this, Judge,' Thomas said to O'Brien. Thomas frequently addressed men as 'Judge' (a lawyer became 'Mr Chief Justice'). The Congressman was at least as honey-tongued as Yarborough. Today, as yesterday, he was the ideal conciliator, and in his square-toed, old-fashioned shoes he walked spryly towards the rear of the aircraft, where the President, still smarting from his perusal of the Texas press, was holding forth in the little tail compartment. 'It's bad,' he said, holding one newspaper aloft to Kellerman, Hill, and McHugh. 'What's worse, it's inaccurate.' He had come to the state as an umpire, not as an antagonist. Godfrey said, 'If you think that's bad, Mr President, wait till you see the Dallas *News*.' 'I *have* seen it,' Kennedy said heavily. He paced forward along the corridor outside his bedroom and paused in the doorway. On a narrow bench outside, O'Donnell was sitting with Connally. Taking no chances, he and O'Brien were keeping the Governor and the Senator at opposite ends of the plane. Ken hadn't made an inch of progress. Logic, even wheedling, was wasted on the Governor. The real factional bitterness was between Johnson and Yarborough, Connally insisted; as Johnson's protégé he had been caught in the middle.

'I've got problems in Texas you don't understand,' he was saying, 'just as you'd have problems *I* wouldn't understand if I came to Massachusetts.'

Kennedy didn't enter the discussion. He had left that to his lieutenants. Besides, his mind was still on the morning papers. 'What kind of journalism do you call the Dallas *Morning News*?' he fumed at Ken. 'You know who's responsible for that ad? Dealey. Remember him? After that exhibition he put on in the White House I did a little checking on him. He runs around calling himself a war correspondent, and everybody in Dallas believes him.' The President added a highly derogatory statement about the publisher.

He saw Thomas approaching and motioned him into the bedroom. Sergeant Joe Ayres entered with a dish of fresh pineapple and a cup of coffee; the plane heaved, and Kennedy, shifting his weight, ladled in four heaping spoons of sugar. 'What can I do for you this morning, Congressman?'

'Mr President, it's the other way round. If I can't win after what you did for me in Houston, I don't deserve to get elected.' There was a tap on the door. Dave Powers handed Kennedy his Trade Mart speech. Thomas added gravely, 'But if I were you, I'd be careful what I said in Dallas. It's a tough town.'

Kennedy let it pass. Nothing he had seen this morning had encouraged him to soften a word. The Washington correspondent of the Dallas *Times-Herald*, who had seen an advance copy of the speech, had warned his office that it was 'a withering blast at his right-wing critics'. The President intended it to be just that.

'Why don't you give Kenny a hand?' Kennedy said, glancing at the door.

'That's why I'm here,' said the Congressman, and went out.

Assaulted on two fronts, Connally began to thaw. He conceded that he had been dazzled by turnouts for Kennedy. That was a language any politician could understand. Minutes before they landed he slapped O'Donnell on the back. 'All right,' he boomed.

'I'll do anything the President says. If he wants Yarborough at the head table, that's where Yarborough will sit.'

It was an uncertain victory. Nellie's reception had been discreetly bypassed. Her vow stood; she wasn't going to have the Senator in the Governor's mansion. And neither O'Donnell nor Thomas was aware of the Governor's plan for a two-tiered head table. If Connally meant to stick to that, they had won nothing. Nevertheless they believed they had won, and when the President emerged in a fresh shirt, combing his hair, Ken exultantly told him Connally had surrendered.

'Terrific!' Kennedy grinned. 'That makes the whole trip worthwhile.'

From his burrow of brightly coloured knobs and switches Jim Swindal blinked out through 26000's plastic nose and watched the ribbon of shining concrete race under his landing gear. Air Force One touched down, and he noted the time for his log: 11.38. Taxiing to the left of the green and red terminal building, he crept towards a building marked 'International Arrivals'. They were to park there, where, penned behind a cyclone fence, the welcome crowd leaped and jumped. Obviously security was tight. You could see it from here. Armed policemen stood on every rooftop of the airport's eastern concourse, and an elderly, hawk-faced agent (it was Sorrels) was chasing a photographer back behind the barrier. But to Swindal it looked like another *viva* throng. Maybe Dallas had been libelled. Viewed from this cockpit the people seemed to be typical Texans, ready to give Kennedy his most boisterous reception since San Antonio.

It wasn't that simple. In San Antonio the President had been greeted by an entire city. Here the greeters were members of the local underground. Unquestionably that underground was out in force. Liberals were making a valiant showing, here and all along the route. A row of school truants held an American flag and a brave 'WE LOVE JACK', and a little Negro boy waved a square of cardboard reading 'HOORAY FOR JFK'. In numbers and noise the libs were anxious to outshout Kennedy's audiences in Houston and Fort Worth. The very fact that they were swamped in Dallas elections, estranged from the majority, and scorned by the city's most powerful men seemed to have kindled a new spirit in them. It wasn't easy to be a liberal in Dallas, or even a moderate. Loyalty to Kennedy demanded courage, and the Kennedy supporters of Dallas had poured into the streets to prove their fibre. The effort was gallant. From a window in 26000 it seemed to eclipse everything else. But they weren't the voice of Dallas. Love Field was a new kind of country. There were differences here, and perceptive Texans spotted them.

Henry Gonzalez noticed how people would start to wave, then jerk their hands back and glance nervously over their shoulders. Ronnie Dugger, editor of the *Texas Observer*, saw a Confederate flag held high above the crowd, and he noted that here and there spectators who hadn't come to applaud were standing grimly with 'braced stance, a pipe that was being puffed too rapidly, brows knitted in frowns'. Liz Carpenter thought that the signs that were hostile were the ugliest she had ever seen. 'CAN THE CLAN', read one. 'HELP KENNEDY STAMP OUT DEMOCRACY', read another. A man whose face was contorted with some inner emotion held a placard which simply said, 'YOUR A TRAITER' (*sic*). A board fastened atop a small foreign car declared, 'MR PRESIDENT, BECAUSE OF YOUR SOCIALIST TENDENCIES AND BECAUSE OF YOUR SURRENDER TO COMMUNISM I HOLD YOU IN COMPLETE CONTEMPT'. Others were: 'IN 1964 GOLDWATER AND FREEDOM'; 'KENNEDY—GUS HALL, LEADERS OF COMMUNIST PARTY WANT YOU RE-ELECTED', 'LET'S BARRY KING JOHN', and 'YANKEE GO HOME AND TAKE YOUR EQUALS WITH YOU'. A large group of hostile teenagers was here despite the school ruling; an entire delegation from Thomas Jefferson High School had come to hiss the President.

The twelve-man official reception committee reflected the peculiarities of Dallas. Not a single representative of organized labour was present, which for a Democratic President was extraordinary. The local unions had been eager to participate in the ceremonies here and at the luncheon, but after a series of exasperating encounters with the Republicans and right-wing Democrats who dominated the host committee they had given up. The delegation waiting to greet the President consisted of nine Republicans, two Dixiecrats, and a lone liberal, Barefoot Sanders. Appropriately, they had assembled an hour earlier outside the Republic National Bank and driven to the field in long black air-conditioned limousines, and it was equally appropriate that the first man to bound through their reception line should be, not the President, but Governor Connally. The Governor was violating protocol, but this, after all, was his hand-picked team, just as he was their man. Kennedy couldn't carry Dallas. It was doubtful that he would even make a respectable showing here next November. The Democratic Governor, however, was a local hero. Archconservative Dallasites could find no socialistic tendencies in him. They knew he wasn't traitor to their values, and they were prepared to push a Goldwater–Connally ticket in '64.

Awaiting the ramp, Kennedy bantered with his valet. George Thomas came from Berryville, Virginia, a tiny crossroads. In the tail compartment the President said quizzically, 'You know, George, I think this is a bigger town than you come from.' He winked and stepped out on the top step, narrowing his eyes as he sized up the crowd in one sweeping glance. Mrs Kennedy appeared beside him, and the underground roared its approval. Dave Powers, the inveterate note-taker, scrawled, 'They look like Mr and Mrs America.' At the bottom the Johnsons had been waiting patiently for five minutes. For the fourth time in less than twenty-four hours they were welcoming the Kennedys to a new city in their best nice-of-you-to-come manner, and both couples felt slightly silly. Moreover, there would be two more such landings today, at Bergstrom Air Force Base and at the ranch. Lyndon looked up at Jackie, shrugging comically at the absurdity of it all, and she laughed. But ludicrous or not, Johnson never left a job half done. The geyser of energy within him wouldn't permit it. If being Vice President meant pumping hands, he would greet every passenger to leave Air Force One, and he did just that. Kilduff, at the end of the line, said, 'Sir, I'm sure if you shake my hand one more time you'll be ill.' Johnson squeezed his shoulder. 'Don't be ridiculous, Mac.'

Yet once the reception line broke up, the Vice President's Dallas work was done. His next scheduled performance wouldn't come until 3.15, when they reached Bergstrom. The massed cheerers on the other side of the chain fence were for the President. Johnson made a token appearance there, but when he saw that the hands were straining towards the Kennedys he led Lady Bird to the grey four-door convertible which Sorrels had borrowed from a local Ford dealer for his use. Hurchel Jacks of the Texas Department of Public Safety was behind the wheel. Joining Jacks in the front seat, Rufe Youngblood tuned his DCN hand set to Baker channel, the Vice Presidential wavelength; with it, he could maintain contact with Agent Lem Johns in the Vice Presidential follow-up car. Apart from Signalmen, Rife and Lem were probably its only listeners. Everybody else with a set was tuned to the Charlie frequency, the radio link with the Presidential car. That was where the excitement would be, and those familiar with Secret Service code could follow the progress of Lancer and Lace from the dialogue between Roy Kellerman in the car's front seat and Art Bales in the Signals car at the end of the parade. Bales was methodically checking out all networks. The high points here were the Lincoln and the two Secret Service follow-up cars. In transit there would be a constant link with Jim Swindal on Air Force One and the small Signals switchboard in the Sheraton-Dallas, which had twenty extensions and ten trunks binding the Presidential party to the Fort Worth board and thence to the

Secret Service field office in Kansas City, Andrews Field, the Pentagon, and the White House and its thousand extensions.

Ordinarily Art Bales would have been a mere passenger. Radio frequencies were normally the domain of Colonel McNally. But the Colonel wanted a break. Like many other members of the party, he had decided to skip the trip into town and have lunch in the terminal restaurant. Muggsy O'Leary was there; so were the baggagemen and the aircraft crews, except for Colonel Swindal, Sergeant Ayres, and the guards posted around 26000 and 86970. The Colonel asked Ayres to make him a roast beef sandwich and stepped into the aircraft's communications shack, turning on the Charlie frequency there. In the staff area Kilduff's two secretaries had stayed behind to type press releases. Aft of them, George Thomas was sorting out clothes. On the inboard bunk he laid out a complete change for Austin: shirt, socks, shoes, and a lightweight blue suit. Then, reflecting that the President would be tired when he returned to the plane, he thought it would be nice to leave a reminder that tonight at the ranch there would be a respite from speeches and parades. Beside the shirt he put a pair of khaki pants, a light sweater, and a sport shirt.

Beyond the plane's left wing the Kennedys were ducking puddles left from the night's rain. By Love Field's Gate 28 the President leaned over Annie S. Dunbar, an eighty-five-year-old loyal Democrat and an arthritic who had come in a wheelchair; then he and Mrs Kennedy walked about fifty yards of fence, smiling and touching fingers. Both had turned away when, on impulse, he turned back. 'There he goes,' his wife said fondly, adjusting Dearie Cabell's bouquet of red roses in the crook of her left arm. 'How do you like campaigning?' Chuck Roberts of *Newsweek* asked her. 'It's wonderful!' she said. The crowd surged towards her. 'Where's my husband?' she asked quickly. Then, relieved: 'Oh, there he is.' To her inexperienced eye Dallas seemed unexceptionable, but those who knew and distrusted the city remained on edge. With a half-smile Gonzalez said to Young, 'I sure wish somebody had invented a spitproof mask.' He looked at the Confederate flag and added, 'And I forgot my bulletproof vest.' At the fence tall Roy Kellerman remained inches behind the President, studying faces and cameras. A local reporter told Roberts, 'The Dallas police have learned their lesson. After Kennedy leaves here they won't let anybody within ten feet of him.' Hugh Sidey, who, as a rule, disregarded airport crowds, left his press bus seat to join them; he felt a general air of tension. Still the Chief Executive continued down the line; he had wandered so far from the main party that Bill Greer moved the Lincoln towards him, shadowing him in order to save time when he decided to quit. The President lingered at the fence for another five minutes. Ronnie Dugger wrote in his notebook: 'Kennedy is showing he is not afraid.'

To Greer the big convertible was like 26000, a flagship, and he liked to make the arrival of the captain on board an occasion for ceremony. On the right front fender he unhooded the small American flag. Kellerman held the door for the President, and Greer removed the cover from the blue Presidential flag on the left with a flourish. He always made a ceremony out of it, and it always irritated the younger agents. In their judgment this was a time to be especially vigilant. The driver should be behind the wheel when the President slid in, ready to take off in case of trouble. Somebody else could unfurl the tiny flags. They regarded the chauffeur with affection, but felt that he was too fussy. He ignored them. The Chief of State was entitled to full honours, and his driver intended to make certain that he got them.

The captain was aboard, Greer was at the helm; they should have cast off all lines and sailed for the Trade Mart at once. Unexpectedly, there was a lot of last-minute running around. The pool car wouldn't start, and for a sickening moment Kilduff thought he had another dead battery. Then the engine turned over. In the interval Dave Powers had appeared beside the Lincoln. 'Lunchtime,' he told Kennedy merrily, 'we're going to hit that captive audience again.' He reminded Mrs Kennedy, 'Be sure to look to your left, away from the President. Wave to the people on your side. If you both wave at the same voter, it's a waste.'

On the plane word had been passed that since the flight was so brief no new plans would be issued for the Dallas motorcade; it would be identical to the motorcade in Fort Worth. If a passenger had ridden in the ninth car there, say, he would be in the ninth car here. It didn't work. The vehicles were unfamiliar, and there was an undignified scramble for seats. Ted Clifton and Godfrey McHugh found an empty station wagon and jumped in. Gonzalez saw Congressman Wright Patman's son in the crowd and thrust him in the second Congressional convertible. The losers wound up in the lowly VIP bus, and Dr Burkley and Evelyn Lincoln were again among them. They had talked their way into the Secret Service follow-up car jump seats in Fort Worth, but since O'Donnell and Powers wanted to ride there now, they had been bumped to the end of the line.

'It's not right,' Dr Burkley kept repeating in a shaky, indignant voice.

The doctor wasn't concerned about status. He was perhaps more anxious to avoid notoriety than any man there. His code name was

Market; it should have been Modesty. The White House press corps, which had dwelt at great length on Dr Janet Travell's treatment of the President's back injuries, was scarcely aware of him. Very few people realized that he was a rear admiral. On social occasions he didn't even identify himself as a doctor. He preferred to be introduced as plain George Burkley, and the details of his private life—the fact, for example, that he was a devout Roman Catholic—were treated by him as though they were state secrets. Sensitive, introverted, and self-effacing, he would have been delighted to leave all limelight to O'Donnell and Powers. But even on a political trip, he felt, politicians should remember that John Kennedy was more than the leader of a party.

'The President's personal physician should be much closer to him,' he told Evelyn. 'I don't see why they can't put me in that lead car. I wouldn't mind sitting on an agent's lap.'

Of course, there was only an outside chance that he would be needed. But that chance was Dr Burkley's sole reason for being here. He wouldn't be in the way. At the very least, he thought, he could perform little personal services for the President. Kennedy had lost countless pairs of dark glasses; people were for ever pinching them for souvenirs. The doctor carried several spares in his black bag. He contemplated the sun, now blinding. This was a day when a man in an open car might need occasional shelter from the glare.

Evelyn glanced around disconsolately. Most of the faces in the bus were unfamiliar to her. Barefoot Sanders was pacing up and down the aisle. Valenti, whom none of the President's people knew, was rubbernecking. Liz Carpenter had led Marie Fehmer and two Dallas women to seats; with irrepressible gaiety she was directing their attention outside to the famous Larry O'Brien.

As they watched, O'Brien broke into a run. Larry had assumed that the Yarborough problem was solved. Suddenly he realized that the Senator had mentioned nothing about riding with the Vice President here. Simultaneously he saw the President staring at him and cutting his eye meaningfully towards Yarborough, who appeared to be looking for another car. It was the Hotel Texas all over again. Larry grabbed the Senator's arm, shoved him on to the seat beside Lady Bird, and slammed the door. The motorcade was beginning to move; O'Brien was about to be left. He looked around wildly and jumped into a convertible with Congressmen Mahon, Rogers, and Thornberry.

All the morning the floor-laying crew had been working on the cleared section of the Texas School Book Depository's sixth floor. Now it was time for a midday break, sandwiches, and, afterwards, the spectacle at the front door. Their feelings about the motorcade were mixed. There was little sympathy among them for the President's uncompromising stand on behalf of equal rights for Negroes. Roy Truly, who didn't believe the races were meant to mix, later doubted that 'half my boys would have gone out to see the parade if it hadn't been lunchtime'. He explained, 'Except for my niggers the boys are conservative, like me—like most Texans.'

Still, a parade was a parade. Fifteen minutes before noon the men used both of the building's antiquated elevators to go down to the street level. As they passed the fifth floor, Charles Givens, a thirty-eight-year-old former Navy steward and senior Book Depository employee, saw Lee Oswald standing by the gate on the fifth floor watching them go. Their departure left the top storeys unoccupied. In effect, the upper part of the warehouse had now met the Secret Service's definition of the classic sniper's perch—it was a deserted building.

Yet no gunman can be certain that he will not be interrupted by a casual intruder whose memory will later place the killer at the scene. It happened to Oswald. Someone—it was Givens—came back. Downstairs he discovered that he had left his cigarettes in his jacket pocket. Returning, he encountered Oswald on the sixth floor. 'Boy, aren't you coming downstairs?' he asked, surprised. 'It's near lunchtime.' 'No, sir,' replied Oswald, respectful as always. Possibly to allay suspicion, more likely to prepare the way for his escape, he said, 'When you get downstairs, close the gate to the elevator.' He meant the west elevator, which could be summoned from above only when the gate was down. 'OK,' said Givens, turning away.

Now Oswald was alone, with over a half-hour for his final preparations. His own movements excepted, the only sound in the upper part of the building came from the roof above. They were innocent and familiar: the scratching of birds. On the rear of the roof stood a fantastic structure resembling an enormous, deteriorating boxcar. Once it had been a boiler. After the building had abandoned steam heat it had been left to rust, and now it served as home for upwards of a thousand band-tailed blue pigeons who hopped around, preening themselves and blinking sightlessly at the activity in the plaza below. They were ignored here and, though naturally jumpy, they were serene. The traffic below was too far away. Only a sudden, sharp noise very close to them would create a stir in this forgotten flock.

Charles Givens rode downstairs and discovered that he couldn't close the west elevator's gate. The elevator wasn't there. It was stuck upstairs somewhere. Givens strolled away, thinking no more about it. It is his recollection that the time was 11.55 a.m.

At 11.55 a.m. the van of Kennedy's procession moved through a section of Love Field fence which Forrest Sorrels had ordered removed for the occasion. Two motor-cycle policemen cleared the way for:

The lead car, an unmarked white Ford driven by Chief Curry. Agent Lawson sat beside Curry. In the rear, Sheriff Bill Decker was on the left, Sorrels on the right. Three more motor-cycles trailed the back bumper and led the rest of the procession by five car lengths.

SS 100 X, the Presidential car, District of Columbia licence number GG 300. Its six passengers were in their usual places: Kellerman beside Greer; the Connallys in the jump seats, John to the right of Nellie; the Kennedys in the rear, with the roses between them. Four motor-cycles, two on each side, flanked the rear of GG 300.

Halfback, the follow-up convertible, District licence number GG 678. Agent Sam Kinney, at the wheel, kept his eyes on the back of the President's head. Emory Roberts, Halfback's commander, was next to Kinney. Clint Hill stood on the left front running board. Agent Bill McIntyre was behind him. John Ready was on the right front running board, Agent Landis behind him. Dave Powers was in the right jump seat, Ken O'Donnell in the left. Agent George Hickey sat in the left rear, Agent Glen Bennett in the right rear, and on the seat between them lay an AR-15 .223 automatic rifle, with a muzzle velocity so powerful that should a bullet strike a man's chest it would blow his head off.

The Vice Presidential convertible. Two-and-a-half car lengths separated it from Halfback, to indicate that the appearance of the Vice President was a separate event. Ralph Yarborough, who loved parades, was under the impression that Lyndon Johnson wasn't enjoying the distinction. The Senator, in the left rear, was waving jubilantly. Johnson stared glumly ahead.

Varsity, the follow-up hardtop, was driven by a Texas state policeman. Cliff Carter was in the middle of the front seat. Agent Jerry Kivett was on his right. Agent Lem Johns was in the right rear, Agent Taylor in the left rear.

The pool car was on loan from the telephone company, and the driver came with it. Kilduff and Merriman Smith of United Press International were in front, Kilduff on the right. As the senior White House correspondent Smith always rode in the middle. Thus he was the newspaperman closest to the radiophone on the transmission hump under the dashboard. Jack Bell of the Associated Press, Baskin of the Dallas *News*, and Bob Clark of the American Broadcasting Company were in the back. In a crisis they could report nothing hard from this car unless Smith surrendered the phone, and

Smith, with his hard, pocked face, was one of the most competitive men in journalism.

The photographers' convertibles came next. The bulk of the motorcade trailed them.

They passed the airport's 'Spirit of Flight', a graceful statue of a figure whose arms stretched upward, and turned north-east, or left, at Mockingbird Lane.

On a map the Love Field–Trade Mart–Love Field motorcade route resembled a crude bottle. Mockingbird was the base. Lemmon Avenue, which ran perpendicular to it, became the left side. Turtle Creek and Cedar Springs sloped inward and then straightened at Harwood, forming the left flank of the neck. The mouth comprised twelve blocks of Main Street, where the heaviest downtown crowds would be. At the end of Main the cars would avoid an awkward traffic island by jogging a block north—here, at the Book Depository, the mouth was chipped—and then cruise westward, on a gently descending incline, into the triple underpass. A sharp right up a ramp here brought them on to Stemmons Freeway, which was the opposite side of the neck. The Trade Mart was at the junction of Stemmons Freeway and Harry Hines Boulevard. After the luncheon the procession was scheduled to move down the boulevard, the bottle's right side, picking up speed as it passed the straggling, yellow-brown brick buildings of Parkland Hospital. At Mockingbird it would turn right, re-entering the base of the bottle, closing the geometric figure, and returning to Love Field for the hop to Austin.

At the beginning there wasn't much to see. John Connally hadn't expected any people here, however, and there were some. Barefoot Sanders recalled that when Kennedy and Johnson drove down Lemmon Avenue on September 13, 1960, it had been deserted. It wasn't now. But Kennedy had been only a candidate then. As President he was bound to be a greater drawing card. To O'Donnell and O'Brien the spectators outside the low, flat, automated factories—Haggar Slacks, IBM—looked like curious but indifferent white-collar workers. Nevertheless there were many blank stretches. Mrs Kennedy found herself waving at billboards advertising 'Stemmons Freeway, Market Place of the Southwest', 'Real Sippin' Whisky', 'Home of the Big Boy Hamburger', and a raffish sign inviting her to twist in The Music Box.

She began to wilt. The reading on a thermometer outside a Coca-Cola bottling plant was dismayingly high, and the sunlight was so bright that she instinctively closed her eyes. She slipped on her dark glasses. The President asked her to remove them. People had come to see her, he explained; the spectacles masked her face. Nevertheless she toyed with the lenses in her lap, sneaking them up when the sidewalks were barren of spectators. On Lemmon Avenue the Lincoln passed beneath an underpass. She liked that; the brief bar of shadow was a relief, a chance to catch her breath.

Twice the motorcade halted at Kennedy's order. At Lemmon and Lomo Alto Drive a line of very small children stood behind a placard: 'MR PRESIDENT, PLEASE STOP AND SHAKE OUR HANDS.' 'Let's stop here, Bill,' Kennedy called to Greer. He stepped into the street and was nearly swept off his feet by a surge of shrieking youth. The scene was affectionately watched by a loyal couple named Gaudet. Towards the end of it, Mrs Gaudet had an unsettling recollection: that morning she had heard a local radio programme devoted to details of the Lincoln assassination, and now she told her husband about it, saying, 'President Kennedy ought to be awarded the Purple Heart just for coming to Dallas.'

Kellerman and his men gently broke up the demonstration of children. So far the city seemed harmless enough to them. In the lead car Lawson murmured a word of commendation to Chief Curry. Lawson had suggested that underpasses be cleared of everyone except uniformed policemen, and the first underpass indicated that his advice had been followed. Everything, indeed, appeared to be on schedule. When the President dismounted the second time, the agents, though vigilant, avoided a show of force. He wanted to greet a group of nuns. He was always alert for a glimpse of Sisters, and it was a familiar scene. Only a tactless bodyguard would have intruded upon it.

In the Vice Presidential car Lyndon Johnson abruptly leaned forward.

'Turn the radio on,' he ordered, indicating the dial on the dashboard. Hurchel Jacks did, and a local station blared strongly, broadcasting an account of their progress.

At Reagan Street, three blocks before the bottle began to narrow, Father Oscar Huber was standing with some young men from his parish. 'I know why you're here,' he was teasing them. 'Don't kid me—you don't care about him. It's Jackie you want to see.' Just then he heard the drone of motor-cycle engines. Leaping up and down, the elderly priest saw Kennedy's head. But it was turned the other way. He wanted to see his face, too. The young men were jumping all around him, however, and he sensed defeat; the Lincoln had slowly drawn abreast of them and was passing on. Then—perhaps he had seen the reversed collar in the corner of his eye—the President spun in his seat, looked directly at Father Huber, and smiled. 'Hurray!' shouted the priest, completely carried away. He continued to bound until the boys grinned at him. He didn't care. He trudged back to his rectory, short of breath but contented. At last he had seen a President, and he could scarcely wait to tell those lazy Fathers lounging around the rectory television set.

Around the corner, in the neck of the bottle, Ted Dealey was watching television in a corner room on the nineteenth floor of his exclusive apartment building at 3525 Turtle Creek. Ted had just returned from a physical checkup and changed into a sports shirt. He was boycotting the Trade Mart luncheon; his son could represent the *News*. Below him he heard a sputtering of engines. He looked down, The motorcade was passing through Oak Lawn Park. Squinting, he made out a flash of colour. Pink, he thought. Some woman wearing a pink hat.

In the park the lead car passed the statue of Robert E. Lee. Forrest Sorrels felt nostalgic. He thought about the day that statue was dedicated by Franklin Roosevelt. Sorrels had been a young agent then; he had never been charged with the protection of a great man before, and he remembered his anxieties. Now it had become routine. All the same, he wished there weren't so many open windows today.

The crowds were thickening now. Every inch of kerb was occupied, and up ahead there was a flurry of excitement. On the west side of Cedar Springs Warren G. Harding, the six-foot-one, 225-pound County Treasurer, was standing outside Dallas County's Democratic party headquarters. The President passed within four feet of Harding, who was struck by what he thought was a preoccupied expression in Kennedy's eyes. He had just asked a nearby judge whether he had the same impression—the judge confirmed him—when he observed two young men on the opposite side of the street holding a large Goldwater sign. Infuriated, Harding shook his fist at them, and after the motorcade had passed he crossed over and demanded to know why they were injecting politics into a visit by a President of the United States. The men felt equally belligerent. In a few ugly phrases one gave a profane description of this President. Harding stepped forward, crowding him. Then he heard a call. The judge was pointing at his watch. It was 12.15. They were due at the Trade Mart in fifteen minutes; even taking the back way, they were going to have to hurry if they expected to beat the President there. Harding glared at the men, glared at their sign, and turned on his heel.

At Live Oak Street, two blocks north of Main, the roaring began. People were standing eight, ten, even twelve deep on the sidewalks, and secretaries were hanging out of windows overhead. Every Kennedy voter in the county seemed to be there. Barred from the luncheon, they were paying tribute in the only way left to them. A dense mob to the left, many of them with dark, Mexican faces, surged into Harwood Street. In the crush Greer decelerated from twenty miles an hour to fifteen, then to ten, then to seven. The overflow crowd forced Motorcycle Policeman B. W. Hargis, riding two feet from the left near fender of the Lincoln, to drop back. It was on Mrs Kennedy's side—each time she lifted her white glove her fluttering fingers evoked an undulating 'Jackiiieee!'—and Clint Hill, the most active agent in Dallas that day, leaped off Halfback's running board and dashed up to replace Hargis, shielding her with his body.

They were at Main. Diagonally across the intersection, to their left, loomed the grey stone pile of the Dallas city jail, Chief Curry's headquarters. The chief turned right, and as Greer pivoted behind him John Kennedy looked ahead down a twelve-block-long human canyon. This was the mouth of the bottle, fifteen hundred yards of baying office workers, fluttering bunting, and incredible heat. Far above the din the eight skyscrapers of downtown Dallas raised their mammoth shoulders against a stainless sky. Atop the Republic National Bank Building a revolving searchlight, now still, jutted into the blue like an oversized cherry picker. The clock on the glittering new spire of the Mercantile Bank read 12.21 p.m.

That was Central Standard Time. The qualification is significant. A century earlier, on April 15, 1865, Abraham Lincoln had died in the Tenth Street Washington house of William Peterson, a tailor, at 7.20 a.m., and though Eastern Standard Time as it is now understood was nearly four years old, no one observed the distinction. It would have been irrelevant. Men elsewhere lived in separate worlds then. Time and space had genuine meaning. By the time distant communities learned of the assassination and grasped its implications, local conditions and individual circumstances had altered, and they viewed the President's death with perspectives quite different from those of Washingtonians.

By November 22, 1963, all that had changed. Few thought about it, for in the absence of shattering developments people were insulated from events on the other side of the horizon by work, families, and friends. Yet the potential for simultaneous experience was there. Television alone had shrunk the dimensions of the globe until the impact of a great tragedy would be felt coinstantaneously by hundreds of millions of people in the Western Hemisphere and, through Telstar, the relay satellite, by remote Russians for whom Central Standard Time's twelve o'clock noon was twelve o'clock midnight.

The age, moreover, was an age of unprecedented mobility. The average nineteenth-century American never left his native state.

Often he died without ever having travelled farther than thirty miles from his birthplace. Everything he saw he saw over his harness reins. His great-grandson of a hundred years later had very likely grown up in one part of the country, married a girl from a second, and was employed in a third. During the early 1940's he had fought in Africa, Europe, or Asia. Now he could easily fly from Boston to New York, say, on the hourly shuttle, or span the entire country during a short summer vacation. Some careers made a man a virtual nomad, and the more powerful and affluent he was, the more he resorted to air travel. Because powerful individuals have strong feelings about any President, and because President Kennedy was a man of great personal wealth, it was inevitable that many whose lives and thoughts were linked with his should have been on the move that Friday noon—in airports, or aloft or on distant continents which, to them, were scarcely more than overnight stops.

In London, where it was 6.21 p.m., Jacqueline Kennedy's sister Lee was in her home at 4 Buckingham Place. Her husband, Prince Stanislaus Radziwill, an exiled Polish nobleman, was at the St James's Club. The Radziwills were stationary for the moment. But they also had a home in Manhattan and were accustomed to crossing the Atlantic almost as casually as the Prince's grandfather had crossed the street. The clock in the lobby of Rome's Eden Hotel stood at 7.21 p.m. There the Most Reverend Philip N. Hannan, Auxiliary Bishop of Washington, who had flown over for a conference at the Vatican, was chatting with an American Catholic layman. In the United States, Senator Barry Goldwater, the Republican most likely to lose to President Kennedy in 1964, was flying to Muncie, Indiana, for the funeral of his mother-in-law. The idol of the Dallas Right, retired Major General Edwin Walker, was in another airliner halfway between New Orleans and Shreveport, Louisiana, and Democratic Chairman John Bailey was approaching Austin on his Delta flight.

Friends and antagonists alike, they were far closer than they realized to the intersection of Harwood and Main, and in a crisis all could move to Dallas, to Washington, or to any other point in the United States in a matter of hours. The most isolated was Mrs Paul Mellon, a gentle patrician who watched over the executive mansion's Rose Garden at the President's request. Bunny Mellon was in the British West Indies. She had gone down to confer with the architect of a new estate she was building. Conditions were primitive, communications were by runner. There were no telephones on the island, and no telegraph. American radio stations were out of range. A rising storm was about to ground the nearest commercial airline. Yet even Bunny Mellon could not escape the rule of twentieth-century concurrent experience. Her radio set could pick up French-language broadcasts from Martinique, which could relay Paris bulletins. And as a Mellon she had her own private plane and pilots in New York.

At Love Field itself Candy McMurrey, sister-in-law of Senator Edward M. Kennedy, the President's younger brother, was awaiting the 12.45 departure of American Airlines Flight 58 to Washington. The gigantic wing span of Air Force One was clearly visible from the gate, and Candy, who had flown with the Chief Executive last summer, was describing the lovely interior to her husband, a Houston attorney. He listened attentively; as a Texan he would feel somewhat strange at Ted's and Joan's anniversary celebration in Georgetown tonight, and this would serve as a conversation piece. The celebration was to be an elaborate affair. At the moment the *Caroline* was over New Jersey, winging southward from New York with most of the Senator's twenty-six guests. In the morning the *Caroline* would again be airborne. The entire party had tickets to the Harvard–Yale game and were going to spend the remainder of the weekend at Hyannis Port with Mr and Mrs Joseph P. Kennedy.

Hawaiian time, as Bill Greer spun the wheel of the big Lincoln, was 8.21 a.m. The Cabinet plane, Aircraft 86972, had left Hickam Field and was bulling its way through strong head winds towards Japan. Secretary of Agriculture Orville Freeman was finishing his breakfast and talking to his wife Jane. Rusk of State, Dillon of the Treasury, Hodges of Commerce, Wirtz of Labour, and Udall of the Interior were poring over their black briefing books. Pierre Salinger gazed absently out the window at the endless blue-grey seascape. In the cockpit the pilot took a reading and made a calculation. The results were annoying. The wind was holding them below 450 m.p.h. He had planned to make Tokyo in one jump; now he realized he would have to refuel at Wake, 1,874 miles away. The change of plan meant little to his distinguished passengers. In Washington each of them was a prisoner of his appointments secretary; if a Cabinet member stepped into the hall for a word with a subordinate, the fact was carefully noted in his official diary. Here they could read and daydream. It was a rare luxury, and they were enjoying it. Even Salinger forgot the silent AP and UPI teletype machines in the communications shack. A White House telephone stood beside it, but there seemed to be no reason why it should ring. In fact, no one had remembered to bring a code book.

Five thousand miles to the east, in Washington, half the men on the streets wore topcoats, half did not. The decision was a toss-up. In the capital November 22, 1963 was a day out of season, filled with echoes of summer and warnings of fall: a day of musk, tang, sunlight, and sudden chill, for the wind had a slight bite. The White

House had enjoyed one of the quietest mornings in memory. It was 1.21 p.m. in Washington, and the mansion's outstanding event of November 22 appeared to be the logging in of 1,339 tourists. The East Gate had been closed on the last of them at noon. With the President and Mrs Kennedy away, J. Bernard West, the chief usher, was spending the afternoon at home with his children. Provi Parades, the First Lady's maid, was Christmas shopping in Silver Spring, Maryland. In the State Dining Room Charles Fincklin, the Maître, had mobilized his six butlers to clean the gold vermeil tableware for Monday's Erhard dinner, and on the second floor of the East Wing Nancy Tuckerman and Sandy Fox were frowning over the dinner's seating plan. Protocol on such occasions was thorny, and Nancy, with the last dozen cards in her hand, was worrying over where they should go. At the opposite end of the mansion, in the west basement's staff mess, Captain Taz Shepard and Dr Jim Young, George Burkley's assistant, were eating alone. The room's big round corner table was more noisy. It had been reserved for Kennedy's Foreign Intelligence Advisory Board, and Clark Clifford, salad fork in hand, was presiding over an intense debate.

There were perhaps a thousand similar colloquies in progress, each of which would be a subject of official interest to the handsome young President now making the slow turn into Dallas' Main Street. In Washington—indeed, along the entire Atlantic seaboard—this was the hour of the working lunch. Nearly every Kennedy appointee, ally, or adversary was leaning over a plate somewhere, canvassing a matter of policy. At 1.21 Acting Secretary of State George Ball was on the telephone with Acting Secretary of the Treasury Henry Fowler, discussing the wheat sale; Fowler hung up and entered the Treasury dining room to review fiscal reports with his aides. In State's eighth-floor dining room, the Ambassador for Indonesia was Deputy Under Secretary U. Alexis Johnson's guest at one table while Under Secretary Averell Harriman, at another, entertained a Congressional delegation. Across the Potomac John McCone, Director of the CIA, was eating with several spies. The Chilean Embassy was host to Senator Hubert Humphrey, whose aspirations for national office had been crushed by John Kennedy in the West Virginia primary of 1960, and to Ralph Dungan, one of Kennedy's ablest aides. On the Hill John McCormack, the second man in line of succession to the Presidency, had just entered the House restaurant with a group of cronies.

Most of the luncheons weren't official. Whenever possible men liked to get away from the office early in the afternoon and hole up for an hour or two in a club, a hotel, or a private home. Former Secretary of State Dean Acheson and Former Ambassador to Russia

Llewellyn Thompson were in the Metropolitan Club. Fred Holborn was at the Statler, Ted Reardon at the Continental, Chief of Protocol Duke at the Carlton. Nick Katzenbach, the Deputy Attorney General, ate in a cheap seafood restaurant on Pennsylvania, between Ninth and Tenth streets. At O'Donnell's, Washington's seafood shrine, Secret Service Chief James Rowley had begun speaking to a class of new agents. Ted Sorensen, at 1.21 p.m., had just left the hotel suite of Roy Roberts of the Kansas City *Star*. Roberts, though a Republican, was an admirer of John Kennedy. He had pressed Sorensen about the rumours that Lyndon Johnson would be dropped from the ticket. All month Presidential aides had been denying this gossip; it was becoming something of a bore. Ted emphatically told Roberts that Johnson was Kennedy's choice. Then, in the back of his mind, he remembered something. Once Kennedy had pointed out to him that beginning in 1860 every President elected in a twenty-year cycle—Lincoln, Garfield, McKinley, Harding, and Franklin Roosevelt—had died in office. It was an historical freak; Kennedy had laughed at it. That was one tradition, he had said, that he intended to break. Sorensen didn't take it seriously either—it was merely a striking series of coincidences—but Roberts' mention of the Vice Presidency did trigger a flickering, peripheral recollection of it.

That world of 12.21 was astonishingly uniform. A Telstar camera poised in the sky with a magical Zoomar lens would have photographed identical patterns of behaviour in men who thought they had nearly nothing in common. It was almost as though society, in contracting, had mysteriously imposed a rigid conformity upon its leaders. As Dwight Eisenhower, a critic of the administration, lifted a spoon at a 'UN We Believe' luncheon in New York, Steve Smith, meeting with an Ohio politician who had become convinced that Kennedy was going to carry the state next fall, was laying down a knife in La Caravelle restaurant a few blocks away. Fidel Castro had no use for either Republicans or Democrats. He would cheerfully have sent both Smith and Eisenhower to the wall. The mere reminder that he shared the same time zone with them would have irritated him. Nevertheless, there he was, and as a North American executive he was entertaining a visiting French journalist at a business lunch seventy-five miles from Havana. They were talking about President Kennedy.

An exception to the culinary rule was Richard N. Goodwin, the *New York Times* Man in the News that November 22. Goodwin was the victim of last night's Latin-American party. He had awakened with a hangover and elected to stay home, drafting the announcement of his new appointment. Goodwin was among those

Presidential advisers whose memorandums and *aide-mémoire* would require executive action today, over the telephone, or shortly after Kennedy's return to the capital. They were a large company. In the Georgetown house of Bill Walton the host had spread sketches for the President's proposed renovation of Pennsylvania Avenue on a luncheon table and was inspecting them enthusiastically with Charlie Horsky of the White House staff and Assistant Secretary of Labour Pat Moynihan. Walton, about to leave on a cultural mission, had booked a 5 p.m. seat to Moscow; in his absence he expected Kennedy to approve this triumvirate's decision. In the E Ring of the Pentagon the indefatigable Robert S. McNamara, his ball-point at the ready, was advancing resolutely on a fifty-billion-dollar defence budget. Around him Mac Bundy, Kermit Gordon of the Budget Bureau, and Jerry Wiesner, Kennedy's scientist-in-residence, were loading adding machines and checking fields of fire in their special sectors. By Friday, the day after Thanksgiving, they had to be in Hyannis Port with final proposals.

Some men, of course, were eating simply because they were hungry. David Ormsby-Gore, the British Ambassador, was dining alone on Massachusetts Avenue; so were the French Ambassador and Madame Alphand, on nearby Kalorama Road. Hale Boggs, famished after a gruelling House Ways and Means session, and Walter Jenkins, Lyndon Johnson's right-hand man, were on their way to quick meals. George Reedy, the Vice President's aide on Capitol Hill, was still in his office. He thought he would take a break in about a half-hour. (It was to be twenty-four hours before he could spare a minute for a sandwich.) Other Washingtonians were using the lunch hour for personal affairs. Mary McGrory of the Washington *Star* and Frank Wilson, Roosevelt's retired Secret Service chief, were in doctors' offices for checkups. Ben Bradlee, *Newsweek*'s chief capital correspondent and a close Kennedy friend, was browsing in Brentano's book store. Angie Novello, the Attorney General's private secretary, had decided to clean his office. It had, she thought, become altogether too junky. Every panelled wall was adorned with the crayoned drawings of Robert Kennedy's children and Angie was carefully peeling off their Scotch tape and filing them away.

Another Kennedy, the President's sister Eunice, was savouring an unexpected delight. She was actually lunching with her husband. Eunice, expecting another child in February, had come downtown with her four-year-old son Timmy; she had just left the office of Dr John Walsh. On a sudden whim she called Sargent Shriver. Shriver rarely had time for a break, but today he made the time, and they were sitting quietly with Timmy in the dining-room of the Hotel

Lafayette. Eunice was wearing a black knit suit. She always wore black during pregnancies; she thought it slimming.

In Washington men of power tend to do everything at least an hour after everyone else. They come to work later, eat later, quit later. Lesser men live by different timetables. Occasionally they even take a day off during the week. Joe Gawler, Washington's most prestigious undertaker, was cutting the grass in his back yard. Sergeant Keith Clark, the bugler who played taps in Arlington National Cemetery on important occasions—the last time had been Armistice Day, before President Kennedy—was home going through his collection of rare books. Jack Metzler, Arlington's superintendent, was about to leave for a long weekend. He was checking Monday's funeral list. It looked like a normal day: twenty-three burials.

At 1.21 Army and Navy posts around the capital had already messed. In Anacostia a young seaman named Ed Nemuth was decorating a hall for an enlisted men's ball. At Fort Myer a husky blond private named Arthur Carlson, who had been told that he would lead a riderless horse behind a caisson when the next distinguished general died, was stuffing his soiled uniforms into a coin-operated laundromat, and behind the great gates of Arlington itself First Lieutenant Sam Bird was conducting a colonel's funeral on a plot in the cemetery's Section 35, near the Tomb of the Unknown Soldiers. A lean, sinewy Kansan, Sam Bird was the kind of American youth whom Congressmen dutifully praise each Fourth of July and whose existence many, grown jaded by years on the Hill, secretly doubt. The Lieutenant was a square, unsophisticated patriot. The strains of the national anthem still thrilled him. He had joined the Regular Army because he wanted to serve his country, and he considered it an honour to be stationed in the national capital. As a tourist he had visited the Washington Monument, the Lincoln Memorial, and the White House, and he had gazed down reverently at the original copy of the Constitution in the National Archives. The routine of a military burial was never routine to him. He treated each one with gravity and solemnity, and as taps sounded and the clock crept towards 12.30 he watched the colonel's elderly widow slowly descend the slope beside his grave. Her two sons were assisting her. In her arms she carried the flag from the coffin, folded in its traditional triangle. One son, thinking to lighten her burden, offered to take the colours from her. Wordlessly she shook her head and hugged the banner to her breast. Lieutenant Bird was proud of her.

Not all executives were dining. Some preferred to eat early and plunge quickly into the afternoon's work, which, for key men, often extended until nine or ten o'clock in the evening. J. Edgar Hoover had been back at his desk for twenty minutes. The U.S. Supreme Court had moved into the long, panelled conference room in the rear of its marble temple behind the Capitol. The justices were pondering ten reapportionment cases. Since 1 p.m. they had been in their high-backed green leather chairs, each with a brass name plate on the back. At the head of the baize-covered table sat the Chief Justice. Arthur Goldberg, the newest member of the Court, was nearest the door. No outsider was permitted to intrude upon these conferences under any circumstances. If an urgent message arrived, it would be written out and brought to the door by a page. Goldberg would answer the knock.

Tight security was also enforced in the Pentagon's Gold Room, down the hall from McNamara, where the Joint Chiefs of Staff were in session with the commanders of the West German *Bundeswehr*. General Maxwell Taylor, the Chiefs' elegant, scholarly Chairman, dominated one side of the table; opposite him was General Friedrich A. Foertsch, Inspector General of Bonn's armed forces. Everyone was dressed to the nines—the Germans out of *Pflicht*, the Americans because they knew the Germans would be that way—and the meeting glittered with gay ribbons and braid.

For sheer colour the generals would have put the Supreme Court in the shade; in pageantry the military takes second place only to the Church. There, however, the brightest martial baubles are hopelessly out-classed, and at 1.21 p.m. that afternoon a Prince of the Church was preparing to make precisely that point. Richard Cardinal Cushing was waiting to receive the new naval commander of Boston. The admiral was about to make a courtesy call, and His Eminence was going to receive him in full splendour. Surrounded by golden holy statues, ornate *prie-dieux*, and oil paintings rich in medieval imagery, the Cardinal stood erect in his magnificent robes. With his warrior's shoulders, square jaw, and penetrating eyes, he looked more like a Cherokee than a saint. He carried himself like an ancient Hamite chieftain, and he spoke in the imperious tones of command. He only hoped he didn't have to talk too much. He suffered much from asthma and emphysema, and had to sleep with two tanks of oxygen in his bedroom. 'Don't tell me. I know,' he growled to a lay sister. 'I sound like Lazarus after four days in the tomb.'

Of all the Kennedy acquaintances who were toiling at that hour, the man with the least ostentatious office (and the most mellifluous voice) was David Brinkley of NBC. Brinkley's workshop wasn't much larger than a washroom in a filling station, and he was bowed over an old-fashioned rolltop desk. He wasn't on the air; there were no network programmes at that hour. The local NBC station, whose manager was out to lunch, was running what Brinkley regarded as a remarkably silly fashion show. Unlike Cardinal Cushing, General Taylor, and Chief Justice Warren, Brinkley was not a maker of history; he merely commented upon it. His presence on the job is worth noting because eighteen years earlier, as a twenty-five-year-old correspondent, he had been alone in NBC's Washington office when word arrived that Franklin Roosevelt had died in Warm Springs, Georgia. He still remembered mispronouncing the word 'cortège' during the Roosevelt funeral and being reprimanded for it.

The weekday lives of most women had nothing to do with offices and working luncheons. They were busy with housewifely chores—feeding children, shopping—or amusing themselves. Mary Ann ('Andy') Stewart, in Washington, and Pat Kennedy Lawford, in Santa Monica, California, were changing dresses with the help of their maids, Jacqueline Kennedy's mother, Mrs Hugh Auchincloss, had just returned from the Chevy Chase Country Club and was seated at her desk in her golf clothes, catching up on correspondence. Joanie Douglas was packing; tonight Justice Douglas would address New York's Yale Club on the eve of the game. Metzler's wife, in Arlington; Nina Warren, in the Chief Justice's Washington apartment; and Rosemary Kennedy, in a Wisconsin home for the retarded, were watching television. Jean Kennedy Smith was with Lem Billings, who had been the President's room-mate at Choate, in downtown Manhattan. Jean had just selected three Christmas presents, identical paintings of the Kennedy boat *Victura*, for the President, the Attorney General, and the junior Senator from Massachusetts. The Senator's wife Joan was in the Elizabeth Arden beauty parlour on Washington's Connecticut Avenue, putting on a face for tonight's anniversary dinner. In Hyannis Port a cousin, Ann Gargan, had just put Joseph P. Kennedy down for his afternoon nap. They had watched the one o'clock news together—though an invalid, the tough old Ambassador wanted to know which of his children were making headlines—and Ann was about to leave the Cape for a visit with her sister in Detroit. The President's mother was also lying down. Ann was being zipped up by the Ambassador's nurse, Mrs Rita Dallas.

Six hundred miles to the south the United States Senate was dozing through a soporific debate on the need for federal library services, and the floor, at present, belonged to bespectacled Senator Winston L. Prouty of Vermont, who looked a little like a librarian himself. Occasionally he glanced up from his gleaming mahogany desk towards the great chair of the President of the Senate, which, framed dramatically against a background of red Levanto marble pilasters and a heavy blue velvet drape embellished with a gold embroidered border, stood beneath the white marble motto '*E Pluribus Unum*'. Since the President of the Senate was also the Vice President of the United States, he was out of earshot. At the moment he was hunched in the convertible on Harwood Street, listening to the Dallas radio as Hurchel Jacks prepared to make the ninety-degree swing into Main Street. In his absence his seat on the rostrum was occupied by President Kennedy's younger brother, Senator Edward M. Kennedy.

Just off the fluted Senatorial chamber was the President's Room, so called because Chief Executives from Lincoln to Hoover had come there to sign bills into law. Under Franklin Roosevelt the room had fallen into disuse. Then individual Senators began using it for private meetings with members of the press, though some demurred; when Jacqueline Bouvier, then a reporter for the now defunct Washington *Times Herald*, interviewed Senator-Elect John F. Kennedy of Massachusetts in 1952, for example, he talked to her elsewhere. (She asked him what he thought of the Senate pages. He told her he thought they ought to change places with the Senators, because they were more distinguished-looking and, in his case, older.) Today Richard L. Riedel, a press liaison officer, sat alone in the President's Room reading the Washington *Post*. Riedel was admiring a cheerful spread of pictures showing the Kennedys in San Antonio and Houston. Now and then he would stride into the Senate lobby and glance at the AP teletype there. A partisan, Riedel preferred the AP machine because it was at the Democratic end of the lobby; he avoided the UPI ticker on the Republican side.

Sitting in the Vice President's chair was regarded as an honour, but Ted Kennedy, like his brother before him, regarded it with mixed feeling. The Kennedys were active. They all liked rough games, competition, challenge; and Attorney General Kennedy was undoubtedly more serene than Senator Kennedy at that moment. All day Thursday and throughout Friday morning the Attorney General had been holding marathon meetings in the Justice Department on ways to combat organized crime. The sessions were to resume in the afternoon. Meanwhile he had brought two luncheon guests to his McLean, Virginia, home—United States Attorney Robert Morgenthau of New York and Morgenthau's assistant. Robert Kennedy had taken a quick dip in the back yard swimming pool, changed to dry shorts, and joined his wife and their two guests around a table by the shallow end of the pool. As they ate chowder Morgenthau idly watched a man in overalls working on the mansion's new wing, which had become a necessity with the Attorney General's growing family. The workman was hanging shutters with one hand and holding a transistor radio in the other. His painter's hat was jammed over his ears; he seemed completely divorced from reality. Few men were closer to reality than his employer. Because of Robert Kennedy's unique position in the government the Signal Corps had installed a battery of White House phones in and around this house. NAtional 8-1414 reached Robert Kennedy as quickly as John Kennedy. While Lyndon Johnson had only one line to the mansion switchboard, this yard alone had two: Extension 163, housed in a small green wooden structure at the foot of the pool, and, in another box by the tennis court on the far side of the rolling lawn, Extension 2324.

In one sense the Kennedys were an anachronism. The mobile society of the 1960's loosened familial ties more and more each year, but their clan remained tightly knit. Intimacy with cousins began at a very early age, and John F. Kennedy, Jr.'s playmates at 1.21 p.m. were little Edward M. Kennedy, Jr. and his sister Kara. Teddy and Kara were busy with a fire engine. Young John had flung his legs over the brown rocking horse in his second-floor room. He was shouting lustily and whacking its already battered head. Maude Shaw looked wistfully at the clock. In nine minutes Teddy and Kara's Irish nurse would take them home to Georgetown. Miss Shaw could then tuck John in for his 1.30 nap and hope he would drop off. Sometimes she felt she was getting too old for such a vigorous child. As often as not he would writhe beneath the covers for a quarter-hour and then come charging out, a toy plane in his hand, ready to pursue her. Caroline was so different, quiet and pensive like her mother. Miss Shaw was going to miss Caroline tonight. Momentarily she hoped the girl would miss her, too; then she dismissed the thought as selfish.

The White House school had ended its daily session at 1.15. Downstairs on the South Portico the President's daughter was standing in a powder-blue coat and new red lace-up shoes, patiently holding her suitcase in one hand and her pink bear in the other. With her were Agatha Pozen and two other class-mates. They were awaiting Agatha's mother, the Friday car pool driver, who was about to become Caroline's overnight hostess. It was a familiar social ritual for girls approaching their sixth birthday, and in most ways it resembled thousands of similar partings on other, less imposing American porches. There was one conspicuous distinction. As a member of the First Family Caroline had to be guarded. Tom Wells, a dark young agent, would follow Mrs Pozen in a black Ford linked by radio to the White House network. The Ford was ready to go, Wells was ready, and so was Betsy Boyd, the school's kindergarten teacher. Miss Boyd had to catch a train, but she wanted to see Caroline off first. Alice Grimes, the head of the school, and Agent

Bob Foster urged her to go ahead. 'Mrs Pozen's always late,' Foster said. 'Why don't you just take off?'

A few minutes later Liz Pozen's Country Squire station wagon swung through the White House Southwest Gate. A guard in the sentry box called a friendly greeting, but she couldn't hear him; she was listening to station WGMS on her car radio.

In Texas 12.21 crept towards 12.22 as Dean Gorham, director of the state's Municipal Retirement System, raced westward along Route 71 in his blue Buick. Gorham was fighting the clock. Last evening he had attended the Albert Thomas testimonial and registered at a Houston motel. He had intended to sleep late. This morning, however, he had been awakened by a frantic call from a fellow Democrat. Through an oversight the programmes for tonight's dinner in Austin had been left in the shop of the Houston printer. People paying $100 a plate were entitled to souvenir menus. Could Gorham pick them up and deliver them to Austin's Municipal Auditorium in time?

He was doing his best, but the rain hadn't slacked until he reached the junction of Routes 90 and 71 at Columbus. He was still east of Smithville, and he knew the expected arrival of Air Force One at 3.15 p.m. would snarl traffic for miles around the state capital. To keep posted on the progress of the Presidential party, he was listening attentively to his car radio. He wished something would delay it for a few minutes, just enough to take the pressure off him. So far it was moving along smoothly on schedule. Gorham had stopped for a vanilla malted and was sipping it as he drove, substituting it for lunch. On the seat beside him lay the bundled programmes, each with a welcoming message from Governor Connally to the Kennedys which ended, 'This is a day to be remembered in Texas.'

The President's advance man for Austin, Bill Moyers, Kennedy's brightest young Texan and Sargent Shriver's Deputy Director of the Peace Corps, was lunching after having double-checked preparations there. The programmes excepted, Moyers had found everything ready for tonight. Places had been set, a ton and a half of tossed salad had been mixed, and fires were being banked for eight thousand steaks. (Steak is not what Catholics usually eat on Friday, but it was too late to do anything about that.) Ticket sales had brought $350,000 into the Kennedy–Johnson war chest, and since mid-morning the ticket holders had been converging on Austin from all over the state. Most were still on the road. A few hadn't left home, among them National Committeeman Byron Skelton, who had just slipped into his tuxedo in his Temple home and was peering into his mirror, adjusting his black tie.

The tempo at Volcano, as the Secret Service called the LBJ Ranch, was also beginning to quicken. Agents from the White House Detail had set up their advance post in a Johnson City motel. At 8 p.m. they planned to seal off Volcano; after that no one would be allowed to enter without a pass. On the banks of the river Bess Abell was now supervising a final dress rehearsal of the whip-cracking and sheep-herding entertainers. Hundreds of freshly baked pies were cooling on a long wooden table outside the kitchen. Inside, Helen Williams, a maid, followed the progress of the Dallas motorcade over the radio as she worked.

In Fort Worth Marguerite Oswald was watching her sixth straight hour of television; during commercials she had bathed and changed into her white practical nurse's uniform. Marguerite had forgotten the President's visit. She was wholly engrossed in her favourite programmes. Marina Oswald was similarly intent upon the Zenith television screen in Irving; Ruth Paine was in the kitchen preparing lunch. Kennedy's visit was very much on the mind of Ruth's husband Michael, however. Michael Paine was eating with a student named Dave Noel in a restaurant between Fort Worth and Dallas. It seemed to Paine that he had heard nothing except malicious assassination jokes for the past two days. They oppressed him, and over sandwiches he and Noel—afterwards he couldn't remember which of them had introduced the subject—talked about the emotional make-up of assassins. After a few false starts they dropped the topic, agreeing that neither knew enough history to discuss it sensibly.

Friday is payday in Dallas, which, to Parkland Hospital, meant an exceptionally large number of patients injured in drunken brawls. But the tide of casualties wouldn't hit the emergency room until late evening, and the noon-hour atmosphere was relaxed. The chief surgeon was in Houston; the chief nurse had driven to a nursing conference fifteen miles away. Jack Price, Parkland's administrator, was standing at the window of his office, admiring the golden weather on Harry Hines Boulevard. He was trying to decide whether or not he should allow some of his employees to step out and watch the passing motorcade. In an adjoining room an assistant had been working all morning on Parkland's budget for the coming year. He stepped in and tossed it on Price's desk. 'It's in balance, Jack,' he said.

At the Trade Mart, within walking distance of the hospital, an organist was warming up with several choruses of 'Hail to the Chief'. Agent Stewart Stout's four-to-twelve shift—so called because those were their working hours at the executive mansion; when travelling they were on call around the clock—had taken up their stations there, preparing to relieve Emory Roberts' eight-to-four shift when the motorcade arrived. Two hundred Texas law enforcement officers had ringed the building. They were in a no-nonsense mood; Sergeant Robert E. Dugger of the Dallas Police Department watched plain-clothes men carry away three of the men with anti-Kennedy placards. Chief Curry's decision to concentrate his heaviest force in and around the luncheon sheds some light on the Dallas leadership's self-distrust. The invitation list consisted largely of powerful civic leaders. The President should have been entirely safe with them. But many belonged to extremist organizations—the editor of the Dallas *Times-Herald* was standing with an avowed member of the John Birch Society—and the Trade Mart had been made one of the two strongest links of the local security chain, second only to the airport.

The weakest link in downtown Dallas was Dealey Plaza. East of there on Main Street, the police had anticipated a crowd; every block was under the surveillance of an inspector. To the west of the plaza, beyond the triple underpass, the speed of the motorcade on Stemmons Freeway would assure safety until the President reached the embattled Trade Mart. There had been 365 Dallas policemen at Love Field, there were 60 at the Mart. In the two blocks from the Main-to-Houston turn to the underpass there were scattered patrolmen, but both organization and speed would be absent. The gap had been justified because there would be few spectators along the Main–Houston–Elm zigzag.

Certainly the lines of onlookers were thinner around the Book Depository than in the shopping district. Nevertheless it was a large gathering for the neighbourhood. Abraham Zapruder's secretary, looking down from the Dal-Tex Building, was impressed by the number of people crowding the kerbs and shouldering their way to the edge of the plaza grass. Some had brought children. Charles Brend, a young Dallas father, kept repeating to his five-year-old son, 'Be sure and wave at the President, and maybe he'll wave back.' In front of the Depository Roy Truly and his boys were listening for the growl of approaching motor-cycles. To their right a tall pine oak spread its branches up to the fourth floor, and thirty feet to the right of the tree, above a cluster of route signs, stubby Abe Zapruder crouched on a low concrete abutment between the Depository and the underpass. He had snapped a telephoto lens on his camera and was explaining jovially to a stenographer behind him, 'Hey, Marion, if I feel around, I'm not trying to play with you. I'm just trying to get my balance, understand? This Zoomar distorts things, it's hard to see.'

At that moment an alert policeman, scanning windows, could have altered the course of history. For Lee Oswald was in position now, clearly visible to those below. A youth named Arnold Rowland, who knew guns, had been watching from below with his wife since 12.14 p.m. (The Hertz sign, so conspicuous, made possible the establishment of exact times.) He saw Oswald silhouetted in the window, holding what appeared to be a high-powered rifle mounted with a telescopic sight. One of Oswald's hands was on the stock and the other was on the barrel; he held the weapon diagonally across his body at port arms, like a Marine on a rifle range. A police officer stood twelve feet from the Rowlands, but it never occurred to Arnold to speak to him. Assuming that Oswald must be protecting the President, he said to his wife, 'Do you want to see a Secret Service agent?' 'Where?' she asked. 'In that building there,' he said.

On the west side of Houston Street Robert Edwards and Ronald Fischer of the county auditor's office had been waiting since 12.20 p.m. They had been told they needn't return to their desks until the President had passed, and they were enjoying the warm weather. Suddenly Edwards pointed and said, 'Look at that guy.' Fischer followed his finger. The weapon was below their line of sight; what had attracted Edwards' attention was Oswald's stance. Fischer agreed that it was peculiar. He was transfixed, staring to his right, away from Main. To Fischer it seemed that 'he never moved, he didn't even blink his eyes, he was just gazing, like a statue'.

The closest known eyewitness, Howard L. Brennan, the frail pipefitter, had headed for the plaza at 12.18 p.m.—again the Hertz sign on the Depository roof pinpointed the moment—and settled down on a three-and-a-half-foot-high white cement wall on the edge of the plaza, directly across from Roy Truly's group at the warehouse entrance. There, at the intersection of Houston and Elm, Brennan was forty yards beneath Oswald. Waiting in the sun, he dried his forehead on the sleeve of his khaki work shirt and then peered up, hoping Hertz would tell him the temperature. But that part of the sign was obscure from here. His eyes dropped to the warehouse's sixth floor, to the pinched face of Lee Oswald, now in profile. He, too, wondered why the young man was standing stock-still.

There was a sound of distant shouting from Main Street. Brennan, Rowland, Edwards, and Fischer forgot the strange figure in the open window and pivoted. Edwards said excitedly, 'Here it comes.'

To Jacqueline Kennedy it was Mexico all over again—hot, wild, loud, with the blazing sun strong in your face and the cheers washing over you like a brighter light, the waves of affection engulfing you until you forgot this rather ordinary street and the faded red, white, and blue convention bunting strung overhead and the advertisements for Thom McAn Shoes, Hallmark Cards, Hart Schaffner & Marx Clothes, Walgreen Drugs—giving yourself to the spectators as they gave themselves to you: beaming, laughing, greeting strangers who at the moment of greeting were strangers no longer, who in their ardour became close friends for a fraction of time as the glittering blue convertible, its fender flags fluttering, breasted the breakers of noise and moved steadily ahead past the police barriers marking each intersection.

12.22. Main and Ervay.

A dozen young people surged into the street; from his kerbside command post Dallas' husky Inspector Herbert Sawyer gave a signal and a clutch of patrolmen closed in, pressing them back. The Secret Service showed signs of activity. Clint Hill jogged alongside the First Lady, and Jack Ready had leaped off Halfback's right fender to block an enthusiastic amateur photographer. In Varsity Lem Johns cracked his door, holding it open a few inches so he could break out quickly if anyone rushed Lyndon Johnson.

On the left loomed the Mercantile Building and the Neiman-Marcus department store. Lady Bird, wedged between Lyndon and Ralph Yarborough, looked up at a Neiman-Marcus window and recognized Mary Griffith, a dressmaker who had fitted her in that store twenty-five years before. The two women exchanged frantic feminine wigwags.

The seventh floor of the Mercantile Building was the headquarters of H. L. Hunt, Dallas' billionaire. Flanked by two secretaries, Hunt stared down as the President gaily saluted the mob in front of Walgreen's.

12.23. Main and Akard.

Forrest Sorrels, in the lead car, heard shouts of 'The President's coming!' He craned his neck and muttered to Lawson, 'My God, look at the people hanging out the windows!'

Clint Hill was watching the windows. So was Yarborough, and he didn't like them. The Senator was delighted by the throngs on the sidewalks. Next to the President, he was the most exuberant campaigner in the motorcade. Ignoring the raucous radio and the Vice President, who continued to appear saturnine, Yarborough kept bellowing lustily, 'Howdy, thar!' He searched for familiar faces and spotted a surprising number of friends from rural east Texas. But there were no friends in the office windows. The men there, he noticed, weren't cheering at all. He squinted up, trying to read their thoughts. To him it seemed that their expressions were hard and disapproving; he had the impression that they were outraged by the display of Kennedy support on the sidewalks.

The spectators at Akard were ten deep, and among them, in the rear row, stood Managing Editor Jack Krueger of the Dallas *News*. Krueger wasn't working. For the first time in his life he was on federal jury duty. He could have offered a professional excuse, but he considered jury service a civic responsibility and had been absent from his desk for six weeks. If a big story broke, the paper would have to cover it without him; he couldn't leave the courtroom unless the elderly judge dismissed him. Now, during the noon break, he had slipped over to his bank. Unlike Ted Dealey, Krueger was tall and physically impressive, yet in this jam he could catch a glimpse of the President only by standing on tiptoe.

12.24. Main and Field.

Jim Hosty, the local FBI agent in charge of Lee Oswald's file, had his wish. He saw Kennedy from the kerb and then stepped into the Alamo Grill for lunch. His day, he felt, was made.

12.26. Main and Poydras.

Marie Fehmer saw her mother standing on the left, semaphored to her from the VIP bus, and wondered whether she had been seen. Liz Carpenter, listening to the echoing roars, crowed, 'Well, this pulls the rug out from under the Dallas *News* and Barry Goldwater!'

Not everyone was so sure. Henry Gonzalez, like Yarborough, continued to be sceptical of the city. But the Congressman and the Senator were exceptions. Mac Kilduff decided that his fears had been unfounded. This was turning out to be one of the best receptions Kennedy had had all week, including Florida. The street had begun to remind Larry O'Brien of New York's Broadway. The canyon of buildings was the same, and so was the feverish tumult. Ken O'Donnell was on his feet, taking a professional reading. Maybe these were the only Kennedy backers in Dallas, but their fire was real enough, and as people on the President's side called pleadingly, 'Jackie, over *here*! *Over here, Jackiiieee!*' O'Donnell's instinct told him that the First Lady was going to become increasingly valuable in the months ahead.

In SS 100 X the President waved again. The roar swelled, rising and rising, and Nellie Connally heard him saying, 'Thank you, thank you, thank you.' *They can't hear him*, she mused. *Why does he bother?* She supposed it was habit. He had been brought up to be gracious.

Clint was on the running board, back in the street, on again, off again. He had lost track of the number of times he had hit the pavement. He began to breathe heavily. Ready, after his one foray, clung to the running board. None of the other agents left the car.

Lamar Street, Austin Street . . .

12.28. Main and Market.

The neighbourhood began to deteriorate. They were entering a seamy section of bail-bond shops, bars, a public gym. It occurred to Yarborough that anyone could drop a pot of flowers on Kennedy from an upper storey. *It will be good to have the President out of this*, he thought, and then he saw that they were nearly at the end. Two blocks ahead on the left lay the ugly Gothic sandstone court-house, and, on the right, the dingy county Records Building. Beyond them the green of Dealey Plaza was visible. *My, that open sky looks good*, the Senator thought. He remembered that he had some friends among the county bailiffs and squirmed around, looking for them. Then he saw the lead car ahead was turning right at the Records Building. Mistakenly he believed they could reach Stemmons Free-way directly from Main. Unaware of the traffic island ahead, which made the detour to Elm Street necessary, Yarborough gaped. Why right? It was the wrong direction. What was over there?

12.29. Main and Houston.

The crowd around the corner was smaller. After the zig off Main and on to Houston, Clint hopped back on the running board and took a deep breath. Yet even here the people were clapping hard, and Nellie, surprised and delighted at Dallas' showing, twisted in her jump seat. 'You sure can't say Dallas doesn't love you, Mr President,' she said jubilantly. Kennedy smiled and answered, 'No, you can't.'

Chief Curry spun the wheel of the lead car left, entering Elm Street, the sharp zag after the zig. It was easy for him. He had done it a thousand times. But the turn was 120 degrees. Bill Greer, swinging the Lincoln around, nearly had to stop in front of Roy Truly. Sam Kinney in Halfback and Hurchel Jacks in the Vice Presidential car would have the same problem. 'Hell,' Jacks said under his breath, sizing it up, 'that's going to be practically a U-turn.'

12.30. Houston and Elm.

The motorcade now resembled the figure Z. Curry, at the top, was approaching the overpass. Three drivers—Greer, Kinney, Jacks—trailed him on Elm. The Book Depository was situated at the point of the sharp angle. The second section of the procession was proceeding towards it on Houston. The third section—a station wagon, the VIP bus, and the Signals car—was still on Main.

Sorrels was saying to Curry, 'Five more minutes and we'll have him there.' Noting that there was only a handful of spectators ahead, Lawson alerted the four-to-twelve shift. He radioed the Trade Mart that they would reach there in five minutes. Then he automatically scanned the overpass. There were railway workmen on top, a security breach. Through the windshield he motioned urgently to a policeman there in a yellow rain slicker, indicating that he wanted the area cleared. The officer was unresponsive. He didn't understand.

Greer, recovering from the difficult turn, started to relax. The strain was over. Then he, too, noticed the workmen. Puzzled, he studied the unfamiliar street to see whether he could veer at the last minute if necessary and take the President beneath a deserted part of the span. The Lincoln was now passing the pine oak, which momentarily screened John Kennedy from the muzzle in the sixth-floor corner window. Abe Zapruder, hunched over his Zoomar lens, was photographing SS 100 X as it approached him. Nellie pointed to the underpass and said to Jackie, 'We're almost through. It's just beyond that.' Jackie thought, *How pleasant the cool tunnel will be.* Everything seemed very quiet here. She turned to the left. Charles Brend held his son aloft: now was a good time to wave at the President.

Kinney, hugging the bumper of SS 100 X, was still keeping his eyes on Kennedy's head. Ken O'Donnell returned to his jump seat. 'What's the story on the time, Dave?' he asked Powers. 'I've got 12.30,' Powers replied. 'That's not bad, considering the crowd. We're only five minutes late.' In the front seat Emory Roberts radioed the Mart, 'Halfback to Base. Five minutes to destination.' He then wrote in his shift report: '12.35 p.m. President Kennedy arrived at Trade Mart.'

Rufe Youngblood, fingering the leather strap of his portable Secret Service radio, was also aware of the time. The Hertz sign told him, and he remembered that 12.30 was their estimated time of arrival at the luncheon. Behind Youngblood, Lady Bird had been gazing idly at the red brick of the Dal-Tex Building and then the rust-coloured brick façade of the Book Depository. Lyndon was still listening to the car radio. Yarborough, now that they had changed direction, felt reassured.

Varsity was making the 120-degree turn.

The pool car was approaching it. Kilduff, misreading the sign on the front of the warehouse, said to Merriman Smith, 'What the hell is a Book Repository?'

Back on Main Street Evelyn Lincoln was saying, 'Just think—we've come through all of Dallas and there hasn't been a single demonstration.' One of Liz Carpenter's local friends laughed. 'That's Dallas,' she said. 'We're not so bad.'

The Lincoln moved ahead at 11.2 miles an hour. It passed the tree. Zapruder, slowly swinging his camera to the right, found himself photographing the back of a freeway sign. Momentarily the entire car was obscured. But it was no longer hidden from the sixth-floor corner window. It had passed the last branch.

Brend's five-year-old boy timidly raised his hand. The President smiled warmly. He raised his hand to wave back.

There was a sudden, sharp, shattering sound.

Various individuals heard it differently. Jacqueline Kennedy believed it was a motor-cycle noise. Curry was under the impression that someone had fired a railroad torpedo. Ronald Fischer and Bob Edwards, assuming that it was a backfire, chuckled. Most of the hunters in the motorcade—Sorrels, Connally, Yarborough, Gonzalez, Albert Thomas—instinctively identified it as rifle fire.

But the White House Detail was confused. Their experience in outdoor shooting was limited to two qualification courses a year on a range in Washington's National Arboretum. There they heard only their own weapons, and they were unaccustomed to the bizarre effects that are created when small-arms fire echoes among unfamiliar structures—in this case, the buildings of Dealey Plaza.[1] Emory Roberts recognized Oswald's first shot as a shot. So did Youngblood, whose alert response may have saved Lyndon Johnson's life. They were exceptions. The men in Halfback were bewildered. They glanced around uncertainly. Lawson, Kellerman, Greer, Ready, and Hill all thought that a firecracker had been exploded. The fact that this was a common reaction is no mitigation. It was the responsibility of James J. Rowley, Chief of the Secret Service, and Jerry Behn, Head of the White House Detail, to see that their agents were trained to cope with precisely this sort of emergency. They were supposed to be picked men, honed to a matchless edge. It was comprehensible that Roy Truly should dismiss the first shot as a cherry bomb. It was even fathomable that Patrolman James M. Chaney, mounted on a motor-cycle six feet from the Lincoln, should think that another machine had backfired. Chaney was an ordinary policeman, not a Presidential bodyguard. The protection of the

[1] The plaza is an acoustical freak, and this writer, like the Warren Commission, could not determine how many shots were fired by the assassin. Two found their mark. A majority of witnesses say they heard three detonations, and three spent shells were found in the sniper's perch. Yet several witnesses closest to the scene—e.g., Mrs Kennedy, Clint Hill, Zapruder—heard only two shots. And it would have been typical of Oswald's laxity to have come to the warehouse with an expended cartridge in the breech, which would have required removal before he could commence firing.

However, three shots may well have been fired. Indeed, three could have been fired within the crucial time span. Afterwards it was argued that this was impossible, since fewer than six seconds elapsed between the first shot and the third, and tests demonstrated that at least 2·3 seconds were required to operate the bolt on Oswald's rifle. The arithmetic went: 2·3 + 2·3 + 2·3 = 6·9. It was a trick. A correct calculation would run as follows: the first shot is fired, 2·3 seconds pass; the second shot is fired, 2·3 seconds pass; the third shot is fired. Total elapsed time: 4·6 seconds.

Chief Executive, on the other hand, was the profession of Secret Service agents. They existed for no other reason. Apart from Clint Hill—and perhaps Jack Ready, who started to step off the right running board and was ordered back by Roberts—the behaviour of the men in the follow-up car was unresponsive. Even more tragic was the perplexity of Roy Kellerman, the ranking agent in Dallas, and Bill Greer, who was under Kellerman's supervision. Kellerman and Greer were in a position to take swift evasive action, and for five terrible seconds they were immobilized.

Hill, though mistaken about the noise, saw Kennedy lurch forward and grab his neck. That was enough for Clint. With his extraordinary reflexes he leaped into Elm Street and charged forward.

Powers, in Halfback's right-hand jump seat, shouted at O'Donnell, 'I think the President's been hit!'

In the Vice Presidential car Yarborough thought he smelled gunpowder. 'My God!' he yelled. 'They've shot the President!'

Lady Bird gasped, 'Oh, *no*, that can't *be*!'

Above the car radio Lyndon Johnson had heard what he knew to be an explosion. Before he could define it further he saw Youngblood coming over the front seat towards him.

Youngblood was less positive than he seemed. In the back of his mind he was thinking that if he was wrong this was going to be very embarrassing. But his voice was firm. He snapped at Johnson, 'Get down!'

Kilduff, in the pool car directly under the gun, asked, 'What was *that*?'

Bob Baskin, in the seat behind Kilduff, knew what it was; he was an infantry veteran of the 85th Division, and he looked around wildly for cover.

Captain Stoughton automatically reached for his telescopic lens.

'Is that a motor-cycle backfire?' asked Congressman Young. Henry Gonzalez, who had been hunting only last Sunday, cried, 'No, it's gunfire!' The policeman driving their car immediately said, 'You're right,' and Gonzalez, who had been in Congress when Puerto Rican nationalists opened fire from the gallery, thought, *Can this be another Puerto Rico?*

On Main Street Ted Clifton said, 'That's crazy, firing a salute here.' Godfrey McHugh said, 'It *is* silly.'

In the VIP bus Dr Burkley was staring out absently at store windows. The President's physician had heard nothing. He was too far back.

The President was wounded, but not fatally. A 6.5 millimetre bullet had entered the back of his neck, bruised his right lung, ripped his windpipe, and exited at his throat, nicking the knot of his tie.[2] Continuing its flight, it had passed through Governor Connally's back, chest, right wrist, and left thigh, although the Governor, suffering a delayed reaction, was not yet aware of it. At the moment, in fact, Connally was glancing over his right shoulder in the direction of what he had recognized as a rifle shot.

As the Lincoln emerged from behind the freeway sign, it reappeared in Abe Zapruder's line of vision. Abe saw the stifled look on the President's face and was stunned. Continuing to train his camera on the car, he wondered whether Kennedy could be pretending. It was as though he were saying, 'Oh, they got me.' Abe thought, *The President is to joke?*

Nellie Connally twisted in her seat and looked sharply at Kennedy. His hands were at his throat, but he wasn't grimacing. He had slumped a little.

Roy Kellerman thought he had heard the President call in his inimitable accent, 'My God, I'm hit!' Roy looked over his left shoulder—Greer, beside him, was looking over his right shoulder; the car, wobbling from side to side, slowly veered out of line—and they saw that Kennedy *was* hit.

At this instant the impact of John Connally's wound hit him. It was as though someone had jabbed him in the back with a gigantic fist. He pitched forward, saw that his lap was covered with blood, and toppled to the left, towards his wife. Both John and Nellie were aware that the Lincoln was slowing down. Huddled together, they glanced up and saw the astounded faces of Kellerman and Greer, inches from their own.

Suddenly the Governor felt doomed. He panicked.

'No, no, no, no!' he shrieked. 'They're going to kill us both!'

Jacqueline Kennedy heard him. In a daze she wondered, *Why is he screaming?*

[2] In the summer of 1966 a former Cornell graduate student published a book which suggested that this first bullet followed a different trajectory. The implication was that a second assassin had aided Oswald. The issue is resolved by the X-rays and photographs which were taken from every conceivable angle during the autopsy on the President's body. Because this material is unsightly, it will be unavailable until 1971. However, the author has discussed it with three men who examined it before it was placed under seal. All these carried special professional qualifications. Each was a stranger to the other two. Nevertheless their accounts were identical. The X-rays show no entry wound 'below the shoulder', as argued by the graduate student. Admittedly X-rays of active projectiles passing through soft tissue are difficult to read. Yet, the photographs support them in this case—and reveal that the wound was in the neck. Finally, the recollections of all doctors present during the autopsy, including the President's personal physician, agree unanimously with this overwhelming evidence. Thus the account in the above text is correct.

Already she had started to turn anxiously to her husband.

Greer turned back to the wheel. Kellerman, hesitant, glanced over his shoulder again. Neither had yet reacted to the crisis.

And now it was too late. Howard Brennan, open-mouthed, saw Oswald take deliberate aim for his final shot. There was an unexpected, last-moment distraction overhead. The first shot had alarmed the birds. As the sound ricocheted in the amphitheatre below, the band-tailed pigeons had begun to depart, first in twos and threes, then in swarms, until now there were a thousand wings flapping overhead, rising higher and higher until they had formed a great ragged fluttering fan overhead, a deep blue V blending into the gentler blue of the overarching sky.

Crooking his arm, Oswald drew a fresh bead with his Italian rifle. *Ready on the left, ready on the right, all ready on the firing line,* his Marine Corps instructors had shouted on the San Diego range, signalling the appearance of rapid-fire targets. He was ready now. They had also told him to hold his front sight at six o'clock on an imaginary clock dial. It was there, and steady. His target, startlingly clear in the cross hairs of his telescopic sight, was eighty-eight yards away.

He squeezed the trigger.

The First Lady, in her last act as First Lady, leaned solicitously towards the President. His face was quizzical. She had seen that expression so often, when he was puzzling over a difficult press conference question. Now, in a gesture of infinite grace, he raised his right hand, as though to brush back his tousled chestnut hair. But the motion faltered. The hand fell back limply. He had been reaching for the top of his head. But it wasn't there any more.

3

MARKET

Lee Oswald, watched by the stupefied Brennan, steps back into the shadows in the deliberate lock step of a Marine marksman retiring from the range.

Below him he leaves madness.

The plaza resembles nothing so much as a field which has just been swept by a mighty wind. Charles Brend has thrown his son to the ground and is shielding him with his body. From his station behind the right fender of SS 100 X Officer Clyde Haygood rams the north kerb with his motor-cycle, overturns, leaves the wheels spinning, and scrambles up the grassy side of the overpass embankment, pistol in hand. A man, thinking to save a woman, tackles her from behind. Bob Jackson, a photographer for the Dallas Times-Herald, *has just seen the rifle barrel being withdrawn. He gapes, unbelieving, at the open window. Motor-cyclist Marrion Baker, riding right beside the Lincoln, is staring up at the pigeons. A policeman near Roy Truly mutters hoarsely, 'Goddamn.' Abe Zapruder screeches over and over, 'They killed him! They killed him! They killed him! They killed him!'*

From the rear of the follow-up car Agent Hickey raises the barrel of the AR-15 and points it about aimlessly. In the jump seats Ken O'Donnell and Dave Powers have heard the sickening impact of the fatal bullet, and Dave has seen it. O'Donnell crosses himself. Powers whispers, 'Jesus, Mary, and Joseph . . .' Sam Kinney, seeing the back of the President's head erupt, stamps on his siren button with his left foot to alert Kellerman and Greer; Halfback's fender siren opens up with an ear-shattering wail. Simultaneously, Sam swerves to the right to avoid Clint Hill. Clint is in the street between Halfback's front bumper and the rear bumper of SS 100 X. His head is low, he is about to leave his feet.

The Lincoln continues to slow down. Its interior is a place of horror. The last bullet has torn through John Kennedy's cerebellum, the lower part of his brain. Leaning towards her husband Jacqueline

Kennedy has seen a piece of his skull detach itself. At first there is no blood. And then, in the very next instant, there is nothing but blood spattering her, the Connallys, Kellerman, Greer, the upholstery, Clint running up behind, the kerb alongside. Gobs of blood as thick as a man's hand are soaking the floor of the back seat, the President's clothes are steeped in it, the roses are drenched, Kennedy's body is lurching soundlessly towards his wife, and Motorcycle Police Officer Hargis, two feet from her, is doused in the face by a red sheet. To Kellerman it appears that the air is full of moist sawdust; Nellie wonders if she is being sprayed by spent buckshot; but John Connally knows, John suddenly recalls his boyhood in the Model T, in a flash he remembers his father and Carlos Estrada and as he slides bleeding into Nellie's lap he fills his lungs and screams again and screams again and screams again in agony; in terror she begins to scream too and they are saturated in Kennedy's bright blood; and one fragment, larger than the rest, rises over the President's falling shoulders and seems to hang there and then drift towards the rear, and Jackie springs up on her stained knees, facing towards the sidewalk, crying out, 'My God, what are they doing? My God, they've killed Jack, they've killed my husband, Jack, Jack!' she cries and sprawls on the sloping back of the car, defeated, tumbling down towards the street and Halfback's approaching wheels and Kinney knows he cannot stop.

Incredibly, the tawdry Hertz clock overhead still reads 12.30. The motorcade has retained its fish-hook formation. All the birds have departed. The sky is again the same faultless blue. Everything beyond the immediate scene looks as it did. Dallas, the country, and the world have not had time to respond. But they are not the same, they can never be; the thirty-fifth President of the United States has been assassinated; John Kennedy is gone, and all he could do for his country is history.

By now there had been a reaction in the front of SS 100 X. 'Move it out,' Kellerman told Greer. To the microphone he said, 'Lawson, this is Kellerman. We are hit. Get us to a hospital.'[1]

[1] Colonel Jim Swindal, monitoring the radio in 26000's communications shack, thought he heard Kellerman say, 'Lancer is hurt. It looks bad. We have to get to a hospital.'

It is Kellerman's recollection that he ordered Greer to leave the scene and radioed the alarm to Lawson just before Oswald's final shot. In his words to the author, 'Greer then looked in the back of the car. Maybe he didn't believe me.' Kellerman is mistaken. Although Greer's memory is vague, the Zapruder film and the recollections of Lawson, Mrs Kennedy, and the Connallys contradict Kellerman's version. Moreover, had he alerted Lawson, the agents in Halfback—Kinney among them—would have heard him over their Charlie set.

The back of the Lincoln was equipped with metal grips on the trunk for agents and a step on each side of the spare tyre. Clint had his fingers in the left grip and his toe in the left step 2.6 seconds after the last shot; he had just begun to surge up when Greer rammed the accelerator to the floor. The Lincoln's 8,000 pounds of steel sprang forward, dislodging Clint's foot. He was dead weight and dragging. Desperately he tightened his fist on the grip. His other arm flailed at nothing. Mrs Kennedy pivoted towards the rear and reached for him; their hands touched, clenched, and locked. It is impossible to say who saved whom. Neither remembers,[2] and the Zapruder film is inconclusive. She drew him up, and he, vaulting ahead, pushed her down until she tumbled back into the car. The window beside her had been raised a few inches. Clint anchored his left hand there, hooked his right foot on the opposite side of the car,[3] and spreadeagled his body across the back of the Lincoln. With his powerful muscles he could hold on now, whatever the speed. It was small consolation to him; from the street he had seen Kennedy's head wound. He knew it was mortal, knew the Secret Service had failed; and in anguish and frustration he hammered the trunk with his free hand.

Chief Curry's Ford was equipped with a souped-up engine, but it couldn't match the powerful machines of SS 100 X and Halfback. Kinney was plunging after Greer, and in the darkness of the underpass the three cars nearly collided. Curry careened to the left, Kinney slewed to the right. They were nearly abreast, with the white-faced motor-cycle policeman frantically competing for the little space left. The police chief hadn't heard Kellerman's mayday to Lawson, and he shouted to a motor-cyclist, 'Anybody hurt?' 'Yes,' the man shouted back. Curry radioed his headquarters dispatcher, 'Go to the hospital—Parkland Hospital. Have them stand by.'

The motorcade was disintegrating. Curry, Greer, and Kinney had scarcely untangled their jam when Hurchel Jacks came hurtling into the underpass with Lyndon Johnson. The Vice Presidential back-up car had momentarily dropped behind; as the echoes of the final shot reverberated in the plaza Lem Johns had shouldered his door open and pounced into Elm Street. Pumping his legs to keep from falling, he drew up by the long crack in the grey asphalt which marked the place of Kennedy's sacrifice. He looked ahead and saw the proces-

[2] Indeed, Mrs Kennedy has no recollection of being on the trunk at all. She was in deep shock. Later she looked at still frames developed from the Zapruder sequence. They brought nothing back to her. It was as though she were looking at photographs of another woman.

[3] A *Time* caption (November 29, 1963, page 23) incorrectly identified the foot as Kennedy's. The President's body, invisible to all photographers, was sprawled across the back seat.

sion was speeding up. 'Go ahead!' he yelled, waving Varsity on. The pool car raced past him. He flagged the first photographers' convertible. 'How about a ride?' he called. Most of them were Texans. He was a stranger to them. They were veering by when a Washington photographer shouted, 'Hey, stop—it's Johns.' The driver braked, Johns hurdled the door. The wheels hardly stopped rolling, but the pause was enough to break up the procession. The first five cars, bound for Parkland, had skidded right in racing turns and vanished up the ramp to Stemmons Freeway. The rest of the drivers were left on their own. Except for the Signals car, which was at the tail of the parade, they lacked White House radios. Unaware that the party's destination had changed, they headed for the Trade Mart.

Parkland Memorial Hospital, four miles away on Harry Hines Boulevard, was as pedestrian as its name. From a distance it was easily mistaken for a drab apartment complex. Dun-coloured, rambling, thirteen storeys tall, it was situated on a low rise overlooking the plain that stretched westward towards Fort Worth. Outside on Harry Hines Boulevard the traffic rushed by feverishly day and night, and now and then a driver miscalculated, bringing the ambulance service a high profit for a short haul. Inside were 607 beds. Parkland specialized in mass production. The emergency area of any major hospital is its slum—a warren of offensive odours and numb-faced men and women whose work has hardened them—and Parkland's was especially unattractive. Nevertheless it was efficient. It did its work, and there was a lot to be done. Each day the emergency area treated an average of 272 cases—one every five minutes. At the instant of John Kennedy's murder twenty-three people were receiving attention for automobile injuries, animal bites, delirium tremens, infections, and suspicious discharges. The twenty-fourth, a woman, was admitted at 12.31. Now the two most famous patients in the hospital's history were approaching at top speed, sirens squalling, from the underpass four miles away. Accompanying them were their stricken wives, the thirty-sixth Chief Executive of the United States, the Secret Service, and the White House press. Presently the distinguished passengers in the rest of the motorcade would be searching for them, and in an astonishingly short period of time the switchboard would be the helpless victim of inquiries from all over the world. Until today any Dallas police sergeant had carried enough rank to clear the board. In a few minutes an incoming call from a Cabinet member would be swept aside as insignificant.

But Parkland didn't know that the blow was imminent. According to the Dallas police log, Curry's first alert—'Go to the hospital,

Parkland Hospital; have them stand by'—was received at 12.30. Actually Dispatcher No. 1's microphone button was stuck, his transmissions were garbled, and three minutes elapsed before Parkland was notified. The first word there was received by Mrs Anne Ferguson, the operator on Parkland's switchboard position No. 2. She heard the dispatcher say, '601 coming in on Code 3, stand by.' This was an alarm of the very highest priority. '601' was the call number of the President's motor-cycle escort. 'Code 3,' rarely used, meant extreme emergency. The time was 12.33 p.m. Mrs Ferguson requested details and was told, 'The President has been shot.' The Lincoln reached Parkland at 12.36, three minutes later. The hospital wasn't ready.

The van of the motorcade was approaching Harry Hines Boulevard at frightening speed. Bill Greer's palms were clammy, he took a fresh grip on the wheel. But he had been a professional chauffeur for thirty-five years. There wasn't a road trick he didn't know. As they passed the Trade Mart the way seemed to be blocked by two slowly moving six-wheel trucks. The trucks were nearly abreast. Bill watched Chief Curry thread his way around them; then, as the trucks moved closer to one another, he swiftly measured the distance. He spun the wheel left, spun it right, and passed between them.

Greer at least had something to do. Roy Kellerman wasn't so lucky, and his inactivity was a torment. Kellerman was a physical giant. Ordinarily he moved and spoke slowly—he was so soft-spoken that other agents had sardonically christened him 'Gabby'—but he was an active man. He was aroused now, yet he couldn't act. In the back Jackie and Nellie were holding their wounded husbands. There was no way he could help them. If he leaped into the rear, he would be worse than useless. The best he could do was to make certain, in his words, that 'they were comfortable, if there was comfort in this. Mr Hill was taking care of Mrs Kennedy. Mrs Connally was over the Governor; there was no action.'

There was little motion, though Kellerman couldn't see it, because each individual's range of vision was extremely limited. The Connallys didn't know that Clint was on the trunk, and Clint was unaware that the Governor had been shot until, half-way to Parkland, he saw blood on John Connally's abdomen. Till then he had thought that all the blood spilled had been Kennedy's. The splotch on John's shirt was too large for that, however. In fact, it was huge. The Governor had lapsed into unconsciousness, and as his eyes closed he had believed he was dying. So had his wife. Putting her mouth to his ear, Nellie whispered, 'It's going to be all right, be still.' Yet she didn't believe it. She doubted that anything would be right again. For a while she thought he was already dead. Then one of his hands trembled slightly. Quickly she put her own over it.

Nellie heard a muted sobbing from the back seat. In a strangled voice Jacqueline Kennedy was saying, 'He's dead—they've killed him—oh Jack, oh Jack, I love you.' There was a pause. Then she began again. Nellie and Clint could hear her, but Mrs Kennedy could not hear herself. In shock she was nearly as comatose as the Governor. Reality came to her in dim flashes. She had heard Kellerman on the radio and had wondered why it had taken the car so long to leave. Next, in her red daze, she had become preoccupied with the President's head. Huddled on the ruined cushion, cradling her husband's shoulders in her arms and his head in her gloves, she crouched over him. Trying to heal the unhealable seemed to be all that mattered; she couldn't bear the thought that others should see what she had seen. The Lincoln flew down the boulevard's central lane; her pillbox hat, caught in an eddy of whipping wind, slid down over her forehead, and with a violent movement she yanked it off and flung it down. The hatpin tore out a hank of her own hair. She didn't even feel the pain.

During the frantic six-minute race to the hospital—up the ramp from the underpass, north on Stemmons Freeway, and northwest on Harry Hines—certain patterns of behaviour began to emerge which were to endure throughout the coming weekend and beyond. Most were vivid forerunners of the patterns which were about to appear all over the country. Some are obvious: incredulity, outrage, grief, distraction. Others are more subtle. Like Abe Zapruder and Jacqueline Kennedy, no one could credit the tragedy to a single assassin. The President was always described as the victim of 'them', never of 'him'. The crime seemed too vast to be attributed to a single criminal. Ford's Theatre was remembered as the building in which one man shot Lincoln, but Dallas became the city where 'they' killed Kennedy.[4]

There were also the beginnings of irritationalism. Mrs Kennedy's tragic attempt to heal the wounds and Zapruder's astonishing performance in continuing to photograph the Lincoln until it passed out of sight—even as he was screaming 'They killed him'—were instinctive. The widow and the garment manufacturer were responding to the law of inertia. Life, one felt, must continue, even though life had clearly ended. Chief Curry's shout to the motor-cycle

[4] There were larger variations on this theme. The uses of personal pronouns are infinite. Some Americans blamed all Texas; some foreigners, all America. Washington an Englishwoman said to this writer, 'You get a good President and what do you do? You shoot him.' The absurdity of this does not, of course, preclude a plural responsibility for the tragedy.

policeman is less comprehensible. The underpass at that moment was no place for conversation. The chief had forgotten the uses of radio, and when he did remember, his headquarters didn't relay his message for five minutes. The normal process of thought had been severely ruptured. Certain people had literally taken leave of their senses. Later that afternoon there was to be much more of this sort of thing, at Parkland, aboard Aircraft 26000, and in Washington.

The most stable mind can absorb just so much. The fate of the President, of his constitutional successor—who was riding a few feet away—and of a gravely wounded Governor kept everyone fully occupied. Furthermore, no one in the Presidential party had heard the name of Lee Oswald. It was impossible for them to define the dimensions of the plot against the government. Where were the plotters? Who were 'they'? The reputation of Dallas as the centre of American fascism led men to assume that the shots in Dealey Plaza had been the signal for a rightist uprising, or, at the very least, an outburst of immeasurable segregationist violence. Yarborough, Gonzalez, and Teague believed themselves confirmed. Those who had deprecated them became instantaneous converts. Lyndon Johnson, almost alone, blamed international Communism. But it didn't really matter. Whoever 'they' were, they could be lurking anywhere. No precautionary measure could be too great. Later the smog of ignorance would clear and perspective would return, but in those first hours visibility was zero. Every concern not directly related to Kennedy, Johnson, and Connally became superfluous. Even wives were expendable. Nothing could be done to remove Jackie, Lady Bird, and Nellie during the headlong dash to Parkland. The moment brakes were applied and tyres stopped whining, however, they would be treated as women who were in the way and left to fend for themselves.

One of the earliest consequences of the catastrophe was to become one of the most searing: a schism among those who were close to the Presidency. Later in the capital Arthur Schlesinger would note the deep division between those whom he thought of as 'loyalists' and 'realists'. The loyalists, mourning John Kennedy, could not adjust to the death of the President. Realists accepted the succession. Schlesinger, a loyalist who admired the flexibility of realists, had the Chief Executive's official family in mind. But the split was evident everywhere. It affected the military—General Clifton became an advocate of realism, while General McHugh forfeited his career to his loyalism—and it tore the Secret Service asunder. Indeed, the first realist was Agent Emory Roberts, a greying, round-shouldered former Baltimore County policeman who made a tough but necessary switch in allegiance while Kennedy's heart was still beating.

From his seat beside Kinney, Roberts had seen the last shot strike Kennedy's skull. He was certain the wound was mortal, and he had assessed the implications at once. Like every other agent, he carried in his pocket a commission book directing him 'to protect the President of the United States'. Since a dead man could not serve as President, the Vice President, Roberts had reasoned, was already the new Chief Executive. Further guarding of the Lincoln would be wasted effort. Roberts' decision had come too late to stop Clint Hill, but when Jack Ready had poised to leap after him Roberts had shouted, 'Don't go, Jack!' Ready had hesitated, then he drew back. As the car picked up momentum Roberts had said to Agent Bill McIntyre, who had been standing behind Hill, 'They got him. You and Bennett take over Johnson as soon as we stop.' In the light of duty, Roberts felt, his responsibility was clear. He had to think of Johnson, and of him alone; the Service's professional obligations towards the body in the Lincoln had ended.

The safety of Lyndon Johnson was, of course, the immediate concern in the Vice Presidential car. The sequence of events there is unclear, however. According to Johnson, Rufus Youngblood hurled him to the floor before the fatal shot. Youngblood himself doubts that he moved that quickly. Ralph Yarborough goes further: he insists that Youngblood never left the front seat. It is the Senator's recollection that the agent merely leaned over the seat and talked to Johnson in an undertone. He contends that there was insufficient space in the rear for Youngblood. Dave Powers, who glanced back, confirms the Senator. But Powers was in another car, and Yarborough, by his own account, was agitated. The reason he was watching the Vice President was that he didn't want Johnson to appear to be braver than himself. He kept reminding himself that he was a Senator from Texas, that he mustn't seem cowardly in an election year, and that it would be bad form to duck out of sight. Lady Bird and Hurchel Jacks—Jacks could see the back seat in his rear-view mirror—agree that Youngblood's head and shoulders were in the rear, with Johnson beneath him.

'Get *down*!' the agent kept shouting in his Georgia drawl. Lady Bird leaned to the left, against Yarborough. She was thinking, *There isn't much down to get.*

Clutching the shoulder strap of his portable radio, Youngblood wriggled his hips, forcing himself farther back. He was grateful that Johnson, long-legged, had told him to slide the front seat to its forward position. They were going to be cramped enough in the rear as it was. Swivelling around, he saw Halfback swinging after the Lincoln. He called to Jacks, 'Follow that car.' Then he signalled

Varsity over his set: 'Dagger to Daylight'—Daylight was Agent Kivett's code name—'I'm shifting to Charlie. Do the same.'

Tuning in the Presidential wavelength, Youngblood heard Emory Roberts' voice: 'Dusty to Daylight. Have Dagger cover Volunteer.'

'He's already covered,' said Kivett, who could see the commotion in the back of the Vice Presidential car.

Youngblood listened to the staccato exchanges between Dusty, Digest, and Daylight. He heard that Lancer had been critically wounded, that they were going to hospital, that Dandy (Lem Johns) had been left stranded, and that Halfback and Varsity were each assigning two agents—with Johns gone, Varsity had only two—to the Vice President. Adding Youngblood himself, that would make five bodyguards. Breaking in, he requested a sixth agent for Victoria when things settled down.

Lady Bird was bewildered. Wedged between burly men she wondered, *What on earth are they saying on that talking machine?* Yarborough, equally curious, shouted at Youngblood and Johnson, 'What is it?' There was no reply. In reality the Vice President knew as little as the Senator. The code was gibberish to him, and Youngblood had decided that it was pointless to spread panic. To Johnson he merely whispered, 'An emergency exists. When we get to where we're going, you and me are going to move right off and not tie in with the other people.'

'OK, partner,' Johnson said in a muffled voice.

'What *is* it?' Yarborough shouted again. Everyone ignored him. Frustrated, he yelled once more, 'They've shot the President!'

Lady Bird still refused to believe it. *This is America*, she was thinking. *There are no assassins here*. She peered over the front seat. A grassy traffic island lay ahead. In the middle of it stood a metal sign, white letters on a green background: PARKLAND MEMORIAL HOSPITAL NEXT LEFT. She couldn't make it all out. Had it said Southland or Parkland? She had seen the word 'hospital', though. It was, she thought, 'one more nail pinning down the lid'; something dreadful had happened, or could have happened. Hoping against hope, refusing to think the unthinkable, she consoled herself with the argument that this was merely a precautionary measure. There had been some sort of accident. They were going to this hospital—Southland or Lakeland or Parkland or whatever. Well, what could be more natural? she asked herself. They were just going to stop and see whether or not anyone had been hurt.

Dagger, Dusty, Daylight, and Digest continued to mutter over the Charlie circuit in their strange tongue. Elsewhere they might have maintained their conspiracy of silence successfully. But Lady Bird's wishful dreams were ill-starred. Here—even here—there could be no sanctuary from mass media. As the car drew up the dominant sound in the car continued to be the squawky commercial radio on Hurchel Jacks' dashboard. After an interval of utter pandemonium, with studio furniture toppling in the background and technicians calling to one another in hysterical stage whispers, a breathless announcer had pulled himself together. He was beginning to fit together bits of information. It was still piecemeal. But there was no mention of backfires, firecrackers, cherry bombs, or railroad torpedoes. He was talking about gunfire.

The announcer's source was Kilduff's pool, fifty feet behind Lady Bird. Earlier the correspondents there had been even closer. The pool car, the sixth and final vehicle in the aborted motorcade, had hugged Varsity's rear bumper as they shot up the freeway ramp. Since passing the Trade Mart it had begun to lose ground and was now weaving dangerously. Actually, the chauffeur was doing well to keep the road. He was driving in the middle of a furious scramble.

Merriman Smith had seized the radiophone while they were still on Elm Street. His Dallas UPI bureau heard him bark: 'Three shots were fired at President Kennedy's motorcade in downtown Dallas.'

Smith was not as astute a reporter as he seemed. Despite extensive experience with weapons he had thought the sounds in the plaza were three shots from an automatic weapon, and in a subsequent message he identified them as 'bursts'. But his speed was remarkable. That first bulletin was on the UPI printer at 12.34, two minutes before the Presidential car reached Parkland. Before eyewitnesses could collect themselves it was being beamed around the world. To those who tend to believe everything they hear and read, the figure of three seemed to have the sanction of authority, and many who had been in the plaza and had thought they heard only two reports later corrected their memories.

Of the driver's five passengers, Kilduff, Baskin, and Clark of ABC could do nothing until the car stopped. Smith and Jack Bell of AP were a different breed. They were wire service reporters; they dealt in seconds. Smith's seniority had given him a clear beat, the greatest in his career, and the longer he could keep Bell out of touch with an AP operator, the longer that lead would be. So he continued to talk. He dictated one take, two takes, three, four. Indignant, Bell rose up from the centre of the rear seat and demanded the phone. Smith stalled. He insisted that his Dallas operator read back the dictation. The wires overhead, he argued, might have interfered with his transmission. No one was deceived by that. Everyone in the car could hear the cackling of the UPI operator's voice. The relay was perfect. Bell, red-faced and screaming, tried to wrest the radiophone from him; Smith thrust it between his knees and crouched under the dash, and Bell, flailing wildly, was hitting both the driver and Kilduff.

'What's that big building up ahead?' Kilduff yelled at the driver.

'Parkland Hospital,' the driver shouted back.

Smith surrendered the phone to Bell, and at that moment it went dead.

The buff brick entrance was illumined by two red neon signs: 'EMERGENCY CASES ONLY' and 'AMBULANCE ONLY'. Of the three parking bays which led to its loading dock only the first was occupied, by one of the fleet of white dual-purpose vehicles which served Vernon B. Oneal, an enterprising Dallas undertaker, as both hearses and ambulances. SS 100 X skirted the bays, swerved left, and drew up on a diagonal outside them, its trunk towards the building. The other five vehicles skidded into odd angles of repose on the circular driveway beyond.

Doors flew open. Smith grabbed Clint Hill.

'How is he?' he panted.

Hill swore and blurted out, 'He's dead, Smitty.'

Smith, swarthy and piratical, dashed inside. On the left of the corridor a clerk was sorting slips in the emergency room's cashier's cage. He burst in on her and snatched up her telephone. 'How do I get outside?' he demanded. 'You—you dial nine,' she stammered. He dialled it, dialled the local UPI number, and quoted Hill.

Clark of ABC had found a second phone in the blood bank office, and Bell was looking for a third. But the wire service war of seconds had grown to minutes, and AP was falling farther and farther behind. Bell had approached Ken O'Donnell, who couldn't talk. Then, when he found a line at the admissions desk and reached his Dallas bureau, the little information that he did have was hopelessly garbled by a grief-stricken operator. On the machine 'KENNETH O'DONNELL' came out 'KENNETH O';$9,,3))', 'BLOODSTAINED' was translated 'BLOOD STAINEZAAC RBMTHING', and 'HE LAY', in a tragic stutter, as 'HE LAAAAAAAAAAA'.[5]

[5] That was only the beginning. All afternoon the Associated Press was a source of misleading and inaccurate reports. Two highlights came at 1.18 p.m. CST, when the AP circulated an unconfirmed report that Lyndon Johnson had been 'wounded slightly', and at 2.14, when AP teletypes chattered that 'A Secret Service agent and a Dallas policeman were shot and killed today some distance from the area where President Kennedy was assassinated.' This seemed to support theories of an elaborate plot. It wasn't corrected until 3.33 p.m. Inevitably, word-of-mouth transmissions embellished errors. In a Nevada motion picture theatre the lights went up and the manager took the stage. He announced, 'We have just learned that the President of the United States, The Vice President, the Governor

Outside in the Vice Presidential car Youngblood had extricated himself. Johnson alighted, rubbing his arm (that gesture, witnessed by a spectator, became the basis for the report that he had been injured), and found himself being borne firmly along by the five agents, the nucleus of the future White House Detail. Momentarily Mrs Johnson was unescorted. She hurried along behind. From the loading dock she peered over the heads towards the Lincoln and saw what appeared to be a graceful drift of pink falling towards one side—her first glimpse, as America's thirty-second First Lady, of her predecessor. She fled inside.

Everyone else had converged on the Presidential car—everyone, that is, except litter bearers. There wasn't an attendant in sight. Kellerman, Sorrels, and Lawson looked at one another, aghast.

'Get us two stretchers on wheels!' Roy bawled.

There was no movement from the hospital.

The failure of the police radio—for it was the dispatcher's stuck button which was largely accountable for this appalling situation—played no role in the passion of John Kennedy. Had his injuries been less grievous, the delayed alarm would have become a proper matter for a searching inquiry. So would the decision to put Dr Burkley at the end of the motorcade. But the Chief Executive was past saving, and had been now for six minutes. Burkley, gowned and masked and supported by the entire staff of Parkland, could have done nothing for him after 12.30. In fact, had he been anyone but the President of the United States, the first physician to see him would have tagged him 'DOA'—'Dead on Arrival.' There was no discernible respiration. His pupils were dilated and fixed. His brain was quite destroyed.

Still his wife held him in her arms, embracing him and moaning.

As Lawson vanished within the building, Powers and O'Donnell bounded towards the Lincoln. Powers heard Emory Roberts shouting at him to stop but disregarded him; a second might save Kennedy's life. He wrenched open the right-hand door, expecting to hear the familiar voice say, 'I'm all right.' They had been through so much. There had been so many crises. It couldn't be, Dave was thinking; it couldn't *be*. Then he saw the staring eyes and knew it was.

'Oh, my God, Mr President!' he cried and burst into tears.

O'Donnell drew up by the left fender, erect and rigid, a figure of stone. His hands were by his sides. He was at attention.

Emory Roberts brushed past O'Donnell, determined to make sure

---

of Texas, and a Secret Service man have been murdered. We now continue with our matinee feature.' The lights went down. No one in the audience stirred. One wonders whether they could have been thinking.

that Kennedy was dead. 'Get up,' he said to Jacqueline Kennedy. There was no reply. She was crooning faintly. From this side Roberts couldn't see the President's face, so he lifted her elbow for a close look. He dropped it. To Kellerman, his superior, he said tersely, 'You stay with Kennedy. I'm going to Johnson.' He followed Lady Bird.

Greer was helping Lawson arrange the stretchers in tandem. The Kennedys and Connallys lay entangled in their abattoir. The others stood about, limping a little, like casualties. Shock had disabled them, and ignorance. Seven minutes ago they had been en route to a luncheon. Now they were milling around in the driveway of a nameless hospital. Few knew who had been hurt, or how badly. One man saw the blood on Mrs Kennedy and gibbered, 'My God, they shot Jackie!' The remark was heard and passed along to patients in the building. Yarborough and Kilduff simultaneously observed a clot of blood on John Connally's head. They assumed that it was his, that he had been shot in the forehead. His face was yellowish-grey. Each of them separately concluded that he was dead.

Meanwhile the Governor, who had been reconciled to death, was recovering consciousness. The jarring of brakes had roused him. His lids fluttered open. He became aware of the movement around the car, and the thought occurred to him—it was occurring to several others at the same moment—that no one could reach the President until the jump seats had been cleared. He tried to heave himself up. His wife, misunderstanding, restrained him. Since the car had stopped Nellie had become visibly agitated. As long as they were moving her self-discipline had been admirable, but now a pendulum was swinging within her. To her the situation here seemed obvious. The man behind her was dead. She had seen the gore; no one could live after that. Yet everybody was fussing over the back seat. They were fretting over a corpse and paying no attention to her John. They were just letting the Governor of Texas lie there, leaving him to bleed while they poked and fooled around, and it was outrageous.

The focus of attention was, in fact, the President, but no one was ignoring the Governor. They couldn't; even if they had been indifferent to his suffering, the stark fact remained that he was in the way. Therefore attendants, who had appeared at last, were leaning over Nellie from her side while Dave Powers, choking back his tears, was lifting out Connally's legs. The transfer was easily accomplished. His condition was far less serious than it then seemed. The Governor's muscles were tense; he could brace himself, and being conscious he could help his bearers. They placed him on the first of the two stretchers and carried him inside, Nellie stumbling after them.

Now it was the President's turn.

Mrs Kennedy hadn't budged. It would seem that in the pitiless exposure of the open car, surrounded by eyes, nothing was left to her; nevertheless she was trying to preserve a cantlet of privacy. Bowing her head, she continued to hold her husband. If she released him, the harrowing spectacle would reappear, and she couldn't endure that. Avoiding the faces around her she crumpled lower and lower, pressing her husband's stained face to her breast. There was a strained hush. The men could hear her making little weeping sounds.

Clint and Roy mounted the steps on either side of the spare tyre, Clint directly behind her.

'Please, Mrs Kennedy,' he said.

He touched her shoulders, and they trembled convulsively. Four seconds passed, then five. Ralph Yarborough had an inkling of what was happening. He didn't understand the crux of it, for he hadn't seen the wound, but he sensed that she was determined not to let the mob see her anguish. The Senator was part of that mob. He was gawking with the others. He couldn't help it. Yet he admired her defiance of him and those around him, and he stepped back involuntarily as she stifled a final sob and controlled herself with a single, violent spasm. Her proud head rose, the face a mask. Still she didn't move.

'Please,' Clint mumbled again. 'We must get the President to a doctor.'

Inaudibly[6] she moaned, 'I'm not going to let him go, Mr Hill.'

'We've got to take him in, Mrs Kennedy.'

'No, Mr Hill. You know he's dead. Let me alone.'

Suddenly he realized what was troubling her—because he had seen the back seat in those first moments he was the only other person there who could know it—and rearing up he ripped off his suit coat and laid it in her lap. Tenderly she wrapped the President's head in the lining as Clint, Roy, Dave, Greer, and Lawson drew him towards the second stretcher. She had another, brief moment of panic; they were moving too fast, the coat was slipping away. Scrambling along the wet seat, she seized it in white-knuckled fists while they grappled with his hips and thighs. It was a formidable struggle. Unlike Connally, his body lacked tension. It was rubbery, and as a former practising lawyer Yarborough recognized the signs. Horrified, he thought, *His legs are going every whichways.*

Now the President was on the litter, and they were rapidly

[6] Hill says he heard 'no verbal reply'. There was one, though. The source is her own recollection. It is the best possible source, for at this point her recovery was instantaneous and complete. From this moment forward her retention—which had been checked against the memories of everyone who was with her during this period—is astonishingly accurate.

wheeling him past a black 'NO LOITERING' sign, through scuffed double doors. Beyond lay another world. There was no sunlight. The air reeked. The corridor was walled in dreary tan tile, the floor was a dingy brownish-red linoleum, and on either side lay a maze of cubicles assigned to Pediatrics, Triage, OB, Gynaecology, X-Ray, Admittance. Emergencies were guided by a broad red stripe in the centre of the floor which swung left, then right down a long hall to a wide single door in the right hand wall bearing the meaningless digit '5'. Inside 5 after a short break, the red stripe was replaced by a green one. This was the surgical subdivision of Major Medicine. White sheeting hung on either side, partitioning booths. A final left, and they were in a passage scarcely wider than the rear of the Lincoln. To their left was Trauma Room No. 2. John Connally was inside, groaning. Nellie stood silently in the doorway, her face swollen, her eyes averted. The President was wheeled right, into No. 1. An arm seized Jackie, and there, on the threshold, she relaxed her grip on Clint's coat and stepped back. Her hopeless vigil had begun.

Grief has no single shape. Some men—among them the most deeply affected—weep within. Ken O'Donnell was of these. He had the appearance of a deaf mute. Next to Jacqueline Kennedy, perhaps, he bore the deepest scars there, and his response was total withdrawal. Never voluble, he had now become catatonic; he wandered from the trauma area to the nurse's station and back again, a dark little man with a peculiar, hammered look. Questions were put to him. He didn't reply, but no one thought that remarkable; he had always been terse. Enmeshed in their own distress, they didn't grasp the profound change in him. O'Donnell had been the most dependable of Kennedy's squires. Now that he had lost his knight he was bereft and helpless.

Dave Powers scribbled three lines:

> 12.35 I carried my President on stretcher
> ran to Emergency Room #1 (10×15 ft.)
> Jackie ran beside stretcher holding on

Ralph Yarborough had been bred in the fulsome tradition of Southern oratory; he thought in rolling phrases, and they were as genuine from him, and as moving, as the silence of O'Donnell. When the first reporters encountered the Senator, he began brokenly, 'Gentlemen, this has been a deed of horror.' He filled up and turned aside, whispering, 'Excalibur has sunk beneath the waves. . . .'

But it was too early for most people to react. Jack Price, Parkland's administrator, was accustomed to mayhem, and as a conservative Republican he had not been bewitched by the Kennedy aura, yet even he could not fashion a meaningful link between the present horror in his halls and what had been, until this moment, a remote, immaculate concept of the American Presidency. Price had been helping with Connally. Standing in the corridor, trying to organize his staff, he had seen the second stretcher fly past with roses on the body's chest. Litters were part of his trade; he dismissed this one, and since the patient's head was swaddled in a suit coat he saw nothing striking there. 'Oh, my Lord, they have shot President Kennedy,' someone moaned. It didn't register. Price simply couldn't absorb what had happened. Then he glimpsed the girl hurrying behind. He recognized her from her pictures, and as her crouched figure darted through the doors that led to Major Medicine he whirled for a second look. But something was wrong. In the photographs he had seen she had always been faultlessly dressed. Now she was blotched and dishevelled. And he couldn't imagine how her stockings had become coated with thick red paint.

Parkland was still recoiling from this first invasion when the second, denser wave arrived from the Trade Mart. The interval was bound to be brief because the buildings were so close, and two circumstances virtually eliminated it. The first was the motorcade schedule. Drivers had been told that the procession would pick up speed after leaving Main Street, and in the excitement which followed the shots they accelerated so rapidly that during the twelve seconds of Officer Clyde Haygood's pistol-in-hand ascent of the overpass embankment every vehicle in the caravan, including the Signals car, swept past him. The second factor was communications. Curry's alarm had been intercepted by all Dallas police radios at the Mart. The men there who had heard it were preparing to escort any member of the Presidential party who could establish his credentials.

Thus Agent Lem Johns, who had broken the motorcade chain by debouching on Elm Street, never stopped moving, and since he felt indebted to the photographers who had picked him up he started a stampede. Outside the Mart he flashed his commission book at a motor-cycle policeman. The officer pulled him into his sidecar. 'Can we come?' called one of the photographers. 'Sure,' Johns called back. 'Turn on your lights and follow us.' Captain Stoughton, in the other cameramen's convertible, was sitting beside a Dallas *News* man. As they hesitated outside the Mart Stoughton shouted at a policeman, 'Where did they go?' The reply 'Parkland' meant nothing to the captain, but the *News* man said, 'God, that's a hospital—let's take off.' The stars on the shoulders of Ted Clifton and Godfrey McHugh attracted an honour guard with sirens and flashing red lights. The first Congressional car executed a U-turn and roared in their wake; it moved so quickly that Henry Gonzalez was alighting in the emergency area driveway while the President's body was being removed from the Lincoln.

There were some stragglers. The two press buses unloaded as scheduled between the Furniture Mart and the Apparel Mart, on Industrial Boulevard; the bulk of the White House press corps showed their Polaroid identification cards, entered the Trade Mart, and heard the news either from officers or luncheon guests who had picked up Merriman Smith's flash over transistor radios. Among the last to learn that anything had gone awry were the passengers of the hapless VIP bus. They had been instructed to go directly to the rear of the Trade Mart. But there were no Dallas policemen at the rear entrance. The guards were Texas state policemen who weren't tied into the radio network and didn't know what had happened. None of them, moreover, had ever seen a White House pass. They had been told that Secret Service agents would vouch for bona fide Kennedy people. But most of the agents had left for Parkland after picking up Kellerman's distress signal over the Charlie network. The result was an icy reception for Dr Burkley, Evelyn Lincoln, Pam Turnure, Mary Gallagher, Jack Valenti, Liz Carpenter, and Marie Fehmer. A Ranger who knew Barefoot Sanders offered to admit him. No one could go with him, however. As a Texan Liz was mortified. 'This is Evelyn Lincoln, the President's personal secretary,' she said indignantly, thrusting Evelyn forward. The guard inspected Evelyn's pass and handed it back to her. He said impassively, 'I'm sorry, lady.'

Suddenly Dr Burkley vanished. Burkley had never deserted Evelyn before, but he sensed that something terrible had happened. The atmosphere was ominous. Strangers were reeling around in circles. Doug Kiker of the *Herald Tribune* was sobbing passionately, 'The goddamned sons-of-bitches.' With his chief pharmacist's mate in tow, the doctor flagged Agent Andy Berger, who was about to leave in a police cruiser. The physician had just tossed his black bag on the floorboard when Chuck Roberts of *Newsweek* ran up. 'Let me go with you,' Chuck begged. Burkley, usually gentle, slammed the door in his face; the cruiser skirred into Harry Hines Boulevard and dropped the doctor outside Parkland's emergency entrance minutes after the President's disappearance within.

That left Valenti with five women, all of them approaching hysteria. He himself was becoming highly agitated. His face flushed, he sprang at Ranger after Ranger, demanding information. No one would tell him anything. Where was the President? Inside. Why couldn't they enter? No Secret Service. Where was the Secret Service? A shrug. Then, from the corner of his eyes Valenti saw a luncheon guest in a business suit emerging from a telephone booth. The man appeared disabled. His arms hung slackly, his legs were wobbling. He addressed them as a group. 'Are you the White House people?' he asked in falsetto. Without awaiting a reply he said, 'The President's been shot,' and wobbled off. 'What a bad joke!' Marie Fehmer gasped. Liz laughed—a high-pitched, mirthless laugh. 'Why should anyone start a rumour like that?' she asked Evelyn. Valenti, damning all Texas Rangers, fell on a passing Dallas policeman. The officer nodded gravely; it was true. All the cruisers had gone, but a deputy sheriff was parked nearby. He was off duty, driving his own car. Moments later Valenti and the deputy were transferring tools, toys, and a stack of dry cleaning from the rear seat to the car's trunk. They wedged themselves and the five women inside and rocketed away. Mary Gallagher was plucking wildly at rosary beads and whispering, 'If I ever needed them, I need them now.' Marie, a Catholic herself, had no beads. She squeezed her eyes shut and recited Hail Marys.

Parkland's grounds had begun to resemble an automobile graveyard. Marooned cars were strewn along its driveways and lawns, some with motors running, most with at least one door open, all of them parked at random angles. Inside, the emergency area had been overwhelmed. Aesthetics aside, a metropolitan hospital is better equipped to handle a panic than almost any other public place, but no institution in the world could have weathered this one satisfactorily. There were too many people with too much rank, and there was an almost total collapse of discipline.

The press, surprisingly, was the most docile group there. Their presence frightened Jack Price; he signalled Steve Landregan, the hospital's public relations man, who led them to classrooms 101–102, on the other side of the building, where most of them patiently awaited a briefing. (They weren't being selfless. They had their pool, and experience had taught them that if they stuck together until a press secretary appeared none of them would be left out.) A greater cross for Price was his own staff. He found himself begging them to return to their own wards. They argued, with some logic, that they were needed to control patients. Ambulatory cases were hobbling in every door, deaf to entreaties to turn back. One man told a nurse, 'If the President's dead, why can't we see him? A dead body won't know the difference.' Unwisely she suggested that Mrs Kennedy was entitled to privacy. '*Jackie's* here?' he cried. 'Where?' He had to be restrained.

The Secret Service should have thrown up a security screen. But the disaster had exposed a hidden weakness—the allegiance of individual agents to a man, not an office. As long as Kennedy had been in command the lines of authority were clear. Now the old order had been transformed into hopeless disorder. Theoretically Roy Kellerman was still the agent in charge. Emory Roberts had already defied him, however, and when Roy issued instructions that all the agents who had been riding in Halfback were to guard the hospital's entrances, nobody bothered to point out that Roberts had undercut him by reassigning them.

In fact, few agents bothered to tell Roy anything, which was probably just as well, inasmuch as a showdown would have led to no real decision. Since Presidents pick their chief bodyguards, and since Kellerman was a stranger to Lyndon Johnson, Kellerman was already a lame duck. The identity of his successor was not so clear. Roberts was with Johnson, but Youngblood had been there before him and was a Johnson protégé. Thus the Secret Service, which should have been a symbol of continuity, was riven by disunion. The agents were as leaderless and perplexed as the rest of the Presidential party. A few (Kellerman, Hill) remained near Kennedy. Others (Youngblood, Roberts, Johns) went with Johnson. Most were following personal loyalties. There was no over-all plan, no design, and the inevitable consequence was anarchy. The impressions of Shirley Randall, a nurse's aide, are instructive. A few moments after 12.35 p.m. she found herself surrounded by strangers 'barging in with big guns'. Her first thought was that she was in the hands of 'some underworld characters'.

The atmosphere of tension was heightened by what appeared to be a communications crisis. Parkland's switchboard operators saw their lines pre-empted—apparently by people dialling 9 on hospital extensions—until all twelve switchboard alarm lights were ablaze, indicating an absolute overload. The implication was that demand had completely outstripped facilities, cutting off the emergency area from the outside world. This was untrue. During the first half-hour, when pressure was at its greatest, members of the Presidential party repeatedly placed calls to Washington and elsewhere. The telephone in the nurse's station, which became the Secret Service command post, was in constant use. At no point was the Presidency threatened by isolation.

After leaving President Kennedy's stretcher in Trauma Room 1, Kellerman, Hill, and Lawson entered the station, a glassed-in office just across the green line from Mrs Kennedy. An attendant secured an outside line for Kellerman. Roy asked Lawson, 'What's the Dallas White House number?' 'RIverside 1-3421,' said Lawson. Hill dialled it. Kellerman identified himself to the Sheraton-Dallas board as Digest and said, 'Give me an instant circuit to Washington, and keep this line open—don't pull the plug.' The White House Signals board relayed Digest to Duplex; in the East Wing of the executive mansion Jerry Behn picked up his office phone. 'Look at your clock,' Roy told Jerry. 'It is now 12.40 here.' (Behn's clock read 1.39 EST—that is a minute earlier.) 'We're in Parkland Memorial Hospital,' Roy said. 'The man has been hit.' Dumbfounded, Behn asked, 'What do you mean?' 'Shot,' Roy said. 'He's still alive in the emergency room. Both he and Governor Connally were hit by gunfire. Don't hang up. This line should be kept open, and I'll keep you advised.'

The line was even kept open when Behn moved downstairs to the larger office of Jack McNally, Special Assistant in charge of staff administration, for the first of the *ad hoc* sessions which were to begin in the East Wing, end in the West, and continue all weekend. Behn, chalk-faced, was at one end; Kellerman and his group of agents were at the other. Furthermore, the White House Communications Agency was capable of expanding this single connection into a conference call at any time. While Clint was listening to Behn's breathing (which grew progressively more irregular), he heard a click, followed by a familiar feminine voice saying, 'Wait a minute.' It was Ethel Kennedy in Virginia. A moment later she was followed by her husband, inquiring for details. The interruption was so unexpected, and the Attorney General sounded so much like the President, that Clint grabbed a clipboard hook for support. At another point Godfrey McHugh entered the nurse's station. He wanted to talk to the west basement Situation Room. 'OK, but don't hang up when you're through,' Kellerman warned. Godfrey thoughtlessly did. Yet when Roy snatched up the receiver the connection was still intact. Signal's operators were listening, and although discreetly silent they were very much on the job.

For the most part the virtuosity of the Signal Corps was unappreciated.[7] Parkland's switchboard girls didn't realize that they were being unobtrusively knocked out of action by a single individual, Chief Warrant Officer Art Bales, who didn't have time to explain what he was doing or why. He was racing through the

[7] Partly because not all Presidential aides knew it. As late as 2.15 p.m. the tape of Dallas police dispatcher No. 2 recorded a message from Patrolman J. E. Jennings at Parkland, who reported that certain members of the White House staff were asking 'if it would be possible for your office to make a collect call to deliver a message for them'. Dispatcher Gerald Henslee replied, 'I'm sorry, all my phones are tied up.'

It should be added that both police channels were frequently clogged with unnecessary traffic: demands for police dogs, confusion over wrong arrests and incorrect addresses, and—this from Inspector Sawyer—speculation over whether overtime pay would be authorized for forty patrolmen who would normally have been relieved by now.

hospital with a hastily assembled posse of policemen from the Trade Mart. He would keep dialling 9 until a dial tone broke flatly. Then he would establish a direct circuit to the Signals board in Washington through the Sheraton-Dallas, hand the open receiver to a waiting officer, tell him to guard it, and systematically move on to commandeer the next instrument. Meanwhile he had alerted Colonel McNally and Jack Doyle of American Tel & Tel, who was the company's liason man for the trip, at Love Field. Bales' fellow technicians were on their way from the airport. They were under instructions to relieve the policemen and set up a second switchboard, three additional dial trunks, and four new long-distance trunks. Because of the ingenuity of Tel & Tel, Doyle could avoid the presently overloaded trunks that linked Dallas with the capital by routing Parkland-to-Washington calls through Chicago and Los Angeles. Bales, on the spot, was aware of all this, and he knew that should all his other emergency measures fail he would have recourse to the motorcade itself, four of whose vehicles—SS 100 X, Halfback, and the pool and Signals cars—were capable of contacting the White House through radio patch.

So the switchboard crisis was largely illusion. But under certain circumstances appearances are more important than reality. Parkland's operators, who never laid eyes on Bales, couldn't know that they were being by-passed for a reason—that there was a method in the madness which confronted them. They saw only hubbub and chaos. Their outgoing lines were mysteriously vanishing one by one, and incoming calls were forming a composite nightmare. Already UPI bulletins were stimulating cranks all over the world. In the next two hours one girl, Phyllis Bartlett, would log conversations with England, Canada, Australia, Venezuela, France, and Mexico. She wrote: 'Every call coming in long distance is urgent and everyone seems to have a title that demands priority.'

Some of the titles were legitimate. Most weren't. Genuine insiders went through Signals, as Ethel Kennedy had. The bulk of the direct-dial long-distance calls came from the curious, the disturbed, the downright demented. A woman in Toledo identified herself as 'The Underground'; she asserted that she had occult powers which would keep Kennedy alive. A man said, 'You nigger lovers, you killed our President.' Another man threatened an operator: 'I know who you are, and you'd better be careful when you start your car.' Most disquieting was a young boy who called three times, talking to a different operator each time. His approach never varied. 'I want to talk to my Daddy,' he would begin plaintively. Asked who his father was, he would say, 'My Daddy—President Kennedy.' Then he would giggle and ring off.

Perhaps all these grotesque calls were placed in mental wards, but during that first hour hysteria was far more widespread than men could bring themselves to acknowledge. In retrospect many later constructed accounts of how they felt they ought to have behaved—with emotion, but with control. The facts are more jagged. There was little control, and there were many aberrations which made no sense whatever. It is not necessary to trace anonymous telephone calls for proof of this. Abundant evidence lies in the conduct of those who were present in Parkland's emergency area. All were able. All were accustomed to strain. Yet nearly everyone, in the minutes before or after one o'clock, acted in a fashion that on any other afternoon would have been considered most odd. None of their quirks deserves ridicule, yet a few examples are useful; otherwise an understanding of the general mood is impossible. Those who would pass judgment on the demeanour of any individual should remember that singular behaviour was endemic—that it was so commonplace, indeed, that it briefly became the norm. Even when it wasn't, it seemed so to others.

Consider Ted Clifton. He was a general officer, a combat veteran, the President's senior military aide. Of all men there, Clifton should have been the likeliest to grasp the capabilities of the Signal Corps. However, he was under the impression that those facilities were not immediately available. Instead, he presented a priority card to a Parkland operator and told her that he wanted to make a long-distance call to the White House. Miraculously, he got through to the National Command Centre, briefed them, and then switched to the Situation Room in search of intelligence. A later, second call, in the presence of Godfrey McHugh, the second aide, who apparently hadn't heard the first call, was placed to Clifton's own office. He asked that Mrs Clifton, Mrs O'Donnell, and the other wives be informed that their husbands were uninjured, and then inquired as to further intelligence. The order of precedence seemed unusual to McHugh, but he raised no question about it. A bachelor himself, he concluded that husbandly solicitude was correct at a time like this.

Or take Clint Hill, a man of exceptional presence of mind who had just demonstrated it on Elm Street. Roaming the emergency area, he realized that he was without his suit coat. It suddenly seemed important that he be properly dressed, and he approached Steve Landregan, who was just his size, and asked to borrow his coat. The public relations man promptly surrendered it, though he wondered—quite reasonably—what possible difference shirt sleeves could make at a time like this.

Dave Powers, like Clint Hill, was preoccupied with clothes. Leaving the stretcher in Trauma Room No. 1 he noticed bloodstains on his sleeve. He remembered telling his wife that when you travel with the President it doesn't matter what you wear; everyone will be looking at him. So he had worn his cheap brown suit, and it was vaguely comforting to realize that only an inexpensive garment had been ruined, that it could be easily replaced.

Outside the trauma room, Sergeant Bob Dugger was scowling fiercely. The bespectacled Sergeant was a towering bullock of a cop, with a beefy face and piercing eyes; to Jacqueline Kennedy he looked rather ugly. She had no way of knowing that he was worried sick about an automobile. He had heard the news at the Trade Mart and had driven here in the deputy chief's car. There hadn't been time to acquire permission, and now anxiety was gnawing at him. What would Chief Batchelor think? Would he report a stolen vehicle? Would charges be filed? This was a serious matter. The Sergeant glowered. Mrs Kennedy, observing him covertly, wondered what his thoughts about the President had been, whether he could be a Bircher.

A message for the wives; a clean coat for Clint; a chief's borrowed car—thus men turned from the unwieldy central event and seized upon details with almost pathetic gratitude. One by one they could be wrapped with understanding and tucked away on the narrow shelves of the mind, postponing that awful moment when all the wrapping and tucking would be done and the enormous fact that would not fit must be faced.

Almost any diversion was welcome. Mac Kilduff strolled outside and saw that Halfback was deserted. Here was an opportunity for two chores. He would use the dashboard radio to inform the White House that the President had been shot. (Kilduff, it will be remembered, had been sitting beside Merriman Smith when Smitty dictated his account in the pool car.) First, however, he must run the engine. He recalled the dead battery yesterday in San Antonio. That mustn't happen again. The pointless message to Washington concluded, Kilduff noticed SS 100 X. Suppose photographers took pictures of the bloody back seat? Presidential press secretaries were supposed to prevent that sort of thing. Kilduff briskly summoned Bill Greer and Sam Kinney and briskly ordered them to put up the bubbletop at once.[8]

[8] There weren't enough useless jobs for everyone; some were duplicated. A few moments later Lem Johns appeared and issued the same instructions to the two drivers. Chuck Roberts, watching the top go up, said bitterly, 'Why now?' One of the drivers said numbly, 'You can't look.' An inaccurate story reported that they washed out the back seat with a bucket of water. Actually this was contemplated. Nurses's aide Shirley Randall was asked whether she would 'come and wash the blood out of the car'. Miss Randall agreed, but in the excitement she forgot.

Individual conduct varied wildly in situations that were virtually identical. Jacqueline Kennedy and Nellie Connally stood a few feet apart awaiting news of gravely wounded husbands. Both knew that the President's injuries had been mortal, and if there is such a thing as decorum in these circumstances, the Governor's wife should have been the first to speak. She wasn't. Jackie gently inquired about Connally. At first Nellie said nothing. She was thinking that this woman was almost a total stranger to her. She replied abruptly, 'He'll be all right.' And that was all.

Ralph Yarborough started yelling and couldn't stop. He was taken into the office of the blood bank director on the other side of the main corridor. Over and over he kept screaming, 'He's *dead*! What a *terrible* thing! What a *terrible* thing!'

Mayor Cabell of Dallas, on the other hand, became almost as quiet as O'Donnell, and when he did speak he denied reality. To those who could hear him he was whispering, 'It didn't happen.'

Hugh Sidey took furious notes, half of which, he later found, were illegible. Bob Baskin simply left. He rode downtown to the city room of the Dallas *News* to talk to friends and find out what, if anything, was happening elsewhere in the world.

The absence of an effective security screen invited intruders. Luckily, Parkland's bewildering floor plan insured the privacy of Lyndon Johnson. He was so far back in Minor Medicine that when the time came for him to leave a guide would be needed. Major Medicine, the trauma area, was nearer the corridor, and the most spectacular incursion occurred at the double doors which separated the red line from the green line. Nurse Doris Nelson was just passing through them when a tall man in a light grey speckled suit shouldered his way past her, shouting, 'I'm FBI!' He appeared violent, and Andy Berger, the closest agent, knocked him down. Sprawled on all fours the intruder gurgled, 'You're not in charge now. What's your name?' 'What's yours?' demanded Kellerman, moving in. Credentials and commission books were whipped out; it turned out that the man really was from the Bureau's Dallas office, though his presence in the hospital was unauthorized. Dragging himself away, he protested, 'J. Edgar Hoover will hear about this!' Hoover did, and the unfortunate agent vanished into the limbo reserved for FBI men whose blunders embarrass the Director.

He was wrong. Berger was right. Nevertheless both had been spurred by the same impulse: the need for action. To active men immobility was literally intolerable; therefore they issued fatuous orders, placed or attempted to place unnecessary long-distance calls, bellowed (Yarborough), abandoned posts (Baskin). If an excuse for action didn't come to mind, they invented one and persuaded themselves that it made sense. This was largely a male reaction—Evelyn Lincoln, Pam Turnure, and Mary Gallagher sat helplessly in the cubicles of Major Medicine—but it was a vigorous woman, Liz Carpenter, who achieved a pinnacle of rationalization. Liz and Marie Fehmer had been left in Parkland's administrative offices with aspirin and water. They had no idea what was happening and were growing increasingly restless. A passing employee called out that Kennedy had been shot. Liz thereupon jumped to an extraordinary conclusion. The President had been scheduled to address a luncheon at the Trade Mart. If he were wounded, he obviously couldn't talk. Therefore, she explained to Marie, the Vice President would have to speak in his place, and as members of the Johnson staff they should be present. There wasn't a moment to spare; he might be at the lectern already. Marie, impressed by Liz's logic, ran after her. At the hospital entrance they explained the situation to a traffic policeman. He looked doubtful, then beckoned to a cruiser, which careened into Harry Hines Boulevard at terrifying speed—the driver himself may have welcomed the chance to act—and deposited them at the Mart's front door. To their amazement only a handful of people were wandering about. All looked dazed. It looked as though the Vice President's remarks would be poorly attended. Liz began to have second thoughts.

The epidemic of irrationalism wasn't confined to the Presidential party. Parkland's staff was also affected. A telephone rang in the emergency area. As nursing supervisor, Doris Nelson—who would presently demonstrate her own lack of immunity—picked up the receiver. To her surprise, a Parkland physician on the other end asked her what she wanted. 'The President has been shot,' she replied, and he said, 'Yes. What else is new?'

Governor Connally felt fingers plucking at his clothing. A voice said, 'I've got his coat and shirt off.' Another muttered, 'I'm having trouble with his pants.' The Governor felt a painful jerking around his hips. Exasperated, he groaned, 'Why not cut them off?' There was silence. Without realizing it he had just reminded them of the hospital's established procedure.

The Parkland employees least in touch with reality were the clerks. The importance of paperwork had been drilled into them, and now, seeking a haven from the general disarray, they fell upon the familiar rituals of routine. 'Kennedy, John F.' was neatly logged in at 12.38, identified as a white male, and assigned the emergency room No. 24740. His 'chief complaint' was described as 'GSW'—gunshot wound. 'Connally, John,' No. 24743, had the same problem, and he was entered three spaces below, after a white female with a bleeding mouth and a coloured female with abdominal pains. (The

Governor, of course, had been admitted before all of them.) This sort of thing went on all afternoon. Price, enraged, threatened to fire one zealous clerk. It solved nothing. Everything had to be recorded and filed; there could be no exceptions. Larry O'Brien entered the hospital with Congressmen Albert Thomas and Jack Brooks. Taking a wrong turn, he found himself alone, facing a counter. On the other side was a bespectacled woman. 'Just a minute!' she said smartly and handed him a form and a ball-point pen. In a stupor he laboriously began to print 'O'Brien, Lawrence F.' Then he came to a dead stop. Suddenly the idiocy of the whole thing struck him. Dropping pen and form, he blundered down strange corridors, searching blindly for his President.

The body of John Kennedy lay at the centre of the storm, insulated from it by the magnitude of the task which preoccupied everyone in Trauma Room No. 1. There was no need for sham activity beyond that threshold. The men and women who were gathering could not doubt the urgency of their work, and discipline invested it with a kind of peace. Blades and catheters were lifted automatically, dials spun instinctively; rubber-gloved hands reached, clenched, and moved in rhythmic pantomime. This was an old battle for them, fought with familiar weapons and with every stratagem they could summon even when they knew they could not win.

They could not win now. The throat wound—which was then assumed to be an entry wound, because there was not time to turn him over—was small, and it exuded blood but slowly. The damage to the posterior cranium, however, could scarcely be exaggerated. That was the origin of the massive bleeding, which had begun on Elm Street, had continued throughout the ride to the unloading dock and the trip down the corridor, and which was unstanched even here. Doris Nelson was smeared; so was everyone who had been near him. By now, one would think, Kennedy would have been bled white, but his great heart continued to pump; some 1500 c.c. of blood—three pints—had flecked the aluminium hospital cart, its sheeting, the floors, the walls beyond. And mingled with it were vast amounts of fine tissue.

Diana Bowron, SRN, and Margaret Hinchcliffe, RN, undressed him swiftly, removing all his clothes except his undershorts and brace and folding them on a corner shelf. Nearly nude, his long body, unmarred below the head, lay on its back across a three-inch black leather pad. The fixed eyes—dilated and divergent, deviated outward with a skew deviation from the horizontal—were raised sightlessly towards the solitary fluorescent lamp glaring overhead. The first physician to arrive, Charles J. Carrico, a second-year surgical resident in his twenties, examined him rapidly. There was no pulse, no blood pressure at all. Nevertheless he was not quite gone. His body was making slow, agonizing efforts to breathe, and an occasional heartbeat could be detected. Carrico commenced emergency treatment, inserting a tube through the mouth in an attempt to clear the airway. Lactated Ringer's solution—a modified saline solution—was fed into the right leg via catheter. In a hurried undertone the resident inquired about blood type.

A nurse darted out. 'What's the President's blood type?' she asked Hill and Kellerman. Clint started to reach for his wallet. Roy said, 'O, RH Positive.'[9]

Returning, the nurse discovered that Trauma Room No. 1 was filling rapidly. Although Doris Nelson stood in the doorway, screening the staff, fourteen doctors surrounded the cart. That was too many. The place was less than twice the size of Kennedy's private bathroom on the second floor of the executive mansion. Only three of the physicians were absolutely necessary: Malcolm Perry, the thirty-four-year-old surgeon who had just stumbled down the flight of steps from Parkland's cafeteria to relieve young Carrico; Burkley, because he was acquainted with the patient's medical history, carried his special drugs in his black bag, and knew the proper dosage levels; and Marion T. Jenkins, chairman of the hospital's department of anaesthesiology. The rest—neurosurgeons, internists, urologists—had come because they were determined to be there if needed. As it turned out, their most useful function was to mask the stark surroundings.

The room was singularly plain. Its grey tile walls were as impersonal as IBM, which had actually manufactured the wall clock. Entering from the passageway in which Mrs Kennedy was just now sitting down—Sergeant Dugger had found her a folding chair—one encountered a solid door, which swung to the right. Within, the initial impression was of utility and durability. This was a chamber of suffering, but it had been designed for doctors, not patients. To

[9] In the *Texas State Journal of Medicine* (January 1964, p. 61) it was stated, 'Blood was drawn for typing and crossmatching. Type O RH negative blood was obtained immediately.' In fact, the President was given O RH negative because there could be no reaction to it, whatever his type. The article, which was prepared by Parkland's medical staff, contains another minor inaccuracy and a startling omission. One of the senior doctors declared that he believes it 'evidence of the clear thinking of the resuscitative team that the patient received 300 mg. hydrocortisone intravenously in the first few minutes'. This medication (Solu-Cortef) was necessary because the President suffered from Addison's disease, but it was provided by his personal physician, Dr Burkley, who also passed along word of his blood type. Dr Burkley is mentioned nowhere in the article. Doctors, too, may become victims of irrationalism.

the layman's eye it had the brutal functionalism of a stockyard. There wasn't an inch of softness, nor a mote of subdued colour. Apart from sheets and cotton every item was noncombustible. The pedal-operated waste can was of stainless steel. The floor was black rubber. Cabinets and drawers were grey metal. There were many electrical outlets in the grey tile walls, but there was no window, no natural light, no gentle shading; wherever one looked, only the harsh, efficient, unsubtle, bland, monolithic apparatus of modern medicine could be seen. The sterility was absolutely necessary, of course, but it made No. 1 an impersonal crypt, and the physicians, simply because they were alive, were a relief.

Mac Perry dominated them. Like his patient he was a bold figure of a man, and with him he occupied the centre of this toneless stage. Angular, big-boned, the grandson of a Texas country physician, Perry was still chewing croquette from the hospital cafeteria when he entered, yet he was already at work. He flung his lightweight blue plaid sports coat to the blood-puddled floor and thrust his big hands into rubber gloves. There was no time to scrub in. There was scarcely time for thought. Two impressions danced across his mind: *The President's bigger than I thought he was* and *He's the most important man in the world.* Then everything kaleidoscoped for him. He saw the bleeding first, of course, and noted 'a rapid loss of great magnitude'. Next he observed that Kennedy's chest wasn't moving. He felt for a femoral pulse, and his strong, probing fingers encountered only Kennedy's rigid back brace. Blood transfusion leads, he saw, were under way. There was one venesection on the President's right leg, and Nurse Bowron was removing the President's gore-encrusted gold wristwatch to clear a space for another on the left arm. Burkley had produced three 100-mg. vials of the Solu-Cortef from his bag, murmuring, 'Either intravenously or intramuscularly.' Everything that could be done with fluids was being done. The great need, however, was for some sort of breathing passage. The tube the resident had inserted wasn't working, apparently because of the wound in the neck. Analgesics were unnecessary. Kennedy was in coma. 'Scalpel,' Perry muttered. A nurse slapped one in his rubber palm. Incising the President's throat just below the mediastinal wound, he began a five-minute tracheostomy ('a mouth in the throat'). Meanwhile the tube between Kennedy's lips had been connected to a respirator in an attempt to start him breathing again.

It was at this point that Jacqueline Kennedy decided to enter the room. She had been in the drab hallway for approximately ten minutes, each worse than the last. Bull-necked Dugger had stared at her, Nellie Connally had drawn away, Doris Nelson had tried to take her gloves off, passing orderlies had attempted to persuade her to rest in one of the sheeted cubicles. The enormity of what had happened had just begun to hit her, but she had already determined that she would not leave here. Parkland's staff didn't understand the strength of the will behind the decision. They knew only her reputation, and like Robert Kennedy she was a very different person than the public imagined. He was gentler and more sensitive than he was thought to be; she was far firmer than people believed. Inevitably both had been overshadowed by the President. Until this hour that hadn't mattered. In the void he was about to leave they would emerge, however, and for Mrs Kennedy the time to assert herself was now.

During the first few minutes she had been quietly watchful. She couldn't understand why all the doctors were running in; she was certain her husband had been killed. Then she had heard the early talk about fluids. Physicians assume that laymen are awed by medical terminology. Usually they are right. This time they were wrong. The President had been ill since marriage; his wife had spent much time in hospital waiting rooms. She knew what a saline solution was, and when she heard a voice from the trauma room say 'resuscitation', she understood that, too. *He's still alive,* she thought in amazement. It made no sense. She was convinced that he had been killed. *Could there be a chance that he could live?* she thought; and: *Oh, my God, if he could, I'd just do everything all my life for him.* The words 'If only' crossed her mind, and 'Maybe', and 'Just anything'. 'Hoping is a thing with feathers,' wrote Emily Dickinson, 'that perches in the soul.'

Jackie glanced up at Larry and Ken, a few feet away. She whispered, 'Do you think . . .?'

They said nothing. There was nothing to say. They drifted away among cubicles, and O'Donnell, stirring from his trance, whispered to O'Brien, 'God, it's a thousand-to-one chance he can live.'

For her it had been a fleeting wish. It was followed by an impulse. She said, 'I'm going in there.'

Doris Nelson heard her and barred the way. The nurse was a starched white dragon with strong muscles, and she had been imbued with the doctrine that relatives should be kept as far as possible from patients. One purpose of the policy was to prevent the very sort of false encouragement which had just been aroused in Mrs Kennedy. Doris said sharply, 'You can't come in here,' and set her rubber-soled shoes. Unintimidated, Jackie said, 'I'm coming in, and I'm staying.' She pushed. Doris, much stronger, pushed back.

Each time her husband had been sick Jacqueline Kennedy had been turned away by doctors. At Columbia she had heard him calling for her after his back operation; she had tried to go to him then, but no one would admit her. Then, when one specialist's treatments had begun to fail, she had wanted to bring in a consultant. She had been persuaded to change her mind, and the President had suffered through four months of intense pain and discouragement. Until then she had bowed to medical advice. She had been young and deferential; the doctors, she had thought, must know best. But after those four months she had sworn a private vow. Henceforth she would at least be at his side when he needed her; never again would she let doctors or nurses cow her. Now, struggling harder, she whispered fiercely to Doris Nelson, '*I'm going to get in that room.*'

It seemed unlikely. She was much frailer than the nurse. But the commotion attracted Burkley's attention. He came over.

'Mrs Kennedy, you need a sedative,' he said shakily.

'I want to be in there when he dies.'

He nodded understandingly, then ran interference for her. 'It's her right, it's her right, it's her prerogative,' he kept saying, leading her past the woman in stained white, who reluctantly stepped aside under the impression that he was a Secret Service man. Inside Burkley held an arm on either side of Mrs Kennedy to prevent anyone from dragging her away.

The room had become even denser with people. Cramped by the pressure, Kennedy's wife and his doctor were forced into the corner immediately to the left of the entrance. Behind her ranged trauma room hardware: grey tile, a green oxygen tube, a steel cabinet packed with gauze. She leaned forward and rested her spattered cheek on Burkley's shoulder. Then she dropped briefly to the floor, knelt in the President's blood, and closed her eyes in prayer. She rose again and stood erect, her eyes intent upon the weaving hands of Mac Perry.

It seemed impossible, but another doctor had shouldered his way in. He was William Kemp Clark, the hospital's tall, bald chief neurosurgeon. Clark had rank; the other physicians made way for him. He and Perry exchanged desolate looks. Both knew there was no chance of saving the patient. They were merely going through motions. Clark saw Jacqueline Kennedy and asked her, 'Would you like to leave, ma'am? We can make you more comfortable outside.' Her lips moved almost soundlessly, shaping the word 'No.' Perry had just finished the tracheostomy when Clark arrived; he was inserting a cuffed tube in the windpipe. Jenkins attached it to an anaesthesia machine, the controls to which were more delicate than those of the respirator. Clark stood vigil over the electrocardiograph. Perry, nearly at the end of his repertoire, desperately opted for closed chest massage. He had to do something to stimulate the chest. But he couldn't get leverage. He stood on his toes, and still the

President's chest was too high. 'Somebody get me a stool,' he panted. Somebody did, and perching on it he began ten minutes of hunching and kneading.

Everything Parkland had was going for Kennedy now. Ringer's solution, hydrocortisone, and the first pint of transfused blood were entering his vessels through the two catheters. A nasogastric tube, thrust through Kennedy's nose and fitted behind his trachea, was clearing away possible sources of nausea in his stomach. Bilateral chest tubes had been placed in both pleural spaces to suck out chest matter through the cuffed tube and prevent lung collapse. Now, in a treatment older than the invention of the most primitive medical device, predating even William Harvey—a technique no more sophisticated than the shaking of a stopped watch—Perry was stroking and palpating the tough, well-muscled flesh over the President's rib cage, trying to coax a single beat from the heart until his own sinews ached and begged for relief.

It wasn't working. The spasmodic respiration had ceased. The gushing from the huge laceration on the right side of the head had ended only because he had no more blood to give. The new liquids excepted, his veins were empty, his skin shockingly white. The brief flutter on the electrocardiograph had ended; the squat ekg machine stood by the hospital cart, gleaming dully. Mac Perry crouched lower, his face clenched. He was breathing harder.

Outside the murmur of voices rose and fell in undulations. Twice before going in Jacqueline Kennedy had beckoned to Powers and said, 'Dave, you better get a priest,' and over the telephone the Attorney General had made the same request of Clint. Agent Jack Ready had made the call. Twenty minutes had passed, however, and no pastor had appeared. Pointing at his watch, Dave kept pressing Ready: 'What's the story on the priest? Listen, we're not going to make it!' Nor did it seem that they could; a cardiac pacemaker machine was being wheeled into the trauma room and prepared for use, but no one was under the illusion that it would be needed. Roy Kellerman, who had been lurking outside the door, crossed to the nurse's station, where Clint was holding the open line to the White House. In a whisper Roy said, 'Tell Jerry this is not official and not for release, but the man is dead.'

Sergeant Dugger, standing alone by the empty metal chair beside the trauma room threshold, heard everything. The sergeant had forgotten Chief Batchelor's car. He was thinking of Mrs Kennedy, and of his own inadequacy. Dugger was far more sensitive than he seemed. He was painfully aware of his appearance—big, red-necked, tough, unfeeling; a poster of police brutality. His incongruous horn-rimmed glasses didn't help. They gave him the look of an angry owl.

He had never been able to correct the impression, partly because he was so inarticulate. Repeatedly he had stood in this hospital with stricken relatives in need of a word of comfort. He had none to give. He didn't know what to say. Afterwards he would explain to his Episcopalian minister, 'I was all left feet.'

He wished now that he had been able to murmur a word, just one word of solace to Jacqueline Kennedy. He wanted her to know that he was a Kennedy Democrat, that he didn't share the segregationist opinions of so many of the other green-shoulder-tabbed men in Dallas' elite Patrol Division. He wanted to tell her that he had been in the Navy in the Southwest Pacific in World War II, and had once served on a PT boat. Most of all he was thinking: *Why not me?* Bob Dugger had been born in Waxahachie, Texas, thirty miles south of Dallas on Route 77; he was forty-three years old, and the most spectacular thing in his future was likely to be a plain-clothes desk job. So he was wondering, *Why couldn't they have killed me?* The Sergeant felt certain that his death would have been little trouble to anyone. Despite his big body, he was sure, he didn't have that much blood to spill.

These were only impressions, unexpressed and, because he was the man he was, unexpressible. Dugger stood rooted by the door in his green tabs and polished badge, his visored cap (he had forgotten to remove it) squarely on his head. To all outward appearances he was impassive and unmoved, a great long gallows of a man with thick, stiff thighs. Behind the horn-rims his eyes were hard and unblinking. Yet he was suffering. Over and over the medley rang through his mind, *The President of the United States. The President. The President ...*

It was 1 p.m. on the IBM clock. The ekg needle was still motionless, and Kemp Clark heaved up from it and said heavily, 'It's too late, Mac.' Perry's long hands crimped in defeat. He slowly raised them from Kennedy's unnaturally white breast, slipped off the stool, walked blindly from the room, and slumped in a chair, staring off into space and absently worrying the nail of his little finger with his teeth. From the head of the hospital cart Dr Jenkins reached down and drew a sheet over the President's face.

Clark turned to Jacqueline Kennedy. He said, 'Your husband has sustained a fatal wound.'

The lips moved again: *I know.*

Burkley reached over to check Kennedy's pulse—they were that close—and felt nothing. He swung back, bracing himself on the tiled walls, and held his square, florid face next to her face. He had to be sure she understood. He tried to tell her, 'The President is gone.' But his voice was indistinct. He had treated a thousand Marine

Corps gunshot wounds in the Pacific, he was a Regular Navy admiral, yet he couldn't control himself. He swallowed hard and in a clotted voice managed to say, 'The President is dead.'

There was no audible response, but she inclined her head slightly and, leaning forward, touched his cheek with her own. The doctor began to weep openly. Embarrassed, he turned to the others and lapsed into navalese. 'Clear the area!' he commanded hoarsely. 'I want this area cleared!'

Doris Nelson took him literally and began a clean sweep down. Elsewhere in Major Surgery new cases had been accumulating. A boy named Ronald Fuller was bleeding from a fall. A man, Carl Tanner, had severe chest pains which required diagnosis. One Ada Buryers complained that she was nervous, and a newcomer suffered from the inability to void. Subordinate nurses were dispatched to fetch a plastic shroud to Trauma Room No. 1 and two paper bags, which looked much like shopping bags, were brought for John Kennedy's belongings. Outside, Doris asked what arrangements should be made for the disposal of the body. Then she prepared a death certificate for Kemp Clark, who, as senior physician in attendance, would have to sign it.

Ken O'Donnell sleepwalked past pediatrics to tell Lyndon Johnson. Powers scrawled:

> 1.00 Mr President pronounced dead by Dr William Clark

By 1 p.m. Dallas time, according to a University of Chicago study conducted the following winter, 68 per cent of all adults in the United States—over 75 million people—knew of the shooting.[10] In that first half-hour information was meagre, imprecise, and distorted, but it was clear from the outset that the crime on Elm Street was the most spectacular single American disaster since Pearl Harbor. An entire nation had been savaged, and the nation realized it; before the end of the afternoon, when 99.8 per cent had learned that the elected President had been murdered, the country was in the grip of an extraordinary emotional upheaval. Over half the population wept. Four out of five, in the words of the report, felt 'the loss of someone very close and dear', and subsequently nine out of ten suffered 'physical discomfort'.

The discomfort—deep grief—followed confirmation of the President's death. In those first, indecisive thirty minutes there was a dissonant medley of response: dread, hope, prayer, rage, and incre-

[10] The investigation was conducted by the National Opinion Research Centre (NORC) of the University of Chicago. NORC had the facilities for a nationwide flash survey. By Monday, November 25, the questionnaire was ready, and by the following Saturday 97 per cent of the 1,384 interviews had been completed.

dulity. Parkland's disorder and distress were being repeated in every community with a television set, a transistor radio, a telephone, or a primitive telegraph, and virtually no one was beyond the reach of one of them. America, at the moment of the President's death, was one enormous emergency room, with the stricken world waiting outside.

The swiftness of the blow intensified the national trauma. There is no way to cushion the shock of an assassination, but the knowledge that fantastic events were in progress at that very moment, coupled with the maddening uncertainty, had created a havoc which had swept up tens of millions of Americans. The immediacy of a running account, however piecemeal, outstrips any report of an accomplished fact. If a thing is done, it is done; if it is being done, the spectator feels that the outcome may be altered—may even feel that he himself may alter it. Audiences are under the illusion that they are on stage. In a sense they are. Their yearning puts them there.

Friday's boundless national audience had begun to gather six minutes after Lee Oswald ceased firing. At 12.36 CST Don Gardiner of the ABC radio network cut into local programmes with a relay of the embattled Merriman Smith's first precede, torn off teletype machines two minutes before. At 12.40—when Kellerman was telling Behn 'Look at your clock'—CBS interrupted 'As the World Turns,' a soapland daydream. Viewers beheld Walter Cronkite announcing that 'In Dallas, Texas, three shots were fired at President Kennedy's motorcade. The first reports say that the President was "seriously wounded".' At 12.45 NBC, the champion of news coverage, became the last of the three to reach the public. NBC was relying heavily upon the Associated Press, that bumbling giant, and to make matters worse the network was 'down'—there were no national programmes at the moment; local stations were in control.

This was the hour of David Brinkley's private ordeal. With every teletype hammering out history, the monitor in his office was continuing to present a fashion show. The manager of NBC's Washington affiliate was out to lunch. No one knew where he was, or would assume responsibility for bouncing the models. In New York Chet Huntley had scuttled 'Bachelor Father', WNBC-TV's marshmallow, but Brinkley's hands were tied, and when he finally reached the air he was in a state of what another NBC newscaster described as 'controlled panic'. British television approached the news more soberly, regularly interrupting programmes to announce the shocking news, but not immediately giving the mass of detail that was to follow.

During the first critical hour in the United States the ratio between the public and its true informants was roughly 38,000,000 : 1.

The Cronkites and Huntleys were as out of touch as their demoralized listeners; the best they could do was pass along details from Smith, at Parkland's cashier's desk, and Jack Bell, in admissions. As commentators the television newscasters would normally have commented. At the moment any gloss would have been highly inappropriate, and their chief contribution was to realize that and remain unruffled. Since most of them had known the President personally, their impassivity that afternoon was no small feat. Even for men with training and long experience it was difficult, and composure vanished off camera. Bill Ryan and Frank McGee dissolved when relieved. Cronkite, taking his first break, numbly answered a studio phone. A woman on the other end, not recognizing his voice, told him, 'I just want to say that this is the worst possible taste to have that Walter Cronkite on the air when everybody knows that he spent all his time trying to get the President.' He replied, 'This is Walter Cronkite, and you're a Goddamned idiot.' Then he flung the receiver down.

Until their elaborate staffs began to function they were marking time. America's multimillion-dollar communications empire had been reduced to a crude, truncated megaphone with two-thirds of the nation at the listening end and, at the shrunken mouth, two wire correspondents clutching commandeered hospital telephones. Smith and Bell shared the same desperate plight. They weren't learning much where they were. Yet should either surrender his outside line, the chances of finding another were negligible. They were dependent upon the co-operation of colleagues and tolerant passers-by who, hopefully, would be reliable. It is a fact, and it is something of a miracle, that the megaphone worked. Fellow reporters were exceptionally generous, scrupulous, and resourceful; most of the groundless rumours circulated in the country that afternoon came from viewers and listeners who heard correct versions and embellished them in the retelling.

Here speed was an asset; before the deceived could spread the deceptions, they themselves had joined the great audience that was forming. Lacking that celerity, lies could have been sown beyond hope of uprooting. Even as it was, most of the 76 million first heard of the tragedy through hearsay. It was a workday. The reputation of daytime television was low; for every housewife who enjoyed the pabulum of 'Bachelor Father' or 'As the World Turns', there were perhaps a score who were occupied otherwise, and who were therefore alerted by her, sometimes at second or third hand. Word-of-mouth was the initial form of communication nearly everywhere, including the White House, whose private news agency was the U.S. Secret Service.

In theory the executive mansion had access to more complete information than any other house, not because agents are better reporters than correspondents, but because they were better situated—Smith, twenty-five yards away from the wide door of the emergency area, couldn't compete with the Kellerman–Hill team inside. As a publisher, however, the White House Detail was inept. Its service was, after all, secret. The scraps Smith and Bell did pick up and dictate were rephrased by professionals, beamed across all fifty states in even, well-modulated tones, and received by sets which were familiar furniture at every American address, including 1600 Pennsylvania Avenue. The voice of the Secret Service was the rasping cop's accent of Jerry Behn. First from his own desk, and later, after his office had grown hopelessly overcrowded, from the conference table in the larger office of Jack McNally, Behn would repeat aloud everything he heard over the open line from the nurse's station. Volunteers would then dash down corridors repeating it again, much as the predecessors, on August 24, 1814, had rushed about shouting that the British were on their way from Bladensburg with torches.

In this haphazard fashion the Chief Executive's home had learned that the head of the household lay gravely wounded in a Texas hospital. The butlers polishing tableware heard it from a government carpenter; a guard told the agent on the south portico; a White House Police sergeant shouted it across the west lobby; Jack McNally told Clark Clifford in the staff mess; a Navy yeoman blurted it out to Taz Shepard, who then thrust his head into the East Wing office where Nancy Tuckerman was putting the finishing touches on the seating plan for the Erhard dinner. Like so many women of the New Frontier, Nancy had led a genteel, sheltered life. Now, because of her position as social secretary and her twenty years of friendship with Jacqueline Kennedy, she had to serve as a grim courier. Among others she telephoned Maude Shaw, upstairs, and Mrs Auchincloss, on O Street; and dealt with a bewildered inquiry from Lee Radziwill in London. Nancy's approach, like Nancy, was gentle and thoughtful. 'What are you doing?' she would begin cautiously, and then she would proceed in stages, explaining that the President had been hurt, that he had been badly hurt, that his condition was critical, that it would be wise to prepare for the worst. It was a valiant attempt at tact, though the enormity of what had happened crushed it; in two instances the result was hysteria.

Since the first UPI bulletin had preceded Kellerman's call by six full minutes, and since every government communications centre was equipped with wire service machines, powerful officials who were in their offices had known of the shooting before Secret Service headquarters. The ragged yellow strips of paper—'Dallas, Nov. 22

(UPI).—Three shots were fired . . .'—were handed to George Ball at the State Department and J. Edgar Hoover at the FBI; to Ted Sorensen, just returning from lunch after a stop at his apartment; to Walter I. 'Bill' Pozen, who was minding the store at the Department of the Interior during Secretary Udall's absence on the Cabinet plane; to Dean Rusk, the senior minister aboard that plane, nine hundred miles out of Honolulu; and to Robert McNamara at the Pentagon. Simultaneously the Pentagon's command centre sounded a buzzer, awakening General Maxwell Taylor, who was napping in his office between sessions with the Germans. McNamara had a tremendous reputation, and he deserved it. Despite his deep feeling for the President—the emotional side of his personality had been overlooked by the press, but it was very much there—he kept his head and made all the right moves. An ashen-faced aide came in with the bulletin. Jerry Wiesner studied the man's expression as the Secretary read it. Wiesner thought: *The Bomb's been dropped.* McNamara quietly handed the slip around—Wiesner felt momentary relief; anything was better than a nuclear holocaust—and then the Secretary acted quickly. Adjourning his conference, he sent Mac Bundy back to the White House in a Defence limousine and conferred with Taylor and the other Joint Chiefs. Over the JCS signature they dispatched a flash warning to every American military base in the world:

> 1. Press reports President Kennedy and Governor Connally of Texas shot and critically injured. Both in hospital at Dallas, Texas. No official information yet, will keep you informed.
> 2. This is the time to be especially on the alert.

By every readable signal the situation was very red. Assassinations generally precede attempts to overthrow governments, and General Taylor issued a special warning to all troops stationed in the Washington area. At Interior Bill Pozen had assumed that this was the first stage in a coup. Never within his memory had the capital been so wide open. Six Cabinet members were over the Pacific, and both the President and the Vice-President were in Dallas. There was another chilling aspect, which struck Pozen with special force: the President's daughter had just left the mansion. She was somewhere in the District of Columbia with Pozen's own daughter and his wife. Trying number after number, he attempted, unsuccessfully, to locate them. Then all lines went dead. The Department of the Interior was cut off.

Secretary Rusk, standing in the stateroom of Aircraft 86972, fingered the two-line bulletin and asked all ladies to retire to the rear of the plane. Beckoning to a steward, he ordered him to summon

Dillon, Freeman, Udall, Wirtz, Hodges, Salinger, Heller, Assistant Secretary of State Robert Manning, and Mike Fieldman of the White House staff. Rusk waited until all were present, hoping that his face wouldn't betray him. It did. Orville Freeman decided that some momentous international development had caused the President to cancel their Japanese visit. Douglas Dillon's thoughts were more specific. Like Wiesner, the Secretary of the Treasury concluded that a thermonuclear device had exploded over an American city.

By now three bulletins had arrived. All the men were present, and Rusk said quietly, 'We have just received a ticker report, which may or may not be accurate, that the President has been shot in Dallas, possibly fatally.'

'My God,' Freeman said. Luther Hodges began to sink towards the floor; he grabbed the table top with a flapping motion and swung himself into a chair. Pierre Salinger, still holding his briefing book open to the section on Japanese economics, leaned over Rusk's upper arm, reading. Wordlessly he took the bulletins from him and read them again. Willard Wirtz, stepping beside Salinger, spoke up. In his opinion, he said, the messages were 'quite garbled'.

In the plane's central compartment Alvin M. Josephy, Jr. was scribbling:

> 8.50 Jean Davis of State just whispered in my ear that word has come over [word indecipherable] that President Kennedy has been shot. Suddenly notice that all the Cabinet members & Manning & Salinger are in forward cabin with Rusk & Dillon. It is true. Terrific, stunned condition up here. No one knows how badly President is. Scty Rusk apparently has a news ticker up in his forward cabin. We are 2 hrs out of Honolulu. Gov. Connally has been shot too. Manning & Salinger running back & forth to Rusk's cabin & to us. President shot in Dallas.

Back in the front cabin, Pierre said, 'We've got to turn back right now.'

Rusk said, 'We ought to have some confirmation.'

Confirmation of a press report was clearly Pierre's job. He entered the communications shack, and it was then, as he confronted the Signal Corps sergeant on duty, that he missed his small code book.

'Get me the White House,' he said. As an afterthought he added, 'See if you can get me Admiral Felt at CINCPAC, too.'

In less than a minute the mansion came through. Commander Oliver Hallett, in the Situation Room, was on the other end. The only code name Pierre could remember was his own, so he said, 'Situation, this is Wayside. What's the word on the President?'

Hallett was receiving relays from Behn through the Signal Corps operator. He said, 'We are still verifying. The President has been shot, we believe in the head.'

'Is he alive?'

'Our information is that he is alive.'

Pierre, like Behn, was repeating each sentence. In the stateroom Rusk turned to the group and asked, 'What shall we do?'

'We've got to turn this plane around,' Dillon said decisively.

There was a twenty-second discussion, then everyone agreed. The word was passed to the pilot, and Wirtz, looking out, saw the southern wing dip in a 180-degree arc. Josephy scrawled, 'Sudden sharp bank—wing turning . . .' Tokyo was no longer their destination. The new destination, however, was uncertain. 'Word is we're going to Dallas,' Josephy wrote. In the shack Rusk called George Ball: 'We got the flash. We're coming back. Should we go to Dallas or Washington?' he asked him. Ball didn't know. 'We'll be at Hickam Field in forty-five minutes,' the Secretary said. 'I'll call you from there.' Pierre, beside him, was connected to CINCPAC. He arranged to have a jet on a Hickam runway with full tanks to fly himself and Rusk directly to Love Field. The more the Secretary of State thought about it, the more sensible this plan seemed. But it was pure improvisation. He had no concept of the situation in Dallas and didn't even know that the Vice President had accompanied the President there.

Salinger, switched back to the Situation Room, was hanging on. Like Sorensen at lunch, he recalled, and nervously mentioned, the twenty-year cycle of Presidential deaths. It didn't hold, one member of the Cabinet objected—they were actually taking the coincidence seriously—because Roosevelt's four terms had disrupted it. Suddenly everyone was talking at once. The tone was one of strenuous optimism. Freeman, especially vehement, insisted that a head wound wasn't necessarily fatal; as a Marine officer he himself had survived one on Bougainville.

'Wayside, stand by on this line,' Commander Hallett said. 'We are trying to verify information.'

Thirty seconds passed.

'Situation to Wayside. We are still verifying. Stand by.'

Thirty seconds.

'Wayside, stand by.'

'I'm standing by,' Pierre said.

It went on and on, every thirty seconds.

Pierre was remembering all the crises in which he had stood at

Kennedy's side. Now, when he was needed most, he was eight thousand miles away. Rusk's thoughts were almost identical. He had never felt so helpless. His President and his country were in agony, and he was locked in a sealed tube 35,000 feet above the ocean.

On the fifth floor of the Justice Department Building at Ninth Street and Pennsylvania Avenue, J. Edgar Hoover had picked up his direct line to the Attorney General's office. It was answered by Angie Novello, who was staring across a desk at a frayed UPI page held aloft by a weeping press office secretary.

'This is J. Edgar Hoover.' His delivery, as always, was staccato, shrill, mechanical. 'Have you heard the news?'

'Yes, Mr Hoover, but I'm not going to break it to him.'

'The President has been shot. I'll call him.'

A White House operator connected him with Extension 163, at the end of the swimming pool behind the Virginia mansion. In response to the ring Ethel Kennedy left the men. The operator told her, 'The Director is calling.' Ethel didn't have to ask which one. In official Washington there were many directors, but only one Director. She said, 'The Attorney General is at lunch.'

At the other corner of the pool her husband had just glanced at his watch. It was 1.45 p.m. They had been away from the office over an hour. He picked up a tuna fish sandwich and said to Morgenthau, 'We'd better hurry and get back to that meeting.'

'This is urgent,' the operator told Ethel.

Ethel held out the white receiver. She called, 'It's J. Edgar Hoover.'

Robert Kennedy knew something out of the ordinary had happened; the Director never called him at home. Dropping his sandwich, he crossed to the phone, and as he took it Morgenthau saw the workman with the transistor radio whirl and run towards them, gibbering.

The Attorney General identified himself.

'I have news for you. The President's been shot,' Hoover said tonelessly.

There was a pause. Kennedy asked whether it was serious.

'I think it's serious. I am endeavouring to get details,' said Hoover. 'I'll call you back when I find out more.'

The Director hung up. The Attorney General hung up. He started back towards his wife and his two mystified guests, who were just beginning to understand the workman's babbling. Midway towards them Kennedy stopped. It had hit him. His jaw sagged; to Morganthau it seemed that his every muscle was contorted with horror.

'Jack's been shot!' he said, gagging, and clapped his hand over his face.

Ethel ran over and embraced him, and Morgenthau and his assistant hurriedly withdrew into the house. Their instincts were correct; leaving him alone was the most that anyone except his wife could have done for him. Unfortunately, solitude was impossible. His obligations were too great. Grief was an indulgence which must be postponed, or, more accurately, restrained, for absolute control was impossible. He nearly brought it off. Like the President, he disapproved of public displays of private feeling, and none of the friends who were about to gather in the yard at Hickory Hill saw him break. Nevertheless there were intervals when he had to turn his back and look away towards the bathhouse, the tennis net, the gnarled trees, the tree house—to wherever there were no eyes to gaze back.

These intervals were brief. His first thought was to fly to the side of his wounded brother, and after alerting McNamara to the need for immediate transportation he darted upstairs to change his clothes. Meantime telephones were ringing incessantly; during the first quarter-hour calls were received or placed at the pool, the court, the upstairs study, and the downstairs library. Taz Shepard offered help in informing members of the family. Kennedy politely thanked him; that was his own responsibility. While instructing Clint Hill to make sure a priest reached the hospital he asked, 'What kind of doctors do they have?' and 'How is Jackie taking it?' He held several subsequent conversations with McNamara (who had been told that his own information was coming from the DIA, the Defence Intelligence Agency, and who in the confusion thought that the source was the CIA), and once he took a call from John McCone of the CIA (who was actually watching Walter Cronkite).

The CIA building was a five-minute drive from Hickory Hill. Kennedy asked McCone, 'Jack, can you come over?'

In his limousine McCone, the governmental director immediately concerned with international plots, wondered, as he had been wondering since a breathless assistant broke the news to him, whether this could be the result of one. He had received no intelligence; he could reach no judgment. All he could do was speculate over the bigotry which had been cropping up in certain American cities, notably Dallas.

Wandering from extension to extension, Robert Kennedy murmured to himself, 'There's been so much hate.'

At the Republican end of the Senate lobby the UPI ticker, ignored, had clattered out its lengthening page of historic bulletins. The AP machine stirred and clanged. In the torpor induced by the federal library debate it, too, would have been overlooked had not Senator Wayne Morse's hunger for news been insatiable. Phyllis

Rock of his office was maintaining a vigil near the AP teletype. At 1.41 she checked it and cried out. Richard Riedel tossed down his newspaper, came over, and read:

> ... AP Photographer James W. Altgens said he saw blood on the President's head.
>
> Altgens said he heard two shots but thought someone was shooting fireworks....

In the half-century since he had come to the Senate as a nine-year-old page boy Riedel had never before committed the breach of running out on the Senate floor. Now he raced up to Senator after Senator, spluttering, 'The President has been shot—the President—he's been shot!' Holland of Florida gaped at him, Dirksen of Illinois sagged. His face empty, Riedel looked up to the rostrum for help and saw Kennedy of Massachusetts. In a cloakroom the strained rumours had just reached the Majority Leader, Mike Mansfield. Mike remembered that Ted had been presiding when Patrick Kennedy died, and he moved towards the chair. Riedel beat him there. On the dais he began, 'The most horrible thing has happened! It's terrible, terrible!'

The Senator had been signing correspondence. His pen wavered. He asked, 'What is it?'

'Your brother.' Riedel remembered that Ted had two brothers. 'Your brother the President. He's been shot.'

The Senator stared at him as though through a veil, then looked at Holland, who was deftly approaching from the other side to relieve him of the gavel. 'How do you know?'

'It's on the ticker. Just came in on the ticker.'

Ted hastily gathered up his papers, and Riedel put his hand on his shoulder. 'Maybe you can take a jet to Texas. Is there anything I can do?'

'No,' said Ted, and quickly departed.

Behind him he left pandemonium. Parliamentary procedure fell apart. Morse asked Prouty to 'yield for a quorum call for an emergency', and on the other side of Constitution Avenue quorum buzzers sounded in every Senator's office. (Through this extension of word-of-mouth, supplemented by a secretary's phone call, Church of Idaho was informed while attending a formal luncheon on the eighth floor of the State Department. He then made the announcement to Averell Harriman and the assembled diplomats.) Morse's move should have prepared the way for an adjournment motion from the Majority Leader. But Mansfield was overcome, he couldn't speak. Dirksen made the move as Minority Leader. He forgot to provide a reason for the record, however, and so, with Holland presiding, the Senate just stopped.

In the lobby Ted Kennedy broke his stride between the teletype machines. It was impossible to see anything. Crowds had thickened around both. He swerved towards Lyndon Johnson's office and dialled the Attorney General's office from there—government code 187, Extension 2001. Nothing happened. There was no dial tone, no sound at all. He dialled again and received a busy signal. Unaware of his direction, he reeled into the street. There a legislative assistant who had been listening to his own car radio recognized him and drove him the half-block to his suite in the Old Senate Office Building. On the sidewalk Claude Hooten of Houston, a Harvard classmate of Ted's, was waiting. Hooten had arrived for the Senator's anniversary celebration. The first reports had reached him, and he led the Senator into the suite, where, it seemed to Ted, countless portable table radios were squawking in horrid concert.

The telephone crisis was growing queerer and queerer. Calls could come in—Martin Agronsky of NBC was inquiring whether the Senator planned a flight to Dallas—but when Ted retired to his private office and tried again to reach his brother, either at Justice or through the White House, all the lines were dead. After a pause one did briefly come to life. The White House switchboard, however, told him that the Attorney General was talking to Dallas, and since Ted Kennedy, unlike Bob, didn't have an executive mansion extension, there was no way of splicing him into the call. The conversation was with Clint Hill, but Ted didn't know that. He didn't even know that the President was in a hospital. Like Bill Pozen at Interior, he was left with a useless black plastic receiver and the task of trying to assess the scope of the calamity. In retrospect its boundaries are clear: there was an assassin at large in Dallas, two victims at Parkland, and reaction everywhere else. That clarity did not exist then. The wounding of John Kennedy was the largest cloud in the sky, but it did not exclude the possibility of others, and the Senator thought of his wife. He wanted to be sure Joan was safe. He asked for his Chrysler. It was unavailable; an aide was using it to run errands. Milt Gwirtzman, another Harvard classmate and a member of his staff, offered his Mercedes, and in it Ted, Milt, and Claude streaked down Pennsylvania Avenue, around the White House on South Executive, out E Street, Virginia Avenue, and the Rock Creek Parkway, into Georgetown. Milt ignored red lights. Beside him Ted pointed warningly to onrushing cars with one hand and, with the other, clutched a transistor radio he had borrowed from a secretary. Claude sat in the back, his head in his hands. As they threaded their way past a jungle of construction outside the State Department, the radio reported that the President was still alive. Milt breathed a prayer of thanks. Claude said, 'My God, my God, the President shot—and in *my state*!' Ted said nothing.

Twelve minutes after leaving the Hill the Mercedes skidded against the kerb outside 1607 Twenty-eighth Street, and the Senator, searching his house for his wife, learned from a maid that she was having her hair done. Milt volunteered to get her. Careening off again, he reached Elizabeth Arden's Connecticut Avenue studio before anyone there told Joan. They knew. Preparing to pay her bill she had become aware of a sudden quietness around her. Then, before cashier or customers could speak, he appeared. 'Why, Milty, what a surprise!' she said. She really was taken aback; it was so odd to see a man in a beauty parlour. She kept glancing at him expectantly until, as they sped away, he explained that the President had been hurt. 'It's a shooting,' he said carefully, trying to keep his voice even. 'We have no news except for that.' Thinking of Patrick—it was inconceivable to her that her brother-in-law would never recover—she said, 'Oh, they've had so much trouble this year!'

On the Twenty-eighth Street threshold Ted awaited them. His face was taut and drained. 'All the phones are gone,' he said. He and Claude had been going through the house, picking up extensions. They had been unable to get a dial tone. The Chesapeake & Potomac Telephone Company was deaf and dumb. It was as though Alexander Graham Bell had never been born. They began to wonder whether the failure of the system could be more than an accident; Joan, scared, said, 'There must be some national reason.' Ted decided to conduct a door-to-door search, asking permission of strangers to test instruments until they found one that worked. It seemed to be the only solution. He had turned on his television set, but despite their many excursions since he left the Senate rostrum the commentators were still exasperatingly vague. He had to reach Hickory Hill. Bob had talked to Dallas; he would know something. On the sidewalk Ted said to Claude, 'We'll split up. You try the doors on the right. I'll take the left. If you get something, let me know.'

The President had been shot, had been raced to Parkland, and had been in Jacqueline Kennedy's arms outside the ambulance ramp when, at 1.37 p.m. Washington time, Liz Pozen had drawn up outside the South Portico of the exclusive mansion. She had switched off her radio as the children jumped in, squealing. Caroline and Agatha climbed towards the rear of the station wagon. 'We're going to sit in the very backest seat,' Caroline called, stowing her suitcase and pink teddy bear there. Counting the children, Liz watched her covertly. Caroline was a sophisticated child; in many ways she carried her emotions as easily as an adult. Obviously she was a trifle nervous about her first night away from home, but she seemed game.

Behind them Agent Tom Wells switched on the ignition in his Secret Service Ford. Unhooking the microphone under the dashboard, he radioed headquarters control, 'Crown, Crown. This is Dasher. Lyric is en route to her destination.'

The exact route to the destination was up to Liz Pozen, and she was pondering choices. Usually her house on Raymond Street was the first stop on the car pool route. Her first thought was to drop Caroline and Agatha off there and let them play while she continued on with the other children. There was an alternative. Because the school was in Caroline's house, she had never ridden in the pool before, and she might enjoy the entire circuit. Entering the Rock Creek Parkway, Liz was still debating with herself when she noticed that the giggles and chatter behind her had begun to die down. Caroline and Agatha were no longer babbling excitedly about the prospect of having tea with her this afternoon at Lord & Taylor's, and the other first-graders had exhausted their small sources of gossip. A pall was settling over the station wagon. Motherly instinct told Liz that this could be the silence before a storm of quarrelling. Music might divert them. Remembering that WGMS had scheduled a musical programme for this hour, she switched on her radio.

Watching traffic, trying to decide whether to turn towards her house, Liz heard the voice of an unfamiliar announcer coming on:

'. . . shot in the head and his wife Jackie . . .'

She instantly switched it off. To the best of her later recollection, the volume was low and those were the only words spoken. The children, she was convinced, heard nothing. Caroline's subsequent remarks to Tom Wells suggest that there may have been more to the broadcast than Liz thought, but at most it would have been hazy; all bulletins were hazy then. Certainly the President's daughter could have had no grasp of what had really happened; Liz herself did not know.

'*War of the Worlds*,' she thought, remembering the realistic 1938 radio drama of invading Martians. She looked wide-eyed into her rear-view mirror and tried to read Tom Wells's expression. From here it was unfathomable.

The agent's commercial radio was on, but he heard nothing from his station until they had left the parkway and turned north on Connecticut Avenue. They were passing the National Zoo when the programme to which he was tuned was interrupted for the nebulous flash, 'We have an unconfirmed report of a shooting in the area of the Presidential motorcade in Dallas.' In the year since Wells had joined the White House Detail the possibility of such a situation had never been far from the surface of his mind. Through his windshield he rapidly scanned the station wagon, but Liz, dark and petite, was too small to be seen from here, and the children, below window level, were invisible. It was as though all the occupants had been mysteriously spirited away, leaving the station wagon to cruise madly towards Chevy Chase Circle under its own power.

Liz Pozen was out of touch. Switching her set on again was unthinkable; she had to remain in the dark until every child, including her own, had been settled down. At the same time, the question of which route she would take had been resolved for her. She would have to pass Raymond Street, keeping Caroline and Agatha with her. The only risk in remaining on the road was that a passing car, hearing the news on his own radio, might see Caroline, recognize her from her pictures, and act rashly. She peered out furtively at southbound drivers. Like Wells, they were impassive.

His station had resumed its regular programme. Four blocks beyond the zoo there was another break—the network was speculating that some members of the Presidential party, perhaps even President Kennedy himself, had been shot. Nothing was firm. Station routine was abandoned for a running account of developments in Dallas, but the announcer was being exceptionally guarded.

Stopping did not occur to Liz, and in the absence of any sign from her Wells could only cling to her rear bumper. They passed through a half-mile of green lights before one turned red; then, braking together, they flung open their doors and met between the two cars.

'Did you hear the broadcast?' he asked.

She nodded once quickly.

'Turn off your radio.'

'I already did.' She searched his face. 'What should I do?'

'Nobody knows whether or not it's serious. Keep going.'

The traffic signal changed; they drove on. Using his microphone, the agent called: 'Crown, Crown from Dasher. Request immediate instructions regarding Lyric in view of the present situation in Dallas. Over.'

Crown was silent. Then: 'Stand by.'

The Ford's commercial radio was describing how a policeman had chased two people up 'a knoll'—the overpass. The announcer interrupted to confirm the shooting of the President.

'Crown, Crown from Dasher. Request immediate—repeat immediate—instructions in connection with my previous inquiry. Get in touch with Duplex or Dresser. Over.'

An answer: 'Duplex's lines are tied up. Stand by for Dresser.'

Crown was stunned. Due to UPI's speed, Liz Pozen and Tom Wells, cruising towards Maryland, knew more than those who should have advised them. Jerry Behn's lines were tied up because he was talking to Roy Kellerman, and Agent Foster, for whom Wells was standing by, hadn't a clue to what had happened. He had just strolled into Post F-5 after an admiring inspection of the new rug in the President's office, and he was preoccupied with the design of a small flight jacket for young John.

In Chevy Chase, near the intersection of Connecticut and Western, Liz let off the first child. In the street she and Wells held their second conference. Since he had no 'procedural instructions', he told her, they would continue with the pool.

His own thoughts were beginning to jell, however, and by the time Crown connected him with Foster, who had merely been informed of 'an emergency in Dallas', Wells had convinced himself that he must spoil Caroline's visit to the Pozens'. His next task was to convince Foster, his superior.

'Dasher to Dresser. I feel the danger has grown. We don't know whether this is an isolated thing, a plot, or a coup. If it's a coup, Washington is sure to be part of it, and I want Lyric back in a secure setting.' Raymond Street, he remembered, was a kidnapper's dream. 'We'd be primed for a snatch, and in lieu of anything to the contrary from you I'm taking Lyric back to Crown.'

It was not an easy judgment, nor would it be popular. Nevertheless it made sense to Foster. He agreed that 'They might be trying to kill the whole family.' Upstairs he conveyed the decision to Maude Shaw, who was sceptical of it. The greatest sceptic, however, was going to be Liz Pozen. Wells, expecting her to be difficult, reached a second judgment; to avoid discussion he would say that he was acting under orders.

In letting out the second child she made a U-turn. He turned off his commercial radio and waved her down. Their third huddle, which followed, was both distressing and hectic. He was so distracted that he forgot his emergency brake, and halfway towards her he caught a horrified glimpse of the Ford slowly rolling downhill. He caught it after a sprint, set the brake, and returned.

'I have to take Caroline back to the mansion.'

'Why?' she cried.

'Security reasons.'

She was even more stubborn than he had anticipated. In their two previous talks she had been more agitated than he was. But now that they were out of heavy traffic, she reasoned, the chances that Caroline might be spotted had diminished. Liz very much wanted to keep her. She had a case; it was inconceivable that an outsider could have discovered these arrangements, and this was no time to upset Caroline.

'It's not my decision,' he said. 'I have no alternative.' Stepping past her, he put his head in the station wagon and said, 'Caroline, you have to go back to your house. You better bring your overnight bag. Maybe you can come out a little later.'

His nervousness heightened the tension. To Liz he seemed needlessly brusque and businesslike. The girls, she thought, looked like two fish—their mouths were open, and they were ready to cry. Caroline shrank back. She said, 'I don't want to go.'

He opened the rear door and picked up the suitcase. 'We don't have any choice. Something has come up, Miss Shaw will probably tell you.'

'Yes, I know what it's about,' she said. He gathered that she had heard a broadcast.

Hugging the bear and fighting back tears, she climbed over the seat towards him. Liz kissed her; Wells put her on the front seat beside him and left. At the first intersection he started to make a right turn. Preoccupied, he had lost his sense of direction. Liz saw his indicator light flashing and shouted, 'Are you sure you know where you're going?' Through his open window he shouted back, 'I want Connecticut Avenue.' 'Then turn left,' she called.

A quarter-mile south of Chevy Chase Circle Caroline looked up at him. 'Why do we have to go home?' she asked. Before Wells could reply she said again, 'Never mind. I know.'

She couldn't know much. Still, his first explanation, he reflected, had been inadequate. She was entitled to something better than that. 'Mommy has changed her plans and will probably come back to the White House tonight,' he said. 'She wanted you and John to be home.'

Caroline again fell silent. She withdrew into her own thoughts, which was not unusual for her. Wells observed that she had become very quiet, but he had no time to coax her into conversation. Reentering the Rock Creek Parkway—which Caroline's Uncle Ted and his two classmates had left a few minutes before—the agent became absorbed in a new, frightening complication. The spectre which had plagued Liz Pozen became a reality: another motorist recognized Caroline. They were passing a light green sedan when the driver glanced over and started visibly. He was a burly man in his early fifties, wearing a hat and what appeared to be a lumber jacket. The agent's description is sketchy, because he immediately began trying to shake him; once the man had recovered he decided to give chase.

He was taking a chance. Tom Wells was one of the finest marksmen in the White House Detail, and he was in a dangerous temper. Yet the anonymous driver is a sympathetic figure; his response was courageous and understandable. The black Ford carried no official markings, and anyone seeing the President's six-year-old daughter speeding away with an unidentified man (Wells may have looked burly to *him*) in the minutes after the shooting might easily have concluded that she was being abducted. The agent, on the other hand, had no way of determining the motives of his pursuer. In taking Caroline from Liz Pozen he had inherited the obligation to keep his commercial radio silent. He couldn't even ask specific questions of Crown without alarming the child beside him. Perhaps his fear of a coup was being vindicated at this very moment; perhaps the strange sedan was part of it. Wells damned the White House garage for failing to provide him a car with a Secret Service 'fireball'—a red light under the car frame—or with a portable, pistol-grip flashlight that illuminated the black-on-red letters 'POLICE'. In its absence he was left with but one choice: flight. Driving his accelerator to the floor, he swerved to the left. His pursuer also accelerated, and was at one point a few feet from his right rear bumper. Gradually Wells drew away. He cut in and out skilfully, allowing other traffic to filter between them, and when he reached the parkway's Virginia Avenue exit there was no trace of the green sedan in his rear-view mirror.

'Crown, Crown from Dasher. Lyric is five minutes away.'

Even that was enough to awaken Caroline's curiosity. She asked, 'Why are you telling them we're coming home?'

He concentrated on driving; there was no satisfactory answer. But he had to be sure that the south portico and Miss Shaw were alert.

'Crown, Crown from Dasher. Lyric is two minutes away.'

At 2.13 Washington time, forty-six minutes after their departure, Tom Wells swept Caroline, her overnight bag, and her stuffed bear past the pallid guards at the Southwest Gate.

For all who had been tuned in between 1.36 and 1.45 Washington time, automobile and home and office sets had provided the first spark in the firestorm. Dean Gorham, still slowly sipping his vanilla malted, had heard it on Texas Route 71. He kept speeding towards the Austin auditorium to deliver the souvenir programmes for the great banquet which would never be held. Helen Williams had heard in the kitchen of the LBJ Ranch. She flung her apron over her face and ran out blindly past the hundreds of pies which had just become garbage. Bernard Weissman, the young right-wing salesman who had signed the full-page advertisement in that morning's Dallas

News, had heard while driving in downtown Dallas with a friend. According to his testimony, fearful that he would be blamed, he had been holed up in a bar for four hours, saying of the assassin, 'I hope he is not a member of the Walker group—I hope he's not one of Walker's boys.' H. L. Hunt had heard over the large console television set in his office. He left the set on and vacated the room for those members of his staff who might be interested in subsequent developments.

Ted Dealey and Marguerite Oswald had both been tuned to Ted's Station WFAA. An announcer, evidently out of breath, ran in front of the camera and gasped, 'I've got some terrible news. The President has been shot, I don't know if fatally.' Dealey was offended by the man's unprofessional conduct. His television reporters, he felt, should be more suave. Marguerite was interested. This was real news. Tomorrow it would be all over the Fort Worth papers, like Lee's defection to Russia in 1959, and she could read about it while watching the 'Today' show. She felt no personal involvement. 'I wasn't upset emotionally—I'm not that type of person,' she said afterwards. 'I have this ability of accepting things. I never let my sleep or eating habits get disturbed.' In Irving Marina Oswald and Ruth Paine had heard it over the Zenith set Lee had been watching the evening before. Ruth translated for her friend and lit a candle. 'Is that a way of praying?' Marina inquired. 'Yes, it is, just my own way,' Ruth replied. Marina went into the yard to hang some clothes. The newscaster reported that the shots had come from the Texas School Book Depository, and Ruth went out to translate this, too. Marina said nothing, but she furtively checked the blanket roll in the garage. Seeing it there, not knowing it was empty, she whispered to herself, 'Thank God.' Ruth did not connect Lee with the shots, though she thought it gripping to know someone who was downtown and could give a firsthand account of what had happened.

In Washington J. Bernard West, the White House Chief Usher, had heard the first bulletin over his home radio, which he had just turned on two minutes before. He ran into his bedroom to change his clothes. Traphes Bryant, President Kennedy's dog handler, had heard it on his car radio on West Executive Avenue. He stopped, put his head on the steering wheel, and prayed. The wife of Arlington's superintendent, seeing one of the first television bulletins that interrupted soap operas, called her husband. 'Just as the doctor was about to operate we saw it on TV,' she cried. He had no idea what she meant. Mrs Earl Warren had also seen the bulletin, on the Warrens' apartment set at the Sheraton-Park. She also phoned the office of her husband, whose secretary, Mrs Dorothy McHugh, rapidly typed on a blank slip of paper: 'There is a report that the President and

Governor Connally have been shot in Dallas and taken to the hospital.' She gave the slip to a page, he rapped on the conference room door and handed it to Arthur Goldberg, and Goldberg gave the message to the Chief Justice, who rose, his eyes bright with tears, and read it aloud. The other justices rose together. They stood paralysed; then Potter Stewart stirred and murmured that there was a transistor radio in his office. It was brought to the room and placed on the huge baize green table top, where it lay, tiny and incongruous, a flat plastic box from which assorted voices swelled and faded in concert while nine clay-faced men in dark suits bowed over it.

Nina Warren had obeyed the universal impulse of the moment—to tell someone, preferably someone close, but, lacking that, anyone who had not yet been told. Dick Goodwin, holed up with his typewriter, and Sergeant Keith Clark, browsing over rare books, remained uninformed only because they had departed from their normal routines and their whereabouts were unknown. The breakdown of the telephone system, which seemed so menacing, was an inevitable consequence of this compulsion to spread the word. It is impossible to estimate how many of the 1,443,994 phones in service in the Washington metropolitan area on November 22 were snatched up in that first half-hour, but the Chesapeake & Potomac's Friday record of over a quarter-million long-distance calls is staggering, and locally the phenomenon of what communications engineers call 'the slow dial tone', a result of overloaded exchanges, became frightening.[11] Lines would go dead, return to normal when a sufficient number of people had hung up, and go dead again and return to life, over and over. The pattern was repeated throughout the country. It became obvious that in a national emergency this would be the first link to snap. The phoners likeliest to get through immediately were those who called as soon as they heard the first flash; Byron Skelton's daughter, knowing that he was about to leave for Austin, dialled him at once and caught him at the front door. After that it was a matter of persistence and luck, because remote acquaintances, distant relatives, and estranged friends were searching for one another's numbers by the millions. Even total strangers called—in Georgetown a ghostly voice told Bill Walton, 'Turn on your radio, the President's been shot.'

Strangers were the most frequent source for those in public places. A fellow shopper stopped Provi Parades in Maryland, a fellow American drew Bishop Hannan aside in Rome, a passing neighbour called to Joe Gawler in Gawler's back yard, a New York policeman

[11] The number of long-distance calls climbed again on Saturday, reached a peak on Sunday, when Oswald was shot, and plunged 30 per cent below normal on Monday, the day of the President's funeral.

approached General Eisenhower and his aide in New York. Fred Holborn, who was wondering why motor-cycle policemen should be roaring down West Executive Avenue at breakneck speed, heard from a sobbing woman in Lafayette Park. Ben Bradlee glanced out Brentano's window and saw pedestrians stumbling around 'like penguins, or a gaggle of geese'. His first thought was that there had been a terrible automobile accident in the street just outside; he hurried to the sidewalk to find out whether anyone he knew had been hurt and learned that someone he knew had been—a thousand miles away. Taxi drivers told Richard Nixon, in downtown Manhattan, and former Secret Service Chief Frank Wilson, in suburban Washington. Washington waiters, ordinarily taciturn, babbled excitedly to Hale Boggs, Ted Reardon, and Nick Katzenbach. (Reardon had patronized the same place for three years because he was confident that no one there could identify him as a Kennedy aide. At 1.40 on November 22 he discovered that everyone there could. Katzenbach, like many others who were dining, was never again able to bring himself to enter the same lunchroom.) A waitress in Dallas' Alamo Grill whispered to FBI Agent Jim Hosty that shots had been fired from the Book Depository, where, Hosty knew, a certain Lee Oswald was employed. A captain at La Caravelle restaurant whispered it to Steve Smith. Jean Kennedy Smith, his wife, on a New York street overheard a girl shrieking, 'Haven't you heard the news?' Jean encountered a friend who was parked nearby. They listened to the car radio together, and then, hearing that her brother was in a critical condition, Jean turned away and walked through twenty blocks of Manhattan to her home on upper Fifth Avenue.

Hearing an announcer, or reading a teletype bulletin, nearly always guaranteed acceptance of the fact as a fact. There were exceptions. At 1600 Pennsylvania Avenue Sergeant Leon Bodensteiner had answered the UPI flash bells, looked at the White House Communications Agency's wire service monitor, and concluded that this was an operator's prank. But Bodensteiner was in the Signal Corps. He knew how such things are done. Laymen are more trustful of devices, less trustful of other people. Ben Bradlee believed the news the moment he was told. Not many did. The assassination was so fantastic that the general reaction was utter incredulity. 'George, I've just heard something wild,' a colleague called to George Reedy on Capitol Hill, and Reedy agreed that it was absurd. He rose to check only because it was his duty to telephone Lyndon Johnson's Walter Jenkins if anything unusual had happened in Texas. When Bill Moyers was told in Austin, 'The President has been shot and the Vice President will want to see you immediately,' he at first dismissed it as a bad joke. So did Llewellyn Thompson, at Washington's Metropolitan Club; Seaman Ed Nemuth, in Anacostia; and Arthur Schlesinger, who was attending a *Newsweek* luncheon in New York with Kenneth Galbraith and Kay Graham; Schlesinger concluded that the report was 'some repellent form of intramural humour'. In Texas Michael Paine thought it was another anti-Kennedy quip, though when Paine heard the Book Depository mentioned he, unlike his wife, thought of calling the FBI about Lee.

The very vehemence with which people scouted those early reports is suspect. It was almost as though they hoped that if they denied it with sufficient vigour, it would go away. 'Don't be ridiculous!' Justice Stewart's wife snapped at her maid, and in the basement of the Supreme Court Building Joannie Douglas, who had driven down to meet her husband, raged at a guard, 'Don't you ever tease about such a thing!' On the West Coast an officer tried to break the news gently to Acting Secretary of the Navy Fay by saying, 'I think the President's been shot.' Fay whirled on him. 'Don't tell me what you *think*, Captain,' he snapped. 'Tell me what you *know*.' In the Justice Department Barney Ross, hearing almost identical words, replied, 'The president of what?' Across the Potomac Lietutenant Sam Bird said 'Oh, really,' took two steps and asked indignantly, 'The *who*?'

One form of rejection was to ignore unimpeachable sources, or to assume that Kennedy's recovery would be painless and swift. Justice Douglas, finding that the rest of the Court had lost interest in the conference, shut himself up in his office and buried himself in legal briefs; he wouldn't even come out to see his wife. Aboard American Airlines Dallas-to-Washington Flight 58 the captain switched on the public address system and announced, 'Ladies and gentlemen, we have just intercepted a radio broadcast from Miami, Florida, saying that President Kennedy has been assassinated and Governor Connally seriously wounded. We do not have any further details at this time.' Candy McMurrey wondered aloud what 'assassinated' meant —was it killed or wounded, or was it merely an attempt?—and her husband said, 'Oh, well, Miami, they have all those kooks and Cubans; you can't trust what they say.' In Cuba itself, Fidel Castro greeted the report that Kennedy had been wounded with the cry, 'Then he's re-elected!' In the Lafayette dining room Sargent Shriver was summoned to a phone and told by his secretary. He returned to the table and said to his wife, 'Something's happened to Jack.' Eunice asked, 'What?' 'He's been shot,' Shriver said. She asked if her brother was going to be all right. 'We don't know,' her husband replied. Eunice thought a moment and then said, 'There have been so many crises in his life; he'll pull through.' Here were two people in conspiracy against reality. They calmly studied the menu and ordered lunch; it arrived, and Eunice ate the bread and drank a cup of soup before a second telephone call destroyed their fragile façade.

There were other façades. Although the facts were set forth in a few stark words, a handful managed to misinterpret them. Joe Dealey and Warren Harding at the Dallas Trade Mart independently decided that 'The President's been hit' meant that he had been hit by rotten fruit. Reardon and Mary McGrory thought another plane had opened fire on Air Force One. Angier Biddle Duke took 'shot' to mean 'shot at'—in other words, a miss. In her Dallas classroom Marilyn Dailey, one of the schoolchildren who had held the 'MR PRESIDENT, PLEASE STOP AND SHAKE OUR HANDS' sign at Lemmon Avenue and Lomo Alto, heard the principal's announcement over the loudspeaker and thought, *Oh! He's only wounded!* Marilyn didn't react until the principal's voice had been followed by organ music; then, in a matter of seconds, she developed a splitting headache. Even after repeated verification there was a tendency to work and rework the concise sentences, looking for the hole that, people felt, had to be there somewhere. This disposition was strongest among those who, like Eunice, remembered the many times the President had cheated death in the past; Arthur Schlesinger recalled PT 109 in the Solomons and felt 'an insane resurgence of hope'.

In Ambassador Joseph P. Kennedy's Hyannis Port home the maid, Dora Lawrence, shouted up from the first floor at Ann Gargan, 'Ann, Ann! Did you hear? Did you hear?' Ann, about to leave for Detroit, turned from her uncle's nurse with irritation. The maid was always panicking. If the poodles slipped outdoors, she would wring her hands. But this was too much—her shrillness was apt to waken Uncle Joe or Aunt Rose. Hurrying to the head of the stairwell, Ann asked crossly, 'What is it?' Dora gave her own version of the first flash: 'Someone has taken a shot at the President!'

Back in her room with Rita Dallas, Ann switched on her television set. The bulletins were pouring in, and in her own panic she committed the sin for which she had been about to reproach the maid: she increased the volume to an alarming pitch. The President's mother appeared in the doorway. 'Please turn the TV down, Ann,' she said. 'I'm taking a rest.'

Her niece and the nurse gestured at one another and reached for the knob, too late; Rose Kennedy had heard that her son had been hit by gunfire. She sank into a chair, trembling. Yet at most she would have been spared no more than a few moments. The telephone rang. It was Bob Kennedy in Virginia. He told his mother that 'It looks bad'—that 'As far as I know Jack can't pull through.'

Rose hung up and hugged herself, as though to ward off the coming chill. She looked haggard. 'I can't stand it,' she said. 'I've got to keep moving.'

Two doors away they heard pacing up and down, pivoting at each corner and returning deliberately. Ann remembered the President's father, asleep down the hall, and began to cry softly. The nurse puckered. Since girlhood she had been told that her face was a map of Ireland, and it was; it was as Celtic as the Sinn Fein. But now she was preoccupied with her name. 'Dallas . . . Dallas . . . Dallas,' the hideous set kept saying, and as her pucker deepened she thought in astonishment, *Why, that's my name.*

The name had another significance in Washington's F Street Club, where Senator Fulbright and Gene Black, former head of the World Bank, had been finishing their lunch. Black was among those with appointments to see Kennedy immediately after the President's return from Texas. He and the Senator were drinking coffee and discussing economics. Elspeth Rostow, wife of the State Department's counsellor, entered the room moments before a man appeared and blurted out what had happened, and where it had happened. Mrs Rostow saw Fulbright throw down his napkin and jump to his feet. 'God*damn* it!' he shouted. 'I *told* him not to go to Dallas!'

Just as water piles up behind a keel in a typhoon, baffling the screws and forcing the helmsman to violate every principle of seamanship to avoid broaching to, so anguish foils the human mechanism. In their struggle to preserve sanity that Friday men and women suspended the laws of normal behaviour. In the White House a member of the President's staff blacked out for two hours. Afterwards he had no recollection of where he had been, but since no one saw him he was probably one of those for whom privacy was an absolute necessity. Rose Kennedy had to go to her room. Jean Kennedy Smith had to walk those twenty blocks. Dave Hackett, who had known Bob Kennedy since boyhood, couldn't bear to be among friends; he left a meeting and scoured the neighbourhood for a taproom where he would be unknown and where he could down a stiff shot unnoticed. In Dallas, Judge Sarah Hughes, hearing of the shooting, quietly walked out of the Trade Mart and drove home. In Washington a lady in Lord & Taylor's suddenly realized that there were no other customers, no clerks, no floorwalkers; she could have walked off with the whole store.

She didn't become a shoplifter, but had she acted queerly she would have been in a large company. Eisenhower's secretary was talking long distance from Gettysburg to a woman at Twentieth Century–Fox who was idly watching a teletype machine beside her desk. The keys rapped out the first flash; without explanation the woman filled her lungs and screamed into the receiver. She kept shrieking—the secretary replaced the call an hour later, after she herself had learned what had happened and had collected herself, and was again greeted by hysteria. On the Pennsylvania Turnpike a filling station attendant was making change for a driver with Texas licence plates. A radio beside the cash register broadcast the bulletin, and the attendant returned to the car and flung the fistful of silver in the driver's face. Mary McGrory, in the middle of a physical checkup, submitted to a routine blood-pressure test immediately after her doctor's nurse had told her the news. She was in excellent health, and there ought to have been nothing unusual about the reading, but under these circumstances it was so appalling her physician wrote her a prescription for hypertension.

After the initial blow had been absorbed, after the first bruises had begun to darken, broadcasts from Dallas were unquestioned. The difficulty was that not everyone had immediate access to them, and it was during this period that trespassers slipped into unoccupied automobiles and turned on dashboard radios, or invited themselves into strange homes with muttered apologies, or entered raffish bars because bars were known to be equipped with television sets, or polled fellow workers to determine who had transistors. The radios turned up in unexpected places—desk drawers, pockets, purses. Afterwards this was a source of embarrassment for some owners, who would go to elaborate lengths to point out that ordinarily they were never brought into the office, just as educated housewives, telling how they happened to call their husbands, would carefully preface their accounts by explaining that usually they didn't look at such soporifics as 'As the World Turns'; it was pure chance that they had tuned in on November 22. At the time, however, no questions were asked. If a set was available it was used. In the staid Metropolitan Club television was never watched except during the World Series. The rule was ironclad, and when the screen there flickered to life, members who didn't understand the reason tottered to their feet with outraged splutters. Then Dean Acheson stepped into the room, his eyes brimming, and silenced them with a glance. Ted Kennedy's expedient of temporary confiscation from a member of his staff was widespread. Chairman John W. Macy, Jr. of the U.S. Civil Service Commission appropriated a portable radio belonging to one of his 230,000 employees in the Washington area and charged around his office propping it on desks and tables until he found a narrow ledge where it emitted a faint signal. At the British Embassy David Ormsby-Gore retired to his bedroom with another portable and lay there alone, wrestling with private agony. The phantom voice which had advised Bill Walton to turn on his radio assumed that he had one. He didn't, so he and his two guests moved into the maid's room to watch her television set.

In another bedroom at the executive mansion Maude Shaw, a non-driver, worriedly asked Agent Foster, 'Oh, dear, what will I do now without White House cars?' Like Sergeant Dugger, fretting at Parkland about his unauthorized use of a cruiser, she was genuinely concerned. The majority focused upon the central tragedy immediately. A minority, of whom Miss Shaw was typical, seized fetishistically upon an insignificant corner of it, and seen in that light her question is entirely understandable. Her next move was to stand watch over the door of the President's sleeping son, but if she had ordered a car and taken him for an afternoon drive through Montrose Park, that, too, would have been explicable. She might even have glimpsed familiar faces there. Nicole Alphand, intently studying the expression on her husband's face as he heard the news over a telephone at the other end of their luncheon table, leaped to the conclusion that President de Gaulle had been assassinated. Set straight, she sent for the embassy chauffeur and drove off to call upon the Robert Kennedys. Nicole was the wife of the French Ambassador and was accustomed to paying her respects; to her, at that moment, it was as simple as that. On O Street the wife of the Peruvian Ambassador, second in seniority in the diplomatic corps, similarly called upon Jacqueline Kennedy's stricken mother. Countless others also took refuge in habit. Two designers at the Bureau of Engraving and Printing, feeling utterly lost, neatly laid out their tools and doodled away at a John F. Kennedy commemorative stamp. (Though meant to be tentative, those Friday sketches were flawless; four days later they were in the hands of the Postmaster General, and the stamp was issued the following spring.) Writers wrote tributes. Composers fingered keyboards. Doctors—e.g., Mary McGrory's—methodically met their patients. A petty functionary at the Library of Congress, clinging to a pet prejudice of librarians, refused to believe a word until it had been confirmed by the *New York Times*. He tried to call the *Times* Washington bureau, found he could not get through, and prickled with the sense of alarm which was terrifying telephoners elsewhere.

The devout prayed. On his way back to the White House, Reardon bowed his head in the rear seat of a taxi and chanted over and over, 'Dear God, just let him be wounded.' Mrs Auchincloss crossed to a quiet Episcopal church on the other side of the street and was amazed to find every pew full and the minister at the altar. The desk of Acting Secretary Joe Fowler became an improvised altar; he shut the door of his Treasury Department office and fell to his knees beside it. And in Boston Cardinal Cushing, the priest closest to the President, was mobilizing his every ecclesiastical resource. The aged prelate sent word to the four hundred parishes of his archdiocese to 'Pray, pray, *pray* for him.' He shepherded the nuns who attended him into his private chapel, and while they said their beads he himself mounted his golden *prie-dieu,* faced a golden statue of Christ, and begged God to spare the life of America's first Catholic President.

His prayers continued. The nation's suspense continued. So did mute phone lines, official fears of a plot, and, through the Joint Chiefs' global alert, the quick knotting of the Pentagon's awesome fist. Erratic reactions also continued, triggered by unsuspected inner quirks. The pathetic refusals to accept the facts persisted, though they were being defeated as each passing minute eroded individual defences of denial and misunderstanding. Those who needed solitude paced their lonely rooms and streets, those who required company forged intimate friendships with strangers they would never encounter again, and those capable of speculation wondered about the source of the shots. Nearly all the conjecture led in the same direction. There was little doubt about the political convictions of the sniper. It was assumed that he and his accomplices, whose existence was also assumed, were agents of the Radical Right. This was true even of the surmises of members of the John Birch Society, and next morning thousands of communities would be retelling the story of the local rightist who had been indiscreet enough to express his elation in public. Elation was unwise, anywhere. America was in no mood to tolerate its haters. Men were assaulted, or at the very least insulted, for less than he had done—driving home from the Trade Mart, Treasurer Warren Harding noticed a riflemen's association sticker on the windshield of the automobile behind him; swerving around, Harding blocked the street and placed the driver under citizen's arrest.

On Washington's Massachusetts Avenue Hubert Humphrey, listening to the radio of his parked car, was swept by alternate waves of anger and pity. The targets of his anger were the 'refined Nazis' of Dallas, as he thought of them, and his pity was for the rest of the city, which needed so much 'sympathy and understanding'. Liberty, he wrote in a memorandum to himself the following day, had become licence. Freedom of expression had been 'perverted and abused'; it had been converted into a 'vehicle for vicious propaganda and hatred that inspired people to do such things as happened in

Dallas to our President'. Humphrey was still among the incredulous as he listened to his car radio, but he was beginning to gather the fragments of fact together with perception. He felt sorrow for the Kennedy family, and especially for the widowed First Lady, and in his Saturday memorandum, while events were still fresh in his mind, he recalled his anxieties about the Vice President's health: 'I knew that this would be a terrible blow for him, and I was deeply concerned lest it literally overwhelm him.'

Within a few minutes of 1 p.m. Dallas time, when Kemp Clark pronounced John Kennedy dead, the set in Humphrey's car, like those everywhere, reported that 'Two priests have gone into the hospital where the President is.' The announcement that the President had been shot in the head had been sombre, but this was the first concrete sign of what was to come, and because of the peculiar nature of the communications megaphone the country outside knew it before the emergency area towards which the clergymen were headed. Dr Clark's words had been inaudible outside Trauma Room No. 1. Members of Kennedy's staff in the surgical booths a few yards away were unaware of what had happened, yet the audience of 75 million heard that the clerics had arrived at the entrance of the building. No names were available. They would have been meaningless anyhow. Unlike Cardinal Cushing, Father Oscar Huber and Father James N. Thompson were not towering figures in the Church. Neither had presided at pontifical Mass or knelt upon an ornate *prie-dieu*. They were just parish priests in Dallas who had been summoned because their church was closest to the martyred President, and now, as Clark stepped away from his mutilated scalp, they had finally reached Parkland.

Jacqueline Kennedy moved silently forward, brushing past Dr Burkley, and looked down on the hospital cart. There had been some difficulty with the white sheet. The cloth was too short for the President's long body. The face was visible. From her the skull wound was hidden. His eyes excepted, she couldn't see that anything had happened to him. Below the forehead he was almost entirely natural, and there was no fear in his expression, no indication of agony; on the contrary, his features seemed to convey compassion. It was all in his mouth. The sight transfixed her. Elsewhere in the room there were new sounds—the rolling out of equipment, the clatter of the pedal as used gauze was stuffed into the waste can, the sticky rustle of the transparent winding sheet, the thud of soggy clothes in the shopping bags, Burkley's strangled sobs—but beside the cart the widow was utterly still. To Sergeant Dugger she appeared to be as quiet as her husband. Standing by his broad shoulders, his hand clasped in her hand, she gazed down on the face she had loved and continued to love; and she was there, steady and poised, when the first priest entered.

He entered with a priestly problem. *Si capax*, 'if possible', is often heard when extreme unction is celebrated in emergency rooms. It connotes conditional absolution. If possible, if the soul has not left the body, the priest grants the forgiveness of sins. He can do no more; at the instant of death his authority ends. The cruel issue is: when does a man die? It is a vexing theological question, and Father Oscar Huber had given much thought to it. Long ago, when he administered the last rites to his dying parents, he had decided that it was preposterous to leave the answer in the hands of secular physicans. The needle on an electrocardiograph had little meaning for him. The soul was more durable than that. In his own mind he had worked out a complicated formula which measured the endurance of each soul by the stamina of the body which had sheltered it. If a Catholic succumbed after a long malignancy, for example, the soul left within thirty minutes of the pronouncement of death. Had the man been in the full flush of health, it could linger anywhere from two to three hours. Like many other Church propositions, this one is deceptive. It seems fatuous at first, but on contemplation it grows in wisdom, and the events of the next three days were to vindicate the judgment of the elderly pastor who, at a few minutes past one o'clock Central Standard Time, was convinced that the soul of John Fitzgerald Francis Kennedy had not yet fled.

Si capax—the Latin phrase might have been written across that entire day in Father Huber's calendar. The pastor had come as quickly as he could. Before Agent Ready's call Father James N. Thompson, a six-foot, middle-aged priest, had heard the UPI bulletins in the recreation room of Holy Trinity's rectory. Information was fragmentary, but it was enough: the President had been shot and was being taken to Parkland. Shouting out the news, Father Thompson sprinted to the garage, and he had backed out Holy Trinity's black Galaxie—'Built in Texas by Texans', read the rear-window sticker—when Father Huber arrived.

The three-mile drive would have tested Job. Both priests had been awed by legends of the labyrinthine security precautions surrounding the Presidency, and they suspected that their reversed collars would be insufficient identification. Father Thompson raised the subject. 'Maybe Monsignor Brady will phone ahead and take care of it,' Father Huber said hopefully. 'Oh, no, he won't,' said Father Thompson. The Monsignor was responsible for Baylor Hospital; Parkland was beyond his jurisdiction. Holding the wheel with one hand, Father Thompson fished out his wallet, extracted his World War II ID card, and laid it on the seat. Father Huber regarded it dubiously. It was dog-eared; it looked counterfeit. That it would impress the Secret Service seemed most improbable. Then he looked at the street. They had driven only five blocks, yet they were in a suburban neighbourhood he scarcely knew. 'Which way are you going, Jim?' he cried. 'I have a secret way,' Father Thompson said.

Actually, there was nothing wrong with the route. Though narrow and meandering, it terminated within a half-block of Parkland and should have been a splendid detour from the great volume of traffic building up outside the hospital. But their luck was bad. They were blocked by a truck trying to negotiate a tricky driveway. Back and forth the driver manoeuvred, easing in, stopping, easing out, stopping again. Undaunted, he repeated the approach, his hydraulic brakes hissing while the time drew later and Father Thompson flushed a deeper and deeper red. The truck made it, the Galaxie rocketed into Harry Hines Boulevard, and the Father signalled for a left-hand turn. A policeman waved him on. Rolling down his window, Thompson gesticulated urgently. 'You'll have to move on,' said the officer. 'Look, officer,' said the priest, forgetting his ID card, 'I'm Father Thompson and this is Father Huber, the pastor.' The patrolman shook his head. 'I'm sorry, sir,' he replied mulishly. '*Look,*' Thompson said between his teeth. 'The President is in there, and he's either dead or dying. One of us *has* to go.' Determined not to budge, he reached down and switched off the ignition. He had just taken his fingers off the key when another policeman ran up, shouting, 'Are they priests? Let them through!' But now the car was stalled. Maddened, Father Thompson flooded the carburettor. He waited and prayed. The engine turned over, they wheeled left—and found themselves confronted by the biggest traffic jam either had ever seen. It was 12.57. 'You go ahead,' said Thompson. 'I'll park somewhere and follow.' Father Huber, springing towards the hospital as fast as his septuagenarian legs would carry him, lost his direction and arrived, not outside the ambulance bays, but at Parkland's main entrance. There, at last, he was met. Convoyed by patrolmen, then by agents, the pastor was escorted into the emergency area by General Clifton.

For most people there his arrival was the prelude to the finality of the tragedy. Major Medicine was so constructed that vision was limited to a few feet. Policemen had formed a cordon in the red-striped corridor; the eminent few inside were isolated in the chopped-up booths. Lacking definite word, they had been sitting or standing about in helpless attitudes, in an atmosphere of utter unreality. Severe shock had distorted their senses. One woman, hazarding the guess that the time must be at least 4 p.m., glanced at a clock and was flabbergasted to find herself three hours off. In the absence of hard fact they had drifted along on hope or supposition. Now nearly all saw the black habit of a priest, the universally recognized chevron of death. Its significance swept hall and cubicles. Clifton's eyes met Captain Stoughton's; both officers' eyes filled up. *This is it,* Henry Gonzalez thought, staring at the stocky little pastor. Mac Kilduff whispered to Albert Thomas, 'It looks like he's gone.' Kilduff crossed to Pam Turnure. 'They've called a priest,' he said brokenly. Only Mac Perry didn't notice. He was still sitting in the passage, and the Father walked right past him, but Mac was unaware of it. His brown eyes glazed with exhaustion, his features screwed up in a curiously lopsided cast, the surgeon was concentrating intently on a perfectly blank patch of tile wall.

Father Huber went directly to Jacqueline Kennedy. He murmured his sympathies—he was breathing hard—and took up a position next to her. Uncovering the President's head completely, he drew the purple-and-white ribbons over his own shoulders and chanted:

'Si capax, ego te absolvo a peccatis tuis, in nomine Patris, et Filii, et Spiritus Sancti. Amen.'

'If it is possible, I absolve you from your sins in the name of the Father, and of the Son, and of the Holy Ghost. Amen.'

He opened the cloth container, unscrewed the vial of holy oil, and pressed it to his thumb. Anointing John Kennedy's pale forehead in the sign of the cross, he lifted the moist thumb up and down, back and forth, touching the President at each station:

'Per istam sanctam Unctionem, indulgeat tibi Dominua quid-quid deliquisti. Amen.'

'Through this holy anointing, may God forgive you whatever sins you have committed. Amen.'

The Apostolic Blessing followed:

'Ego facultate mihi ab Apostolica Sede tributa, indulgentiam plenariam et remissionem omnium peccatorum tibi concedo, et benedico te. In nomine Patris, et Filii, et Spiritus Sancti. Amen.'

'I, by the faculty given to me by the Apostolic See, grant to you a plenary indulgence and remission of all sins, and I bless you. In the name of the Father, and of the Son, and of the Holy Ghost. Amen.'

The priest stepped back, finished. In cases of sudden death he had always used the short form of the last anointing, and here he had mechanically followed custom. He hadn't referred to his prayer book once. Dr Burkley blurted out, 'Is that *all*?' The doctor had never challenged a priest before, but the brusque ceremony offended him. It bore an uncomfortable resemblance to the rapid by-the-numbers procedures of the nurses. The passing of a President, he felt, ought to be a more solemn occasion. 'Can't you say some prayers for the dead?' he asked.

Father Huber hurriedly chose several in English. Ordinarily he would have knelt, but the floor, he saw, was one vast bloodstain; he didn't know that Jacqueline Kennedy had already been to her knees here, so he merely folded his hands, inclined his head, and began by murmuring the first half of the Lord's Prayer. The widow and the physician, the only other two Catholics present, responded with the second half. The nurses bowed in silence.

'Hail Mary, full of grace, the Lord is with thee; blessed art thou among women, and blessed is the fruit of thy womb, Jesus,' the pastor then recited.

The two replied, 'Holy Mary, Mother of God, pray for us sinners, now and at the hour of our death. Amen.'

A black shoe shuffled on the threshold. Father Thompson, having abandoned Holy Trinity's car, entered hesitantly. He saw Jacqueline Kennedy's apron of blood, and stepping to the side of the pacemaker machine he started to bless himself. His arms were unaccountably heavy. Bewildered, he hunched and strained and offered a lame sign of the cross:

'Eternal rest grant unto him, O Lord,' the pastor was saying, wiping away the oil from the President's head. The cotton came away stained crimson. Burkley faltered, but the voice of the President's wife was firm. She answered, 'And let perpetual light shine upon him.'

Father Thompson genuflected. He put down a hand to steady himself; it came up wet. Once again he crossed himself in crippled slow motion, forcing his disabled muscles to move. He couldn't imagine what was wrong with his arms.

Mrs Kennedy turned and left; the others followed her. Dr Burkley, near collapse, wandered across the green line, saw Evelyn Lincoln's familiar back, and moaned, 'Oh, Evelyn, he's gone!' Jacqueline Kennedy returned to her folding chair, watched over by the stolid Sergeant Dugger and, briefly, by the pastor. Father Huber had been fine during the rites. They were rote to him. Once he had anointed a child who had been horribly mangled in an accident. The body had been in shreds, yet he had maintained a stoical bearing. In the narrow passage between trauma rooms, however, he started to tremble all over. To the widow he said shakily, 'I am shocked. I want to extend my sympathy and that of my parishioners.'

Her eyes were haunted, but her face was expressionless, 'Thank you for taking care of the President,' she said, her voice a clear, dry whisper. 'Please pray for him.'

Since he had anticipated her most pressing concern, he said

swiftly, 'I am convinced that his soul had not left his body. This was a valid sacrament.'

Her head drooped, then tilted forward. Father Thompson signalled a passing nurse for help, and Father Huber asked, 'Do you want a doctor?' She straightened and smiled vaguely. 'Oh, no,' she said. She did, though. She was at the point of fainting. The nurse brought her a cold towel, and leaning over, she held it right against her forehead until the giddiness passed.

From the doorway of Trauma Room No. 2, vacated since Governor Connally had been moved upstairs, Father Thompson beckoned to Father Huber. They had a professional problem. Physicians could change into mufti and quietly slip out of the hospital. Priests couldn't. Beyond this sanctuary they would be recognized and asked about the President's condition. The wiser course was to wait here as long as they could. Unfortunately, that was not long. The emergency area was resuming its high pitch of activity. Every facility was needed. There could be no exceptions. Everyone who could must leave, every useless article had to be removed. Even Mac Perry was obliged to come back for his sports coat. He asked a nurse to retrieve it from the floor beside the hospital cart, and it was then, at 1.10, that he saw Father Huber for the first time. The two priests were reluctantly emerging into the passage. They brushed against a hatted Franciscan, Father Peter H. Azcoitia from Our Lady of Perpetual Help. The Franciscan, a Mexican, was among the many pastors who had heard news bulletins and hurried to Parkland on their own. In broken English he stammered, 'Glad it was you—not me.'

Father Thompson hovered over Jacqueline Kennedy. He intended to offer his condolences. Like the Sergeant, the priest became conscious of his own clumsiness. He marvelled at her tranquillity and couldn't quite believe in it. No one could be that composed, especially a woman so young. Perhaps, he thought, he should volunteer to return to Washington with her as a silent companion. He dismissed the idea; surely there were others here who were closer to her. Then he wished that he could pick her up and tell her that all this hadn't happened, that it was just a frightful dream.

'Mrs Kennedy,' he began, and ended right there. He lunged back into Trauma Room No. 2 to collect himself.

Father Huber led him out past the cubicles. At the wide door an agent stepped in front of the pastor. He said meaningfully, 'Father, you don't know anything about this.'

Both priests nodded. Yet it wasn't that easy. In the corridor they managed to be as imperturbable as deaf mutes. At the car, however, a group of reporters on the way to the improvised press room sighted their inverted collars. Hugh Sidey led the chase. Father Thompson was behind the wheel, and the old pastor had opened the door, when the correspondents surrounded them. Father Thompson refused to give his name. 'Is he dead?' Sidey asked. Father Huber took a deep breath. He said, 'He's dead, all right.'[12]

He spelled his name for them, and they scurried off. For a long moment the priests sat motionless, the unused Navy ID card between them. Then Father Thompson attempted to shift a leaden wrist. His left palm was sticking to the wheel. Absently he yanked it free and examined it. He said under his breath, 'The blood of a President. *My God.*' He started to bless himself once more and checked the motion. His hand had tightened in anger; it would be sinful to cross himself in such a mood. More to himself than to Father Huber he said, 'Why, you can't even wash blood off a closed fist.' With his right hand he pried the fingers loose. It was difficult. The knuckles were rigid, the fingernails locked underneath; the tendons in his wrist throbbed painfully. Gradually the cramped coil of rage relaxed, and he drove back to the church massaging the joints. To himself he prayed, 'Lord, never let me close my fist again.'

In Holy Trinity's rectory Father Huber opened a shabby black leather volume whose spine bore the gold lettering, '*Sick Call Register*'. The pages were ruled and labelled, like a ledger. Under 'Date' he wrote '22–11–63'; under 'Name', 'Pres. John Kennedy'; under 'Residence', 'Parkland Hospital'. Ministrations were 'Cond. abs., cond. ex., Last B.'—conditional absolution, Extreme Unction, last blessing. The last column, on the far right, was headed 'Remarks'. Usually it was left blank, but he felt this occasion required at least one remark. He thought and thought and then made the simple entry, 'Assassinated in Downtown Dallas'.

No one had thought to switch off the radio in the Vice Presidential convertible, and as Tom Wicker of the *New York Times* walked past the unoccupied car he was startled by a mechanical voice declaiming from its dashboard: 'The President of the United States is dead. I repeat—it has just been announced that the President of the United States is dead.' Wicker vaulted a chain fence and called to Sidey, 'Hugh, the President's dead. Just announced on the radio. I don't know who announced it, but it sounded official to me.' Sidey hung his head. He couldn't talk. Wicker ran on to the press room.

[12] At 1.23 UPI identified Father Huber and reported that he had 'administered the last sacrament of the Church to the President'. His actual words followed. At 1.32 the AP carried the flash, 'Two priests who were with Kennedy say he is dead of bullet wounds.' Father Thompson had said nothing, and bullet wounds had not been mentioned.

There had been no official word, and a report from an unknown priest was not conclusive. Nevertheless a statement could not be postponed indefinitely. It was 1.15 p.m. Death had been pronounced a quarter of an hour ago, and while Father Huber's indiscretion was unknown in the emergency area it was hardly surprising. The secret could not be kept long. Too many people had been in the trauma room.

Kilduff sought out Ken O'Donnell. He asked, 'He's dead, isn't he?'

In a syllable O'Donnell confirmed it.

'This is a terrible time to have to approach you on this,' Kilduff said, 'but the world has got to know that President Kennedy is dead.'

Ken said, 'Well, don't they know it already?'

'No, I haven't told them.'

'Well, you are going to have to make the announcement. Go ahead. But you better check it with Lyndon Johnson.'

An agent guided Kilduff through the white jungle of Minor Medicine. At the end of the last right turn Kilduff saw the broad back of Kennedy's constitutional successor. He cleared his throat and said, 'Mr President.'

It was the first time that anyone had so addressed Johnson. He turned and, according to Kilduff's later recollection, 'looked at me like I was Donald Duck.'

Kilduff asked permission to make a statement. Johnson shook his head. 'No. Wait. We don't know whether it's a Communist conspiracy or not. I'd better get out of here and back to the plane. Are they prepared to get me out of here?'

The Secret Service was prepared, and he knew it, but he wanted to be certain he had left Parkland before reporters were informed. After a flurry of conferences with agents Kilduff understood. At 1.20 he approached Johnson again and told him, 'I am going to make the announcement as soon as you leave.'

'Yes,' said Johnson. 'As soon as I leave you announce the death.'

Kilduff walked out the emergency entrance with him. As soon as they reached the sunlight, reporters bayed, 'What can you tell us?' Lowering his head, Kilduff bulled through them and plodded off across the grass, towards classrooms 101–102. He thought he was alone. He wasn't—Ted Clifton, who hadn't regained his stability, was stalking him with the hazy notion that he might be needed as a witness—and on re-entering the far end of the hospital Kilduff was hailed stridently by Merriman Smith and Jacky Bell. The wire service men had just relinquished their precious phones. Now, learning that fresh news was imminent, they hopped around, demanding answers. Kilduff declined to be goaded. He kept shaking his head doggedly, repeating that he would say nothing until the conference began.

Until an hour ago classrooms 101–102 had resembled a double study hall in a modern high school. The walls were panelled with bright green chalk-boards. Desks stood in tidy ranks, and the sole incongruity, a hospital bed in the left front corner, was covered with a sanitary canopy of plastic. Across the front board someone—perhaps a member of the staff who had heard garbled references to 'Lakeland' and 'Southland'—had neatly written the name 'Parkland'. On other afternoons the chalked words were more clinical. Student nurses sat primly behind the desks and learned hospital drill. Now the hall was crowded with agitated reporters. A few seconds ago Hugh Sidey had told them of his carside interview with Father Huber. There was little doubt in anyone's mind about the nature of the coming announcement. Still, it wasn't official yet, and as Kilduff slowly mounted the dais scattered voices yelled 'Quiet! Quiet!'

There was quiet. And then Kilduff, red-eyed and tremulous, was unable to speak. Incoherently he thought, *Well, this is the first press conference on a road trip I have ever had to hold.* He started to tell them that and held his tongue. It really wasn't news. Instead, he said, 'Excuse me, let me catch my breath.' He caught it. There was another, longer pause. A full minute had passed. Clifton, scrutinizing him with hooded eyes, was of the opinion that he would never be able to talk, that no statement would be issued, that they all might sit there for ever. Kilduff, like Father Thompson, was fighting a cramp. Puckering and rocking slightly, he thought, *All right, what am I going to say, and how am I going to say it?*

The words were framed. They would not be eloquent, but they would do the job. At 1.33 he moistened his lips. 'President John F. Kennedy——'

'Hold it!' called a cameraman, and a lens clicked.

'President John F. Kennedy died at approximately one o'clock Central Standard Time today here in Dallas.'

There was a rush towards the hall. The wire men were off again. Peter Geilich, a Parkland administrative assistant, leaped aside to avoid being trampled. They reminded Geilich of movie reporters rushing out to grab the nearest telephones. Unluckily for them, it wasn't that pat. The nearest phones were useless. All outgoing lines had been snared by Bales; Smith and Bell battled the ensnarled switchboard in vain while a woman out-foxed both. Virginia Payette, a former reporter who had married the local UPI manager, dropped a dime in a second-floor pay phone. At 1.35 UP bells chimed on teletype machines around the world:

FLASH

PRESIDENT KENNEDY DEAD

JT135PCS

'He died,' Kilduff had meantime continued, 'of a gunshot wound in the brain. I have no other details regarding the assassination of the President. Mrs Kennedy was not hit. Governor Connally was hit. The Vice President was not hit.'

Wicker started to ask him about the swearing in of Johnson and broke down. Kilduff, grasping the sense of the question, tried to answer it. He began to cry. Nevertheless the subject seemed too significant to be dropped, and another correspondent rose.

'Has the Vice President taken the oath of office?'

'No. He has left,' Kilduff replied.

He stepped aside for a break. In a show of bravado he lit a cigarette; his lighter flame quivered violently. He yearned for an excuse to adjourn the meeting. It was impossible. Reporters were clamouring for a medical briefing. He saw Sidey's face and hoarsely called to him, 'I can't do it.' Yet he thought it logical; like them he was remembering Eisenhower's heart attack. Actually, the precedent wasn't valid—Eisenhower had survived—but putting a doctor on this platform seemed to be the next step. He nodded listlessly and promised to do what he could. Unhappily, he didn't know the names of any of the physicians who had treated President Kennedy. He couldn't even find his way back through the building. Taking a white-coated attendant aside, he asked directions, and the man led him through the long halls like a keeper.

In the emergency area he explained the situation to Dr Burkley. Burkley, like Clifton, was still adrift. He asked vapidly, 'Did you tell the press I was with the President when he died?' Taken aback, Kilduff replied that he had. Burkley bobbed off erratically and fetched Mac Perry. Three other physicians later joined Perry in 101–102, but he bore the brunt of the briefing, and it was harrowing. The scene was bedlam. Several correspondents were hysterical. A question would be asked, and the doctor would be halfway through his answer when another reporter broke in with an entirely different question. Misquotations were inevitable. Had the scene been calm and orderly, the results would still have been unfortunate, however, for none of the doctors, Perry included, had thoroughly examined the President. Because they had failed to turn him over—in Carrico's later words, 'Nobody really had the heart to do it'—they hadn't seen his back. To them the throat wound suggested that one of the shots had come from the front. Reporters who drew that conclusion weren't to blame. They hadn't seen the body. Perry, who had, was their source.

Under any circumstances the possibilities for muddle in gunshot cases are almost infinite. Abraham Lincoln, like John Kennedy, was shot in the posterior part of the head. Because Booth's nineteenth-century weapon was low-powered his victim survived for nine hours and the .44 calibre derringer ball of Britannia metal did not shatter his head; a one-inch disc of bone was driven three inches into the brain, and the ball lodged in his skull. In other respects the fatal wounds of the two Presidents are similar though, and the medical reports of April 1865, like Perry's, were baffling. Lincoln's assassin had approached him from the right side, yet the derringer ball entered his head from the left. Perplexity and unfounded rumours persisted until the conspirators' trial, when one of the witnesses testified that the President, attracted by something in the pit of the theatre, had twisted his head sharply leftward and downward at the last moment. Medical briefings are supposed to quash such misunderstandings. The one at Parkland did exactly the opposite. Perry was asked whether one bullet could have struck the President from the front. He replied, 'Yes, it is conceivable.' Sidey, realizing the implications, cried, 'Doctor, do you realize what you're doing? You're confusing us.' It was too late. By the following morning millions were convinced that a rifleman had fired from the top of the underpass, and in many parts of the world the conviction is established truth today.

The press rightly divided the bewildering montage of events into two main stories: the assassination and the succession. During Kilduff's trip to the emergency area and again after the briefing they speculated about where Johnson would take the oath. According to Robert Donovan of the Los Angeles *Times*, 'The consensus immediately prevailed, of course, he would take it in Dallas, because in the kind of world we are living in you can't have the United States without a President, even in the time it takes to get from Dallas to Washington.' Here the reporters must be faulted. There is no evidence that any of them challenged the assumption that the office of President of the United States was vacant. In perspective this is amazing, for the seasoned White House correspondents in 101–102 had covered the inauguration on January 20, 1961. They should have recalled that the correct answer to the question 'Has the Vice President taken the oath of office?' was affirmative; he had sworn that he would, to the best of his ability, 'preserve, protect, and defend the Constitution of the United States' that frosty noon on the

Hill nearly three years before. Indeed, he had, in accordance with custom, done so before John Kennedy.

In 1963, when the warning time for nuclear missiles from the Soviet Union had been reduced to less than a quarter-hour, *any* Presidential hiatus was intolerable. There ought to have been no interregnum. That one existed must be traced to men's minds, not to the law of the land. The most brutal murder in American history seemed to be the paramount fact that Friday afternoon. It overwhelmed everyone, and the stunned nation demanded to know the identity of the assassin. No one at the press conference thought to ask the identity of the man who, at that very moment, occupied the mightiest office in the world. Yet there was an answer. The Presidency, like an immortal heart, never stops. America had a new Chief Executive. His name was Lyndon Baines Johnson, and although even he did not realize it, he had been in power for over an hour.

4

VOLUNTEER

In the White House Situation Room Commander Oliver Hallett told Crown to bring the Cabinet plane straight back to the capital, with no Dallas stop, and in the communications shack west of Hawaii Pierre Salinger heard an even voice say—'From Stranger to Wayside. You are to turn around——' the turn had been completed, but the Situation Room didn't know that—'and come back immediately to Washington'. Salinger repeated it slowly. Dean Rusk looked around in bewilderment. 'Who is Stranger?' he asked. 'Who's in Washington?' Lacking a code book, his fellow passengers aboard Aircraft 86972 could only stare. Actually, the cipher would have been of little help. 'Stranger' was literally a stranger. He was Major H. R. Patterson, an obscure officer in the White House Communications Agency's net control. Like their fellow careerists in other sensitive agencies, Commander Hallett and Major Patterson were acting because the need for action was evident and the government was in a state of temporary paralysis. The Presidency abhors a vacuum. Its powers require constant exercise. Should the Chief Executive be inactive, relatively little men start taking over at once. Their motives aren't selfish; they merely believe that certain steps are necessary, that the orb of authority must be wielded by someone. And they are quite right. The alternative is anarchy.

Had Vice President Johnson assumed the office of President at 1 p.m. in Parkland, there would have been no void. The transition would have been immediate. The fact that he failed to do so may be traced to the riddle of Presidential succession, which had confounded constitutional scholars for 122 years. The American Constitution, that imperfect classic, specifies in Article II, Section 1, Clause 5, that 'In Case of the Removal of the President from Office, or of his Death, Resignation, or Inability to discharge the Powers and Duties of the said Office, the Same shall devolve on the Vice President'—a solecism which should have made the Founding Fathers blush. What is meant by 'the Same'? If the phrase to which it refers is 'Powers and Duties', then the Vice President remains Vice President, exercising those powers and performing those duties until the people can choose a new President. We know now that this was the desire of the men who framed the Constitution. The notes of James Madison, published long after his death, provide a cogent record of the secret deliberations of 1787. The founders never intended that any man should become Chief Executive unless he had been elected to that office. The wording they approved stated that in the event of the death of an incumbent the Vice President should serve as acting President 'until another President be chosen'. This unequivocal provision was then dropped by the Constitutional Convention's five-man committee on style, which made constitutional interpretation the art of the impossible. It is worth noting that the most perceptive analysis of the two versions of II, 1, 5 was written by the sixty-eighth Attorney General, Robert F. Kennedy, in 1961.[1] Robert Kennedy concluded that it was the sense of the Convention that should a President die in office 'merely the powers and duties devolve on the Vice President, not the office itself'.

But the Madison papers appeared too late. The second possible antecedent for 'the Same'—'the said Office'—had become hallowed by precedent. In 1841 William Henry Harrison caught cold during his inauguration and became the first American Chief Executive to die in office. His Vice President, John Tyler, learned the news while playing marbles with his children in Williamsburg, Virginia. Tyler, who didn't know about Madison's notes, never doubted that he was entitled to occupy 'the said Office'. Several eminent American statesmen dissented, notably Henry Clay and former President John Quincy Adams, who, on April 16, 1841, seven days after Tyler's inaugural address, made acid reference in his diary to 'Mr Tyler, who styles himself President . . . and not Vice President acting as President'. Tyler, however, had powerful allies, chiefly Secretary of State Daniel Webster, and he had already moved into the White House. Time and custom were working for him. By the end of June even Adams was calling him 'Mr President'.

During the next century death elevated six more Vice Presidents —Millard Fillmore, Andrew Johnson, Chester Arthur, Theodore Roosevelt, Calvin Coolidge, and Harry Truman—and the claims of each to 'the said Office' were uncontested. The Tyler precedent held, despite grumblings that few running mates to emerge from conventions were big enough to lead the ticket. Roosevelt and Truman excepted, the six were an uninspiring and undistinguished group. In

[1] *Opinions of the Attorneys General*, XLII, No. 5 (August 2, 1961), 9–10. Most of Kennedy's scholarly research on this matter was the work of Nick Katzenbach.

the words of one scholar, the Vice Presidency was 'a comfortable sinecure with which to honour some of the country's more able politicians'. The qualifications of the second office in the land bore little relationship to the demands of the first. Nevertheless the silent engine of succession was still there, waiting to be used. Tyler had led the way. Succession had, in effect, become automatic.

Or almost automatic. Tyler did something else which acquired a special significance in Dallas. His action arose from the realization that men like Adams were certain to contest his right to occupy the White House. When he picked up his marbles in Williamsburg, convinced in his own mind that he was already the tenth President of the United States, he was aware that Article II, Section 1, Clause 7, of the Constitution stipulated that a Chief Executive, 'before he enter on the Execution of his Office', must swear or affirm his support of that Constitution. Although he had already done that as Vice President, he resolved to make assurance doubly sure. Leading the Cabinet to the Indian Queen Hotel on Pennsylvania Avenue, he repeated the pledge on April 6, 1841. It was administered by Chief Justice William Cranch of the District of Columbia Circuit Court, who immediately afterwards signed an affidavit setting forth the legal situation. The document declared that Harrison's successor deemed himself qualified to take over 'without any other oath than that which he has taken as Vice President', but that he had asked to be sworn in again 'as doubts may arise, and for greater caution'.

John Tyler has much to answer for. Apart from annexing Texas and taming the Seminoles he did little for his country during the next four years, and in tightening his grip on the Presidency at the Indian Queen Hotel he had left an exasperating constitutional trap for Fillmore, Johnson, Arthur, Roosevelt, Coolidge, and Truman, all of whom fell into it. No one remembered Cranch's affidavit. The document was filed away in the National Archives and forgotten. But everyone recalled the dramatic oath, and each of the six men who was to stand in Tyler's shoes felt obliged to repeat it. An act undertaken 'for greater caution' was magnified out of all proportion. The ceremonies, conducted while the grieving republic mourned its fallen leaders, became folklore, and the very Bibles on which the new Chief Executives rested their hands were integrated into the myth. The Constitution, of course, mentions the Bible nowhere.

In time of crisis the pull of myth increases tenfold. On November 22, 1963, the typical American, like the typical correspondent in 101–102, was under the impression that the oath was mandatory. He still is. His leaders (though lamentably few of them have thought the matter through) are divided. Speaker John McCormack, who with Kennedy's death became next in line of succession, echoes the popular misconception. He thinks Johnson had to be sworn in as soon as possible 'because the country had to have a President'. Chief Justice Warren agrees. The oath is needed in such circumstances, he argues, to put the new leader's dedication to the Constitution on record. Reminded that Johnson had taken the vow at the Kennedy inaugural, he replies, 'But he didn't take it as President.'[2]

The weight of informed opinion lies on the other side. Barefoot Sanders, who was the U.S. Attorney on the spot, thinks Johnson became President the moment Kennedy died. So does Robert Kennedy; so does Nicholas de B. Katzenbach, who followed Kennedy as the sixty-ninth Attorney General. Hubert H. Humphrey, whom Johnson chose as his own Vice President, declared emphatically, 'A Vice President becomes President when there is no President. Later, when he takes the oath, he puts on the cloak of office. But that act is purely symbolic.' Former President Eisenhower takes the strongest position of all. In the view of Eisenhower—who scorns the second oath—Johnson became Chief Executive the moment it was obvious that Kennedy was dying; that is, before Kemp Clark pronounced him dead. The former President believes that Johnson was entitled to sign legislation at any time after 12.30 Central Standard Time. Had a national emergency arisen between then and 2.38 p.m., when he took that second oath, and had Johnson failed to act, Eisenhower holds that he would have been derelict in his duty and subject to impeachment.

The cadre of professionals who serve the Presidency is similarly split, though they, too, are inclined to dismiss the oath as inconsequential. Because the Secret Service White House Detail lacked forceful leadership on November 22, individual agents are vague. Former Chief Wilson is a more vigorous witness than any of them. When Franklin Roosevelt died, Wilson left one man with Mrs Roosevelt and immediately reassigned all others, including those who had been guarding the President's grandchildren, to Truman. 'As far as the Service is concerned,' Wilson declares, 'when a President dies the Vice President becomes President at once, and all protection goes to him and his family.' Colonel McNally of the White House Communications Agency concurs: 'It sounds cold-blooded, but the instant President Kennedy died, communications-wise he disappeared off the face of the earth. Oath of office or not, Lyndon Johnson was President in our eyes and head of the government.'

[2] The implication is that a Vice President's loyalty may diminish during his service in the Vice Presidency. It is possible. But then, a President's loyalty might shrink during his Presidency. If the country cannot assume that a man elected to national office will honour his sworn word, the foundations of the government are reduced to sludge.

It is improbable that Johnson had considered these complex issues before a blaze of gunfire confronted him with them. Over a year and a half afterwards he informed this writer that it was his opinion that 'the Vice President becomes President immediately upon the death of the President. He is obligated thereafter to take the oath of office, but there is no lapse in the powers of the Presidency.' Having taken the second oath, he perhaps felt an obligation to defend it. Otherwise the statement conforms with judicial opinion. However, it was made after the full ramifications of the question had been laid before him. In Dallas, he conceded, he had felt differently. Although 'immediately aware' of his new responsibilities, the 'full realization', the 'subjective identification' of himself as Chief Executive, 'came gradually'.

Perhaps anticipation of the consequences of a President's death should be obligatory for Vice Presidents, but it wouldn't come easily. There is little evidence that Johnson's seven predecessors had given the matter much thought. The attitude of national politicians towards the White House is highly ambivalent; they simultaneously crave it and recoil from it. Vice Presidents, like Presidents, are loath to dwell upon the fact that they are a heartbeat away from the executive mansion, and when the beat suddenly stops they are dumbfounded. 'I don't know if any of you fellows ever had a load of hay or a bull fall on him,' Truman told reporters on April 14, 1945, 'but last night the whole weight of the moon and stars fell on me'.

Truman's reaction should be mulled over if the Dallas transition is to be put in perspective. When the news arrived from Warm Springs, with which he had no connection, he was in Washington. His predecessor had died peacefully. There had been no violence. Johnson's plight, on the other hand, was ghastly. The President had been visiting the Vice President's home grounds, and in twenty-four hours the Connally–Yarborough feud had transformed the trip into a Johnsonian disaster. At 12.29 p.m. his career was at a low ebb. He sat sluggishly in the back seat of his convertible, insensitive to the cheers around him, seeking refuge in the blare of a dashboard radio. His prestige had come apart, and for the moment he had apparently abandoned hope of reassembling it. Then, sixty seconds later, the elected President and his lady lay in a welter of blood, and Lyndon Johnson was the leader of the nation.

In the moment it takes to drive over a crack of grey Texas asphalt his life and his country's history had been transformed. He had no way of knowing why it had happened, but he had been a political creature since youth. The instant his antennae began to sweep the scene he had to deal with the stupendous fact that, in the eyes of the United States and the world beyond, a Texas murder had put a

Texan in power. The catastrophe had struck him harder than any other man in Dallas. If he was mesmerized, if some of his actions were incomprehensible, the nature of that unprecedented shock has to be borne in mind constantly, and to recapture its impact on him the reel of events must be wound back to 12.36 p.m., when Lady Bird, after a frightened glance at the pink blur at SS 100 X, darted into the hospital behind the wedge of agents surrounding her husband.

At 12.36 p.m., Bertha L. Lozano, R.N., had been on duty at the emergency area's Triage desk, where emergency cases were sorted and routed to appropriate treatment areas. This outpost, halfway down the main corridor between the ambulance dock and the wide door leading to Major Medicine, commanded all approaches to surgery. Any unexpected arrival would have to pass here, and Nurse Lozano was a seasoned lookout. Unfortunately, the distraught switchboard had neglected to inform her that President Kennedy had just been shot on Elm Street. According to her account, she was unaware of anything unusual until 'I suddenly heard a door open, and an unaccountable number of Dallas policemen screamed at me for help and to bring a carriage.' Wheeling in a stretcher from O.B.-Gyn., she returned to a corridor packed with yelling policemen. A litter rolled past bearing a patient whose face and head were covered with a suit coat; then she was engulfed by a mass of shoving men. Abruptly the mass parted. She found herself face to face with Lyndon Johnson, 'and when I looked at him, recognizing him, I suddenly sensed who our patient on the carriage might be'.

If Johnson had followed a direct route he would have reached the Triage desk well before the body of John Kennedy, but neither he nor his bodyguards had known which way to turn. Two prominent doors facing the dock from outside were permanently locked. Beyond the real entrance, to the left, lay an exasperating series of choices: a lobby, a waiting-room, the blood bank, two flights of stairs. To Rufus Youngblood and Emory Roberts, preoccupied with thoughts of a plot, every room looked like a trap. Youngblood appealed to Miss Lozano for a quiet place. She led them into Minor Medicine.

Lady Bird followed with mounting alarm. In the car she had discounted Yarborough's cries, but the agents around Lyndon could not be ignored. Until today the Secret Service had provided him with only token protection. Obviously this was the real thing. Their concern was infectious, and the maze they were following multiplied her fear. *Right, left, right, left,* she thought; every gleaming hospital wall was the same. She couldn't possibly retrace her steps without help—they were almost entirely dependent upon the strange woman in starched white. Furthermore, Youngblood, in securing the area, was eliminating the few landmarks which might have been useful. A Negro man lay in a bed to their left. 'Move him,' Youngblood told the nurse, and to Agents Kivett, McIntyre, and Bennett he said, 'Close all blinds.'

When the Johnsons drew up at the end of a ward they had the impression that they had reached the interior of the hospital. Actually they had been following a great circle. Had the shade in the ward's single window been raised, they would have discovered that they were standing just a few feet from the ambulance dock. Nurse Lozano had taken Youngblood at his word: Minor Medicine's Booth 13 was the quietest place on the floor. But the reason it was unoccupied was that it was adjacent to the emergency area entrance. That wasn't quite what Youngblood had had in mind. If a second assassin had trailed the motorcade here—and in the turmoil his only difficulty would have been finding a place to park—his prospects of success would have been fairly good. Although he couldn't have seen his target, the window by Booths 12 and 13 was the only one on the first floor of that side of the building, and its drawn blind attracted further attention to it. Little cunning would have been required to guess that inside, within range of an automatic weapon or a grenade, stood Kennedy's successor.

He stood with his broad shoulders braced against a blank wall, sniffing from a vapour inhaler that he always carried to clear his nasal passages. Bowing his head, he pinched one nostril, breathed deeply, then repeated the process. There was no conversation. He, his wife, and his bodyguards were speechless. Lady Bird was resting her back against the tangential wall, watching him. 'Lyndon and I didn't speak,' she recalled later. 'We just *looked* at each other, exchanging messages with our eyes. We knew what it might be.'

Nevertheless they weren't sure. They waited indecisively, craving information like everyone else. Johnson sent an agent for Roy Kellerman. After the inevitable wrong turns and misadventures the man blundered into Major Medicine and came back with Kellerman. 'Roy, can you tell me the condition of the President?' Johnson asked. Kellerman replied, 'President Kennedy has been hit. He is still alive. The condition is not good.' Johnson asked, 'Will you keep me advised?' and Roy answered, 'Yes, sir.' He meant to keep his promise, but he never saw that part of the floor again; when he returned to Major Surgery, his hands were full.

Ken O'Donnell thrust his head into Booth 13. 'It looks pretty black,' he said. 'I think the President is dead.'

Johnson didn't reply. Now he could only wait.

In the interlude men gravitated towards him. The first newcomer was Agent Johns. Skirting the cashier's cage, where Merriman Smith was holed up dictating, Johns ran past the vacant Triage desk. Outside the wide door leading to Major Medicine he nearly collided with Art Bales. 'Are you the bagman? Stay here,' John gasped, racing on. Bales sent Gearhart, the real bagman, into Minor Medicine, where, because he was unknown to the Vice Presidential detail, he was kept secluded in Booth 8, from which the Negro patient was being evacuated, until Emory Roberts saw him and identified him.[3] Cliff Carter, a more familiar figure to the agents, was sent straight in, and four Congressmen—Thomas, Brooks, Thornberry, Gonzalez—loitered uncertainly in the passage between hospital beds. Henry Gonzalez had been wandering through the labyrinth of halls when Carter plucked his sleeve and said, 'Why don't you go see the Vice President? I'm worried about him.' He pointed the way, and the Congressman peered into Booth 13. There seemed to be nothing wrong. Johnson was just standing there, sniffing. Gonzalez asked an agent, 'Is Mrs Kennedy badly hurt?' The man said, 'No, it's the President. She's all right.' Henry inquired, 'How is the President?' The agent replied, 'Bad,' and Henry said, 'Oh, gosh.'

Others beside Gonzalez had mistaken the identity of the victims. Leaving Larry O'Brien, Jack Brooks had immediately sought out the Vice President. To Carter he said, 'How's Lyndon?' Carter answered, 'He's OK, but the President's pretty bad.' A low voice muttered, 'He's dead, Jack.' Brooks decided to stay put. One place was as good as another, and in those early minutes all accounts were equally valid. Later, sorting out their recollections, individuals would usually remember who first told them that the President was dead. What they forgot was that at the same time they were hearing other, unfounded bits of information, and it was this atmosphere of doubt that sent them scampering towards every corner of the floor, including Johnson's. One of the first rumours to sweep the hospital was simply, 'Everybody's been shot.' It reached Jack Price, and he was systematically checking the entire emergency area. The search was slow going. Nurse Lozano, his sentry, was still absent on vital errands, and her chair had been taken over by a hysterical mother with a two-year-old boy bleeding from a small cut. Peering into Minor Medicine, Price caught a glimpse of Mrs Johnson's white,

[3] During the Eisenhower administration there had been two bagmen, and in January 1961 Captain E. Peter Aurand, USN, Naval Aide to the outgoing President, briefed Captain Tazewell Shepard on the nature of the satchel which had accompanied Richard Nixon. Shepard packed a bag and sent it to the office of the new Vice President by courier. An aide returned it with the explanation that Johnson did not want it.

strained face. As he hurried forward an agent stepped from Booth 13 and said curtly, 'He's OK.'

It was a time of tension, of fright—after Elm Street, anything could happen—and of strangeness. The place itself was strange. Even those members of the Presidential party who were from Dallas (Baskin, Marie Fehmer) were unfamiliar with Parkland. It was inhabited by oddly dressed people. Minor Medicine, like Major Medicine, surrounded the visitors with hundreds of yards of taut white sheets, behind which unidentifiable voices held peculiar conversations. Jack Brooks never found out who had said, 'He's dead, Jack.' Similarly, Henry Gonzalez overheard a man, apparently talking to a telephone, say, impatiently, 'Yes, yes, yes, I saw him. It's all over with, I tell you, I saw the body! It's over!' *What* body? Henry wondered. *What* was all over? He was puzzling over this when a nurse in an operating gown hurried up with two paper bags. 'Who do I give these to?' she asked, her voice muffled by her surgical mask. Gonzalez and Cliff Carter came forward. 'The Governor's personal effects,' she explained, handing a bag to each. 'They have to be signed for.' Carter's signature passed unchallenged, but for some reason she eyed Henry stonily. 'Who are you?' she demanded. 'This is Congressman Gonzalez,' Carter said, introducing him. She stalked off wordlessly, and the Congressman noticed that blood was seeping from the bottom of his bag.

Gonzalez wasn't horrified. He was past that, and grateful to be of use. Here, as elsewhere in the emergency area, the search for something to do had become intense. Carter scurried off to a vending machine and brought coffee to the Johnsons. Lady Bird, who always carried notebooks to record what she called her 'never-to-be-forgotten moments', had produced one from her purse and was rapidly writing down her impressions. Thornberry was also making notes, and Youngblood was in constant motion. He acquired two folding chairs for his charges—Lyndon sat briefly, then resumed his hunched stance, switching the inhaler from nostril to nostril—and he said to Bird, 'I want you to give me the current whereabouts of Lynda and Lucy.' Lucy, she told him, was at Washington's National Cathedral School for Girls, on Wisconsin Avenue; Lynda was in the Kinsolving Dormitory at the University of Texas. Youngblood said to Kivett, 'Call the chief in Washington and the Austin Secret Service office. Put the girls under protection.'

Another agent asked Youngblood to make a call. 'I'm not leaving this man for anybody,' he said crisply. He did, however, want to leave Parkland. From the moment they reached the ambulance dock he had been plotting a getaway. Not only the hospital, but the entire city had become an abomination to him. He was a man of exceptionally strong will, and he felt strongly that he couldn't meet his responsibilities to Johnson as long as they remained here. To Youngblood Dallas was a place of violence and death. Staying in it was an insane risk. Love Field was the obvious escape hatch; they should head there immediately. Emory Roberts was of the same opinion, and the two agents pressed their view on Johnson.

To them the issue seemed simple. Yet in it lay the first germ of what later became a series of misunderstandings. For those who had been close to the slain President, it was impossible fully to appreciate the tremendous shock, the sudden pressure, inflicted on the new President. While he had already succeeded to the office, he didn't realize it, and the slumped figure in Booth 13 bore little resemblance to the shrewd, assured President Johnson the country later came to know. Within a few months he was to become the despair of the Secret Service, the President who rode roughshod over agents and disregarded their advice. In Parkland all that lay ahead. Dazed, silent, he was far readier to take orders than to issue them. His poise had dissolved. In a feeble whisper he said to Thornberry, 'This is a time for prayer if there ever was one, Homer.'

Two factors increased his muddle. Johnson wasn't the only man incapable of coping with the fact of his succession. Kennedy's grieving staff couldn't bear to face it either. As Air Force Aide to the President, Godfrey McHugh was the logical man to co-ordinate air transport back to Andrews Field. Twice agents asked him to speak to Johnson, and each time he refused, merely pointing out that the Vice President had his own plane. The second factor was the absence of Jerry Behn, the Head of the Secret Service White House Detail. In deciding that he would not make each Presidential trip Behin had not only broken precedent; he had left his agents without a leader. Had he been present, the bodyguards in Minor Surgery would never have dreamed of acting without his consent. But Behn was in the East Wing of the White House, gripping a telephone receiver and awaiting news from Roy Kellerman. Kellerman was his deputy. It is conceivable that a more tenacious deputy might have imposed authority over all the Secret Service men in Dallas, though that point is moot; Youngblood had the bit in his teeth. Of all the agents there he had the quickest tongue and one of the clearest minds. He had Johnson's confidence. He and Roberts had a plan, and neither was in the mood to defer to Kellerman. Indeed, they didn't even consult him. Although Roy was the agent in charge at Parkland, he wasn't told that the new President was to be taken from the hospital. During the next half-hour he talked with both Youngblood and Roberts. Somehow the subject never came up. Only later, by chance, did he learn from his men that Johnson had already left.

In Booth 13 Youngblood and Roberts opened the campaign with the new President after Kellerman's return to Major Medicine. Roberts told Johnson that he had seen Kennedy's head wound. 'The President won't make it,' he said. 'Let's get out of here.'

Youngblood said, 'We don't know the scope of this thing. We should get away from here immediately.'

'Is Carswell possible?' Johnson asked hesitantly.

It wasn't; Youngblood sent Lem Johns out to ask a local policeman the route there, and when Johns returned everyone agreed that the SAC base was too far.

'We've got to get in the air,' Roberts persisted.

Still hesitant, Johnson said, 'Maybe President Kennedy will need the aeroplane.'

This was a second germ of misunderstanding. No one asked which aeroplane he had in mind. It may be (as Roberts and Johns later came to believe) that the talk of Carswell had confused them, leading them to think that the Vice President's plane was being moved there. It is equally possible that the agents, like the man they guarded, were drawn by the halo the press had given Angel. In any event, the subsequent discussions in the booth seem to have been based on the assumption that only one Boeing 707 was parked at Love Field. In reality the situation there was unchanged. Neither 26000 nor 86970 had been moved. Each carried the same equipment, both were guarded. Nevertheless, from this point forward the backup plane was forgotten. Johnson and his agents thought only of 26000, Angel, Air Force One—the aircraft identified with John F. Kennedy.

Johnson was reluctant to leave. He did not want to seem presumptuous, he said, and he told the agents that he would not move without approval from a member of Kennedy's staff, preferably Ken O'Donnell. Roberts sought out O'Donnell in Major Medicine. 'Johnson wants to go,' he said. 'Is it OK if he uses the plane?' O'Donnell nodded—a gesture to be borne in mind in the light of the subsequent confusion—and Roberts reported back to Johnson, 'Ken says it's OK.'

Youngblood continued to hammer away. 'We don't know what type of conspiracy this is, or who else is marked. The only place we can be sure you are safe is Washington.'

Over the past half-hour there had been a build-up of information. Kellerman had prepared them for the worst; O'Donnell had appeared in the booth with what Lady Bird described in her notebook as 'that stricken face'. Everyone in the ward knew that Jack Ready had phoned for a priest, and now Roberts recrossed the corridor for fresh reports from Trauma Room No. 1. At 1.13 p.m. he reappeared before Johnson.

'The President is dead, sir,' he said.

The new President felt, as he later put it, 'shocked and sickened'. He glanced at his watch. To Lady Bird and Cliff Carter he said, 'Make a note of the time.' Then he said to his wife, 'We're leaving. We'll go as quietly as possible.'

It was evident that they would also go swiftly. Johnson instructed Carter to round up Jack Valenti, Liz Carpenter, and Marie Fehmer, and Youngblood told Johns, 'Get an unmarked car and find a policeman who knows Dallas like the back of his hand.'

Events were moving rapidly when Lady Bird intervened. Her first reaction to Roberts' announcement had been wild anger. A choking sensation followed. Her emotions were in violent conflict. In her words, 'Nobody ever had to shift gears so fast. One minute I had been thinking about the ranch, and now *this*.'

'Can I——' she began. She paused and said firmly, 'I must go see Mrs Kennedy and Nellie.'

Her husband not only agreed; he wanted to accompany her. Youngblood, however, was still very much in command, and when he told the new President that he could not leave this ward, Johnson dropped the idea. Roberts was sent over once again to ask Jacqueline Kennedy whether she would see Lady Bird. Leaning over her, he asked, 'Is it all right for Mrs Johnson to come and say hello?' She nodded, and he brought Lady Bird over. Congressman Jack Brooks tagged along as a spare guard.

In their absence Ken O'Donnell made a second trip to Booth 13 and confirmed Kennedy's death to Johnson. The conversation that followed is a matter of dispute. According to Johnson, O'Donnell twice urged him to board Air Force One. It is Johnson's recollection that he consented, with the stipulation that he would wait there until Mrs Kennedy and President Kennedy's body were brought to the plane. O'Donnell declares this version to be 'absolutely, totally, and unequivocally wrong'. He says that Johnson raised the possibility of a conspiracy and that 'I agreed that he should get out of there as soon as possible.' Then, he recalls, 'He asked me whether they should move the plane—meaning, I thought, Air Force Two—to Carswell Air Force Base. I said no: It was thirty-five miles to the Air Force base and it would take too long to move the plane. Besides, no one would know that he was going from Parkland Hospital to Love Field anyway; they had no way of knowing.' Concerning 26000, O'Donnell says, 'The President and I had no conversation regarding Air Force One. If we had known that he was going on Air

Force One, we would have taken Air Force Two. One plane was just like another.'

Youngblood supports Johnson, but O'Donnell was clearly dumbfounded when, an hour later, he encountered the Johnsons on 26000. It is entirely possible that Johnson mentioned 'the plane' to O'Donnell in connection with Carswell, and that the new President, remembering Roberts' report of his own conversation with O'Donnell, thought that he and Ken were talking about the same plane. What is highly unlikely is that O'Donnell would have suggested that Johnson await Mrs Kennedy when a second aircraft was available. Ken knew Johnson was anxious to take off immediately. He also knew that President Kennedy's widow would not depart without his body and that she would, therefore, be delayed. Despite his shock O'Donnell would have instantly realized that the two were irreconcilable. The discrepancy between the two versions is probably a consequence of confusion though there is an alternative. The new Commander in Chief may have been determined to maintain the closest possible association with the fallen Commander in Chief during what might well become a national emergency, and he may have supposed that O'Donnell understood and shared his concern. This is subtle and intricate, but Johnson in full possession of his faculties is a subtle and intricate man. There is no way to pinpoint the exact moment that he regained control of himself that Friday afternoon. By all reports, including his own, he was still under Youngblood's influence when they left Booth 13. He did not really become his own man until he reached Love Field. However, he may have had earlier thoughts about the value of identifying himself with what he called 'the aura of Kennedy', and in the light of certain remarks he made to associates the next day this construction upon his exchange with O'Donnell cannot be ruled out.

If Lyndon is inscrutable, his wife and his aides are not. Like the late President's staff, they were obviously heartbroken. Jack Valenti, who until now had been barred from the emergency area by his lack of credentials, hadn't heard that Kennedy was no longer alive when he talked his way past the guards. Cliff Carter found him in the corridor between Major Medicine and Minor Medicine, looking at Jacqueline Kennedy. The dark, gnomelike Houston public relations man was wondering why 'her eyes moved beyond me and through me as though I were an apparition'. Carter took his arm and whispered, 'The President is dead, you know.' Valenti collapsed, sobbing uncontrollably. Carter said, 'You must pull yourself together. You can't let the Vice President see you in this condition.' But his own condition wasn't much better. The two men staggered down the hall, propped against each other like drunks. The question of what

Johnson would think of Valenti didn't arise, because when Carter brought Jack back to Minor Surgery the new President had left.

Nothing in Parkland was quite as it should be. Men sobbed, women were hushed. The confrontation between the two First Ladies was an affair of muffled dread. Looking neither left nor right, Lady Bird followed Roberts into what seemed to her to be 'a hall full of silent people'.[4] She saw a closed door—Doris Nelson was beyond it, working on the President's body. Beside it, in Bird's words, the young widow was standing, 'quiet as a shadow', her eyes 'great wells of sadness'. Painfully conscious of the deathly quiet, Mrs Johnson embraced her and said, crying, 'Jackie, I wish to God there was something I could do.'

Lady Bird tiptoed away. On the second floor, with Nellie, the atmosphere was quite different. The two women had been intimate friends for twenty-five years, the Governor was alive, and the very walls of bright orange tile seemed to encourage hope. Bird put her arms around Nellie and said, 'He is going to get well.' Remembering a recent death in the Connally family, she added, 'Too much bad has happened, he's *got* to get well.' Almost fiercely Nellie replied, 'He is, Bird, he's going to be all right.' Her eyes filled up, and Jack Brooks, sensing that her brave front was about to crumble, handed her his handkerchief and said with a mock shrug. 'Oh, he'll be out there deer hunting at ninety.' She wiped her eyes and smiled faintly.

Below them arrangements for the Johnsons' leave taking were picking up momentum. Lem Johns reported back to Youngblood: Chief Curry had surrounded Love Field with Dallas policemen. Two unmarked cruisers were waiting outside Parkland, with their motors idling and Curry himself behind the wheel of the first one. Johns was sent off again to look for a separate exit from the hospital. In the hall Youngblood met Kellerman, who, though unaware of the imminence of Johnson's departure, had realized the need for increasing the guard around him. 'You take the day shift, Roberts and his men,' he said, forgetting that Youngblood already had them. 'Let me keep Stout's [Steward Stout, the shift leader] four-to-twelve people.' To Kellerman this appeared more than adequate. It gave the new President a complete shift, plus the Vice Presidential agents.

In the nurse's station Godfrey McHugh was smoothing the way for what he believed would be exclusively a Kennedy flight. He

[4] In both her statement to the author and again to Chief Justice Warren, Mrs Johnson vividly describes ascending and descending flights of stairs en route to Major Medicine. This is a striking example of how shock can distort memory. There were no stairs.

phoned Colonel Swindal, ordering him to move to another part of the Dallas airport, as a security precaution, and to draw up a flight plan to Andrews. After talking to a Dallas police captain on the runway, Swindal wisely ignored the first instruction. He was already in Love's safest spot. Even before McHugh's call he had begun other preparations; seven thousand gallons of additional fuel were gushing into the tanks of both 707's—the fuel they had had was adequate for Austin, but not Washington—and he was plotting a course across Texarkana, Memphis, and Nashville for President Kennedy's last trip across America. Like Kellerman, McHugh, and everyone else who hadn't been in Booth 13, the Colonel had no idea that another President would be aboard.

Had the occasion been less grave, Lyndon Johnson's departure from Parkland Hospital might be called convulsive. It resembled one of those Chaplinesque farewells in which the only people who wind up on the mobbed train are those who have come down to see their friends off. Some of the right people left Parkland, but others didn't, and the exodus was accompanied by episodes of disorder, hubbub, and unexpected bungling. 'Suddenly,' said Henry Gonzalez, 'I saw the might and power of the United States Government in complete confusion.' Rufus Youngblood, who until now had maintained a mastery of detail, completely forgot Lem Johns. Scouting all doors, Johns had found one which the press had overlooked and which led right to Harry Hines Boulevard. Delighted, he raced back to the emergency area and learned that for the second time in an hour he had run aground; the Johnson party had gone. Gonzalez was invited to join the group. Regretfully he declined. He was still juggling the blood-soaked paper bag, and decided that he should give it to Nellie Connally. Cliff Carter and Jack Valenti missed Johnson by less than a minute, but they did miss. They would have made it if Valenti hadn't felt responsible for Liz Carpenter and Marie Fehmer. 'Have them paged,' Carter suggested, and the two men were delayed while they waited for the two women who, unknown to anyone, had gone over to the Trade Mart to hear Johnson's address.

Amazingly, Liz and Marie were at the hospital when Johnson pulled out, and seats were found for them. At the Mart they had observed the questioning of a youth by two policemen. 'Do you suppose he's the one who did it?' Liz asked vaguely. Soon afterwards their attention was attracted by a woman across the street with a transistor radio glued to her ear. Suddenly she screamed, and her expression told them everything. Even Liz realized that there would be no speech now. It occurred to her that Johnson might have gone to a hotel, and entering an airline office she borrowed a phone to reach him that way. Marie, more realistic, poured out their story to a sympathetic Dallas policeman. He put them in a state police cruiser, and they careened back to Parkland, pleading with the driver all the way to slow down. Drawing up, they saw Lady Bird in the second unmarked car. She, too, had just made it; after leaving Nellie she had flown downstairs and was trying to catch her breath. With a fluttering hand she signalled them to come along, and they squeezed into the hastily assembled caravan.

Afterwards Liz's ingenuity was much admired. In fact, her presence had been pure luck, which was true of everyone there except the Johnsons, their bodyguards, and Ira Gearhart, who forced himself and his bag into a policeman's lap. Cecil Stoughton was to play a memorable role during the administration of the oath, but he was there for the ceremony only by chance. Stoughton had been among those who were holding telephone receivers for Art Bales. Johnson walked right past him with his long lunging stride, the big hands swinging, and observing Bales in the entourage, Stoughton asked, 'Where's he going?' '*The President*,' Bales hissed, 'is going to Washington.' Immediately Stoughton understood. 'So am I,' he said and handed the phone to Bales, who was thereby left behind. At that, the photographer was late. There was no room for him in the motorcade. Albert Thomas, quite by accident, wound up in the lead car as a human shield. After Johnson and Kilduff parted, Youngblood led the new Chief Executive to Chief Curry. The threat of a plot still obsessed the agent. That was why he had insisted upon two automobiles; if a sniper recognized Lady Bird he would be shooting at the wrong car. Youngblood put Congressman Thornberry beside Curry, got in the back with Johnson, and told the President to crouch below window level. Because Johnson obeyed, Thomas, emerging from the hospital, didn't see him. 'Stop!' he shouted. 'Keep going,' Youngblood called to Curry. From the floor Johnson inquired, 'Who is it?' The agent told him, and Johnson, asserting himself for the first time, said, 'Then stop.' Making the best of the delay, Youngblood decided to use every inch of flesh as protection. He directed Thomas to sit in front, pulled Thornberry into the rear, and arranged Johnson's shoulders so that he was in the middle. Any bullet aimed at the President would first have to pass through Curry, one of the two Congressmen, or Youngblood.

'We took off,' Jack Brooks later recalled, 'like a striped-assed ape.' Lady Bird, more ladylike, remembered that 'we went fast—*fast*'. Actually there were several exasperating delays. Curry had just begun to accelerate when a delivery truck appeared out of nowhere and halted right in front of him. The agents went for their guns, but the deliveryman, though guilty of extremely bad traffic manners, was real enough. Then there was the junkyard of abandoned cars. This obstacle was dodged by hurtling over kerbs and grass. Next Curry destroyed the purpose of the unmarked cars by hitting his siren. 'Stop that!' Johnson and Youngblood yelled together. The chief did. The motor-cycle escort, however, had picked up his cue; the wails were audible for over a mile, and Curry had to radio them to cut it out. Thereafter things went more smoothly, though at times they had to slow to a crawl. The number of red lights was extraordinary. They didn't stop for them, but to avoid collisions they had to treat them as what the Secret Service calls 'pink lights', pausing and glancing each way before speeding up. To those who were listening intently for rifle shots these pauses were almost unbearable, and the trip seemed longer than it was. It was within a minute of the time span of the drive from the triple underpass to Parkland: out the four lanes of Harry Hines, right at a sign reading 'DALLAS LOVE FIELD', right on Mockingbird, and through the break in the airport's chain fence. Three miles, seven minutes; they were there.

In Lady Bird's car no one spoke or moved between the hospital and the airport. In the cruiser ahead, Youngblood, using the portable DCN set which still dangled from his shoulder by its leather strap, radioed ahead to Paul Glynn, Johnson's valet, telling him to move all Johnson luggage from 86970 to 26000—the first notice to anyone at the field of the aircraft switch—and in the car behind Mrs Johnson, Liz Carpenter, the only writer present, made the first notes for the statement which the President eventually would have to make to the American people. She had scarcely begun when the cars braked. As they alighted Youngblood shouted, 'Everybody run up the steps.' Everybody did, and as Lady Bird entered the plane's rear door for the first time she heard Walter Cronkite's reedy voice coming from the stateroom, commenting on Kilduff's statement: '. . . Lyndon B. Johnson, now President of the United States . . .' Although the volume was turned up, it was hard to hear him; in every compartment crew officers, stewards, and secretaries were weeping. Johnson headed for the television set, and Joe Ayres, his rotund face streaming, adjusted the picture for him.

'Close all shades in the plane,' the President was calling. 'Close the shades,' Youngblood echoed—a subtle change from Parkland.

Obeying, Ayres beheld a remarkable sight: an automobile, in violation of all military and civilian safety rules, was racing towards him across the breadth of Love Field. Inside were Johns, Carter, Valenti, Stoughton—the Presidential photographer had finally found a seat with the stragglers—and a terrified Dallas policeman. Each of them knew that the short cut was insane, but in the past hour life had become cheaper; as Carter left the paper bag containing half

Connally's clothes with a nurse she had confided to them, 'The Governor's not expected to live.' So no one protested when Johns, who had thought that the aircraft had been moved to Southwest Airmotive, Love's private plane terminal, cried in exasperation, 'Hell, we're on the wrong side of the airport! Let's shoot the runways.' The control tower looked down in awe as they veered across the expanse of oil-stained concrete, their siren screaming, and swerved up beside the ramp.

'Which one?' asked Valenti, looking at the two 707's. He couldn't tell them apart.

'This one,' said Johns, leading him up.

That was the last car in President Johnson's first motorcade; with its hair-raising arrival from Parkland, the Youngblood breakout, as it might be called, was complete. Parkland didn't know it, though. Most of the agents and aides in the emergency area were under the impression that the group that had begun the grand tour of Texas at San Antonio International Airport the day before was intact. And when they did hear of the lightning move later, they were indifferent to it. The man they still regarded as President lay dead; they couldn't think beyond that.

Had it not been for the hospital's public address system, none of them might have been reminded of Johnson and his staff in the hour after Kennedy's death. It would have been better if they had been allowed to mourn in private. The lodging house across from Ford's Theatre had not been furnished with microphones. For all the phantasmagoria of April 14–15, 1865, Mary Todd Lincoln and her husband's lieutenants had been insulated from intrusion. Not so Parkland in 1963. Besides being a place of tile, plastic, stainless steel, and institutional buff, the hospital was studded with loud-speakers whose metallic voices relentlessly repeated the page Valenti had left:

'Liz Carpenter, please come to the administrative office. Liz Carpenter, please come to the administrative office. Liz Carpenter . . .'

In a cubicle a few yards from the trauma room's closed door Evelyn Lincoln heard it and blocked her ears. She was thinking of the campaigns, the Bay of Pigs, Big Steel, the missile crisis—of all they had been through together, all that had lain ahead. Now it was gone. It couldn't be true. But the nagging PA system insisted that it was:

'Liz Carpenter, please . . .'

Oh God, Evelyn thought, *they're taking over already.*

They weren't really; not yet. To those who loved John Kennedy the transition of power seemed needlessly cruel. Certainly it was harsh. It couldn't be otherwise; the brutal murder had guaranteed that. Consolidating the two groups on one aeroplane was to prove extremely unfortunate, and aspects of Johnson's behaviour in shock may have proved exacerbating, but the difficulty there was largely one of manners and mannerisms. Johnson was not himself that afternoon. In Dallas the national interest required strength, not elegance, and it is arguable that Johnson, far from taking over too quickly, did not take over quickly enough. The United States needed a President, yet neither he nor his advisers had fully grasped the fact of Kennedy's death. Valenti spoke for the majority of them when he burst into 26000's stateroom and said, 'I got here as quick as I could, Mr Vice President.'

Between pink lights on the way to Love Field the wife of the former Vice President, now the President, had glanced up at a building and observed there a flag already at half-mast. It was then, Lady Bird recalled afterwards, that 'the enormity of what had happened first struck me'.

It was striking an incalculable number of Americans at the same time and in the same way. An irresistible, almost telepathic urge to lower the colours swept the country; banners were floating down outside schools, statehouses, prisons, stock exchanges, department stores, office buildings, and private homes. At the White House Commander Hallett sent a man out to reel down the mansion's ensign immediately after he had ordered the Cabinet plane back to Andrews Field, and since the Commander had access to the Kellerman–Behn line, the standard at 1600 Pennsylvania Avenue may have been the first to slide down its pole. The motive for Hallett's swiftness lay in his own youth. He had marched in Franklin Roosevelt's funeral cortège as an Annapolis midshipman, and he remembered that there had been criticism then because several hours had lapsed between the announcement of Roosevelt's death in Warm Springs and the descent of the White House flag.

Elsewhere the compulsion is harder to explain. In the nurse's station Steve Landregan phoned instructions to haul Parkland's flag down at once; at Brooks Medical Centre in San Antonio Dr Welch, who had no military role, dashed out to the spot where President Kennedy had stood the afternoon before and yanked in the halyard himself. Afterwards neither man could explain why that had been his first thought. Whatever their reasons, such sights were to leave an indelible impression on those who witnessed them. Coming after a series of bulletins, each darker than the last, the spectacle of a falling banner was profoundly affecting. In Arlington Lieutenant Sam Bird, who had impetuously driven off to visit the Tomb of the Unknown

Soldiers after hearing of the shooting, had just re-entered Fort Myer's grounds when he saw the post's standard begin its descent. He drew over to the kerb, alighted, and saluted. After this, he thought, nothing could move him so deeply again. (Like everyone else who concluded that the emotional peak of the assassination had been reached, Sam Bird was mistaken, and he was among the first to have an inkling of what lay ahead; as he finished saluting, a captain strode up to him and said, 'You're taking an eight-man army casket team to MATS at Andrews. Pick the best eight on the post. I'm getting you an H-21 chopper—one of those banana jobs.')

At the executive mansion the drama had been heightened by the sudden appearance of an immaculately dressed little girl who really wasn't old enough to be downtown by herself. She walked slowly up the Pennsylvania Avenue sidewalk from the direction of Fifteenth Street, reached through the old black iron fence, and carefully placed a single flower on the White House lawn. The guards at the Northwest Gate looked from the blossom to the flag and retreated into their sentry box like walking wounded. In New York Chuck Spalding, Harvard '40, had been trapped in the office of a real estate consultant since the first word that his old friend was gravely wounded in Texas. To his mounting horror, the consultant became involved in a crass conversation with his broker. The broker had just explained that at the New York Stock Exchange, where the Stars and Stripes had also been lowered, the Dow Jones industrial average was plunging with it; the average was down over twenty points, and the two men were matter-of-factly discussing whether or not this was a 'good time to buy'.[5] Desolate, Spalding walked to the window, and as he pressed his gaunt face against the pane the flag atop Grand Central Station dropped—to him it seemed that it was falling on its own—to half-staff.

'Good-bye, Johnny,' Spalding said quietly to himself.

How many banners had been reefed into mid-point when Kilduff made the official announcement of the President's death is unknown, but certainly there were a great many. A Parkland doctor at the Trade Mart heard the news by phone at 1.18 p.m., and the American and Texas flags on the two poles which had been erected that morning dipped at 1.19. In most of the country Father Huber, not the acting press secretary, reached the great hovering audience first. Following rumours of a bullet wound in the head—which had evoked the image of Lincoln lying unconscious in the house at 453

[5] From their point of view it was an excellent time. A week later the average had rebounded 39.02 points. The fact remains, however, that the instincts of Spalding, himself a man of wealth, were correct. Kennedy's father had been a shrewd dealer in stocks, but he had never cashed in on the martyrdom of a President.

Tenth Street—and reports that last rites had been administered—which was enough to dash all remaining hope—the priest was instantly believed. The public has less faith in official pronouncements than either officials or reporters; to the waiting nation, Kilduff was merely confirming an accepted fact. On the strength of the priest's statement the Harvard *Crimson* had gone to press with an extra, and thousands of flags, including the one that Lady Bird glimpsed, had already plummeted when Kilduff faced his flock of correspondents in classroom 101–102 and struggled for the hardest words he would ever speak, unaware that a gentle, dumpy little man in a black habit, perched on the front seat of a church Galaxie with an oval 'BUILT IN TEXAS BY TEXANS' sign, had already said, 'He's dead, all right.'

Kilduff's press conference ended the most tempestuous hour in the history of American journalism. It was only the first hour in what was to become the greatest simultaneous experience this nation or any other had ever shared, but once the people knew that the President had been murdered a tenuous semblance of form began to emerge. Over the weekend it was to grow and grow until the President's widow, by her gallant devotion, restored the country's sense of pride and majesty at Monday's state funeral. Early Friday afternoon there was no trace of either. Coherence had vanished in a gibbering of teletype keys, a spatter of broadcasts, a chorus of calls from breathless friends and passing strangers; and since everything that was to follow stemmed from those first deranged minutes, a chronology is useful:

Dallas Time	*Developments*	*Reports*	*Washington Time*
12.30 p.m.	Oswald shoots the President, wounds Connally.		1.30 p.m.
12.34 p.m.		UPI flash: three shots have been fired at the Presidential motorcade in Dallas.	1.34 p.m.
12.36 p.m.	Kennedy reaches Parkland Hospital.	ABC breaks into local programme with the first network announcement.	1.36 p.m.
12.37 p.m.	Caroline Kennedy leaves the White House.		1.37 p.m.
12.39 p.m.		UPI says Kennedy has been wounded, 'perhaps fatally.'	1.39 p.m.
12.40 p.m.	Kellerman phones the White House from the nurse's station; Agent Ready calls for a priest.	AP reports: 'President Kennedy was shot today . . .' Walter Cronkite appears on screens with the first CBS flash.	1.40 p.m.
12.41 p.m.		AP describes blood on Kennedy's head.	1.41 p.m.

Dallas Time	*Developments*	*Reports*	*Washington Time*
12.45 p.m.		NBC interrupts programmes to say Kennedy and Connally have been wounded in Texas.	1.45 p.m.
12.55 p.m.		UPI reports Jacqueline Kennedy and Nellie Connally are safe and Kennedy is still alive.	1.55 p.m.
12.57 p.m.	Father Huber arrives at the hospital.	AP quotes Congressman Albert Thomas: the President is in 'very critical' condition.	1.57 p.m.
1.00 p.m.	Kemp Clark pronounces the President dead.	By now 75 million American adults know of the shooting.	2.00 p.m.
1.13 p.m.	In Booth 13 Emory Roberts tells Johnson Kennedy is dead.		2.13 p.m.
	Caroline returns to the White House.		
1.15 p.m.	O'Donnell talks to Johnson.		2.15 p.m.
1.02–1.17 p.m.		Intermittent broadcasts describe the priests' arrival at Parkland.	2.02–2.17 p.m.
1.18 p.m.		AP puts out an unconfirmed report that Johnson has been 'wounded slightly'.	2.18 p.m.
1.23 p.m.		UPI reports that the last sacraments have been administered.	2.23 p.m.
1.25 p.m.		UPI says Johnson is uninjured.	2.25 p.m.
1.26 p.m.	Johnson leaves Parkland.		
1.27 p.m.	Hugh Sidey talks to Father Huber.		2.27 p.m.
1.32 p.m.		UPI quotes Father Huber: 'He's dead . . .'	2.32 p.m.
1.33 p.m.	Johnson arrives at Love Field.		2.33 p.m.
	Kilduff faces the press in the classroom.		
1.35 p.m.		UPI flash: 'President Kennedy Dead'; AP 12-bell flash follows.	2.35 p.m.
1.36 p.m.		NBC says Johnson has been taken to a 'secluded place'.	2.36 p.m.

The first real report of the President's death to the world outside Parkland cannot be pinpointed, because there is no record of conversations over the key nurse's station line to Washington. Logging exact times was far from anyone's mind; the participants were preoccupied with keeping their connections unbroken. It was a few minutes after 1 p.m. on the trauma room's IBM clock when Dr

Burkley stepped into the passage and told Kellerman, who ordered Clint Hill to inform Jerry Behn. Hill suggested that the Attorney General be told at the same time, before he heard from the press; Kellerman nodded and Clint went ahead, asking first for Behn. It is the recollection of Sergeant Philip Tarbell, who was the key Signalman at the White House switchboard, that he monitored this call 'at approximately 2.05 p.m.'—1.05 in the hospital. Anyone the eavesdropping operators chose to tell knew within the next few minutes. Because the Signal Corps naturally gave first priority to the Defence Intelligence Agency, Secretary McNamara was among the first to hear, though he, still under the impression that his Dallas source was the CIA (whose closest base was in Miami), never understood how he had learned so quickly. By the same means the Cabinet plane, five time zones away from the capital, was informed before aides watching Cronkite in Nancy Tuckerman's East Wing office on the floor directly above Behn. Pierre Salinger had remained at his post in the communications shack, listening with one ear to the subdued Cabinet debate over whether or not to obey Stranger's order to fly non-stop to Andrews, by-passing Love Field, and, with the other ear, awaiting fresh word from Stranger, who had been droning his broken-record 'Stand by . . . Stand by . . . Stand by' every fifteen seconds. Then the blow fell. Abruptly the monotonous pitch changed. It rose: 'Situation to Wayside. The President is dead. Repeat, the President is dead.'

'The President is dead,' Pierre told the Cabinet, not really believing a word of it. Who in his right mind could accept such a fantastic statement from an unknown voice, received in an aircraft a thousand miles from nowhere after a guarded verbal exchange between two men who had been addressing one another by aliases? Perhaps Wayside could. But he didn't exist. Salinger, who did, was incredulous.

'He's dead,' Wayside repeated in a low tone.

Dean Rusk moved towards the PA system of Aircraft 86972. It was slow going. His head was down, and he had to walk the length of the fuselage. Reaching the tail compartment, he wet his lips and told the microphone, 'Ladies and gentlemen, it is official. We have had official word—the President has died. God save our nation.'

That was the proper way to do it. But November 22 was not a proper day. Looking down the main corridor, Rusk realized that this solemn announcement had startled no one. Indeed, it had been something of an intrusion; he hadn't told the passengers anything they hadn't known already. Baffled, he tried to imagine how they had found out. The truth—that the other members of the Cabinet who had been with him in the stateroom had ignored his seniority, creeping along in his wake and passing the word *sotto voce* to their wives—did not occur to him.

The whispering had begun as a faint rustle. It grew louder, turned into an erratic buzz, became a whine, and was precipitated by weeping.

Alvin Josephy, who had written down Rusk's words as they were spoken, wrote on:

> Pierre Salinger, in the aisle, grabs his wife, they cling in a terribly tragic embrace—Hodges, now seated across from us, buries his head in his hands and sobs, tears come down his cheeks—others crying—Udall sits next to Lee, stares tough-jawed past her, out the cabin window as he takes her hand—Manning sits opposite us—tears start in his eyes—Myer Feldman crying—Wirtz mad—not a sound or movement in the cabin for 5 minutes.

Phyllis Dillon comforted her husband, who was wondering where Vice President Johnson was. The Wirtzes made a valiant effort to look at each other and failed. Orville Freeman slumped in his seat beside Janie Freeman. 'Poor Jackie,' she said after a while. She reached over and squeezed his hand. 'I'm so glad you weren't made VP in L.A. I'm selfish.'

He nodded. Then his mind raced back forty months, to the convention in Los Angeles. His name had been mentioned then as a possible Vice Presidential candidate. Had events taken a different turn, he reflected, the new occupant of the White House might well be named President Orville Freeman. He mused absently, *Isn't that something?* On a pad he scribbled Janie's remark and added beneath it: 'Thought then in my mind too—What if, what would I do?'

In Salinger's White House office a UPI ticker emitted a sprinkle of chimes and pecked out the 2.35 EST flash, which was instantly ripped from the machine. The ripper was Bill Pozen. His presence there was sheer chance. He wasn't looking for Pierre; he was trying to find his daughter. Despairing of the telephones at the Department of the Interior and untouched by a teacup of whisky which a fellow official had given him to steady his nerves, Pozen had walked the three blocks from his office to the mansion's Southwest Gate, hoping Agatha and Caroline might be here. Caroline was, but Agatha wasn't, and wandering distractedly from room to room he saw, on the teletype, what television viewers in the nearby Fish Room heard seconds later from Walter Cronkite. They watched Cronkite remove, replace, and again remove his horn-rimmed spectacles; a muscle in his jaw trembled violently; he confirmed that the President was gone. One of Kennedy's minor aides said, 'What a shame—just as he was getting so many things going.' Dean Markham, trying to concentrate on larger problems, could only marvel at the incongruity of this scene. The executive mansion, he thought, should have been told before the rest of the country. But for all its guards and gates it had become just another house, watching daytime TV.

The confirmation was the second great blow of that hour. The first, the report of the shooting, had reached a scattered nation preoccupied with business lunches and weekday tasks. In less than sixty minutes the United States had been transformed; a majority of the huge audience was now within earshot of newscasters. William O. Douglas excepted, the Supreme Court had dispersed to television sets in the chambers of Justices Brennan and Stewart; Deputy Attorney General Katzenbach and the Assistant Attorneys General were ranged in a semi-circle before the set in Robert Kennedy's office; Dave Hackett, having decided that bars were inappropriate, was listening to a taxi radio on Constitution Avenue. Mary McGrory, her prescription for high blood pressure in her pocket, was standing in the middle of the Washington *Star* city room. Her national editor was thrusting wads of money into her cupped hands and telling her to go to Dallas. 'If he dies . . .' she kept saying, her voice trailing off flaccidly. The editor appeared to have unlimited assets, and he couldn't seem to stop giving them away; she was holding a fortune in cash. 'If he dies . . .' Mary said for the last time, and then a voice from one of the men keeping vigil over the *Star* machines verified his death.

Another voice, muffled and off-camera somewhere in the back of a television studio, had susurrated a few minutes before, 'Clint Hill says he's dead,' and Bill Walton, Pat Moynihan, and Charlie Horsky, knowing who Clint was, had abandoned hope and left Georgetown for the White House. Angie Duke had also learned prematurely, and mysteriously; dashing back to the State Department from lunch, Angie found that the Japanese chargé d'affaires, who certainly couldn't have been on any list of the Signal Corps or the DIA, or even of the CIA, had already called and left a formal expression of condolences on behalf of his government.

For Walton, Moynihan, Horsky, and Duke, mourning thus began early; for John W. McCormack the confirmation was a private anticlimax. The Speaker had still been in the House restaurant when two reporters came to his table and said that Kennedy had been shot. Other reporters and Congressmen then began to dart up with bits and pieces of information. The appearance of priests convinced McCormack that the President had succumbed. Then, in the next minute, he was told that the Vice President had been shot and, in the minute after that, that Secret Service agents were on their way to the

Hill to protect him. Although the first report was inaccurate, the second was true; under the succession act of July 18, 1947, inspired by Harry Truman's affection for Sam Rayburn, the Speaker (rather than the Secretary of State, as in the past) was second in line of succession, and if both Kennedy *and* Johnson had been murdered, Rayburn's aged successor was now President of the United States. At 2.18 p.m. in Washington the possibility seemed very real. It struck McCormack, he later recalled, with 'a terrific impact'. He rose unsteadily from his chair and immediately suffered a severe attack of vertigo. Linen, waiters, tableware swam before his eyes; he thought he was going to lose consciousness and tumble to the floor. Passing a palsied hand over his eyes, he sank back to his seat, and he was still here, trembling, when a Congressman called over that Johnson was unharmed.

Before that dizzy interval in which he believed that he might be moving from his sixth-floor suite in the Hotel Washington to 1600 Pennsylvania Avenue, on the other side of the Treasury Building, McCormack had said, 'My God, what are we coming to?' Maude Shaw, forgetting her need for White House cars (but remembering that the news must be kept from Caroline, who was in her room shrieking, inconsolable over her separation from Agatha), whispered to Agent Tom Wells, 'Oh, God, what kind of people are these?' Across Lafayette Park Eunice Shriver had phoned her brother Bob from her husband's office. All he could tell her then was 'It doesn't look good.' Later one of the Shrivers' assistants brought in the UPI flash. Shriver put his arms around his wife and suggested a prayer for the President's soul, and with Dr Joseph English, Chief Psychiatrist of the Peace Corps, they knelt around the desk, repeating 'Hail Mary, full of grace . . .' and 'Holy Mary, Mother of God . . .' in unison.

The pious invoked the name of God or went to their knees or meditated. Told by Ann Gargan and Rita Dallas, Rose Kennedy faced the nurse bravely and said, 'We'll be all right.' But she really didn't want to be with them. She didn't want to see anyone just then. Her room was too small for the pacing she must now do, and rubbing her elbows she said to Ann, 'I'll be outside.' Leaving them weeping, the President's mother, the most religious of the Kennedys, went down to the lawn by the sea, to stride back and forth throughout the remainder of the afternoon, a solitary, graceful figure walking over mile after mile of autumnal grass while her invalid husband slept.

The erratic continued to be erratic, and there were still a lot of them. Joe Gawler phoned his funeral home to ask whether there had been 'a contact' from the Kennedy family. Dean Gorham finished his daredevil ride to the Austin auditorium, looked up at the

'WELCOME PRESIDENT JOHN F. KENNEDY' sign over the finish line, and forgot about his bundles of souvenir programmes; the next time he saw them someone had dumped them in the auditorium trash. Wesley Frazier, who had driven Lee Oswald and his rifle into downtown Dallas five hours earlier, calmly polished off his lunch in the Book Depository and then, realizing that there could be no further work in the growing turmoil, drove back to Irving to take the afternoon off. Ruth Paine cried, but Marina, dry-eyed, continued to hang clothes. The federal judge whose jurors included Jack Krueger of the Dallas *News* told the courtroom what had happened. To the horror of the managing editor, who was in the middle of the most stupendous story in the history of Dallas and felt that he should be allowed to leave for his city room immediately, the judge intoned, 'The President is dead, but the business of the United States must go on. Mr Prosecutor, you may proceed.' But the most eccentric performance was probably that of Sergeant Keith Clark. Clark heard of the tragedy when his children arrived home from school and shouted it up the stairs. Suspecting that the President might be buried in Arlington, in which case he would play taps, Clark decided that he should look his best. He hurried to the nearest barber for a haircut.

The efficient became extremely businesslike. Jack McNally was bustling around his office, organizing it as a command post, showing Colonel McNally's men where to put in new lines. Those with talents turned to them. The Boston Symphony Orchestra stopped the Handel concerto and started the slow movement of Beethoven's 'Eroica', which is often used as a funeral march for fallen heroes. The fluent found words for the occasion—Dean Rusk had spoken well, and at the United Nations Adlai Stevenson said with simple eloquence, 'We'll bear the grief of his death until the day of ours.' Those with a conspicuous lack of eloquence became speechless—when Dick Goodwin called Ken O'Donnell's secretary for a trivial fact, she choked, stammered, and at last said apologetically, 'Maybe you don't know it, Mr Goodwin, but the President has been assassinated'; Mrs Auchincloss called her young son Jamie at the Brooks School with the intention of gently breaking the news that his idol had been injured, and Jamie, knowing more than she did, parried her questions awkwardly and finally sobbed, 'Mummy, I think he's dead!'

Some men celebrated for their command of the language were also struck dumb. Walter Lippman reached the Washington *Post* and collapsed. Cardinal Cushing greeted his naval visitors with five hoarse words: 'Jack Kennedy has been assassinated. . . .' He couldn't go on. His lips were working furiously, but there was no sound, and the admiral hastily withdrew. Ted Sorensen had been the rhetorician of the New Frontier, and at 2.35 he was also the most prestigious aide at the White House. Sitting across from Behn in McNally's office he felt that he should assume some responsibility, yet he couldn't. He felt shackled; if he had been standing in the middle of a stadium, he could have done nothing. At length he stirred a little and said with slow bitterness, 'They wouldn't even give him three years,' and left the East Wing for the West. Ted was as acrimonious as a man of his quiet temperament could be. The really aggressive were belligerent. In the West Wing Reardon shouted at Sorensen, 'I'd like to take a fucking bomb and blow the fucking State of Texas off the fucking map!' Barney Ross hunched his shoulder and crashed his fist into a Justice Department wall. Abe Zapruder slammed the door of his office in the Dal-Tex Building and began kicking every object that would move. In Phoenix, Arizona, a thirty-three-year-old man fired two shots through the window of the local John Birch Society office, and at 819 North Eleventh Street in Temple, Texas, Byron Skelton plucked at his black tie and shrieked at his wife, 'I knew it! I knew it! I knew it! If only they had paid some attention to those letters! Why? *Why?—Why didn't they listen to me?*'

'Everything has changed,' Fidel Castro told his luncheon guest uneasily. He was wrong: individual modes of behaviour had not changed, nor had extremism. Barry Goldwater, who had known John Kennedy in the Senate, and who admired and liked him, was as angry as Ross; when his plane landed he expressed his outrage and cancelled all his public appearances. Not all Goldwater admirers shared his wrath, however. An Oklahoma City physician beamed at a grief-stricken visitor and said, 'Good, I hope they got Jackie.' In a small Connecticut city a doctor called ecstatically across Main Street—to an internist who worshipped Kennedy—'The joy ride's over. This is one deal Papa Joe can't fix.' A woman visiting Amarillo, the second most radical city in Texas, was lunching in the restaurant adjacent to her motel when a score of rejoicing students burst in from a high school directly across the street. 'Hey, great, JFK's croaked!' one shouted with flagrant delight, and the woman, leaving as rapidly as she could, noticed that several diners were smiling back at the boy. In Dallas itself a man whooped and tossed his expensive Stetson in the air, and it was in a wealthy Dallas suburb that the pupils of a fourth-grade class, told that the President of the United States had been murdered in their city, burst into spontaneous applause.

Once the identity of the assassin had been established elaborate attempts were made to sponge away the memory of these incidents. The Radical Right wasn't contrite. Its initial glee was confirmed and reconfirmed; during a meeting in the Cosmos Club which was brought to the attention of the FBI in Washington six months after the tragedy a retired Marine Corps general told an admiring group of retired military officers that 'It was the hand of God that pulled the trigger that killed Kennedy.'[6] But the radicals were content to leave the guilt in Oswald's grave. Their goal had been achieved, and they were anxious to avoid the undertow of public disapproval.

Even the facts about Dallas' schoolroom episode were obscured. It was first mentioned in a blistering sermon against hate two days after the President's death. The preacher was the Rev. William A. Holmes of the city's Northaven Methodist church, and Walter Cronkite picked up his text on CBS. The network's local affiliate, receiving advance notice of the network broadcast, followed it with an interview of a public school teacher who explained that her fourth-grade class had clapped after being told that it was being sent home early. The effect of the interview was to burnish the city's tarnished reputation. In point of fact that station had the wrong school. In Dallas proper the announcement of the assassination had been coupled with a suspension of all classes, so the possibility of confusion did exist there. However, not all Dallas children attend the public schools. In the private, rich, racially segregated suburban school system of Park Cities—Highland Park and University Park, where Big D's big money is—the school day continued to the final bell. Since the fourth-grade class mentioned in Mr Holmes' sermon was there, and since the pupils in it were told only of the death, they could have been applauding only that. For those who did not despise the President the episode is distasteful. To some it may still be incredible. Yet there can be no doubt of its authenticity. The source is the teacher herself, who went to the minister that Friday evening for guidance. He discussed it with Superintendent White, who conceded that quite apart from Park Cities the announcement of the President's murder had inspired eleven separate acts of disrespect in the public schools of Dallas proper. Mr Holmes became a highly controversial figure in Texas that week. Because of his sermon his life was threatened, and at the suggestion of the Dallas Police Department he left his house and found sanctuary in the home of a member of his congregation.

The swift solution of the riddle of who had fired the shots was to have the effect of dissipating early reactions. This was lucky for the gloaters. Had the assassin been identified, say, as an agent of the

[6] Here as elsewhere, the author is relying on his own research, not hearsay. The source for the remark is another officer who was present at the meeting.

John Birch Society, Birchers everywhere would have been in for an awkward afternoon. It was also fortunate for domestic tranquillity. Almost as soon as conclusions had been drawn, they were to be confounded, and instead of hysteria the national attitude became one of pervasive sadness. Perhaps hysteria would have lost its momentum in any case. Since Orson Welles' Martian fiasco of 1938 Americans had been through two major wars and the tensions of the Russian armistice; they had become more sophisticated and harder to jar. Conceivably they would have behaved equally well if the riddle had endured or grown more complex.

The early symptoms, however, were not reassuring. In Dallas Muggsy O'Leary had seen people reunning wildly from building to building, tripping, sprawling, picking themselves up, and running on again. On Connecticut Avenue, in Washington, the progress of Bill Walton's taxi was blocked by a crowd which had gathered outside the ABC offices and flowed across the street to the Mayflower Hotel. In the cab Pat Moynihan reached for his billfold, which contained a map of roads leading to the huge West Virginia cave where, in the event of nuclear attack, the sub-cabinet was supposed to assemble. He checked himself and left his wallet where it was; the office of Defence Emergency Planning had estimated that the ride to the cave would take twenty-five minutes, but with this chaos it might as well be in California.

North of Lafayette Park the bell in St John's church, the church of the Presidents, was tolling wildly, like a fire gong. And motorists were going berserk. They were ignoring stop signs, signals, pedestrians, policemen, and other motorists. Cars swerved drunkenly from lane to lane, or spun without warning in crazy U-turns, or were left forsaken in the middle of intersections, their engines idling and their doors hanging open. If the confirmation of the President's death had been followed by a rash of other ominous developments —the assassination of Lyndon Johnson and the disappearance of the Cabinet plane, for example, and the proclamation of a new government by a committee of the Right or Left—the public convulsion could have become uncontrollable. In retrospect the mere suggestion of such a sequence seems preposterous. But at noon the assassination would have seemed preposterous.

Kennedy was still believed to be alive, and traffic had not yet entered its mad phase, when Mac Bundy crossed the Potomac with McNamara's driver, each of them, as Bundy noted in his subsequent memorandum of events, boosting the courage of the other. In the corridor that curves past the oval office Bundy joined Ralph Dungan, whose return from the Chilean Embassy luncheon had preceded his arrival by a few minutes. Neither of them said a word. The scene was studded with small incongruities: Dungan, puffing his pipe, looked serene and ironical, which he wasn't; on the wall hung two Texas Ranger pistols buckled to a piece of ranch fence (a sign above identified them as 'The Texas Peacemakers'); and General Services Administration workmen, having received no new orders, continued to put down the new blood-red rugs in the President's and Evelyn Lincoln's offices.

Walton, Moynihan, and Horsky arrived. Still no one spoke. Then Ted Sorensen came in from the colonnade by the Rose Garden and said hollowly, 'It's over, he's dead.' Bundy—that strange blend of almost brutal realism and almost feline sensitivity—realized that Sorensen was the hardest hit and hurried to his side. Dungan removed his pipe and studied the stem blindly. He asked, 'What have they done to us?'

Presently the men in the hall began to notice the new carpeting. Because it had been conceived as a surprise, none of them expected it, and they were shocked. Fred Holborn came up just as the men were replacing the furniture upon it; he stepped back, stupefied. Moynihan, perceiving the familiar rocking chair in the hall, peered in at the rug; to him 'it looked as though they knew, that someone knew a new President was coming in'. Bundy had left Sorensen to call McNamara from Ken O'Donnell's office, and he, too, was appalled. 'Oh, my God, they're putting scarlet carpets in the President's office!' he said to Bill Walton. 'We must stop it.' Walton disagreed. To stop it now, he said, would be pointless. They argued and finally told the men to finish, but to finish quickly.

Abruptly Walton declared loudly, 'I've got to get out of here.' He glanced at his watch—it was 2.30 exactly, three minutes before Kilduff's official announcement in 101–102 and Johnson's arrival at Love Field—as he left the West Wing lobby with Pat Moynihan. Outside Pat remarked upon the colours, lowered at Commander Hallett's order. 'Bill, you might as well see that,' he said, pointing. Walton sagged. 'Let's walk out the way he would have expected us to,' he said, trying to smooth the wrinkles out of his voice. But he stumbled. He couldn't quite manage it, and at the Northwest Gate Moynihan hailed a cab and helped him into it.

Returning to comfort Holborn, Pat was accosted by a White House policeman who asked to see his pass. He answered acidly, 'What difference does it make now?' It made none; yet he was wrong and the guard right. If there was even a chance of a threat against the government, and the chance certainly existed at 2.30, a single act of carelessness could have become criminal negligence. Hindsight began early. Within the next three hours most of those who had considered this possibility began trying to forget it. They felt that they had been absurd. They hadn't been. Undeniably some impulses were quixotic. Senator Eugene McCarthy's maid began packing the family's belongings on the theory that the lives of all Democrats were in danger; as a South American she was thinking in terms of a purge, which in a two-party country would be impractical. But the apprehension of men like Bill Pozen was entirely reasonable, and they were in good company. 'You'd better get the Watch Committee going,' George Ball had phoned John McCone before McCone's departure for Hickory Hill, and the director had replied shortly, 'I already have.' The committee consisted of the sharpest eyes the CIA could focus on Moscow and Peking. Every member was a technician, expert in the intricate ways of Sino-Soviet agents, and they were to remain on the job all weekend and afterwards, tapping foreign sources to determine whether or not the crime could have been the work of an outside ring.

In the Pentagon McNamara and the Joint Chiefs remained vigilant, though after their conference in the Secretary's office the Chiefs decided they should leave sentry duty to subordinate sentinels and rejoin their meeting. General Taylor in particular felt that it was important to present a picture of stability and continuity, that it would be an error to let their visitors from Bonn suspect the depth of the tragedy until more was known. At 2.30 he and his colleagues filed back into the Gold Room. He told the Germans briefly that President Kennedy had been injured. General Friedrich Foertsch replied for his comrades that they hoped the injury was not too serious. The Chiefs did not reply, and for the next two hours they put on a singular performance. Aware that the shadow of a new war might fall across the room at any time, they continued the talks about dull military details, commenting on proposals by Generals Wessel and Huekelheim and shuffling papers and directives with steady hands. Even for men with their discipline it was a stony ordeal, and it was especially difficult for Taylor, who had to lead the discussion and whose appointment as Chairman had arisen from his close relationship with the President. As America's first soldier he would be expected to make the first military decision should war come. Meanwhile he had to sit erect and feign an interest in logistics and combined staff work. At 4.30 the meeting ended on schedule. The Joint Chiefs rose together and faced their rising guests. Taylor said evenly, 'I regret to tell you that the President of the United States has been killed.' The Germans, bred to stoicism, collapsed in their chairs.

At 4.15, exactly fifteen minutes before the Gold Room adjournment, the Chesapeake & Potomac Telephone Company's Georgetown office, which served the Pentagon, had become the last exchange in the capital to resume normal operations. The phone emergency was then officially over. But though it, too, became quickly forgotten, while it lasted it had seemed unforgettable. Individual diallers, never having encountered this obstacle, naturally placed it in the context of the President's murder; between 2 and 4 p.m. in Washington it required no great leap of imagination to picture the country crawling with sinister figures industriously sabotaging communications. What set this aspect of the crisis apart was its immunity to rank; all flashing lights looked alike to switchboard operators, and automated exchanges could not distinguish between the phone of an exasperated Senator and one in the hands of a child. Completing a call required luck and persistence, and the list of the luckless included a number of men and women who were accustomed to very quick service. Hale Boggs couldn't reach the Speaker's office. Mamie Eisenhower couldn't get Ike. Ben Bradlee's *Newsweek* phone was dead; so was Justice Stewart's; so was Liz Pozen's when she arrived home with Agatha. Mrs Auchincloss did get through to the White House operator, but she was told that there was no way for her to reach her daughter at Parkland Hospital. Communications traffic between the capital and Texas had reached the saturation point. The phone company was doing its best—half the circuits in the entire Eastern half of the United States had been reserved for Washington traffic—but Dallas' eighteen long-distance trunks were all overloaded, and every hospital phone Art Bales had confiscated was needed.

Even Crown was temporarily paralysed. The Signalmen there had never been asked to do so much with so little. Because the President had expected to spend only three hours in Dallas, Signals had no direct lines to the city. Calls from the Sheraton-Dallas were being worked off the temporary board on the seventh floor of Fort Worth's Hotel Texas, and the cascade of words from Clint Hill, Kellerman, Roberts, Bales, Behn, Shepard, Youngblood, and the Attorney General was streaming over this rickety, narrow bridge. In the capital Crown's men were handling Agent Tom Wells' guarded inquiries about Caroline, making arrangements to install five new White House lines in Lyndon Johnson's home, putting in another five lines in Jack McNally's office, and juggling the backlog of local calls to and from Robert Kennedy at Hickory Hill. Both the Signal board in the east basement and the NAtional 8–1414 board on the fourth floor of the Executive Office Building were in a bind. According to Sergeant Tarbell, Hill's disclosure to Behn that the President was dead—which came a full twenty-five minutes before the public knew Father Huber had said, 'He's dead'—triggered an internal crisis. In the Sergeant's words, 'The switchboard went completely wild, with everyone attempting to call out.' The big wave broke within the next half-hour. The Chesapeake & Potomac dial tones grew progressively slower until they ceased altogether. For the first time in memory the Signalmen discovered that 'we could not dial out'.

As expert technicians they realized that the trouble lay in overburdened exchanges. Unfortunately, the very nature of the emergency prevented them from reassuring outsiders, and Senator Kennedy, roaming the 1600 block of Twenty-eighth Street, had reached a frenzy of uncertainty. He and Claude Hooten continued to press buttons in a row of new town houses until Claude found one whose phone was functioning. He explained the situation to the woman of the house while Ted called his brother. Bob told him quietly, 'He's dead. You'd better call your mother and our sisters.' The suggestion seemed sensible. The country hadn't heard from Father Huber, and had Ted had access to a permanent dial tone, he could have followed through. But there were no permanent dial tones. The instant he hung up the housewife's line went dead.

Recrossing the street, he found that the extensions in his home were still out. Milt Gwirtzman said, 'What about my house? Maybe we'll have better luck there.' That, too, sounded logical. The Gwirtzman home was only eight blocks away. But the phones were lifeless there, too. Ted said between his teeth, 'Let's go to the White House.' It was a silent ride. He, deep in thought, did not mention his talk with Bob, and Milt, who had heard the worst over one of the Senator's television sets just before they left Twenty-eighth Street, was tactfully quiet. At the mansion there were new frustrations. A crowd had formed on Pennsylvania Avenue, so Ted directed Milt to East Executive Avenue. The guard at the East Gate, recognizing the Senator, waved them through. Leaving the Mercedes in the driveway, Ted tugged at the centre door. It didn't give. It was the tourist entrance, which was always locked at this hour. He rattled it furiously, crying out. 'Doesn't *anything* work?'

The door beside it yielded, and in the great east–west corridor which bisects the mansion's ground floor he wandered into the office of Dr Janet Travell. The doctor offered him a sedative. He declined; what he really needed was a reliable telephone. She turned her examination room over to him, and there, after an odyssey that had begun on Lyndon Johnson's rostrum and led him halfway across the District of Columbia and back, the President's younger brother began to establish contact with reality. Signals gave him Hyannis Port; he talked briefly to his mother, who said that she had heard from television. 'I'm worried about your father,' she told him, and he said, 'I'll come right home.' Taz Shepard stepped in for a moment and told Ted that Jean, Pat, and Eunice already knew and were safe.

Eunice, indeed, was entering the next room. The Shrivers, violating the most hallowed of White House traffic rules, had entered one-way West Executive Avenue from the wrong end and parked on the south grounds outside the Diplomatic Reception Room. Ted spoke to his sister privately, together they held the first of several telephone conversations with Bob, and Eunice attempted to place a call to Pat—who had left word with her maid that she could not talk to anyone. Eunice then phoned Lem Billings in New York, because Lem was the sort of person you lean on in a time of trouble.

'I'll fly out and bring Pat back,' he said instantly.

'She's on the Coast!'

'It's only four or five hours.'

'Oh, I don't think that will be necessary.'

It wasn't; Bob had reached Pat, and she had booked a flight to Washington. Since their emergence on the national scene the Kennedys had attracted affection and vehement criticism. No one, however, had challenged their stamina, and in this ultimate test the President's brothers and sisters were standing up. The critics had accused them of behaving like royalty (a charge which had also been familiar during the Roosevelt years), but in time of calamity the lot of the public patrician is unenviable. All the Kennedys were denied privacy when they needed it most. Exceptional poise was expected of them, and was forthcoming. In Dr Travell's office Eunice consoled members of the mansion staff and solicitously inquired of Bundy about Governor Connally's condition; while checking airline schedules to Hyannis Ted bucked up the spirits of aides who had rushed downstairs upon hearing that he was here. Since talking to his mother the Senator had recovered. The blow in Dallas could scarcely have been greater. Yet now, at least, he knew its boundaries. There was a picture once more, and he was in it.

Most important, he, his sister, and his brother-in-law here were receiving a sense of direction from Hickory Hill. The new head of the family was crisp. Plans for a commercial flight were abandoned; at this hour they were impractical. Major Mike Cook, Godfrey McHugh's executive officer, was instructed to set up immediate helicopter transport from the South Lawn to Andrews for Ted and Eunice, and Jetstar transport from Andrews to the Cape. *The Cape*, Eunice thought fleetingly as Bob's voice crackled over the line. They would continue to go back each year, but this, she realized, would be her last departure for there in a helicopter.

Bob Kennedy had been dressing for Dallas when he received word that the brilliant world he had known and loved was finished. He had been struggling with his necktie in the upstairs library, pacing beside a wall of photographs of his father, his wife, and his children; of Joe Kennedy, Jr. and Kathleen Kennedy, taken before both of them had died in Europe during his youth; of himself, looking quizzical in an Indian headdress; of the President addressing a joint session of Congress; of the President and Jackie—reminders, all of them, of the Kennedy legacy. Ethel had been standing to one side, squeezing her hands, and John McCone had just entered the room. They had stared at him, he at them.

'Do you know how serious the wound is?' he had asked.

'No, I don't.' Kennedy affixed a PT boat tie pin, the tiny golden symbol of the New Frontier. 'Do you?'

The White House extension on the desk rang. He dove for it.

'Oh, he's dead!' he cried.[7]

'Those poor children,' said Ethel, in tears.

'He had the most wonderful life,' Kennedy said.

Later that would be his wife's most vivid recollection of his response—how, in the starless night, he remembered how bright the sun had been. McCone was struck by the fact that 'through this ordeal, as severe a trial as a man can go through, he never cracked. He was steely. Obviously he was seriously affected, but at no time did he lose his composure.' They descended the stairs in a rank of three and walked to the rear porch. Kennedy poked his head in a window of the living-room, where Morgenthau and several others were watching the television commentary.

'He died,' he said in a low voice and walked towards the pool.

The extension there rang. It was J. Edgar Hoover again. Since 1.48 p.m. he had been on the phone with Gordon Shanklin, the agent in charge of his Dallas office. Until a moment ago he hadn't been learning much (he was among those who thought Parkland was called Lakeland), but the most important of the details which he had promised that he would endeavour to get had just come through.

'The President's dead,' he said snappily and hung up.

He expressed no compassion; he did not seem to be upset. His voice as the Attorney General recalled afterwards, was 'not quite as excited as if he were reporting the fact that he had found a Communist on the faculty of Howard University'. Ordinarily garrulous, he had suddenly turned curt with his superior. It would be charitable to attribute the swift change to the stresses of that afternoon. Yet although Bob Kennedy continued in the Cabinet for over nine

[7] Kennedy thought the caller was Clint Hill. It was Taz Shepard. This was another telephonic phenomenon of November 22. Men who had known one another for years had difficulty recognizing each other's voices.

months, Hoover, whose office was on the same floor, never walked over to offer his condolences. One of his assistants wrote Kennedy a moving letter, and the agents in the FBI's crime squad sent him a message of sympathy, but their Director, unlike the Director of the CIA, remained sphinx-like. He did speak to Bob one day when they happened to enter the Justice Department together, and he accepted a Christmas gift from him, a pair of cufflinks bearing the Justice seal, but those were their only contacts.

It was his brittle consistency which made Hoover unique. The typical reaction to the murder resembled a sine curve, or a parabola. People went one way and then reversed themselves. Ethel Kennedy was crushed at first and righted herself after the funeral. The brooding, Celtic agony that was to darken her husband's life the following spring was postponed that Friday; in his back yard he lost himself in action, attempting to call Ken O'Donnell, who was still unavailable, and getting through to five members of his family and to Steve Smith in New York and Lee Radziwill in London. He touched every base he could think of, weighing the possibility of flying out to Dallas to join Jacqueline Kennedy in accompanying the President's body back and even raising the question of his brother's personal papers with Mac Bundy, who checked with the State Department and learned that when a President dies in office his personal files belong to his relatives. (Bundy ordered the combinations on the locked files changed at once.) In his talks with Pat and Jean, and in the conference call to Dr Travell's office, Bob became, in effect, a kind of family personnel manager, matching talents with assignments. Jean was the sister closest to Jackie; she would come to Washington. Eunice was closest to her mother; she would fly to Hyannis Port. Pat was a continent away and had been unwell; she would come here. Shriver, the born administrator, was to organize the funeral arrangements; Ted was to break the news of the President's death to his father—the most painful task of all.

The calls went on and on. Meantime the number of visitors to Hickory Hill had grown and become a crowd. Morgenthau and his assistant slipped away and were succeeded by successive waves of friends, neighbours who wanted to be helpful, the press, and plain Nosy Parkers. Women reached the house first: Sue Markham, Marian White, Nancy Brown, Ann Chamberlain. Then the cars from downtown Washington turned in from Chain Bridge Road: Dean Markham, Justice White, Dave Hackett, Ed Guthman. A priest stopped in to ask whether he was needed. A lieutenant of the Fairfax County police drove up with twelve men, and Guthman quietly posted them in the bushes surrounding the yard, where they stumbled over newspaper photographers with telescopic lenses.

Outwardly Kennedy was more collected than his callers, most of whom had rushed here on impulse and found on arrival that they didn't know what to say. Byron White touched his shoulder, said vaguely, 'It's hard to understand how these things happen,' and drifted off. Nicole Alphand threw up her hands. 'Bob, there are no words,' she said. Then, being a Washington hostess, she found some: 'You must be brave because you are the chief of the clan now and all the hopes rest on you.'

He nodded. Privately he was wondering what the wife of the French Ambassador was doing here, but it was more polite to look understanding. He had to be the diplomat here, and he was; to some of his friends his manner suggested that he was more concerned with their loss than with his own, an attitude which was to be characteristic of Jacqueline Kennedy throughout the weekend and which, for many, was shattering. 'We don't want any gloomy faces around here,' he told Hackett lightly, and his greeting to Guthman, ten minutes after the calls from Shepard and Hoover, was almost casual.

'How are you doing?' he asked.

'I've seen better days,' Guthman replied, adopting his low key.

'Don't be sad.'

'Pretty hard not to.'

Kennedy took him aside. Guthman was what Shriver called one of the administration's blue-chip men—a Pulitzer Prize winner, a Neiman fellow, and a veteran of the rioting in Oxford, Mississippi. He was a good man to talk to, and Bob told him of Byron Skelton's warnings about Dallas, recalling that although he had sometimes worried about possible assassination attempts, the President never had, and that both brothers had agreed that RFK, not JFK, would be the likelier target for a fanatic.[8]

'Maybe this will reduce hate,' said Guthman, searching desperately for a bright thread.

Kennedy shook his head. 'In a few months it will be forgotten.'

It was 2.40. The networks had just confirmed the President's death, and Ethel was due to leave on her daily car pool route. Little David Kennedy's school ended at 2.45. His older brothers and sister were to be picked up an hour later. Ethel wanted to remain at her husband's side and let others take her place, but he felt she should go. They were bound to have heard the news, he explained. They would be disturbed and would need their mother. In the end there

[8] Robert Kennedy had worried about John Kennedy. Like the President, however, he brushed aside threats against himself. Therefore, Guthman, without consulting him, arranged sundown-to-dawn surveillance of Hickory Hill that afternoon. The Fairfax police guarded the estate until Monday, when they were relieved by U.S. marshals from the District of Columbia. The District had ninety such marshals. Ninety volunteered for the duty.

was a compromise. Dean Markham met David in the family station wagon; Ethel went for the others. At David's parochial school—where the nuns refused to release him until Markham had produced his White House pass—Ethel's substitute became the first New Frontiersman to anticipate a facet of the assassination which was to give the next three days added poignancy. This had been an administration of young men, and it was small children who were to give the parents their cruellest moments. David climbed in sturdily, clutching a toy telephone. He dialled a number, dialled another. Encountering no more success than adults in Georgetown, he suddenly looked over. 'Jack's hurt,' he said with seven-year-old innocence. 'Why did somebody shoot him?' Markham realized that the child didn't know his uncle was dead. He looked away. At Harvard he had been known as the Crimsons' meanest lineman, but he wasn't that tough.

In spite of their inner turmoil the thoughts of individuals turned outward; they pondered the loss to the nation and the world and wondered how the great gap could be closed. On the far side of the Atlantic, Stanislaus Radziwill, the only man in the London club with a PT boat clasp, was thinking back a quarter-century to the ravaged autumn of 1939. He had been a Polish Army officer then, and when Poland was submerged in the Nazi tide and he was captured, he had felt that the Dark Ages were returning. Now he had the same feeling; if the President of the United States could be slain on a crowded street at noon, Western civilization as he had known it must be in great peril.

Dean Markham's first words to Ethel on reaching Hickory Hill had been 'What about the country?' and in New York Dwight Eisenhower's thoughts, like Markham's, had been of America. Like Radziwill, Eisenhower contemplated his own past. He remembered applying for a permit to carry a concealed weapon in 1948, when he became President of Columbia University and had often crossed Central Park evening with a derringer in his pocket as insurance against the violence that lurked around nearly every American corner. Ranging farther back, to the 1930's, he recalled a sunlit afternoon in Haiti when, as a young major, he had strolled alone through a great hall in Port-au-Prince's national palace. The walls had been lined with busts of former chiefs of state, and studying the dates beneath each he had calculated that two-thirds of them had been killed in office. Haiti, he had thought then, was a land of voodoo and savagery; his own country wasn't at all like that. Now he wasn't so sure, and he felt heartsore.

In the British Embassy on Massachusetts Avenue David Ormsby-

Gore wrote a note to Bob Kennedy. By the time it was finished the lines were tear-stained, but he blotted it as best he could and sent it off to Hickory Hill by hand anyhow.

> DEAR BOBBY, 22 Nov. 63.
>
> This has been a horrible, tragic day—for me, for the world but—above all for Jack's family. Knowing the feeling of abject misery, numbness and fury which at the moment consumes my whole body I think I have a (word indecipherable) idea of what you must be going through.
>
> Jack was the most charming, considerate, and loyal friend I have ever had, and I mourn him as though he were my own brother. He still had great things to do and he would have done them. Mankind is infinitely poorer. . . .

That poverty weighed heavily upon those whose duty it was to snatch up the fallen torch. The nation beyond Washington, and the millions abroad who had regarded the murdered President as one of their own could sink into the umbra of deep mourning. They could disregard tomorrow. The Executive Branch of the federal government could not. Already its leaders were speculating about the character of the executive mansion's incoming tenant, and on the whole they were uneasy. Until the inaugural, when he had quietly slipped into the obscurity of the Vice Presidency, Lyndon Johnson had been a creature of the Congress. On the Hill he was admired and respected, but at the other end of Pennsylvania Avenue he was an enigma. During John McCone's five-minute drive from the CIA to Hickory Hill he had totted up everything he knew about the new Chief Executive. The sum was little more than a cipher, and to McCone the prospect of a new leader was frightening.

In the State Department's carpetland Llewellyn Thompson was brooding over Johnson's capacity for foreign affairs. State considered Thompson the nation's Russian expert. He himself did not. Increasingly he had come to lean upon John Kennedy. The President had set out to master the intricacies of Sovietology, and in Thompson's opinion his success had been astounding—'He had drained me dry of all I knew,' he said later, 'and on the rare occasions when there was a difference of opinion between us, he was right and I was wrong.' In a flash the wisdom had disappeared, and the new President didn't have his predecessor's consuming interest in governments abroad.

The anxieties of General Maxwell Taylor were more immediate. Keeping his masklike expression in the Gold Room, riffling through German proposals and NATO charts, the Chairman of the Joint Chiefs had inwardly seethed over the satchel in Dallas. It was there, and it would be safe; he could count on the Signal Corps to put the bagman somewhere near the new Commander in Chief. That wasn't the problem. The difficulty was that Johnson had no idea of what was in the bag. He knew that it existed, but he hadn't been briefed about the contents, and if the thunderbolt of all-out war struck that afternoon, the country's retaliatory arsenal could be spiked until he had been led through Taz Shepard's primers for the first time.

The General's fears appear to have been justified. Had Russia attacked across the DFW line on the afternoon of November 22, 1963, the greatest military establishment in the history of the world might easily have been musclebound during the fifteen fateful minutes of warning time and perhaps even afterwards, when second-strike capacity became a factor. This, of course, is conjecture. The arcane mysteries of command decisions are the private property of the executive mansion's West Wing and the Pentagon's E Ring, and doubtless they have changed many times since then. But Johnson's ignorance of Ira Gearhart's football was real enough, and so were Gearhart's difficulties with the agents of the Vice Presidential detail at Parkland. The assassination did not signal a sneak attack, so the price of folly was unpaid. Instead, the lesson was written on the slate of time in cosmic letters and left to be learned. Llewellyn Thompson's apprehension is another matter. Appraising it must be left to those who evaluate Lyndon Johnson's foreign policy, and an account of the transitional period during which he came to power is clearly not the place for that. Perhaps Thompson's misgivings were completely without foundation. McCone's were, as he readily conceded the following spring. By then—indeed, almost from the moment he reached the capital—Johnson had taken hold with remarkable forcefulness.

He did not take hold in Texas. It is highly unlikely that he could have done so. He was reaching hard, and he had a long arm, but it wasn't a thousand miles long. The setting conspired against an instantaneous shift in authority; as long as he remained at Love Field his grasp would be limited. When Jack Valenti entered the stateroom of Air Force One, the attention of the Vice President, as everyone continued to call the new President, was riveted on the television screen. Johnson was hoping that Walter Cronkite would tell him what was going on. Those who have never been in the eye of an historic storm may find this hard to believe, but the value of even the most perceptive eyewitnesses comes later, when the recollections can be matched against one another in tranquillity. As long as events are still unfolding, the observations of each individual are as meaningless as a single jagged fragment in a thousand-piece jigsaw puzzle.

There are certain situations in which the fitting of grooves can begin at once. That is the job of intelligence, and it would have been possible if the assassination had occurred in the White House, with its magnificently equipped Situation Room. In Dallas, however, there was no Situation Room, only the situation itself. Even after Ted Clifton had discovered that Johnson had driven to Love Field he couldn't tell Washington, because Bales, under these extraordinary circumstances, couldn't provide him with a scrambled line. Lacking security, technicians literally did not dare talk. At 1.35 p.m. the stateroom of 26000 was somewhat like Bastogne in the third week of December 1944, when the 101st Airborne became the last division in Belgium to learn that the town had been invested by enemy troops. If Dallas had been surrounded, the New York studios of CBS would have been a lot likelier to know of it than anyone within shouting distance of the thirty-seventh Vice President, now become the thirty-sixth President, of the United States.

Dallas was not invested. The networks knew nothing Johnson did not know. He turned away, relieved. The big picture was not as frightening as it had seemed in imagination, unless, of course, the commentators were also in the dark. Actually, much was happening which was unknown to either Johnson or Cronkite. Unrecognized for what it was, the key to the puzzle had already appeared. Twenty minutes before the Johnson party boarded the plane, a policeman named J. D. Tippit had been shot to death two miles from the Book Depository, but another forty minutes were to pass before anyone suspected the significance of Officer Tippit's death. At 1.35 it was logical to suppose that the great crime had been committed by a great criminal backed, perhaps, by a criminal nation. If that were true, the grand design would be revealed in a grand fashion, not in the petty killing of a patrolman. Thus far it had remained hidden, and Johnson huddled with his fellow Texan politicians about his next move while the rest of the passengers, like their new President, wondered what was really happening outside.

Although the desire for knowledge mounted steadily in the plane, it remained unsatisfied. Love Field was, if anything, more misinformed than Parkland Hospital. Each offered a massive refutation of the pebble-in-the-pond theory of communication, the fiction that information spreads from its source in evenly spaced concentric circles. To the layman the pattern seems both aesthetic and logical, and any outsider hanging around the airport fence at 1.35 p.m. would have instinctively placed himself in an outer ring, the policemen on the runway in intermediate rings, and the fuselage of

26000, glinting in the bright afternoon sunlight, in the centre. But at Love Field geometry and proximity were irrelevant. In Colonel McNally's words, 'The cops were running around with goofy looks'—McNally believed that 'if this had been a concerted affair, the conspirators could have had the plane and everything'. Those who didn't look goofy *felt* goofy. Jim Swindal, for example, had greeted Johnson at the foot of the ramp with a snappy salute. From the fence he gave every appearance of knowledgeableness. In fact, Colonel Swindal, like Colonel McNally and Sergeant Ayres, knew far less than Americans in distant parts of the country whose access to the nearest television set wasn't blocked by a President, and who were, therefore, privy to the confidences of Cronkite and David Brinkley.

The Presidential party's rear echelon at the airport didn't know what had happened at the hospital, and the best informed among them had only the haziest notion of the motorcade's movements after 12.30 p.m. The last transmissions the aircraft had received from downtown Dallas had been Kellerman's alarm and Roberts' 'Have Dagger cover Volunteer.' Then the plane's Charlie set had gone dead. Swindal had gathered that there was an emergency of some sort, but he could only speculate. Remembering the Adlai Stevenson incident, he had guessed there had been a riot. After McHugh called from Parkland and told him their next leg would take them to Andrews Field he had hazarded that the strain of the trip had been too much for the President's back, and they were going to take him back to Walter Reed or Bethesda Naval Hospital for treatment. Because of the Charlie blackout, and because the Signalmen who could operate the more complex equipment were all in the terminal restaurant (no one aboard remembered the UPI and AP teletype machines), Swindal had turned to the stateroom television set. Sergeant Ayres, George Thomas, and the two secretaries from Salinger's office, Chris Camp and Sue Vogelsinger, had joined him there. As the full dimensions of the tragedy emerged the women had dissolved. Swindal had recoiled, and Ayres tinkered madly with the reception until he got what he later called 'a real good picture'. George Thomas had disappeared into Kennedy's bedroom. The President would have no use for the clothes he had laid out, so George had carefully repacked them.

Inside the terminal, those who were lunching had experienced the sensations which had been shared that moment in a million other American dining rooms. Munching sandwiches and sipping soup, they had become aware of a pervasive tension. Clearly something, somewhere, had happened to someone. Waitresses in far corners had been dropping dishes, and there had been a deafening clamour in the kitchen, as though everything suspended from hooks had fallen at once. Next a puzzling whisper had been passed from table to table; the captain of the Pan American press plane wanted his men to report to him immediately. Concerned, Master Sergeant Joe Giordano and the two men with him had risen to investigate. Discovering that their waitress had vanished, they had pooled their change, flung it on the table, and raced out, passing Colonel McNally, who had eaten early and was waiting patiently at the cashier's desk. She had just received a phone call; he hadn't even noticed her end of it. He had glanced up at Giordano and then noticed that the woman was talking to herself. 'He's been shot, he's in the hospital,' she had been mumbling. She had been confused; she hadn't seemed to know whether or not to take his bill. Speculating that a close friend or relative had been injured, he had asked charily, 'Who?' She had looked vacant. The restaurant's PA system had begun paging the crew members of both 707's. The Colonel had repeated urgently, '*Who?*' She had shaken herself briskly. 'President Kennedy,' she had said and rung up the sale.

As McNally had stumbled into the sun, change in hand, and stared at the puddles on the field—puddles, he had remembered, between which John Kennedy had buoyantly stepped less than two hours before—the unheralded Johnsonian cavalcade had been swiftly moving from Parkland to Love. From his command post at the fence the Colonel had synchronized communications through the Sheraton-Dallas switchboard. Learning that Kennedy was gone, he had begun a few incoherent pencilled notes: 'A President is dead, murdered in a supposedly American city . . . tragic hours . . . One of the blackest days in our Nation's history.' Unknown to him, as he had prepared his agenda of emergency communications action, Chief Curry had been hurrying through the pink lights on Harry Hines Boulevard. To the consternation of those in the rear echelon, the car had been preceded by SS 100 X ('The back seat,' wrote McNally, who couldn't look, 'was described as a horror'). Armed agents from the hospital had fanned out, crying to everyone they recognized that they would have given anything 'to have been able to shoot it out with that son of hell'; that 'he should be torn limb from limb; death is too good for him'. (A change, this, from the ominous 'they'; the literal agents accepted a cardinal rule of ballistics: one weapon, one man.)

In this mêlée Lyndon Johnson had unexpectedly headed for the ramp of 26000. There had been no opportunity to clear the stateroom for him. Swindal had barely had time to scramble down for that welcoming salute. That the television set should be on appeared normal to the new President. To those who had been watching it, however, his unforeseen appearance seemed inappropriate, and in embarrassment they scattered to other cabins and, in some cases, to the runway; Chris Camp and Sue Vogelsinger, concluding that Johnson's presence on 26000 meant Kennedy would be on 86970, elected to switch to the other 707. (The secretaries anticipated no awkwardness between Johnson and the Kennedy group. They merely recalled that it was established policy for the President and his Vice President to ride on different aircraft so that one crash could not kill both. The fact that the assassination had rendered the policy meaningless did not occur to them.) The women were lucky. The runway was far more comfortable than the aeroplane. After McHugh had ordered preparations for an immediate take-off, Swindal had disconnected the ground air conditioner, and the interior was rapidly becoming a kiln.

Rufus Youngblood's hour in history—it lasted almost exactly an hour—was nearly at an end. It was a freak, an outgrowth of the panic and uncertainty which had briefly broken the nation's stride. Once the new Chief Executive felt secure the Secret Service was destined to fade back into the shadows, and for Lyndon Johnson security returned when he had been extricated from the vortex of Dallas. Climbing the ramp ended the threat. Only a return to the city could renew it, and he had no intention of flirting again with whatever dark forces lurked in those sunlit streets. He had been badly scarred. Ten months later he was invited to address an American Legion National Convention in Dallas at the height of the Presidential campaign; to the dismay of the Legion (and the chagrin of the city's civic leaders) he refused. Love Field, although part of Dallas, represented a giant step towards asylum, and the period of the Youngblood protectorate, which had begun on Elm Street, may be said to have ended in the stateroom of 26000 when the agent first insisted that the Johnson family move directly into the White House upon arrival in the capital.

He had crossed a line. To him the suggestion was just another safety precaution. Johnson saw that it had other implications, some of them exceedingly delicate, and he flatly rejected it. That was at approximately 1.45 p.m. Johnson was then firmly in control. In their early moments aboard, however, Youngblood had continued to act as his Ken O'Donnell, with Emory Roberts and agents of the Vice Presidential detail as his staff. Explaining that he himself would be tied down in the stateroom, Youngblood told Lem Johns to identify Vice Presidential advisers for the crew, order the stewards to draw up a passenger manifest, and delay the plane's departure until the arrival of the Kennedys. The first of these was essential. The crew knew Lady Bird from the newspapers, but the rest of the newcomers were strangers. (To complicate matters, some strangers didn't know where they were; Liz Carpenter was under the impression that she was on 86970.) Before nightfall all who had been close to Johnson would be on their way to national eminence, but first Johns had to clear the way to the stage, and his task was not limited to the group from the hospital. One of his first problems was to deal with an A-priority request from Love's control tower. Airport operations reported that 'A Mr Bill Moyers is in a private plane overhead, requesting permission to land'. None of Swindal's men had heard of this Mr Moyers. Johns persuaded them that Lyndon Johnson had; flashing his commission book he promised to vouch for him personally.

'Do you know that we're waiting for Mrs Kennedy?' Johns inquired of Swindal. Swindal didn't. Johns further inquired, 'Do you know where we're going to put the coffin?' Swindal didn't know that either, and Johns tactfully ventured that stewards might remove the seats on the port side of the tail compartment. The colonel asked dazedly, 'Where will we put the seats when we've taken them out?' 'On the backup plane,' said Johns, and Swindal nodded slowly at Ayres, directing him to do it.

Fifty feet away, at the fence, Emory Roberts was speaking crisply into one of McNally's telephones: 'Volunteer and Victoria are aboard. Where are Lancer and Lace?' Of all the unlikely conversations held that Friday afternoon, this one strains credulity most: Mr and Mrs Johnson were ready to leave Dallas. What was holding up Mr and Mrs Kennedy? One sympathizes with Roberts. His assignment was unenviable. To make things worse, he wasn't getting through; the reply was an unintelligible squawk. Undaunted, he tried again and was again unsuccessful. No one could ascertain the whereabouts of the absent Kennedys.

In 26000's communications shack Johns made a discovery which was to grow in importance over the next hour. Jerry Behn, thanks to Colonel McNally's electronic sorcery, was now in direct telephone communication with the plane through the Signal Corps switchboards in the Sheraton-Dallas and Hotel Texas. The link meant that the government in the capital needn't be a slave to television. Furthermore, the splice between the White House and the plane made two-way conversations possible.

The new President had shaken off the torpor of Booth 13; he had already begun accustoming himself to the mantle of authority when he had ducked past Swindal's salute and homed in on the beam of Cronkite's voice. Entering as he did through the tail compartment, he had had to pass the narrow corridor beside the Presidential bedroom. There he had wavered. 'Is there any other place we can use?'

he had asked Sergeant Ayres, explaining to Lady Bird, 'These are their private quarters.' It was then that they had heard the television set and entered the stateroom. The steward brought them water. Johnson was parched; perspiring in the stuffy stateroom as he watched Cronkite, he drained a tumblerful and two bottles of Kennedy's Poland water. His hand was dead steady (every eye was on it; now that he was President, his smallest gestures would be covertly observed by those around him), and although his own eyes were on the screen, he was issuing a spate of orders, reminding Rufus Youngblood to post a lookout for Jacqueline Kennedy, telling him to have the agents make a written record of their movements, and leading a running discussion with aides and Congressmen over the advisability of taking the Presidential oath immediately.

On the couch opposite the stateroom desk Bird fingered her choker of pearls and jotted down her memoirs. They formed a jumbled chromo. She overheard 'the agonized voice' of a Secret Service man crying that the Service had never lost a President before, and she 'hurt for him'. She was aware of Lyndon, moving restlessly from chair to couch to chair. She intercepted a message from Parkland—Mrs Kennedy wouldn't move from Major Medicine without the body. Johnson let it be known that 26000 wouldn't budge; they were going to 'wait on' the gallant lady and the coffin. Television's square eye had become somewhat newsier; there were reports that the President had been the victim of a .30–.30 rifle. The stateroom's occupants kept loosening their collars and mopping their foreheads. Lady Bird alone felt chilled. She nursed her elbows and listened to Lyndon canvassing the men on the question of where he should be sworn in.

His approach, a Johnsonian trademark, was subdued and noncommittal; he was requesting their opinions without disclosing his own. Jack Brooks, an impulsive ex-Marine, was a partisan of the instant oath. Homer Thornberry countered, 'Let's wait until Washington.' Albert Thomas sided with Brooks. 'Suppose the plane is delayed?' he asked Johnson, echoing the convictions of the correspondents at Parkland. 'The country can't afford to be without a President while you're flying all over the country.' Thomas was ignoring the fact that this was no ordinary aeroplane, and that Jim Swindal didn't fly 'all over' any route, but the debate itself was probably of little consequence. Johnson's mind seemed to be made up—he was, Joe Ayres observed, 'very much in command'. To Thomas he said, 'I agree. Now. What about the oath?'

They looked blank. Throats were cleared, limp ties loosened, but no one spoke. Here he was seeking, not a consensus, but hard information, and the Texas Congressmen hadn't any. The best they could offer were fuzzy memories of textbook engravings of Chester A. Arthur or Calvin Coolidge, who, in the dancing illumination of defective lamplight, affixed his hand to a shabby family Bible while strangers in old-fashioned nightshirts stood around gaping. Everyone agreed that there was an official in the picture. His identity, however, was obscure. He could have been a Supreme Court Justice or a notary public. Undoubtedly he was supposed to do more than hold the Bible. Yet the fine print of the oath itself eluded the Congressmen entirely.

It was all very unsatisfactory. Johnson was not limited to the passengers in 26000's main cabin, however. Learning from the agents of the Vice Presidential detail that the communications shack was in contact with Washington, he eagerly looked around for telephones. The closest one hung from a hook on the other side of the aisle. He ignored it. Possibly he could not yet bring himself to sit at Kennedy's stateroom desk, though the more plausible explanation is that he wanted solitude. In any event, the instrument he did use was on another, smaller Presidential desk, in Kennedy's quarters.

Because he had not been briefed, the new President was unaware that conversations to and from 26000, 86970, 86971, and 86972 were monitored at Acrobat (Andrews Field) and automatically taped by the Signal Corps. Unfortunately, as General Clifton later explained to this writer, the device only operated when the planes were airborne. In this age of sophisticated eavesdropping, Angel dialogues were sometimes picked up by a group of zealous amateurs in Colorado, but a check has failed to uncover any such activity between 1.26 and 2.47, when Colonel Swindal took off and the turning reels at Andrews began to record voice traffic from the Presidential aircraft, together with that which was already being received from the Cabinet plane. The absence of an incontestable record and the nature of Johnson's talks mean that the page of history he wrote in 26000's bedroom is blurred. Nevertheless it is partly readable. Although he himself informed this writer that he could not even 'recall the precise sequence of calls' which he made, he was never entirely alone—'I'm sticking to you like glue,' said Youngblood, trailing him inside—and in all important instances the recollections of the person to whom he talked are available.

No consensus on the question of his reanointing could be complete if the government's chief legal adviser were left out. Thus the first issue of the Johnson administration arose. It was a prickly one, because the man to whom the new President must now turn was the one member of the Cabinet who was entitled to sit out the transition. That respite was to be denied him. It was unfortunate that this was so, for the consequence was to be an extraordinary misunderstanding.

Perhaps misapprehension was inevitable. No one was quite normal at that hour, but both Lyndon Johnson and Robert Kennedy were deeply disturbed men, staggering under fantastic burdens. The full weight of the most awesome responsibility in the world had just descended upon Johnson's shoulders; harrowing personal tragedy had fallen on the younger Kennedy. However, the new President had little choice. The question he had asked of the Congressmen was constitutional, which meant that the buck couldn't stop here on the plane. It had to go to the Department of Justice. Conceivably Deputy Attorney General Katzenbach could have been consulted; equally conceivably, Katzenbach would have checked with Kennedy anyhow. Thus the issue had to be laid before the lawyer who had been John Kennedy's, and who was now automatically his successor's, Attorney General. That he should be the dead President's brother was cruel mischance, yet if the incoming Chief Executive were to exercise Tyler's 'great caution' he had no option. Seated at the end of Jacqueline Kennedy's bed, with Rufus Youngblood standing against the wall, he accordingly placed a call to Robert Kennedy in Virginia, and moments later the white phone at the shallow end of Hickory Hill's swimming pool rang.

Johnson was not J. Edgar Hoover. He was a man of tact and sensitivity. He began by expressing his condolences. But he had just become the busiest man in the world, and after a few compassionate sentences he plunged into business. The murder, he said, 'might be part of a world-wide plot'. In Johnson's statement to the Warren Commission seven and a half months later he suggested that the Attorney General had agreed with this interpretation and had 'discussed the practical problems at hand—problems of special urgency because we did not at that time have any information as to the motivation of the assassination or its possible implications'. In fact, Kennedy was unresponsive. He was not among those who suspected a grand conspiracy, and he didn't understand what Johnson was talking about.

'A lot of people down here think I should be sworn in right away,' said the new President, moving closer to the point. 'Do you have any objection to that?'

Kennedy was taken aback. It was scarcely an hour and a quarter since he had first heard of the shooting, less than an hour since he had learned that the wound had been fatal. As Attorney General he couldn't understand the need for a rush, and on a personal level he preferred that any investiture be deferred until his brother's body had been brought home.

'Congressman Albert Thomas thinks I should take the oath here,' said Johnson, citing support. There was no answer, and he pressed on. 'A lot of other people feel the same way.' The phone by the pool remained silent. Kennedy did not dissent, he said nothing. Changing to another tack, Johnson again referred to the plot, and then he requested information. According to Youngblood he asked 'questions about who, when, and how he should take the Presidential oath'. Kennedy heard, 'Who could swear me in?'

'I'll be glad to find out and call you back,' he answered.

He depressed his receiver and asked the operator for Nick Katzenbach. It was 3 p.m., in Washington, according to Katzenbach's secretary's log, when, for the first time since the assassination, Robert Kennedy talked to his Deputy Attorney General. According to Katzenbach, Kennedy's voice was 'matter-of-fact, flat'. He told Nick, 'Lyndon wants to be sworn in in Texas and wants to know who can administer the oath.'

Katzenbach said, 'Bob, I'm absolutely stunned.' There was no reply. He said, 'My recollection is that anyone can administer the oath who administers oaths under federal or state laws. Do you want to hold on while I check?'

Bob did, and using another Justice line Nick called Harold Reis in the Department's office of Legal Counsel.

'That's right,' said Reis. He reminded Katzenbach that Coolidge had been sworn in by his own father, a justice of the peace, and he added, 'Of course, the oath's in the Constitution.'

He was the man Johnson should have been talking to. Telling the Deputy Attorney General was not necessary, but telling the new President was. What was required was someone with a gift for explaining the obvious. Actually, it wasn't as obvious as it appeared to be; a great many eminent attorneys, Robert Kennedy among them, were so shaken that they had forgotten where they could lay their hands on the oath. Reis' instincts were better than he knew. It may have been like pointing out to the Washington Redskins that they were entitled to four downs, but if the Redskin quarterback forgot, somebody would have to come to his rescue. No one had come to Johnson's, and waiting for the Attorney General to phone back he was using other lines in an attempt to find out what was in any copy of *The World Almanac.*

As Kennedy talked to Katzenbach, Johnson had placed two more Washington calls. The first was Volunteer to Vigilant—Lyndon Johnson to Walter Jenkins. The former Vice President's chief aide told him what he already knew, that he ought to return to the capital. Unhappily, Vigilant was uninformed about the oath. Drawing a blank there, Johnson phoned McGeorge Bundy. In each case the inquiry from the bedroom was oblique. Given the nature of the inquirer it could not have been otherwise, and an appreciation of his nature and special talent is essential to a grasp of the misunderstandings which were to be bred by his approach. To men who were accustomed to dealing with President Kennedy, it was like listening to a foreign tongue. Both in public and in private, Kennedy had been as direct as his pointed finger at televised press conferences. Johnson approached a strongly fortified position by outflanking it, or burrowing under it, or surprising the defenders from the rear, or raining down obstacles upon them from the sky, or starving them into submission. Rarely, and then only reluctantly, would he proceed directly from A to B. To him the shortest distance between two points was a tunnel.

His supreme talents were those of the man behind the scenes. But his complexities do not even end there, for few men in public life have found less comfort in anonymity. When the circus catch was made, he wanted the fans to note the LBJ brand on the fielder's glove. They noted it. It could not be missed. Yet the feeling persisted that bat, batter, and umpire had been stamped with the same brand—that the play had been set from the start. It was only a feeling. Nothing was ever proved. His critics called him a wheeler-dealer. They overlooked the subtlety of Johnsonian strategy, his use of wheels within wheels. Put him within reach of a console switchboard and he became an octopus, clutching telephone receivers like bunches of black bananas. As Senate Majority Leader he had made the legislative process work with the virtuosity of statecraft, often relying on intermediaries, who in turn engaged other go-betweens. Typically, a Johnson adviser called a colleague who phoned an associate who made an appointment with a friend, each of whom carefully covered his tracks as he went. Johnson always managed to be out there in centre field at the finish, his mitt outstretched to snag the descending ball.

Given time that Friday he would have turned to this elaborate process. There was no time. He was hard pressed, on an aeroplane, in unfamiliar surroundings. Even so, the refractional quality of his telephone conversations is striking. Bundy's notes of twelve days later are revealing: 'I talked briefly to the new President to say that he must get back to Washington where we were all shaky. He agreed, and I now know that he immediately reached the same conclusion himself.' The Johnsonian tactic—soliciting an answer which is already known—is familiar. It may seem pointless. It isn't. It has the great advantage of putting the answerer on record.

Johnson then confided that he was worried about the oath and uncertain where to take it. Bundy explained that he had his hands full at the moment; he was monitoring the eastward progress of the returning Cabinet plane. Furthermore, he did not lightly deliver horseback opinions, especially when the terrain was strange and, in this instance, extremely forbidding. Mac's undergraduate major at Yale had been mathematics. He wanted life to be that exact. Presidential oaths clearly belonged on someone else's desk spike. He politely suggested that Johnson 'leave that to the Justice Department'. He was right. Oaths are to Justice what weapons are to Defence. Bundy's counsel, like Bundy himself, was flawless. And although the Attorney General, like the new President, would have preferred to let someone else field the question, Justice had the answer. As Johnson talked to Bundy, Nick Katzenbach had checked back with Bob Kennedy and confirmed his earlier opinion.

'Then any federal judge can do it?' Kennedy asked.

'Anybody, including a District Court Judge.' Nick added, 'I imagine he'll want Sarah Hughes.' Sarah was from Dallas, and he remembered Johnson's vigorous lobbying for her appointment.

Inside, in his library, Robert Kennedy signalled the White House operator, who interrupted Johnson's Bundy conversation and connected him with his Attorney General. The crux of their exchange is unclear. This second Johnson–O'Donnell talk at Parkland, has two renditions. The facts are unclear, and a dispassionate observer cannot choose. According to the President's subsequent statement to the Warren Commission, Kennedy advised him 'that the oath should be administered to me immediately, before taking off for Washington, and that it should be administered by a judicial officer of the United States'. Youngblood's memory is foggy. He tends to support his superior, with qualifications, but he explains—quite reasonably—that he only heard one voice. Kennedy, who was on the other end, does not remember recommending an immediate ceremony, and it should be noted that such a recommendation would have been inconsistent with his mood. It is his recollection—and that of Ed Guthman, who was with him—that he said, 'Anybody can swear you in. Maybe you'd like to have one of the judges down there whom you appointed. Any one of them can do it.'

He was asked about the wording of the oath.

'You can get the oath,' he said. 'There's no problem about the oath, they can locate the oath.'

'Fine,' said Johnson, and rang off.

But it wasn't fine. He still lacked a text.

In the stateroom Cliff Carter said to Marie Fehmer, 'You'd better go in, he's making calls.'

She saw Johnson on the bed and sat in the chair facing the door. The desk and telephone were between them.

'Write this down,' Johnson told her. He dictated brief notes of his talks to Jenkins, Bundy, and the Attorney General and said, 'Now. Let's get Waddy Bullion.'

J. W. Bullion was a Dallas lawyer who had been counsel to Lady Bird for twenty-three years. Marie carried a little book with the telephone numbers of the Vice President's oldest friends and allies. Bullion was in it, and she dialled RIverside 1-4721. His secretary said he was in Shreveport on business.

'Get Sarah Hughes,' Johnson said.

At RIverside 8-2251 Sarah's law clerk, John Spinuzzi, explained that she was out—the last he knew she was on her way to the Trade Mart lunch. The new President took the receiver from his secretary. 'This is Lyndon Johnson,' he said tersely. 'Find her.' Then, to Marie: 'Try Irv Goldberg.'

RIverside 1-6252 was the office number of Irving L. Goldberg, another local attorney and veteran of Johnson's Texas political campaigns. He, too, was out. Like Sarah, he had last been seen driving off in the direction of the Trade Mart, and like her he was now at home watching his television set. The phone there rang; his secretary said excitedly, 'The Dallas White House is trying to reach you.' Her voice faded and was succeeded by static—it was a very poor connection—and then a faint but familiar voice came on. 'This is Lyndon. Do you think I should be sworn in here or in Washington?'

Irv thought rapidly. Maybe Johnson was already President, but he wasn't clear about the Constitution. It was best to make sure.

'I think here.'[9]

'Who should do it?'

'Sarah Hughes.'

'We're trying to get her here. You try, too.'

Goldberg wanted to be helpful. 'The Dallas White House,' however, meant nothing to him. All he knew was that Johnson must be somewhere in the city. He asked cautiously, 'Where are you?'

'Love Field. And you'd better get out here.'

Irv knew he would never make it. He would make every effort, and he could reach the field quickly, but experience had taught him that he wasn't adept at talking his way past policemen. (He was right. He and his wife raced to the airport and were stopped at a barrier.) Still, he thought, he could do something about Sarah, and hanging up he called Barefoot Sanders. To Goldberg, unschooled in the Florentine intrigues of the federal government, it seemed that a U.S. attorney with jurisdiction over one hundred north Texas

[9] According to Johnson's recollection—nine months older than Goldberg's—the lawyer 'advised' that he should be 'sworn in at once, and undertook to locate Judge Sarah Hughes to administer the oath'.

counties ought to have sufficient authority to provide Sarah with an honour guard of Secret Service and FBI men. Even on a normal day it was more complicated than that. Sanders was without authority over either the Service or the Bureau's Dallas office, which, although it was as much a part of Justice as he was, had a maddening habit of referring reports to him with notes explaining that they 'might be of interest to the Justice Department'. And this day wasn't normal. The U.S. Attorney had hitchhiked back to his office from the Trade Mart and was chest-deep in lawbooks, trying to put his finger on a statute under which the President's murderer could be charged. U.S. attorneys in San Antonio and Fort Smith, Arkansas, were on the phone offering counsel, and Sanders had appealed for advice to both his Fort Worth office and Justice's Criminal Division in Washington.

He needed all the help he could get. Oswald had created a legal nightmare. In Washington J. Edgar Hoover was proceeding on the assumption that the sniper on Elm Street had violated a federal law. Thirty-seven years before, when an FBI man was slain in Illinois, Hoover had pushed through a statute protecting his agents. He hadn't dreamed that Presidents of the United States weren't already covered. The Director was in for a shock. Since 1902 every Secret Service chief had urged Congress to outlaw Presidential assassination, and all had failed. Threatening the life of a Chief Executive was illegal, but if the threat were carried out, if the bravo succeeded, the U.S. Code was silent. There was one exception. Should the assassin be part of a plot, the FBI could move in. This assassin had acted alone, however, and as soon as that became clear local authorities had exclusive jurisdiction. He was guilty only of a Texas felony. Technically, there was no difference between the shooting of the President and a knifing in a Dallas bar-room.

Barefoot was desperately trying to bridge this unbridgeable gap. He had already drawn up five separate forms of complaint. All of them were to prove invalid, but at the time he was hoping that one of them would put the killer in the hands of federal policemen. In his hands were three versions of 18 U.S.C. (United States Code) 2385, advocating the overthrow of the government; 18 U.S.C. 372, the general conspiracy statute; and 18 U.S.C. 1114, Hoover's law covering federal law enforcement 'officers and employees'. This would stand up if the AP's 2.14 p.m. report of a dead Secret Service agent, which had just come in, were true. The FBI couldn't arrest a President's killer, but it could hold the killer of a Presidential bodyguard.

This pettifoggery was interrupted by a call from Goldberg, who summarized his conversation with the Dallas White House, explaining that he had suggested that the oath be administered by Sarah Hughes and that Johnson had agreed.

'That's fine if we can find her,' Sanders said. 'I'll do what I can.'

Her office was directly above his. He bolted upstairs and arrived just as Sarah, independently of Johnson, Goldberg, or himself, phoned in to inquire whether there had been any messages for her.

He took the receiver. 'This is Barefoot. The Vice President wants you to swear him in as President. Can you do it?'

She said she could. At that moment her secretary started to wig-wag frantically to him on the other line. A call was coming in from a Johnson aide on the plane. Sanders nodded. He knew what it was all about. He was handling it.

'Where do I go?' Sarah was asking.

'Love Field. I'll clear you with the Secret Service. How soon do you think you can get there?'

'Ten minutes,' she said rashly. 'But what about the oath?'

'I'll have it at the airport when you get there.'

Barefoot was promising more than he could deliver. His role in the ceremony ended with that call. The fact that he didn't do more wasn't entirely his fault; the general bedlam had hobbled everyone. The instant he hung up, the phone rang again. It was Rufus Young-blood, calling on Johnson's order to offer Sarah an escort. Barefoot explained that she had already left for the field. An escort would have been of dubious value. Arranging a rendezvous would have just delayed her. The motor-cycles might have gone to the wrong address, or, conceivably, to the wrong official. Three messages from the Dallas police tapes indicate the range of chaos. At 1.56 p.m., the police radio had put out an incorrect home address for J. D. Tippit, who was a member of the department, and whose wife needed the commiseration of his brother officers. At 2.24 a dispatcher broadcast, 'A Mr Bill Moyers is on his way to swear in Mr Johnson'; correcting himself at 2.35, he told cruisers, 'We now have information that Judge Sarah Hughes is en route from Parkland to Love to swear President Johnson in.' Moyers was ineligible to preside over the induction of a notary public, and Sarah wasn't near the hospital. At the same time, both errors are understandable. Even in Texas, members of the Johnson team were largely obscure, and it is a con-spicuous weakness of the telephone system that the whereabouts of callers are easily confused. In Dallas and elsewhere that afternoon men took what they thought were long-distance calls when the callers were, in fact, just a few offices away. Similarly, the police department, learning that Sarah had phoned her office, had con-cluded that she was with the party left behind at Parkland.

The oath is another matter. The U.S. Attorney should have been able to provide that. But Barefoot had become so immersed in 18 U.S.C. 2385, 18 U.S.C. 1114, and 18 U.S.C. 372 that he had become overwhelmed by finer points of law. He couldn't imagine where the Presidential pledge could be, and was rummaging through statute volumes from three libraries—his own, Sarah's, and that of Judge Joe Estes—when a clerk said, 'Hey, what about the Constitution?' 'Of course,' said Barefoot, feeling foolish. He needn't have blushed, though. As U.S. Judge for the Northern District of Texas Sarah had more legal rank than he did, and she not only had forgotten the Constitution; she had decided that since the essentials of every oath are pretty much the same, the exact wording didn't matter. 'I was not afraid,' she recalled afterwards. 'I could do it without a formal oath—I could make one up.' Driving towards the airport in her red sports car, she was more concerned about speed. She had known Lyndon Johnson since 1948 and 'I knew he would want things in a hurry; that's the way he is.'

He also liked things to be done properly, however, and, fortunately for those who do not view the wording of the U.S. Constitution so lightly, he was covering all bases. At 2.20—3.20 in Washington—Nick Katzenbach's phone rang. It was the Dallas White House, continuing its tireless search for a lawyer who knew precisely what a President should say on assuming office. 'Hold on,' Nick said, 'and I'll dictate it.'

Aboard the Presidential plane Cliff Carter told Marie Fehmer, 'Get on the phone in the staff cabin and read it back to him.'

Laying down his receiver, Katzenbach crossed to a bookcase, opened the glass doors, and took a heavy blue volume from the lower shelf. It was the Government Printing Office's 1953 edition of the annotated Constitution, edited by Edward S. Corwin. Riffling through it, Nick put his finger on the bottom of page 384.

Back at his desk he read, 'I do solemnly swear, parenthesis, or affirm, unparenthesis, that I will faithfully execute the, capital, Office of President of the United States, comma, and will to the best of my ability, comma, preserve, comma, protect and defend the Constitution of the United States period.'

Marie's fingers moved lightly over a pad, and as she wrote, Lyndon Johnson, who had remained in the bedroom, moved into the stateroom. Valenti, Carter, and Congressmen Thomas and Thornberry had been sitting with Lady Bird, watching television. Glimpsing the tall figure in the entrance, they rose together. Now it had hit them. Now they knew who he was, and now Albert Thomas became the second man to call him by his correct title.

'It's a terrible burden, but we all know you can do it, Mr President.'

Valenti heard the title; it made him 'all goose-bumpy'. Then he heard Johnson speaking to him.

'I've just talked to the Attorney General, and he has advised me that I should be sworn in here.' He pointed towards Marie. 'I want you to check the oath.'

Swiftly cranking a blank 3 × 5 file card into one of the aircraft's two electric typewriters, she had already transcribed her notes. Valenti bounced in from the stateroom, took both card and phone from her, and read the text back.

'That's it,' said Nick.

Marie joined the group in the stateroom. The television announcer's voice was indistinct, and she gradually became aware of the reason. Someone was hammering in the plane's tail compartment.

'What's that noise?' she asked Cliff.

'They're taking out seats to make room.' He came to a full stop.

'Oh,' she said uncomprehendingly.

His eyes looked poached. He averted them and finished, 'Room for the casket.'

'*Oh.*'

There was a momentary silence; the sound of the television set a few feet away became conspicuous, as though someone had just turned up the volume. At present the commentators were confused, but in downtown Dallas the news had just taken a dramatic turn. The police had entered a theatre and arrested a man for the killing of Policeman Tippit. Five minutes before Katzenbach began dictating the oath to Marie, the homicide squad had learned that their new prisoner worked as a stockman in the Texas School Book Depository and was, in fact, the only Depository employee to have been missing when Superintendent Truly counted heads a half-hour after the assassination. The first faint light was entering what had, until now, been a pitch-black maze.

The flight and arrest of Lee Oswald must be seen in context, which is asking a lot. The mind instinctively rejects any connection between him and the nation's martyred Chief Executive. One feels that he slew in the criminal hope that reflected glory from the Kennedy nimbus might brighten his own anonymity—'Everybody will know who I am now,' he told a police captain after he had been caught—and justice demands that while the deed cannot be undone the spoils should be destroyed. He shot the President of the United States in the back to attract attention. Noticing him, and even printing his name in history books, therefore seems obscene. It is an outrage. He is an outrage. We want him Out.

Still, there he is. He will not go away, any more than John Wilkes Booth and Vidkun Quisling will go. They stain the pages of our texts, and so will he. Crucified and the crucifiers, Balder and Loki, Eichmann and his Jews are united in time's unscrupulous memory, and righteousness cannot divorce them. Yet inspecting opposite sides of a coin is difficult, especially when they must be examined at the same time, and in this crime coeval observation is necessary. The events of November 22, 1963, were synchronic. It was as though the Axis powers had surrendered and Adolf Hitler and Franklin Roosevelt had died in the hours between noon and mid-afternoon in Washington of a single day in 1945.

People can absorb just so much, no more. On November 22 the assassination blotted out nearly everything else. The announcement of Kennedy's death was a saturation point, and the scattered patches of consciousness left were reserved for thoughts of those who had been closest to him, concern for the country, and feelings of personal deprivation. Even Lyndon Johnson was discordant. One surveyor of feeling among college students found that many reported 'an immediate reaction of resentment against Johnson, partly because of his Texas background, partly because he seemed ("irrationally", the students acknowledged) to be somehow usurping the presidential role'. The transition was accepted in the way an unpleasant cathartic is accepted. Americans had learned the facts of succession—or, more precisely, the accepted version of those facts—as schoolchildren. They knew the thing had to be done, and were reconciled to it. But they didn't want to think about it. The slain President's successor was thrust into the background, behind his widow, his children, his parents, his brothers and sisters, and his chief aides, all of whom were more familiar than his relatively colourless Vice President. Johnson was expected to mumble 'I do' at the end of the oath and then retire into the scenery. Having acknowledged his induction into office, the public quickly moved on to matters which, at the moment, seemed far more compelling.

If the new President was relegated to a walk-on role and then rudely hustled into the wings, the murderer was shoved straight out the stage door. He wasn't even the object of much curiosity. Later, after a decent interval (and, incidentally, his own murder) he was readmitted. The sequel was dismal. In death as in life he conformed to type. His ghost put on a vulgar performance, mugging, upstaging, and hogging the limelight with, regrettably, the co-operation of the President's Commission on the Assassination of President Kennedy. That was unavoidable. Under the terms of its mandate the Commission had no choice. Yet the Warren Report might be subtitled 'The Life of Lee Harvey Oswald'. It is largely a biography of him, and he would have gloated over it; the index lists nearly four times as many references to him as to Kennedy and Johnson combined.

Among those who keep faith with the myth that murderers are more fascinating than their victims, Oswald was eventually assigned the star role in his own existentialist extravaganza. Reality requires ventilation of the compartment in which he has been sealed, and, after the airing, a sense of perspective. Perspective doesn't do much for his stature. In panorama he shrinks to his former size (which is extremely small), while his environment, having been nothing before, can only grow (its magnitude depends upon the spectator). Nor does his aberrance diminish. He is more of a gargoyle than ever, and the barbarous obbligato he played that Friday measures, as Tomas de Torquemada and Lazarillo de Tormes measured in other ages, the potentialities of human depravity. A man can set any course. His capacities are boundless, and the coexistence of Oswald and the Kennedys in the 400 block of Elm Street at 12.30 p.m. provides an unparalleled illustration of the uncharted spaces within the human soul.

Lee Oswald has been repeatedly identified here as the President's slayer. He is never 'alleged' or 'suspected' or 'supposed' or 'surmised'; he is the culprit. Some, intimidated by the fiction that only judges may don the black cap and condemn, may disapprove. The managing editor of the *New York Times* apologized to his readers for a headline describing Oswald as the murderer, and four months after the appearance of the Warren Report the Washington *Post* continued to refer to him as 'the presumed assassin'. But enough is enough. The evidence pointing to his guilt is far more incriminating than that against Booth, let alone Judas Iscariot. He is the right man; there is nothing provisional about it. The mark of Cain was upon him. From the instant he dropped his mail-order rifle on the top floor and fled down the enclosed stair well—leaving a tuft of fibres from his shirt wedged in the butt plate and a profusion of finger and palm prints on the weapon, on the paper bag which he had used to conceal the gun during the drive from Irving with Wesley Frazier, and on one of the cartons he had stacked as a gun rest—there could be no doubt of his ultimate conviction.

. . . Provided, of course, he was brought to trial. On November 22, his speedy arrest had been considered an achievement. What is really remarkable is that he managed to elude Jesse Curry's men for an hour and twenty minutes. When he opened fire, uniformed officers were standing on the sidewalk below and riding in the street. One of them, Marrion L. Baker, was directly under the gun. As Oswald left the Mannlicher-Carcano between two rows of boxes and headed down the stairwell, Baker abandoned his motor-cycle and headed up with Superintendent Roy Truly. Arriving on the second-floor landing, the policeman saw the assassin twenty feet away, entering the warehouse lunchroom. Oswald was walking away from him, and Baker had the impression, doubtless correct, that he was in something of a hurry. Drawing his revolver, the patrolman commanded, 'Come here.' Oswald came. Baker asked Truly, 'Do you know this man? Does he work here?' The superintendent vouched for him, and the policeman turned away. 'Truly okayed Oswald,' a Dallas inspector explained to this writer, 'and Baker naturally assumed that anybody who worked there was OK.'

Because of Oswald's epic stupidity—and his panic; it is highly likely that he lost his head when Officer Tippit beckoned to him—the assassin's movements after the murder can be reconstructed with precision. Placing them in rough context, however, requires another cyclic chart:

Dallas Time	*Oswald*	*Dallas Police Activity*	*Developments Elsewhere*	*Washington Time*
12.30 p.m.	Shoots JFK from 6th floor of Book Depository.	Chief Curry orders Parkland alerted, orders search of triple underpass area.		1.30 p.m.
12.31½ p.m.	*Is halted at gunpoint by Motor-cycle Officer Marrion L. Baker in Depository's 2nd floor lunchroom; Superintendent Truly explains to Baker that Oswald is an employee.*			1.31½ p.m.
12.32 p.m.	Depository's clerical supervisor speaks to him on 2nd floor by front stairway saying 'Isn't it terrible?' and he mumbles a reply.	Baker continues on to the Depository roof, convinced from the sound of the pigeons that the shots have come from there.		1.32 p.m.
12.33 p.m.	Leaves Depository by front entrance, pausing to tell NBC's Robert MacNeil he can find a phone inside; thinks MacNeil is a Secret Service man.			1.33 p.m.
12.34 p.m.		Police dispatcher on one channel mentions Depository as a possible source of the shots; cruisers hear sirens and garbled transmissions on other channel.	Robert MacNeil reaches NBC by long distance from Depository. First UPI flash about shooting.	1.34 p.m.

Dallas Time	*Oswald*	*Dallas Police Activity*	*Developments Elsewhere*	*Washington Time*
12.35 p.m		Motor-cyclist Clyde Haygood radios headquarters he has 'talked to a guy who says the shots were fired from the Texas School Book Depository with a Hertz Drive-a-Car sign on top.'		1.35 p.m.
12.36 p.m.			JFK reaches Parkland.	1.36 p.m.
12.37 p.m.		Officer Haygood radios, 'Get men to cover the building, Texas School Book Depository – believe the shots came from there . . .' Inspector Herbert Sawyer arrives and orders front door of Depository sealed off.	Caroline Kennedy leaves the White House with Liz Pozen.	1.37 p.m.
12.40 p.m.	Boards bus at Elm and Murphy, seven blocks from Depository in downtown Dallas.		Kellerman tells Behn of the shooting; says, 'Look at your watch'; agent Jack Ready calls for a priest.	1.40 p.m.
12.44 p.m.	Asking for a transfer, leaves traffic-bound bus.	Code 3 emergency is broadcast – all downtown cruisers ordered to proceed 'to Elm and Houston with caution'.		1.44 p.m.
12.45 p.m.		Oswald's description, based on observation of eyewitness Brennan, is broadcast over Channel 2 by Inspector Sawyer from a radio car in front of Depository. Officer Tippit ordered to patrol Oak Cliff area.	J. Edgar Hoover tells Attorney General President has been shot.	1.45 p.m.
12.47–12.48 p.m.	Enters cab at Greyhound bus station, $3\frac{1}{2}$ blocks from bus. Rides in silence beside the driver, who thinks he's 'a wino 2 days off the bottle'.	Rebroadcast of Oswald's description to all cruisers.	Hoover establishes contact with Dallas FBI office.	1.47–1.48 p.m.

Dallas Time	*Oswald*	*Dallas Police Activity*	*Developments Elsewhere*	*Washington Time*
12.50 p.m.		Secret Service Agent Sorrels finds rear door of Depository unguarded by police; asks Truly to draw up a list of his employees.		1.50 p.m.
12.54 p.m.	After 2½-mile ride leaves cab at Beckley and Neely, a 5-minute walk from his rooming house.	Tippit reports in from his cruiser; dispatcher orders him to be 'at large for any emergency'.		1.54 p.m.
12.55 p.m.		Third broadcast of Oswald's description to all cruisers.		1.55 p.m.
12.57 p.m.			Father Huber arrives at Parkland.	1.57 p.m.
12.59–1.00 p.m.	Arrives at rooming house, unresponsive to housekeeper's greeting.		JFK is pronounced dead. Joint Chiefs begin emergency meeting. 2-hour phone crisis begins in Washington.	1.59–2.00 p.m.
1.03 p.m.	Leaves rooming house with pistol, zipping up his jacket. Back at Depository, Superintendent Truly notices his absence.	Truly tells policeman, 'We have a man here that's missing'; officer says, 'Let's go tell Captain Fritz'; Fritz cannot be found.		2.03 p.m.
1.05 p.m. (approx.)			Hill tells Behn JFK is dead; Shepard tells Attorney Gen.; DIA tells McNamara; Stranger tells Salinger on Cabinet plane.	2.05 p.m. (approx.)
1.10 p.m.			McNamara joins meeting of Joint Chiefs.	2.10 p.m.
1.12 p.m.		Deputy Sheriff Luke Mooney finds 3 empty cartridge cases near the 6th-floor window.		2.12 p.m.
1.13 p.m.			LBJ in shock is told JFK is dead; says, 'Make a note of the time.' Caroline Kennedy is returned to the White House.	2.13 p.m.
1.15 p.m.	*Is stopped by Tippit less than a mile from his rooming house, beside a drugstore; Oswald kills him with 4 revolver bullets; 9 witnesses subsequently identify Oswald.*		Joint Chiefs broadcast alert to all U.S. world commands.	2.15 p.m.

Dallas Time	*Oswald*	*Dallas Police Activity*	*Developments Elsewhere*	*Washington Time*
1.16 p.m.		A pickup truck driver breaks in on Tippit's radio to say, 'Hello, police operator – we've had a shooting out here. . . .'		2.16 p.m.
1.18 p.m.			AP circulates report LBJ wounded; Speaker McCormack believes he may now become President McCormack.	2.18 p.m.
1.22 p.m.	Still carrying pistol in hand, cuts through Patton St. to West Jefferson Blvd.; comes out by a Texaco Station across from a parking lot and drops his jacket there.	Dispatchers broadcast fresh description of Oswald based on observations of 2 women who saw him. Rifle is found by police on Depository's 6th floor by Deputy Sheriff Eugene Boone; Truly reports to Captain Will Fritz, 'I have a man missing.'		2.22 p.m.
1.26 p.m.			LBJ leaves Parkland.	2.26 p.m.
1.27 p.m.			Father Huber says: 'He's dead, all right.' First flags are lowered to half-mast. Joint Chiefs resume meeting with Germans.	2.27 p.m.
1.32 p.m.			Father Huber is quoted on teletypes: 'He's dead, all right.'	2.32 p.m.
1.33 p.m.			LBJ arrives at Love Field.	2.33 p.m.
1.35 p.m.	Runs past the Bethel Temple and accompanying signs – 'PREPARE TO MEET THY GOD' and 'JESUS SAVES'.		UPI flash confirming JFK's death.	2.35 p.m.
1.36 p.m.			MacNeil of NBC broadcasts, 'Shots came from the building called the Texas School Book Depository'; Ruth Paine tells Marina this; Marina quickly checks the garage, sees the blanket roll is still there,	2.36 p.m.

Dallas Time	Oswald	Dallas Police Activity	Developments Elsewhere	Washington Time
			and thinking the rifle is inside, whispers to herself, 'Thank God.'	
1.40 p.m.	Runs into the Texas Theatre, 8 blocks from Tippit's body, without buying a ticket.			2.40 p.m.
1.45 p.m.		Police dispatcher on Channel 1 broadcasts: 'Have information a suspect just went into the Texas Theatre on West Jefferson.' Cruisers begin converging on the theatre.	Dean Markham picks up David Kennedy.	2.45 p.m.
1.50 p.m.	*Oswald is seized in movie after a scuffle in which he tries to shoot a second officer; cries, 'Well, it's all over now!' and then shouts, 'I protest this police brutality', as he is taken out.*			2.50 p.m.
1.51 p.m.		Sergeant in Cruiser No. 2 reports: 'Suspect in shooting of police officer is apprehended and *en route* to station.'		2.51 p.m.
2.00 p.m.		Dispatcher on Channel 2 orders Code 2 escort (red lights and sirens) to Parkland for Jacqueline Kennedy.	Marina Oswald finds husband's wedding ring in china cup. LBJ calls Attorney General about oath; he calls Katzenbach.	3.00 p.m.
2.08 p.m.			JFK's body leaves Parkland.	3.08 p.m.
2.15 p.m.		Capt. Fritz returns from Depository to homicide bureau and orders arrest of Oswald, missing Depository employee; is told, 'There he sits.'		3.15 p.m.
2.20 p.m.			Katzenbach dictates text of Presidential oath to Marie Fehmer.	3.20 p.m.
2.30 p.m.	*Interrogation of Oswald begins in Room 317; Sorrels of Secret Service and Hosty of FBI are present.*		Cabinet plane lands in Hawaii.	3.30 p.m.
3.15 p.m.			Networks broadcast news of a suspect's arrest.	4.15 p.m.
3.23 p.m.			Networks identify Oswald by name; his age is given as 24.	4.23 p.m.

Dallas Time	*Oswald*	*Dallas Police Activity*	*Developments Elsewhere*	*Washington Time*
3.26 p.m.			Networks tell of Oswald's 1959 application for Russian citizenship; the public links Tippit's murder with the assassination; Marguerite Oswald, leaving for work, turns on car radio and hears her son has been arrested.	4.26 p.m.

Marguerite wheeled her ancient Buick 180 degrees, drove the seven blocks back to her house, and telephoned Bob Schieffer, a reporter on the Fort Worth *Star Telegram.* For the first time since her son's attempt to turn his coat in Moscow she was a public figure. She was, in her words, 'the accused mother'.

The accused mother's subsequent movements seem to have been motivated by a remarkable interest in publicity and finance. According to Marina, whom she joined after Schieffer and another newspaperman drove her to Dallas, her 'mania' was 'money, money, money'. Marguerite afterwards remembered how she had tried to bargain with them. 'Mamma wants money,' she told Marina. She extended her hand towards the men and rubbed the thumb against the fingers. 'Boys, I'll give you a story—for money,' she told one of them, who had identified himself as 'Tommy' Thompson. Mamma was not as shrewd as she appeared to be. She was not paid for the pictures. To make things worse, they were unflattering. The photographer neglected to warn her when he was going to snap his shutter, and while she was making herself comfortable he shot her sitting with her stockings rolled down, exposing her fleshy legs. She never forgave him for that. A year later the memory still rankled.

In the first hours it was hard for Marguerite to know what approach she should take. She hadn't found her bearings. Unexpectedly she had become a celebrity, but she had no agent, and dealing with mass media was exasperating. There was little time for other details; when Lee telephoned from jail and asked to speak to Marina, his mother curtly terminated the conversation. To Ruth Paine, who was taken aback by this episode, she explained her dilemma: 'Well, he's in prison, he doesn't know the things we are up against, what we have to face. What he wants really doesn't matter.'

Marguerite Oswald is the most implausible individual in her son's life, himself excluded, and she may be *sui generis,* but then they are all implausible. It would be too facile to dismiss the public's desire to quarantine Lee as mere smugness. The men and women he knew *are* odd. Indeed, Oswald is rather like a Dickensian caricature. He bears a striking resemblance to the title character in *Barnaby Rudge*. Born on the day of his father's death, Barnaby was twisted by the maternal blunders of Mary Rudge, a woman whose life, like Marguerite's, had been one of hardship and sorrow. Half-witted and highly susceptible to his environment, the youth was swept up in the No Popery mob that marched on Parliament, hooted at Edmund Burke, and burned most of London in 1780. Rudge, like Oswald, was friendless—his only confidant was a raven—and Oswald, like Rudge, was unable to cope with the most obvious consequences of his actions. Leaving Tippit's corpse, he fled into a movie, thinking that he would find asylum in its sheltering darkness. It never occurred to him that the flick of a switch could turn up the house lights, exposing him there in the tenth row.

The film was *War Is Hell*, a bad B-movie. Oswald's own incredible tale is authentic, and America knows it, for the national audience was there. Because television squeezed a hundred million people under the canopy of that theatre marquee as he was being led out and then took them to Captain Fritz's Room 317 while newscasters fed the country scraps of data about his past, that authenticity was established during his first hours in custody. The nation knew as much as the interrogation team. Some individuals knew more; Commander Hallett heard the suspect's name and said, 'I wonder if that's the guy I knew in the Soviet Union,' and Hallett's sixteen-year-old daughter Caroline, arriving home from Stone Ridge School, saw Oswald's picture on their set and cried, 'He was in Moscow!' The Halletts had recognized him before the networks put his Soviet record on the air. When it was broadcast, George Ball turned away from his twenty-four-inch screen on the eighth floor of the State Building. The Acting Secretary was worried. He checked the department's files to see whether there was anything there, and found there was a lot.

Oswald's Russian adventure was avidly seized upon. If America couldn't shuck him, the Reds could be saddled with him. In reality his absence from Texas had been brief. He had been in the U.S.S.R. thirty-two months, and during most of that time he had been trying to get out; after the first year he wrote in his diary: 'I am starting to reconcider my desire about staying. The work is drab. The money I get has nowhere to be spent. No nightclubs or bowling allys, no places of recreation acept the trade union dances. I have had enough.' So he returned to the state which must accept the fact that it was his home, just as Americans must learn to accept him as a figure in American history.

Dallas was especially anxious to forget that the assassin had prowled its streets, read its leading newspaper, watched the patriotic programmes on WFAA, and listened to the anti-Kennedy stories of his fellow employees in Dealey Plaza. Bernard Weissman testified afterwards that when he heard Oswald had called himself a Marxist—that he hadn't been 'one of Walker's boys' after all—he 'breathed a sigh of relief', and Bob Baskin of the Dallas *News* was 'relieved that he was not of the right wing'. Yet even then there were Dallasites who were afraid that the world would be sceptical. A Parkland physician said warily, 'Dallas has had several incidents that have been very unfortunate'; a Texas Ranger said, 'Dallas will have a real black mark now'; a salesman told a *Newsweek* correspondent, 'I hope you guys don't think too bad of Dallas'; and Merriman Smith riding from Parkland to Love Field, heard the police driver say, 'I hope they don't blame this on Dallas.' Someone in the car replied, 'They will.'

The fact that they would troubled Dallas. Big D brooded about its image, unaware that the watching country would regard that very anxiety as suspect. In the Baker Hotel's Club Imperial and in the Republic and Mercantile Bank buildings there was a deepening worry that the bad publicity might get worse. Civic leaders were glum. The Dallas Chamber of Commerce issued a statement of regret over the President's death. Later Friday afternoon District Attorney Henry M. Wade, the man responsible for the assassin's prosecution, departed his office for a social function and failed to leave a number at which he could be reached, but his second assistant, William F. 'Bill' Alexander, prepared to charge Oswald with murdering the President 'as part of an international Communist conspiracy'. Perhaps that canard would have absolved Dallas. The indictment could have had grave repercussions abroad, however, and although it had already been drawn up, when Barefoot Sanders heard of it from the FBI he phoned Nick Katzenbach, who persuaded two members of the Vice President's Washington staff to have their Texas contacts kill it.[10]

Mayor Earle Cabell's first reaction to the arrest was sanguine. That Friday he expressed confidence that the assassination 'would not hurt Dallas as a city'. The *News*, on the other hand, was saturnine. In an editorial which would be published in its next edition the paper declared, 'It cannot be charged with fairness that an entire city is in national disgrace, but certainly its reputation has suffered regrettable damage.' Actually, no thoughtful critic was pre-

[10] Shanklin of the FBI was especially helpful in aborting Alexander's folly. Alexander himself subsequently played a key role in the trial of Jack Ruby, Oswald's killer.

pared to fault the entire city. At noon Main Street had been solid with liberal Kennedy Democrats, and the riders in the motorcade would never forget their enthusiasm. What was suspect was the cult of absolutists whose polemics could have swayed a deranged mind. The leader writer for the Dallas *Times-Herald* understood this. He reminded his readers that before the shots could have been fired, 'first there had to be the seeds of hate—and we must pray that Dallas can never supply the atmosphere for tragedy to grow again'. Yet any criticism, even self-criticism, was rejected by many in Dallas. 'What on earth did we do to deserve this?' a bewildered man asked Warren Leslie, a New Yorker who had become a member of the city's mercantile elite—he would soon resign from it—and in the Club Imperial there were complaints that the city was being victimized, that left-wing Eastern liberals and intellectuals were ganging up on Dallas conservatism.

There was no remorse among the city's rightists on the afternoon of November 22. At 3.05 p.m., when 80 per cent of the American people were in deep grief, an NBC camera panned towards a group of spectators outside Parkland's emergency entrance and picked up a young man with a placard that read, 'YANKEE, GO HOME'.[11] Barefoot Sanders was astounded to learn that although next day's Harvard–Yale game had been called off, interrupting the oldest football rivalry in the country, most Dallas County high schools were going ahead with plans to play under lights that Friday evening. When Warren Harding arrived home, a child who lived in his block said, 'Mr Harding, I'm sorry your President died.' Harding didn't know what to say. He puckered and then replied, 'Son, he was your President, too. He was everybody's President.' The child shook his head. 'He wasn't ours,' he said. 'My Mom and Daddy didn't vote for him. He didn't mean anything to us.'

In the White House Ralph Dungan removed his pipe. He leaned forward against his desk and buried his head in his arms.

'And the hell of it is, they'll blame it all on that twenty-four-year-old boy,' he told Pat Moynihan.

[11] This strains credulity, but there it is, on page 10 of the National Broadcasting Company's programme log of November 22–25, 1963.

5

GO, STRANGER

'Liz Carpenter, please come to the administrative office,' Parkland's PA system had barked for the last time and then quit, coughing static. In the lull that had followed, President Kennedy's wife sat outside Trauma Room No. 1 in unique isolation. An hour ago she had been America's First Lady, encompassed by panoply and special privilege, all of which had vanished in the speed of a full-jacketed cartridge. Officially she no longer existed. Every other member of the Presidential party had retained his title and gauds of power. Her own secretaries were still White House secretaries, but she herself was a widow, and the government had no G.S. classification for that. Everything that she had been had stemmed from John Kennedy's position. Ted Clifton and Godfrey McHugh had stayed at Parkland; Roy Kellerman was keeping the four-to-twelve shift at the hospital —six agents and Bill Greer—but the generals and Roy were acting without authorization and technically, without justification. Their commissions and commission books did not mention her. There was no provision in either the U.S. Constitution or the U.S. Code for a dead President's wife. Indeed, had the law been observed literally, even Kennedy's closest lieutenants, Ken O'Donnell, Larry O'Brien, and Dave Powers, should have been aboard Aircraft 26000. The entire apparatus of the Executive Branch of the federal government belonged to Lyndon Johnson now. When he left for Love Field at 1.26 p.m., it was their legal duty to follow. Jacqueline Kennedy was entitled to neither aides nor bodyguards. She wasn't a Chief Executive, and wasn't related to one.

'I'm not going to leave here without Jack,' she whispered to Ken.

'Let's get a coffin,' he said to Clint Hill, Andy Berger, and Dr Burkley, and Burkley said to Jack Price, 'I want the best undertaker in Dallas and the best bronze coffin.'

'You don't mean it,' a woman's voice moaned.

It was Mary Gallagher. No one had told her of the death. She was standing on the other side of the green line, clutching the pillbox hat with the tuft of Jackie's black hair and the stain in back. 'I mean it,' the doctor said. He saw Evelyn Lincoln crying in the next cubicle; he kissed them both and told them, 'Don't change your expression for Mrs Kennedy.'

They were all thinking of her, wishing they could do something to ease her pain. Wouldn't you like some more water? she was asked. Would you like a cup of coffee? A pill? A place to lie down? In the softest of voices she declined. The door of the trauma room was closed. Inside, Doris Nelson was washing the body with Margaret Hinchcliffe while David Sanders, an orderly, mopped the floor and removed the dirty instruments. Even they wanted to cosset the widow. Doris put her head out and said, 'Can I get you a towel?' Jackie shook her head politely. 'Why don't you remove your gloves?' Doris persisted.

'No, thank you. I'm all right.'

Those who had been in the motorcade were racking their brains with *if only* this, *if only* that. One of them came to her. Bill Greer, his face streaked with tears, took her head between his hands and squeezed until she thought he was going to squeeze her skull flat. He cried, 'Oh, Mrs Kennedy, oh my God, oh my God. I didn't mean to do it, I didn't hear, I should have swerved the car, I couldn't help it. Oh, Mrs Kennedy, as soon as I saw it I swerved. If only I'd seen in time! Oh!' Then he released her head and put his arms around her and wept on her shoulder. Henry Gonzalez also wept. Henry hadn't meant to; he had come to pay his respects and had every intention of behaving with dignity. But when he came up she looked so alone, and so frail, that he choked and cried, 'Oh, Mrs Kennedy! Is there anything I can do?' She shook her head and bowed it. As she did he saw the blood clotted in her hair, and he knelt at her feet, praying, the soggy bag containing half of Governor Connally's clothing in his hands and his face in her stained skirt. Then he crept back, retreating across the green line. After that no visitors got by O'Donnell until 1.30, when the undertaker arrived. Ken, once more at the peak of his efficiency, stood before the folding chair as a sentry. Some of the women, notably Dearie Cabell, were bent upon consoling her, but he diverted them all. After a time they stopped trying. He had an intimidating look about him. His head was cocked to one side, and there was a curious puckered expression on his face, as though he were constantly wincing.

Stiff-faced, the young widow sat as thin and straight as a spire of smoke from a dying fire. She still felt faint—three times she swayed slightly and nearly lurched to the floor—but that was physical weakness; she retained her heightened sense of awareness. She was thinking clearly, and she was thinking ahead. There was one thing that someone could do for her. After the nurses had finished she wanted to be with the President's body a moment, to touch him, and give him something. It would have to be something of hers, something that would stay with him.

Ken would see to it.

'You just get me in there before they close that coffin,' she said to him quietly, and he nodded.

Juggling the paper bag, Gonzalez thought of John Kennedy in the antiseptic little cell and Jacqueline Kennedy in the drab passage, separated from him by the closed door, each in utter solitude, and he remembered a line he had learned as a boy from the works of Gustavo Adolfo Bécquer:

> *¡ Dios mío, que solos se quedan los muertos!*
> Oh God, how alone the dead are left!

Jack Price was being cagey. He didn't want to show preference towards any mortician, and when Dr Burkley requested his advice he stalled. 'Well, you can get a casket from a military installation or a private home,' he answered noncommittally. Burkley said, 'We just want a casket or a basket—something you can carry a body out with.' Steve Landregan passed by, and Clint Hill caught his arm. 'We've got to get a casket,' Clint told him. Price said to Steve, 'Hold up; they haven't decided what they want yet.' The President's physician was becoming impatient. 'Just get us one as fast as you can,' he said grittily. Still evasive, Price inquired, 'What kind should I ask for?' Exasperated, Burkley said, 'I don't give a damn! Just get one!'

'Get one,' Price echoed to Steve.

Trailed by Clint, Steve hurried to the hospital's Social Service department.

'Where's the nearest funeral home?' he asked a woman there.

'Oneal's, in Oak Lawn,' she replied and gave him the number.

'We can make the call here,' Steve said.

He couldn't. Bales had released lines, but Dallas' Southwestern Bell, like Washington's Chesapeak & Potomac, was crippled by overloaded exchanges and circuits. Steve ran from office to office, picking up receivers, and he didn't get a dial tone until he reached Price's private office upstairs.

'*Now,*' he panted to Clint, dialling Oneal's LAkeside 6-5221.

Vernon B. Oneal is a cumbersome figure in the story of John Kennedy. Squat, hairy, and professionally doleful, with a thick Texas accent and grey hair parted precisely in the middle and slicked back, he was the proprietor of an establishment which might have been invented by Waugh or Huxley. It had a wall-to-wall-carpeted Slumber Room. There was piped religious music, and a coffee bar for hungry relatives of loved ones. There was the fleet of white hearses—white, because the owner felt that death should never be depressing—which doubled as ambulances. The transformation was easy and ingenious. A driver put a red 'AMBULANCE' sign in a side window, turned on his siren, and he was ready to haul the living. Identical vehicles conveyed the same individuals to Parkland and, after slumber, to memorial parks. A hustling businessman, Oneal had seven radio-equipped ambulance-hearses and his own dispatcher. The dispatcher was tied into the police network, because the concern had a contract with the city. In effect, it was a concession. Vernon Oneal handled tragedies east of the Trinity River, and Dudley M. Hughes, his chief competitor, worked the west bank. That was how the maimed were moved to emergency rooms in Dallas, and the only thing wrong with the arrangement was that on the early afternoon of November 22 seventeen of Oneal's staff of eighteen men were out to lunch. The exception was his dispatcher. The two of them had stayed behind to mind the store. They had anticipated that the Presidential parade would reduce traffic and, therefore, automobile accidents. There had been no reason to expect a big job.

'You're kidding!' Oneal had gasped when the dispatcher told him that 601 was reporting a Code 3. The undertaker had yanked out a transistor radio from a desk drawer and had been following bulletins like everybody else when his phone rang.

Steven Landregan identified himself. He said, 'I'm going to give you a man, and I want you to do what he says. This is confidential.'

There was a pause. Then another voice: 'This is Clint Hill of the Secret Service. I want you to bring a casket out here to Parkland. I want you immediately.'

'Hold on—hold on!' Oneal said. 'We've got merchandise at all prices.'

'Bring the best one you have,' said Clint. 'Any questions?'

'Well, what about a police escort?'

'Get a police escort if necessary.'

Oneal promptly forgot the escort. He had too many other matters on his mind. Running into his selection room, he chose his most expensive coffin, the Elgin Casket Company's 'Britannia' model, eight hundred pounds of double-walled, hermetically sealed solid bronze. He couldn't carry it alone. Hurrying out to his driveway, he stood vigil there until he had collected three returning employees. The four of them eased the massive coffin into the pride of his vehicular fleet—a snow-white, air-conditioned 1964 Cadillac which he had bought at the October convention of the National Funeral

Directors in Dallas. It was less than a month old, had exactly nine hundred miles registered on the dashboard indicator, and was furnished with light-green window curtains.

At Parkland's ambulance dock Oneal and Ray Gleason, his bookkeeper, opened the back of the Cadillac. Agents and White House correspondents sprang forward to help them; the coffin was laid on the rubber cradle of one of the undertaker's portable, lightweight carts—known in the trade as church trucks—and wheeled down the long corridor. At the double doors the correspondents stepped back. Andy Berger signalled Ken O'Donnell; they were here.

'I want to speak to you,' Ken said to Mrs Kennedy in an undertone, motioning her to follow him down the passage.

She followed him to a door there, and then Pam Turnure saw her reach out like a cat and grab the knob to be sure it was open. She hadn't seen the church truck, but she had guessed correctly what was arriving, and that they didn't want her to see it. Ken had made a promise. She intended to see that it was kept.

Kemp Clark appeared beside Ken. She appealed to the physician. 'Please—can I go in? Please let me go back.'

'No, no,' he mumbled.

She leaned towards him. 'Do you think seeing the coffin can upset me, Doctor? I've seen my husband die, shot in my arms. His blood is all over me. How can I see anything worse than I've seen?'

Clark capitulated. 'Ah, oh, all right, I know.' He stepped aside. Dave Powers noted:

1.30 Undertaker—Vernon B. O'Neal [*sic*] to Emergency Room #1

She was right behind Oneal. Crossing the passage, she continued to ponder what she could put with the President, and she had the odd feeling of reliving a moment in her own past. She remembered: it had been at her father's funeral. That had been the first time she had seen anyone dead, and she had been heartbroken. That day she had been wearing a bracelet; it was a graduation present from him. He had been so proud of her the day he had given it to her, and standing by his coffin she had unfastened it on impulse and placed it in his hand. She wanted to do the same thing now. But what could it be? Until this summer he had carried a St Christopher medal, fashioned as a bill clip. She had given it to him when they were married, and it would have been appropriate now. It wasn't here, however. They had put it in the little coffin with Patrick. Afterwards the President had asked her for another one, so on their tenth wedding anniversary when he had presented her with a slim ring set with green emerald chips, she had given him a medal of gold. It would be here in his billfold; Kenny or one of the nurses could find it. Then she changed her mind. The new St Christopher's, she decided, would be wrong. It was only two months old. It hadn't been with him long enough to be really a part of him. Besides, it was his, not hers. It already belonged to him. It couldn't be a gift twice.

Suddenly she thought of her wedding ring. Nothing had ever meant so much to her. Its very plainness made it dear. Unlike the circlet set with emeralds, it was unadorned. It was, in fact, a man's wedding band. The President had bought it in a hurry in Newport just before their wedding. There hadn't even been time to put the date in; she had taken it to a jeweller and had that done later. The ring would be exactly right—provided she could get it off. She attempted to unfasten the left one and couldn't even work the snap.

They were inside the room now. Apart from the disinfectant and the blistering artificial light overhead, the place was much altered; it was nearly immaculate and almost empty. The audience of a half-hour ago had dispersed. Oneal was there, leaning over his burnished coffin, adjusting it on its truck. O'Donnell stood in the doorway. Sergeant Dugger had followed her across the threshold. He looked competent, and drawing herself up she held her wrist towards him. He understood. He found the snap with his thumbnail and unpeeled the glove.

She moved to the President's side and lifted his hand. An orderly succeeded in working the ring over Kennedy's knuckle with cream, and she looked down tenderly. She yearned to be alone with him. If only these people would go away. They would never leave her, of course: she knew that. They would be frightened for her and what she might do, terrified of unspoken and nameless perils. To ask them would only upset them, so she withdrew in silence. In the passage she asked Ken, 'The ring. Did I do the right thing?'

He said, 'You leave it right where it is.'

Now the waiting began, a dreadful time, a time of small acts of callousness and, at the end, a great, ugly eruption. The President had come to Parkland in one clamorous outburst; he was to leave it in another.

The door had been closed again. Within, Vernon Oneal was plying his craft. He was concerned about the Britannia's pale satin upholstery; it was immaculate now, but could easily be stained. Motioning to Orderly David Sanders, Oneal directed him to line the inside of the coffin with a sheet of plastic. Nurses Doris Nelson and Diana Bowron swooped around, wrapping the body in a second plastic sheet. Then the undertaker asked Doris to bring him a huge rubber sheath and a batch of rubber bags. Placing the sheath over Sanders' plastic lining, he carefully cut the bags to size, enveloping the President's head in them one by one until he had made certain that there would be seven protective layers of rubber and two of plastic between the damaged scalp and the green satin.

All this took twenty minutes. Jacqueline Kennedy had returned to her chair, looking, Henry Gonzalez thought, 'like a wounded rabbit'. To Henry, and to the rest of the Presidential party, John Kennedy's slender young widow had become a mystic symbol; they had never felt so close to another human being. They supposed that everyone felt the same, and those who learned that they were mistaken were deeply shocked. Henry was the first of them. He was looking down the narrow hallway, towards a room which physicians used to take emergency calls. A fragile nurse patting a well-cherished head of blonde hair and a youth with a thin, conceited face were standing there together. They had their arms around one another, a gesture, Henry assumed, of commiseration. Then the nurse smirked. The youth murmured something in her ear, and she giggled. Henry called indignantly, 'Show a little respect, can't you?' They looked up, startled, and vanished.

To suggest that frivolity or incivility was dominant at Parkland would be a gross injustice. Most members of the staff were as bereft as their bewildered visitors, and were doing their best to shape order out of unprecedented chaos, but accident rooms, like drunk tanks, are unlovely places; some employees inevitably became hard-bitten, and while the nurse and her escort were a flagrant exception to the general rule, there were other incidents which grated: the resonant sound of baritone laughter echoing down one corridor, horseplay between two orderlies in a second, an exchange of colourful language from opposite ends of a third hall.

Jacqueline Kennedy noticed none of this. By now Major Surgery's carnival-house floor plan had been mastered by the mafia, the agents, and the military aides. They had her thoroughly sealed off. None of them liked the place, and there was a general feeling that waiting for the body was unnecessarily cruel for her—a viewpoint she did not share; 'You could go back to the plane now,' one of them said to her, and she replied again, 'I'm not going back till I leave with Jack'—but they believed that she was safe from intruders. Only a freak of chance could break the box they had built around her.

But it was a freakish hour. A Catholic clergyman was probably the one stranger who could slip through the concentric circles of sentinels around her. The other guards would conclude that the Catholic widow had sent for him; the Boston Irishmen who were closest to her would defer to him. And this is precisely what happened, exposing Mrs Kennedy to what would be remembered as 'the episode of the priest'. Later O'Donnell, O'Brien, and Powers wondered whether he had been a real priest. No genuine cleric, they felt, could have behaved the way he did.

He was authentic enough. Father Thomas M. Cain was the superior of the Dominican Fathers at the Roman Catholic University of Dallas, six miles from Parkland. At the same time, he was undoubtedly eccentric. An energetic, bespectacled cigar smoker with thinning grey hair and a turkey gobbler neck, Father Cain was, even on serene days, a man of erratic mannerisms. He talked a great deal, sometimes disjointedly, gesticulating loopingly with his long arms, and he tended to swing between cycles of impulsive activity and remorse. When the academic dean of the university had called him at his priory and told him of the shooting, he had but one thought: a Catholic President had been wounded, and he belonged at the President's side. The fact that other priests would be closer was irrelevant, for he had something they did not. In a green bag in his office he kept an ornate crucifix containing within it a minute splinter from the True Cross, encased in plastic. Changing to his robe and collar, Father Cain pocketed the bag, bounded out to his car, and headed for the hospital. He drove the accelerator straight to the floor. It was, he admitted afterwards, something of a miracle that he wasn't killed. Pausing only to pick up a newspaperman, he left the car in the anarchy of badly parked automobiles and dashed in past the Dallas policemen, the Kellerman shift, the two uniformed generals, and the mafia. On the way he heard someone say that the President was dead.

Mrs Kennedy looked up and saw him hovering over her. His eyes were wild.

'When did he die?'

'In the car, I think,' she said haggardly.

Father Cain loosened the bag string. 'I have a relic of the True Cross.'

He held it out and asked her to 'venerate it'. She kissed the crucifix, not quite understanding what this was all about. Then he said he wanted to take it into the President. She thought, *This must mean a lot to this man,* and *If he wants to give it to Jack, how touching*. O'Donnell nodded; the priest went in. But he didn't leave the relic. He merely walked around, waving it ceremoniously in the air above Vernon Oneal, the nurses, the orderly, the plastic and rubber sheeting and the seven rubber head bags.

Coming out he said, 'I have applied a relic of the True Cross to your husband.'

She stared. It was still in his hands. She thought, *You mean you didn't even give it to him?*

O'Donnell edged towards him. Father Cain, however, wasn't to be dismissed that easily. He was moving around in a state of excitement, his larynx bobbing. He pressed her hand and tried to put his arms around her, addressing her by her first name, calling her endearing names, and promising to write her a letter. Just as Ken—and Larry and Dave, who were closing in from the other side—thought they had the priest cornered, he jerked away from them. Skirring back into the trauma room, he walked around Oneal, pranced out, confronted a group of hospital employees standing against a wall, and led them in a recitation of the Lord's Prayer.

He returned to Mrs Kennedy and reached for her hand again.

She yanked it away. 'Please, Father. Leave me alone.'

Now O'Donnell stalked him in earnest, and now he backed away, clutching the bag. They could hear his voice drifting across a cubicle wall, chanting prayers feverishly. They thought they were rid of him, but he was only a few feet away, and he had no notion of leaving.

The long burnished coffin was closed and poised on its church truck. Jacqueline Kennedy smoked her last cigarette, smoked one Dugger borrowed for her, stamped it out—fumblingly he produced an ashtray, too late—and began to fidget. She was ready. The undertaker was ready. Parkland, having done all it could, had turned to new emergencies. Yet they weren't moving. The trauma room door was propped open, and the IBM clock there revealed that they had been in the hospital for over an hour.

'Sergeant, why can't I get my husband back to Washington?'

Bob Dugger knew why. He had overheard certain conversations; the nature of the fresh development was clear to him. He wasn't going to brief her, however. It made Dallas look like a hick town, he thought; as a Texan he felt humiliated. The other men had tacitly agreed to keep it from her, and, amazingly, they were successful; it was the loudest and longest uproar of the afternoon, it raged all around her for over half an hour and nearly ended in a fistfight a few feet from her, yet not until much later, in Washington, did she understand just why they had been delayed so long.

Roy Kellerman had been the first agent to scent trouble. Shortly before the coffin arrived, Roy had been standing with Dr Burkley in the nurse's station, hanging on to the Behn line, when a pale, freckled, wall-eyed man in shirt sleeves entered, reached for another phone, and flipped the receiver off snappily, like a gunman in a

Western. 'This is Earl Rose,' he said. 'There has been a homicide here. They won't be able to leave until there has been an autopsy.'

Father Cain had been a temporary distraction; Rose was a stage heavy. The priest had meant well. At most (as he himself believed afterwards) he had been a victim of the national distress. Rose was not a man to be plagued by self-doubt, and he was unaccustomed to criticism from others. He was the Dallas County Medical Examiner, with an office in the hospital. He was, moreover, an official of strong convictions. Pedantic and brittle, he had a way of wagging his finger and adopting the stylized tone of an overbearing schoolmaster. He seemed to invite hostility. His colleagues thought him arrogant and smart. He was certainly bright; he knew a great deal of Texas law, and he treated it as revealed religion. '*Dura lex, sed lex*'—'The law is hard, but it's the law.' That was his attitude. Unlike the priest, the doctor was to suffer no feeling of shame afterwards. He worked himself into a white-hot anger that afternoon, and he was so sure he was right that his wrath never ebbed; a year later the mere mention of the battle he had fought on November 22 was enough to make him tremble. As a physician and a Dallas appointee he represented both the medical and legal professions. He could be an obstacle of formidable bulk if he chose to be, and he so chose. To him the situation at Parkland was clear, and clearly outrageous. A man had been killed in Dallas. Other men were trying to remove the corpse, in open defiance of Texas statutes. They were flouting rights of which Dr Earl Rose was the appointed guardian. Strong action was required, and he meant to take it.

He hung up and turned to leave the nurse's station.

Kellerman blocked the way. In his most deliberate drawl Roy said, 'My friend, this is the body of the President of the United States, and we are going to take it back to Washington.'

'No, that's not the way things are.' Rose wagged his finger. 'When there's a homicide, we must have an autopsy.'

'He is the President. He is going with us.'

Rose lashed back, 'The body stays.'

'My friend, my name is Roy Kellerman. I am Special Agent in Charge of the White House Detail of the Secret Service. We are taking President Kennedy back to the capital.'

'You're not taking *the body* anywhere. There's a law here. We're going to enforce it.'

Dr Burkley argued with Dr Rose, physician to physician. It was useless. Kellerman, who hadn't moved from the doorway, gathered his million muscles and loomed forward.

'My friend, this part of the law can be waived.'

Rose, stonewalling, shook his head.

'You will have to show me a lot more authority than you have now,' said Kellerman.

'I will,' Rose said scathingly, reaching for the phone.

He could, too. Now that John Kennedy was no longer a living President, his mortal remains were in the custody of the state. The examiner's position was impregnable, unless he abandoned it, and he was digging in deeper every moment. He phoned the sheriff's office and the homicide bureau of the police department. Both agreed that an autopsy was mandatory. Under the law they had little choice. Given the uncertainty of the hour and the absence of federal jurisdiction, Rose had an ironclad case. Assassination is murder, murder is a felony, and in felonious crimes he had a legal obligation to Dallas County. That was why he had an office in Parkland Hospital. Justice must be served; when and if captured, the assassins or assassin had rights, among them the right of access to the findings of an impartial post-mortem examination. The point is arguable, of course, because by now it ought to have been categorically clear to Rose that the Secret Service would maintain a vigilant watch over Kennedy's body, and had he been realistic he should have realized that an assassination without a scrupulous post-mortem was unthinkable. Nevertheless, there was area for reasonable debate. His error, which was grave, was that he was not behaving reasonably.

Burkley begged him to reconsider. 'Mrs Kennedy is going to stay exactly where she is until the body is moved. We can't have that.'

What Mrs Kennedy did was of no concern to Rose. She could come or go as she liked. She was alive and had been accused of no infraction of the law. His sole interest was in the cadaver. 'The remains stay,' he said flatly. 'Procedures must be followed. A certificate has to be filed before any body can be shipped out of state. I can release the body to a Texas JP who will function as coroner, or hold the body and have an autopsy here.'

'It's the President of the United States!' Burkley cried.

'That doesn't matter. You can't lose the chain of evidence.'

The dispute spread outside the nurse's station. Dave Powers heard about it and came over, incredulous. Rose explained everything to him in detail, then shook his head impatiently when Powers urged him to make an exception in this case.

'Regulations,' the examiner said, his voice frozen in B-flat.

Godfrey McHugh approached Rose and was told, 'There are state laws about removing bodies. You people from Washington can't make your own law.' Godfrey appealed to Mayor Cabell, who said that he had no authority to intervene; then to a member of Parkland's administrative staff, who said that Rose was absolutely right; then to a policeman in civilian clothes, who suggested that a justice of the peace might be able to do something. 'How long will that take?' Godfrey asked. 'Ten or fifteen minutes,' the man said. 'When we're ready, we're leaving,' Godfrey said indignantly.[1]

Burkley suggested that Rose come along on the plane. Rose shook his head; the law made no provision for such a trip. Ted Clifton remembered that he had talked to Attorney General Waggoner Carr of Texas on Aircraft 26000 during the flight to Dallas from Fort Worth, and he asked that he be paged over the PA system. The page was broadcast. Carr did not materialize. Although the party which had landed at Love Field less than three hours earlier had included virtually every Texan of rank, all of them had dispersed or headed for Love Field except the Governor, who was in surgery (and who, when he heard of Rose's position ten months later, found it astonishing). In retrospect the furore that the medical examiner raised seems remarkable. He was a man of authority, but there ought to have been some way of diverting him. His strength was largely a strength of will. He was firm; while other Texans floundered or shrank from responsibility, he knew exactly what he wanted. The only Parkland doctor to side openly with the dead Chief Executive's staff was Kemp Clark. 'Jack, is there a JP in the building?' he asked Price. 'Earl Rose has raised the question.' Clark explained the dilemma and added, 'For God's sake find someone—I'm trying to calm them down.'

The PA system inquired whether there were any justices of the peace within earshot. None stepped forward. Mayor Cabell and individual members of the staff began calling outside on their own initiative. JP after JP was reported to be out to lunch. The first caller to reach one was a woman in the admittance office. At Dallas County Precinct 3 she found Judge Theron Ward in his office. She sketchily filled him in and said, 'We need you here immediately.'

Theron Ward could not comply immediately, or anything like it. Precinct 3 was in Garland, Texas, fourteen miles away. Pushing all the way, he made Parkland in twenty minutes. Had anyone there been in the mood to make allowances, he should have been congratulated. He wasn't; by then no one there was making allowances for anyone. The row around Earl Rose had grown in intensity, and nearly everybody had become involved in it. Dr Rose had talked to District Attorney Wade, who had advised him to step aside and let

[1] Approximately ten minutes later a uniformed patrolman, C. E. Jackson, went ahead anyhow. At 1.44 p.m. he radioed Dispatcher No. 2, 'We need a justice of the peace at Parkland Hospital, Code 3.' Code 3 —emergency, red lights and sirens—might have been of immense help, but here, as in so many other crucial moments, Dallas police communications broke down. The next message on the dispatcher's tape is hopelessly garbled.

the Secret Service handle everything. A less combative man would have welcomed the escape hatch, but Rose didn't want to escape. Instead, he became if anything more vehement. Burkley and McHugh were hopping up and down with frustration. O'Donnell and O'Brien, to whom Powers had reported everything, were standing off to one side and eyeing the medical examiner icily. But the mafia wasn't going to intervene unless all the others had failed, and they were confident that would be unnecessary. Surely they felt, there must be someone in Texas who could dispose of this prodigy.

Kemp Clark was still trying. He and Rose had exchanged bitter words, and afterwards Clark had taken the worried Price aside and advised him that he favoured using force. 'It may come to pinning him down and sitting on him,' he warned, adding that he would be delighted to be among the sitters. He was one of many. If Rose had intended to pre-empt the centre of the stage, he was meeting with spectacular success. Except for Jacqueline Kennedy, whose human shield had grown more dense since Father Cain's intrusion, every eye was upon him. Even Vernon Oneal briefly left his Britannia casket to see what was going on. The medical examiner's inflexibility surprised Oneal. Rose had always co-operated 100 per cent with Dallas funeral directors, providing them with quick service and immediate autopsies. The undertaker, who was under the impression that the President was going to be cosmetized by him and conveyed to a local memorial park in one of his funeral coaches, couldn't understand what the cavil was all about.

Outside Parkland, Theron Ward added his tan Buick coupé to the tangled junkyard. He might as well have arrived in a tumbrel. He was on his way to an execution of sorts. A justice of the peace could make no peace between the militants in Major Medicine, he could only mangle his own reputation. Ward was nearly saved from his fate—at the entrance he introduced himself to a Secret Service man as 'the JP' and was promptly ejected. The misunderstanding arose from the title. On the Eastern seaboard a JP was a minor functionary, a rung or two above a notary public. In Texas he was an elected magistrate, with a courtroom and a daily docket. Judge Ward was accustomed to a more dignified reception, and when he presented himself at another entrance he got it, from a nurse who led him to the nurse's station. She knew about the battle there. She looked grateful to see him and said so, which was the last kind word he was to hear for some time.

Earl Rose recognized him. His eyes lit up; he crooked his finger 'peremptorily'—the adverb is Ward's—and cried, 'Judge Ward, you are under the gun! This case must be handled as no other case in history has been handled. If you allow this body to be moved, it will be moved illegally.'

During the hasty introductions which followed, Ward attempted to explain his role to the glowering federal officials who flanked the medical examiner. 'I'm the JP who will be handling the case,' he said to Dr Burkley, attempting to take Burkley's arm. The arm was withdrawn. The President's physician, in tears, was too outraged to debate legal points. Rose's attitude had discredited Ward in advance, creating a violent revulsion towards local law. To the Washingtonians, moreover, the judge didn't seem to be much of a jurist; Kellerman, like the agent who had turned him away, was unimpressed by the title of JP. Ward's physical presence was no help. In primitive situations, and this one had become stark, physique may count for a great deal. A prepossessing newcomer—a Texan with the lordly bearing of a Connally—might have dominated the quarrel. The judge was short, slight, sandy-haired, and young. Finally, he appeared to be indecisive.

'I'll handle everything as quickly as possible,' he assured Kellerman and Burkley. They eyed him sceptically and felt vindicated when, in the very next breath, he marched back down the hill. He begged for 'a few minutes to check a point of law'.

Actually, his request was entirely reasonable. He was in strange country and plainly needed a guide. He would have been a remarkable magistrate had he been able to act without one. Even in Texas a justice of the peace is far down the bar, an arbiter of petty misdemeanours. The issue here would have taxed a Supreme Court Justice. Elsewhere in the same city at that very moment a federal judge and the U.S. Attorney for a hundred counties were vexed by the relatively simple question of the Presidential oath. During his début, at least, Ward deserved a sympathetic hearing.

He didn't get it. The men with whom he was pleading were in a fever of resentment. Their tempers couldn't take another degree of heat. Shattered by the murder, antagonistic towards all Texans because of it, they had been harried past endurance by the inimical medical examiner. They looked upon Ward as Rose's confederate until he proved himself otherwise, and to them an appeal for time was anything but proof.

Kellerman displayed his commission book. 'My friend—Your Honour—isn't there something in your law that makes a waiver possible?'

'I'm sorry,' Ward said unhappily. 'I know who you are, but I can't help you under these circumstances.'

'I'm sorry, too,' Roy said greyly.

As Ward was talking Kellerman had noticed that the church truck was being rolled into view. He quickly paced across the green line to lead it out. Jacqueline Kennedy was standing behind it, her hand resting lightly on the bronze top. Clint Hill, Godfrey McHugh, Dugger, and Oneal were bunched around her; O'Donnell, O'Brien, Powers, Clifton, Gonzalez, and Andy Berger flanked the church truck.

Earl Rose stood at the double doors, embattled. It had come to that.

At this point, everything becomes confused. Judge Ward, who watched the beginning of the scene from the nurse's station, afterwards believed that the encounter was over in a matter of moments. In fact, it was prolonged. According to the nurses who were watching Parkland's IBM clocks, Rose's last stand lasted ten minutes. Since it was a direct confrontation between a diehard defender of state sovereignty and the representatives of the national government, with the body of the thirty-fifth Chief Executive lying between them, and since the medical examiner's vehemence generated a sense of panic in the Presidential staff which persisted after they left Parkland and led to fresh scars at Love Field, the episode is worth a detailed chronological account. Regrettably, that is impossible. Only the highlights are clear. Each man has his own story, and all clash, because all are saturated with emotion. Mrs Kennedy, who had the clearest eye there, would be an invaluable witness, but she was deliberately sequestered. Ken O'Donnell saw Rose's arms defiantly akimbo and huddled with Powers.

Rose spotted the coffin. Gonzalez saw him hold up one flat hand, like a traffic cop. 'We can't release anything!' he said. 'A violent death requires a post! It's our law!'

Ken O'Donnell, the leader of Rose's opposition, had been in the nurse's station with Burkley, trying to get District Attorney Wade on the phone. Wade's secretary had stalled and Ken had hung up. He thought he was the angriest man there. Then he glanced at Dugger. The huge sergeant was in a heavyweight's crouch; his eyes were damp with tears; his fists were knotted and arching back and forth, like the warm-up swings of a batter. *He's going to belt him,* Ken thought, *he's really going to do it*. Dugger was thinking the same thing. 'I'd like to have hit him,' he said later.

Rose himself looked as though he were ready to hit someone. The Dallas medical examiner seemed to be in a tantrum. His arms were flapping, his shirt was dishevelled. The blood had left his freckled face, giving him the complexion of cold oatmeal. He was speaking rapidly in a shrill, animated voice, which to Gonzalez sounded like a screech. Following the thread of his thought was hard, but he appeared to be lecturing them on the protection of the innocent, the accused's day in court, the credo of the physician and—he always returned to his central theme—the sanctity of the Texas statutes which federal employees were attempting to profane.

The men around the coffin decided to adopt Kemp Clark's suggestion; if necessary, they would hold him down. A signal was passed, O'Donnell to Kellerman to the four-to-twelve shift. Rose was surrounded by muscle.

'You can't leave now!' he said to Ken, bounding up and down to keep the coffin in view. 'You can't move it!'

Ken was beginning to doubt that anything could move. A crush of sweating men had developed around the double doors. The doors had been forced open, and people were wedging their way in from the red-striped corridor beyond; Theron Ward estimated the crowd at forty. Until now Rose had been a lonely figure, but this was still Dallas, he was still a public official, and despite Sergeant Dugger's defection a medical examiner's natural allies were Dallas policemen. One of them was among the arrivals from the outer hall. He took up a position at Rose's side. It looked as though they might have to hold more than one man down, and if the patrolman intervened actively, he would be no pushover; he was wearing a pistol and was fingering it.

As O'Donnell and O'Brien were shouldering their way towards Rose they were stopped by Burkley and McHugh, who proposed another solution. They explained that a local justice of the peace was present. He had the power to overrule the medical examiner. Everyone waited while the judge was summoned; then he arrived and disappointed them. He could do nothing, he said. If a JP suspected a homicide, it was his duty to order an autopsy. There were plenty of grounds for suspicion here, and he couldn't overlook them. *Ergo*—he guessed the procedure wouldn't take more than three hours.

O'Donnell asked that an exception be made for President Kennedy.

Although the din was atrocious, both he and O'Brien heard the justice of the peace say, with what they regarded as a distinctly unsympathetic inflection, 'It's just another homicide case as far as I'm concerned.'[2]

The effect on O'Donnell was instantaneous. He uttered a swart oath recommending monogenesis. Thrusting his head forward until their noses nearly grazed, he said, 'We're leaving.'

The policeman beside Rose pointed to the medical examiner and the justice of the peace and told O'Brien, 'These two guys say you can't go.'

[2] The judge believes he was more compassionate, but it is three to one; Ted Clifton also heard the exchange.

'One side,' Larry said cuttingly. Jerking his head, Ken said, 'Get the hell over. We're getting out of here. We don't give a damn what these laws say. We're not staying here three hours or three minutes.' He called to Dave, who had backed Jackie into a cubicle, 'We're leaving *now*.' To Kellerman he snapped, 'Wheel it out!'

At this juncture, in O'Donnell's words, 'it became physical—us against them.' Kellerman, who hadn't even heard Ken, had begun to pull the church truck on his own, butting flesh with his shoulders; the agents and Dugger were pushing. It is impossible to say who was obstructing them, because in the mêlée several men who seemed to be barring the progress had been daunted and were simply trying to get out of the way. Earl Rose wasn't among them. His patrolman had capitulated, and he had been shoved away from the threshold. Neither was Theron Ward. He was in the nurse's station, calling the District Attorney. As the number rang he saw Mrs Kennedy emerging from the cubicle behind Dave. He had a vivid impression of the bloodstains on her clothes, and then he was talking to Ward. To Ward, as to Earl Rose earlier, the District Attorney explained that he had no objection to the removal of the body. Holding the receiver with his right hand, the judge waved towards the puddled humanity at the door with his left hand, motioning them to go ahead. The value of the gesture is doubtful. It was like signalling to a bowl game scrimmage from a cheap seat. The scrap was already resolved. The last havering human obstacle faded away, and the coffin rolled into the corridor. The widow was walking directly behind it, her gloved right hand once more on the gleaming cover.

As they approached the ambulance dock an orderly raced up and handed an agent a blank certificate of death, signed by Kemp Clark. It was swiftly pocketed. By now the formation was moving forward in a rush, and in the disarray two Kennedy men had been left behind. Dr Burkley and Bill Greer had separately returned to the trauma room, each with the thought that something might have been forgotten. Quite a lot had been left. Greer arrived before Burkley. Margaret Hinchcliffe gave him the two paper bags containing the President's personal effects, and while he was folding the tops over, Doris Nelson handed him Clint Hill's stained blue suit coat. After he had hurried out Diana Bowron thrust her hand in her uniform and encountered an unfamiliar lump. It was Kennedy's gold watch, still covered with his dried blood. Fleeing down the hall, she turned it over to an agent.

The President's physician entered the deserted room alone. He inspected it carefully and found nothing until he reached the stainless-steel trash can. In tidying up David Sanders had crammed the container to the brim with the debris of emergency surgery—intravenous material, gauze, sponges, plastic vials, empty cartons bearing the labels of pharmaceutical houses. The doctor was pressed for time. He didn't have time to sift through the rubbish, but strewn through it, he saw, were bright red petals of what had been Jacqueline Kennedy's bouquet of welcome from the city of Dallas. Two dying blossoms were within reach. The orderly had left one lying on the floor beside the can pedal; the other stuck out from the lid. Burkley picked up the first rose, broke off the stem of the other, and carefully slipped both into an envelope.

Earl Rose, swept aside, nursed the galling conviction that he had been bilked by everyone, including Theron Ward, who he felt had been pusillanimous. Ward himself departed to complete a batch of official forms with his registrar. In his precinct log he docketed the inquest he had never held as No. 210; 'Burial-Transit No. 7992,' authorizing 'the removal of John F. Kennedy, male, white,' was belatedly drawn up and sent, for some reason, to Oneal's, Inc.; Kemp Clark's death certificate turned out to be inadequate under state statutes, so Ward signed another. Accuracy was not a forte of official Dallas that afternoon. On the new document—the deceased's 'usual occupation' was given as 'President of the U.S.'—Kennedy's Washington address was erroneously recorded as 600, not 1600, Pennsylvania Avenue. The transit permit incorrectly listed his age as forty-four. The Dallas Police Department completed a homicide report later in the day and it, too, was imprecise, stating that headquarters had received word of the shooting at 5.10 p.m. With that the local rites were over. Ceremonial homage had been paid to the letter of the law.

The forms were filed; the medical examiner and the JP, meanwhile, had lurched off history's stage. Father Cain, however, had remained. He had dodged ahead of the procession in the corridor and stationed himself on the loading dock. He continued to vibrate with prayers. Over the past half-hour he had scored a complex litany—scales, harmonics, and full chords of benedictions: *Cum spiritu tuo sursum corda; Dominus vobiscum; Gratias agamus Domino Deo nostro; Dignum et justum est*—and he was standing between the emergency area entrance and Oneal's spotless vehicle awaiting his cue.

Different participants saw the coffin's emergence variously. The White House press corps, clustered below, completely missed the priest. Chuck Roberts scribbled that Mrs Kennedy was 'still wearing the raspberry-coloured suit in which she had started the day's campaigning—and still looking beautiful'. Hugh Sidey noticed that Godfrey McHugh, who had joined Kellerman in front, came to attention as the sunlight struck him, and that a single tear rolled down Larry O'Brien's cheek. To Tom Wicker they were all 'stunned, silent, stumbling'. Jacqueline Kennedy, above the reporters, saw only the casket top. Her head bowed, she stood apart. Sergeant Dugger knew that this was the zero hour of his life. Now, *now* he must reveal some shred of his grief to her. Vernon B. Oneal was annoyed. His driver had neglected to remove the red ambulance sign from the side window of the Cadillac. Nobody would be able to identify it as a hearse. The correspondents would misreport it. The undertaker shook his head waspishly, and as he did his attention was distracted by Father Cain, who had become a cynosure for O'Donnell, O'Brien, and Powers. There was no way around him. Dave Powers took a deep breath and invoked the name of the Saviour.

The priest was already chattering a paternoster, swinging his green bag by its drawstring as he tuned up his voice. But he was about to be surprised. His second appearance was to be a damp squib. He had exposed himself earlier inside. The piety of the mafia had been sorely tested, and they weren't going to give him another opportunity to come near Mrs Kennedy. Everyone here was a stranger to them, and every hand seemed to be against them. Just as there was no way of ascertaining that the assassin had been a stray dog, so was it impossible to tell that Rose was not a representative of Texas authority acting under instructions. It was hard to believe that a minor functionary would take so much on his shoulders. They had heard a lot of static; they had seen a great deal of muscle and a policeman's gun. There might be worse to come. To the Presidential staff—Kennedy's lieutenants, aides, and agents were unanimous in this—it appeared highly probable that a superior force was on the way to intercept them. If they loitered in Dallas, they couldn't put anything in the field to match it. Their only chance was to hurry. They had temporized too long as it was. Perhaps that had been Rose's purpose, some of them thought; perhaps he had been sent to delay them. They had to move quickly, and Father Cain was no help. As Catholics the Irishmen were grateful for his blessing, but his timing was most inopportune.

At the wide door O'Donnell had been the strong man. On the dock it was O'Brien. During his years with Kennedy he had become so suave that even his wife Elva had forgotten that Larry's glibness was a veneer, that he was the son of a Springfield, Massachusetts, bartender. Underneath he hadn't changed, however; he had the ovoid torso of a bouncer. In his present frenzy he was capable of bouncing a priest, and in essence that is what he did. Dugger and the agents were exchanging grimaces and rolling their eyes; O'Brien acted. 'I was in a panic to get out of there,' he recalled afterwards.

'That little lady just couldn't stand there with her husband's body that way.' Father Cain was propelled to the dock edge, where he continued his incantations while the staff, coached by Oneal, eased the President into his ambulance-hearse's cargo compartment. There was a door on the right-hand side, leading to a jump seat beside the coffin. Dugger, who was nearest, opened it for Jacqueline Kennedy.

'Thank you,' she whispered.

The sergeant started, and he began to weep. He still felt tongue-tied, but by speaking to him the President's wife had given him a feeling of identity. He remembered that he had a name. He looked at her as directly as his clouded spectacles would permit; he held out his clumsy hand, she touched it lightly, and he said, 'Bob Dugger, Ma'am.'

Then he closed the door. It was exactly 2.08 p.m. Burkley, who entered the hearse by the rear doors, squeezed his chunky frame behind Mrs Kennedy. He had to make himself very small. Clint Hill and Godfrey were there, too, and three agents were cramped in front. Kellerman was on the right as usual, but Andy Berger was behind the wheel. This was the only time in these last days that Bill Greer did not chauffeur the President. Preoccupied by paper bags, he was temporarily lost in the warren of halls, and Kellerman was unwilling to wait. The prospect of a pitched battle in the presence of the young widow had intimidated them all. They were determined to reach the airport and take off before the imaginary reinforcements could arrive and overpower them.

'Do you know the way to my mortuary?' the undertaker called to Roy. 'I'll meet you there.' Roy replied, 'We're not going there. We're going to Love Field. Follow us and you can pick up your ambulance.' 'Hearse,' Oneal instinctively corrected him. Then he turned to Hugh Sidey and expressed concern over who would pay him.

Sidey just stared at him. The correspondent had no way of knowing that the long weekend ahead was to demonstrate just how splendidly the memory of a President could be extended beyond death. Sidey glanced from the funeral director and the small semicircle of curiosity seekers in front of the tangled parking lot to the wintry pile of the hospital overhead and then out to the neoned boulevard, where the six-lane stream of blatting traffic halted and moved, halted and moved as the signal lights mechanically turned red, amber, green. *Sordid*, he thought, *what a sordid place for the glory of the Kennedy era to end.*

The passengers in the white Cadillac and the four-car column that trailed it felt the first stirrings of relief as they tore out Harry Hines and Mockingbird. The vehicle immediately behind the hearse was a convertible, a relic from the motorcade which now seemed to belong, not merely to another day, but to another age, as in a sense it did.[3] Pam Turnure was there with Mac Kilduff, Evelyn Lincoln, Mary Gallagher, and several others—nearly a dozen people sardined together. *It's like a circus car*, Pam thought, fighting for air. But the greater the distance between them and the hospital, the safer they felt. Their apopemptic ride was an escape, and because pursuit was assumed—because the men at the doors to Major Medicine had been told that they were fugitives from Dallas justice—it took on the character of a stampede. At breakneck pace they passed a Slick Airways hut, spun right, and right again. Braniff and American Airlines hangars came into view, shimmering in the mid-afternoon heat on the opposite side of the concrete and tarmac desert of Love.

There were two warning signs:

RESTRICTED AREA

And:

Slow
DANGEROUS
Trucks

Andy Berger was inattentive. No hearse had ever travelled at such speed. They were travelling at least as fast as the Johnson party had, and they took the unpaved patch by the fence gap as though it were as hard as a highway. Greer, with his Old World courtesies, had never given them such a ride.

Jacqueline Kennedy, talking to Clint, became conscious of a movement behind her, and pivoting in the jump seat she saw Burkley, squeezed in his meagre space. He was burrowing into his clothing. She peering back, wondering what could be the matter with him. Then his hand appeared with the two roses intact. 'These were under—were in his shirt,' he panted, red-faced, and she took them and put them in the pocket of her suit.

At Gate 28 Berger was braking beside Aircraft 26000, which they still thought of as their plane. There was no discussion as they disembarked. Kennedy was going aboard first; everyone knew that. Early in his administration he had held a door for Eleanor Roosevelt. 'No, you must go first,' she had said. 'You are the President.' He had laughed and said, 'I keep forgetting.' And she had said gently, 'But you must never forget.' He had never really forgotten, but sometimes protocol had become a bore and had been disregarded. Not now, though; the Secret Service, Ken, Larry, and the military aides prepared to carry the coffin up. 'It's awful heavy,' Ted Clifton said

[3] Conceivably this had been Vice President Johnson's convertible.

anxiously, and looking at the steep steps of the ramp leading up to the rear door, he said, 'Do you suppose we can get it up there?' The others were silent. It was going to go, they were going to do it, that was all.

In their haste they damaged the Elgin Britannia. Not being undertakers, they did not know that a device automatically pins a coffin to the floor of a modern hearse. There was a catch which released the lock, but they didn't see it. The four-to-twelve shift bounded for the doors and unlatched them in double-quick time, and when the coffin wouldn't budge they made it budge. Heaving and straining, they felt a tremor. They yanked together and heard two brittle cracks. Vernon Oneal's most expensive coffin had been damaged; a craggy piece of trim from the lower hinge and the entire top of the handle housing behind the head had snapped off. Dave Powers stepped into position to bear his share of the weight. He wrote:

2.20 I helped carry casket aboard Air Force #1.[4]

To Pam, standing beside Jackie, the manhandling seemed to take for ever, but the men were holding nearly half a ton and going straight up, with scarcely an inch on either side of the narrow steps for manoeuvre. It was an exercise in desperation and brute strength. Yet there were no grunts, scarcely any words at all; the airport, Pam noted, had become 'strangely quiet'. Colonel McNally wrote that people were standing about awkwardly, that Air Force personnel saluted, and that some policemen bowed their heads. 'Give us a hand,' Roy Kellerman called to Joe Ayres, and the stewards and Colonel Swindal ran down to help. Dave Powers, realizing that he was really too old for this, stepped to one side and signed himself with the Cross. Mary Gallagher saw him and fingered her rosary. Foot by foot the coffin rose, Godfrey in front twisting it for the turn, and though the men in back were doing everything they could to keep it level, the smashed handle housing presented a serious obstacle; they couldn't find a grip. Their mighty burden tilted a little in the back and then tilted quite a lot. Evelyn Lincoln worried. She thought, *He's wedged down, it's so uncomfortable for him.*

The refitting of the tail compartment was complete. Ayres and two master sergeants, Joe Chapel of Air Force One and Deroy Cain from the backup plane, had finished removing the partition and the four seats from the port side. Larry O'Brien felt almost absurdly

[4] It was closer to 2.15, though not as early as the new President thought. In his statement to the Warren Commission President Johnson estimated that Mrs Kennedy and the coffin arrived 'just after 2 o'clock'. The President was mistaken. At 2 p.m. he had been on the telephone with Attorney General Kennedy, and the calls to Bullion's office and to Goldberg, Katzenbach, and Sarah Hughes were still to come.

grateful—it was the first sign of planning he had seen—and the exhausted body bearers, with Godfrey McHugh acting as foreman, eased the coffin over until it lay flush against the bulkhead. Godfrey's uniform and Ted Clifton's were splotched with dank patches of perspiration; their ribands and gold and silver left-shoulder aiguillettes were askew. They stood back with Larry, Ken, Dave, and Roy, surveyed the results, and then leaned down to make small symmetrical adjustments.

The cabin was dark and suffocating. The effect of the closed shutters and the disconnecting of the air conditioning had been cumulative. In the semi-darkness there were shufflings and mutterings, and for a moment the pallbearers were unaware of another passenger across the aisle. In one of the two light plaid seats on the starboard side Mrs Kennedy sat alone, watching intently. She had slipped in right behind them. Evelyn, Pam, and Mary had entered afterwards, and Pam had fallen back to embrace her, but now at 2.18 p.m. all the secretaries were in the staff cabin; of the Kennedy women, only the President's widow remained. Her resolve held: she was as near her husband as she could be.

They saw her, and Clifton and McHugh exchanged a look.

'One of us should stay,' Clifton said. To the others this meant nothing; to the two generals it was obvious. Since the beginning of written history military tradition has required that should a Commander in Chief be slain, a high-ranking officer must remain with the body until burial as a guard of honour. 'I will,' Godfrey said, and they explained the custom to O'Donnell, who nodded.

Few guardians have been more faithful than McHugh was to be. He couldn't begin his vigil quite yet, however. He had another pressing duty; he was the Air Force aide, and this was a plane.

'Should we get airborne?' he inquired of O'Donnell.

Ken nodded. 'Are we ready?'

'I'll check the fuel,' Clifton said.

'It's done,' said Godfrey. 'I did it by phone.' Turning towards the cockpit, he broke into a run.

As the stewards locked 26000's rear door, Jacqueline Kennedy quietly rose. She wanted to be by herself for a few minutes. She wouldn't leave the coffin, but the bedroom was adjacent to the tail compartment. The last time she and Jack had been alone together, she remembered, they had been in that private cabin. A recollection of the happiness they had known there swept over her, and she decided that would be the right place for her to compose herself. Stepping softly, she moved down the dim dark corridor. Because she regarded the bedroom as hers, she did not knock; she simply grasped the latch and twisted it. Facing the door, in the desk chair, sat Marie

Fehmer. Reclining on the bed was Lyndon Johnson, dictating to her.

Mrs Kennedy came to a dead stop. The new President heaved himself up and hastily lumbered past her. Marie swiftly gathered her notebooks and pencils and followed Johnson out.

The widow stared after them. For an instant she paused indecisively on the bright blue carpet with the golden Presidential eagle worked into it; then she returned to the corridor and took a blind step towards them. Again she wavered. Sergeant Ayres stood at the forward end of the corridor. He was looking directly at her, and his heavy face, she saw, was ashen. The relentless tension of the past two hours was beginning to lift. The galley had been opened, and someone had ordered vegetable soup. Immediately it had become a fad. A half-dozen others had agreed that vegetable soup was just the thing. Now Johnson called for a bowl. In Marie Fehmer's words, he 'just inhaled the soup and crackers—they were gone in a flash.' Putting the dish aside he sighed, 'It's been a year since I got up.'

Mrs Kennedy returned to the tail cabin. Godfrey McHugh, meantime, had reached the nose of the aircraft. Johnson had been behind the closed door of the bedroom as the General passed there, and in the murk Godfrey had not noticed Lady Bird or any of the other new passengers. The General was preoccupied with the need for immediate departure. Entering the staff cabin, he was relieved to hear a familiar whine; Jim Swindal, on his own, had started the No. 3 engine, the sign that a hop was imminent. Calling ahead Godfrey shouted, 'Take off! The President is aboard!'

Two Presidents were aboard, though Godfrey had not thought of it that way. Once Johnson had made up his mind to return to the capital in the Presidential plane (and it cannot be denied that this was his right and perhaps his duty, because of Air Force One's symbolic significance), there was no way strain could have been avoided between the Kennedy and Johnson people. His decision to take a second oath of office in Dallas was to make it more pungent. During the past two hours the Kennedy staff had lost a President and battled to remove his coffin from the hospital—more buffeting than most people experience in a lifetime. Their tempers were tinder. If Johnson had directed them to take the plane parked alongside, they would have been spared the climax of their anguish. Yet perspective suggests compassion. Johnson *was* the President, whether or not they could bring themselves to acknowledge him as such. And as Robert McNamara observed later, 'You must remember that *he* was in a state of shock, too.' To his credit, he was now acting decisively. To theirs, they concealed their scars, realizing that any public rift with the emerging administration would be a disservice to the country and, in consequence, to the man they mourned.

Had the man they mourned arrived on 26000 alive, his very appearance would have been the signal for an instant take-off. He nearly did it in death. That was why Jim Swindal cranked up engine No. 3. The moment the President boarded the aircraft and Joe Ayres latched the rear door behind him they were supposed to depart. The Chief Executive's time must not be wasted. Swindal's crew was enormously proud of the speed with which they could become airborne, and drilled constantly to shave seconds. Godfrey McHugh assumed that the first engine whine would be followed by a quick taxiing into position and a lifting sensation. It had always been that way. This was to be an exception, however. Swindal couldn't leave yet. He was just warming up. The forward hatch had been left open; the ramp there had yet to be withdrawn.

The Johnson party and the Kennedy party were milling around in the staff cabin. Godfrey was diverted by aisle traffic, and in that interval he was primed for a collision of authority. His antagonist, oddly, was Mac Kilduff, a Kennedy man who had ridden to the airport in the breakneck caravan behind the hearse. Kilduff wasn't looking for trouble. He had been summoned and commissioned by the new President. During the positioning of the coffin in the tail compartment Mac had been standing at the foot of the forward ramp, talking to Agent Lawson and the two secretaries from Salinger's office. 'I'm the first Secret Service advance man ever to lose a President,' Lawson had said heavily, and the girls had been trying to console him.

A crewman had called down the steps to Kilduff: Johnson wanted to see him at once. Mac had run up the steps. He was baffled. Unlike the secretaries, he hadn't heard that Lyndon was aboard, and he couldn't imagine what he was doing here. Larry O'Brien was similarly perplexed. O'Brien had just seen the President emerging from the bedroom with Marie Fehmer. Remembering the rhubarb at the hospital, Larry had wondered, *How did he know we would appear? What would he have done if we hadn't come?*

Johnson had been incisive with Kilduff. Watching him in the stateroom, his wife had thought him 'absolutely a graven image. His was a face that looked carved in bronze.' He had known exactly what he wanted: he wanted the acting press secretary, whose calmness at Parkland had impressed him, to take the lead in setting things up for Sarah Hughes. To the new President he seemed an ideal liaison man, a vigorous Kennedy aide and an expert in mass media. As Vice President he hadn't been told that this trip was supposed to be Mac's swan-song.

Johnson had sketched his plans. He had said, 'I've got to be sworn in here. I've talked to the Attorney General.'

Mac had reacted quickly. The flight to Washington, he realized, would have to be postponed. He had headed for Swindal, and as he darted forward he must have passed McHugh—one of several near misses for Godfrey, which can only be understood in the light of the turmoil in the staff area.

'Cut it off!' Mac had told Swindal. He offered no explanation, but he was a member of the Presidential staff. The pilot had obediently reached for his instruments.

Kilduff had trotted down the ramp steps in pursuit of reporters. Godfrey approached the nose of the aircraft seconds later, and it was at this point that he called, 'Take off! The President is aboard!'

'No, we can't,' Swindal called back.

'Let's *go*.'

'Mr Kilduff says we can't.'

'It doesn't matter what anybody says. *Move*,' McHugh commanded. He was a general, Swindal was a colonel. He returned aft assuming that he would be obeyed.

Johnson's bags had just been delivered from the backup plane. Mrs Kennedy had resumed her seat across from the coffin, and the new President, who had been inquiring of Kilduff whether there were any photographers present, entered the bedroom's powder room to change his shirt and comb his hair. For the second time Godfrey missed an encounter by seconds, though it is doubtful that his attitude would have changed much if they had met. To him Lyndon Johnson was still Lyndon—the Vice President—and Vice Presidents, far from issuing decrees to the men surrounding Presidents, defer to them. Johnson had tacitly acknowledged this at Parkland when he turned a deaf ear to Youngblood and Roberts, refusing to leave what they regarded as a potential death trap until O'Donnell had given him permission to go. Since then he had grasped the enormity of what had happened and had become President Johnson in his own eyes. But Godfrey McHugh saw things differently. He was an emotional man, he had already decided to renounce his Texas citizenship—and under the present circumstances he would regard an instruction from Johnson as an impertinence.

The cabin in the tail grew more humid. Jacqueline Kennedy said, 'It's so hot. Let's leave.'

'Didn't you tell them?' Ken asked McHugh.

'Yes, but Mac Kilduff told them something else. I'll go up again.'

In the communications shack he ran into Kilduff. Mac was out of breath. He had been attending to assorted details, assembling a makeshift press pool—two of the men had flipped a coin to see which would go—and rehearsing Cecil Stoughton and his cameras for the ceremony. Even so his unintelligibility with Godfrey is remarkable. He could hardly have been more obscure had he tried.

'What's going on?' McHugh demanded.

'We're waiting for newspaper people.'

'The hell with newspaper people! We're going to go.'

'We have to wait for Lady Bird's luggage; it's not here yet.'

'What? She's on her own plane.'

'No, she's here, and we're waiting for a Texas judge. A lady.'

Back to the rear compartment. Ken asked, 'Well?'

'*I* don't know what's happening. We're waiting for a woman judge, some reporters, and Mrs Johnson's baggage,' Godfrey reported. He knew it sounded idiotic, but that was what he had been told.

O'Donnell's face drew to a point, as though the muscles had been tightened by a single drawstring within. '*You leave right now.*'

'This time we're going,' McHugh promised grimly. He could replace Swindal and fly the plane himself if he had to.

In the corridor outside the bedroom he hesitated. Mac had specifically mentioned Lady Bird. It seemed preposterous to Godfrey, but perhaps something had happened to the backup plane; perhaps Johnson was here, too. On his two round-trip sprints Godfrey had seen no sign of him. Maybe the Vice Presidential agents were hiding him somewhere. The safest course was to check. He went in and looked around. Nobody was there. It never occurred to him that Johnson might be behind the closed powder room door, and he sped ahead, convinced that Kilduff was mistaken.

By now Godfrey had become part of a task force. He had struck out twice, so while he was inspecting the bedroom O'Donnell had dispatched Ted Clifton, Roy Kellerman, and Clint Hill to the front of the plane. As it turned out, all three learned the correct explanation before McHugh. Valenti, Stoughton, and Homer Thornberry crowded around Clifton, saying, 'We can't go yet,' 'We've got to find a federal judge,' 'Lyndon has word from the Attorney General, he called Washington.' Kellerman and Hill heard none of this; they were barging up the aisle after Swindal. Roy burst into the communications shack and saw the ramp. Wondering why it hadn't been wheeled away, he descended the steps. Just then Kilduff flashed by.

'You'd better get aboard, we're going to take off,' Roy warned him.

'No, we can't, we have to have the oath,' Mac replied. Over his shoulder he called to Clint, who was standing at the stair head, 'A judge is going to swear in Johnson. Bobby requested it.'

He had justified the delay to everyone except Godfrey McHugh. There is something marvellous about the General's continuing ignorance. By his own account he made five journeys through the length of the aircraft before he found out why they weren't moving. Even O'Donnell and O'Brien knew before Godfrey did. Wandering into the staff cabin, Larry heard someone ask Marie Fehmer if she had typed the Presidential oath of office. She nodded and he comprehended everything. At about the same time, O'Donnell overheard a discussion in the stateroom, and when someone called out, 'We need a photographer and we're waiting for a judge,' Ken, though he disapproved, understood what was meant. McHugh alone remained in the dark. Ted Clifton would have enlightened him. Somehow they missed connections. Clint and Roy could have quickly briefed him, but they had become bogged down in Secret Service details; Johnson's decision to travel on 26000 meant that Roy's shift assignments were fouled up. The four-to-twelve Trade Mart men, whom he had designated as the new President's bodyguards, were on 86970; the weary eight-to-four agents were here. Roy threw up his hands. A reversal now would add to the muddle; it was safer to stand pat.

Roy had another problem. Passing through the staff cabin he had been struck by the unusually large number of passengers and by the unfamiliarity of their faces. On any other trip he would have recognized them all—would, in fact, have known who they were in advance. The one difference between Air Force One and Air Force Two was that Air Force One always carried a passenger manifest. It was a basic precaution; no matter how short the flight, a Presidential guest could not mount either ramp unless his name had been typed on that sheet. Stepping into the cockpit with Clint, Roy worriedly said to Swindal, 'There are a lot of people on this plane.' The Colonel said. 'We can carry them.' Kellerman saw Rufus Youngblood entering the communications shack. He asked him, 'Do you know all these people here?' Youngblood assured him that Lem Johns had already started a manifest.

This was a confrontation between opposites—between Kellerman, Kennedy's chief bodyguard, and Youngblood, head of the Johnson detail. Mystified by the bustling around him, Roy felt thwarted, while Rufus' briskness had continued unabated. He had dealt with the manifest. He had sent Jack Ready to the gate to meet Sarah Hughes, and he had asked Chief Curry to accompany Ready and identify Sarah when she drove up. But no one could anticipate every problem that afternoon, and the Youngblood men were as worried about possible overload as the Kellerman men. Before the arrival of the hearse Emory Roberts had carefully calculated the probable number of passengers. He reckoned on a coffin and Jacqueline

Kennedy, and that was all. As he later confessed, he hadn't realized that Mrs Kennedy would bring her husband's aides with her; the presence of O'Donnell, O'Brien, and Powers dismayed him. Counting both waves, there were twenty-seven people, and despite the pilot's assurances the Johnson agents became anxious. As a consequence Johns asked several minor members of the Kennedy party to leave, and other passengers who had ridden on 26000 since leaving Washington were turned away before they could mount the ramp. One was Ralph Yarborough. For two days everyone had been trying to lure Yarborough to the Vice President's side. Suddenly he was an outcast. He asked for a reason, and Ted Clifton told him, 'Maximum security.'

Clifton had swiftly adjusted to the transition. His reasoning was clear. As a general he held the 'special trust and confidence' of the President. The occupant of the Presidency had changed, and Clifton had to change, too. His duty was to the office, not to the man. Following a talk with Valenti and Thornberry he functioned as President Johnson's military aide.

Meanwhile McHugh, who felt otherwise, was building up steam. The conflict had become irreconcilable. The Kennedy party, on the one hand, believed that Air Force One's chief passenger was their fallen leader; since he could not give them orders, they looked to Mrs Kennedy, who shared their feeling that they must quit Dallas, and who was bewildered by the delay. The attitude of the Johnson party, on the other hand, was summed up by Youngblood, who drew Lem Johns aside during the turmoil and emphatically told him, 'When the boss says we go, *then* we go.'

After the Kellerman–Youngblood huddle had broken up Godfrey had reached the front of the plane for the third time. He spotted Mac Kilduff. Bounding towards him—Kilduff had the impression that he was 'galloping'—he said hotly, 'We've got to take off immediately.'

'Not until Johnson has taken the oath,' said Kilduff.

'Johnson isn't here. He's on the backup plane.'

'Then you go back and tell that six-foot Texan he isn't Lyndon Johnson,' Mac said. 'We're not going to Andrews until the President has been sworn.'

McHugh flushed. Pointing towards the tail compartment he cried, 'I have only one President, and he's lying back in that cabin.'

It was a dramatic remark, and the plane was small enough so that his words were quoted to virtually every passenger before they landed at the capital. Ken O'Donnell heard them and was proud of the General. 'This morning you were this tall,' he said, holding his hand a few inches from the floor. Then he raised it as high as he could reach and said, 'Now you're up here.' But Lyndon Johnson had ears, too. That brief exchange in the communications shack altered the destinies of the two men; Kilduff, whom O'Donnell had dismissed, had laid claim to a job in the new administration, while the General had forfeited his hope for another star. Indeed, even Godfrey's days in uniform were numbered.

After the new President had changed his shirt and combed his hair, Joe Ayres laid out some blue Air Force One towels for Jacqueline Kennedy. She thanked him and entered the bedroom, and the Johnsons came in to offer their condolences. He felt that words were inadequate; he called her 'Honey,' put his arm around her and shook his head, but he left expressions of commiseration to his wife. Mrs Johnson was a woman, and Mrs Kennedy liked her.

Her face crumpling with tears, the new First Lady said, 'Oh, Jackie, you know, we never even wanted to be Vice President and now, dear God, it's come to this!'

'Oh, what if I hadn't been there!' Jacqueline Kennedy said. 'I was so glad I was there.'

Johnson's instinct had been correct. Words were inept. Lady Bird was ordinarily the essence of tact, yet here she slipped. 'I don't know what to say,' she sobbed, and then she said it: 'What wounds me most of all is that this should happen in my beloved State of Texas.'

She had scarcely finished before she realized that her tongue had tripped. 'Immediately,' as she said later, 'I regretted it.' This was no day for Texas chauvinism; Kennedy's death should be what wounded her most. Her eyes wavered and fell, and she saw the stained glove. She had always envied the way Jackie wore gloves. She herself usually felt awkward in them, and couldn't wait to take them off. As always, this one seemed a part of Jackie. And it was caked with her husband's blood. Bird filled up. She suggested, 'Can we get someone to help you put on fresh things?'

'Oh, no,' Mrs Kennedy replied. 'Perhaps later I'll ask Mary Gallagher. But not right now.'

The three of them sat on the bed, Mrs Kennedy in the middle. After a pause Johnson said uncertainly, 'Well—about the swearing in.'

'Lyndon,' she began, and took a quick breath. Of all those who had been with her husband, she was the first to accept the future. 'Oh, excuse me. I'll never call you that again,' she said. 'I mean, Mr President.'

'Honey, I hope you'll call me that for the rest of your life,' he said.

She was silent. Words were difficult for her, too. The fact was that he was now the Chief Executive, and she resolved never again to address him by his first name.

'About the swearing in,' he repeated, trying again.

'Oh, yes, I know, I know,' she said quickly. She thought she knew. She, too, had seen the old engravings, and she remembered that during her televised tour of the White House for CBS she had pointed out that Rutherford B. Hayes, whose inauguration day fell on a Sunday, had taken the oath in the Red Room. The ceremony didn't have to be on the east steps of the Capitol. It could be anywhere. It could be held right here, and evidently it was going to be. She said, 'Yes. What's going to happen?'

'I've arranged for a judge—an old friend of mine, Judge Hughes—to come,' he answered. 'She'll be here in about an hour. So why don't you lie down and freshen up and everything? We'll leave you alone.'

'All right,' she said mindlessly, and they went out, closing the bedroom door.

Alone, she smoked a cigarette, staring vacantly into space. Then the full force struck her. *An hour*, she thought. *My God, do I have to wait an hour?*

In the stateroom a note awaited Johnson: 'Mr President, I am here if I can be of any help—Bill Moyers.'

Moyers was one of two passengers whose presence seemed almost supernatural. The other was Marty Underwood, who had advanced Houston and who, when Oswald opened fire on the blue Lincoln, had been sound asleep six hundred miles away in the Rice Hotel, exhausted by his ten days of politicking there. One of Max Peck's assistants had entered the room with a pass-key, told Underwood of the shooting, driven him to the airport, and put him aboard a Braniff plane which was just leaving for Dallas. Love's control tower had given the scheduled flight a green light; Underwood had sprinted to the eastern concourse and was sitting groggily in the staff area. Afterwards he would have only the haziest recollection of how he had got there. The shock had left him in a state of semi-amnesia. There was really no reason for him to be aboard. He was nowhere near as important as the Rice management had thought him to be. Except as a dazed witness to the coming ceremony he was useless.

Bill Moyers was most useful, and his trip had been more remarkable, because he had come by a more unorthodox route. Two hours ago, when the first UPI bulletin had been broadcast, he had been lunching in Austin's Forty Acres Club with Frank Erwin, Chairman of the State Democratic Executive Committee. An hour later he had been over Waco, Texas, in his hastily chartered plane when he heard Bob Trout announce Kennedy's death. Acquiring permission to land, the pilot had parked beside the two huge 707's, but Moyers, ignorant of Johnson's whereabouts, had vaulted into a state police car and peremptorily ordered the trooper to take him to Parkland—he had heard the hospital's name from Trout. Halfway there the police revealed that the new President was at Love. Executing a tight U-turn at top speed, the trooper returned him to the airport. There Moyers hesitated. He couldn't tell 26000 and 86970 apart. Their wings were almost touching. Neither had been moved since noon, but he assumed that the similarity was a security manoeuvre, designed to outwit anyone stalking Johnson. He saw a Texas Congressman at the foot of 26000's front ramp, bounded aboard unchallenged, was stopped at the stateroom door by an agent who didn't know him, and rapidly scribbled his note at a staff cabin desk.

Johnson promptly sent for him—a Texan who was also a friend of the Kennedy family was an invaluable ally—and nodded slightly as Moyers entered. They didn't speak. The President seemed pale and wan. There was a distant look in his eye, and he was subdued, which was unlike him. Moyers' description of his demeanour is very like the accounts of those who had been in Booth 13. It was only a momentary relapse, however, triggered, perhaps, by his encounter with Mrs Kennedy. Johnson was gaining confidence and momentum, and within the next few minutes he began dealing with Kennedy's chief lieutenants.

Like the widow, they were bewildered. Unlike her, they had not been brought up to be courteous in adversity, however, and the meeting was strained. McHugh was there. Seeing Johnson, he guessed correctly that he had erred in not opening the powder room door earlier. Lyndon was aboard. If an oath had to be administered on the plane, the General now inquired, why couldn't the ceremony be held in the air?

It was a reasonable question. He received no satisfactory answer. Instead, a maddening discussion about lens angles and close-ups had begun. The concern was arising in several minds that they were about to witness a spectacle which was bound to involve President Kennedy's widow. Independently of them she was reaching the same conclusion; after the Johnsons' departure she noticed that her Austin clothes had been carefully laid out on the other bed: a white dress, white jacket, and black shoes. A number of people could have removed them from the hang-up closet—Mary, Evelyn, Ayres, George Thomas—but none had, and she was left with the feeling that they wanted her to look immaculate in the inaugural picture.

Johnson had given careful attention to his own appearance. But this preoccupation may easily be misinterpreted. If the oath was to dramatize the stability of the American system of government, both for Americans and for allies and antagonists abroad, then the show had better be a good show. And if continuity was to be the theme, Jacqueline Kennedy's presence was desirable, however tormenting it might be for her.

In the stateroom O'Donnell and O'Brien were sitting opposite the new President and First Lady. 'The Constitution puts me in the White House, but you two are free to make your own choices,' he said to Ken and Larry. 'I want to urge you to stay and stand shoulder to shoulder with me. I need you more than you need me—and more than Kennedy needed you.'

O'Brien was squirming. He had been chivied enough. *Hell, let's talk about this later*, he thought. Larry was beset by the vision of Earl Rose storming aboard with the Dallas Police Department and carrying off the body of his fallen leader at gunpoint. But Johnson, as he recalled afterwards, 'was very definitely in a take-charge mood.' Lady Bird, who was to have no memory of the contretemps, felt that 'everybody was doing his utmost best in a difficult situation'. The others were to recollect that they did their best to interrupt her husband and that he, wound up, continued to steamroller ahead. But the Irishmen were skilled politicians, too. They perched tensely, awaiting an opening. O'Brien found one first. He broke in to describe the coroner's behaviour and the need for immediate departure.

'No, I've talked to the Attorney General, and it's his opinion that I should be sworn in here,' Johnson replied. With each passing moment his vision of his conversation with Hickory Hill was growing stronger. 'I'm expecting a judge, a woman, a friend,' he said, and he added: 'She's a Kennedy appointee.'

Then the realization hit O'Brien: *This man is President of the United States*. Larry's opposition ceased. He closed his eyes, praying that the judge arrived before the police.

O'Donnell was harder to shake. He couldn't see why Kennedy people should be involved in a Johnson ceremony. In his opinion the presence of the two groups was a matter of pure chance. The new President kept insisting that he would have held the plane for Mrs Kennedy. There can be little doubt that he had intended to do that from the outset, but Ken was sceptical. He was convinced that had the judge reached the airport before the hearse Johnson would have taken off without them. He kept remembering the struggle at Parkland, and his face tightened more; to Ted Clifton he looked wolf-like. Clifton heard O'Donnell saying over and over, 'We've got to go,' 'We've got to get out of here,' 'We can't wait.' Each time Johnson's reply was the same: 'No, I have word from the Attorney General.'

Later, when Clifton learned that Attorney General Kennedy disavowed advising a Dallas oath (a disavowal strongly supported by Kennedy's opening words to Katzenbach: 'Lyndon wants to be sworn in in Texas. . . .'), he concluded that the new President must have meant Attorney General Waggoner Carr of Texas. But both O'Brien and O'Donnell clearly heard President Johnson say 'Bobby.' Bob Kennedy was the one man who could have persuaded O'Donnell to withdraw his objections. If Bob wanted the new President sworn in in Dallas—and the Kennedy people never dreamed that Johnson might have misunderstood the Attorney General (though he apparently did)—they would just have to sweat out the judge's arrival. They only hoped she would hurry. They literally prayed for her swift arrival. To Clifton, as to O'Brien, the Parkland ogres had sprouted to colossal size. The possibility that the slain President's body might be kidnapped seemed very real.

President Johnson crossed the aisle, settled into the yellow upholstery of the Presidential chair, and ordered more vegetable soup from Joe Ayres. Kilduff was in and out, briefing him. He had been unable to find a Signal Corps technician who would record the oath, but the Dictaphone on the desk by the soup bowl would probably serve. He himself could hold its microphone near Johnson and the judge during the ceremony. Afterwards the Dictabelt, transferred to quarter-inch tape, could be distributed to the networks. Cecil Stoughton had prepared two cameras, one a 35-millimetre Alpa Reflex, which did not require a flash, and his Hasselblad, which did. The Hasselblad was equipped with a wide-angle lens, nearly 90 degrees; with it, Stroughton could photograph the whole stateroom. The fluorescent light overhead was bad, but he had loaded his reels with extremely fast film—Tri-X, ASA 400. Development should present no problems.

The soup craze had been succeeded by an iced water craze. Every throat was parched. The stifling air seemed thick enough to congeal. If they waited another five minutes, Johnson would have to change his shirt again.

The bugbear of blackshirts obsessing the mafia was entirely hallucination. Only one Dallas man had come to Love Field from Parkland; Vernon Oneal was standing by Gate 28, waiting to reclaim his Cadillac. By coincidence the undertaker's parents had once rented a duplex from Sarah Hughes, and he, not Chief Curry, became the first person to note her arrival at the airport. Oneal had overheard the chief and Jack Ready discussing her. He saw her gay sports car swerve around the 'Spirit of Flight' statue and shouted, 'There she is!'

Curry greeted her and took her arm. 'Barefoot Sanders wants you to call him about the oath,' he told her. 'There's a phone on the plane.'

She nodded absently and hurried after him to the ramp. Jim Swindal took over there. He escorted her up the steps and introduced her to Ted Clifton. She said, 'I have to use your telephone. The U.S. Attorney has the oath of office.'

'Here it is,' said a voice, and a hand thrust Marie Fehmer's 3×5 card at her. Pocketing it, Sarah followed Clifton through the staff cabin, into the stateroom. She embraced the President, Mrs Johnson, and her fellow Texans, and Johnson said, 'We'll get as many people in here as possible.' He dispatched men to round up witnesses. Valenti, Youngblood, Roberts, and Lem Johns were sent into the staff area to extend a general invitation, and then he himself went in.

Gesticulating broadly, he announced, 'If anybody wants to join in in the swearing-in ceremony, I would be happy and proud to have you.'

There was no stampede. Johnson's friends and allies excepted—and since he had just acquired possession of the aircraft, they were a minority—26000's regular passengers hung back. Their aloofness can only be understood in the context of 2.35 p.m. Though the assassin had been caught, forty minutes would pass before the networks even announced that 'a suspect' had been arrested. In the absence of information there was a general revulsion, not only towards Dallas, but towards the entire State of Texas. Lyndon Johnson, the most famous of Texans, was the innocent victim of that visceral reaction, and Cecil Stoughton's subsequent negatives are stark evidence of what Larry O'Brien called 'the tension on the plane'. The spectators who were to be framed in Stoughton's lens were a lopsided group. Despite the width of the Hasselblad lens, the photographer did not record the presence of a single major Kennedy aide. Dr Burkley stood behind someone else. There were two agents, there were Kilduff and his two pool reporters. There was Underwood, and there were three Kennedy secretaries—Evelyn, Mary, and Pam—each of whom was led in by Jack Valenti and Lem Johns. The new Chief Executive thanked them effusively, kissed Evelyn's hand and Pam's and called Pam 'little lady'.

Godfrey McHugh was beside John Kennedy's coffin, standing rigidly at attention. Ken O'Donnell withdrew to the corridor. O'Brien participated in setting up the ritual which Lyndon Johnson had said Bob Kennedy wanted; then he retreated behind Sarah

Hughes. The feeling extended to members of the permanent Presidential staff. Stoughton himself wished he were elsewhere. In his prints two tiny points of light identify the spectacles of Ira Gearhart, but the bagman and his football had to be there; the thermonuclear threat was no respecter of tragedy. Gearhart was alone. The crewmen had quietly retired. Boots Miller of the baggage detail was in the staff cabin with his face averted, cradling in his arms a paper bag containing Jacqueline Kennedy's ruined pillbox hat, and Jim Swindal recoiled down the aisle to Clint Hill's side and pressed his face against Roy Kellerman's broad back. As 26000's pilot the Colonel should have been present. Nobody had known that he took politics seriously. But beneath his Milton Caniff air the dapper Alabaman had idolized John Kennedy. He had not known he could suffer so. He felt as though he had a stone in his chest. It would have taken every Johnson agent to drag him into the stateroom. As he explained afterwards, 'I just didn't want to be in the picture. I didn't belong to the Lyndon Johnson team. My President was in that box.'

President Johnson did not deserve this. To a man of his hypersensitivity such treatment was deeply wounding. More important, it was an affront to the Presidency. But those who abstained from the ceremony meant no disrespect, and all Air Force One's passengers were in shock. Martyrdom had transformed the John Kennedy they had known. The politician who had flown west to woo votes no longer existed, even in memory. The manner of his death had clothed him in romance, investing him with a magic more powerful than Prospero's, so that

Nothing of him . . . doth fade,
But doth suffer a sea-change
Into something rich and strange.

Prospero's conjury raised a tempest. The coexistence of the two administrations in an oppressive aeroplane, and the fact that most of these same individuals had battled one another three years earlier in Los Angeles, made tempest inevitable here. There were no villains aboard. The villain was downtown at police headquarters.

The public, poring over the print which Stoughton was to relay within an hour over an AP drum at the Dallas *News*, saw a hazy human frieze in the background and the Johnsons in the foreground, but the focus of attention was the classic, pain-torn profile of Mrs John F. Kennedy. It was her presence that the man about to be sworn in had coveted most. He wanted her beside him and he said so to everyone within earshot. In the end she appeared, but the decision was hers. Three years in the White House had given her an abiding respect for her husband's office. She understood the symbols of authority, the need for some semblance of national majesty after the disaster, and so she came.

They were waiting for her. O'Donnell and O'Brien, prowling the corridor, exchanged solicitous looks. First one and then the other gently opened the bedroom door and peered inside. No sign of her; she must be in the powder room. They couldn't venture there, and Ken went for Mary and Evelyn. Neither man contemplated a role in the ceremony for her. O'Donnell, in fact, was vehemently opposed to it. But they were afraid she might have collapsed. At the same time, Johnson was concentrating on the stateroom tableau which Stoughton would record. 'How do you want us? Can you get us all in?' he asked him. 'I'll put the judge so I'm looking over her shoulder, Mr President,' the photographer replied. The President told Sarah, 'We'll wait for Mrs Kennedy. I want her here.' Stoughton suggested that she stand on one side of him and Lady Bird on the other. Johnson nodded. He was becoming impatient, though. Looking at his wife, he asked that someone summon her. He glanced at the bedroom door, glanced again, and said decisively, 'Just a minute. I'm going to get her.' At that instant the door opened and the widowed First Lady stepped out.

During this sequence of episodes—Johnson's talk with Ken and Larry, the arrival of Sarah Hughes, and the posing in the stateroom—Jacqueline Kennedy had been out of touch with events elsewhere in the plane. This was possible, just as Johnson's earlier camouflage from Godfrey had been possible, because the President's personal quarters had been devised to provide him with a maximum of privacy. All Mrs Kennedy had known was that she was supposed to wait an hour. She had no intention of spending any part of it changing into her Austin dress. Out of curiosity she sent for George Thomas, but her husband's valet hadn't laid it out; he left hurriedly, explaining that he was 'too tumbled up' to talk. Really it didn't matter. With a foresight which eluded all those who had urged (and would continue to urge) her to shed the violated pink suit, she sensed how utterly wrong that would be. To stand beside her husband's coffin in that clean white frock would have been incongruous, a profanity.

She paced between the beds, passing and repassing the hated Austin clothes, and then entered the powder room. There was an overhead light, a mirror tilted upward for the convenience of the beholder, a vanity shelf furnished with accessories and a switch controlling the light and, facing it all, a low stool upholstered in saffron leather.

After washing her face and combing her hair with the precision of a robot she laid the powder room comb aside and gazed blankly at the result. She saw nothing; her thoughts were elsewhere. She was thinking about time. It was *such* a long time. If she were to follow Johnson's suggestion and change, an hour might be appropriate, but inasmuch as she had no intention of removing this suit, it seemed interminable. Suddenly solitude was unbearable. She decided to spend the rest of the hiatus with someone who had been close to him: Ken, perhaps, or Larry. Probably they were nearby. She stepped into the corridor, looked towards the stateroom, and saw everyone waiting. Their expressions were expectant and then, when they saw her, relieved. It was unbelievable: *they* had been waiting for *her*. She hurried towards them, wondering, *Why did he tell me the judge wouldn't be here for an hour? I could have just stayed in there!*

Albert Thomas embraced her. 'You're a brave little lady,' he whispered. Jesse Curry told her the Dallas Police Department had done everything it could. Johnson pressed her hand and said, 'This is the saddest moment of my life.' He leaned down, introducing her to Sarah Hughes, and then drew her to his left side. 'Is this the way you want us?' he inquired of Stoughton. The little photographer, drenched with perspiration, was crouched on the seat directly across the aisle from the Presidential chair. He called out instructions, asking witnesses to move left, right, up, down. All the time his mind was racing. Doubtless this would be the most important picture he would ever take. He was naturally a worrier, and he had some cause for concern. He had failed with the Hasselblad before. In addition he was apprehensive about Ken O'Donnell. With the ambivalence of everyone aboard, he called Johnson 'Mr President' while looking to President Kennedy's chief lieutenant as the man he must please. One sure way to displease Ken would be to photograph Mrs Kennedy's stains. *Bloodwise I'd better be OK*, Stoughton thought anxiously.

He was ready. The Chief Executive and the two First Ladies were ready. The first woman to preside over a Presidential oath was as ready as she would ever be—Sarah was shaking all over, but she felt certain she could make it—and Kilduff was holding the Dictaphone mike by her mouth, his thumb tensed to depress the control button. Then a voice from the semi-circle of witnesses asked, 'What about a Bible?' The Scriptures had always been part of the ritual. There was a pause in which everyone looked at everyone else, hoping that Lem Johns' manifest included someone of exceptional piety. Then Joe Ayres reassured them. President Kennedy always carried his personal Bible under the lid of the table between the two beds in his private cabin, and Ayres went to fetch it.

It was an unusual copy, and very personal; even Larry O'Brien, to whom Ayres handed it, had never seen it before. The cover was of tooled leather, the edges were hand-sewn; on the front there was a gold cross and, on the inside cover, the tiny sewn black-on-white initials, 'JFK'. On flights alone the President had read it evenings before snapping off the night light. Larry carried the white box in which the President had kept it down the corridor, and as he re-entered the stateroom and stepped behind Sarah Hughes she nervously began the oath. Her voice quavered, 'I do solemnly swear that I will——'

'Just a minute, Judge,' Larry said, slipping the Bible from the box and handing it to her.

She regarded it dubiously. Kennedy, she remembered, had quoted the Bible a lot. This must be his—after all, this was his plane—and that meant it was probably Catholic. She hesitated and decided it would be all right.[5]

'I do solemnly swear . . .' she began again.

The oath lasted twenty-eight seconds, the judge leading and the new President responding, his left hand aloft and his big right hand resting lightly over President Kennedy's black initials. His spruced hair, cut only the day before, his tie and his breast-pocket handkerchief were all correct, yet nothing could efface his rough bulk; he was clearly the tallest man in the cabin. Lady Bird looked bird-like. And Jacqueline Kennedy, on the other side, was a silhouette from another world. Stoughton held his camera high. The stains did not show. Stunned, defeated, she fixed her sightless expression upon the Dictaphone mike.

'. . . that I will faithfully execute the office of President of the United States . . .'

President Johnson's audience was not rapt. The years edit memory, omitting awkward recollections, but the witnesses to this historic occasion are surprisingly unanimous. Their thoughts, they agree, were wandering. Most of them didn't hear a word. The photographer, hunched on the seat behind Sarah, had good reason. Stoughton was almost drowning in his own sweat—his sports coat and slacks clung to him limply—because he had discovered that his misgivings were justified; the Hasselblad was defective. His first frame was a dud; nothing snapped. Recovering rapidly from the sickening silence, he guessed that a small pin inside had failed to

[5] The myth of 'the Catholic Bible' endures in Protestant America. Although such editions do exist, neither the obsolete (Douay) version nor the current (Confraternity of Christian Doctrine) rendition differs to any discernible extent from the one familiar to non-Catholics. Ecclesiastical scholars could distinguish between them, but Sarah Hughes couldn't. Neither, in the opinion of Bishop Philip M. Hannan, could John Kennedy, and it is unlikely that the question had ever crossed the President's mind.

make proper contact. He twisted the film advance lever forward and back, jiggled the works, and heard a click. Dancing on the seat like a dervish he took sixteen pictures, three of them with the Alpa Reflex. As he crouched for a close-up of Johnson, he could hear the leathery thump of his two camera cases; the other spectators, he realized, weren't making a sound.

They were thinking, though, mostly about each other. Albert Thomas decided Jesse Curry was a lens hog; the chief, beside him, was standing on tiptoes and obscuring those behind him. Mary Gallagher and Marty Underwood were watching Ken O'Donnell, who was pacing the corridor outside the bedroom like a caged tiger, his hands clapped over his ears as though to block the oath. Ken was thinking of Jackie, *She's being used, she's being used.* Larry O'Brien stared at Jack Valenti. This was the first time Larry had seen Jack since yesterday's wind-up conference in Houston before the testimonial dinner for Albert Thomas. He was the same Valenti—alert, intent, straining for some unseen bait—but there was a new zeal about him. He was Sammy Glick in Sammy's graduation photograph, and O'Brien, noticing the throbbing veins in his neck, thought, *Well, he's on his way now.* Muggsy O'Leary saw Valenti, too. At the same time it occurred to Muggsy that there had never been so many Texans in the stateroom. He thought, *It's all over for us.*

Everyone was suffering from physical discomfort. Although the ceremony lasted less than a half-minute, it seemed much longer. The pressure of dank bodies, the soaring temperature, and the stuffiness of the cabin gave it the oppressive atmosphere of a sudatorium. Under their shirts and slips they felt beads form and trickle. Lady Bird alone was unconscious of the humidity. Her reflections were elsewhere, and were fanciful. She was thinking, *This is a moment which is altogether dreamlike, because the thing is so unreal; we're just like characters in a play; this is the beginning of something for us that's dreadful and heavy, and you don't know what it holds. We're stepping into a strange new world. It has the quality of a dream,* she thought again, *and yet it isn't a dream at all.*

'. . . and defend the Constitution of the United States,' her husband repeated after the judge, his voice almost inaudible.

Those were the last words on the card, because that was all the Constitution required. Sarah felt something was missing. Impulsively she added, 'So help me God.'

'So help me God,' Johnson repeated slowly, his lidded eyes searching hers.

The words were almost lost in a jet scream. Jim Swindal had vaulted through the communications shack, affixed his seat belt, and revved up No. 3 again.

The President embraced his wife and Jacqueline Kennedy. Lady Bird, her eyes brimming, stepped over and squeezed Mrs Kennedy's hand. 'Now sit down here, honey,' Johnson said to the widowed First Lady, steering her towards the seat Stoughton had just vacated. Sarah Hughes put her arms around him and stammered, 'We're all behind you.' Her congratulations had to be quick, because it was obvious that departure was a matter of seconds. Swindal's engines were shrieking, and Johnson, sinking into the Presidential chair, said to Lem Johns, 'Let 'er roll.' Three passengers fled down the front ramp as it was wheeled away: Sarah, Chief Curry, and Cecil Stoughton. Mac Kilduff had flipped out the pink Dictabelt and slipped it over the extended fingers of Stoughton's left hand. In his right hand the captain was gripping the odds and ends of photographic equipment. Audio and video, he thought, tottering down the steps with his two cameras swinging from his neck; he was the sole repository of the records of the ceremony.

It was 2.47 in Dallas when Jim Swindal lifted 26000's hundred tons from Love's yellow-striped concrete and braced himself for an initial six-hundred-feet-a-minute climb over the hooded blue and yellow airstrip lights. Swindal's head was splitting; it was as though a gigantic sledge-hammer was pounding his skull. He marked the time in his log, Dave Powers jotted it down, and on the ground Emory Roberts, holding the line to Behn, told him the plane was up. Hugh Sidey and Colonel McNally, standing near Roberts, glanced at their wrists and consulted their notes. For all of them it was a moment of extraordinary poignancy. Sidey, watching the Presidential plane gain momentum, felt that a part of himself was leaving. He had never been so lonely in his life. McNally, coming to the end of his chronicle, observed that the hissing blast from the four engines rippled the surface of the oily puddles near the chain fence. In the turbulence a half-dozen discarded signs, remnants of the morning's jubilant reception, struggled to rise. One made it. It stood erect for a fraction of a second, long enough for McNally to copy the neat hand lettering 'WELCOME JFK', it read. Then the gust passed, the four jets passed, and the placard slid back into slime.

The plane was picking up momentum. The shaded cabins deprived the passengers of a view, but from the nose Swindal looked down on hangars, a parked cluster of privately owned Jetstars, a complex of rust-red gantries, and, in the distance, the phallic skyline of downtown Dallas. Though the sky was of palest blue, the jumbled landscape below took no hint of gentleness from it. Under Swindal's right wing three distinctive buildings loomed. The first read 'Ramada Inn,' the second 'Executive Inn.' The third bore no sign; though vastly larger than the others, it was colourless from this height and as shapeless as a Rorschach blot. The Colonel, who hadn't been there, couldn't identify it as Parkland Memorial Hospital.

In the stateroom Johnson said with satisfaction, 'Now we're going.' He rang for Joe Ayres and ordered a bowl of bouillon. Lady Bird had crackers.

Mrs Kennedy rose. She said politely, 'Excuse me.'

She didn't want to offend the Johnsons, but a refrain kept running through her mind: *I'm not going to be in here, I'm going back there.* Scurrying down the corridor, she saw Ken, Larry, Dave, and Godfrey standing around the coffin; she sat in one of the two seats opposite, and Ken joined her on the other. Their eyes met, and she began to cry. It was the first time she had wept; the tears came in a flood, and for a long time she couldn't speak. When she straightened out her voice she said, as though this were 12.30 and the blow had just fallen, 'Oh, it's happened.'

'It's happened,' O'Donnell repeated in a dead voice.

'Oh, Kenny,' she cried, 'what's going to happen . . .?'

'You want to know something, Jackie?' Ken said. 'I don't give a damn.'

She took a deep breath. 'Oh, you're right, you know, you're right. Just nothing matters but what you've lost.'

It was a tiny vestibule, the smallest on the plane. Because it was in the tail it was the compartment most affected by sudden shifts in the airstream. On any other trip it would have lacked status, but President Kennedy was here, and Mrs Kennedy was with him, and everyone knew it. In effect, this was to be the stateroom until they debarked at Andrews. All the Kennedy men and women in the staff cabin wanted to be there. That was impossible—there wasn't room—so a series of individual pilgrimages began, each individual moving slowly back past the Presidential chair now occupied by President Lyndon Johnson.

Dr Burkley came first, or, more accurately, his was the first attempt; he wanted to see how Jacqueline Kennedy was bearing up, but on this trip he halted a few feet short of her. Whatever her state, he sensed, George Burkley would only make it worse. The change in him had been a sudden thing. He had been composed enough as he set out and passed Johnson. Then, in the corridor, something caught his eye. The bedroom door was ajar. Inside, lying on a newspaper, was her second glove. It was as though she had never removed it, for in two hours the blood had completely dried; the glove was like a cast of her hand. To him it depicted 'all the anguish and sorrow and desolation in the world'. He began to shiver, as though caught in a frigid draught. Returning to the staff cabin, he beckoned to Mary

Gallagher, who became the second pilgrim. In the bedroom he raised an arm, exposing a shirt sleeve—itself bloodstained—and pointed to the stiff gauntlet. 'Put it away somewhere,' he said. 'Don't crush it.'

Mary plucked a fistful of Kleenex. As she lifted it from the newspaper she saw the headlines beneath. It was the front page of the *Times-Herald*'s first edition.

DALLAS GREETS PRESIDENT

Security Boys Play It Cool	Jackie Sparkles, Ladybird Too	Crowds Cheer Wildly For JFK

In the staff area Mary handed the shaped glove to Clint Hill, who sheathed it in a manilla envelope. Remarkably, almost none of the Kennedys' objects had been mislaid. In spite of the two-hour anarchy virtually every article they had brought to Dallas was leaving with them; the President's clothes, wallet, and watch, and Mrs Kennedy's gloves, hat, and handbag were all safely stowed aboard. There was one exception. Tripping down the ramp steps towards Earle and Dearie Cabell, who were waiting on the field, Sarah Hughes was hailed by a self-assured man—she remembers him as 'rather officious'—who pointed at the black binding in her hand and asked, 'Do you want that?' She shook her head. 'How about this?' he inquired, fingering the 3×5 card with the text of the oath. Neither belonged to her, and so she surrendered them, assuming that he was some sort of security man.

He wasn't. His identity is a riddle. How a cipher could have penetrated Jesse Curry's cordon is difficult to understand, but he did. The venture required enterprise and luck. The spoils, however, were priceless; he left the airport with a pair of unique souvenirs. The file card is the less valuable of the two. It is an archivist's curiosity, of interest only to collectors and museums. The book, however, is something more. It was private property, and at this writing it remains untraced. President Kennedy's family is entitled to it and would give a lot to have it back. By now, however, the anonymous conzener may have disposed of it. Either way, the fact remains that the last item of Kennedy memorabilia to be left in Dallas, his most cherished personal possession, was his Bible.

The stragglers at Gates 27 and 28 dispersed slowly. The Cabells shook hands with the Texas Congressional delegation who had been left behind and rode off in a station wagon. Ralph Yarborough, five Congressmen, and the Kennedy staff members who had been ejected from 26000 entered the vacant cabins of the backup plane, where, as on the Presidential aircraft, there was friction between the Texans and the non-Texans.

Apart from the jabbering of reporters in a row of portable glass phone booths which had been quickly set up for them by the Signal Corps, Love Field's eastern concourse was unnaturally quiet. In this hush, broken only by the creaking of gears, a crane hoisted SS 100 X aboard a C-130 cargo plane to be refitted for future Presidential motorcades, and Kennedy's seal and Presidential flag were brought from the Trade Mart and laid, furled, in a compartment on the press plane. By 3.35 p.m., when the C-130 departed for Andrews, the field had begun to return to normal. The correspondents flew away; the confetti and the hand-lettered placards that littered the fifty-yard stretch where the crowds had cheered wildly for JFK four hours earlier were dumped in metal containers beside the terminal building; the dignitaries who had wished LBJ Godspeed forty-eight minutes before had returned to their offices and homes. Among the last to go was Vernon Oneal. The undertaker wanted to inspect his Cadillac thoroughly. He checked every inch of the upholstery to make certain that it had been left in trim condition. It was tidy. Nevertheless he drove back to Oak Lawn Avenue dissatisfied.

Win Lawson was driving downtown with Chief Curry. As they approached the triple underpass the traffic thickened, and in the plaza vehicles were bumper to bumper. Before entering the Secret Service Lawson had been a salesman of carpets and Carnation milk products. He was unwise in the ways of crowds; the dense mass puzzled him, and he said so. Curry explained it. Dallasites who hadn't been downtown at 12.30 naturally wanted to look at the scene of the crime, he said. Their headlong charge towards the centre of the city had prevented motorcade spectators from leaving, and the congestion had been building up steadily. Curry guessed that this was just about the worst glut of automobiles he had ever seen. It didn't diminish. An hour later, when Managing Editor Krueger persuaded the federal judge to release him from jury duty, Krueger thought it 'incredibly bad'; the nosing cars reminded him of 'worms crawling around in pain'.

The chief and the editor looked forward to reaching their offices, anticipating sanctuary. Both were deceived, and for the same reason. Journalism is the fastest of businesses. Every American publisher knew that this was the biggest story of his lifetime and wanted a man on the spot; Felix McKnight of the *Times-Herald*, who had been handling press arrangements for President Kennedy's visit, later estimated that as Air Force One took off over three hundred out-of-town reporters and newscasters were converging on Dallas. The *New York Times* alone was flying in six men to reinforce Tom Wicker. Since the *Times-Herald*, an afternoon paper, didn't close until 3.15 p.m., it was too busy for visitors, so they headed either for the *News* or police headquarters. In the chief's words, his office was 'just pandemonium'. The hubbub had begun while he was at the airport, and when he stepped off the elevator at the third floor he saw television cables snaking across the corridors.

Krueger's experience was much the same. As he walked into his city room telephones were jangling incessantly. Here the messages were different, however. At headquarters the outsiders were asking insiders what was going on; in the city room the phoners were telling them, sometimes profanely. To the consternation of staff, the *News* was being subjected to unprecedented, spontaneous abuse. Big out-of-state advertisers were cancelling contracts, and local readers were dropping their subscriptions. The chain had begun. Dallas was blaming the *News*; Texans were blaming Dallas; Americans were blaming Texas; and the world was blaming the United States. Yet not all links in the chain were identical. Some people, and some cities, were searching their own souls. The editor of the Austin *American* was writing: 'Hatred and fanaticism, the flabby spirit of complacency that has permitted the preachers of fanatical hatred to appear respectable, and the self-righteousness that labels all who disagree with us as traitors or dolts, provided the way for the vile deed that snuffed out John Kennedy's life.' That sort of self-criticism found no echo in the Dallas establishment. The *Times-Herald* was the more reflective of the city's two dailies, but the publisher's tribute to his staff when November 22's final edition was locked up was a singular exhibition of complacency. 'Today you performed superbly,' he declared in a statement posted as the Presidential aircraft flew towards Washington. 'No newspaper in this country could have done a better job within the severe time limitations. All of you took difficult assignments and came through without faltering.' As an afterthought he added, 'It is a sad day.'

He added something else which illuminates the haze of Dallas *Angst*: 'We must handle this story with the best of taste in the next few days. We are sort of on trial because it happened in our city.' They were very much on trial, and painfully aware of it. Civic pride was in jeopardy. Big D was in danger of becoming little d. It felt that it had, in the words of a *Times-Herald* sports writer, 'been penalized half the distance to the goal line'. Under the circumstances there was no point in protesting that the referee had made a mistake; the crowd wouldn't understand. The only solution was to get back in there and regain the lost yardage. Re-establishing the city's prestige would take a lot of doing, but the big businessmen who lived in the northern suburbs were big doers. Certain sacrifices would have to be made. The local fringe groups must be publicly disowned. Bruce Alger would have to be led to the altar—a forfeiture easily borne, because he could be replaced next fall by Cabell, a Guelph for a Ghibelline. And for the present Dealey's editorial voice must speak *sotto voce*. The people who were landing at Love Field with each incoming flight weren't wanted, but telling them that was unthinkable; they must be shown how hospitable Dallas could be. Outside correspondents would be accommodated with *News* desks, *News* phones, and introductions to people who could tell them what the city was really like.

President Kennedy had been a reader of Thucydides. One of his favourite quotations was a comment on the weakness of the Peloponnesian policy-making body, each member of which, the Greek historian related, 'presses its own ends . . . which generally results in no action at all . . . they devote more time to the prosecution of their own purposes than to the consideration of the general welfare—each supposes that no harm will come of his own neglect, that it is the business of another to do this or that—and so, as each separately entertains the same illusion, the common cause imperceptibly decays.' Kennedy had also observed that in Goethe's great poem Faust lost his soul because of his preoccupation with the passing moment. Dallas was preoccupied with the moment, Dallas was concerned with its own purposes, Dallas was pressing its private ends. The heat—the scorching heat which only the city's mercantile élite could generate—was on every public servant in the country. They were expected to toe the mark, and they were told exactly what that mark was.

The man most likely to be caught offsides was Chief Jesse Curry. Curry had already bruised the treasured image, and now he was entrusted with the custody of Lee Oswald. Any affront to the journalists who were swarming through the five police bureaux on his third floor would be intolerable. Both he and District Attorney Henry M. Wade were expected to put up with intruders and bear inconvenience. No information about the prisoner in the maximum-security cell block on the fifth floor must be withheld. None was. Trapped in this deadly fire, Curry and Wade acquiesced, and in so doing they ran into an institutional difficulty. The trouble with surrendering to reporters is that there are never any terms. Capitulation is total. You are lucky if your birthmarks are unnoted. The conflict between due process and freedom of the press had been going on since the trial of John Peter Zenger. Neither side can yield, and neither should. As events in Dallas were to demonstrate, the abdiction of authority can lead to a slough. Veteran reporters there were appalled—'You have the nicest policemen to the press I have ever seen,' Henri de Turnure of *France-Soir* told a Neiman-Marcus executive: 'God help you!'—and so were experienced lawyers. By evening the official co-operation with newspapermen and telecasters had become so enthusiastic that in Washington the Deputy Attorney General, staying at his post during the Attorney General's absence, began to entertain serious doubts that any conviction of the suspect could survive appeal. Curry and Wade were trying the case over the networks, with no opposing counsel. Their drawing card was displayed to the press on fifteen occasions; Jim Hosty of the FBI compared the resultant crushes to 'Grand Central Station at the rush hour' or to 'Yankee Stadium during the World Series games.'

It was a travesty of justice, and Katzenbach phoned his forebodings to Barefoot Sanders. He told him, 'It would be a nightmare if the President's assassin were found guilty and the Supreme Court threw the case out because he had not had a lawyer. That would be about as low as we could sink.' Sanders tried to intercede. But a federal official had no status at the jail. While the red carpet had been rolled out for every free-lance writer, the U.S. Attorney did not belong to the fourth estate, and he was virtually ignored. The pageant went on. As long as Aircraft 26000 remained airborne it had no competition; commercials had been cancelled until after the President's funeral; there had never been so many viewers. Suddenly Curry's force was the most famous police department in history.

The most remarkable aspect of the spectacle was unknown to those outside headquarters. Katzenbach, mulling over the legal rights of an accused man and the ghastly contingency of a subsequent reversal, assumed that all the unfamiliar figures romping around the uniformed men on his screen were bona fide correspondents and commentators. But November 22, 1963, was the first of four days during which anything was possible, and as it turned out Katzenbach was taking too much for granted. Avid for approval, fearful of incurring displeasure, Curry had suspended what is standard operating procedure in any police station when public interest in a crime is at fever pitch; his men weren't checking press credentials. It was open house. Video tapes preserved by NBC-TV, WFAA-TV, and KRLD-TV resemble an M-G-M mob scene. The extras included complainants and witnesses who happened to be in the building, prisoners, relatives of prisoners, relatives of police officers, known criminals, and drunks who wandered in off Harwood Street. Any crank who wished to ogle the most famous department's most famous captive could have attended the Curry–Wade–Oswald press conference which was set up in the jail basement late Friday, when Oswald was displayed on a platform for better viewing, and one crank did attend it.

He had come equipped with horn-rimmed spectacles, a notebook, and the lie that he was a translator for the Israeli press. Lying was unnecessary. It was first come, first served. There was no room for Captain Fritz of Homicide, who arrived late, but the impostor mounted a table top unchallenged. Once he even participated in the questioning, and the tapes reveal that he had a close look at the suspect. The watcher and the watched were unalike physically, but emotionally they bore a certain resemblance. Both were misfits with twisted personalities, outcasts who craved attention, nursed grudges, were prey to wild impulses and fits of murderous temper, couldn't relate to other people—women especially—and were indifferent to public affairs. Later the bogus translator insisted that he had idolized the President. He may have convinced himself that this was true, but it is hard to credit it. At 12.30 p.m. he had been at the Dallas *News*, placing weekend advertisements for his two striptease joints, yet he hadn't bothered to walk over and see the motorcade four blocks away. His professed admiration of Kennedy, like Oswald's simulated Marxism, was a patent fraud, a figment of self-delusion designed to dignify his motive. In reality neither of them had the civic conscience of a cat. Each man's absorption with his ravaged inner self eclipsed any other interest; each was terribly alone.

While the horn-rimmed humbug had come to see one individual, the performance in Curry's cellar offered other diversions. It is not too much to call Henry Wade's question-and-answer session a broad farce. Indicating Lee Oswald, he told the listeners of radio station KLIF and the viewers of television sets tuned to KRLD, WFAA, and the NBC network that 'I figure we have sufficient evidence to convict him'; that Curry's sleuths had lined up 'approximately fifteen witnesses'; that there were no other suspects; that the prisoner was mentally competent and had been formally charged. One man asked him whether or not the prisoner was represented by a lawyer. The District Attorney of Dallas County replied, 'I don't know whether he has one or not.' Wade revealed that the accused man would be transferred to the county jail—he would keep viewers posted on details—and he slyly suggested that Oswald had been in Dallas 'only two months'. A man called, 'That's a good job, Henry.'

It was not a good job. It was an atrocity. It was inaccurate and misleading—Oswald had lived in Dallas as a boy and had landed at Love Field when he had returned from Russia with Marina, for example, if that was relevant—and the review of specific items of evidence and the assertion of guilt by a district attorney were flagrant violations of principles sacred to the courts. Wade, speaking into the battery of microphones in front of him, was addressing the men and women from whom a jury would have been chosen had not police blundering led to another murder and rendered the trial unnecessary. It was unbelievable at the time; it is even less believable now.

The District Attorney noticed the moon-calf face of the counterfeit Israeli translator in the audience and placed it. He had seen him within the past three days while trying a sex case. After the klieg lights had been darkened and the prisoner had been led back to his fifth-floor cell the intruder ran up to the stage. 'Hi, Henry!' he cried. They shook hands. The man said, 'Don't you know me? I'm Jack Ruby, I run the Vegas Club.' Possibly out of curiosity, Wade inquired, 'What are you doing here?' Ruby waved his hand about and said grandly, 'I know all these fellows.' Those fellows were Dallas patrolmen. This time he wasn't shamming. He really did know them. After Sunday Europeans were to puzzle over the ease with which Ruby had strolled in and out of Curry's headquarters. The men and women who had surrounded President Kennedy were equally baffled; they were unacquainted with the maggoty half-world of dockets and flesh-peddlers, of furtive men with mud-coloured faces and bottle blondes whose high-arched over-plucked eyebrows give their flat glittering eyes a perpetually startled expression, of sordid walk-up hotels with unread Gideon Bibles and tumbled bedclothes and rank animal odours, of police connivance in petty crime, of a way of life in which lawbreakers, law enforcement officers, and those who totter on the law's edge meet socially and even intermarry. There is no mystery about Jack Ruby's relationship with Dallas cops. His type is depressingly familiar in American police stations. All police reporters know at least one Ruby. He worships patrolmen and plain-clothes men, and the fact that he is occasionally arrested doesn't dim his ardour. Often he is proud of his record. It is proof of his virility. He is usually overweight, middle-aged, has puffy eyes, wears broad lapels and outrageous neckties, and decorates his stubby fingers with extravagant costume jewellery. He is recognized by the spicy smell of his shaving lotion, and by the way he keeps touching officers, and handing them things, and combing his hair in front of them like an oarsman sculling.

That Friday Ruby, having abandoned the pretence that he had been entitled to attend the conference, was busy handing out cards giving officers free privileges at his two striptease establishments. The cards were wordlessly pocketed. The policemen saw nothing improper in this. Like their District Attorney, they knew Jack, and when off duty they frequently dropped into the Vegas or the Carousel in mufti, occupying reserved seats and consuming free setups—usually rye and 7-Up, the wine of that strange country—while hoarsely urging mascaraed women to peel off black net lingerie. One thirty-year-old detective, August Eberhardt, had been acquainted with Ruby for five years. The detective had met the strip boss while a member of the vice squad, and although he kept a professional eye on the Vegas and the Carousel, and had booked one of Jack's trulls for drug addiction, he was a regular patron of them. He had, indeed, taken his wife to both joints. Mrs Eberhardt preferred the entertainment at the Vegas. You could always start a debate about that on Harewood Street, but while each of the two enterprises had its partisans, and every girl out of stir was followed by her claque, there was general agreement on the force that Jack could always be counted on to provide a lively performance.

Eberhardt glimpsed Ruby at the press conference. They gossiped; among other things, Ruby inquired about Mrs Eberhardt. Jack trotted out his yarn about being a translator. As an old friend the detective knew Ruby spoke Yiddish, though he didn't think much about it. Jack said he had brought coffee and sandwiches for the reporters—'Nothing but kosher stuff is all I bring.' After that, according to the detective, he 'talked a little bit about the assassination'. Jack said, 'Mike'—he always called Eberhardt by his middle name—'it is hard to realize how a complete nothing, a zero like that, could kill a man like President Kennedy was.' He remarked dolefully that Kennedy's death was unfortunate for the city of Dallas, 'and then', in the detective's words, 'he left'. As Eberhardt recalled later, 'I didn't notice where he went.' Nor did other officers pay much attention to the departure. They knew Jack Ruby would be back, and they were right.

Book Two
CASTLE

6

ANGEL

Goaded by a mighty tailwind, the Presidential aircraft hurled eastward at a velocity approaching the speed of sound. Beyond the airport Jim Swindal had looked down on a flat tan-and-green plain criss-crossed by parallelograms of cyclone fences and highways, a tract blank as a plate. Ahead lay a navy blue blob of water and, in the distance, a crinkling of mountains. The pilot radioed Andrews Air Force Base his estimated time of arrival—'2305Z': Air Force 'Zulu Time'—Greenwich Mean Time. It would be 6.05 p.m. in Washington when they breasted Andrews. In the old propeller-driven flying boxcars Jim had shuttled over the Hump against the Japanese the thirteen-hundred-mile flight would have taken at least five hours, but in the great flagship he could make it in scarcely more than two.

He reset his watch; 3 p.m. in Texas (2100 Zulu) was 4 p.m. in Washington. Then, spitting flame, Angel climbed steeply. Swindal's rate of ascent leaped from 600 feet a minute to 4,000: he was burning a gallon of fuel every second. The colonel was cleared to 29,000 feet. He was determined to go as high as he could, however, higher than anyone had ever taken President Kennedy, and reaching out he spun his small black trim-tab wheel clockwise, rising another 12,000 feet before levelling off. At this tremendous altitude, nearly eight miles straight up, the sky overhead was naked and serene. Its tranquillity was deceptive. Andrews was relaying reports of tornadoes below—he leaned over and saw black combers of wind-swept scud freckled with hurrying rain—and behind him a cold front was moving in from Arizona. Already wild squalls were lashing the Panhandle. At Love Field the temperature was plunging, and the western sky was livid. Kennedy weather had left Dallas with him.

Instinctively Swindal ticked off the landmarks which he knew lay under the churning clouds: the scribbly banks of the Mississippi, the tartans of Memphis and Nashville. He was glad he couldn't see them. He wanted to flee every familiar cairn, and his instruments seemed to offer a way to improve upon nature. He poured on the oil, riding the tailwind. He soared, and by his very celerity he hastened the end of illusion. There could be no escape, nor even a healing lacuna under the sun, for he was going the wrong way, racing away from it.

At 535 mph, night approaches swiftly. Less than forty-five minutes after their departure shadows began to thicken over eastern Arkansas. In the southern sky he saw a waif of a moon, a day and a half off the quarter, hanging ghostlike near the meridian. At the outset he thought of the darkness as a blessing. Returning this way it would be best to land in gloom. The inkier Washington was, the better. But as the light failed, the crescendo of the day hit him harder and harder. He and John Kennedy had been exactly the same age. John and Jacqueline Kennedy, he reflected, had been 'the best we as a country had to offer'. He had brought the President to Texas in exuberant spirits, at the height of his remarkable powers; and now he was ferrying him back in a box. Swindal slumped in his harness. Since boyhood he had been in love with aeroplanes. He had progressed to flight school, to MATS, to the post of personal pilot for the Secretary of the Air Force, and then to this, the ultimate accolade. Now the spell was broken. The passion of his life had been spent. Henceforth flying would be commuting, like driving a bus. His deracination deepened as the sky deepened until, over Tennessee, he 'felt that the world had ended'. Behind him (as he thought of it then) were the President, the First Lady, the Vice President, and Mrs Johnson. No aircraft commander had ever been charged with so grave a responsibility, yet he wondered whether he could make it to Andrews. He was near collapse. 'It became,' in his words, 'a struggle to continue.'

His co-pilot was, if anything, in worse shape. Lieutenant Colonel Lewis Hanson was normally a buoyant young New Englander. His mother-in-law lived in Dallas; she had been recovering from a stroke, and he had decided to call on her during the motorcade. When she had greeted him with the cry, 'Kennedy's been killed!' he had thought she had lost her reason. Then, after turning on her television set, he had begun to doubt his own. Back at the airport he had become obsessed with the desire to leave Texas immediately—at any moment he had expected the fuselage to be raked by machine-gun fire—and twice during the wait for Sarah Hughes he had started the engines on his own. Now, as Swindal manipulated the controls, Hanson mechanically fingered his headset, pinpointing 26000's rapidly changing position for Andrews. The fliers didn't speak to one another. Roy Kellerman came up briefly and sat in the jump seat. The three men started to speculate about motives behind the assassination and gave up. The fliers didn't trust their voices. They fell silent again, and Roy quietly crawled back.

—The magenta twilight turned to olive gloaming and became dusk. The last thin rays of sunlight glimmered and were succeeded by early evening. The colonels looked out upon th overarching sky. There was a lot to see. In the last ten days of autumn the firmament is brilliant. Saturn dogged the moon. Jupiter lay over the Carolinas, the Big Dipper beyond Chicago. Arturus was setting redly behind Kansas; Cassiopeia and the great square of Pegasus twinkled overhead. But the brightest light in the bruise-blue canopy was Capella. Always a star of the first magnitude, it seemed dazzling tonight, and as the Presidential plane rocketed towards West Virginia it rose majestically a thousand miles to the north-east, over Boston.

Aft of the cockpit Signalman John Trimble was too busy to brood. He had three phone patches going in the communications shack, and he was using Hanson's UHF and VHF sets, yet it wasn't enough. Every official in Washington, it seemed, wanted to talk to Air Force One. Usually Signalmen here were technicians, airborne switchboard operators. From the instant Swindal had retracted his landing gear, however, the unprecedented demand for lines meant that Trimble had to decide who would speak to whom, regulating voice traffic between Angel here and Acrobat and Crown and Castle in the capital. At his elbow were requests from Market, Digest, Wing, Warrior, Watchman, Dazzle, and Dagger; in Washington there was a backlog from Duplex, Vigilant, Domino, and Witness. Trimble had a good knowledge of the Kennedy team. He knew which members of the old administration carried rank, and he knew Lyndon Johnson. Johnson's people, however, were strangers to him. He couldn't tell which ones could be fobbed off with excuses. All he could be sure of was that they were members of the new President's staff, that each said that his business was urgent—and that Trimble, an enlisted man, had to choose among them. It was an impossible quandary. All he could do was to play it literally by ear; the thicker a man's Texas drawl, the better were his chances of getting through.

Several conversations were trivial. Congressman Albert Thomas wanted his secretary to leave his apartment key under the doormat; Congressman Jack Brooks wanted to get in touch with Mrs Brooks. Some messages dealt with Johnson's plans. Lem Johns was forwarding instructions to the White House Communications Agency, and Bill Moyers was talking to Walter Jenkins and Mac Bundy. (Ted Clifton talked to Bundy, too, asking again whether an international plot was emerging. It was not a discreet inquiry. Trimble's patches were not secure. They could be bugged. Bundy replied crisply that the Pentagon was taking its own steps.) But the bulk of the verbal traffic was about President Kennedy. Clifton had examined the broken handle housing on Oneal's Britannia; the damage made manhandling the coffin down another ramp impossible, he said, and he asked Andrews to have a lift ready on the airstrip. Clint Hill told the kiddie detail to take Lyric and Lark to Hamlet, Mrs Auchincloss' home at 3044 O Street. Dr Burkley suggested that Mrs Kennedy be met by Dr John Walsh, her physician. Behn instructed Kellerman to remain with the coffin until it arrived at the executive mansion, and there was much talk about 'choppering', because the White House assumed that Kennedy would be moved by helicopter.

The assumption was incorrect—it had been decided that Kennedy should be moved by ambulance—and the muddle was compounded by the question of who should move him. Not even a President's death can muffle inter-service rivalry. Burkley directed Taz Shepard to alert Bethesda Naval Hospital; Clifton advised Dr Leonard Heaton, the Army's Surgeon General, that the autopsy would be performed at Walter Reed. (Heaton, sensing conflict, called General Eisenhower and asked his advice; Ike replied that 'since there is no way of knowing who is giving orders', the Surgeon General had better play it safe, go to Andrews, and stand by.) The Air Force didn't have a hospital in the capital, but Godfrey McHugh seemed fated to be in the thick of any fray that arose that afternoon. Godfrey placed the call requesting an ambulance. From somewhere in the Stygian depths of minor bureaucracy a seneschal rejected the request on the grounds that District law prohibited the transfer of corpses by ambulance; the widow would have to settle for a hearse. It was impossible to know who the official was. The voice was being relayed by a chain of operators. McHugh didn't really care. 'Just *do* it,' he snapped. In the most corrosive tone he could summon he added, 'And don't worry about the law. *I'll* pay the fine.'[1]

Behind the shack, in the staff cabin, moods ranged from catatonia to heartbreak to estrangement. Muggsy O'Leary crouched apart in a window seat on the port side, staring down at his hands. Evelyn Lincoln sobbed. But the estrangement was dominant. All anyone here knew about Oswald was that 'a suspect' had been picked up in

[1] There was no fine. The District of Columbia did prohibit the moving of bodies in ambulances without coroner's permits, but the D.C. Police Department acted as the coroner's representative in the District and surrounding Maryland and Virginia counties, and the matter could have been cleared up without troubling anyone on the plane. As it turned out, the law was disregarded entirely. McHugh's conversation merely demonstrates that there was more than one Earl Rose abroad that afternoon.

Dallas. That didn't mean much. Even if he were the right man, his provocation remained obscure.

The first wave from Parkland was looking ahead. They had to anticipate tomorrow; that was their duty. The second wave was looking back, yearning for yesterday. Individual recollections of the flight were to vary sharply. Inasmuch as the shades were still drawn, no one knew when daylight ended. It was like living in a void. Each passenger was left with his own troubled thoughts, and each fashioned his own verity, even his own time. Pam Turnure thought this was the longest trip in her life, a journey without a destination. To Marie Fehmer, swamped with work, it was the shortest of rides. Yet nearly everyone in the cabin felt the smouldering animosity. Valenti afterwards described those two hours as 'absolute chaos', Chuck Roberts as 'soreness'. Mac Kilduff called it 'the sickest plane I've ever been on'. Clint Hill, discarding his ruined clothes for a crewman's, looked down the aisle pensively. In his later words, 'It was undeniably very, very sick, with a great deal of tension between the Kennedy people and the Johnson people.'

'*Fortiter in re, suaviter in modo*'—'Be graceful under pressure.' The man who lay in Oneal's coffin had admired the Roman maxim. Without him his leaderless staff drifted into an ill-concealed enmity. Some made no attempt at camouflage. Ken O'Donnell was particularly vocal. Twice Johnson sent Moyers back to ask O'Donnell and O'Brien to sit with him. They flatly refused, and McHugh strode up to the pool seats, where Chuck Roberts and Merriman Smith were probing each other's impressions of the hospital, to make certain the reporters knew about it. 'I want the record to show,' he said, pounding the table between them to stress each syllable, 'that Ken O'Donnell, Larry O'Brien, Dave Powers, and me spent this flight in the tail compartment with the President—President Kennedy'. Ted Clifton entered that rear compartment on an errand for President Johnson. Ken flashed, 'Why don't you get back and serve your new boss?' Clifton asked McHugh, 'What's eating him? I'm just doing my job.'

The Texans, too, had loved Kennedy, and until today they had had greater reason to distrust Dallas. To them the suggestion that they bore any responsibility for the atrocity was unforgivable. They were prepared to discount sorrow, but this rankled, and they, too, felt a recrudescence of the Los Angeles spirit. Among them only Bill Moyers, the most generous of Johnson's advisers, refused to be aroused. He had long been convinced that O'Donnell's toughness was an act, that under the sardonic veneer he was a tender man. Realizing how deeply Ken had been hurt, he declined the bait.

Moyers wasn't in the staff area, though. There indignation was uncushioned. Paul Glynn, Johnson's valet, stood uncomfortably against the forward bulkhead. He was only watching the President's gripsacks. It was enough; the luggage was unwelcome, therefore its guardian was a trespasser. Though Glynn was a native of Delaware, he might as well have been wearing a five-gallon hat. In the Austin–Boston polarization there were no way stations, no neutrals; everyone was branded either JFK or LBJ. Sometimes the labelling required ludicrous distortions. The Johnsonians presumed that Mary Gallagher's anger was Irish anger—among themselves they spoke of 'Mary's Irish'. In point of fact, Gallagher was merely her married name; she had been born an Italian.

Still, her wrath was genuine enough. As she sorted out her blazing thoughts she heard the drone of the stateroom television set. The broadcaster's voice was inaudible, but above it she heard a Texas Congressman cry, 'Say, that's *great*!' She stiffened. Two of the newcomers saw her expression and scowled at her. The meeting of eyes lasted only a moment. It was enough; it was searing. As a native of Dallas Marie Fehmer felt a special sense of torment, and she made a stab at pacification. She offered to order soup for the Kennedy secretaries. Lips tightened, heads were shaken. They didn't want soup—didn't, really, want an armistice.

During the first hour of flight the most conspicuous drawl in the cabin was Cliff Carter's. Cliff was dictating Lyndon Johnson's minute-by-minute diary, beginning at 12.30 p.m., while Marie rapped it out on one of the two typewriters. On any other occasion Cliff's voice would have been unobjectionable. Actually it was quite soft. The difficulty was his Bastrop County dialect. It was so pronounced that it was almost a separate language. To New Englanders it was more alien than Oxonian; the '*whares*' and '*thangs*' and '*yews*' and '*mahs*' and '*yoahs*', and especially the repeated references to '*Kinnidy*' skirred on Kennedy ears. But then, any sound was jarring. Marie knew it. Conscious of the stutter of her keyboard, she was distinctly ill at ease. She hated the noise, hated the machine. She squirmed, wishing there were another way to print.

Liz Carpenter found another way. The older woman had never felt so much like an intruder, and although she realized that death was the true intruder, she was determined not to attract attention to herself. The clatter of a second typewriter, she decided, would be indecent. Rather than use it she block-printed, even though her prose was far more urgent than Cliff's diary. She was redrafting the statement the President must make to the battery of television cameras which she knew would await him when he debarked. Rummaging in her purse, she found the king-sized 'ladybird card'—a white card with a silhouette of a tiny bird in one corner—that she had used during the frantic ride from Parkland to Love. Much of it was illegible, and she puckered, trying to remember what she had meant to write.

She read:

> This is a tragic hour for
> [indecipherable] a [indecipherable]
> and the U.S.A. and for me and a
> deep personal tragedy for me—
> I will do my best
> that is all I can do
> and I ask God's help—
> and yours—

Laboriously printing a second draft, she passed it in to the stateroom. Johnson showed it to Moyers, asked him to home it, made a few changes of his own, and sent it up to Marie, who copied it on a fresh 3 × 5 card. The typed version dissatisfied Johnson. It still lacked something. As Valenti watched he studied it carefully. Before slipping it in his side pocket the President reversed the two clauses in the peroration. It now ended: 'I ask for your help—and God's.'

Johnson was restless. His big frame hulking against the stateroom's pastel walls, he paced from side to side, telephoning from the desk, conferring with Texas Congressmen on the tawny aisle carpet, and hovering over the television set. The set's reception was poor; the storms below were blurring newscasters' images and garbling their voices. Joe Ayres' deft fingers twirled futilely, and for minutes at a time the President lowered at a blank, silent screen.

There was an incessant stirring around him. The pilgrims trekked to the rear and back; the Congressmen came and went; Valenti, Marie, Clifton, and Kilduff were in and out. Towards the end Cliff Carter entered and stayed. Four companions were constant: Mrs Johnson, Ayres, Rufe Youngblood, and Bill Moyers. To Moyers the President remarked that the world would be watching him carefully during the next few days. Moscow must not detect the slightest shift in Washington's foreign policy, and the West must be steadfast. A stable transition was essential. On the morning of April 11, 1937, Congressman-elect Lyndon Johnson had declared in Austin, 'I don't believe I can set the world on fire and go up there and reform the United States of America right away.' A quarter-century hadn't changed his disposition. He wasn't a man to mount a King Harry charger and pluck flowers from nettles. But he could be firm, he could be decisive. And he could get things done.

With continuity in mind, he made several decisions during the flight. There was some talk of barring the press from Andrews. He shook his head vigorously; it would, he said, 'look like we're panicking'. Upon reaching Pennsylvania Avenue he wanted a series of meetings with key officials. Because of his background he thought of the Congressional leadership. 'Democratic or bipartisan?' Castle crackled. 'Bipartisan,' he replied, and Moyers left to get the names from Larry O'Brien. That, as it turned out, was to be the only conference that evening. At first the President contemplated a full-dress meeting of the White House staff. Bundy advised against it, pointing out that the men there were too bereft. O'Brien told Moyers the same thing; Moyers agreed, and Johnson reversed himself. Precisely how he learned about the Cabinet trip is uncertain. At one point he directed Clifton to have Rusk, McNamara, and Bundy, the three Presidential aides responsible for national security, on the airstrip when he landed at Andrews. Clifton answered that Rusk couldn't make it. Whether he explained why is moot. Johnson may have learned from Bundy, or from Moyers, who had been told by O'Brien. In any event, the news that six ministers were over the Pacific staggered him. He ordered Clifton to see that the Cabinet plane returned immediately and was informed that it was already on its way.

Johnson was learning—learning under the most trying circumstances conceivable—that a Chief Executive has virtually no privacy. Affairs of state and personal details intermingled, sometimes in the same conversation. One moment he was requesting a CIA briefing from John McCone. In the next moment he and his wife were being notified by Rufe Youngblood that their daughters were unharmed. Lucy was safe at the National Cathedral School, and Lynda was in Austin—Lady Bird's motherly pride expanded when she heard that Lynda had gone straight to the Governor's mansion to comfort the two young Connally children. Johnson said he wanted Secret Service agents assigned to both girls at once. Youngblood assured him that they were covered. Rufe still felt that the Johnsons should spend that night at the White House, but Johnson wisely demurred.

'That would be presumptuous on my part,' he said. 'I won't do it.'

The agent argued. He protested that he had 'to think first of security'.

'I realize that,' the President said, 'but you can protect the Elms, too, can't you?' Youngblood conceded that they could.

Familial matters settled, Johnson returned to the bleary screen. It was like a picture seen dimly through a rain lashed window-pane, and the sound was as instructive as a poltergeist. Already the networks had established the pattern which would hold through

Monday. Having cancelled all commercials until the funeral, they were filling in with eulogies from eminent statesmen, interviews of men-in-the-street, and video tapes of highlights in Kennedy's life and administration. From time to time there were bulletins of hard information. Stoughton's still photographs of the oath were being shown. The U.S. commander in Bonn had alerted his troops to a possible invasion from the East, and Oswald's background was emerging. His residence in Russia, his application for Soviet citizenship, and his pro-Castro activity in New Orleans were now common knowledge, though their relevance, of course, remained a matter of conjecture.

Clifton cleared his throat. The man with the football was aboard, he said, explaining exactly what the football contained. Johnson nodded and squinted at the maddening screen. The visitors to the rear passed and repassed. It was macabre; President Johnson occupied President Kennedy's airborne office while President Kennedy's staff, some of them bloodstained or carrying bloodstained clothing, shuttled between him and Mrs Johnson on their way to the widowed First Lady. Lady Bird, sitting alone on the couch where Stoughton had crouched with his cameras, had the extraordinary illusion that she was two people. She felt 'an air of sedation'. It was 'like standing in a rarefied atmosphere on a mountaintop and seeing every detail limned in your mind's eye, and yet part of you was seeing it as a somnambulist'. Obviously all this was happening, but to someone else. She sent for Liz Carpenter. She said she wanted to go over her notes. Liz, however, was under the impression that Bird just wanted company. Thinking ahead, she told the new First Lady, 'You'll be asked to say something when we get there.' Mrs Johnson thought a minute. She said, 'I just feel it's all been a dreadful nightmare and somehow we must find the strength to go on.' Liz said, 'Well, that will be your statement,' and wrote it down.

Johnson instructed Youngblood to be sure that an agent was with the casket. Rufe replied that Behn, at Roy Kellerman's suggestion, had already established a new shift; Kellerman, Hill, Landis, and O'Leary were assigned to the slain President and his wife. Then Johnson beckoned to Moyers. He told him that he had no intention of entering the bedroom now. Perhaps the widow would like to use it to clean up. Moyers, the gentle nexus, went back to tell Jacqueline Kennedy.

Mrs Kennedy, in Moyers' words, 'chose to stay with the body'. In her own words she sat looking at 'that long, long coffin'.

She sat on the aisle seat, closest to the body; Ken O'Donnell brooded beside her. After the hasty reconstruction of the tail compartment to accommodate the casket, those were the only two seats left. Godfrey, Larry, and Dave stood throughout the flight, and the visitors from the staff cabin would stand among them, shifting this way and that to avoid jostling one another. Afterwards an incorrect report was circulated that some of them sat on the casket. They never touched it. Mary Gallagher felt a pervasive desire to kiss it, but knowing that would upset Mrs Kennedy she turned away. Like everyone there, Mary's first thought was to spare the widow, to help and serve her. There was about them an air of consecration; they couldn't even bring themselves to lean over her. When Larry O'Brien first spoke to her, he knelt, and the others followed his example. Approaching Andrews, O'Donnell rose and knelt, too.

This was an entirely new relationship. The day had gone for ever when the polls dismissed the President's wife as Jackie the Socialite. And she herself was a new Jackie, transformed by her vow that the full impact of the loss should be indelibly etched upon the national conscience. She declined Moyers' invitation because she had no need of the bedroom. Remembering the strangeness of the fresh clothes that had been laid out there, she reflected that during her three years in the White House she had learned much about Lyndon Johnson. Their rapport had been excellent, but a great deal depended upon what the press was told when they landed. She sent for Kilduff and said, 'You make sure, Mac—you go and tell them that I came back here and sat with Jack.' Kilduff bowed his head. He mumbled, 'I will.'

The new Jackie contrasted so sharply with the First Lady they had known that even the inner circle of Kennedy intimates were slow to grasp the extent of the *volte-face*. For as long as they could remember she had been quiet and retiring; she had dodged limelight, and when she did appear in public she was the apotheosis of the well-groomed alumna of Miss Chapin's, Miss Porter's, and Vassar. Stoughton had read O'Donnell's thoughts correctly; Ken was furious about the release of the oath pictures, fearful that they would show the stains on her. The feeling that something must be done about her appearance had become universal. In the stateroom the Johnsons and Rufe Youngblood were concerned about it, but so were the standees in the tail cabin. 'Why not change?' Godfrey asked her. She shook her head vigorously. Kilduff saw the rust-red blood caked under the bracelet on her left wrist and recoiled. Mary's first thought, on arriving from the front of the plane, was to fetch a warm washcloth and soap. Speaking in hushed tones, she consulted Godfrey, Clifton, and Clint Hill about it until O'Donnell came over and said, 'Don't do anything. Let her stay the way she is.' Ken now grasped her purpose.

Finally she broke her silence and spelled it out to Dr Burkley. Kneeling, the physician indicated her ghastly skirt with a trembling hand. 'Another dress?' he suggested diffidently. '*No*,' she whispered fiercely. 'Let them see what they've done.'

The last man to realize that she really meant it was Kilduff. He thought long about how they could off-load the coffin at Andrews without pictures being taken. His solution was to open the galley door on the starboard side, opposite the usual exit. That way the great mass of the fuselage would mask both the coffin and the widow; photographers and television cameramen would see nothing. He proposed the plan. She vetoed it. 'We'll go out the regular way,' she said. 'I want them to see what they have done.'

What had been done had unstrung everyone else in the cabin, and they talked disjointedly. Kilduff tearfully told her about his four-year-old son Kevin, who had been drowned while he was abroad on a trip with the President. To Bill Moyers, Larry O'Brien appeared resigned, a man drained of all vitality. Moyers expressed his own sorrow. Larry said haltingly, 'It's incredible—he put all of this into it—he worked so hard for it—and this is what happened—this is how it ends.' Godfrey McHugh kept repeating to himself, 'He's my President—my President.' Dave Powers reminisced about their trip to Ireland in June and the Celtic songs Kennedy had loved there: 'The Boys from Wexford,' 'Danny Boy,' and 'Kelly, the Boy from Killane.' Dazedly Ken O'Donnell said, 'You know what, Jackie? Can you tell me why we were saying that this morning? What was it he said at the hotel? "Last night would have been the best night to assassinate a President." Can you tell me why we were talking about that? I've never discussed that with him in my life.'

She shook her head. She herself had discussed it with her husband; she was recalling a conversation with him the Easter after his inaugural, and how they had concluded that they would have to rely upon the Secret Service. But this was no time to go into that. Really, words were so pointless now; Evelyn Lincoln came back to comfort her, and not knowing what else to say she recited mechanically, 'Everything's going to be all right.' Jacqueline Kennedy said, 'Oh, Mrs Lincoln!'

Abruptly O'Donnell rose. 'You know what I'm going to have, Jackie? I'm going to have a hell of a stiff drink. I think you should, too.'

She was dubious. She had promises to keep, and miles to go, and a drink might trigger uncontrollable weeping. She asked, 'What will I have?'

'I'll make it for you. I'll make you a Scotch,' he said.

'I've never had Scotch in my life.'

But maybe he was right. Bracers were often prescribed for victims of shock. She hesitated, then nodded.

'Now is as good a time as any to start,' she said to Godfrey.

On a signal from him—he had ordered all galleys closed after the vegetable soup saturnalia—Sergeant John Hames produced glasses, and Ken brought her a tall, dark tumbler. It tasted like foul medicine, like creosote. Nevertheless she drank it, and drank another. Indeed, after the funeral, when she had moved to Georgetown, Scotch was the only whisky she would take. She never learned to like it. But always it reminded her of that trip back from Dallas, of the hours she wouldn't permit herself to forget.

The clutch of men standing around her emptied glass after glass, and in the staff cabin Kilduff was setting something of a record. Mac was drinking gin and tonic as though it was going out of style. He later calculated that between Dallas and Washington he consumed nearly two-thirds of a bottle of gin. Like the Abbé Sieyès, who regarded the Reign of Terror as something to live through, each of them was trying to survive the hideous ride, and if liquor would help they wanted it.

Liquor didn't help. It didn't do anything. Nothing testifies more persuasively to the passengers' trauma than their astonishing immunity to alcohol. O'Donnell's instinct had been correct; in time of stress, when emotions have been ravaged and shredded, spirits are usually medicinal. Up in the control cabin Colonel Swindal, who couldn't touch anything now, was promising himself a tall jigger when he reached his MATS office at Andrews. He would keep that promise—and discover that it was like drinking tap water. Kilduff, having downed more than enough to anaesthetize him, gave up in despair. He was still cold sober. And when Ben Bradlee met Mrs Kennedy and her escorts at Bethesda Naval Hospital, he was outraged; from their conduct he assumed that no one had had sense enough to give them something to drink.

The decision to move to Bethesda was made by her. Dr Burkley, kneeling in the aisle, explained that because the President had been murdered there would have to be an autopsy. 'Security reasons,' he said, required that the hospital be military. The option lay between Bethesda and Walter Reed.

'Of course, the President was in the Navy,' he said softly.

'Of course,' said Jacqueline Kennedy. 'Bethesda.' It was then that Godfrey left to place his exasperating call stipulating an ambulance.

'I'll stay with the President until he is back at the White House,' Burkley promised, and he, too, left.

Sergeant Hames made sandwiches, but no one could eat them; after a few nervous nibbles they were thrust aside for conversation, and the Irishmen made a rudimentary start on what was to be the chief topic of the next twenty-four hours, the site of the grave. Their unanimous choice was Boston. All three remembered Kennedy standing on the cemetery knoll after the rites for Patrick. They thought he should be there with his son, in the Massachusetts soil they all loved. It was, as O'Donnell put it, 'the kind of feeling you have for a close friend'. He told Jackie, 'He must be buried in Boston, and don't you let them change it.'

She nodded absently. In the syncope of grief her own thoughts were turning inward. She was vividly recalling a conversation with the President towards the end of their first year in the executive mansion. She had just returned there from the funeral of Tony Biddle, and she had brought up the subject of their own funerals.

'Where will we be buried when we die, Jack?'

'Hyannis, I guess. We'll all be there.'

'Well, I don't think you should be buried in Hyannis, I think you should be buried in Arlington. You just belong to all the country.'

Then he had looked at her with a gently mocking expression and passed it off with a light comment about great mausoleums and Pharaonic tombs. And she had thought he was so right. And, indeed, it *had* been absurd to sit there talking about where their graves should be when they were still so young.

She turned towards Godfrey. 'This is my first real political trip,' she said. She told him, as she had told Lady Bird, 'I'm so glad I made it. Suppose I hadn't been there with him?'

She didn't look directly at McHugh. She had always had a way of looking off in the distance as she spoke, and during the flight this cachet seemed more pronounced. Those who were with her blessed her for it, for if her deep dark eyes had met theirs, her words would have been unbearable. They were difficult enough as it was. She asked for Clint Hill. She had regarded him as the brightest agent on the White House Detail, and because, like her husband, she really cared about excellence, she had sometimes brought him up to the mark. 'Oh, you know, Mr Hill,' she said, 'if I ever gave you a lecture'—her tears were falling now—'it was just because you were always just one of us.' Clint left stumbling. She collected herself and consoled the mafia: 'You were with him at the start and you're with him at the end.' Larry O'Brien thought giddily, *She's* worrying about *us*. In his later words, 'That frail girl was close to composure, bringing to the surface some strength within her while we three slobs dissolved.'

At the time, Mrs Kennedy did not contemplate a ceremonial funeral, but the ritual that was to come was to give the country a finer final last memory of her husband. His aides had perceived one side of him. They had campaigned and worked with the vibrant, shrewd young politician and President whose key had always been C-major. His wife had been closer to him. She had seen the dark star which had followed him through life. Since boyhood, she knew, he had been dogged by physical illness. The stamina which had sustained him was not the vitality of boundless health. It was a vigour of the spirit, an abiding vine of faith in man's ability to determine man's fate. In his bedridden childhood he had read the legends of valour; as a man he had written of courage. He had believed in heroes star-crowned and all golden, had fashioned a dream of leadership and fashioned himself to fit it. Perhaps another lonely little sick boy might read Marlborough and Sir Thomas Malory and become exalted as he had been. Afterwards she would think: *History made Jack what he was.*

On the aircraft, however, these reflections lay ahead—the riptide of anguish ran too strongly for coherence. Yet the implications of her still shapeless mood were to be vast. Jacqueline Kennedy was thinking of one President, but because the Presidency is a continuum her decisiveness affected the office herself, and therefore the nation. The Constitution, as Johnson had told O'Donnell and O'Brien, was putting him in the White House. It could not put him in the hearts of the people. That lay in the future, and in his hands. For the present the focus of public attention would be the widow of the slain Kennedy. Martyrdom, in transforming the country's concept of him, had elevated her to a kind of temporary regency. How she behaved during the transition would have lasting implications for the United States. The power of the government had passed on to Lyndon B. Johnson, but Mrs John F. Kennedy possessed a far greater power, over men's hearts, and like Johnson she could not shirk it. By what she did or left undone she herself would write history.

In the cramped tail compartment the men swayed and grasped at bulkheads for support while she, her eyes brimming again, gazed at the long, long coffin gleaming dully in the dim light.

Slumped in his co-pilot's seat, Hanson continued to radio position reports ahead as Air Force One climbed yet higher into the starlit night. The names on his flight chart read like an atlas of small-town America—Rockwall, Hope, Carthage, Stuttgart, Henderson, Hartsville, Paintsville, Louisa, Gassaway, Clendenin. The Presidential plane was passing above half the country, and on the map the route from Love Field looked like a dark blue curving scar. Unlike the passengers, who hadn't the faintest notion of where they were, he had to know 26000's precise location on the arc that swung up through eastern Texas, Arkansas, Tennessee, Kentucky, West

Virginia, and Virginia, towards Washington and Andrews, in Maryland, although like Swindal—like everyone else aboard—the co-pilot gave no thought to the land eight miles down.

But the people below were thinking of them, and only of them. Beneath Angel's swept-back wings the United States was in the throes of an unprecedented emotional convulsion. As Air Force One climbed over the border states, pivoting slightly north of Murfreesboro for a three-hundred-mile leg which would carry it directly towards Cape Cod before Swindal swung right for the capital, approximately 110 million Americans knew it was aloft and would reach its destination at about 6.05 p.m. Its exact route, of course, was secret. This was an elementary security precaution. Even on normal trips the pilot's long zigs and zags were clandestine. The directions were the subject of highly classified messages to key Air Force officers. On this flight the plane lacked the customary ground network of local Secret Service agents, stationed in unmarked automobiles to confirm its passage overhead with detection gear. Angel's sole contact was Acrobat, which was monitoring the co-pilot with exceptional care and listening intently on other frequencies for reports of 'unidentified, unfriendly' aircraft on the radar screening the south-eastern quadrant of the country. If the assassination of Kennedy were the first blow in a Soviet or Sino-Cuban machination, the airborne Presidential aircraft would be a prime target for a second blow. Air Force One, its backup, and the Cabinet plane not only were unarmed; all three lacked escorts. The U.S. Government was exceedingly vulnerable. The Pentagon had placed every Air Force base along 26000's route on stand-by, ready to scramble jet fighters; pilots were actually belted in and ready to go.

Thus the American people knew only that President Kennedy and his successor were somewhere in the sky above. How many of the 110 million were following commercial broadcasts is a matter of speculation. Pearl Harbor, the last thunderbolt of comparable magnitude, belonged to another communications era. Radio was in its heyday then, but most radios had been large and cumbersome. Now they had been replaced by television and the transistor. The University of Chicago's NORC study suggests that at the moment of Swindal's Murfreesboro pivot only two-tenths of one per cent of the population was unaware of the murder. Obviously, not everyone who knew of it was hovering over a loudspeaker. Some were in transit, some were too distressed to hear more, and there is always a subnormal minority which is genuinely indifferent—which would remain so in the thermonuclear war.

Many who were most deeply concerned simply could not spare the time to listen. In Manhattan Jean Kennedy Smith was packing a black dress. The president of Harvard was calling off the Yale game and accompanying functions; the students of Notre Dame had begun preparations to sing one hundred masses for the President's soul. The Chesapeake & Potomac Telephone Company was preoccupied with its own plight, summoning over three hundred off-duty operators. On the Rio Grande, as the Presidential aircraft reached midflight, customs officials were sealing off the Mexican border to prevent any escape there by conspirators.

In Fort Worth, Dallas, and Austin, individuals were picking up debris. Mrs J. Lee Thompson III, whose art exhibition Jacqueline Kennedy had admired so much that morning, was crating it at the Hotel Texas; the suite had to be evacuated for a new tenant. At the Trade Mart a huge electric sign which had been erected to welcome the President and First Lady was being dismantled, and in Austin's auditorium Mrs E. D. Moore, the caterer who was to have managed tonight's triumphal banquet, was confronting a staggering mass of food. Mrs Moore saved the steaks by refrigeration, but the rest was beyond redemption, and she was supervising the dumping of six thousand rolls, four thousand potatoes, a half-ton of fruit cocktail, and a ton and a half of tossed salad.

But even those who were distraught or preoccupied with urgent tasks checked with friends and colleagues from time to time for fresh news. Curiosity alone was an irresistible stimulant. The scene in the LBJ Ranch house was typical—according to Bess Abell, 'the knob of the kitchen TV had been turned as high as it would go, and the kitchen was a sea of bodies'. These were the hours when, all over the United States, a parked car whose radio was audible was sure to draw a crowd—silent crowds, most of them, whispering among themselves. It was also the period when rumours and false reports reached a peak. On Capitol Hill George Reedy had quickly scotched the canard that Johnson had been injured. Reedy had seen the wire report that a 'spectator' had observed Johnson 'walk into the hospital holding his arm'. He knew it was part of the American mythology that a heart attack always starts in the arm, and after calling Walter Jenkins, who had talked to Johnson on the plane, Reedy convinced Congressional correspondents that this was just buzz. Other yarns were harder to put down. The German alert seemed especially ominous, hinting at massive troop concentrations throughout Europe. The linking of Oswald's name with Cuba evoked memories of Castro terrorism; throughout the evening a great many people were to be under the impression that a Cuban had been charged with the crime.

A certain amount of distortion was inevitable. Erratic individuals are eager to credit the incredible. A century after Lincoln's death his assassination is still being laid at the door of a member of his Cabinet, and years after Kennedy's death there would be those who would reject any information which did not fit their preconceived theories about the crime. These people did not want facts; they merely wanted to feed their own ravaged emotions. But that Friday stable persons were being misled too. The erratic performance of the Associated Press was responsible for much of the confusion. The AP was an American institution. Deservedly, it was regarded as a pillar of accuracy. When it followed its twelve-bell confirmation of the assassination with the report that an unnamed Secret Service man had been killed and added cryptically that 'no other information was immediately available', Bill Greer's wife, in suburban Washington, believed the worst. She knew that Bill always drove the Lincoln, and although a denial of the rumour from the Treasury Department was on the printer two hours later, she assumed throughout the flight that her husband was dead.

There were other lapses during the afternoon. Most were inconsequential. Over an hour after 26000's departure from Love Field, NBC was broadcasting that 'LBJ is remaining in Dallas'. The flash that a red-shirted man with black curly hair had been arrested 'in the Riverside section of Fort Worth in the shooting of a Dallas policeman' was quickly forgotten when the truth about Oswald began to pour in an hour later. An entirely inaccurate story of how the President's parents had learned of his death from a Hyannis Port workman scarcely mattered; neither did a description of 'the President . . . struck in the right temple by the bullet' or of the weapon as 'a German Mauser'. But one account was to cause real mischief later. The AP flatly declared that Kennedy had been shot 'in the front of the head'. It was this report, put out scarcely an hour after the President had been pronounced dead, which became the chief source for the conviction of millions that all subsequent investigations of the tragedy were fraudulent.

Jean Kennedy Smith took the 4 p.m. shuttle to the capital. Everyone who had been close to the President was anxious to be at his side, and during Angel's flight a number of Kennedy relatives and friends were also aloft. The impulse had begun when they knew only that he had been injured; then, like the Attorney General and the cabinet, their first instinct had been to race to Dallas. Theodore H. White, author of *The Making of the President 1960*, was among those New Yorkers who were on their way to New York's LaGuardia Airport, prepared to hire a plane to Texas, when a taxicab radio broadcast Kilduff's announcement from 101–102. White boarded the Washington shuttle instead and was followed by Chuck

Spalding and Adlai Stevenson on subsequent flights. The Coast Guard prepared to fly Assistant Secretary of the Treasury Jim Reed to the capital. Arthur Schlesinger, Ken Galbraith, and Kay Graham came down on *Newsweek*'s Martin 404. Circling over Washington National Airport, Galbraith constricted his six feet, eight inches, fastening his seat belt. After a long silence he said to Schlesinger, 'We let the Right inject this poison in the American bloodstream—and this is the result.'

The swiftness of New York-to-Washington air service meant that the group from Manhattan landed first. Several arrived so early that they didn't know when or where the President's body would be returned; Jean Smith and the three from the *Newsweek* Martin went directly to the White House, and White cruised around in a cab for a half-hour before the radio in the taxi reported that Air Force One was heading for Andrews. He directed the driver out Suitland Parkway and met Mary McGrory at the MATS terminal. So much had happened since lunch that it was difficult to come to terms with the new reality. In one part of their minds men and women realized that John Kennedy was, in fact, no longer alive. Because the rest of the mind revolted, however, they reverted to the more believable moments when they had merely known that he was hurt. President Kennedy was hurt and they were rushing to his side. That was all they could absorb. Later—the exact time and extent of the reconciliation varied from individual to individual—they thought: *The President has been killed, Jacqueline Kennedy needs help.* That realization was eclipsing; any contemplation of Lyndon Johnson or the future was impossible.

Flights from California took five hours and twenty minutes, and while the passengers from New York milled about uncertainly in the capital, those from the West Coast were passing the Rockies. Peter Lawford had been performing in Stateline, Nevada, with Jimmy Durante. He and his agent, Milt Ebbins, were on a chartered plane. Pat Kennedy Lawford and her daughter Sydney were standing by to board an American Airlines jet from Los Angeles—Sydney was Caroline's age, and bringing her proved to be a brilliant stroke; throughout that week she was to give her cousin the kind of companionship no adult could have provided. On another eastbound airliner Red Fay was cradling his own daughter, and like Dean Markham he had to turn away from the devastating, unanswerable remark of a child. The President had participated in the little girl's christening. Approaching the Mississippi, she looked up and asked, 'Daddy, what happens to me now that I don't have a godfather?'

The savage, unpredictable storms lashing the continent confined some Kennedy intimates to the ground. Bunny Mellon's plane was in

Manhattan, and despite the great Mellon wealth she couldn't hire another to take her to Puerto Rico. In Antigua she paced the terminal frantically, looking out gloomily at the most ferocious cloudburst she had ever seen. Others, debarking at the capital, weren't sure they should have come. At 3.30 p.m. Candy McMurrey telephoned her sister from Washington National to suggest that she and her husband return to Texas on the next flight. Joan Kennedy begged her to stay. The White House had just called to say that Ted wouldn't be home tonight. Joan was in bed, prostrate, and she knew that the family would need all the help it could muster to cope with callers. The McMurreys immediately took an airport cab to Georgetown.

High above Washington Lieutenant Sam Bird was riding towards Andrews in his H-21 helicopter with eight casket bearers from Fort Myer's south drill field. Disregarding seniority, Bird had picked the strongest, most reliable enlisted men on the post. As the rotors chattered over Pennsylvania Avenue he peered down on the White House, the federal triangle, the memorials, the Roman complex of the Hill. This was the first time he had ever ridden over the city, and he thought its beauty breathtaking. He remembered all the tours he had taken, all the souvenirs he had bought and sent home to Kansas. None matched the splendour beneath him. The Capitol dome reflected the day's dying light, and a million flickering reflections glittered and shimmered below. It was the most spectacular panorama the Lieutenant had ever seen. He wished this were some other day.

The Cabinet plane faced the longest journey. Its initial leg, from the Pacific turnaround to Hawaii, was an hour and forty minutes, almost the length of Swindal's entire flight. Aircraft 86972, like Aircraft 26000, carried on a ceaseless stream of conversation, first with Honolulu and then, after refuelling at Hickam Field, with the capital. Like the messages from Angel, these were guarded, because there was no way to scramble voices. On 86972 there was another reason for hesitation. The men aboard were uncertain of their new status. President Kennedy once observed that a number of governmental institutions have grown independently of the Constitution. His favourite example was Congressional seniority, but the Cabinet is another. Both are rooted in precedent; they are part of our unwritten constitution, and in time of crisis their status is equivocal. Until Truman's law of 1947 the President's foreign minister had been the Vice President's legal successor. Now the position of Rusk and his airborne colleagues differed from those of O'Donnell, O'Brien, Sorensen, and Bundy only in that their appointments had been ratified by the Senate. All were the servants of a national leader who no longer existed.

Throughout this maddening interregnum—and it must be remembered that the presence of an AP teletype in the communications shack meant that during much of the first lap the passengers thought co-conspirators had killed a Secret Service agent and a Dallas policeman, and were under the impression that Lyndon Johnson might also be a casualty—they could only act on the assumption that they were principal advisers of the American Chief Executive, whoever he might be. Most of them could wait for clarification from President Johnson or, if it should come to that, from President McCormack. Rusk couldn't. The nature of events required that he be the busiest man in the conference room. As their senior he drafted missives of condolence for Jacqueline Kennedy and support for Kennedy's successor; as Secretary of State he had to weigh implications abroad.

Lacking a secure line he wisely decided against placing a call to McNamara. Instead, he filled a yellow ruled page with instructions for George Ball, to be relayed as soon as they reached CINCPAC on Oahu. Some directions were obvious. The diplomatic corps must be reassured, and formal notes must be sent to each of the fifty state governors—the United States is, after all, a federal union. One directive arose from the uncertainty of the moment. Anticipating the needs of the thirty-sixth President, Rusk requested a country-by-country 'inventory' from his department's desks, assessing precisely what the assassination would mean 'externally and internally' in every world capital, with a breakdown of danger spots. One apprehension was so delicate that the Secretary didn't even commit it to paper. To those around him he wondered 'who has his finger on the nuclear button'.

Pierre Salinger and Douglas Dillon were bent over identical pads. Pierre was drafting a joint statement for the correspondents he knew would be waiting at Hickam; Dillon, the one Cabinet member here who had been close to the First Family, was preparing a personal wire to Mrs Kennedy. Among others, Luther Hodges, Orville Freeman, and Walter Heller were also writing, though not for transmission. Each was struggling to frame his own thoughts. It was a kind of therapy, entirely understandable for public men who dealt in words. Yet critical eyes watched them. The tensions of 26000 and 86970 were here in diluted form. The most absonant of human emotions had been uncaged; it was impossible for any given individual to please everyone. The notetakers were resented by those who were not taking notes, one of whom felt that 'this was no time to compose memoirs'. Really they weren't memoirs. They were in-choate attempts to measure the pervasive anguish. Heller noted a 'complete grief-stricken silence . . . for a period that no one can measure by the clock'. Even as Secretary Wirtz, a non-writer, was silently reflecting that they all seemed to be 'under a blanket', Secretary Freeman was scrawling:

> Dead silence—Tears—Mostly stunned
> Gloom
> . . . deep affection I hold—tragedy. As Jane said the sense of firm progress and direction of last 3 years meant so much. . . . what a crime. . . . My thought: What a diff. place the W.H. will be. . . . What an incredible unbelievable tragedy.

They landed in flawless Honolulu sunshine. Five time zones to the east darkness was approaching, but here it was still mid-morning. Admiral Harry Felt came aboard with what Hodges described as 'some of the terrible details', telling them that the assassin had used 'a high-power rifle and scope'—Freeman, the ex-Marine, had guessed this—while Rusk, Salinger, and Bob Manning hurried across the airstrip. The others kept their belts fastened. The men wanted to refuel as quickly as possible, and they were anxious to shield their distraught wives from staring strangers. Manning handed Salinger's statement to Felt's press officer for distribution to reporters; the Secretary talked to his Under Secretary (and discovered that Ball had anticipated most of his orders); the Situation Room informed Pierre that Johnson had been sworn in. Thirty-five minutes later they took off with three new passengers—two members of the press and a physician.

The physician had been Rusk's idea. The Secretary believed he detected signs of emotional collapse in several of the women, and pausing in his descent of the ramp he had requested a Navy doctor of the ascending admiral. Felt ran a trim ship. Twenty minutes later a Navy doctor scooted up, black bag in hand. As it turned out, Rusk was to be the only man to know that medical attention was available, because one of the Secretary's colleagues was so worried about *him* that he put him asleep. In Rusk's thirty-four months at State he had never taken a sedative. The chances of sudden shifts in the world situation were too great. He could not risk grogginess. He had had to be ready to carry out Kennedy's commands at any instant. Now, however, Douglas Dillon decided that a sleeping pill was imperative. Dillon knew that Kennedy had largely acted as his own foreign minister, giving Rusk the lead. Studying the Georgian's posture, normally so erect, he thought he could almost see the weight of responsibility coming down on his shoulders. Obviously he was very, very tired. On a gesture from her husband Phyllis Dillon dug out a capsule, and together they persuaded Rusk to swallow it and curl up under a blanket in the tail compartment. Later, when a low-priority call came through from Ball, Dillon went up to the shack and handled it.

For the Secretary of the Treasury to double as Secretary of State was an act of exceptional thoughtfulness. Conflicting themes were clashing wildly: passengers were indignant with one another for jotting down impressions, and simultaneously, were solicitous of one another. Mental collages were dream-like, incongruous; Freeman wept and, while contemplating the Oahu beach below, wrote:

> Waikiki beautiful as we took off—surf break & diff. colour blue & green.
> But no heart to take a picture as Rusk, Hodges, Dillon & I sit in compartment in heavy silence & sorrow——
> It doesn't seem possible——
> Enroute 1.50 Hawaii time—I just completed a little cry, hanky under glasses. . . .[2]

There was surrealistic behaviour here, too. Liquor was no more effective over the Pacific than over Appalachia, but there were several heroic attempts at oblivion. Among the men Dillon and Salinger were the most upset. The others had been acquainted with the President; they had been his friends. So Pierre did something which at first seems wondrous. He beckoned to five other men and organized a poker game. The stakes, Josephy noted with amazement, were '$100 worth of chips each to start'. Actually, it wasn't at all fabulous; it was a passkey to Salinger's raddled personality. Behind his Levantine façade lay the sensitive pianist who had been a child prodigy. In politics he had camouflaged sensitivity with a tough manner. Tough men smoked strong cigars, drank deeply, and gambled, and these became part of Pierre's virile masquerade. The true index to his internal agony on November 22 was the way he played his cards. Throughout the eight-hour flight to Andrews he tossed out money with senseless abandon. He had never done that before, he never would do it again. This once, however, recklessness seemed important. And it was. It worked; it preserved his sanity. Between hands he would turn his back and bury his head in his hands (everyone did that; those pauses were the bad moments; in this extraordinary game no one watched the dealer); yet he never cracked. The make-up of the game changed—at its height there were seven players, with Mike Feldman, Manning, and two corre-

[2] This is unclear. According to the pilot's log, they departed Hickam at 11.05 Hawaii time (2105 Zulu). The likeliest explanation is that Freeman had become confused by the zones.

spondents, John Scali of ABC[3] and a *Time* man, staying longest—but Pierre never missed a bet. At the end of the journey he was to survey a crumpled mass of bills and silver. In a semicoma he counted it out. He had won over $800, and he was appalled.

While Dean Rusk slept and the poker players bluffed and raised, another group of men sat in the conference room, fumbling for the future.

Here, too, the number of participants varied; the maximum was ten and included the five wakeful Cabinet members and Walter Heller. There was a period of settling down. After the teletype had spiked the false rumours, after Dillon had voiced the Cabinet's general fear that Americans might demand retribution from Russia and/or Cuba, and after all available facts were in (when the first bulletins had arrived, Heller noted with astonishment, they hadn't even known 'where the Vice President was'), a serious, constructive conversation began. They talked, Hodges wrote, 'in pairs and threes and groups', and the central topic became 'the new President's desires and plans'.

This was probably the first thoughtful assessment of the Johnson Presidency. Angel's passengers were disabled by the horror they had seen, most of official Washington was preoccupied by the imminent return of the Presidential plane, but in this landless void the murder was an abstraction, and for eight hours there was nothing the non-gamblers could do except talk. The sense of strain remained. They had the futile sensation of swimming in clear glue with weighted arms. These were civilized men, but anger showed its fist, and in the beginning there were a few sharp skirmishes. Wirtz, who had campaigned for Stevenson in Los Angeles, said wryly, 'I gather you don't think the world is at an end? I thought so when Kennedy was nominated.' The others bridled at this tactlessness, and when Luther Hodges insisted that the Attorney General had denounced Lyndon Johnson at a recent meeting of the Kennedy family—and then conceded that this was only hearsay—he himself was denounced as a rumour-monger. Immediately Hodges stumbled into another pitfall. He declared that 'the South' regarded Johnson's support of civil rights legislation as treachery. Pressed, he admitted that his informants were all Southern businessmen.

Gradually the level of the conversation rose. There was long deliberation over the Gordian problem of Presidential disability and another sober review of the line of succession. When the prospect of

[3] Scali, as ABC's Statement Department correspondent, had quietly served as the President's personal representative thirteen months earlier, persuading an official at the Soviet Embassy that Russian missiles must be removed from Cuba.

either McCormack or Hayden in the White House was raised, two Secretaries winced in unison, as though on signal. Then, having skirted the edges of the real issue, they grappled towards the core. In the improvised shorthand of one Cabinet member, they talked 're LBJ & what kind of Pres'. This Secretary's own view was that LBJ was a 'strong man & will rise occasion . . . this is a strong take-charge man'. Heller declared that Johnson was ignorant of the balance-of-payments problem. There was a pensive silence. No one could say much for LBJ's grasp of economics. They weren't even sure he understood the Keynesian theory behind the proposed tax cut. But Dillon pointed out that a State Department representative, acting on Kennedy's instructions, had provided the Vice President with a daily summary of incoming cables. The note-taker scribbled: 'Up on int'l affairs.'

Again he scrawled, using capitals, 'WHAT KIND PRES'. For they were back on the fringes. The essential question was how Johnson would act, not what he knew, and the answer lay in the tortuous logogriph of his personality. Hodges had scarcely spoken to the man. The Secretary of Commerce threw up his hands. He couldn't even make an educated guess. Wirtz was better informed, but that merely meant that he knew the dimensions of the enigma; he confessed that he had no idea what direction the new President would take. Like Wirtz, Udall knew Johnson and could assure them that whichever way he went, he would be decisive. Over the past three years he and Freeman had been the two Cabinet members who had seen the most of the Vice President. In fact, as Freeman remarked, they were the only ones who really knew him. The Secretary with a pencil reminded them of Johnson's devotion to Kennedy, his parliamentary ability, and his party loyalty ('Lyndon skilled in pol. . . . his best compliment—he got on train and stayed'). In addition, he said aloud, he thought Johnson had benefited from Kennedy's 'magnificent training'.

They listened attentively, hoping he was right. Lyndon Johnson was the only President they had, and unlike McCormack and Hayden he was at the height of his faculties. Yet none of them responded enthusiastically. The writing Cabinet member himself had doubts. In his notes to himself he observed that Lyndon 'does not have this sense of the time and the age and the forces which John F. Kennedy had to such an unusual degree'. The cachet was gone. It had been odd: 'Jack Kennedy was never really outgoing in a sense with people that you felt close to him, but yet he had that peculiar quality that so endeared him and commanded such loyalty and devotion . . . that quality was there until I could almost say that you love that man [despite] his somewhat taciturn New England attitudes.' And undeniably his administration had been brilliant: 'We were making progress and the national economy was moving ahead. In the international field we were making progress. There was enlightenment. . . . He would have won that election in '64.' The writer felt closer to Johnson, and had sympathized with the Vice President, who 'wasn't . . . completely accepted by the illustrious crowd around Pres'. Nevertheless he concluded: 'Hard to tell what he will do.'

On that agreement was universal. Yet even as they parried and probed they were reaching for their dispatch cases. To them this seemed entirely natural. In reality it was a remarkable achievement in the chronicles of government, and during the following weeks observers abroad, usually so quick to chide the United States, admitted to astonishment at this aspect of the transition. On this point foreigners had reason to be impressed. Here were John Kennedy's ministers quietly contemplating the administration of a man they hardly knew under circumstances which, if the lessons of world history meant anything, clearly pointed, not to a lone killer, but towards a savage lunge for power.

The difference was that these were Americans. They weren't thinking of the world's past. Bred to insularity by the remoteness of their continent, they were interpreting the violence in Dallas in the light of the American experience. At times this insular quality is a weakness. Here it was strength, reflecting the continuum of the U.S. Presidency. In the six generations since George Washington's first inaugural on Wall Street the government had never been comminuted by a coup. Each of the three previous assassinations had been a psychotic deed—Booth's 'plot' was no plot by European standards; it had been a cabal of impressionable weaklings led by an Oswald with charm. The union had been threatened by secession, but it had never been menaced by *Jacobins* or *Carbonari*, and the possibility of such a conspiracy occurred to no one on Aircraft 86972. When Castle and Acrobat relayed Angel's directive for a Cabinet meeting at 2.15 p.m. the following day, men in the conference room thumbed through their papers. In Hodges' words, they were preparing 'as a matter of custom and courtesy to submit resignations, as I understand is done at the end of a President's first term, but we will await President Johnson's reaction and comment'.

Like Franklin Roosevelt, John Kennedy had been a man of wealth and a zealous defender of capitalism. Neither had won much gratitude from capitalists. In the early 1960's, as in the 1930's, the men in Manhattan's financial district had regarded the White House with captiousness and enmity. Kennedy was no more a traitor to his class than Roosevelt had been. But as the son of a financial buccaneer who had become one of FDR's ablest advisers on fiscal reform—the Securities and Exchange Commission and the integrity it brought modern markets were largely creations of Joe Kennedy—JFK had been alert to the vulnerability of the economy to blind panic. During his first week in the executive mansion he had designed an intricate prearrangement to safeguard against such panic. On February 3, 1961, he had sent his proposal to the Congress as a major message, and on the afternoon of November 22, 1963, it lay on the desk of Joe Fowler, Douglas Dillon's surrogate.

Historically the relationship between the Treasury and the mansion had always been intimate. The United States was, after all, the oldest and greatest capitalistic democracy, and the two great buildings, standing on either side of East Executive Avenue, were actually linked by an underground tunnel. Since 1902 the Secret Service, as an arm of the Treasury Department, had tightened the bond. Fowler thought first of the Service; he called Chief Rowley and asked that adequate security arrangements be made for the Vice President and the Speaker of the House. Rowley assured him that this was being done. Fowler's second call was to Robert McNamara, the ranking Cabinet member in Washington.[4] Like the men in the White House, he wanted to be sure that 86972 was reversing course. The Secretary of Defence was talking to the Attorney General on another line, but an aide relayed word that the aircraft was on its way back. They hung up, and it was then that Fowler remembered the plan Kennedy had drafted for just such an extremity as today's.

Briefly, the President's strategy was this. The first step was to see that all government security markets suspended trading at once. Second, Fowler instructed Alfred Hayes, president of the Federal Reserve Bank of New York, to call Keith Funston of the New York Stock Exchange and Ted Etherington of Amex, requesting them to close down. The gongs rang, and just in time; the assassination of the President, coupled with a shocking vegetable oil scandal which had been exposed earlier in the day, had sent the Big Board into a dizzy spiral. Clearing the floors provided a respite. In itself it was no exploit. Funston, in fact, had anticipated the Treasury. The crux of Kennedy's design lay abroad. The major risk was speculation against the dollar. Such piracy is easy to detect. Sharks buy gold, betting that the price will rise from $35 an ounce to $40, say, or $45. Stopping them is not so easy, and no solution can be improvised after the balloon of fear has gone up.

To prevent them from turning world markets into casinos, with the United States as the heavy loser, Kennedy had set up what he

[4] Protocol for the big four is State, Treasury, Defence, Justice.

called a 'swap arrangement' with the central banks of other countries. The U.S.A. literally swapped its money for theirs. He had ordered the Treasury to accumulate enormous stocks of pounds, marks, lire, yen, pesos, rands, guilders, French francs and Swiss francs—of every form of international currency. These had then been locked up. They constituted a kind of insurance: the President left a standing order that in any emergency they should all be released at once, with massive offers for foreign exchange being made to counter any dollars thrown on the table. The first occasion for the measure was to be his own violent death.

It worked magnificently. The key man was Al Hayes, because New York's Federal Reserve is more than a reserve bank; it also serves as the government's fiscal agent. Luckily for Hayes, foreign exchanges had closed before the assassination. Nevertheless America's great vaults were opened that afternoon, and next day the bales of bills were to be used. On Saturday a few European gold markets opened, notably London's and Zurich's. On both, corsairs reached for the panic button. The Kennedy swap blocked them completely. Their dollars were taken, but in return they received other tender, not gold. (On Monday the Jolly Roger was hoisted again—after a few passes the speculators realized the extent of America's preparations and withdrew. Meanwhile in the United States Wall Street was given the weekend plus an additional twenty-four hours of breathing time. Declaration of a bank holiday would have been alarming, so David Rockefeller, a friend of the Kennedys, persuaded his brother Nelson to halt trading as 'a special mark of respect' for the late President. By Tuesday everything was steady.) The entire operation was a financial masterpiece, conducted on so high a plane that the oil and gas men of Dallas who had traduced JFK as a 'Comsymp' enemy of free enterprise never even understood what was happening.

Fowler, who was to succeed Dillon in 1965, was functioning Friday afternoon as a member of what Washington calls 'the sub-cabinet'—under secretaries, deputies, and key aides. In the absence of the six Secretaries and the attenuation of the Attorney General these men were carrying on superbly. Katzenbach was wrestling with Texas law. Bundy, who wore a sub-cabinet hat because of his national security role, was setting up new locked files in the West Wing for Lyndon Johnson. George Ball and Acting Secretary of Agriculture Charlie Murphy were conferring with Macy over the telephone impasse; they concluded that the solution to the Chesapeake & Potomac's plight lay among Macy's quarter-million Civil Service employees in metropolitan Washington, countless thousands of whom were attempting to dial their home phones while their wives tried to call *them.* Here again the answer was a Kennedy answer, this time a design of Robert Kennedy's. Three months earlier, while preparing for the August 28 civil rights March on Washington, the President's brother had suggested that government workers be released early on a staggered basis, in nine separate waves. With a fresh wave being disgorged every fifteen minutes the flow of traffic would be even, there would be no congestion, and the federal triangle—the great Corinthian complex between the Mall, the White House, the Hill, and Pennsylvania Avenue—would be cleared out. At 3.05 p.m., eighteen minutes after Swindal's take-off from Love Field, Macy checked with the District police and then acted on his own responsibility. The rapid recovery of public communications during the next hour and a half suggests that setting the Attorney General's plan in motion may have been the turning point for the frantic telephone company.[5]

As Angel darted over the Cumberland River's verniculating shore, Washington's most furious official activity that afternoon was on the Potomac segment of the Pentagon's E Ring—for obvious reasons its nature cannot be described here—and in Foggy Bottom. In the New State Department Building, as the capital still called it, Angier Biddle Duke was putting out a condolence book and a silver tray for envoys' cards. Cables were being dispatched to American legations around the globe, instructing them to prepare other books. The sole copy of the funeral ceremonies for FDR was exhumed from the department's archives. Harlan Cleveland wrote out a proclamation of mourning for Lyndon Johnson—the new Chief Executive was to adopt it intact—while U. Alexis Johnson drafted a list of what had been accomplished and what remained. Both papers were then set aside for presentation at Andrews.

The second read:

November 22, 1963

MEMORANDUM FOR THE PRESIDENT

Following are suggested steps and procedures based upon historical precedents, including most recently the death of President Roosevelt:

1. The issuance of a proclamation by you appointing the day of

[5] Emergency planners have yet to learn the lessons of November 22. A study of that afternoon suggests that in any disaster on a workday commercial telephones would become highly unreliable. The public could be reached by television and radio, but the homes of all vital officials should be knitted into a government system similar to the White House Communications Agency. The Signal Corps has the equipment and the expertise to do this; it lacks only a green light.

the late President's funeral as a day of national mourning and prayer.—Draft proclamation attached for your consideration.

2. A circular telegram from the Secretary of State to the Governors of all States and Territories, informing them of orders with respect to a period of thirty-day public mourning, information with respect to the funeral services, and requesting notification if they intend to be present at the funeral ceremonies.—This will be done as details are available.

3. On your order, the issuance of instructions by the Secretary of State, closing all Executive Departments and Agencies on the day of the funeral and instructing the Secretary of Defence that all military commands and vessels under the control of the Secretary of Defence fly flags at half mast for a thirty-day period of mourning.—This will be done.

4. Notification of the death of President Kennedy to all Chiefs of Mission in Washington by the Acting Secretary of State.—This has been done.

5. Notification by the Acting Secretary of State to call Chiefs of Mission in Washington that you have taken the oath as President, and announcing funeral arrangements for the late President. This will be done as soon as arrangements are known.

GEORGE W. BALL
Acting Secretary

U: GWBall/vh

That completed, the State Department's principals debated more delicate issues. For the first three hours the probable explanation of the killer's provocation seemed clear. All the under secretaries were familiar with the political climate in Dallas. Then, at 4.25 p.m., an urgent Secret Service message arrived through channels. Treasury wanted to know whether State had a dossier on one Lee Harvey Oswald. Within minutes the networks were broadcasting the fact that Oswald had applied for Soviet citizenship, and George Ball's demand for a check followed the Treasury's. The dossier arrived; it was thick. Obviously Oswald had been to Moscow. Johnson ordered an investigation 'to see if our handling of the case had been OK'. At the same time a spirited discussion began over the possibilities of war. To Ball, Tommy Thompson declared vigorously that the Communists didn't work this way. The U.S.S.R. would kill defectors, but not chiefs of state. They would never set a precedent which might be awkward for them. Averell Harriman, like Thompson a former ambassador to Russia, gave him eloquent backing. As a nuclear attack did not materialize, the two Russian specialists were vindicated and Alex Johnson observed that a revulsion in the country against Oswald's professions of Marxism—professions which Harriman regarded with mounting scepticism—could undo all Kennedy's careful work towards a *détente* with the U.S.S.R. Johnson requested that the District police provide an unobtrusive cordon around the Russian Embassy. One was set up, but it proved unnecessary. Like Harriman, most Americans on the East Coast found a Marxist Dallasite scarcely credible. At that very moment a mobile television unit was interviewing in Rockefeller Plaza. All assumed that the crime had been inspired by what one called 'the ultraconservatives that spread hate in the South'.

Despite his age, Harriman had felt himself bound to John Kennedy by a special tie. The tall, elegant patrician had long been a departmental maverick; he was notorious for filing State directives in his wastebasket. When FDR died he had been in Moscow. Convinced that no one in Washington could give Harry Truman an intelligent appraisal of Russia's plans for postwar aggression, he had, without authorization from anyone, charted a nonstop course that would take him over Rumania, directly to the capital in forty hours—a world's record at that time. (Afterwards he said, 'The Department thought me very naughty. But they always say no. So I never ask them.') One of the staunchest of the original New Dealers, he had had another reason to remember FDR's death. The recollection of Muscovites weeping outside the Kremlin as he left Molotov and Stalin that day had never been far from the surface of his mind. For sixteen years he had waited for another Roosevelt to rise. Then, in 1961, it had happened. 'Franklin Roosevelt had talked over the heads of government to the hearts of people,' he said six months after Dallas. 'The same was true of John Kennedy. He also had been an expression of the ideals that the world hoped us to live up to. His inaugural and his subsequent speeches were read everywhere, and the world felt that a new FDR had come to power.'

Now, suddenly, the magnificent gift had vanished. Harriman felt crushed: 'Roosevelt's death was shattering to me because I had hoped that he would play a role in building the peace. Then, with Kennedy, I had felt that his handling of the Cuban situation had materially changed the Russian policy. Khrushchev had used the threat of nuclear war against us and had told Robert Frost that democracies were too liberal to fight. I was terrified that he underestimated our willingness to fight and that there would be a showdown in Cuba. Kennedy convinced him that he would have to take his weapons out of Cuba—or else. Furthermore, the President had been sensible and wise enough to give Khrushchev a way out. Khrushchev had looked down that long nuclear barrel and he—and we—knew that President Kennedy had the Communists' number.

Most important, and this revealed his magical flair for statesmanship, *other countries were on our side.*'

Abruptly it was over: 'No two Presidents before had had world opinion and affection centred upon them as had Roosevelt and Kennedy. In both cases people abroad felt they had lost a personal friend.' Franklin Roosevelt had been Harriman's personal friend. In 1945 his loss had been almost insupportable. He hadn't believed that he was capable of suffering that way again. Yet the assassination of John Kennedy was really worse: 'You must remember that at Yalta President Roosevelt had been a sick man. The fact that he died, although a shock, was not so startling because one had wondered about his health. Besides, it was wartime, and death was not unusual. The Kennedy affair, on the other hand, was something I had never contemplated. . . . Then came the stunning fact, and the reaction in one's self, one's country, and in the world was in some ways more vocal and more intense than the reaction to Roosevelt's death. This was particularly true among youth. Someone had cared about them . . . genuinely cared, and was doing something about it. Youth knew and was responding. Suddenly . . . he was gone, gone, gone.'

Harriman abruptly walked out of the under-secretarial meeting and informed his staff that he would meet his afternoon schedule. They were astounded. One assistant, William H. Sullivan, encountering him in the foyer outside Ball's office, protested, but Harriman shook his head doggedly. 'No,' he replied, 'the world must go on.' He was among those who had pondered what the President would have expected of him and concluded that Kennedy would want him at his post. He went there. Very shortly he regretted it. First on his schedule was a meeting with a group from Standard Oil of New Jersey. The agenda called for a conference on measures which might improve the firm's worsening position in South America. The talk was wobbly from the outset, and it dove beyond hope of recovery when a zealous junior executive suggested that since a dead President couldn't help them, the new President should send a letter to the President of Argentina. That blew the discussion wide open. In Sullivan's words, 'I think all of us on the government side were adequately disgusted with that attitude so that we moved, with the collaboration of more senior and sensible executives, to a rapid closure of the meeting.'

Coming less than two hours after the announcement of Kennedy's death, the mere term 'the new President' was, to Sullivan, 'particularly bad taste'. There were more unfortunate lapses that afternoon in Washington. Those who had disliked the Kennedy Presidency were adjusting to its end with amazing speed. They had never forgiven him his victory over Big Steel the year before. His appeal had eluded them, as Roosevelt's appeal had baffled their fathers. Their failure to gauge the loyalty he had aroused became startlingly evident in several insensitive remarks which were casually passed Friday afternoon. While Air Force One was still climbing over eastern Texas Fred Holborn had received a telephone inquiry from a writer for a business periodical. Holborn had a 3.30 appointment with the writer at the White House. The journalist merely wanted to confirm the time; he saw no reason why they shouldn't proceed. Holborn thought there was a reason, and he tartly suggested an indefinite postponement. Later he received another call from a slight acquaintance. At first he assumed that the caller wished to express sympathy. To his dismay—and utter disbelief—he realized that he was being asked whether he would use his influence, as Special Assistant to President Kennedy, to secure two fifty-yard-line tickets to the Army–Navy game.

Jersey Standard's company man, the business writer, and the football fan are hard to fathom. Yet it was a capricious time. The disguises which individuals wear in society, the lubricants that make day-to-day encounters bearable, had been swept away. Some men became meaner, some nobler; all were guileless. For three days men were to be transparent. During that weekend which they would afterwards seal off in the attic of their minds they were artless, whole-souled, and, for once, unashamed of emotional display.

In the Capitol Congressman James Roosevelt, ordinarily bland, proposed that John Kennedy be awarded the Medal of Honour. Across the Hill's lovely old park Earl Warren, the rightists' Public Enemy No. 2, issued a blunt indictment of the apostles of hate.[6] Senators Mansfield, Bible, and Byrd were in deep shock. At 3.48 David Brinkley noted that people were weeping freely on Nebraska Avenue. In the White House Hubert Humphrey was stumbling from one White House policeman to another, wringing hands and embracing them. Already a crowd had gathered across the street in Lafayette Park. No one knew what the men and women there expected. They didn't know themselves; reporters found them incapable of speech. They kept peering anxiously at the mansion's North Portico as though hoping to see the President emerge, smile, and wave.

Speed explained much of the response. The panorama of events

[6] Two weeks later, on December 6, the House Republican Policy Committee denied that 'hate was the assassin that struck down the President'. Instead, it charged, the true criminal was 'the teachings of Communism'. Expanding this theme, Senator Millard L. Simpson of Wyoming took the floor that day to attack people seeking 'political advantage from warping the uncontestable truth' and blaming 'rightists and conservatives'. The murderer, the Senator said, 'was a single kill-crazy Communist'.

whirled faster and faster; Friday afternoon was like one of those Pete Smith movie features of the 1930's in which trick photographers trebled, quintupled, and then sextupled the movements of celluloid figures. Everywhere, everything was continuing to happen at once. Less than a minute after Angel's wheels had left Love, while Colonel Swindal was still adjusting flaps and dive brakes, the Russian radio was playing funeral music, the House of Commons had adjourned, and Prime Minister Lester Pearson was finishing a nationwide broadcast to Canada eulogizing the President. Before Air Force One reached the Mississippi all Ireland was in prayer. As the Colonel passed Mammoth Cave National Park formal statements had been issued by President Hoover, President Eisenhower, Governor Rockefeller, Winston Churchill, and Pope Paul VI, and as the sweptback 707 wings swooped high over the dark craggy mass of West Virginia, where Senator John F. Kennedy had nailed down the Democratic nomination nearly four years before, the eight-year-old daughter of K. O. Mbadiwe, Nigeria's Minister of State, was reciting Kennedy's entire inaugural address to him from memory (he slumped, in tears), and Mayor Willy Brandt was asking his burghers to light candles in their windows that evening. The Berliners did more. '*Ich bin ein Berliner*,' Kennedy had told them, and they remembered. Down the narrow streets wound dense formations of youth holding blazing torches high against the night.

That was reflexive, and its spontaneity was moving. In Washington something else was required: competence and calm judgment. Some men were incapable of it. On the Constitution Avenue side of the Justice Department Barney Ross sat in a stupor. Over an hour passed. Then he roused himself and called his home in Bethesda. His sixteen-year-old daughter answered, sobbing; the family had been trying to reach him, she said, but all the telephones seemed to have broken down at once. They wanted him with them. He mumbled that he understood, sat immobile for another hour, took the elevator to the street, bought a newspaper, read every story carefully, and boarded a No. 32 bus. All the way home he kept remembering that other ride twenty years before, when Lieutenant Kennedy had brought him through the Japanese lines to safety. But most key individuals and institutions stood the strain well. The Watch Committee was alert. The Pentagon was ready. The subcabinet was engrossed in its tasks. The President's burial site had not yet been selected, but on a hunch Superintendent Jack Metzler of Arlington National Cemetery called for his file on state funerals—the most recent had been for the Unknown Soldiers of World War II and Korea. At Fort McNair the Military District of Washington was also alert, calling in police, State Department, and Navy liaison officers, though MDW's high state of efficiency was largely luck. Herbert Hoover had been ill, and on September 9 a command post exercise (CPX) had guaranteed readiness in the event of his sudden death.[7]

Angie Biddle Duke, Chief of Protocol, was performing well. The crux of his difficulty, and that of everyone in the upper echelons of government, was that he didn't know to whom they were all answerable. The Presidency is a very personal office. From a distance it tends to merge with the entire Executive Branch; its powers seem to be divided among the faceless members of a team. In crises this comforts those who feel that anonymity suggests impersonal precision. They delude themselves. The most vivid perception of those who have been close to a Chief Executive is of the man's solitude. It cannot be otherwise. He and his understudy are the sole men for whom we all vote; without a President there could be no United States. On Friday Duke knew only that the President was dead. He hadn't thought beyond that and didn't even know whom to talk to. Legally the men in power were the former Vice President's aides, but they themselves didn't want that. Indeed, they weren't prepared for it. George Reedy called Walter Jenkins, who suggested they meet in Jack McNally's White House office. Reedy and Willie Day Taylor of Johnson's staff drove down Pennsylvania Avenue in Johnson's white Lincoln. They didn't know where to park, so Willie Day continued on to the Cathedral to look after Lucy Baines Johnson. Inside the mansion, Reedy realized that he had no idea where McNally's office was. In the west basement he asked directions and was led to the East Wing, where he found Jenkins in a meeting of Kennedy aides. The two of them sat in silence. Reedy was conscious of 'some strain between the two groups, the Kennedy group and the Johnson group. . . . Walter and I felt like intruders. We had the authority, I guess, but we lacked the know-how. In practice we ratified the decisions made by Kennedy men.'

The technicians (broadly interpreted, the term may include most members of the sub-cabinet) were adroit because they were following predetermined patterns of behaviour. If you were accustomed to plugging a switchboard or planning funerals—or calculating foreign exchange rates—you instinctively picked up the thread of habit. Those who were thrust into new situations were far likelier to falter or, in some cases, to turn their backs. They had been struck, said John McCormack, 'by a thunderbolt out of a clear sky'. McCormack

[7] In Europe anti-American journalists seized upon the obvious readiness of the soldiers who were to parade in Monday's funeral to charge that Secretary McNamara had been rehearsing troops for the funeral before the assassination.

was among those who turned away. Throughout 1964 his refusal to weigh proposals to alter the law of succession was universally interpreted as a token of ambition. Since Johnson's death would make him President, his angry dismissal of such discussions as 'indecent' were given but one interpretation; pundits inferred that he was brooding over that single heartbeat. The truth was 180 degrees the other way. He not only wasn't brooding; he couldn't even bring himself to think of it. The prospect, to McCormack, was literally unbearable. The Speaker was fully aware of his age and his limitations. Each morning and each evening in the Hotel Washington he repeated a simple prayer for Johnson's health: 'May the Lord protect and direct him.' That was the best he could do. He was incapable of facing the fact that should prayer fail Congressional legislation would make him the thirty-seventh President. On the afternoon of November 2, as Aircraft 26000 approached mid-flight, a detail of Secret Service men presented themselves at the door of the Washington Hotel's Suite 620. They never crossed the threshold. The Speaker coldly informed the special Agent in Charge that 'The Capitol provides me with all the protection I need. This is an intolerable intrusion in my private life and Mrs McCormack's, and I won't have it.'[8]

When the Georgetown switchboard's last light winked on, resuming normal service, nine AT & T jets were in the air rushing emergency units from San Francisco, Milwaukee, Philadelphia, Harrisburg, Norfolk, New York, Cincinnati, Huntington, and Charleston; some had taken off before the Presidential aircraft left Dallas, and boosters from nearby Baltimore were already being feverishly installed. At that moment (4.15 p.m. EST), as Angel traversed the Confederate-grey oxbow of the Arkansas River three miles north of Pine Bluff, Lyndon Johnson asked Sergeant Ayres to connect him with President Kennedy's mother by radio patch. Castle put the Sergeant through to the compound and Rose Kennedy was summoned from her lawn to the phone. She answered, 'Hello?'

Ayres started to say, 'The President wants to speak to you,' and checked himself. Instead he said, 'Mr Johnson wants to speak to you,' and handed the receiver to him.

Lady Bird, studying her husband's face, realized that this was the most difficult call of his life. Muffling the instrument with his big

[8] And he didn't. When Johnson reached Washington McCormack insisted that the Secret Service must discontinue all interest in him at once. Because of the Speaker's political power his extraordinary demand was honoured that Friday. Thus the man next in line was without security protection for fourteen months. It was one of the best-kept secrets in the government. Those who knew of it did not even mention it to one another until Hubert Humphrey had been sworn in.

hand, he whispered, 'What can I say to her?' Then he removed his hand and said, 'I wish to God there was something I could do.'

Rose Kennedy replied, 'We know how much you loved Jack and how Jack loved you.'

'Here's Lady Bird,' said the President. To Liz Carpenter it seemed that he was thrusting the stateroom phone at his wife 'like a hot potato'.

'Oh, Mrs Kennedy,' the new First Lady began and paused. Dropping her voice, she said—it was precisely the right thing to say to a mother—'We must all realize how fortunate the country was to have your son as long as it did.'

'Thank you, Lady Bird,' Rose said.

Joe Ayres then set up a second patch, and both Johnsons talked to Nellie Connally at Parkland. Listening to their end, Cliff Carter gathered that Nellie was in good spirits. Apparently her husband was recovering. Cliff was astounded. From what the emergency area nurse had told him he had assumed that by now the Governor would be dead.[9]

Running ahead of the wind, Angel revved up to 635 mph; Aircraft 86972 passed the 150th meridian; the AT & T's improvised fleet approached the capital with its tons of now useless equipment; Red Fay crossed the Middle West; Lieutenant Sam Bird's helicopter fluttered over Anacostia Flats; and Senator Edward Kennedy and Eunice Shriver, the two principals who had left the capital when everyone else was converging on it, reached Otis Air Force Base on Cape Cod. They were met by Jack Dempsey, an old friend. The family chauffeur drove them to Hyannis Port.

Meanwhile Joseph P. Kennedy had awakened from his nap, and Ann Gargan had gone in to tell him of his son's death. He had been surprised to see her; he thought she had left for Detroit. Standing at the foot of his bed, she had begun, 'As you see, I haven't left. There's been an accident. . . .'

She bit her lip. Nurse Rita Dallas had just entered and was tugging at her elbow. Rose had just told Rita, 'If anything happens to him, I couldn't stand it. Tell Ann to wait till one of the boys gets back.' In the hall the nurse had whispered this message to Ann.

[9] That Friday Lyndon Johnson did not know that John Kennedy had ordered the taping of all Angel conversations while the plane was in flight. On April 21, 1964, this writer learned that the Love-to-Andrews tape still existed. Since security was not involved, it was first thought that a complete transcript of it would serve as a useful appendix to this book. Presidential consent was withheld, however. On May 5, 1965, the author was permitted to read an edited transcript at the White House. Doubtless the tape will be available to future historians.

Returning to her uncle, the girl said lamely, 'My car got banged up—that was the accident. That's why I can't go. So I'm staying.' The old Ambassador had squinted at her with what, to her, had seemed a distinctly suspicious look.

The burden of dealing with his parents therefore fell upon the junior Senator from Massachusetts. Arriving, he crossed to the grand piano downstairs and stood, arms akimbo, intently examining the keyboard. He was still there when Ann's brother Joe bounded in. He was breathless; he had just broken every speed record between Boston and Hyannis. Ted studied him absently and murmured, 'Hi, Joey.' Joe swallowed. 'Hi. Teddy.'

The President's mother had just finished talking to Air Force One; she wanted to walk again. Rose, Eunice, and the two men donned heavy sweaters and strolled along the beach to the Squaw Island causeway and back. A brisk gale was whipping around the white-shingled houses and lashing the weathered wooden fences and green hedges that separated the manicured Kennedy lawns. The strollers flapped their arms for warmth. Rose said obliquely, 'Joey, you should read more.' He nodded. 'Yes, Aunt Rose.' 'Read Marlborough, Fox, and Burke,' she persisted. The wind tore at them, and she added, 'Like Jack.' That was it: Now there could be no dodging of the central issue, and they plunged into a discussion of where the burial should be.

The consensus was Boston. Back at the big house Ted called Cardinal Cushing. The Cardinal vetoed Brookline as unsuitable. The narrow streets made traffic there congested enough as it was, and a Presidential funeral would create an impossible jam. Either His Eminence or a member of his staff—several were on the line, and he had no later recollection of this—suggested a tomb in the centre of Boston Common. The Senator left the matter open. He replaced the receiver, and his mother asked his advice about her own plans. Should she pack for Washington? 'Stay here till Dad's been told,' he suggested. That brought up the dreaded question of when he should be told. 'Wait till tomorrow morning,' she begged. 'Give him one more night.'

It wasn't easy. Joe Kennedy customarily watched television when he awoke from his nap, and the networks were carrying nothing except assassination news. He couldn't talk, and he wasn't in the mood to read. Upstairs Ann had been evasively insisting that she couldn't get any channel. She had played his favourite phonograph records, and during the long Squaw Island walk Rita Dallas had set up a 16-millimetre movie for him in the basement theatre. He squirmed, restless. The nurse gave him a milk shake with sedation in it, but the sedative proved as ineffective as the liquor on the

Presidential aircraft; the Ambassador was wide awake and vigilant. Back in his bedroom he fidgeted, and when Ted, Eunice, and Joe entered he looked up expectantly.

'Hi, Dad,' the Senator said carelessly. 'I had to give a speech in Boston, so I thought I'd say hello.'

The absurdity was growing. Joe Kennedy was old and afflicted, but behind his withered features he remained canny. His children were putting on a charade, and he seemed to know it. Ted and Eunice engaged in animated argument while an early supper was served. Their father thrust his plate aside and gestured at the television set.

Ted turned his back to the bed and disconnected it. 'It doesn't work, Dad.'

The Ambassador's eyebrows rose owlishly. He pointed accusingly at the dangling cord. Desperate, Ted went to his knees. He obediently inserted the cord in the wall socket, and then, in the twenty seconds before the sound could warm up, he ripped the wires from the back of the set.

He spread his hands. 'Still no good. We'll fix it in the morning.'

Rita Dallas came in with a glass of milk. She had fortified it with another, more powerful opiate. Joe sipped it slowly, running quizzical eyes over them. By this time they had all reached a peculiar understanding. Obviously he knew that something momentous had happened; he was waiting to be told what. They knew he knew, but because of Ted's commitment to his mother nothing could be said until tomorrow. So Ted and Eunice exchanged droll comments while their hearts were aching and their father sprawled in his lair of rumpled sheeting, a wary spectator. Finally the drug took hold. The parchment lids drooped. He fought to raise his lashes, twisted this way and that, and then capitulated, turning his drawn face into the pillows.

While Joseph P. Kennedy had awakened from one nap his most famous grandson had roused from another. The President's son was struggling to swing his leg over the side of his crib in the blue bedroom on the second floor of the executive mansion. Caroline had wakened him. Maude Shaw had changed her to pyjamas and put her in her yellow room next door, hoping she, too would sleep. It hadn't worked. She was punching the mattress and screaming for Agatha. Miss Shaw now realized that the separation of the two first-graders had been a mistake. Ethel Kennedy, Mrs Auchincloss, and Jacqueline Hirsch, the French teacher, had offered to shelter the children, but in the absence of instructions from their mother the nurse wasn't budging. She did decide to reunite the two girls. She telephoned Liz

Pozen. Liz said at once, 'I'll let Agatha come to the White House to keep Caroline company. I'll bring her right away.'

'No, I'll send a White House car for her,' said Miss Shaw.

That was a mistake. On any other day it would have been quicker, but she hadn't counted on today's bizarre traffic. Liz could have made a one-way trip. The chauffeur, starting from the Twenty-second Street garage, faced a round trip. Moreover, the driver was unaccountably obtuse. Parking outside the Pozen house, he left his commercial radio blaring. The whole neighbourhood could hear it. Liz scampered out, indignant, and even then he couldn't see why it was important that Agatha should not know of the assassination; he complied grudgingly.

Back at the mansion the Presidential apartment was almost deserted. Apart from John's lusty shouts there was no sound. Miss Shaw was the only adult upstairs. Charles Fincklin and his fellow servants couldn't bear to face anyone in the family, which, to them, included the children's nurse. Ben and Toni Bradlee were the first friends to arrive. They came—after the usual parking problems—at the suggestion of Nancy Tuckerman, who begged Toni to 'Send off Jackie's mother.' Toni replied, 'I can't do that to Mums.' Nor could she. Nancy's concern was understandable. Mrs Auchincloss was emotive, as she herself was the first to admit. Nevertheless she was the President's mother-in-law. They would simply have to wait, hope, and cope.

Agatha was delivered at the South Portico at 3.30 p.m. Her father embraced her, took her upstairs, and sprawled in a chair, limp with relief. Caroline was appeased, and the two girls began to play in the oval study. John, however, was now fully awake. His leg wasn't quite long enough to span the slatted crib side. He attempted to vault over it, failed, and bellowed louder.

In presenting his christening cup, the Irish Ambassador had read a poem:

. . . When the storms break for him
Make the trees shake for him
Their blossoms down;
And in the night that he is troubled
May a friend wake for him . . .

In the broad central hall a friend stirred. Hearing the calls from the blue bedroom, Bill Pozen crossed and turned the knob.

'Hello, John,' he said gently.

'Hello, Mr Pozen!' John held up his arms and crowed.

Pozen carried the boy to Miss Shaw and went downstairs. He decided that he shouldn't stay with the children; he wasn't that close to the First Family. But Ben Bradlee was. Ben had been two years behind Kennedy at Harvard. He knew John and Caroline well, and although he had been unable to carry Caroline lately—like the President, he suffered from a bad back—that didn't matter; she was busy with Agatha. So he played with the boy. Lying on the floor beside him, he marched his fingers up and down the rug, entertained him with stories about a three-year-old boy named John who had great adventures, and watched as the President's son proudly showed the salute Dave Powers had taught him. John was an amusing saluter. His parade-ground stance had always delighted his mother. He would stand at exaggerated attention, chest puffed out and the sturdy legs rigid, his face tense with solemnity. Then his right fingers would stiffen and he would begin his swing. Somehow he always missed. If he were wearing a hat, he would knock it off; just as frequently he struck his nose. This afternoon he was especially diverting. Nobody smiled.

Nancy, Toni, and Miss Shaw watched from the sofas beneath the muted mantel clock. The nurse kept squeezing her hands. 'I haven't the heart to tell them,' she kept whispering. 'I can't do it.' Toni distributed bubble gum among the children. She shouldn't do it, she thought; it wasn't good for their teeth. But gum was the only thing in her purse they could possibly want, and she had to give them something. Pleased, they champed away, John listening to Ben's stories and pausing from time to time to smite his nose, Agatha earnestly gossiping over dolls, and Caroline listening. All four adults thought the President's daughter exceptionally withdrawn. For long periods she was completely silent. Once, however, she spoke up clearly. Agatha had been talking about her nurse, Ann Connally, an Irishwoman. Caroline's eyes turned dream-like. Peering over her playmate's shoulder, she said, 'A long time ago my father's people came from Ireland because there was nothing to eat. They all had to crowd on a big boat because you couldn't eat the potatoes.'

Abruptly the stillness of the room was ruptured by the whirl of rotors. A brown Army helicopter was taking off from the mansion's South Lawn. John left Ben, Caroline left Agatha. The President's children raced to the windows. 'That's Mommie and Daddy!' they shouted gleefully. 'Mommie and Daddy are coming home!' John swung up his arm, grazing his right cheek, and beamed at Ben. He said, 'Daddy's here!'

Ben felt like a criminal. In desperation he said, 'Daddy will be back later.'

The three groups resumed their places: the man with the boy, the six-year-old girls crouched over their dolls, the women on the divans. Then there was another fluttering; a second chopper was departing, hovering over the Rose Garden like a gigantic insect.

'*There* they are! Mommie and Daddy are home!' Caroline and John cried in chorus.

Ben took his wife aside. He said grimly, 'I'm going to tell those children.'

'No, you aren't,' she said. 'You don't have the right.'

Below, the tumult grew: a third helicopter, a fourth, a fifth. 'It was ghastly,' Nancy remembered afterwards, and Ben would never forget 'those bloody great choppers, one after another, drowning everything out. The evening,' he said later, 'grew progressively worse.' There had never been anything like this fleet of rotors before. No one came upstairs to explain, and the adults were baffled. After a while Caroline also grew perplexed. 'Why are there so many?' she asked. They turned away: they could only shrug and avoid her inquiring eyes. But John never abandoned hope. Each time he fled tirelessly down the long rug, piping, 'Here they come! Here they come!'

It was five o'clock. Darkness had gathered, yet no one reached for a switch. Caroline stopped speaking altogether. In utter hopelessness the nurse, Nancy, and the Bradlees waited for something to happen. Something did: the white princess telephone by the fireplace purred. Miss Shaw answered. It was Bob Foster, downstairs at Secret Service Station F-5. He had just received a coded message from the plane. Clint Hill had instructions for Foster and Tom Wells. Lace wanted Lyric and Lark taken to Hamlet, the Auchincloss home, before Angel reached Acrobat. The agents at F-5 had no way of knowing that Clint and Ken O'Donnell had reached this decision on their own. Foster and Wells did remark to one another that it seemed unlike Mrs Kennedy, and it was; she had always remembered how, when she was a girl in Central Park, the presence of a Secret Service man had made Kate Roosevelt uncomfortable, different, and lonely, and she had been determined to mitigate that sense of isolation in her own children. Clint, however, had convinced himself that she would want them in a secluded place. O'Donnell had agreed, and he had also agreed that mentioning the move to her would be unwise. Had the call come from any other agent, the kiddie detail would have disregarded it, but Clint was Lace's agent; if he said it, it must be so. Foster told Miss Shaw to pack.

Ordinarily the Secret Service was as precise about time as Colonel Swindal. This time a muddle arose over that, too. The two men at F-5 were under the impression that they had just ten minutes in which to act—that Mrs Kennedy and the coffin would arrive at the mansion within a quarter-hour. John and Caroline were still in their nap clothes. Miss Shaw had to change them and quickly pack an overnight bag. Meantime Foster and Wells were organizing transportation. Four hours had now passed since the assassination without fresh developments, and the possibility of a co-ordinated conspiracy was steadily diminishing. Nevertheless they had to remain on full alert. Taking the children from the sanctuary of the mansion was clearly hazardous. They checked their .38 calibre side arms, packed a twelve-inch shotgun in a case, and laid the case on the front seat of Well's Ford. Foster put Miss Shaw and the children in a Country Squire station wagon; the Ford followed. Before turning on the ignition, Wells unlatched the case to make certain the shotgun's pistol grip would be within quick reach. At 5.33 p.m. they glided behind the EOB for the eleven-minute drive to Mrs Auchincloss' house.

But Mrs Auchincloss, unaware of the signal from Clint, was en route to the White House with her husband. And the ten-minute estimate was a fantastic error. At that moment the Presidential aircraft was above the Guyandot River, over three hundred miles to the west. Swindal had slowed to cruise speed. He wanted to be sure he didn't land early. He had just been told that a large delegation was gathering at Andrews.

That was what the helicopter fleet had been all about. The sub-cabinet, the Supreme Court, and the Congressional leadership were arriving at the airport in relays. Some were being ferried by chopper and some by limousine, and all were going against the advice of Robert Kennedy. At 4.30 p.m. the Attorney General had been on the telephone with Sargent Shriver, discussing how the President's body should be moved from Andrews. Shriver favoured a helicopter; a chopper would avoid curious crowds in downtown Washington, which, he pointed out, would be especially distressing for the widow. Bob said, 'Have both things ready and she can decide.' Then Shriver called again. Everybody wanted to go to Andrews, he reported; they were discussing which officials had priority. Kennedy was appalled. He didn't think anybody should be there except himself, McNamara, and General Taylor. The prospect of a crowd hadn't occurred to him, and he said, 'I don't think it's a very good idea. It's unnecessary.'

Consternation at the White House. Arthur Goldberg came on the line.

'Bob, this is not right. This is something more than personal. This is the President of the United States. I think we should all go.'

'The last thing Jackie wants to see is a lot of people.'

'We owe this gesture to the President—and even to her. It can't be private. Newsmen will be there in any event, and so will the diplomatic corps. How will it look if only foreigners are there—no Americans?'

Silence. Then: 'If you want to go, go. I'm not going to get into an argument about it.'

Unknown to him, there had already been a heated argument about it at the mansion. Angie Duke, as the official arbiter of protocol, had first ruled that no one should go to Andrews. That word was passed, and immediately there were repercussions. Harriman characteristically decided to ignore it. Humphrey phoned Duke from the East Wing. 'The hell with you,' he said. 'I'm going to the airport.' Dungan thought Jenkins, Reedy, and those who had worked with Kennedy had to be there. Ted Sorensen was undecided over the propriety of going, but if the others went, he would too. Bundy pointed out that he had to be at the ramp; Clifton had called him from the plane and told him the new President wanted him there. Duke had begun to have second thoughts. He realized that Goldberg was right; you couldn't stop the ambassadors. So he reversed himself.

By now Fairfax County police had surrounded Hickory Hill. The press was staying beyond their lines. The children were subdued, but Dave Hackett had contrived to engage them in a game; he lay beside the jungle gym, his eyes shut, and let them creep up on him. At twilight the Attorney General made a final call to McNamara, changed his shirt once more, and set out for the Pentagon with Ed Guthman. On the front lawn Nicole Alphand was thinking of Jacqueline Kennedy. A refrain was running through her mind: *Her husband, the father of her children, her President—three losses in one for her*. As Kennedy and Guthman drove off Nicole noticed that the day, which had been beautiful, was touched by a sudden chill. Taking Ethel by the arm, she led her inside.

In the car with Guthman Robert Kennedy talked about every aspect of the disaster except one—his own incalculable loss and shattered career. He discussed the enormity of the tragedy, the impact on Jackie, the blow to his parents, and the country's uncertain future. The liberal convictions of Attorney General Kennedy, like those of President Kennedy, were far more deeply held than most liberals had suspected, and they surfaced during the drive. 'People just don't realize how conservative Lyndon really is,' he said as they rode up in the Secretary of Defence's private elevator. 'There are going to be a lot of changes.'

McNamara greeted them in shirt sleeves. The two Cabinet members gripped hands in a long, tight handshake, and the Secretary slipped on a coat. Taylor joined them—another silent greeting—and Guthman remained in the E Ring while they walked out to the Pentagon's south helipad and flew across the Potomac to Andrews. There was no conversation in the helicopter. The three passengers were men of identical, anthracite temperament. They didn't have to lean on others; they were strong enough to lean on themselves. What each really wanted was to be alone, and despite their friendship they separated at the airport. In Taylor's words, he 'wandered about aimlessly, thinking gloomy thoughts'. There was one brief exchange between Kennedy and McNamara. The Attorney General suggested that the Secretary board 26000 with him when it landed. McNamara shook his head. 'It's not my place to do that, Bob,' he said gently. 'I'm not a member of the family.' Then he walked away, seeking asylum in shadows.

Air Force One was thirty minutes away, manoeuvring over the Shenandoah, as Bob Kennedy looked out across the plain of oil-stained concrete. Andrews had never been an attractive base. The hangars were exceptionally squat, the bulbous red and white water towers were ungainly, the grass by the wire fence was unmowed crabgrass. Most of the field was now cloaked by night, but Kennedy glimpsed a group of television cameramen by the MATS gate. He resolved to avoid them. Yet he was equally determined to be at Jackie's side the instant the plane stopped rolling. Casting about, he saw a deserted Air Force truck and vaulted over the tailgate. Sitting in almost total darkness among pieces of unfamiliar gear, he remembered the last time he had been here. It had been at noon on Saturday, October 20, 1962. The missile crisis had just begun; U-2 reconnaissance had confirmed the presence of Russian sites in Cuba, and the President, alerted by phone, had flown home from Chicago on the pretext that he was suffering from a cold. The Attorney General had stood on this same barren stretch, waiting for his brother. But that had been morning. Now he was hiding in the back of a truck, and it was night.

To those who had known President Kennedy intimately everything, even inanimate objects, seemed to kindle memories of him. Sargent Shriver, arriving at the mansion, had hung his topcoat in Dr Travell's office and left it there while he saw Ted and Eunice off. When he returned it was gone. His thought was that theft was impossible in the White House. Doubtless a guard had put the coat in a closet. Later in the afternoon, when it developed that it really had been stolen, he began to fume. It was irreplaceable, superbly woven of charcoal grey cashmere, and it was less than three years old. Then he remembered with a pang—he had bought it for the inauguration.

He remembered. And then he forgot. As the family's representative-in-residence at the White House he had become wholly engrossed in details and decisions. Americans, accustomed to swift action, saw nothing remarkable in the announcement that the President would be buried Monday. Europeans who specialized in pomp were astonished. In London the Duke of Norfolk had been working on arrangements for Winston Churchill's state funeral since the early 1950's, and he had allocated a week for rehearsals once Churchill did succumb. After Kennedy's interment in Arlington the Duke repeatedly inquired of visitors from the United States, 'Three days—*how?*'

The answer lay partly in America's national temperament, partly in the fibre of the men who had gathered around Shriver and Ralph Dungan that Friday afternoon. They were not automatons. For an hour and a half after the first bulletins from Dallas they had been immobilized by grief. The group in McNally's office clustered ineffectually around Behn, listening in a stupor as he repeated reports from Kellerman and Hill. Most of their colleagues were down in the Situation Room, watching television on the room's wall-sized, Orwellian screen. The only aide then functioning at the peak of his proficiency was McGeorge Bundy.

At three o'clock Washington time, when President Johnson was calling Robert Kennedy for the first time, McNally saw Shriver returning from the helicopter take-off. He approached him, told him of the gathering in the East Wing, and suggested that he join it. Shriver shook his head. 'I'll use Ralph's office,' he said. That was the beginning of the metamorphosis. Dungan brooded behind his desk, sucking on an unlit pipe; Sarge sat in front on a straight-backed chair. Between them they reached the first funeral decisions during the next two hours. They were never alone. One of their fellow planners described the meeting—which was to continue nonstop through three successive nights—as 'Jack's last campaign'. It was a lot like a campaign; a man almost had to be a political veteran to function in it. The room filled up quickly Friday. At one point the standees included Mac Bundy, Ted Sorensen, Jerry Behn, Walter Jenkins, George Reedy, Jack McNally, Fred Holborn, Taz Shepard, Averell Harriman, Angie Duke, Bill Walton, Ted Reardon, Dick Goodwin, Arthur Schlesinger, Ken Galbraith, Kay Graham, Jerry Bruno, Dr Joseph English, Dean Markham, Chief Stover of the White House Police, Monsignor Cartwright of St Matthew's Cathedral, and Lieutenant Colonel Paul Miller, MDW's short, spare ceremonies officer. It was difficult to breathe; secretaries would eavesdrop on conversations and relay the gist of them to other secretaries.

The right of several individuals to be there was clearly marginal.

Galbraith, for example, was a former member of the administration. Kay Graham had never belonged to it. And Bruno was simply trying to find out what was going on. As the man who had advanced Texas, he had been monitoring the progress of the motorcade over the telephone from his office at the Democratic National Committee. Shortly after 12.30 the Signal Corps operator had broken in to say, 'Somebody's been shot—I've got to cut you off.' Since then he had grasped the essential facts, but he was anxious for details. He wasn't learning much—short and stubby, he couldn't even see over Galbraith's shoulders by leaping in the air—and he was one of the first to be motioned out.

It was Shriver's special talent to find a job for every volunteer. Several men were sent off to draw up separate lists of the President's friends; Adlai Stevenson, when he arrived later, was asked his views on protocol. The key advisers there were Angie Duke, who had brought State's book on the Roosevelt Funeral, and Colonel Miller. At 3.42 p.m. Shriver and Dungan knew that Aircraft 26000's destination would be Andrews; by 4.30 they had begun specifying who should go to the airport and Duke was dispatching a protocol officer to handle foreign diplomats there. Then they held the first tentative deliberations on the burial itself. Colonel Miller explained that state funerals are reserved for Presidents, Presidents-elect, and anyone designated by a President.[10] The chief difference between them and other official funerals is lying in state, and Miller had drawn up plans for this in both the mansion's East Room and the Capitol's great rotunda. In the event of a Boston burial, he said, three possible departures had been laid out: 'rail, air, and destroyer'. The Navy, he added, was already holding a destroyer in readiness. It remained on stand-by throughout the next day, though from the tempo of the meeting Miller had already concluded that a sea voyage was unlikely; if President Kennedy were taken to Massachusetts, it would probably be by air. The prospects of any long-distance movement appeared dim to the Colonel, however, and he was right. Unlike his wife, Shriver never seriously considered Boston. Independently of Mrs Kennedy he was focusing on Arlington. Shortly after 5.30, at about the time Robert Kennedy found haven in the truck at Andrews Field. Shriver phoned Metzler to ask whether there was any rule prohibiting 'a Catholic burial in a national cemetery or the burial of children'. The superintendent answered, 'Negative to both. We have Catholic ceremonies almost every day,

[10] All the five-star generals and admirals have been so designated and notified. Some, like the late Douglas MacArthur, displayed a keen interest in the arrangements. Only two have declined a state funeral, Omar Bradley and Chester Nimitz.

and minor children are with their parents.' With this call Metzler was convinced that his hunch was justified, and he proceeded on the assumption that Arlington would be chosen.

That was a good guess. There were bad guesses, too. Clint Hill and Ken O'Donnell weren't the only men to misinterpret Jacqueline Kennedy's mood during those first hours. Shriver, Dungan, and Metzler, for example, were sure she would want the funeral mass held in the Shrine of the Immaculate Conception, Washington's largest and most prestigious Roman Catholic church. They erred; she was vehemently against it. They were also guilty of one conspicuous oversight. Captain R. O. Canada, Jr., Bethesda's commanding officer, wasn't informed of the role his hospital would play. And Godfrey McHugh's tart order for an ambulance had been ignored. Canada did send one to Andrews, but that was sheer chance. Because Lyndon Johnson had served in the Navy, he had been Canada's patient after his massive heart attack on July 2, 1955; the ambulance was dispatched against the possibility that the new President might be stricken again during the flight. The Captain learned from his office television set that it would carry President Kennedy.

The White House had talked to Canada's staff about another matter which was almost unknown at the time, even among members of the Kennedy family. One would have thought that Vernon Oneal would be the last undertaker to see the President's body—that once it had been landed it would become the sole responsibility of the government. Not so. The funeral industry had attained a kind of metapsychic domination over all who dealt with death. They had even adopted its jargon; Metzler, Miller, and the doctors at Bethesda referred to 'the remains', not 'the body', and Fort Myer's Old Guard had abandoned the more dignified 'pallbearers' for 'casket team'. All of them had been seduced by the curious myth that only licensed morticians could prepare 'the remains' for burial. It was untrue, and there should have been no undertaker in Washington. But everyone at a responsible position at Arlington, MDW, Fort Myer, and Bethesda was under the impression that there had to be one. Indeed, so unanimous were they that the issue would never have arisen had it not been for the publication of Jessica Mitford's *The American Way of Death* six months earlier. Robert Kennedy had read Miss Mitford's carefully documented exposé of the gouging of bereaved relatives, and so had Dr Joseph English, the Peace Corps psychiatrist who stood at Sargent Shriver's elbow Friday afternoon.

Among the immediate concerns in Dungan's office had been questions of who would receive the body, whether or not an autopsy would be held, and, if so, where it would be performed. Dr Burkley solved these by relaying Mrs Kennedy's instructions to Taz Shepard. Captain Canada was in the dark, but his staff wasn't; Bethesda was getting ready. Then Colonel Miller told Shriver that a private funeral home would be necessary.

Shriver bridled. 'Why? Why can't the government do it?'

'There are precedents,' said the Colonel, visibly disturbed. 'It has to be private. The military isn't equipped to prepare the remains.'

Shriver hesitated. He asked Miller to recommend an undertaker. The Colonel shook his head.

'Why not?' Sarge demanded.

'I'd be offending the other sixty-seven morticians,' the Colonel said. Then, after an awkward pause, he said, 'Gawler's.'

'Why Gawler's?'

'It's among the best. It's been used in other official funerals.'

Someone suggested that everything could be done at Bethesda. Shriver stared at Miller. 'I thought you said the military couldn't do it.'

Miller squirmed. Taz Shepard said to him, 'Paul, let's check on another line.' They did, and Shepard reported back to the meeting, 'Bethesda says they can do the embalming, but not preparing the remains.'

'Colonel, I guess you feel a lot better,' Shriver said.

'I sure do,' said Miller, and at 4.25 he alerted the funeral home.

In his absence, however, Dr English reported to Shriver that he had made inquiries of his own and discovered that the first suggestion had been correct; there was no need to offend any of the morticians or involve them in any way. 'Cancel the arrangements that have been made,' Shriver snapped. He and English thought this had been done. Nine months later they were startled to learn that they had been wrong—that the funeral home had, in the words of one of its executives, 'cosmetized, clothed, and casketed the remains'.

Colonel Miller's alert had been received by Bill Gawler, a cousin of Joe and the head of the firm. Bill entered it on his 'first call sheet' and spread the word. The funeral home felt deeply honoured. Within an hour the house—a huge red brick edifice on Wisconsin Avenue—was occupied by a detail of troops in dress blues. The soldiers were members of the Old Guard's ceremonial outfit. They called themselves the Death Watch, because in state funerals they took up positions at the corners of the coffin. On watch, they stood at rigid attention; approaching and leaving the bier they moved in double-slow cadence. By 5.30 p.m. they were rehearsing in what the funeral home advertised as its 'French', 'Green', and 'Georgian' rooms.

The firm had been established in 1850 on Pennsylvania Avenue, just a block from the White House, in 1962 it had moved to this new emporium. Colonel Miller's information about it was correct. Gawler's belonged to the undertaking aristocracy. Its eminent clients had included President Taft, John Foster Dulles, and James Forrestal, and it handled the Washington arrangements for Franklin Roosevelt's funeral. It was especially favoured by officers of high rank and civilians of wealth; some tourists even included 'the viewing hours at Gawler's' on their capital itineraries. Joseph H. Gawler, the dignified director of the establishment, and Vernon B. Oneal, the hustling Texan, were as far apart as two men in the same business could be. But it *was* the same business, and in 1963, when the young President had been leading a vigorous crusade to erase colour bars, it had remained the most segregated business in the country. 'I guess they feel more comfortable among their own people,' a Forest Lawn salesman explained to Jessica Mitford, conceding why there were no Negroes in his cemetery. 'Actually, the coloured funeral directors would prefer not to have us bury them,' a Gawler's executive told this writer. The blunt truth was that during the 113 years of its history the firm which was to act as President Kennedy's mortician had never buried a Negro.

As the Death Watch went through its solemn ballet on Wisconsin Avenue, Lieutenant Sam Bird was smoothly integrating the armed forces at Andrews Field. Debarking from his helicopter, the Lieutenant had discovered that the Air Force had already posted a ceremonial cordon. He put his own men inside it. Then the Air Force sent a detail of pallbearers. Bird estimated each man's physical strength and set up two teams, half Air Force, half Army. Marine, Navy, and Coast Guard contingents arrived. Fortunately, all were enlisted men. Because he was the only officer present, the Lieutenant's authority was unchallenged. He continued to form and reform his two teams until each had at least one soldier, sailor, Marine, airman, and Coast Guardsman. The men left over were hastily placed in ranks between the Presidential aircraft's parking space, the Kennedy helicopter, and the helicopter Lyndon Johnson would board.

Hurry up and wait: it was routine to the enlisted men. At the MATS terminal it applied equally to the Supreme Court, subcabinet, Congressional leadership, and diplomats. All were victims of the jet age. They had been raised in a more leisurely period, when men had been granted time to put their emotions in order. As children they had read of the assassination of Abraham Lincoln, and the parallel was very much on their minds that evening. But Lincoln's funeral train had moved across the countryside at a stately pace. Angel's four mighty Pratt-Whitney engines were bringing

John Kennedy home from Texas in 136 minutes. And no one could be sure that the estimated time of arrival was correct. As it turned out, they could have driven to Maryland with time to spare, but they weren't taking any chances, and so, as the President's children peered out eagerly from the second-floor windows, there had been an incessant scurrying around the helipad beside Caroline's tree house. Choppers were faster than cars; everybody had wanted a seat on one.

Most succeeded. Taz Shepard went with the Goldbergs, Ralph Dungan with Ted Reardon and Lee White, Sorensen with Jenkins and Reedy. Harriman, Fowler, and Celebrezze flew together; so did the Congressional leadership. Angie Duke was crowded out. He rode in a White House Mercury with Schlesinger. Two under secretaries slid over to give Galbraith a seat. Fred Holborn sat alone at the tail of the black motorcade; he had decided to go at the last minute. Four key men—Shriver, Goodwin, Markham, and Walton—remained behind with Colonel Miller, deep in the therapeutic work of planning the order of the parade. Later they were envied. No one was to cherish the memory of that night at Andrews. It was noisy with the incessant flap of the olive-drab rotors; the huge klieg lights glared; the moonlit cement apron had never seemed so white, or people so strange.

None of them, of course, was normal. Natural behaviour there would have been aberrant. Angie Duke stumbled up to the ambassadors, saw them waiting robot-like in a roped-off area, and shrank away without a word. Three of Dr John Walsh's woman patients passed him repeatedly. Each looked directly into his eyes without seeing him. Galbraith was under the impression that he had ridden here beside Under Secretary Roosevelt, one of his oldest friends. At the end of the half-hour drive he turned, started to say 'Frank', and saw that the man was Under Secretary Robert Roosa. Individuals stood alone, in trances: Chief Rowley of the Secret Service; the new Postmaster General, looking forsaken; Mac Bundy, intent, a dispatch case under his arm; Harriman, hollow-eyed and suddenly very old.

Though there were literally miles of room, Earl Warren, John McCormack, and Hale Boggs were bunched together protectively, in a kind of wedge; farther down the apron Senators Humphrey, Mansfield, Dirksen, and Kuchel had formed another such group, and from time to time Dirksen cast a wary eye about, his ruined face clay-white. Spectral figures appeared from nowhere, spoke a few words, and vanished. Taz Shepard was separately approached by the Secretary of Defence and the Chairman of the Joint Chiefs. Each muttered furtively that he must brief the new President on the satchel;

he nodded, and they disappeared. Ted Sorensen stared out across the field. He appeared to be straining to glimpse something in the void beyond the lights, though there was nothing there to see.

Between the wire fence and 26000's parking area there were approximately fifty dignitaries. The most conspicuous object in front of them was an ugly, bright yellow piece of machinery. Ted Clifton had specified a 'fork lift' for lowering the coffin here. That would have been small and practical. Instead, Andrews had wheeled out a monstrous truck lift, a roofed device mounted on greased hydraulic columns. The platform had been hoisted about twelve feet above the concrete, resting on double braces which formed a double X. Everything about the lift was wrong. The platform couldn't be lowered to the ground—the closest it could come was five feet—and there were no adequate steps. MATS called such trucks 'catering buses'. Ordinarily they were used to place hot meals aboard transport planes, and that was exactly what this one looked like. In the intermittent winking of the grey Pontiac ambulance's red emergency light those on the left could even read its number: '61 C 305'. Lieutenant Bird had stationed himself and his first team on the platform; his second team was ranged around the braces. They didn't help. The thing remained atrocious.

Behind the fence, unnoticed, three thousand people stood in the moist, chilly night. On any other flight they would have caught John Kennedy's eye, and even now, before his splendid plane appeared, the more august greeters would have been aware of them; they would have been murmuring excitedly among themselves, and agile youths would have been leaping high for a first glimpse of the Presidential seal. Tonight they were utterly quiet. Here a shoe shuffled, there an eyeglass glinted; a cigarette glowed, shrinking to its doom. That was all. Unentitled to helicopter seats or limousines, they had driven out to Suitland Parkway in their own cars, and afterwards they were to leave as silently as they had come. Yet their inconspicuous presence was far more significant than the conspicuously hideous yellow truck. They were the vanguard of the greatest throng ever to pay tribute to a martyred President, and they invested the ghastly scene with gentleness, dignity, and meaning, for they were what a President's life is all about.

During their ride here Schlesinger had said to Angie Duke, 'You know, the Radical Right has never been taken seriously in this country,' and Sorensen had told Jenkins and Reedy on their helicopter ride, 'I feel sorry for your position. I'll help as best I can. But I hope you don't mind if I don't think too much of the State of Texas.' Reedy said softly that he felt the same way. The conduct of the two Johnson aides was above reproach. They had been hit as hard as the Kennedy aides and showed it; Schlesinger reflected that if Lyndon Johnson could command the loyalty of men like Reedy and Jenkins, there must be more to him than he had thought. Bundy went farther. He was inclined to exculpate Dallas on the ground that 'one madman doesn't make a madhouse'.[11]

Front Royal, Manassas, Falls Church . . .

Over Dulles International Airport Jim Swindal knifed down through a thin overcast, and for the first time since leaving East Texas he saw land. The lights of metropolitan Washington loomed ahead; beyond lay Upper Marlboro and the dark reaches of the Chesapeake Bay. Crossing the Potomac, he lost altitude rapidly. The Tidal Basin became visible from the cockpit, then the massive square dome of the National Archives and, beneath the No. 1 engine pod, Capitol Hill. Swindal eased out his flaps and dive brakes and lowered his landing gear. The pilot's head was still throbbing, but he knew this would be the last time he would take the President down. He wanted it to be right.

Bolling, St Elizabeth's Hospital. They were gliding in over rural Maryland: Oxon Run, Silver Hill, Suitland, Morningside . . .

Lyndon Johnson was in the Presidential bedroom, shaving, combing his hair, and changing his shirt again. In the staff cabin corridor Clint Hill approached Roy Kellerman and said, 'She wants to see you.' Back in the tail compartment Dave Powers told Roy, 'Mrs Kennedy wants you agents who were with the President to carry him off, and she wants Greer to drive.' Knowing how the chauffeur was suffering, Kellerman was struck by the thoughtfulness of the gesture. Mrs Kennedy herself was speaking to Evelyn Lincoln, Mary Gallagher, Muggsy O'Leary, and George Thomas, who had also been summoned. 'I want you near the coffin,' she said to each, and to Godfrey McHugh she said, 'I want his friends to carry him down.' Ted Clifton came back to tell Ken O'Donnell, 'The Army is prepared to take the coffin off.' O'Donnell replied shortly, 'We'll take it off.'

Ken passed the word in the staff area that Mrs Kennedy wished to have those who had been closest to her husband accompany him upon debarkation. But there was a second President aboard, and it does seem clear that everyone had priority over the new Chief Executive, including stewards. Fifteen people were wedged into the tiny corridor. Kilduff saw that the President was left standing there in the stateroom.

[11] A slippery analogy. One criminal doesn't make a penitentiary either. Madhouses and prisons are the places to which men are committed *after* the fact.

The acting press secretary was humiliated. Later in the evening his embarrassment increased. At the EOB he discovered that Johnson continued to be annoyed and that he held Kilduff responsible. The new President was still brooding over the incident the following afternoon. After presiding over the Cabinet for the first time he confided to one of its members that he had 'real problems with the family'. According to this Secretary's notes, set down later that same day'

> He said that when the plane came in . . . [they] paid no attention to him whatsoever, that they took the body off the plane, put it in the car, took Mrs Kennedy along and departed, and only then did he leave the plane without any attention directed or any courtesy towards him, then the President of the United States. But he said he just turned the other cheek . . . he said, what can I do, I do not want to get into a fight with the family and the aura of Kennedy is important to all of us.

'Let's remember the happy things, not the sad things,' Jacqueline Kennedy said to Clint Hill as they taxied towards the MATS terminal. Colonel Swindal's landing had been a triumph. None of his passengers had known when they touched the ground. The crowd waiting by the chain fence had realized that arrival was imminent because they heard the whining jets. They couldn't see its silhouette, however; the klieg lights blinded them. At 6.03 p.m. these were abruptly cut off. The reason was commonplace. The pilot had to see his way. The effect was nevertheless dramatic: under the dim fragment of November moon the plane looked like a great grey phantom slowly creeping upon them from a quarter-mile away. They couldn't even hear it any more, because the Colonel had switched off three of his pods, and the fourth was drowned out by the warm-ups of two of the wasplike helicopters. Closer and closer the huge ghost crawled until Swindal, looking down, could identify two of the waiting men. Robert McNamara was facing him, looking peculiarly tall. Robert Kennedy had just left the sanctuary of his truck and was posed in a tense half-crouch, to spring aboard.

Swindal paused momentarily for the croucher. The eyes of the crowd were on the rear hatch, the President's. A ramp had been readied for the front entrance, and the Attorney General vaulted on it, unseen; he was pumping up the steps while it was still being rolled into place. Leaping in, he darted through the communications shack, the staff cabin, and the stateroom. Liz Carpenter, recognizing his gaunt features, reached out to pat his shoulder. He didn't notice her or the Johnsons—next day the President observed to one of his advisers that Kennedy hadn't spoken to him—because he was intent on reaching one person. 'I want to see Jackie,' Liz heard him mumble. In the tail compartment he slid behind and then beside Mrs Kennedy. 'Hi, Jackie,' he said quietly, putting an arm around her. 'I'm here.' Those around them started: his voice was exactly like his brother's. 'Oh, Bobby,' she breathed, and she thought how like Bobby this was; he was always there when you needed him.

The aircraft glided forward once again and parked. Outside the floodlights went up. Swindal and Hanson scooted down the ramp, stationed themselves under the port wing, and faced the rear door, saluting stiffly. The ponderous yellow lift was wheeled up. The door swung open, Larry O'Brien's round face peered out. The officials below saw the haggard profile of the Attorney General and were astonished; they hadn't known he had been in Dallas. He was holding the widow's fingers; her purse was dangling from her other hand. Presently they saw the stains on her. And then in the next moment Kellerman, Greer, O'Leary, Hill, and Landis manhandled the casket into place in front of the two Kennedys. The light fell full upon it, it glinted uglily. Theodore H. White yearned for 'a cry, a sob, a wail, any human sound'. Earl Warren saw 'that brave girl, with her husband's blood on her, and there was nothing I could do, nothing, *nothing*.' Taz Shepard saw the skirt; he looked up into her haunted eyes and felt a stone in his chest. Ted Reardon prayed to himself, *Jesus, Mary, and Joseph, I wish I hadn't come.* Yet all these were unspoken monologues. There wasn't a single voice. Speechless, they were incapable of taking their eyes off the dark red-bronze coffin. All afternoon they had been thinking about it; now it was here. And that made it irrevocable. Now they knew, now it was true.

Unable to follow Dr Burkley, Sergeant Ayres had been stranded in the corridor outside the bedroom midway between the Kennedy group and the Johnson group. Out of habit he stepped into the room for a final check. Crumpled in a corner lay the issue of the Dallas *News* which the President had reread that morning on the hop between Carswell and Love. During the wait for Sarah Hughes his widow had apparently touched it, for it was smeared with his blood. Ayres snatched it up and bunched it in his fists. Squeezing crablike past President Johnson, he bounded down the ramp and threw it away.

7

LACE

Atop the moving lift Lieutenant Sam Bird, approaching the coffin, raised his white-gloved hand in a salute. For the Lieutenant, Air Force One's arrival was followed by a chain of small surprises. The truck, with his second team marching alongside, had begun to roll the instant the lights went up, and from the corner of his eye he had glimpsed the quiet crowd beyond the fence. He was amazed; he hadn't known anyone was there. Then he had seen the Attorney General and had joined the general perplexity: why, he wondered, hadn't the accounts from Dallas reported that the President's brother had been with him when he died? At the sight of the casket Sam Bird's throat became congested. It disturbed him for a special reason: its cover was bare. Accustomed to the pageantry of Arlington, he missed the national colours. A fallen chieftain should be shielded by a flag, he thought, and he wished he had brought one with him. Then the lift halted by the hatch and he looked up into the face of Godfrey McHugh. The Lieutenant hadn't seen many generals, but he recognized McHugh from his newspaper photographs. He saluted again. To his dismay Godfrey ordered, 'Clear the area. We'll take care of the coffin.' Sam Bird and his body bearers scrambled unceremoniously down a yellow metal ladder.

Looking over McHugh's shoulder, Roy Kellerman spotted Agent Floyd Boring on the ground. 'Floyd! Can't they raise this thing any higher?' he called down. 'It isn't flush.' Boring inquired and called back, 'It's as high as it can go.' The lift was a total failure; it couldn't even reach the Presidential door. Kellerman on one end, Greer on the other, the five agents and Godfrey McHugh twisted Oneal's Britannia on to the truck bed. Jacqueline and Robert Kennedy stepped after it; the others followed, the swollen faces of Evelyn, Mary, Burkley, and O'Donnell forming a stolid rank behind the widow. As the lift began its descent Mac Kilduff precipitantly decided that he couldn't be left behind; he lunged forward, was nearly caught between the frame and the bed, and was pulled back to safety by a steward.

Bob Kennedy explained the transportation choices to his sister-in-law. 'There's a helicopter here to take you to the White House. Don't you want to do that?'

'No, no, I just want to go to Bethesda.' She saw the grey ambulance, assumed it was the one she had requested, and said, 'We'll go in that.'

With five feet to go the lift reached its limit and stopped. The men could jump, the women couldn't. Pam, feeling faint, fell forward and was caught. Mrs Kennedy was helped down by Taz Shepard and Ted Clifton—like Kilduff, Clifton couldn't bear to be excluded, and had made his way here from the front ramp. The last man off was Burkley; the President's physician hovered near the coffin as it was being removed from the platform. The transfer was awkward. Lieutenant Bird's second team swung in and was waved away by McHugh. But they were needed; there was no one else to receive the casket. Struggling and writhing, a union of Presidential aides, agents, and enlisted men from the five armed forces shouldered the chipped bronze box and eased it down. For a moment it wobbled wildly. 'Grotesque,' wrote a reporter in the press pen.

Kellerman brushed past Boring and explained to Chief Rowley that SS 100X would be arriving from Dallas in two hours; it, too must be met and taken to the White House garage for a detailed Secret Service–FBI examination. Major General Philip C. Wehle, Commanding Officer of the Military District of Washington, was making a final check with the MDW helicopter pilot who had been assigned to President Kennedy. The pilot told him he had just heard of a change of plans—the body was going by car. General Wehle's first thought was of security. In this he was typical; never having been assigned to an assassinated President before, agents and soldiers were thinking of Presidential protection. Wehle set off to inform McNamara.

The Secretary nodded. The General rounded up Sam Bird and six members of his second team and led them aboard the helicopter. Having failed to provide a proper military escort here, he was determined to be on hand when the coffin reached Bethesda. The enlisted men were awestruck—they had never ridden on an H-21 with cushioned seats—and the pilot raced across the capital (passing directly over the Greenlawn Drive home of Barney Ross, who ran out in time to see its familiar belly lights); then, with a cough of engines, the rotors settled down on the hospital's heliport. In 1961 Burkley had requested the pad, hoping he could persuade the President to inspect Washington's naval hospital. Kennedy had never found time. This was the first time the heliport had been used, and like so much else between 6 and 6.30 it was an occasion for bizarre misunderstanding. As Lieutenant Bird stepped to the ground, a score of Speed Graflex bulbs exploded together. Newspaper photographers assumed that the casket was right behind him.

During the seething movement of humanity at Andrews Jacqueline Kennedy had been temporarily stranded. Clint Hill assumed she would sit on the ambulance's front seat and went that way. She balked. 'No, I want to go in the back,' she said, and pivoted aside. She tried the rear door, tried again and wrestled with it. It was fastened from the inside. *Why doesn't somebody help her?* Mary McGrory wondered. Jim Swindal saw the difficulty and sprinted over, but just as he arrived the driver reached back and released the lock. Mrs Kennedy wrenched it open and scrambled in.

Beside the driver, gaping, were the heart specialist and nurse who had been sent to attend Lyndon Johnson. At Roy Kellerman's request all three slid out wordlessly and Greer, Kellerman, Landis, and Burkley scrambled in, Burkley on Landis' lap. The Attorney General entered the back, sitting opposite his sister-in-law; Godfrey perched beside her. The rest of the Bethesda cavalcade lined up swiftly, Clint and Dr Walsh in the second car; the mafia in the third; Evelyn, Pam, Mary, Muggsy, and George Thomas in the fourth. Before the truck lift could be removed and a ramp brought up for the new President, the body of President Kennedy had begun its forty-minute drive to the hospital.

Bob Kennedy slid open the plastic partition separating the rear of the ambulance from the front and asked, 'Roy, did you hear they'd apprehended a fellow in Dallas?'

Roy hadn't. For two hours Lee Oswald had been news in the rest of the nation, but of 26000's passengers only those who had been watching the stateroom television set knew of it.

'That's good,' Kellerman said.

'It was one man.'

'At the hospital I'll come up and talk to you.'

'You do that,' said Bob, and closed the partition.

Jacqueline Kennedy told him, 'I don't want any undertakers. I want everything done by the Navy.'

He asked Godfrey to see to that. Then a disjointed discussion ensued, touching upon the probable future of Kennedy aides, the delayed take-off from Love Field, McHugh's role in that, and the explanation which the new President had offered at the time. 'He said he'd talked to you, Bobby,' Jackie told her brother-in-law, 'and that you'd said he had to be sworn in right there in Dallas.' The

Attorney General was startled. There must be some misunderstanding, he said; he had made no such suggestion.[1]

Leaning gently on the coffin, Mrs Kennedy whispered, 'Oh, Bobby—I just can't believe Jack has gone.'

Her eyes fixed on a grey curtain over his shoulder, she described the motorcade, the murder in the sunlight, and the aftermath. For twenty minutes he listened in silence. Afterwards he said, 'It was so obvious that she wanted to tell me about it that whether or not I wanted to hear it wasn't a factor. . . . I didn't think about whether I wanted to hear it or not. So she went through all that.' Still, it could only have been an ordeal for him. Jacqueline Kennedy and Robert Kennedy were different, too. She was entirely feminine, he masculine; she was Gallic, he a Celt; she had to share her grief, he had to camp alone with his. But he could take hers, too. It was part of being the new head of the family, and so, without comment or expression, he heard the full horror of Dallas; heard the tale told in that husky voice which came to him softly across the scarred casket.

So she went through all that. . . .

He looked out between the curtains. Until now the landscape had been either nondescript or coarse. Leaving the base Bill Greer had taken Westover Drive and Suitland Drive, driving through forested land to Suitland Parkway's four lanes. Except for the rolling hills they might have been on a Texas super-highway. 'Speed Limit 45, Speed Radar Checked,' the signs had warned; 'No Trucks', 'Keep Right', 'Caution Construction Work Ahead', 'Entering Washington'. Crossing into the District they had passed through a labyrinth of viaducts and industrialization: a gasworks, a trumpery of motels, package stores, billboards, and Gulf and Esso ('Happy Motoring!') filling stations. A few people had been waiting for them—Pam Turnure saw children standing in pyjamas—but the groups were random, because the motorcade to Bethesda had been unexpected right up to the moment of its departure.

At the South Capitol Street Bridge the first downtown landmark appeared, the jutting Washington Monument, and Bob Kennedy saw it. To the right, and then dead ahead, shone the Capitol. The open circuit of his consciousness picked up another line; Jackie retained his attention, but part of his mind turned inward in retrospect. He was remembering the late 1950's on the Hill when Senator John F. Kennedy sat on the McClellan Committee and Robert F. Kennedy had served as chief counsel with Kenny and Pierre as staff assistants. Greer turned west from Canal down Independence and the Mall.

[1] The author invited President Johnson to comment on this misapprehension. He replied that he had nothing to add to his statement to the Warren Commission.

Now everything was evocative. The Federal Trade Commission: Big Steel. NASA: Glenn. The red gingerbread of the Smithsonian: his brother's love affair with America's past. His own office at Justice: Oxford, the Cuban prisoners. Internal Revenue: the tax cut. The Labour Department: Reuther and the March on Washington.

They passed between the twin wings of Agriculture. Greer swung north towards Seventh Street, and Bob peered north across the Mall and the Ellipse. On the left the unlovely mansard roof of the Executive Office Building hulked briefly, a bad Ronald Searle joke. Then, through the spidery late autumn foliage of Grover Cleveland's maples and Theodore Roosevelt's daimio oak, the Attorney General saw the gleaming South Portico of the Executive Mansion. For 1,036 days it had been the home of President John Kennedy. But this was the last of them. The thousand dawns were memory. The light had glimmered and died, and as Greer began the tortuous approach to the construction around the State Department, the Pan American Union Building intervened, eclipsing the pale vision.

Leaving the Mall, Greer had twisted his wheel to avoid a tall, narrow green truck parked by an open drain, into which a party of workmen were feeding coils of thick metal rope. Television technicians were already preparing funeral coverage; the Chesapeake & Potomac had begun laying what ultimately became nearly six miles of temporary video cable. By the following evening, when Bunny Mellon returned from the Caribbean, she would have the impression that 'all Washington was being wired'. Certainly all downtown Washington was. Ultimately everything from the Hill to the Potomac was to be under electronic surveillance, with a CBS producer co-ordinating tripartisan network broadcasts. The forerunner of all this had been the brief scene at Andrews, when the national audience glimpsed for the first time the principals in the drama which had begun four and a half hours before. Unknown to the passengers in the Pontiac ambulance, each of the public buildings they passed was crowded with officials who had watched the descent of the truck lift—Guthman and the Assistant Attorneys General at Justice; the Assistant Secretaries of Freeman, Wirtz, and Hodges; and the Interstate Commerce Commission at Twelfth and Constitution.

That was the federal triangle. It had been no different elsewhere; Bill Greer took the Rock Creek Parkway, then Waterside Drive to Massachusetts Avenue, then Massachusetts to Wisconsin, and there was hardly a home in north-west Washington which did not know as much about the history of the day as he did—which did not, in fact, have more information about the assassin who had observed Greer through the cheap telescopic sight five hours earlier. At Jacqueline Kennedy's mute appearance in 26000's doorway the Ormsby-Gores had wept in the British Embassy, the Alphands in the French. They had known the President well, but there were also tears in the legations of nations so small that most of John Kennedy's constituents couldn't have placed them on a map. Out Massachusetts and along Kalorama Road this was normally the prime hour for weekly cocktail parties. There had been none today. Ambassadors hadn't even advertised the fact that they were cancelling them; that in itself would have been considered undiplomatic. In a state of semihypnosis the envoys who hadn't driven to the MATS terminal had beheld the black and grey images flitting across the squares of glass. Indeed, it is possible to divide almost everyone in the District at that time into two groups: those who went to Andrews and those who monitored broadcasts of it. Lucy Johnson cried at the Elms, Mrs Harriman in Georgetown, Mrs Greer—with relief—in suburban Maryland. Even Agents Foster and Wells had seen some of it. Storing their shotguns on a high shelf in the Auchincloss kitchen, they had carried Caroline's old crib down from the attic, rapidly improvised substitutes for two missing parts, and set it up for John. While the children played with young Jamie Auchincloss the men had hunched furtively over a set, keeping the volume knob down until, when Caroline ran in with a question, they had to switch it off altogether.

The capital was typical of the nation. Colonel Swindal had approached his landing strip at six o'clock there, five o'clock in the midwest, four o'clock over the Rocky Mountains, and three o'clock on the West Coast. All America had been out of touch with the Presidency since the take-off from Love Field, and those who could feign disinterest or suppress curiosity were exceedingly rare. In Houston the staff of the Rice Hotel had assembled in Max Peck's office, identifying among the Andrews pall-bearers their Secret Service advance man, who had been among them twenty-four hours before (they had been worried about him; the denial that an agent had been killed had not yet caught up with the story), and in Dallas Marie Fehmer's family saw her come down the MATS ramp after the new President and embraced one another, certain now that she was safe.

Seven screens had been alight in the White House alone: Nancy Tuckerman's, Salinger's, the Fish Room's, the Situation Room's, and, in the Presidential apartment, those in the West Sitting Room, the Treaty Room, and the third-floor hall. In the absence of the First Family and its retinue they were watched by servants. After Andrews the help continued to gaze. It was part of the national fever. Television, in Justice White's words, had become 'a hypodermic, an emotional bath'. Men who never watched regularly scheduled programmes became helpless witnesses of whatever was shown; Justice Goldberg had hardly used his set before, yet all weekend he was either participating in funeral functions or home, staring at shadows. At the time few doubted the wisdom of the networks' policy. One did; Dwight Eisenhower thought the experience was upsetting to the American people. Eisenhower considered the renunciation of commercials a proper gesture of respect, but felt that a five-minute hourly summary of recent developments would have provided adequate news coverage, and that the familiar television diet would have been less disturbing. Perhaps the people needed to be disturbed. There is no doubt that they were. The marathon went on and on until White's little daughter asked him, 'Daddy, when are we going to be happy again?'

One unforeseen consequence of the ban on commercials was that programmers were hard-pressed to fill the time. Almost anyone with a eulogy to the slain President, or a memorial concert, or the haziest recollection of his assassin was instantly put on camera. Lacking those, producers dug into their video-tape libraries, running and rerunning every reel which was remotely relevant. One minute a viewer might see a still photograph of Jack Kennedy, Harvard '40, in his black silk swimming suit. Moments later Lieutenant (jg) Kennedy would be decorated for valour in the Pacific (1943), Congressman Kennedy would be campaigning in Boston (1946), Senator Kennedy would be moving for Estes Kefauver's Vice Presidential nomination by acclamation (1965), and President Kennedy would be informing the nation that the Soviet Union was installing a billion dollars' worth of warheads in Cuba and that he had therefore ordered the island blockaded (1962). The sequence might be reversed, scrambled, or interrupted by films of Franklin Roosevelt's funeral, which, in turn, might be succeeded by an amateur cameraman's record of the abortive attempt on President-elect Roosevelt's life in 1932. Since announced distinctions between tape and live camera were infrequent, and since television was the chief—sometimes the sole—tie with reality, individual recollections of that weekend are often an idiotic pastiche; Ted Sorensen returned from Andrews, walked into the Fish Room, and found himself listening to familiar words spoken by a familiar voice: it was the President delivering his Houston speech of yesterday evening, the text of which Kennedy and Sorensen had reviewed here in the West Wing yesterday morning.

Upstairs one picture was dark. The Oval Room had been deserted since 6 p.m. Twenty minutes before Air Force One landed, a small group of friends and relatives had been bracing themselves to console Jacqueline Kennedy there. After seeing the children off Nancy Tuckerman and the Bradlees had received Janet and Hudi Auchincloss. The strain had been conspicuous; all five had sat in constricted postures. Unsummoned waiters had arrived with chicken sandwiches, which were unwanted, and drinks, which were drained. Conversation had been spasmodic, schizoid. Mr West, dignified and discreet, had entered occasionally to tell Nancy of the plane's progress. Abruptly Jean Kennedy Smith, unheralded, appeared in the doorway holding the overnight bag in which she had packed her black mourning dress. She looked about uncertainly, her face white and pinched. Conversation stopped entirely. There really hadn't been anything to say anyhow, and now they abandoned pretence and retired into private reveries. Less than a minute later Mr West glided in behind Jean with word that the widowed First Lady would be going directly to Bethesda.

Nancy wavered. To Toni Bradlee she seemed unsure of her position; despite her long friendship with Mrs Kennedy, Nancy had only been White House social secretary since early summer. 'You don't want to intrude,' she said hesitantly. 'But maybe everyone will take that attitude and no one will go.' Then, decisively: 'I'll order a car.'

Jean left her bag in the Lincoln Room; Provi Parades hurried down from the third floor, where she had been listening to Frank McGee's description of her mistress' defiled suit over NBC, with a make-up case and a suitcase of clean clothes initialled 'J.B.K.' Nancy took them, though neither was destined to be opened that night. Squinting down they saw that the Rose Garden was thick with reporters who had guessed that the coffin might be brought directly here. To avoid the press Nancy ordered Carpet (the White House garage) to take her party out through the East Gate.

Carpet, the garage; Crown, the mansion; and Castle, the White House headquarters where all Signal Corps ganglia met, were straining at the tether, and their eagerness to be of service to the family is the only rational explanation for the wild ride which followed. Everything was overdone. It was sensible of Castle to warn Captain Canada that 'the First Lady's parents' were on their way, but the rest of it was entirely unreasonable. A platoon of white-helmeted motor-cycle policemen led the car to the District line, where Maryland state troopers took over. Every officer was winding his siren, and from passing cruisers and firehouses, some of them blocks away, other sirens echoed the strident wails. It was baroque. It was Ray Bradbury. It was a perpetual fire alarm—if every house in greater Washington had been ablaze, the noise would have been identical.

At the approach to the Bethesda the sidewalks were solid. Because of the passengers' stupor the dense crowds made little impression. The instinct of self-preservation is unquenchable, however, and their speed was as fantastic as it was needless. None of them had seen an automobile travel this fast on urban streets. As Greer moved steadily up Suitland Parkway, observing the 45 m.p.h. limit out of habit, they were hurtling along Wisconsin at over 90. Ben and Hudi in front and the four women cowering together in the back were literally frightened for their lives. They saw one near fatality. A motorcyclist overturned, sailed over his sidecar, landed on his feet, and scrabbled into the silent mass of kerbside witnesses. 'That ride was so bad,' Ben recalled later, 'that it took your mind off everything else. It was an assault on a man's senses. It added a new dimension. Before there had been sadness and the suffering with the children. Now there was darkness and this unbelievable velocity. The gaping bystanders began to look like ghouls to me; I had the feeling that we were racing towards our doom.'

The chauffeur chose one of the hospital's three gates at random, and they were met by a civilian guard and a sedan bearing a Catholic chaplain and a senior nurse who had been told to watch for Mrs Kennedy. The reception at either of the other two gates would have been the same. Since the Secret Service had dislodged the regular driver at Andrews, Captain Canada had no idea where the ambulance would enter. Therefore he had stationed chaplains and nurses at all of them. The guards were under orders to admit no one except employees, patients in serious condition, their relatives, and cars with White House clearance. Canada was worried about crowds. Minutes after the televised announcement that President Kennedy was en route here multitudes had begun to surround the grounds. Their sheer numbers were overwhelming, and unprecedented; Bethesda had not had this many visitors in all its history. Effective precautions were impossible. The sole barrier linking the gates was a low fence of four parallel green pipes. A child of six could scale it. Children did, and so did the infirm. The lawn was covered with a shapeless blur of onlookers.

The Captain had sent a distress signal to Fort McNair, without luck. General Wehle was at Andrews, and his MDW deputies were awaiting his return. Canada had exactly twenty-four Marines. Frantic, he deliberately misled the press, announcing that the President's body would be taken to the emergency entrance. Then he mobilized all off-duty corpsmen at the heliport. He expected the worst. As it turned out, he couldn't have been wider of the mark. The huge mob was to grow huger, but it was docile. Like the three thousand at Andrews, those here simply gazed. After the first hour most of the insiders forgot they were here. Ben Bradlee, who didn't, continued to regard them as ghouls 'or the kind of people who show up at society funerals.' That was unkind. Like Ben they were here out of respect, touched by what Lincoln called 'the better angels of our nature'. They didn't want to bother anyone, and they weren't a bother. Not knowing how else to express themselves they just stood, some all night.

Bethesda Naval Hospital was dominated by its soaring stone tower. Nancy's hotspurs led them there, and they alighted, grateful to be in one piece. Captain Canada greeted them; officers in blues swarmed around and ushered them to the elevator. The hospital had two VIP suites, on the sixteenth and seventeenth floors. In 1949 James Forrestal, the first Secretary of Defence, had leaped to his death from the first. They were taken to the second, a set of rooms shaped like a short-stemmed T. The stem was a corridor, separating a bedroom on the left and a small kitchen on the right. The T was crossed by a long narrow drawing-room. Perhaps because it was unnautical—the only salty touch was an engraving of a sea serpent beset by four puffing winds—Bethesda was proud of the décor. It was certainly an expensive suite, generously equipped with air conditioning, wall-to-wall carpeting, and bedroom television, but it was drab; walls, furniture, jalousies, and carpeting were uniformly coloured a shade of tan perilously close to institutional buff. Toni thought it 'sanitized and cold'. On the brightest day the effect would be depressing, and this was not that.

'Do you like it?' an officer inquired.

'It's nice,' Nancy replied, thinking it not at all nice.

'This is where Forrestal committed suicide,' he said inaccurately.

'Oh,' she said, understandably wondering why he had told her. He left, and Jean Smith nervously applied lipstick. Toni watched her and nudged Nancy. In an undertone she asked, 'Do you think we should?'

The social secretary looked despairing. 'What does it matter now?'

Jiggs Canada had once been George Burkley's shipmate, and he should have known him better. Posting three teams of chaplains and nurses had been superfluous. Though Burkley made light of his rank, he *was* a rear admiral in the Regular Navy, and a stickler for form. 'The President of the United States always enters by the main gate,' he firmly told Greer as they followed the Tuckerman race out Wisconsin. Even the team there was by-passed. 'Don't stop,' Burkley ordered. This time there were no flashing lights or orchestration of braying sirens, because those close to the President knew he had despised them, but there was a motor-cycle escort. Greer accelerated, the policemen roared ahead, and the ambulance and its train of shadowing Mercurys swept up to the entrance. Canada saluted; a commander opened the door. Burkley struggled off Landis' lap.

There he found everything shipshape. On the blue-and-gold anchor-embellished welcome mat were the captain; Rear Admiral Calvin Galloway, the commanding officer of Bethesda's medical centre; and a fourth chaplain—Canada was the kind of seaman who carries spare anchors everywhere. He and the Attorney General helped Mrs Kennedy out. Clint, Pam, and Dr Walsh approached from the other cars, and in an uneven rank they crossed the marble lobby and vanished into the dark brown elevator.

Admiral Galloway lingered on the walk, detained by General McHugh. 'We're going to the morgue for the autopsy and the embalming,' Godfrey said. 'Mrs Kennedy doesn't want an undertaker.'

'We don't have the facilities. I highly recommend a funeral parlour.'

Godfrey pressed him. 'Those are the family's wishes. Isn't it possible?'

'It's not *im*possible,' said the Admiral frowning. 'It's difficult, though. And it might be unsatisfactory.'

O'Donnell and O'Brien came over, and the matter was laid before them. 'You've heard the decision from the General,' Ken said curtly, and the Admiral left perturbed. They then headed for the elevator. Godfrey stayed by the coffin; as the honour guard, he meant to remain with the President's body, wherever it went. To his dismay it went nowhere for five full minutes. Everyone seemed to have gone. Even the Mercurys had driven off. McHugh, Greer, and Kellerman and the coffin had been left among the motionless spectators. In the deflected lobby light their eyes shone like cat's eyes. The General started counting them and then gave up. He looked down uneasily. He couldn't move the coffin alone. He didn't know what to do. He had been prepared for everything except inactivity.

The muddle was the consequence of a failure in interservice communication. The Army had been as vigilant as the Navy; General Wehle had stationed himself beyond the cornerstone in a staff car, with Lieutenant Bird and his body bearers right behind him in a truck. They had observed Mrs Kennedy's arrival, but the darkness, the great blocks of silent people, and the many moving vehicles distracted them. It had confused two naval physicians, too. When an ambulance drew away from the kerb they called, 'That's it—we'll guide you to the morgue.' At the morgue Wehle, Bird, and the six enlisted men debarked and inspected each other's uniforms while awaiting some movement from the ambulance. It was still as still. The Lieutenant crept up and peered inside. It was empty. Even the driver had gone. Panicky, they fled back and saw, among the shining cat's eyes, the uneasy face of Godfrey McHugh. Wehle and Bird coloured. The Military District of Washington was meticulous about ceremony; for a casket team to leave a Commander in Chief's casket was an astounding lapse, and after casting about bitterly—and vainly—for the two doctors, they reformed the tiny escort.

The morgue was fronted by a concrete jetty approached along the left side by a short flight of cement steps. Since coffins were the most precious burden to pass this way the stairs should have been designed for them. They weren't. They were too narrow, and a steel handrail was an impediment to bearers. The railing thwarted a gesture of McHugh's. This once, he thought, it would be appropriate for a general to join hands with five enlisted men, and he relieved the Coast Guardsman in the team. But navigating the ponderous Britannia required exceptional dexterity on the left. McHugh was too old. He tried, and kept trying until his eyes filled with frustration. It was no use. He was holding them all up, and motioning to the lanky Coast Guard youth he capitulated. The others moved quickly then, inside and sharp left through double brown doors labelled 'RESTRICTED—AUTHORIZED PERSONNEL ONLY'. Lieutenant Bird decided that he wasn't an authorized person. After his men had lowered the casket to a wheeled gurney he shepherded them into the corridor and mounted guard. Two Navy corpsmen passed, rolling a litter. Nothing appeared to be on it except a small lump wrapped in sheeting. 'What's that?' he inquired. 'Baby. Born dead,' one mumbled. The Lieutenant whispered, 'Oh.' It occurred to him that Bethesda wasn't going to be at all like Arlington.

Actually a morgue—any morgue—is starker than any cemetery, more forbidding than even an emergency room. Within its severe limits this one was a model of cleanliness and efficiency. The anteroom, from which Sam Bird had retreated, was furnished with eight reefers (neatly labelled 'Remains') and twin gurneys. The spotless tile walls of the main chamber were lined with specialized equipment: medical scales, a cylindrical sterilizer, a washing machine for rubber gloves, and a sawing machine which looked curiously like a hobbyist's jigsaw. Dominating them all was the eight-foot-long autopsy table in the centre. The table resembled nothing encountered in ordinary experience. It was high, constructed of stainless steel, and perforated with hundreds of holes. Tubes, faucets, and motors jutted from the sides; enormous drainage pipes swooped down from the surface and disappeared into the cement floor. Such frames are so obviously what they are that some medical schools have adopted the practice of administering tranquillizers to students examining one in operation for the first time. The layman recoils, and long after he has left he remembers the stench of the chemicals.

Two laymen, Generals McHugh and Wehle, watched the Navy's autopsy crew open the Dallas coffin and carefully lift the body of the President to the perforated table top. Godfrey couldn't take it. Giddy, he sank to a bench, and Roy Kellerman tiptoed in and sat beside him. MDW's CO remained, standing at attention at the foot of the table. Husky, jut-jawed, a 1930 graduate of West Point, Philip Wehle looked like a cartoonist's concept of a brass hat. But labels are deceptive. General Wehle's ideal had become a politician, a man younger than himself and a former naval person. To him John Kennedy had been a gallant officer, tried in combat. He had voted for him and enthusiastically approved of his foreign and domestic policies. Eleven days ago the General had pulled his rank to acquire a first-hand view of him in Arlington. He had watched the President stride vigorously at the head of the Veterans Day parade, his small son at his side, and that evening he had decided that everything he had learned on the Hudson about leadership and character had taken on new meaning.

Now he thought—and he thought of it that way—*the nation's Commander in Chief has been killed in action.* He felt 'a great welling love, an unendurable sadness, the cruelty of a personal loss'. He stood erect, shoulders back, thumbs tight along the seams of his creased trousers in the Academy posture he had learned at the Highlands, his eyes on the tall table's punched steel surface. Two naval officers had sliced away Vernon Oneal's rubber and plastic envelopes with flashing scalpels and stripped Kennedy entirely. The Chief Executive lay naked on his back. At this angle the throat was invisible to Wehle. He observed a slight discoloration over one eye. Otherwise the President appeared unmarred. The General became oblivious of the steel slab and its immaculate machinery. He saw nothing except Kennedy. He thought, *What a magnificent body he had, the physique of a Greek god.* From deep in his past, from over a third of a century, the strains of A. E. Housman's 'To an Athlete Dying Young', memorized in a childhood classroom, came to Wehle's mind:

The time you won your town the race
We chaired you through the market-place;
Man and boy stood cheering by,
And home we brought you shoulder-high.

Today, the road all runners come,
Shoulder-high we bring you home
And set you at your threshold down,
Townsman of a stiller town.

He couldn't recall it all. The lines came in disjointed fragments. But the penultimate stanza sprang to his mind intact:

So set, before its echoes fade,
The fleet foot on the sill of shade,
And hold to the low lintel up
The still-defended challenge-cup.

Then, groping, he remembered the next couplet:

And round that early-laurelled head
Will flock to gaze the strengthless dead. . . .

Four minutes after the ambulance's departure from Andrews the unwieldy truck lift had been removed and President Johnson had descended the MATS ramp. The first man to greet him was Secretary McNamara. To Mike Mansfield, who was standing behind the Secretary, the new President said pensively, 'It's terrible, terrible.' He gave Jenkins and Reedy a nod of recognition and plodded forward with his peculiar stride, brushing by Schlesinger, who impulsively took his hand and blurted, 'I'll do all I can to help.' Hubert Humphrey, Earl Warren, and Averell Harriman also reached out, but several men hung back. Arthur Goldberg's eyes met Johnson's, yet he did not step up, because 'I was not there for that. I had come to pay my respects to the body. I felt it was appropriate just to stand and be there.'

At 6.14 p.m. the President drew up before a cluster of microphones in front of the press pen. According to his later recollection he silently asked 'for God's help that I should not prove unworthy. . . .' He wasn't getting much secular help. The setting could hardly have been less auspicious. Though the truck was gone, the dreariness of Andrews remained, and he was competing with a clamour of discordant sounds. A few feet away Hubert Humphrey and Mrs Mansfield were sobbing uncontrollably. Two turbojet H-21's were whooshing away; with professional disapproval Colonel Swindal noted that one had both its fore *and* aft rotors going. Lady Bird at his left elbow, Johnson read his statement: 'This is a sad time for all people. We have suffered a loss that cannot be weighed. For me it is a deep personal tragedy. I know the world shares the sorrow that Mrs Kennedy and her family bear. I will do my best. That is all I can do. I ask for your help—and God's.'

The television audience, though baffled by the sound—the helicopters were off-camera—heard the President. Few at Andrews did. Even Mrs Johnson didn't seem to be listening; she was looking away, and her eyes had a veiled look.

The Congressional leadership gathered around the President; Humphrey, Mansfield, Dirksen, Smathers, Kuchel, Hale Boggs, Carl Albert, Charlie Halleck, Les Arends. His quarter-century as a parliamentarian made the men of the Hill his natural allies; unlike Kennedy, who had never been a member of the Senate's inner club, Johnson would lean on them heavily. Nevertheless he now headed a separate branch of the government. He needed friends there, too. McNamara's welcome had touched him. As Vice President he had attended meetings of the National Security Council and the Cabinet, and he knew Kennedy's two strong men had been the Attorney General and the Secretary of Defence. Summoning McNamara, he said he wanted him, Mac Bundy, and 'someone from State' to accompany him to the White House.

The Secretary replied that George Ball was here; Ball came forward and presented his department's memorandum and proclamation draft. In the front compartment of the H-21 there was a polite Alphonse-Gaston dispute over protocol. The Presidential chair was on the port side of the craft, facing front. The antipodal seat, facing the Chief Executive, was traditionally reserved for his senior adviser. McNamara suggested Ball take it; Ball suggested McNamara. After a colloquy the strong man capitulated and sat; Mrs Johnson was led to a starboard couch, flanked by Ball and Bundy. Jenkins, Valenti, Liz Carpenter, Moyers, and the Vice Presidential Secret Service agents occupied the rear compartment, and then there was a scramble for the other helicopter. The winners were Reedy, Marie Fehmer, Cliff Carter, Kilduff, and the bagman. The big loser was Ted Clifton, who rode back to the capital alone.

George Ball was under the impression that the new President was still in shock. Johnson's face twitched; to the Under Secretary his movements seemed like those of a drugged man. McNamara, on the other hand, thought him 'surprisingly stable—much more so than I would have been in his situation'. Certainly the President said all the right things. During the ten-minute ride over Anacostia Flats he suppressed any feeling that he had been slighted at the airport. Instead, he spoke of Mrs Kennedy's courage in Dallas. 'I have never seen anyone so brave,' he said to Ball. He told the three of them that he admired them and then added a comment which Ball found especially moving. 'Kennedy did something I couldn't have done,' Johnson said. 'He gathered around him the ablest people I've ever seen—not his friends, not even the best in public service, but the best *anywhere*. I want you to stay. I need you. I want you to stand with me.'

He asked each for a report on what had been done and what decisions must be made. Bundy said he thought there would be nothing urgent for the next forty-eight hours. The President turned to the Secretary of Defence. 'Any important matters pending?' he asked. McNamara outlined the disposition of American forces around the globe, their degree of readiness, and allied power available to the United States. Should the murder in Texas prove to be the prelude to any enemy strike, the military establishment was ready with an overwhelming counterstrike. Ball spoke briefly about the impact of the assassination on foreign governments.

It was 6.25. They were over the White House south grounds.[2] Earlier the big brown wasps had used the grass, but now the steel pad had been set up, and the first H-21, shining in the beams of lights held by servants and correspondents, eased towards it. Seventy feet away the passengers could see the tree house and young John's swing and slide set. The children were first in the thoughts of those on the ground, too. They had always been the helicopter's chief greeters, and as Lyndon Johnson stepped on to the lawn, arriving at the executive mansion for the first time as President, he looked about and discovered that no one was looking at him; as though in response to a silent command all had pivoted towards the balcony, where Caroline and John would normally have been. Three years ago, when President Kennedy had won his race, he had been borne here shoulder-high; now President Johnson was arriving in a tragic time of mourning. It was without doubt the most painful assumption of power in American history.

Crossing the lawn he talked to McNamara and Mac Bundy. Even Bundy, the most precise man in the government, seems to have been unclear whom he meant by 'the President'. He said, 'There are two things I am assuming, Mr President. One is that everything in locked files before 2 p.m. today belongs to the President's family, and the other is that Mrs Kennedy will handle the funeral arrangements.' Johnson said, 'That's correct.' He strode past the Rose Garden, past Evelyn Lincoln's office and the Cabinet Room, through the entire West Wing and over West Executive Avenue to his Vice Presidential office on the second floor of the Executive Office Building. Juanita Roberts, his chief secretary, was waiting for him, and he

[2] The chronology here is interesting. Comparing the shift reports of the Presidential agents who were in the ambulance with those of the Vice Presidential detail, it is evident that the body of the slain President passed the mansion within minutes of the new President's landing. The two events were almost simultaneous. Establishing which occurred first is, however, impossible.

went straight to work. Ted Clifton, arriving at the EOB fifteen minutes later, suggested to Bill Moyers that Johnson should use Kennedy's oval office. Moyers mentioned it, and Johnson sharply vetoed it. 'That would be presumptuous of me,' he said. He reached for his telephone, remembered that Marie Fehmer had the little book with all his numbers, and he asked Juanita, 'Where's Marie?'

She was lost. In fact, the bulk of his party had disintegrated between the pad and the mansion. His aides were bewildered by the enormous house. George Reedy entered the Diplomatic Reception Room, took several wrong turns, and finally asked a White House policeman for directions. Jack Valenti and Cliff Carter were avoiding guards. Neither had a White House pass, and they raced frantically up and down the red-carpeted basement corridor until they blundered outside and sighted the Executive Office Building. But Marie had the worst time; like them she was painfully aware that 'I had no clearance, no identification, no way of proving who I was. I had worked in Lyndon's Capitol office, so I didn't even have EOB clearance. The only time I'd been in 274 was during the Cuban crisis.' Utterly lost, she explored the White House carpenter shop, florist shop, swimming pool, and theatre before she, too, found the way out to West Executive. When Marie returned to her Washington apartment late that night, her room-mates told her that during her period as a missing person the President had phoned there twice, trying to locate her.

The new First Lady didn't pause at her new home. Anxious about her younger daughter, she asked to be driven straight to the more familiar house at 4040 Fifty-second Street, NW. Lucy Baines was waiting for her on the front steps. 'Oh, Mother, I go to the most wonderful school!' she cried. 'We all said prayers in the gym when it happened, and then they took me aside and told me the President was dead.' Inside, the Elms was crowded with people. Lady Bird was surprised and touched; she had forgotten that they had so many friends. She had also forgotten that the house had this many television sets. Screens seemed to be in every corner of every room, blaring away. Excusing herself, she went upstairs with Liz Carpenter, telephoned her older daughter in Austin, and changed her clothes. Hugging a dressing gown to her, she looked speculatively at Liz. 'How do you feel?' 'Chilly,' Liz answered. 'I'm *freezing*,' Lady Bird said. She switched on the bedroom television—it was really the only way to find out what was going on—and lay down, heaping coverlets and blankets on herself. They didn't help. Her teeth were chattering. She couldn't remember a November this cold.

McNamara and Ball had dropped out of Johnson's wake in the West Wing. He told them he had invited the Congressional leadership to join him here when they returned from the airport, so they swerved right, into the Cabinet Room, and sat talking for twenty minutes. It was the first time they had discussed the Kennedy Presidency together, and they found that they had been thinking along the same lines since the inaugural. Both felt that his narrow mandate in 1960 had been a cloud, that the driving force in his first administration had been a desire to unite the country. Each had cherished great hopes for the autumn of 1964. They had believed that Kennedy would win by a large margin, and that if the opposition nominated Goldwater the landslide would be unprecedented. Then, they had believed, the President's vision would guarantee four of the most exhilarating, innovative years America had ever known.

They parted as the last of Johnson's staff members were assembling on the second floor of the EOB. Awaiting them, the President told Jenkins and Ted Reardon, the Kennedy aide responsible for the Cabinet liaison, to set up a Cabinet meeting for tomorrow. Kilduff was told of Presidential displeasure with the Andrews debarkation; Lem Johns was instructed to fetch soup from the White House staff mess. Johnson, Reedy noticed, hardly mentioned Dallas. At one point he did murmur, 'Rufe did a very heroic thing today. He threw me on the floor of that car and threw himself on top of me.' But that was an aside. He was concentrating on the future. 'There must be no gap,' he said emphatically, and 'The government must go forward,' and 'We've had a tremendous shock, and we have to keep going.'

Marie entered, breathless; the phoning started, with Moyers placing the calls. At 7.05 the President talked to Harry Truman. At 7.10 he spoke to Eisenhower in New York, offering to send a plane for him. Eisenhower explained that he had his own plane and could fly down immediately. But that, they agreed, would be unnecessary; they could meet in the mansion tomorrow morning. At 7.20 Johnson expressed his sorrow to Sargent Shriver, who was still toiling by Ralph Dungan's desk. Hanging up, the President wrote the first of two notes on White House stationery, and at 7.25 he telephoned J. Edgar Hoover. The Director was home. Unaware that regular programmes had been suspended, he had waited until seven o'clock before turning his television on, thinking to catch NBC's nightly newscast on Channel 4. He was watching a re-run of Kennedy's October 22, 1962, missile speech and wondering whether this was the best Huntley and Brinkley could do when the phone rang. His old neighbour said he wanted a complete FBI report on the assassination. Depressing the receiver, Hoover called his office, ordering a special assistant and thirty agents to Dallas.

Juanita Roberts reported that the Senators and Congressmen were waiting in the anteroom. The President murmured that they would have to wait a little longer. He had to finish that second note. In each of them the bold, angular Johnson scrawl was missing. His handwriting was cramped and diminished—some words were so small they seemed micro-filmed.

THE WHITE HOUSE
WASHINGTON

November 22, 1963
7.20 Friday Night

DEAR JOHN—

It will be many years before you understand fully what a great man your father was. His loss is a deep personal tragedy for all of us, but I wanted you particularly to know that I share your grief—You can always be proud of him—

Affectionately
LYNDON B. JOHNSON

The second was a little longer. Himself the father of two girls, he had been particularly fond of the President's daughter.

THE WHITE HOUSE
WASHINGTON

November 22, 1963
Friday Night 7.30

DEAREST CAROLINE—

Your father's death has been a great tragedy for the Nation, as well as for you, and I wanted you to know how much my thoughts are of you at this time.

He was a wise and devoted man. You can always be proud of what he did for his country—

Affectionately
LYNDON B. JOHNSON

He would never be a simple man. He was capable of tactlessness and tenderness, cunning and passion. Wordlessly he handed the letters to his secretary, heaved himself up and strode into the anteroom to greet the leadership.

The meeting was brief and accomplished little. They discussed no legislation. Turning deliberately from face to face, the President said that he was speaking to them 'as one friend to another'. He asked for their co-operation, counsel, and assistance; and it was warmly pledged. To Mike Mansfield and Everett Dirksen he expressed the hope that a new, stronger bipartisan leadership group could be forged. 'Then,' in Mansfield's words, 'we broke up.' But one Senator remained. As Hubert Humphrey observed in his memorandum to himself the following morning, he stayed back for just a moment and had a private word with President Johnson. I think of him as Lyndon, as a dear friend. I assured him of my whole-hearted co-operation, of my desire to be of all possible assistance, and asked him to feel free to call upon me. He put his arm around me and said that he needed me desperately. A little later, Bill Moyers, who is close to Lyndon Johnson, told me that the President would need me very, very much. He thought even more so than President Kennedy had ever needed me, if that was the case. I told Bill Moyers, who is close to President Johnson, that I stood ready to serve in any capacity, however he wanted me.

Jean Kennedy Smith had been looking out a window of the tower suite at Bethesda, watching the darkness press hard against the cold panes, when a muted voice said, 'She's here.' She turned, and Mrs Kennedy was standing in the centre of the drawing-room. 'There,' in Ben Bradlee's words, 'was this totally doomed child, with that God-awful skirt, not saying anything, looking burned alive.' She crumpled into Ben's arms with a moan, half-sob; he had never heard a sound like it before. Under his breath he said, 'Cry, *Cry*. Don't be *too* brave,' and transferred her to Toni, who didn't really believe it was happening. But despite the unreality Toni was capable of coherent thought, and she felt that Janet Auchincloss was being ignored. 'Here's your Mother,' she murmured. Jackie turned to Mrs Auchincloss with a wan smile and kissed her. Her mother said, 'Oh, Jackie, if this had to happen, thank God he wasn't maimed.'

The widow embraced Nancy Tuckerman. 'Poor Tucky,' she said quietly. 'You came all the way down from New York to take this job, and now it's all over. It's so sad. You will stay with me for a little while, won't you?'

Nancy was stricken: *Jackie* was thinking of *her*. In the little hall between the bedroom and kitchen, where the others had hung back, Canada whispered to Burkley, 'Does she always speak in that soft voice?' 'Always,' Burkley whispered.

Behind her stood Robert Kennedy. He stepped to the telephone, made a brief call, and quickly returned. To Bradlee he was 'the strongest thing you have ever seen. He was subdued, holding Jackie together, keeping everyone's morale up when his own couldn't have been worse. He was just sensational.'

Beckoning Jackie aside, Bob told her, 'They think they've found the man who did it. He says he's a Communist.'

She stared. *Oh, my God*, she thought, *but that's absurd*. Later she would think about hatred and the highly charged atmosphere of Dallas; at the moment, however, she just felt sickened. It was like existentialism, entirely purposeless, and she thought, *It even robs his death of any meaning*. She returned to her mother. 'He didn't even have the satisfaction of being killed for civil rights,' she said. 'It's—it had to be some silly little Communist.'

Janet Auchincloss invited her daughter to stay with her in Georgetown. There was no response. Then Mrs Auchincloss said casually, 'You know that the children are at O Street.'

Puzzled, Mrs Kennedy asked, 'Why are they there?'

'Why, because of your message from the plane.'

'I sent no message. They should be in their own beds. Mummy, my God, those poor children; their lives shouldn't be disrupted, now of all times! Tell Miss Shaw to bring them back and put them to bed.'

Mrs Auchincloss called Maude Shaw, but the nurse already knew. The softest whisper travelled fast in that suite; Clint Hill had overheard the exchange and phoned Agent Wells from the nurse's desk outside.

'I thought she wanted them away from Crown,' Wells said.

'So did I,' said Clint. 'I'll explain later.'

Agatha Pozen had already left. At 6.15 Foster had put her in a black White House Chrysler with a policeman. Now the Auchincloss' Italian butler, who had been clearing the dinner table, whisked the unused crib back to the attic while the kiddie detail loaded Caroline, John, Miss Shaw, and the cased shotgun into another car. At 7.43 they left Hamlet, and at 7.56 they were back inside the mansion grounds. Foster and Wells escorted the nurse and children to the second floor; they rode down to F-5, where a White House policeman handed Foster a heavy brown paper bag. 'Joe Giordano gave me this,' the policeman said. 'He told me to turn it over to you and to nobody else.' Foster stepped into Franklin Roosevelt's old map room and opened it. He needed only one glance. Inside was a pink pillbox hat spattered with blood and brains. Rapidly folding over the bag's top, he examined the side. Printed there in large capital letters, was 'HILL'. Foster called the guard. In bitter fury he asked, 'What do you think my name is?' 'Clint Hill,' the man said positively. He saw Foster's expression and became less positive. 'Why, I always thought you were Hill—aren't you Hill?' 'No.' Furious, Foster gave him his own and added another for the guard.

Upstairs Maude Shaw faced a far more difficult trial. At Bethesda Mrs Auchincloss had confronted her daughter with the fact that the news must be broken to Caroline and John.

'Jackie, are you going to tell the children or do you want me to, or do you want Miss Shaw?'

Mrs Kennedy asked for an opinion.

'Well . . . John can wait. But Caroline should be told before she learns from her friends.'

'Oh, yes, Mummy. What will she think if she suddenly . . .' She thought a moment and then said something which her mother thought wise. 'I want to tell them, but if they find it out before I get back ask Miss Shaw to use her discretion.'

Janet Auchincloss didn't quite do that; she used her own discretion. Jacqueline Kennedy's mother was determined to remove one last—perhaps crushing—duty from her daughter's shoulders today. Phoning the nurse again, she began, 'How are the children doing?'

They were fine, Miss Shaw replied. A trifle confused, perhaps, but at their age they were resilient; they had been fed and were drowsy. She herself was not at all fine. Self-control had become an iron struggle. Sometimes she lost it and would have to turn her back until she had regained composure.

'Mrs Kennedy wants you to tell Caroline.'

Miss Shaw was speechless. She couldn't cry aloud—the children were in the next room—but she wanted to. Instead, she said in a low, desperate voice, 'Please, no. Let this cup pass from me.'

'You must. There's no one else.'

'I can't take a child's last happiness from her. I don't have the heart—I can't destroy her little happy day.'

'I know, but you have to.'

Until today the nurse had thought that last August was the low tide in her life. In the first hours of Patrick's life Caroline had been ecstatic at the thought of having another baby brother. Then the blow had fallen. Mrs Kennedy had been in the hospital, the President had been too grief-stricken to speak to his daughter, and so it had been left to the nurse to look into those wide eyes—'the Bouvier eyes', as she always called them—and say that Patrick had gone to heaven. She had been convinced then that nothing could be harder. This, however, was on another plane entirely. They hadn't known Patrick. Neither Miss Shaw nor Caroline had ever seen him. But the President had been the most important figure in their lives. He and his daughter had been particularly close; remembering how proudly he would introduce 'My daughter, Caroline' to visitors, the nurse begged Mrs Auchincloss, 'Please, *please*, can't someone else do it?'

'No, Mrs Kennedy is too upset.' There was no more to say; they hung up.

Miss Shaw was probably the best choice. There was no real substitute for Caroline's mother, of course. Next to her was Robert Kennedy. With his discipline, his feeling for children (he was far warmer among them than with adults), and his resemblance to his older brother he would have been admirable. Miss Shaw, however, was there. Moreover, she had been with Caroline since the President's daughter was eleven days old.

She put John to bed. Now it was the girl's turn. In Caroline's bedroom Miss Shaw said slowly, 'Your father has been shot. They took him to a hospital, but the doctors couldn't make him better.'

There was a pause.

'So,' she continued, 'your father has gone to look after Patrick. Patrick was so lonely in heaven. He didn't know anybody there. Now he has the best friend anyone could have.'

She paused again.

'God gives each of us a thing to do,' she said. 'God is making your father a guardian angel over you and your mother, and his light will shine down on you always. His light is shining now, and he's watching you, and he's loving you, and he always will.'

The little girl buried her face in the pillow, crying. Miss Shaw stood by the bed, her rough hands fighting one another, until the child slept. Then she tucked her in, crossed to John's room, tucked him into his crib, and sat alone in her room between them. She tried to knit. It was no good. Her fingers wouldn't work properly. She laced them together and sat rocking in the dark, alert for the slightest movement from the yellow bedroom, throughout the night.

On the second floor of Parkland Hospital John Connally slept soundly under the orange tile walls, watched by Dr Jenkins, Nellie, and twenty members of the Connally family, and guarded by a troop of armed Texas Rangers. The Governor's operation had been successful. It had been a surgical feat, however, and the possibility of a downturn was very real. To assure recuperation Jenkins had placed him next to his office. The Rangers approved. None of the windows faced out; a second gunman could not penetrate here.

This concern over other assassins later seemed like the belated shutting of a barn door, but it was impossible to be certain that Friday evening, and everything with hinges was being closed. In his White House office Arthur Schlesinger was writing: 'No one knows yet who the killer is—whether a crazed Birchite or a crazed Castroite. I only know that the killer has done an incalculable disservice to this country and to all mankind. It will be a long time before this nation is as nobly led as it had been in these last three years.' Oswald had then been under interrogation for over five hours. That he alone could be responsible for his act appeared highly unlikely, and in the context of the time Schlesinger's uncertainty and the vigilance of the Rangers made excellent sense.

The sleep of children and patients, like the floodlit high school football games, was abnormal. America's nerves had never been tauter; the networks' national audience did not diminish, even though the commentators had little to report. A man wearing a swastika was arrested in the state capital at Madison, Wisconsin, after he had announced that he was 'celebrating Kennedy's death'. It was A-wire news on every ticker. Almost anything became the occasion for a chime of teletype bells. The family's desire that floral tributes be omitted and the money be contributed to charity, and the announcements that a special Mass was being held at Georgetown University, that Washington's Episcopal Cathedral would remain open all night, and that Cardinal Cushing would celebrate the funeral Mass in Washington Monday was treated as flashes. When the Cardinal's decision was broadcast at 8.30 p.m., the bulletins about Oswald had already begun to be stale. Nearly everything of significance had been learned so quickly. What was left was an intolerable vacuum.

Now, as at Parkland six hours earlier, men with jobs were lucky. Under Secretary Johnson presided all night over a State Department task force assembling scraps of data about Oswald (a scene he would have relished). At Gawler's the Death Watch rehearsals continued with an innovation; their commander, First Lieutenant Donald W. Sawtelle, had been informed that Mrs Kennedy wanted members of the honour guard to stand with their backs to the coffin. It couldn't be done. The watch was silent; the enlisted men moved on visual signals. They had to be stationed so that they could see the officer in charge out of the corner of their eyes. But trying it was something to do, and Sawtelle persisted. In the basement of the EOB Joe Giordano and Boots Miller furled and refurled Kennedy's Presidential flag before storing it with his seal of office in Room 89½; then they went to work on his silk American flag, carefully adjusting each fold. Chief Rowley assembled his Texas agents in the White House staff mess. He grilled them individually and issued an order that they and the men still on duty with Johnson or with Kennedy's body must submit detailed reports before leaving for home. In the mansion Charles Kincklin told his six butlers that in view of Mrs Kennedy's uncertain plans they would all remain on duty throughout tonight and tomorrow. The staff would pass the time by making sandwiches. He hadn't counted on the servants' eagerness. By 9 p.m., when Sawtelle transferred his command post from Gawler's to the White House, all available space in the State Dining Room was covered with towering platters, and tables were being cleared in the President's theatre downstairs for more of them.

Again, as in the hospital, some of those without work invented it. Policemen couldn't sit idle, so they criss-crossed the capital in tight motor-cycle formations, and it became a quite ordinary thing to see these grim V's of helmeted men roaring aimlessly across the city. The firehouses continued to scream. Even in Georgetown, normally so quiet, one heard their banshees till dawn; had there been a real fire, one felt, every unit in the District, southern Maryland, and northern Virginia would have responded pell-mell. The writers wrote. In Schlesinger's office he and Ken Galbraith drafted separate letters to Mrs Kennedy. Galbraith's note was brief but poignant in its pledge of devotion.

Schlesinger's was longer, and almost illegible:

Friday evening

DEAREST JACKIE:

Nothing I can say can mitigate the shame and horror of this day. Your husband was the most brilliant, able, and inspiring member of my generation. He was the one man to whom this country could confide its destiny with confidence and hope. He animated everything he did with passion and gaiety and wit. To have known him and worked with and for him is the most fulfilling experience I have ever had or could imagine——

Dearest Jackie, the love and grief of a nation may do something to suggest the feeling of terrible vacancy and despair we all feel. Marian and my weeping children join me in sending you our profoundest love and sympathy. I know that you will let me know when I can do anything to help.

With abiding love
ARTHUR

Others drank, and learned what those who had been aboard the Presidential aircraft could have told them: there were no intoxicants on November 22. Pat Moynihan and a friend split a fifth of whisky. Their senses remained undulled; they examined the label with astonishment. Mary McGory tried to get drunk with Teddy White and quit at the same time that Jim Swindal was giving up at Andrews. Swindal telephoned his wife in Falls Church and encountered another aspect of the assassination: the countless women who had loved Kennedy from a distance were inconsolable. The Colonel's wife was among the few who had met him. A Stoughton photograph of her with the President was her most treasured possession, and she was hysterical. So was Marie Fehmer; so was Marie Harriman. Mrs Harriman was valiantly trying to serve as hostess to a brilliant group of guests which was headed by Adlai Stevenson and which later included Schlesinger and Galbraith, but she wasn't up to it. In the thirty-three years of their marriage Harriman had never seen her so upset. His wife was caught up in a terrible, vindictive rage. She had been one of those who had dreaded the Dallas Right, and now she was beyond comfort.

Many men who had thought themselves at loose ends became busy answering telephones. The chief telephoner was the new Chief Executive. The Johnsonian era had begun. With the two White House switchboards at his disposal he found fulfilment; one hand was wrapped around the receiver in a stranglehold—no one has succeeded in covering so many inches of plastic—while the other played deftly over the colourless buttons of the Signals console. Two of the men he reached Friday evening were Arthur Goldberg and Ted Sorensen. Justice Goldberg's home phone rang at 9 p.m. The President had recognized him at Andrews; he asked why Goldberg hadn't come forward to shake his hand. The justice explained that he had gone to meet the coffin of President Kennedy. He agreed to come to Johnson's office tomorrow for a further talk. Sorensen heard from the President at approximately 9.30, just as he was finishing dinner. Like Goldberg, Sorensen was asked to call tomorrow. Automatically Ted replied, 'Yes, Mr President.' Then the implications of what he had just said reached him. He would never call John Kennedy 'Mr President' again. He replaced the receiver and collapsed.

Lyndon Johnson was perhaps the most active telephoner in the city, which is saying a lot, because Chesapeake & Potomac records indicate voluminous activity in every exchange. These were the hours when long-distance dialling began to climb steeply. Congressmen were especially in demand; their constituents were calling them. The Texans were out of action, knocked out by exhaustion. After long-distance conversations of their own, to relatives, they went to bed and sank into a deep sleep from which they could not be roused. Any Senator or Representative in the buildings flanking the Capitol was almost certain to hear from home, however. He would find himself listening to members of his party, of the opposition; even to foreigners who felt a compelling need to speak to someone in public life.

Hubert Humphrey had the impression that he had half the state of Minnesota on the line. After discussing Lyndon Johnson with George Smathers (who' thought I was going to be needed very much by the President') Humphrey went to his desk in Suite 1313 of the New Senate Office Building. He felt forsaken. Then the ringing began. The callers were

> people who merely wanted to tell me how sorry they were ... plain people who would weep over the telephone. I recall one particular phone call from a Minneapolis or St Paul cab driver

who had just finished work, and he wanted to tell me that his whole family wanted to be remembered to . . . Mrs Kennedy and the children and how sorry they were that they had lost their great friend President Kennedy. That was characteristic of all the calls. Not a single one was anything but filled with sorrow and sympathy and understanding. How wonderful it is that the people of the country felt so close to the President.

Reaching Senators was relatively easy. Barney Ross was obscure. Nevertheless he heard from two former crewmen of PT 109, one in Louisiana and one in New Hampshire. Twenty years after their shipwreck they remembered the young officer who had rescued them, and they wanted Barney, the other officer who had been aboard, to know that they were on their way to the funeral. Fitful, Barney herded his wife and children into the car and drove slowly around Bethesda, observing the crowd. The Rosses thus joined the capital's army of roamers—those who had gathered at Andrew's Field or outside the hospital or in Lafayette Park, who went to the office or explored strange taverns, who walked the streets. Humphrey abandoned his suite and showed up on three network broadcasts. Sorensen had encountered Burkley's chief petty officer in the West Wing. 'Did he suffer?' he asked. Chief Hendrix assured him that the President couldn't have felt anything; death had been instantaneous. Ted nodded silently and wandered off, winding up in his brother's apartment. The wife of the French Ambassador paced West Executive Avenue with her husband in tow. Hervé Alphand had come reluctantly. It was against his professional intuition; he never came to the President's residence unless formally invited. But Nicole was adamant. She must be at Jackie's side, she insisted, and she gave up only after Taz Shepard, on his way to brief Johnson in the EOB, told her Mrs Kennedy was remaining at the hospital with the President's body. At about the same time there was a flurry of activity on the opposite side of the mansion; a car was stuck in the middle of East Executive Avenue. Behind the wheel was Ed Guthman. A writer like Schlesinger and Galbraith, he had been trying to set down his impressions of the day in his Justice Department office, and had just quit. The language had never seemed so inadequate. So now he was here. Anything odd in that sensitive neighbourhood stirred suspicion Friday evening, but the explanation was embarrassingly simple. Guthman's car was out of gas.

The legitimate workers, those who invented busy work, the telephoners and writers and wanderers were a minority. The majority maintained its television vigil, and late in the evening their new President rejoined them. Leaving George Reedy to prepare tomorrow's agenda, Johnson raced out MacArthur Boulevard to Spring Valley with Moyers, Valenti, Cliff Carter, and Horace Busby, a former Texas newspaperman who subsequently joined his staff. Behind the wrought-iron gates of the Elms, patrolled by agents with shotguns, the President restlessly strode from set to set. Lady Bird came down to the terrace and sat beside her husband for a while. Then Busby left and everyone else trooped up to the master bedroom and studied the screen. Their comments were sporadic. Once the President said softly of Mrs Kennedy, 'At a time when we showed the world our seamy, ugly side, she revealed and symbolized our nobler side. We should always be grateful to her.' But most of the time he just looked. Later Valenti recalled that the networks 'were re-enacting scenes of Dallas and of Texas, and of the world-wide reactions to the assassination; they would show the parade and the motorcade and then they would show films of John Kennedy making statements and speeches in the past. Lyndon Johnson watched this with interest.'

Eventually the man of the house turned off the light, and the conversation continued in the dark until he fell asleep. His three aides then tiptoed out. The first night of the Johnson administration was one of the few in which the President was not the most rapt viewer in the capital; many Washingtonians remained attentive through the night, switching from television to radio and back. The nonstop broadcasts of that weekend were to leave Americans with the feeling that new coverage could not have been more complete. Actually, it was random. Some of the most significant developments were deliberately (and wisely) concealed, and insignificant sidelights were ignored by the press, not because of their unimportance but because broadcasts were unaware of them. The public did not know, for example, that President Kennedy and Officer Tippit were not the only people killed in Dallas on November 22. At 10.40 that evening there was a third murder, unrelated to the others. The victim, a thirty-two-year-old woman, was stabbed to death by her lover. In police language he 'picked up and grabbed a butcher knife and started cutting up on the deceased'. She was pronounced dead at Parkland.

The arrival of the Kennedy party in Bethesda's suite had set in motion a strange ritualistic dance. Groups formed, parted, and re-formed; partners were changed; speaking in metallic voices, the participants watched each other covertly and swiftly glided to the side of anyone who displayed signs of distress. Certain individuals detached themselves. Evelyn Lincoln sat on a window sill clutching the President's worn black alligator briefcase, drifting in a private world of thought; Jean Smith, similarly withdrawn, stood off to one side; and Bob Kennedy was frequently on the telephone, talking to Officer Tippit's widow, to Nellie Connally, to Lee Radziwill in London, to Shriver. Otherwise the drawing-room ballet was continuous. Dave Powers had set the stage by ordering drinks, beer, and coffee. The hospital galley sent up sandwiches—thick, crusty cheese sandwiches, the antithesis of the dainty wafers which were traditional at the White House—and with these props the show went shakily on. At one point the Attorney General even ordered a record player. That was too much for Ben Bradlee. He protested. Kennedy looked around vacantly. 'She'd like it,' he said, pointing at Toni, and instructed a yeoman to bring the music. Ben awaited anxiously, but the yeoman did not return. Bob apparently forgot about it.

In the danse macabre certain themes recurred. At one time or another nearly everyone present urged Mrs Kennedy to change her clothes. To each such suggestion she shook her head tightly. Then it was felt that she ought to take a sedative, and attempts were made to enlist Captain Canada's support. Here, too, she was inflexible, and Dr John Walsh supported her. He said, 'If she doesn't want it, OK. Leave her alone, let her talk herself out.' She was talking a great deal—he thought she was 'on a talkathon.' To him she recounted her recollection of what had happened in the Presidential Lincoln. She told Ben and Toni the story of the ring at Parkland and recalled the death of Patrick. Always the two deaths were intertwined. For the country the assassination of the President stood alone; for her the two acts of the double tragedy were inseparable.

All afternoon her mother had been afraid that she would feel a revulsion against the United States. Since the age of twelve Jackie had lived most of her life in the capital. Washington, Janet Auchincloss believed, was the proper home for her older daughter, and she wanted her grandchildren brought up as Americans. In the bedroom she said, 'I hope you will never live any place but in this country, because Jack would want that.' Mr Kennedy looked amazed. She replied, 'But of course. I'm going to live in Georgetown, where Jack and I were.'

In Mrs Auchincloss' words, 'Jackie knew how the President's funeral should be, and there were no wrong notes in it.' At Bethesda the widow seemed to be conscious of her new responsibilities. She was, as she recalled afterwards, 'sort of keyed up in a strange way'. Seeing Pam Turnure in tears, she put her arms around her and said, 'Poor Pam, what will become of you now?' She worried about all of them and worked at bracing their spirits, even those of Dave Powers, the professional jolly. 'Do you know what we should have in the Kennedy Library?' she asked, smiling faintly. They waited cautiously. 'A pool,' she said, 'so Dave can give exhibitions of how he swam with the President.' Powers was delighted, and envious. He could not have done so well.

The spectators shifted partners, the brittle talk continued. Between calls the Attorney General reaffirmed to Ken O'Donnell and Larry O'Brien that he had not urged Johnson to take the oath on the plane. They exchanged wondering looks, not appreciating the possibility that Johnson may have wished to emphasize the continuity of the Presidency. It was one more piece of 'senselessness', which, to them, was the dominant theme of the tragedy. Throughout that weekend Mac Bundy could not get the German word '*Unsinn*'—'absurdity'—out of his head. Ken had much the same thing in mind when he asked those around him, over and over, 'Why did it happen? What good did it do? All my life I've believed that something worthwhile comes out of everything, no matter how terrible it is. What good can come out of this?' The meaninglessness threatened the anchor of Ken's faith.

O'Donnell asked questions. Ethel Kennedy asked none. Ethel had lost both her parents in the crash of a private plane. Extreme unction had been impossible. For a woman of her piety the raising of the faintest shadow of doubt would be disastrous. Therefore she did not inquire. She simply accepted. At 7.15 she arrived in the suite after an unpleasant ride—Dave Hackett had slowly driven her over in the Attorney General's Cadillac, whose controls he didn't understand, and at the gate a Bethesda guard had flashed a bright light in her face to identify her. Running up to the widow, she embraced her and cried, 'Oh, Jackie!'

Her sister-in-law told her she felt certain that the President had gone straight to heaven and 'is just showering graces down on us'.

'Oh, Ethel, I wish I could believe the way you do.' Then: 'Bobby's been so wonderful.'

'He'll always help you.'

Really there was no option. The President's widow and the new head of the Kennedy family had to make decisions jointly. With a single exception, which arose later in the evening, they were of one mind. They certainly never disagreed about the issue of an undertaker. She repeated to him, 'I don't want Jack to go to any funeral home,' and he nodded vehemently.

Sitting down, she faced Toni Bradlee across the round drawing-room table.

'Do you want to hear?'

Toni had never wanted anything less. Still she assented. Like Bob Kennedy, she felt that what she wanted was irrelevant. And so she heard.

'How can she *do* it?' whispered Ethel.

'It's her French blood,' Ben said. 'She's purging herself.'

John Walsh said, 'It's the best way. Let her get rid of it if she can.'

Shortly before 7.30 the Secretary of Defence reached the hospital. Bob Kennedy had talked to him at his home minutes after his return from the White House, and his arrival at the hospital was typical of McNamara; to the annoyance of Admiral Galloway and Captain Canada, who thought the Secretary should travel in an official limousine, with an escort, he drove a dark blue Galaxie, the last model manufactured by the Ford Motor Company before he resigned its presidency to come to Washington. He had bought it in October of 1960, he was proud of it, and he refused to be shunted into a gleaming Cadillac. Expecting to stop in for a few minutes, he left Mrs McNamara in the front seat. Discovering that Mrs Kennedy wanted him to stay, he rode down and reminded his wife that their thirteen-year-old son must be picked up at his Boy Scout meeting before 8.30. The Navy was speechless. No panoply, no colour—he might as well have been an accountant. The McNamaras didn't care; like Ethel Kennedy, Margie McNamara drove her own car pool shift, and she and her husband were active in civic activities and parent–teacher groups. To Ben Bradlee the Secretary's very presence in the suite was electrifying: 'After Bobby he was the second towering person there. There was no subterfuge in that man, no special smile; just naked strength. He was a man without guile, and it was that kind of occasion.'

McNamara walked through the suite and reached a decision: 'She was in that suit with the bloody skirt and blood all over her stockings, and it was fantastic, but she just wanted someone to talk to. I felt I had to be calm for her and listen to her. We were in the kitchen, Jackie sitting on the stool and me on the floor. It went on for hours. I was concentrating entirely upon her, because she needed me and I felt, the hell with the others; let them take care of themselves.'

She talked about the murder. Finally she asked, 'Where am I going to live?'

The executive mansion was no longer a Kennedy residence, and she remembered that she didn't own the Georgetown house either. Late in 1960 the President-elect had said, 'Why sell it?' It was ideal, and after two terms they would need a permanent home. But eight years seemed such a long time. It was practically a decade, so he had put it on the market. Now she needed it, or might. She was indecisive. Sleeping in that bedroom alone would be unbearable, she thought, and then she reflected, *I must never forget Jack, but I mustn't be morbid.* So: she would move back to Georgetown, preferably into the same address.

'I'll buy it back for you,' McNamara said.

Later that scene excluded everything in the Secretary's memories of the hospital. It would seem to him that he had never left the kitchen. In fact, he did more. When Shriver encountered a snag in acquiring a detail of ceremonial troops for the North Portico, McNamara issued an order, and he joined the debate which was shaping over the burial site. The mafia's position had become firmer. Jean also preferred Brookline, and the Attorney General, who hadn't committed himself, remarked to Bradlee, 'Everybody from Boston favours there.' Ben said, '*I'm* from Boston, and *I'm* not in favour of it.' Bob studied him quizzically. 'Our people don't think of you as a Bostonian,' he said. Ben was nonplussed—Bradlees had lived in Beacon Street when O'Briens and O'Donnells were across the sea—and then McNamara drew Kennedy aside and said forcefully that he agreed with Ben. Bob replied, 'If you feel that strongly, why not say something to Jackie?'

McNamara did. He returned to the kitchen and explained to her that while he understood the tie to Massachusetts, the President shouldn't belong to one section of the country. He wasn't arguing for Arlington. At that time he really didn't know much about it; to him it was merely one of several national cemeteries. But he was convinced that any one of them would be more fitting than the Brookline plot. 'A President, particularly *this* President, who has done so much for the nation's spiritual growth and enlarged our horizons, and who has been martyred this way, belongs in a national environment,' he said. 'I feel this is imperative. Boston is just too parochial.'

Although she had been thinking along the same lines, she reached no final judgment that night. Bethesda was ill-suited to deliberation. The dismal furnishings; the unreal, almost stately mazurka in the drawing-room; the efficiency apartment kitchenette; the sea of spectators below; the suddenness of it all—every concomitant blurred resolution. The very floor plan was congesting. At one point Toni felt a sealed coffin was important, but she couldn't get through to Mrs Kennedy; there were too many people in the intersection of the T. Early editions of the following afternoon's newspapers created the impression that the widow had been a super-executive, issuing rapid-fire commands in the manner of her husband. They erred. She did ask Jean, 'Where are you staying? Where did they put you?' and after her sister-in-law had replied that her bag was in the Lincoln Room she suggested Jean have it moved across the hall to the Queen's Room—so called because Queen Elizabeth had once stayed there—because the Attorney General was the President's brother;

having him there seemed appropriate. And early in the evening she also solved the lying-in-state question. Few of the million tourists who filed through the mansion's first-floor rooms each year knew that the White House Historical Association's dollar guide had been largely the work of the First Lady. At the bottom of page 39 she had had reprinted an engraving of Lincoln's body on its catafalque, and when Bob gently pointed out to her that they would have to think about what they were going to do when they left here, she answered, 'It's in the guide-book.' That was the basis for the myth that she had made a series of snappy judgments. According to one widely published version she had been busy as a whipsaw during the flight from Dallas, starting parade plans the moment Air Force One left Love Field. 'From the hospital,' the Associated Press reported, 'she asked artist William Walton to find a certain book on a certain shelf in the White House library containing sketches and photographs of Abraham Lincoln lying in state.' She didn't speak to Walton, and there was no such book. 'From Bethesda Hospital during that first long night,' wrote *Life*, 'she began a series of astonishingly detailed plans and decisions, many drawn from history, the rest of them of her own devising . . . she remembered her husband's keen interest in the Special Forces, the guerrilla-trained troops he had sent to the jungles of Vietnam. She asked, "Couldn't the honour guard include a member of the Special Forces?" ' She did not remember her husband's keen interest in the Special Forces; she did not ask such a question. Her sole contribution at the hospital was her reference to the White House guide, and even there her memory was vague. Later she rechecked the engraving and was appalled to see that Lincoln had lain on what appeared to be a teratoid, golden oak, four-poster bed.

The Kennedy who was really in charge in the tower suite was the Attorney General. He made the call about the catafalque. He requested a representative from the Special Forces. He asked that the President's personal possessions be removed from the West Wing before their return, so that Jackie would not see them and be upset, and he was responsible for the strains of the 'Navy Hymn', which would haunt the President's countrymen long after the eulogies had been forgotten. To them two passages would endure—the opening 'Eternal Father, strong to save', and the concluding:

O hear us when we cry to Thee
For those in peril on the sea.

He remembered a third. In 1945 he had served as an apprentice seaman aboard the destroyer *Joseph P. Kennedy, Jr.*, christened in recognition of his oldest brother's heroism. Young Joe had been a

Navy flier. Earlier in the war the military services had revised their traditional music to include pilots. The 'Marine Hymn's' 'on the land as on the sea' was changed to 'in the air, on land and sea', and sailors sang:

O God, protect the men who fly
Through lonely ways beneath the sky.

The national tragedy of November 22 made the long-ago death of another Kennedy seem remote to most of those who knew of it, but it wasn't remote to his brothers. Young Joe had been the Kennedy destined for a political career; because Joe had been killed, Jack had run for Congress; Jack's murder meant that the staff had fallen into Bobby's hands; should he die, Teddy would be next. The President had never forgotten Joe. Bob, knowing that, and knowing that he would have approved, asked for the hymn. Like nearly everything else, it was attributed to the widow. Men who talked to Bob Kennedy subsequently convinced themselves that they had spoken to Jackie; men who had heard Bob's wishes relayed through Shriver told the press that they were acting at the request of Mrs Kennedy. On the plane she had displayed unsuspected stamina, eclipsing O'Donnell and O'Brien, and that strength would reappear after they had returned to Pennsylvania Avenue, but on the night of November 22–23 the commanding figure in Bethesda Naval Hospital was Robert Kennedy.

As Ralph Dungan put it, there were 'two circuits that night: here and there'. 'There' was Bob Kennedy. 'Here' was Dungan's office, where Shriver continued to preside over the marathon meeting, discussing preliminary arrangements for the funeral Mass with Richard Cardinal Cushing and trying to absorb Colonel Miller's copy of the turgid *State, Official and Special Military Funeral Policies and Plans*. Both the tower suite and the West Wing were vexed by an exasperating uncertainty: no one knew when the President's body would be ready to be moved from the morgue. From a telephone on the nurse's desk outside the suite Clint Hill periodically checked with Roy Kellerman; Ted Clifton, at Shriver's elbow, called Godfrey McHugh. Kellerman and McHugh weren't doctors, so they asked Dr Burkley, who repeatedly replied, 'It's taking longer than they thought.' The first estimated time of arrival at the White House was 11 p.m. This then became midnight, 1 a.m., 2 a.m., 3 a.m., 3.30 a.m., and 4 a.m. The reason it was taking longer was never specified, but since even laymen could guess what 'it' was, they didn't inquire.

At the hospital the two most impressive men were the Attorney General and the Secretary of Defence; in the mansion they were

Shriver and Walton, both of whom joined in the response triggered by Mrs Kennedy's recollection of the guide-book.

Shriver, juggling telephones, turned the lying-in-state task over to Dick Goodwin. Goodwin phoned Schlesinger at the Harriman house, and at approximately 10 p.m. Roy Basler of the Library of Congress received a call from Schlesinger, who said he was 'relaying an urgent personal request from Mrs Kennedy'. This was typical; three men—Kennedy, Shriver, and Goodwin—stood between him and the widow, but Schlesinger gave Basler the definite impression that he had just talked to Jacqueline Kennedy. In this case, however, the deception was doubtless wise; as an historian Schlesinger knew how refractory archival bureaucracies could be. Further dialling summoned David C. Mearns, the chief of Basler's manuscripts division, and James I. Robertson, a scholar of the Lincoln funeral. Mearns, Robertson, and a third librarian met in the cavernous library. The library's master switch was off, locked in that position by a timing device. Flashlights were fetched, and the three men ran up and down the gloomy warrens, assembling a truckload of reports from century-old newspapers and magazines. The most precise accounts were delivered to the North-west Gate of the White House, and on a table in the mansion's marble entrance hall Goodwin laid out two, from *Frank Leslie's Illustrated Newspaper* and the May 6, 1865, issue of *Harper's Weekly*. Walton riffled through them, found an Alfred Waud sketch in *Harper's*, and went to work.

There was little wasted motion in Dungan's office. There was some: on his arrival from Boston, Frank Morrissey, a roly-poly friend of the Kennedy family and something like a character out of *The Last Hurrah*, did begin a night-long series of long-distance calls which began boomingly, 'This is Morrissey at the White House,' and the point of which eluded those within earshot. The Democratic National Committee did send a man to the marathon meeting, though the need for a professional politician was unexplained. And General Clifton was misinformed about the Lincoln catafalque. The original was stored in the Capitol basement, and a replica was available, but Clifton was frantically attempting to get the White House carpenters to build a new one. These, however, were exceptions. The Jackie–Bob–Sarge–Goodwin–Schlesinger–Library–Walton chain was the rule. At 1 a.m. Pierre Salinger showed up red-eyed, his pockets stuffed with the $800 in unwanted bills and change, and immediately began holding press briefings. (Pierre assigned himself to the President at Bethesda; he told Kilduff to serve as press secretary to the President in Spring Valley.) Dean Markham was notifying Kennedy friends that a short Catholic service would be held in the East Room at 10 a.m., and that the Rev. J. J. Cavanaugh was planning it.

Down in the executive mansion's theatre, where Lieutenant Sawtelle's honour guard had resumed rehearsals, Special Forces men were being integrated into the Death Watch. This was a greater challenge than Lieutenant Bird's reshuffling of body bearers at Andrews. The Attorney General's recognition of the guerrilla fighters moved them deeply. As one of their officers told Clifton, 'These boys regard the President as their godfather.' They came anxious to serve with dignity. But the Death Watch was unusual duty. Refitting them in Army dress blues, leaving them their distinctive green berets, was relatively easy.[3] And the visual signals were swiftly learned. The real problem would come in the morning, when the men stood by the coffin. Experience had taught Sawtelle that the fragrance of wreaths could be nauseating, that a soldier who kept his eyes fixed on one point could become hypnotized and swoon, and that a man's greatest struggle would be with his own emotions. It was hard enough to remain rigid when visitors wept over the coffin of a stranger. All the men in the joint guard of honour had held the young President in special regard, however, and the reverence of the elite Special Forces made them particularly vulnerable. The Lieutenant cautioned them never to look directly at a candle, the quickest mesmerizer. He warned them that they must think about other things—about anything except the murdered President. Even so, he was worried. Obviously the husky guerrillas were tense. They were primed for combat, but standing motionless hour after hour required a different sort of discipline. Sawtelle decided to hold them back until the East Room watch had been established for some time, and then to assign an additional soldier to each shift as insurance against fainting.

The chief activity in the corridor outside Dungan's anteroom was the drawing up of *ad hoc* lists, and it was to continue all weekend. There were guest lists for each phase of the funeral: seating plans, standing plans, marching formation, lists of lists—the Executive Branch, the Legislative Branch, the Supreme Court; Special Assistants to the President; visiting heads of state; the diplomatic corps; friends of the family; former Presidents; distinguished Americans. The average member of the national television audience never gave this aspect of the burial a thought, but the speedy solution of it baffled the Duke of Norfolk more than anything else, because in any state funeral the most harrying problem is whom to exclude. Markham began by telephoning Steven Smith for names of intimate

[3] After the funeral a black band was added to Special Forces berets, signifying perpetual mourning for President Kennedy.

friends, and Ken Galbraith was asked to submit a list of Presidential acquaintances in the academic community. He resolved upon a summary solution: only professors who had been invited to White House dinners would be invited. Markham began to accumulate mounds of paper—he had a master list of lists of lists—and plunging into them he was resigned to the fact that some feelings would be ruffled. He comforted himself with the reflection that those who really loved the President would understand. If they didn't, they weren't worth worrying about.

By late evening, Angie Duke said later, 'We began to feel the presence of Mrs Kennedy' (i.e., Robert Kennedy). They knew that the family wished a Navy escort for the caisson, four men from each service flanking it, and muffled drums. Apparently the demand for drummers was going to be great. Clifton wondered whether he could mobilize enough qualified military musicians to accompany the caisson from the mansion to the Hill. The past three years had taught him much about Kennedy improvisation, however, and he was prepared to fill the ranks by issuing uniforms to drummers who weren't entitled to wear them.

The prickliest issue was the question of religious services. Colonel Miller was of no help whatever here; the funeral of a Roman Catholic President was without precedent. For hours they skirted the topic. At midnight Angie Duke artfully raised it. He suggested the possibility of a secular funeral, observing that, 'The President believed in the separation of church and state, and I believe he would want a service in the White House.' Duke wasn't serious. Himself a Catholic, he knew it was unthinkable. His purpose was to provoke a serious discussion, and he succeeded brilliantly. As he put it, 'At once I could feel the electricity.' He dwelt upon the advantages of a nondenominational ritual until he began to sound like a Unitarian, and the more he talked, the more Shriver and Dungan bridled. Sarge cut him off. He said tautly, 'The family will not permit a non-religious funeral.'

Duke had antagonized them, but had made his point. 'When he suggested a burial service in the White House,' Shriver said afterwards, 'I realized that we would have to have a Mass for Jack, and I felt that it would be appropriate to have a funeral Mass in the White House.' Because the line between the things of God and the things of Caesar had been sharply drawn in 1960, the Kennedy men were far more aware of it than the aides of any Protestant President would have been. John Kennedy must be buried as a Catholic. Nevertheless, as Chief Executive he represented all Americans, and Shriver ordered two *prie-dieux* for the East Room, manned by pastors from all faiths, including the Greek Orthodox. To his surprise, Clifton spoke up and said the clergymen were here—actually in the mansion, ready to kneel. Chaplains representing every denomination had called him and volunteered. Each had read Kennedy's Houston declaration; they understood his position perfectly. They had thought of him, not as a Catholic President, but as the President of the United States, and each of them wanted to pray to his God for his President. To Bill Walton they seemed to be 'nice, kind, gentle men, trying not to be in the way and not knowing quite what to do, because there wasn't anything for them to pray over yet'. In fact, they had already done something remarkable just by coming; in death John Kennedy had convened a kind of spontaneous ecumenical council.

'Trying to fight off the appalling reality,' Schlesinger noted jerkily. Yet the work was more than therapy. Already the broad outlines of the funeral were clear: the East Room on Saturday, the great rotunda of the Capitol on Sunday, and the funeral Mass and burial on Monday. Thousands of details were still unresolved. No one knew, for example, just what sort of Mass Cardinal Cushing would celebrate or even where it would be held. The merits of St Matthew's, St Steven's, the Shrine at Catholic University, and the Shrine of the Immaculate Conception had been reviewed again and again. Dungan was strong for Immaculate Conception: 'What was bugging me was space; I was already thinking about foreigners, and then there was the Congress.' Since everyone in the meeting, including the man from the National Committee, had his little list, Dungan didn't have to elaborate the point. He won it. As matters stood at midnight, when Duke left to meet the Cabinet plane, a Pontifical Requiem Mass was to be held for the President on Monday at the Shrine of the Immaculate Conception. The fact that the Shrine was not within walking distance occurred to none of them, and had it been raised, it would have been disregarded as an inapt *démarche*; no one then dreamed that Mrs Kennedy would want to walk.

At 12.35 a.m. November 23, the first full day of the Johnson administration, Aircraft 86972 ended the twenty-four-hour flight which had begun when the Cabinet plane left Oahu for Tokyo and taxied up to the MATS terminal. As the plane entered its glide pattern Dean Rusk walked the length of the fuselage, giving detailed instructions on the order of disembarkation. Cabinet members would leave first in a body, and he would make a statement in their behalf. Wives and lesser officials would follow; then assistants with security material. The scene at the wire fence might have been a rerun of Angel's pantomime six and a half hours earlier. There was the gigantic 707; the dazzling klieg lights and microphones; the press in its pen; clusters of waiting Under Secretaries and Assistant Secretaries, and chauffeurs standing by cars. Many of the greeters were the same—Angie Duke, George Ball, Frank Roosevelt. But this time there was no crowd and, of course, no yellow truck lift.

Standing where President Johnson had stood, the Secretary of State said that he and his colleagues fully shared 'the deep sense of shock, the grievous loss we have suffered. Those of us who had the honour of serving President Kennedy value the gallantry and wisdom he brought to the grave, awesome, and lonely office of the Presidency. President Johnson needs and deserves our fullest support.'

Ball whisked Rusk into a limousine. The Freemans rode home to watch television, the Dillons to their medicine cabinet—both the Secretary of the Treasury and his wife took sleeping pills and then lay awake through the night, listening to the sirens on Massachusetts Avenue, wondering where the fire was. At Andrews the Under Secretaries and Assistant Secretaries who weren't needed dispersed slowly. Among them was Pat Moynihan. Moynihan was glum, and troubled by foreboding. Drinking black coffee in the MATS mess before the plane landed, he had overheard several other members of the sub-cabinet anxiously inquiring of one another whether anyone there knew George Reedy. One reminded the others that the Cabinet was meeting tomorrow; he expressed the hope that 'some of the more important Under Secretaries will be invited'. Pat turned away in disgust. The conversation, he thought, confirmed his suspicions about the New Frontier's second echelon. Too many of them were ambitious young men who were greedy for American power without understanding America itself.

He didn't belong with them. It is difficult to say where he did fit. A child of New York's worst slums, a self-taught intellectual and author with a Ph.D. from the Fletcher School of Law and Diplomacy, he was a stranger to Washington's elite. He was Irish but something of an outsider; no one had thrown him into a swimming pool or even invited him to Hickory Hill. Young, handsome, and highly articulate, he could have been mistaken for a Kennedy intimate, but he wasn't one; he found Lyndon Johnson attractive because he felt that both he and Johnson had started from the bottom. Moynihan had been a Manhattan longshoreman, a saloon owner, a tough. He had been arrested on New York's West Side and beaten up in a police station. He remembered several unpleasant encounters with Boston patrolmen, and extrapolating from experience he was entertaining grave doubts about the Dallas Police Department.

Before the arrival of 86972 he had spoken heatedly to Under Secretary Ball; afterwards he talked to Secretary Wirtz. With each he made the same point: 'We've got to get on top of the situation in Dallas,' he said. 'American cops are emotional. They don't believe in due process, and they are so involved in corruption that they over-compensate when they run into something big. You can't depend on them. The most profound national interest can't be left in the hands of policemen. The facts here are so confused that if we don't move quickly there will be no end of trouble later establishing a case against the Communists, against fascists, against the President himself, against anybody. It might be an anti-Khrushchev faction, it might be a Chinese faction out of Cuba—you couldn't construct a cast with a wider range of possibilities. But you can be sure of one thing. Nobody can predict what the Dallas police will do, and their saying a man is a Commie doesn't make him one.'

George Ball replied, 'You're right, I'll talk to Rusk.' Yet Moynihan had the impression that Ball hadn't understood what he had been talking about. Wirtz also promised to speak to Rusk, and he was equally hazy. Moynihan wouldn't quit. At Andrews he cornered Bob Wallace, an old friend and the Assistant Secretary of the Treasury in charge of the Secret Service. Defensively Wallace replied, 'We *are* in charge of the situation. My best man is in Louisville or Nashville, on his way to Dallas.' Unsatisfied, Moynihan pressed his case with others. Most of them misinterpreted his concern. They thought he was arguing the existence of a right-wing plot. He wasn't. 'I only want to know the facts,' he kept saying. 'I have no convictions of any kind, but what keeps a republic together is procedure, and we have chaos in Dallas; we have to move fast.' One man replied, 'That's far out.' Pat exploded: 'You stupid son-of-a-bitch! The freely elected President of the United States is lying dead in a box, and you're telling me I'm far out! It's the far-out events that make history. It's far out to say that Caesar is going to be stabbed in the forum today.'

At the airport and back in the capital he kept trying, making a pest of himself without results. A few, like Ball and Wirtz, agreed that something must be done. Nothing was done, and from the evasiveness and vagueness of their assurances Moynihan guessed that nothing would be. This, he thought, was the Achilles' heel of most of the Kennedy team. They had been prepared for anything except this. They had everything but direct knowledge of the brutal side of the United States. Their grace and their airy *flânerie* had removed them from the world of police stations, trouble, and an understanding of how rough Americans couldn't believe in it. Pat had; he could; he did; and since he went on record with everyone who would listen to him, there is no doubt that he, like Byron Skelton earlier in the month, felt an uncanny premonition. He was convinced that unless the federal government acted vigorously the country must expect a second catastrophe in the Dallas jail.

At 7.10 p.m. Dallas time Lee Harvey Oswald had been formally charged in the third-floor office of Captain Will Fritz with the murder of Patrolman Tippit. Justice of the Peace David L. Johnston presided. At 1.30 a.m. (2.30 in Washington), following repeated parades before newspapermen, including his basement press conference, he was arraigned in the fourth-floor identification bureau for the assassination of John Kennedy. David Johnston was again the officer of the court; on both occasions he had come to the police station for the closed session. The definition of a star-chamber proceeding, it will be remembered, is one held in secret.

After the first arraignment Oswald told correspondents that he had protested to the justice of the peace (whose name he hadn't quite caught) 'that I was not allowed legal representation during that very short and sweet hearing. I really don't know what the situation is all about.' It was a lie. Oswald certainly knew what the situation was about. Circumstantial evidence, the very best kind, convicts him ten times over. He was merely playing the scene for all it was worth. Thanks to local authority, however, it was worth a great deal, and what he may have really meant was that he could not believe petty officials anywhere could be this clumsy. Even the Russians had been smoother. Pat Moynihan, when he learned the truth, was aghast. He realized that he had been wrong to extrapolate from New York and Boston. Dallas was in another league entirely.[4]

Here was the greatest crime in the city's history, and here were myrmidons in complete charge. The District Attorney was available for television appearances; otherwise he was out of touch, even for the United States Attorney. Friday evening a delegation of American Civil Liberties Union lawyers visited headquarters to ascertain whether Oswald was being deprived of counsel. Policemen and the Justice of the Peace assured them everything was on the up and up. But they weren't permitted to see Oswald. Despite relentless pressure from the Deputy Attorney General in Washington—and the

[4] The author recalls a colloquy between three lawyers of the Warren Commission staff on June 27, 1964, when the Commission's report was being drafted. Here are notes of it: 'X: "How critical of the Dallas police should we be?" Y: "We can't be critical enough." Z (senior man): "That's just the problem. If we write what we really think, nobody will believe anything else we say. They'll accuse us of attacking Dallas' image. The whole report will be discredited as controversial. We've just got to tone it way down."' There was a spirited discussion, after which X and Y consented.

pressure of the Johnson men he enlisted—the Dallas Bar Association was inactive that night. Meanwhile the chaotic questioning continued. Its casualness even exceeded the insouciant standards which are customary during the investigation of petty crimes in the Southwest.[5] Oswald was being simultaneously interrogated by Dallas homicide men, county sheriffs, Texas Rangers, FBI agents, and the Secret Service. For all the wealth in Dallas, the city budget was niggardly. With a tiny fraction of the sum spent each year on the Cotton Bowl festival, Will Fritz might have been provided with a recording device, but his repeated requests for one had been turned down. (The department also lacked modern photographic equipment; each time officers wanted to see Abe Zapruder's film of the assassination they had to go to his office.) For some reason which has never been satisfactorily explained the department's secretaries had been sent home. Thus the historian is deprived of even a shorthand transcript of these vital sessions. The best we have is a composite recollection of the interrogators.

The following afternoon, when the Bar Association's president drove to the station, Oswald declined his assistance, declaring a preference for John Abt, a New York lawyer celebrated for his defences of political prisoners, or for an American Civil Liberties Union attorney. No one told him that the ACLU had attempted to see him the previous evening and had been turned away.

The Attorney General became impatient. At 10 p.m. Godfrey McHugh assured him they would be ready to leave Bethesda at midnight, but at midnight the embalming hadn't even begun. During the delay several occupants of the tower suite roused from their stupor. Jean Smith told George Thomas to bring the President's favourite suits and ties from the White House; he left for the mansion with two agents. Ken O'Donnell gave Bob Kennedy the President's wallet. Then Ken said determinedly—it had been preying on his mind since Parkland—'Jackie, I'm going to get that ring back for you.' Down in the morgue he spoke to Dr Burkley, who worked the ring free and brushed past him. On the seventeenth floor Burkley explained to the Attorney General, 'I want to give it to her myself, so I can be sure she has it.' Wordlessly Bob Kennedy stepped aside, and in the little bedroom the Presidential physician handed her the ring and tried to voice his anguish.

The fact was that he had never been quite sure of his position with

[5] This writer once spent a year observing those easygoing procedures in the Oklahoma City Police Station. During that time the policemen there handled the most minor offenders more carefully than Dallas treated the most notorious American criminal of the century.

the Kennedys. Janet Travell had overshadowed him in the newspapers, and being Navy he had sometimes appeared preoccupied with fussy service routine and interservice rivalry. Last spring it had been assumed that the infant she was expecting would be delivered in Washington, and the issue was whether she should be confined at Bethesda or Walter Reed. Dr Walsh had been in the Army, so Walter Reed was the obvious choice. But Burkley had been obtuse. He had set about reserving this very suite for the expectant mother until she, hearing about it, wrote him a sharp letter. Though the public never saw it, Jacqueline Kennedy's temper could be formidable. Burkley therefore had maintained a respectful distance until today. But she was also capable of instinctive compassion, and when he handed her the ring and awkwardly attempted to express himself—he could think of nothing but clichés—she told him how much his attentiveness had meant to the President and her. Then she reached into her jacket pocket, took out one of the red blossoms the doctor had handed her in Oneal's ambulance-hearse, and held it out.

Burkley bowed his head. He mumbled, 'This is the greatest treasure of my life.'

The population of the suite reached its peak during Friday's penultimate hour. At 10 p.m. Margie McNamara returned from the Boy Scout meeting. John Nolan, Robert Kennedy's administrative assistant, came up. Ethel had called Charlie and Martha Bartlett, and with a score of occupants crammed into it the suite was approaching capacity. To Charlie 'Jackie was poised, unreal. She was talking about the murder—I gathered she had been talking about it for some time. She told me about red roses and the new rug they were to have put in the President's study that day and the blood. She wasn't sobbing. Tears were just a breath away, but they never came. Bobby was watching, silent, ready. He was terrific, low-key as always.'

The bedroom television was on, nobody knew why. There were the endless film clips of the President's past, deep organ music, selections from a massive orchestra; a lugubrious encomium from Governor George Wallace of Alabama; a smug, infuriating video tape of Jesse Curry, made that morning, describing Dallas' airtight security precautions; pictures of Oswald's press conference; and, at 11.35, NBC's announcement that 'Mrs Jacqueline Kennedy and her two children went to the Naval Hospital and will remain there overnight'. The sensible thing would have been to switch the set off. Since no one knew who had turned it on, however, no one would take the responsibility. Instead the bedroom was evacuated.

The men and women tended to segregate, the men congregating in the kitchen, the women around the large drawing-room table. McNamara leaned against the refrigerator and talked, as he had to George Ball, about how splendid Kennedy's second four years would have been. Charlie Bartlett asked him whether he knew that he was supposed to be Secretary of State in that term—Charlie had heard it from the President. The Secretary of Defence nodded slowly. 'I don't know what I could have done about policy, but I could have helped with the administration,' he said. Jackie, at the big table with Martha, Margie, Toni, Jean, and Ethel, had stopped speaking of Dallas. She was trying valiantly to entertain them, to act as the gracious hostess while declining fresh offers of sedatives and shaking off her mother's renewed suggestions that she change her clothes. Martha thought, *It's almost as though she doesn't want the day to end.*

'Suddenly,' Ben Bradlee said later, 'we'd been there too long.' He and Toni drifted towards the door. Mrs Kennedy urged Evelyn, Nancy, Mary, and Pam to drive home and get some sleep. 'Somehow we've got to get through the next few days,' she told them. Mary's lips framed the question, '*How?*' 'Be strong for two or three days,' she was told. 'Then we'll all collapse.' Of herself Jacqueline Kennedy said to Martha, 'I'm not leaving here till Jack goes. But I won't cry till it's all over.' Dr Walsh was also escorting people out. He had been worrying about 'the big, nebulous, indefinite something—when they'd be ready downstairs'. The postponements were provoking. Given sufficient strain any constitution will snap. The widow, he decided, must have some rest. Only Bob Kennedy seemed reluctant to see the number of guests dwindle. 'Why go?' he inquired as they moved in a group towards the big elevator. They murmured excuses; they fled.

Mrs Kennedy had a special request for her mother and stepfather.

'Will you stay at the White House, Mummy?'

Janet Auchincloss said that she would be happy to stay.

'Will you sleep in Jack's room?'

'Anywhere you like,' Mrs Auchincloss said. But she felt it was sacrilegious. Tentatively she suggested they use a sitting-room couch instead.

'No, I'd like it if you slept in Jack's bed.'

'Of course.'

'Would Uncle Hugh stay, too?'

'Of course.'

Then it struck Janet: her daughter wanted company. The southwest corner of the second floor was very large. The President's bedroom, the First Lady's bedroom, the First Lady's sitting-room, and the passages linking them formed a separate apartment, cut off from the rest of the mansion by the Oval Room and the bisecting east–west hall. With the President gone, his wife would be there all alone; Miss Shaw, the children, and Bob and Jean might as well have been in a separate building. Mrs Auchincloss said to her husband in an undertone, 'We'll stop in Georgetown for toothbrushes,' and they slipped away.

Ken, Larry, and Dave, like Mrs Kennedy, weren't leaving without the President. There was no discussion. It was understood. They withdrew from the apartment and stood behind Clint Hill. The nurse showed Ethel and Jean to other rooms down the hall. Dr Walsh gave Jean a sleeping pill, and he, Bob McNamara, and Bob Kennedy remained with Jackie. An hour later Jean was back. The pill had been ineffective, and she had forgotten something. Bob went into the kitchen with McNamara, and the President's wife and his sister wandered aimlessly through the drawing-room, into the bedroom. The television was broadcasting a Mass. The two women knelt by the screen until the service was over. Abruptly the images altered and became unbearably familiar—the channel was starting one of those long sequences of Kennedy's life. Mrs Kennedy rose with one motion and twisted the knob. The light shrank to a square point and vanished, and Jean stumbled back to her room.

In the drawing-room Dr Walsh prepared a syringe; he detected signs of utter exhaustion in her. Considering the past two days, it was incredible that she should still be on her feet—Bob Kennedy and Bob McNamara were men of extraordinary stamina, but they hadn't been in Texas—and while the doctor had no way of knowing how much more would be expected of her, he suspected that it would be a lot. At a bare minimum she needed one hour of complete relaxation. She hadn't been able to talk it out. Just before Jean arrived Bob had suggested she return to the mansion; she had shaken her head and said she would lie down. Now she wasn't even doing that. He loaded the needle with 100 milligrams of Visatril, a formidable dose, and showed it to her.

She eyed it dubiously, then wavered. 'Maybe you could just give me something so I could have a little nap,' she said, holding out her arm. 'But I want to be awake when we go home.'

Walsh had complete confidence in the drug; he felt sure she would coast off within thirty seconds. Settling her down, he returned to the drawing-room, sat in a chair, and instantly fell asleep.

Mrs Kennedy waited and waited. Ten minutes passed and nothing happened. She looked around for a cigarette. There weren't any here, so she strolled into the living-room in search of a package. As she passed the doctor's chair he awoke and looked up in disbelief.

His astonishment was so evident that it was comic. She smiled down at him and strode on with a firm step. Walsh stared after her, thinking, *I might just as well have given her a shot of Coca-Cola.*

Major General Wehle raced home, changed from greens to blues, raced back and was confronted by Lieutenant Sam Bird, who reported that the Dallas Coffin was marred. He advised the general that the family be notified.

The call to the seventeenth floor was made by Godfrey McHugh. He said, 'Bob, the casket we have is cheap and thin, it's really shabby. One handle is off, and the ornaments are in bad shape.'

'Get another,' Kennedy said.

'I'm not going to leave here.'

'I want you to.'

McHugh refused; he was, he explained, a guard of honour. 'But I know a place near here. It's only a few blocks down Wisconsin. It's Gawler's.'

Kennedy had heard of Gawler's. A friend of his had been buried from there recently. McHugh suggested a bronze or mahogany coffin. But Robert Kennedy was tenacious, too; both he and his sister-in-law had rejected a private funeral home on principle, and upon reflection he decided that the military ought to handle the whole thing. There was no reason to bring in an undertaker. This conversation, like all others, was being screened through Clint Hill, and the mafia was listening. Ken O'Donnell and Larry O'Brien huddled and agreed that Bob was in a daze. He was going through enough; he shouldn't be asked to worry about this, too.

Ken cut in. 'We'll take care of it, Bob.'

Thus Gawler's, which had been vetoed by the Kennedy family, became part of the Presidential funeral. The damaged coffin was largely responsible—largely, but not entirely, for the issue of whether or not it was to be closed had not been resolved, and should the coffin have been open during the lying in state, the special arts of the undertaker would have been essential. Quite apart from that, however, the Attorney General was in a dilemma. He could scarcely permit a state funeral to proceed with a battered casket. A subsequent examination revealed that the lieutenant and two generals had exaggerated the extent of the damage to Oneal's Britannia, and that the casket was neither cheap nor thin, but Kennedy could not have guessed that, nor could he have been expected to come down and make his own inspection. He had been right the first time; they must get another. And O'Donnell was also correct: the mafia must spare him the actual choice.

Dave Powers squiggled:

Around midnight Ken, Larry, and I picked
out a coffin for our President

Dave omitted another Irishman. Muggsy O'Leary had been summoned from the morgue. In a night sated with sentiment the journey of this quartet was especially touching. Dave was naturally reminded of a story; it was about himself. 'You know, the Irish always measure the importance of people by the number of friends who come to their wakes,' he said in the car. 'All my life I've thought of my wake being held in a Boston three-decker tenement. I just assumed he'd live longer than me, and I'd be so proud to have the President of the United States at my wake. And now here I am, going to get a casket for him.'

Gawler's selection room contained thirty-two coffins that night, each of them mounted on a velvet-skirted estrade which in turn stood upon thick, cream wall-to-wall carpeting. Flush overhead lights gleamed softly; a tape recorder provided appropriate background music. Joe Gawler led them in. According to O'Brien, 'I said to the man at the display room, "Would you show us the plainest one you have in the middle price range?" I don't know why I asked him that, but I think it was because I wanted the coffin to represent the American people. Therefore I thought it should be plain. And that's what we got. He said, "Here." He showed us several, and we took the one with the simplest interior. I never asked the price.' According to O'Donnell, 'The coffin we chose was the second one we looked at. I know that Larry and I had both reached the same decision simultaneously—that that would be the one we would use. It was plain.'

Tampering with their moving account is a pity, but the Irish, as John Kennedy once noted wryly, are not noted for their accuracy, and the casket in which he was to be buried is obviously a matter of some historical interest. Undoubtedly O'Brien's recollection of their intention is correct. Robert Kennedy was thinking along the same lines. He believes he spoke to O'Donnell about the price while Ken was at the funeral parlour; and he has a clear memory of talking to a girl who told him, 'You can get one for $500, one for $1,400, or one for $2,000.' She went on about water proofing and optional equipment. Influenced by the Mitford book, he shied away from the high figure. He asked for the $1,400 coffin, and afterwards he wondered whether he had been cheap; he thought how difficult such choices must be for everyone.

But all this is mysterious, because no one on Gawler's staff recalls talking to the Attorney General about price or anything else. Moreover, the casket O'Donnell and O'Brien picked—it was immediately to the left as they entered the selection room—could hardly be called plain. Known to the trade as a Marsellus No. 710, it was constructed of hand-rubbed, five-hundred-year-old African mahogany upholstered in what the manufacturer described as 'finest new pure white rayon'. Gawler believed his visitors wanted 'something fitting and proper for the President of the United States', which does not give with O'Brien's impression that they had purchased an ordinary coffin. It was unusual, and it was very expensive. In 1961 Jessica Mitford had found that the average bill for casket and services in the United States was $708. Muggsy O'Leary thought the price mentioned in the selection room was $2,000. Even that was low. Gawler's charged $2,460. In a subsequent decision, the most expensive vault in the establishment went with it. The total bill, as rendered and paid, was $3,160.

Joe Gawler and Joe Hagan, his chief assistant, supervised the loading of the coffin in a hearse, or, as Hagan preferred to call it, a 'funeral coach'. The firm's young cosmetician accompanied them to Bethesda. The two caskets, Oneal's and Gawler's, lay side by side for a while in the morgue anteroom; then Oneal's was removed for storage and the undertakers, Irishmen, and George Thomas were admitted to the main room. The autopsy team had finished its work, a gruelling, three-hour task, interrupted by the arrival of a fragment of skull which had been retrieved on Elm Street and flown east by federal agents. The nature of the two wounds and the presence of metal fragments in the President's head had been verified; the metal from Oswald's bullet was turned over to the FBI. Bethesda's physicians anticipated that their findings would later be subjected to the most searching scrutiny. They had heard reports of Mac Perry's medical briefing for the press, and to their dismay they had discovered that all evidence of what was being called an entrance wound in the throat had been removed by Perry's tracheotomy. Unlike the physicians at Parkland, they had turned the President over and seen the smaller hole in the back of his neck. They were positive that Perry had seen an exit wound. The deleterious effects of confusion were already evident. Commander James J. Humes, Bethesda's chief of pathology, telephoned Perry in Dallas shortly after midnight, and clinical photographs were taken to satisfy all the Texas doctors who had been in Trauma Room No. 1.

The cosmetician then went to work. In Hagan's words, 'He was really under the gun. There were about thirty-five people, led by General Wehle, breathing down our necks. We were worrying about the skull leakage, which could be disastrous. We did not know whether the body would be viewed or not.' The application of cosmetics required nearly three hours. It was quite unnecessary, but that was not the undertakers' fault. Neither McHugh nor Burkley, who were in constant touch with the tower suite, could guarantee that the coffin would be closed. McHugh told Hagan it was better to take the time and be on the safe side. 'The family may change their minds at any time,' he said. Burkley had spoken to Mrs Kennedy. He knew her wishes, 'but', he explained afterwards, 'I was determined that the body be fully dressed and that the face be just right in case people opened the coffin a thousand years hence.'

Dave Powers picked the clothes. From the eight suits and four pairs of shoes George Thomas had brought Dave chose a blue-grey suit, black shoes, and, after an extensive debate between Ken and Larry, a blue tie with a slight pattern of light dots. Lieutenant Sam Bird, standing beside General Wehle, saw the embroidered 'JFK' on the white silk shirt sleeve; then it was hidden by the coat. The Presidential valet recalled that his dislike of flamboyant monograms had extended to handkerchiefs. Kennedy had carefully folded them so that the initials would not show, and Thomas did it for him now, slipping the handkerchief into his coat pocket. Completely dressed, the body was wheeled into the anteroom, beside the waiting coffin. A naval officer told Lieutenant Bird, 'Clear the area. We don't want anybody in here under any circumstances. The Secret Service are going to put him in.' Even General Wehle left, but the body was transferred by physicians and undertakers, not agents. Joe Hagan arranged the President's hands and placed a rosary in them, and Godfrey McHugh, ignoring a naval officer who had ordered him out, carefully watched Joe Gawler close the coffin. The lid latched, he noticed, with a faint, almost imperceptible click. Should it ever be re-opened, Godfrey wanted to do it himself.

In the corridor outside the morgue one of the undertakers handed Lieutenant Bird an American flag. It was standard Veterans Administration issue, 5½ by 9 feet; funeral parlors regularly acquired them from the VA for veterans' burials. Because so many military families used Gawler's, the firm had a stock of them, and this one had been kept on hand for the funeral of the next man who had worn the uniform. The flag was folded, as usual, in a triangle. The lieutenant didn't have to be told what to do with it. Flag drill is as familiar to men stationed at Arlington as the manual of arms is to Marines. After the casket team had carefully packed the floor of the ambulance with blankets—the ambulance lacked the rubber pins and rollers of a hearse, and Gawler was determined that his coffin not share the fate of Oneal's—the team formed two facing ranks. When the casket had been wheeled between them, the flag would be neatly handed from man to man, unfolding as it went until, fully unfurled, it was being held above the lid. Then it would be draped over the coffin and all hands would salute.

Waiting there, Lieutenant Bird suddenly recalled the colonel's widow in Section 35 of Arlington the previous noon. He remembered her stumbling down the slope just before he heard the President had been shot, and how she had refused to let her son relieve her of the flag. She had clutched it tight against her heart with both forearms. He realized that he was holding this one the same way.

During General Wehle's absence from his customary command post at Fort McNair, the Military District of Washington was gripped by a strange inertia. A martyred Chief Executive was about to be returned to the executive mansion. Every soldier at McNair and Mayer, every sailor at Anacostia, every Marine from Quantico should have been alert. They weren't. They were either in their bunks or watching the atypical late shows. The Secretary of Defence, with two and a half million men under arms, hadn't been able to muster an appropriate guard for the White House. He was bewildered. The Attorney General, also puzzled, said icily, 'If we can get twenty thousand troops to Oxford, Mississippi, we can get enough troops to Washington, D.C., for this.'

It was a reasonable assumption. It didn't work. Sergeant Shriver, who was keeping Kennedy and McNamara posted, was frantic. This was not, after all, Valley Forge; it was peacetime, and the Pentagon was maintaining the largest standing army in history. Yet the only standees at 3 a.m. were Lieutenant Sawtelle's Death Watch and Lieutenant Bird's casket team. The smoothly oiled military establishment had inexplicably clanked to a halt. Orders were issued, but not obeyed. The businessman in Shriver was choleric. 'We have a fifty-billion-dollar defence budget,' he barked at Taz Shepard and Paul Miller. 'The guy in charge of it is coming home. Can't you find *anybody*?'

The Navy Captain and the Army Colonel squirmed, exchanged uncomfortable looks, and hurried off to make calls. They returned. No troops arrived.

In Bethesda Mrs Kennedy finished her cigarette and turned the television on again. More organ music. More pictures of her husband. Another glimpse of the swearing in. Scenes of thousands of Americans praying in churches. She watched a while, crying alone, and then crossed to the kitchen, where Bob Kennedy and Bob McNamara were talking quietly.

Her brother-in-law mentioned Officer Tippit's widow. 'Do you want to speak to her?'

She didn't; it was so hard to concentrate on anything except the

President who lay below. Perhaps Mrs Tippit's loss had been as great as hers, but she couldn't think so. She could only marvel at Bobby's thoughtfulness.

Muggsy O'Leary, just back from Gawler's, peered in. She asked, 'Please, Muggsy—don't ever leave me.'

'I won't.'[6]

While Bob was telephoning in the drawing-room, she broached the issue of the open coffin with McNamara. It was now urgent. Friday had become Saturday. Dawn was approaching. In a few hours President Kennedy would be lying in state. The memory of her father's funeral returned again, and she said, 'I want the coffin closed so badly. You can't have it open.'

He disagreed. 'It can't be done, Jackie. Everybody wants to see a Head of State.'

'I don't care. It's the most awful, morbid thing; they have to remember Jack alive.'

The Attorney General came back, and the three of them perched where they would go—he on top of the refrigerator, McNamara on the sink, Jackie on the floor. She said again that she couldn't stand the idea of what undertakers called 'viewing the remains'. Bob Kennedy, like Bob McNamara, said that this was an exceptional situation. He didn't see how a President's funeral could disregard the public; private preferences had to be set aside. She had always listened to men. These two had been among that select handful whom her husband had trusted completely, and eventually she lapsed into silence—as she put it, 'I just sort of accepted that with such misery.' She didn't really accept it. It was clear that she felt something precious to her was at stake. Womanlike, she was waiting. 'The tension in that kitchen,' McNamara said later, 'was unimaginable'.

Behind the North Portico, still undistinguished by the presence of a single soldier or sailor, the decoration of the East Room was proceding in an atmosphere of controlled frenzy; as the number of people in the tower suite had dwindled, the decorating force had grown. Bill Walton commanded a manifold crew: Shriver, Dungan, Schlesinger, Goodwin, Taz Shepard, Dean Markham, Colonel Miller, Mr West, General Clifton, Dr English, Maître Fincklin and his six butlers; Cecil Stoughton; Traphes L. Bryant, the President's dog handler; Lawrence Arata, the White House upholsterer; and Mrs Arata. Pam Turnure and Nancy Tuckerman had come here from Bethesda, and the Auchinclosses looked in briefly.

[6] Nor did he. After she moved from the capital he was the one Irishman who remained with her and the children.

'How do you like it?' Walton called down to them. He was standing on a steep stepladder, engulfed in crepe.

'Oughtn't there to be a flag?' Mrs Auchincloss inquired.

He looked startled. He said, 'Of course! A flag!' and swayed on, looping great bolts of cloth around a massive crystal chandelier.

Upstairs Janet Auchincloss tapped on Miss Shaw's door. She anticipated that Caroline and John might run into their father's bedroom when they awoke, expecting to find him there. She said, 'Tell the children Uncle Coo and I will be in the President's room.'

The Auchinclosses retired to the President's four-poster. They did not rest. The bed was board and horsehair. Janet had heard about these boards. Contact with one was something else. There was no resilience whatever. It actually hurt, and she thought of the President sleeping all these years in constant pain, bearing the strain of office each day and then stretching out on this. She had been his mother-in-law, but she had not known; it still did not seem possible.

Downstairs the volunteers toiled on, fuelled by vats of coffee. Afterwards their task looked easy. Few appreciated how staggering it had been. 'I was supposed to be a pro about this sort of thing, and I didn't even know how to start,' said Nancy Tuckerman. The East Room of the White House is the largest room in the mansion. Originally known as 'the Public Audience Chamber', it is panelled in white-enamelled wood and illuminated by five great windows and three gigantic chandeliers, any one of which would mash a man to pulp. The sheer dimensions of the room are defeating. To relieve its bare aspect, Andrew Jackson had spent over $9,000, a remarkable sum then, and all Jackson did was fill it up. Walton's challenge was quite different. He had to transform this gay ballroom into a funeral hall.

At the outset he didn't think it possible. He studied the Library of Congress engraving and doubted there was that much crepe in Washington. Luckily that much was unnecessary. The closer Walton examined the sketch, the more he realized that Mrs Kennedy would recoil from such a display. It resembled a grotesque carnival of death. Everything had been overdone. If the engraver had been accurate (it was possible, of course, that he hadn't even been in the capital), the chandeliers had been wholly enveloped in crepe, transforming them into horrid beehives. Borders of crepe would be more appropriate, provided it was available. It was; thick bolts miraculously appeared. Lawrence Arata had been storing them for chair upholstery, and when his supply was exhausted he sent out for more from a shop. Because of the uncertain deadline, the decoration proceeded in phases. Clifton's first word from McHugh had been that the body would be brought through the North-west Gate before eleven o'clock. Between then and McHugh's next call Walton ignored everything except the chandeliers. After the first postponement he turned to the windows, fashioning curtains of black. As delay followed delay Walton, Shriver, and Arata dashed about brandishing cloth and hammers, carpet tacks gripped in their teeth, darkening the mantel and the door. The mansion entrance and the North Portico were to be left until last; they would do them if they had time.

Schlesinger, who was writing more than he was tacking, noted: 'It is now twenty minutes to two. The casket will arrive at the White House around 3.30.' He overheard 'forlorn scraps of conversation' about 'the rooms in which we had had such happy times, filled with memory and melancholy'. The estimated time of arrival was then changed from 4 to 4.30. That proved correct, though down in the theatre the rehearsing Death Watch received the news with soldierly scepticism, and those upstairs were too busy to give it much thought. Between crepe-looping sessions they were dealing with artifacts. Considering the protean group and its lack of experience with funerals, there was remarkably little discussion. Most were intimidated by Walton and Shriver. Walton was the New Frontier's artist-without-portfolio. And Shriver had his own notions about taste. He frowned down at the monstrous East Room piano, which was designed by Franklin Roosevelt and which looks rather like a Byzantine altar. 'We'll move it,' he said briskly. The men around him sagged. It was a Herculean job—what was really needed was a crane—but groaning and perspiring they somehow managed it.

The catafalque replica, which had been arriving in pieces since midnight, was uncrated and erected. It should have been majestic. It looked barren. Accoutrements were needed. Lincoln had had them; they must be provided for Kennedy. Walton thought first of flowers, and pointing to one of Jacqueline Kennedy's East Room urns he told West, 'Fill it with magnolia leaves.' West said he hadn't any. 'Yes, you do,' Walton said. 'Cut them off Andy Jackson's trees, they'll grow back.' Two men from Gawler's arrived, bearing various objects. Walton, a Mitford reader, gave them a wall-eyed stare. Two *prie-dieux* were accepted. The rest—rich satin backgrounds, ornate candlesticks, a five-foot cross of natural wood—was immediately rejected. Walton studied them and then said quietly, 'Well, it's just hideous, Sarge.' Sarge agreed that it was pretty bad, and the undertakers crept out.

Candlesticks fetched from St Matthew's turned out to be even worse than the undertakers', and while wooden sticks from St Steven's were presentable and were adopted, a crucifix from the Shrine of the Immaculate Conception, a gold Saviour affixed to a silver cross, was so dreadful that Walton began to wonder whether they needed any cross at all. He checked the Lincoln engraving. A crucifix was clearly visible. Furthermore, it had lain at the foot of the bier; it would be conspicuous to every visitor. 'Doesn't anyone have one that would fit?' he asked in despair. 'I'll get mine,' said Shriver. He dispatched a White House car to his home in Maryland, and his secretary, who had been watching the Shriver children, gave the driver the Benedictine cross from his bedroom—black, hand-sculptured, with a realistic, Germanic figure. 'Perfect,' said Walton when he saw it. 'It could have been ordered for the occasion.'

Sarge walked out to the portico with Goodwin, West, and Dr English. Across Pennsylvania Avenue the huge, eerie crowd was milling about. They would never see the crepe-bordered East Room, Shriver thought, and the occasion should be made memorable for them, too. Remembering White House parties when the President and Mrs Kennedy had had the grounds lit with little flaming pots, he called a council of the military men present. 'This funeral for a President is going to vary a little bit from the manual,' he said. 'I know he isn't really coming home, but I want it to look that way.' He explained the need for light. They replied that they had none. '*None?*' Sarge repeated sarcastically. 'Not even flashlights?' Hurt, one officer suggested helicopter lights. 'Ridiculous,' Shriver fumed, and telephoned the District Highway Department. He recalled seeing tiny flambeaux set out to warn night drivers of highway construction. They weren't used any more, he was told. The department had been completely converted to electrical equipment. He hung up, abandoning hope. But the old equipment had not been discarded. The right warehouse was located, the man with the key was found, and at 3.30 a.m. pots were situated on either side of the entrance drive and ignited.

Meantime Shriver had turned to the door. It was one of his greatest problems, and he never completely solved it. The entrance to the mansion was handsome. Unfortunately it was obscured by a storm door and framework; both were aluminium, which seemed to him to be cold and ugly. Bill Walton agreed. He further pointed out that in the event that the coffin should be cumbersome, the storm door might not be wide enough for it. Sarge waved his arm. 'Take it off,' he said. The mansion staff huddled. The answer came back to him: 'It won't come off.' Sarge glowered at them. 'Goddamn it, I was in the Merchandise Mart and I *know* it will come off,' he said. He was partly right. The three-sided glass enclosure could be dismantled, and West supervised its removal. But the frame was embedded in concrete. It had to stay. Lawrence Arata and his wife mounted stepladders and tacked crepe around it, and nobody noticed the frame. Shriver and Walton thought it was gone.

Among them they had created a scene of indescribable drama: the flame-lit drive, the deep black against the white columns, the shrouded doorway, the East Room in deep mourning, the catafalque ready to receive the coffin. There was only one omission, and Shriver was now free to concentrate on it. He said to Shepard, 'All right, where are they?'

He didn't identify them. It was unnecessary. Shepard spread his hands. He just didn't know.

'The President of the United States is going to be here any minute,' Sarge said flintily, 'and there's nobody to meet him. God-damn it, Taz, we want some soldiers or sailors who will walk slowly and escort him to the door, reflecting the solemnity of the occasion.'

'Get the Marines,' Dean Markham suggested. Markham had served in the Marine Corps in World War II, and he knew that the Corps' crack drill teams were garrisoned at Eighth and I streets, south-east of the Capitol.

Colonel Miller thought it was an excellent idea. 'That's closer than any Army or Navy post,' he said, 'I'll send a bus.'

Shepard phoned the barracks' duty officer. Under pressure him-self, he spoke with exceptional force: 'Break out the Marines. The Commander in Chief has been assassinated, and I want a squad at the White House double-quick. You better move!'

They moved. At the time of Shepard's call they were in their bunks. Exactly seventeen minutes later they appeared on the South Portico in immaculate dress blues, each man trailing a glossy rifle at order arms. The entire squad had dressed in the bus. Unquestionably the men of any other service would have responded eagerly, but the selection of the leathernecks was particularly fitting for two reasons. Thomas Jefferson had ordered the construction of the barracks at Eighth and I, but John Kennedy had been the first President to inspect them. The Marines remembered that. They remembered something else. Every one of them knew where Lee Harvey Oswald had learned to shoot.

Double-timing through the Diplomatic Reception Room, the squad appeared on the North Portico. Under his breath Shriver said to English, 'They made it.'

Their officer, First Lieutenant William Lee, formed them in ranks, dressed the ranks, and then strutted them down the drive towards the gate. At mid-point he ordered a halt and began speaking to them in a low voice. From the mansion it was inaudible, and after the vexing delay those on the portico were afraid might be lost. Shriver squinted towards the gate. In the flickering torchlight he had an indistinct impression of glittering brass buttons, buffed shoes, choker collars, and visored white caps. Lieutenant Lee's sword shimmered, but the comforting thump of boots had stopped; they were making no sound at all.

'Where's he taking them?' Goodwin asked uneasily. 'What are they doing?'

A voice behind him said, 'They're bowing their heads.'

Lieutenant Bird's pallbearers saluted the flag-draped coffin, and Dr Burkley headed for the seventeenth floor. Ethel and Jean, roused by light knocks, remained in the background with Burkley and McNamara while Jacqueline Kennedy and the President's brother headed the group from the tower suite. Mrs Kennedy was uncertain about their destination; she was under the impression that they would go to another room and wait there—that had been the pattern for fourteen hours. Instead, it seemed, they were going to walk awhile. Leaving the elevator on the third floor, she followed the bobbing hat of a naval officer for nearly two hundred strides over seemingly endless stretches of rolling, red-tiled corridor to a second, push-button lift which carried them down to the basement. The hat bobbed to the right, past an out-patient clinic, left beneath a sign flashing physicians' call numbers, and then she saw the flag outside the morgue and knew they were really going home now.

The purpose of the long trip had been to shield her from photographers. The cameramen were undeceived. They had scouted every exit and spotted the ambulance parked beside Gawler's hearse. She saw them beyond the concrete platform, dim figures prancing behind ropes, and again she murmured to Clint Hill, 'Don't keep them away. Let them see.' They didn't see. Everything happened too quickly. The coffin slid in; she sat on the jump seat beside it; Robert Kennedy crouched on the floor, and at 3.56 a.m. Clint told Bill Greer to pull out. Greer followed General Wehle's staff car in a rapid tour of the hospital grounds, back out the main gate, and down Wisconsin to Massachusetts.

It was the smallest hour of the morning. Hardly anyone spoke. Everything had been said, and they were exhausted. Bob Kennedy saw that they were passing Gawler's and remembered that the new coffin had come from there, but he remained mute. So did his wife, in the car behind the ambulance, though Ethel looked sideways at McNamara and wondered 'what his philosophy could be, what made him strong and sympathetic like Bobby'. Except for the red roof light on the staff car, the cavalcade did not announce itself. Nevertheless the silent witnesses were there. Wehle, McHugh, Dave Hackett, and Lieutenant Bird looked out wearily and saw men in denim standing at attention beside cars halted at intersections, and in all-night filling stations attendants were facing the ambulance, their caps over their hearts. To Hackett his hushed trip back to the mansion was the most moving moment of the weekend, because the roughly dressed workmen heading for the 5 a.m. shift, the attendants and the bareheaded Negroes on the sidewalks were, he thought, 'the people the President had been working for hardest'. They knew it, and they were here. And although traffic was thinnest at this time of day, a tremendous escort had sprung to life. The casket team rode in the last car of the procession. Yet as they turned off Massachusetts at Twentieth Street, Lieutenant Bird looked back up embassy row and saw 'hundreds of automobiles following us, bumper to bumper as far back as the eye could see, their headlights flashing'.

In Lafayette Park the naked elms and beeches above the crowd there glistened with dew and stirred faintly in a southerly breeze as the General turned off his roof light. He radioed a brief report to the rest of the cars that they were entering the North-west Gate and slowing down to pick up an honour guard of Marines. The report couldn't reach the rear of the ambulance. Mrs Kennedy heard 'a slow clank-clanking' outside. The Attorney General thought he could hear the roll of drums, and perhaps the distant strains of music. In reality there was only Lieutenant Lee's squad, moving ahead at port arms, in flawless formation, in that heartbreaking cadence of mourning which the Marine Corps learned at the turn of the century.

The two chief mourners stepped out; Shriver silently clasped their hands. The casket team moved up to the ambulance. Normally the officer commanding military body bearers does not touch the coffin, because he would throw it off balance, but on the portico steps Lieutenant Bird's six men began to lurch alarmingly. Stepping up swiftly, he slid his fingers beneath the coffin and felt a wrenching strain in his arms. The soldier in front of him rolled his eyes back, whispered, 'Good God, don't let go,' and the seven of them carried it across the marble hall, into the East Room, on to the catafalque. Maître Finklin and a doorman lit the tall candles. The hands of both Negroes were trembling violently, and in attempting to ignite the fourth taper the doorman extinguished his torch and had to begin again. Bill Walton handed a sheaf of flowers to Godfrey McHugh, who laid them against the coffin. McHugh did the job awkwardly, but Walton decided that rearrangement could wait. He tiptoed away; he was anxious not to intrude upon the family's grief. Everyone who had joined in the redecoration felt that way. They bunched together on the south side of the room, from time to time looking at the casket almost furtively. Among them was Pierre Salinger, who wrote: 'Our Chief was home. And for the first time since I peered at the yellow piece of paper in the hand of the Secretary of State, I began to believe he was really dead.'

Standing in the doorway of the elegant room she had loved, whose history she knew so well, and which she had last left at the height of Wednesday's judiciary reception, the widowed First Lady recognized the tallest of the men—gaunt, pocked Chuck Spalding. Their eyes met. During that fleeting exchange she saw the harrowed lines of suffering in his face and thought of Abraham Lincoln; Spalding himself thought 'of all the things planned for, all the things fought for, all the things achieved, all the things to do, all the things so suddenly lost'.

'A priest said a few words,' Schlesinger noted. It was a brief blessing. Those at the far end of the chamber could not hear it, Father John Kuhn of St Matthew's was reading the *De Profundis*, Psalm 130:

Out of the depths I cry to you, O Lord; Lord hear my voice! . . .
My soul waits for the Lord more than sentinels wait for the dawn.
For with the Lord is kindness and with Him is Plenteous
Redemption;
And He will redeem Israel from all their iniquities.

To the widow the blessing, like the yards of exquisitely folded crepe, was supremely appropriate. She had been through so much that was sordid and tawdry since her departure from the mansion. Now she knew she was home. Kneeling by the veterans' flag, she buried her face in the field of stars.

'Then she walked away,' Schlesinger wrote. 'The rest of us followed.'

They trooped out to the hall. She mounted the stairway to the second floor, and they stood about uncertainly, awaiting some instruction from the Attorney General. Bob had one. During their moments together beside the catafalque he had whispered to Jackie that he would settle the coffin issue before retiring. To do that, however, he must return to the East Room and ask that the lid be raised for him. While Lieutenant Sawtelle's Death Watch ceremoniously relieved Lieutenant Bird's body bearers, the top was lifted and cocked open on its small hinge by Godfrey McHugh or Joe Gawler. Either could have done it; each recalls it; the recollection of neither is persuasive. Gawler remembers a conference by the bier between Robert Kennedy and Eunice Shriver, who was, of course, in Hyannis Port. McHugh's memory is more circumstantial, but in his mind the incident seems to have blurred together with an almost identical scene Sunday, when Jacqueline Kennedy was present. It was really not a time of clarity. Her spontaneous gesture with the bunting had shattered them all.

The President's brother requested that the service men withdraw from the catafalque, and approached it alone. It was the first time he had seen the body. He made up his mind then: Jackie had been right. Yet it couldn't be entirely a personal decision. McNamara's argument still carried force. John Kennedy had been a husband and a Kennedy, but he had also been the American Chief of State, and others who had been close to him—including O'Donnell and O'Brien—felt a sealed top was improper. Therefore Bob Kennedy solicited several opinions. Emerging into the hall, his cheeks damp, he requested those who were waiting there to go in and return with their impressions. He explained, 'Jackie wants it covered.'

Perhaps this was leading them. Had he not indicated her preference, the results might have been different. This is possible, though hardly probable, for the Secretary of Defence came out a minority of one. Indeed, of those who entered—McNamara, Schlesinger, Spalding, Walton, Nancy Tuckerman, Frank Morrissey, and Dr English—only the doctor and the Secretary considered the President presentable. English said he was opposed to an open coffin on principle, but was 'surprised that his appearance was as good as it was, that he looked well'. He merely wondered why the President's body was 'tilted somewhat to the right, if that was because of the shell and what it had done'. (Actually, tilting is standard undertaking practice. In 'casketing', to quote a trade journal, 'natural expression formers' should always 'turn the body a bit to the right and soften the appearance of lying flat on the back'. This avoids 'the impression that the body is in a box'.)

The verdict of the others was vehement, and because they knew Robert Kennedy's tough fibre, they did not soften it. Arthur Schlesinger and Nancy Tuckerman went in through the Green Room. 'It is appalling,' Arthur reported. 'At first glance it seemed all right, but I am nearsighted. When I came closer it looked less and less like him. It is too waxen, too made-up.' Nancy echoed faintly, 'It really is not like him.' Spalding said bluntly that the face resembled 'the rubber masks stores sell as novelties.' He urged Bob to 'close the casket'.

His eyes full, the Attorney General turned to Bill Walton and whispered, 'Please look. I want to know what you think.' Walton looked as long as he could, with a growing sense of outrage. He said to Bob, 'You mustn't keep it open. It has no resemblance to the President. It's a wax dummy.'

Schlesinger, anticipating questions about a Head of State—the

McNamara argument—assured Kennedy he would be acting on the best of precedents. The Roosevelt coffin had been closed.

'Don't do it,' Walton pleaded.

'You're right,' Kennedy said incisively. 'Close it.' Turning away, he went upstairs with Spalding.

Salinger broke the news to the press, and although the networks were almost at their wits' end for scraps of information they displayed admirable taste in playing the announcement down. Even so it aroused curiosity. Innumerable members of the national audience were convinced that the casket was sealed because there was something to hide. At NBC David Brinkley was 'flooded by letters and wires demanding an explanation. I was repeatedly asked to provide one, and usually I refused, though I sometimes said it was at the request of the family, or for reasons which seemed obvious. To me it *was* obvious. I feel strongly that the coffin should be closed at all funerals.'

One magazine offered a gratuitous elucidation. *Time* (December 6, 1963) reported that 'the casket . . . was never to be opened because the President had been deeply disfigured'. This was wholly untrue. Neither wound had damaged the President's face. His features, intact when his wife examined them at Parkland, had been treated with cosmetics, and this was what gave offence. Her impressions of Sunday morning, when she next saw him, are chronologically out of place here. Yet one of them is pertinent: 'It wasn't Jack. It was like something you would see at Madame Tussaud's.'

Dawn was unmemorable, which is unsurprising, because the moment of daybreak is imprecise anyhow. In the U.S. Naval Observatory at Massachusetts and Thirty-fourth N.W. sunrise was recorded at 6.50 a.m. That was determined by scientific instruments. It is arbitrary on any day, but meteorologically November 23, 1963, was about to smother the Eastern seaboard. Between dawn and dusk not a single ray of sunshine would be discernible to the trained scanners at the observatory at Dulles, or at Washington National. The overcast was solid, an unbroken blot.

Yet even the dimmest sunrise is preceded by what infantrymen call morning twilight. At 4.34, when President Kennedy had been carried up the steps of the North Portico on the aching fingertips of six enlisted men and one junior officer, the sky had been swarthy. Pale streaks were lacing the eastern horizon as the first shift of the Death Watch mounted guard, however, and that first light was oddly translucent. The greyness was not entirely grey. The penumbra was tinged with a sickly yellow which any seaman would have recognized and distrusted. Already storm signals were flapping on the Chesapeake and the lower Potomac. It was going to blow, hard.

An abrupt barometric drop from 29.76 to 29.44—those were the early readings—induces an atavistic tension in people and animals. Farmers know the signs as well as sailors. With the charge of negative electricity that precedes the deluge barnyards become restless. Sheep bleat. Cattle low. It is a primitive warning; trouble is on the way. But Washingtonians who were awake in Saturday's seventh hour don't remember that either. Their nerves were incapable of withstanding another turn of the screw. They couldn't imagine greater trouble, and therefore as the darkness outside merged unobserved into gloomy daylight, the darkness within them went on and on and on. Once—it had been yesterday noon, a staggering thought—life had been normal. At lunchtime one had looked forward to the office, home, dinner, children, sleep. Since then routine had been ruptured and displaced by a grotesque abnormality. Though a full night had passed since then, there had been neither normal work nor meals nor repose.

Only a handful slept at all. Ken Galbraith induced insentience with a mild overdose of sleeping pills; he was shortly awakened by a punishing headache. Mac Kilduff stretched out on the press room cot he had used during the Cuban missile crisis. Chief Usher West tossed on a mansion couch for an hour, General Wehle in his Fort McNair CP for two hours, Lieutenant Bird dozed forty-five minutes in Fort Myer's Bachelor Officers Quarters. Bill Walton drifted off in 'a skin-thin, foxhole sleep; I had been thrust back twenty years into the 82nd Airborne.' An unnatural trance was the best the most phlegmatic could manage. The sensitive couldn't close their eyes, and genuine slumber was a phenomenon. Lieutenant Bird leaped to his feet at the first spatter of rain. His first thought was that he was going to get thoroughly drenched, because he was 'too proud to wear a raincoat'. Taz Shepard heard the drizzle and approved. Any other weather, he felt, would have been an affront. In Georgetown Ben Bradlee lay through the ominous gloaming, listening to the dying of the last sirens. Beside him Toni sprawled weeping, and not because she was a woman or especially emotive; it had been a night of tears; Mac Bundy, the Kennedy–Johnson aide who had made the swiftest transition, later noted tersely, 'Friday and Saturday I cried at home—after that not'.

Bundy then rose and summoned a White House car. 'Jobs,' he wrote, 'were our only comfort.' And a job was not a task performed during specified hours; it was a substitute for void. The impact of the tragedy did not strike everyone with equal force, of course. Though Mac described it as 'deep and general', he also observed that 'The shadings of grief were varied—and the sense of sharing seldom complete. Jackie and Bobby were in a circle all their own; near them were the family; then—in different ways—Kenny and Bob McNamara—and then for different things a lot of us. And in different ways each circle of hurt found it easy to forget that others were also in grief. In particular it was easy to forget that the new President and his circle were hurt, too.'

There were no closed planes; total immunity was almost unknown. With absolutely nothing to do at that unearthly hour, Washington had seldom been busier. Bundy, wretchedly attempting to set up a staff conference, reflected that 'The real sadness . . . was not at predictable moments—but whenever one got hit at some unguarded opening by a fresh thought of loss and change. I remember such states in passing the Rose Garden, in coming to the elevator to the second floor, in admiring the new red rug in his office which he never got to see.' Nor were the afflicted confined to those who had known John Kennedy. It would be hard to find a less susceptible crew than Joe Gawler's undertakers. They were so accustomed to death that they maintained a scoreboard in the funeral parlour basement to keep track of each day's remains. Yet Gawler and his men couldn't go home after the East Room ceremony. Leaving Pennsylvania Avenue, they picked up their unused hearse at Bethesda, repaired an S iron on its side, and began preparations for Saturday's funerals.

On the third floor of the Executive Mansion George Thomas inspected the President's Texas luggage, which had been deposited on a rack outside his room. He couldn't bear to open it, so he became a kind of community valet, polishing shoes and pressing suits for any man who would have him, including, later in the day, another gentleman's gentleman whom he mistook for a distant Kennedy relative. Godfrey McHugh sat alone in his East Wing office, fumbling through dull Air Force orders. He had considered himself relieved by the Death Watch, but since he didn't know what else to do he greeted Saturday by struggling through unreadable military prose. Dr Burkley decided to resign—Arthur Schlesinger subsequently regarded himself as the first Kennedy appointee to try to quit, but the physician beat him. Leaving the mansion after Father Kuhn's blessing, Burkley crossed West Executive and notified Walter Jenkins that he wished to retire. Neither man thought it extraordinary that the other should be functioning at five o'clock in the morning.

The writers went on writing. In crisis literacy may eclipse every other passion. Drunks were sober, lechers chaste, and aspirants for the Presidency—including every Republican who had been mentioned as a candidate—were free of Potomac fever; but the stream of words swelled hourly. By 5.15 a.m. Schlesinger was back at his East Wing typewriter, banging away. With pencil and White House stationery Charlie Bartlett dashed off, not a column, not a letter, but an extraordinary unaddressed tribute:

> We had a hero for a friend—and we mourn his loss. Anyone, and fortunately there were so many, who knew him briefly or over long periods, felt that bright and quickening impulse had come into his life. He had uncommon courage, unfailing humour, a penetrating, ever curious intelligence, and over all a matchless grace. He was our best. He will not be replaced, nor will he be forgotten, for in truth he was a kind of cheerful lightning who touched us all. We will remember him always with love and sometimes, as the years pass and the story is retold, with a little wonder.

One deciphers Bartlett's handwriting with wonder. He had rarely written so well for publication. He was, of course, as close to Kennedy as any writer; he and Martha, 'shamelessly match-making', as Jacqueline Kennedy later said, had introduced the future Mrs Kennedy to the future President. Yet those who had met John Kennedy but once or, more often, not at all were setting down panegyrics as moving. From Torquay seventy-nine-year-old Sean O'Casey was writing a friend in New York:

> What a terrible thing has happened to us all! To you there, to us here, to all everywhere. Peace who was becoming bright-eyed now sits in the shadow of death: her handsome champion has been killed as he walked by her very side. Her gallant boy is dead. What a cruel, foul, and most unnatural murder! We mourn here with you poor, sad American people.

André Malraux cabled Mrs Kennedy: '*Nous pensons à vous et nous sommes si tristes. . . .*' A Frenchman who had never seen either member of the First Family wrote the widow: '*Madame, La mort de votre mari m'a fait un très grand coup au coeur. . . . Votre mari était un grand homme qui restera pour toujours* [word illegible] *dans ma mémoire.*' In the British Embassy in London, where it was now 11 a.m., an unknown Englishman set down in halting script: 'With the death of President Kennedy every man in the Free World is a Kennedy,' and an eleven-year-old British schoolboy wrote Jacqueline Kennedy, 'I thought that he was a peace loving, brave and kind man. In fact, all that a man should be. One day I hope that I will follow his example.'

The English had a special affection for the great-grandson of an Irish potato farmer who had seemed to them to have become the apotheosis of their own moribund aristocracy, a regency figure miraculously reborn. But the glow had spread everywhere; in Italy, which had learned overnight that the assassination weapon was a product of Terni Arsenal, C2766 was already known as '*il fucile maledetto*'—'that accursed gun'. Even those who had chivvied, traduced, and fought Kennedy were also awake and scribbling. Charles de Gaulle was groping for the right words. So was Nikita Khrushchev. So was Fidel Castro. And so, at 810 Fifth Avenue in Manhattan, was the Republican presidential candidate of 1960.

None of the homage was easy. For this man, however, every stroke of the pen must have been excruciating. It was not generally known, but Richard Nixon had admired the President extravagantly. He wrote of his and his wife's thoughts and prayers for Mrs Kennedy and mentioned the role of fate in making the two men political enemies. Somehow the letter conveyed a spirit of what Nixon himself might have called Americanism. It was civil, and it was touchingly gentle.

It is notable that the one man who enjoyed absolute peace that night—the best, he confided to his brother next day, that he had ever known—was the assassin. To Robert Oswald and to his interrogators Lee Oswald trumpeted that he was refreshed. Certainly he looked spry. In Dallas another Texan, a bystander who had witnessed the assassination, also slept soundly. Young Ron Fischer, the bookkeeper who admired Barry Goldwater, said afterwards, 'Sure, I had a reaction. It took me several minutes to drop off. That may have been my digestive system, though. I'd had a real big meal, and I always eat too fast. It's the one thing that's really wrong with me.'

Nevertheless Oswald and Fischer were unusual. America was not a fit nation early Saturday. Across the country, millions, including many who had voted Republican in 1960, arose feeling drugged. Ken Galbraith's hangover may not be attributable to pills. His lethargy was widespread. It was quite ordinary for an individual to stir awake with the sensation that he had just been rescued from a dreadful nightmare. Roy Truly didn't experience it because he was one of the true insomniacs. The Book Depository superintendent had wrestled vainly through the night with a clammy sheet. He had the feeling that his stomach was 'tied up in a huge knot'. He was suffering from violent nausea and diarrhoea and was under medication. Howard L. Brennan, the pipefitter who had seen Oswald fire the fatal shot, was even sicker. Although Brennan, like Truly and Fischer, had violently disapproved of the Kennedy Presidency, he was deeply disturbed. Obsessed with the fear that the assassin's co-conspirators would kill his two-year-old granddaughter, he commenced the first of a long series of therapeutic sessions.

In the White House guest rooms even fitful rest was exceptional. Dr John Walsh was flitting from threshold to threshold doling out red ovoid Seconal capsules, two a customer. They were gulped obediently, if cynically. Hardly anyone expected results. The ineffectiveness of barbiturates and alcohol had been repeatedly demonstrated; they had become a bad joke; in lieu of narcotics the guests conversed with one another. Like Jacqueline Kennedy at Bethesda, they were trying catharsis. Bob Kennedy talked to Chuck Spalding. Sargent Shriver and Jean Smith knelt together by the closed coffin and then talked in the hall. Jean transferred her bag to the Rose, or the Queen's Room, thinking to nap there. She didn't stay long. At 6.25 Pat Lawford and six-year-old Sydney descended an American Airlines ramp at Dulles Airport, and Peter and Milt Ebbins, his theatrical manager, arrived at about the same time. Pat walked in on Jean, and the first moves in a weekend of musical bedrooms were made: Jean, Peter, and Milt went to the third floor, and Pat and her daughter lay down in the room adjoining the Queen's so that Sydney would be close to Caroline. First, however, the sisters had to compare notes, and just as they had wound up and Jean was settling down on her new mattress, her husband arrived on the new day's first shuttle from New York and whizzed in through the South-west Gate. He wanted to talk.

Elsewhere on the third floor O'Donnell and O'Brien, who had been assigned adjoining bedrooms, were not in them. They were combining their persuasive talents to enlist Salinger, who had no bed—not that it mattered—in the faction supporting a Boston burial. Pierre capitulated quickly. Ken and Larry then told of the tensions of the flight from Dallas while three men, attended by George Thomas, shaved. The 10 a.m. Mass in the mansion for intimate friends and associates of the President was their first real commitment, and busy work and cat naps were broken off to tidy up. Inevitably they were inefficient. They were—literally—sleepwalking. In the President's bathroom Hudi Auchincloss' ablutions were interrupted by the Attorney General. Robert Kennedy stepped in apparently looking for something, and stepped out. He hadn't said a word. Auchincloss crossed to his wife, who lay wide-eyed on her back. He said wonderingly, 'You know, I don't think he even saw me.'

The ceaseless, repetitive dialogues went on in bathrooms, dressing-rooms, by the catafalque, anywhere. Dave Powers went home to change his blemished suit and told his wife the most remarkable yarn of his life until the clock warned him he must return to the mansion for the Mass. Nancy Tuckerman and Pam Turnure hurried home, changed, hurried back to the White House, and joined new conversations. In an apartment just off the 6100 block of Sixteenth Street Evelyn Lincoln's husband had greeted her with 'Do you remember what I said about Texas?' She replied groggily, 'You said something was liable to happen in Dallas.' He nodded, and they were off. 'I've got to be at the office at eight,' she finally said—forgetting that her employer was no longer alive. Marie Fehmer, whose employer had become the most active man in the world, alternately wept and chatted with her two room-mates until the hour struck. Then she dressed with such speed that she didn't notice her choice until she had reached the EOB. To her horror she saw that on this atrabilious day she was wearing a skirt of gay Kelly green—at about the same time that Evelyn realized that she had absently dressed in pink.

Marie and Evelyn wrung hands, as Nellie Connally had twenty-four hours before, and as pointlessly. Friday morning Jackie had been the only woman anyone had noticed, and on this Saturday nothing short of indecency would have raised an eyebrow. With a forty-six-year-old President lying in a coffin, the world was transformed. Westminster Abbey's tenor bell tolled each minute in a tribute reserved for monarchs, Brazilian television technicians terminated a bitter strike to transmit news from America, the Japanese captain who rammed PT 109 was inconsolable, the Chairman of the Soviet Union sat dazed in the American Embassy, Norodom Sihanouk of Cambodia ordered his anti-American posters hauled down, and the ruling junta in the Dominican Republic, which the Dallas *News* had endorsed but which President Kennedy had refused to recognize, proclaimed nine days of official mourning.[7]

Under these circumstances, and particularly at this early hour, decorum had no meaning. One of the most searching assessments of the days ahead was held by a Cabinet Secretary and a Special Assistant to the President in the front seat of a private automobile. Arthur Schlesinger, a fast writer, left the mansion to drive Robert McNamara home. As the serpentine murk spread greyly along the stately little complex of residential streets beyond Dupont Circle, Schlesinger parked. According to his journal, McNamara told him that the country had 'suffered a loss which it would take ten years to repair, that there is no one on the horizon to compare with the President as a national leader'. McNamara thought that 'Goldwater was out, that Nixon would be the likely Republican candidate, and that a party fight among the Democrats would be suicidal. He said

[7] Only Peking was consistent. The scrutable Red Chinese broadcast assassination news briefly and gleefully. *Kungjen Jih Pao*, their newspaper, published a cartoon of America's murdered President lying on his face. The caption read, 'Kennedy biting the dust'.

that he did not know Johnson well and did not know his habits of work but supposed that he would concentrate above everything else on the 1964 election.'

Concern over the new President grew, and like the dawn their image of Lyndon Johnson was muddled and smudgy. The Secretary described the helicopter ride from Andrews. Although Johnson had urged him to stay, he said, he was 'uncertain whether the relationship would work'. As he left the car—it was now daytime, soupy but light—Schlesinger declared that he himself would leave the administration immediately. He felt that 'the whole crowd of us should clear out—that is, those of us in the White House', leaving Johnson with 'his own people around him'. Schlesinger observed that 'The Cabinet is different from the White House staff, which is personal. Even there Mac Bundy is an exception and has created his own job.' He was convinced that President Kennedy's official family could not become President Johnson's. The Kennedy Cabinet might become the Johnson Cabinet; that was a separate issue.

For a former Harvard professor Arthur Schlesinger was foxy. The Secretary had speculated innocently about next November, but his driver, usually voluble, had listened with the laconism of an O'Donnell. McNamara was a registered Republican. Schlesinger was a zealous Democrat, and despite his silence on this point his convictions about the campaign were far more partisan than the Secretary's. He wondered whether Lyndon Johnson should be his party's candidate in the coming election. Already he was looking ahead to the convention in Atlantic City. After leaving Dupont Circle he conferred with Chairman John Bailey, asking him whether it would be possible to deny the new President the nomination. John, according to his account, replied that 'it might be technically feasible, but the result would be to lose the election for the Democrats'. Schlesinger suggested that the party was likely to lose anyway, that either Rockefeller or Nixon would win by carrying 'the big industrial states'. He then added perceptively, 'But I suppose that Johnson is astute enough to recognize this too, which means that he may be driven to an aggressive liberal programme.' This judgment was reached on the thirty-sixth President's first full day in office, before he had made a single move in any direction, and it came from a Democrat who was pondering the wisdom of forfeiting the election, 'regardless of merits', to beat him. Yet it would be hard to find a shrewder appraisal of the Johnsonian domestic programme that would later emerge.

The daylight was as broad as it would ever be. In the aoristic haze oak leaves lay in sodden arabesques beside Eisenhower's old putting green, and beneath the three windows of the First Lady's bedroom a lone, bedraggled squirrel scolded his paws. Jacqueline Kennedy did not see him. She was unconscious. That is the only adequate word to describe her condition. She was not asleep; no one in the mansion was as incapable of rest as the hostess. But Dr John Walsh had resolved upon a drastic step. She could not go on this way. He would have to knock her out with powerful medication, administered intramuscularly.

Leaving the East Room, she had debouched in a second-floor vestibule and stumbled into the arms of her maid. Provi was weeping; the two women had embraced and then, in her private quarters, Mrs Kennedy had finally shed her stained clothing. By now the President's blood was no longer damp; the blemishes had darkened as they dried. Even so, the maid was overcome by the extent of the blood. Nothing she had seen or heard on the television reports had prepared her for this. While her mistress bathed, Provi packed the clothes and hid the bag.

Walsh came in after the bath. In the tower suite Walsh had administered one shot to his star patient. It had been worthless. Now he grimly armed another needle, this time with the strongest weapon in his arsenal. She lay down on her side of the double bed, the soft side (the other side was board and horsehair), and he injected a full half-gram of Amytal. He didn't tell her what it was, but it was formidable enough to knock out a prizefighter, and as he and Provi slipped out into the West Sitting Room they were convinced that she was insensible. She wasn't yet. She could cry, and did, but she could not cry herself to sleep. Eventually, the sedative reached her. For the first time since rising in Fort Worth's Hotel Texas, when her husband's voice had drifted up from the parking lot eight storeys below, she was out.

8

CROWN

She was quiet for perhaps an hour. Shortly after six o'clock she asked her maid for orange juice, and then the drug dragged her down for another two hours. That was the limit of its effect, however; too much was on her mind, and she swung up into a sitting position on the side of the bed, determined to resolve two issues before the 10 a.m. Mass. Unaware that Robert Kennedy had agreed with her about the coffin, she asked for him. Meantime she braced herself to talk to her children.

At 7.30 the door of the President's bedroom where Jacqueline Kennedy's mother had just awoken, had swung open and Caroline had entered. In a dreamlike tone the President's daughter said to her grandmother, 'He's dead, isn't he?'

There could be no adequate answer, merely a tight nod. But the little girl did not seem to expect details. To young John Kennedy, Mrs Kennedy said that a bad man had shot his daddy, then added that he hadn't been bad really; he had just been sick. The boy looked blank. For him the full meaning of the assassination was impossible to grasp.

Robert Kennedy assured his sister-in-law that the public would not see the President. Then, while she changed to black weeds—it was the only black dress she owned; in five years she had worn it just twice, at the press conference when her husband announced his candidacy for the Presidency on Capitol Hill and, more recently, at John's christening—he struck off on a lonely walk through the mist-shrouded south grounds. It was just past eight o'clock. In the West Wing Pierre Salinger's phone was ringing. The operator said, 'The President wishes to speak to you.'

Salinger was startled—'I'd had very little sleep, and I was not yet thinking of anyone else as being the President.' Johnson came on the line, gentle and soft-spoken. He understood Pierre's personal involvement with Kennedy, he said, but he wanted him to stay as press secretary: 'I need you more than he needed you.'

The new President's first problem, upon leaving the Elms, was selecting a destination. As Chief Executive he was entitled to occupy the oval office. One may reason that his duty lay there, that any other course would sap confidence in government at a critical time—indeed, several men stated the issue just that way. On the other hand, grief remained the nation's dominant mood. His presence in the White House would inevitably become the source of misinterpretation and resentment. There was no clear option, and Johnson was uncharacteristically indecisive. His first choice was to go to the West Wing.

As Head of the White House Detail, Jerry Behn commanded his convoy of agents. Behn's habitual greeting was, 'What's new?' The gambit was depressingly trite, an office joke. This morning Evelyn Lincoln saw Behn before he saw her, and it is a sign of the widespread antagonism towards the Secret Service that Evelyn looked him in the eye and said bitterly, 'Jerry, there's something new.' He turned away without answering.

Evelyn was packing; Mac Bundy had assigned Maxwell Taylor's old EOB office to her. She knew the Attorney General wanted the West Wing cleared of President Kennedy's belongings, but she felt no sense of urgency, and she even asked Cecil Stoughton to photograph the newly decorated rooms while JFK bric-a-brac was still there. Then LBJ unexpectedly appeared and asked her to step into the oval office. 'Yes, sir,' she said, and obediently followed.

President Johnson sat on one of the two facing divans. Evelyn started towards the rocking chair, veered away, and sank on the opposite couch. According to her recollection he said, 'I need you more than you need me. But because of overseas'—presumably a reference to the necessity for shoring up confidence abroad—'I also need a transition. I have an appointment at 9.30. Can I have my girls in your office by 9.30?'

He was giving her less than an hour. She said faintly, 'Yes, Mr President.'

Muggsy O'Leary, who was standing by Evelyn's desk, admiring the new red carpeting, overheard the conversation. Of Johnson he felt there was 'anxiety on his part to get in'.[1]

Johnson then said to Evelyn, 'Do you think I could get Bill Moyers in Ken O'Donnell's office?'

[1] The President was invited to contribute his recollections of his Saturday morning conversations with Mrs Lincoln and Robert Kennedy, and of the Attorney General's subsequent arrival at the Cabinet meeting. He replied that he did not have any comment upon them.

She didn't know how to reply. She lacked any influence with Kennedy's chief of staff. After an awkward pause she faltered, 'I don't know, Mr President.'

Withdrawing in confusion, she encountered the Attorney General in her own office. She sobbed, 'Do you know he asked me to be out by 9.30?'

The younger Kennedy was appalled. He had just come in from the South Lawn to see how the moving was progressing, but he hadn't counted on this. He said, 'Oh, no!'

In the hall he encountered the new President. This was the first meeting of the two men since the assassination, and it must be viewed in context. Lyndon Johnson was no longer a Kennedy subordinate; it was the other way around. Robert Kennedy had been aroused by the reports of the President's demeanour on the plane, while Johnson, for his part, was in an impossible position. Nothing he did Saturday morning would have pleased everyone. His first obligations were to his country, and it should be remembered that he met those obligations handsomely. To George Reedy he had said, 'There must be no gap; the government must go forward.' It was a wise conclusion. And there was no gap. At the juncture of administrations there would merely be an unsightly scar.

The President was coming out of O'Donnell's office when he saw the Attorney General. He said, 'I want to talk to you.'

'Fine,' said Robert Kennedy. But he didn't want to talk in the Presidential office. They entered a little anteroom opposite the President's washroom, and Johnson told him that he needed him more than his brother had. By now a half-dozen members of the administration had quoted this same line to Kennedy. And he did not want to discuss his continuance in the Cabinet now anyhow. He told Johnson that the immediate issue was more prosaic. It was furniture. Crating his brother's things was going to take time, he explained, and he asked, 'Can you wait?'

'Well, of course,' the new President answered, and in the next breath he began qualifying his reply. In effect he said that while he himself did not want to occupy the White House at once, his advisers were insisting upon it.

The Attorney General was not impressed, and his unresponsiveness seems to have triggered Johnson's prompt decision to switch back to the EOB. The story that he had walked up to the threshold of the new red rug, declared solemnly, 'No, this isn't right,' and spun on his heel rapidly became gospel among lesser Johnsonian aides. It is untrue. Yet he was not exaggerating the pressure upon him to take over—pressure which, after his exchange with Kennedy, he resisted fiercely. He walked down to the Situation Room for a briefing from McCone and Bundy; then, huddled under an umbrella held by an agent, he dashed across West Executive Avenue for meetings with Rusk, McNamara, and the Congressional leadership. To his staff he said tersely, 'Marie will handle the phones, Juanita will handle the people.' There was some discussion of a nationwide television address that evening. He shook his head. Colonel William Jackson, his Vice Presidential military aide, argued forcefully that he ought to go back to the White House. The President ignored him. 'It would give the people confidence,' the Colonel explained. 'People will get confidence if we do our job properly,' Johnson said tartly. 'Stop this. Our first concern is Mrs Kennedy and the family.'[2]

On the other side of the street Robert Kennedy told Evelyn that she needn't hurry. Nevertheless she sped along. Two Kennedy rocking chairs were rapidly roped together and rolled across West Executive on a little dolly. Evacuation by 9.30 was an impossibility, but Evelyn was determined to have everything in cartons by 11 a.m., and although she left briefly for the religious service in the mansion, she made it. Alone the task would have required a full day. From the moment she reached for the first box, however, she was surrounded by an eager crew: her husband, Mary Gallagher, Joe Giordano, Boots Miller, and Muggsy. Ken O'Donnell glanced in briefly, said he approved of the rapid removal of the President's belongings, and slapped his Texas trip folder on his desk. 'I'm going home,' he said in his pithy way; she assumed he was quitting. The folder was packed away with the President's ship models, paintings, the cigar box in front of the Presidential chair in the Cabinet Room, the carved desk from the oval office and the personal mementoes on it—photographs of his wife and children, the coconut shell upon which he had carved the news of his survival after the sinking of PT 109, and a silver calendar noting the dates of the Cuban missile crisis. To Giordano, unfastening the wall set of Paul Revere lamps, a gift from the White House Correspondents Association, was the toughest job he had ever tackled. As one Chief Executive's furnishings departed, another's arrived. Behind Evelyn's desk a huge gold-framed portrait of Lyndon Johnson, brought over from his Vice Presidential office, was swiftly hung.[3]

As Evelyn and her team packed, Schlesinger was completing his letter of resignation in the East Wing, Sorensen was notifying his staff in the West Wing that he intended to quit and that he expected them to do the same, most of the agents who had been in Texas were toiling over their longhand reports, Bill Greer was taking President

[2] Like Godfrey McHugh, the unfortunate officer was soon transferred.
[3] It vanished almost as quickly. Two days later it was gone.

Kennedy's Dallas clothing to Protective Research for a scientific check, Miss Shaw was looking out with brimming eyes on the forest of umbrellas in Lafayette Park, Mac Bundy was on duty in the Vice President's EOB anteroom, Dwight Eisenhower was en route to see Johnson, who was telephoning first Hubert Humphrey, thanking him for his televised tributes over CBS and NBC, and then Ralph Yarborough, to acknowledge his telegram of support. Pierre Salinger wearily screened all the correspondents' requests to see Sorensen and approved two, from Teddy White and Art Buchwald. Sorensen received White promptly and then completely forgot Buchwald, who was left waiting in the depressing west lobby. A floor below him Ken O'Donnell, on his way to the mansion, paused to tell a group of open-mouthed subordinates about the comportment of the coroner and the judge at Parkland. At the eastern end of the same corridor Larry O'Brien stood alone, his stocky neck bowed, blinded by tears.

Despite his woolly head John Kennedy Galbraith decided that someone ought to write a proper obituary for the Washington *Post*. He called the editor, volunteered to do it himself, and set to work in Kay Graham's study. In various rooms of Hickory Hill Ethel Kennedy, her children, and Dave Hackett all awoke stunned. Hackett began sobbing before his feet hit the floor; from bed he telephoned his mother. Six miles away the Old Guard (minus five half-hour shifts of the Death Watch, while were at the White House) fell out on Fort Myer's north parade ground to hear the formal proclamation of mourning the State Department had drawn up for President Johnson. Rain had begun to descend, yet Lieutenant Sam Bird found that every man in ranks had independently reached his own conclusion about raincoats; not a slicker was in sight.

From Texas Byron Skelton telegraphed Robert Kennedy: 'I only wish the warning to you in my letter of November fourth against the Dallas visit could have been heeded'; in Dallas Lee Oswald lay in his fifth-floor maximum-security cell. His wife, his mother, and his two daughters were in suite 905–907 on the ninth floor of the Hotel Adolphus. Thomas B. Thompson of *Life* had whisked them there from the Paine home. The evidence against the assassin had been accumulating through the night. At 4 a.m. CST, executives of Klein's Sporting Goods in Chicago, after poring over their microfilmed records for six hours, found the *American Rifleman* coupon with which Oswald had ordered C2766 eight months before. His rest had not improved the behaviour of the rifle's owner. When Oswald was returned to the 11 × 14 interrogation room, Forrest Sorrels felt he was 'baiting Fritz, hoping Fritz would beat him up so he'd have a police brutality charge'. On the other hand, police interrogation techniques hadn't improved either. The tiny room was again invaded by a convention of city, state, and federal officers, and some of the questions put to the prisoner seem scarcely pertinent. Fritz, for example, asked him if he believed in 'a deity'. The Captain later recalled that Lee said he 'didn't care to discuss that'—a sensible rebuff. He did offer a pitiful fabric of lies about his past. He insisted that he couldn't afford a rifle on the Book Depository's $1.25 an hour. And he was anxious that the standees in the cubicle understand that 'I'm not a Communist, I'm not a Leninist-Marxist, I'm a Marxist,' an effort which, considering the absence of a dialectical materialist among his questioners, seems pointless. None of them knew Hegel. But then, neither did their prisoner.

Of the assassination he remarked, 'People will forget that within a few days' because there would be 'another President'. That, and a passing reference to the Chief Executive's 'nice family', was about all he had to say about his victim; to Fritz he observed that he didn't have 'any particular comment about the President', by whom he meant President Kennedy. Sketchy as the record is (apparently he wasn't asked about Connally), one feels that a full transcript would be equally disappointing. Even when he was allowed to see his wife, mother, and brother he was singularly uncommunicative about the national tragedy. During a five-minute interview with his wife and mother he largely ignored Marguerite. Instead, he asked for news of the children in Russian; at one point his wife laughed aloud and explained to her mother-in-law, 'Mama, he say he love me and buy June shoes.' Marina did not ask him whether he had killed Kennedy. Nevertheless it was very much on her mind. Later she said, 'I could see by his eyes he was guilty.'

That expression had an extraordinary effect on her brother-in-law, who followed them and whose visit lasted twice as long as theirs. According to Robert Oswald's subsequent recollection, his brother 'seemed at first to me to be very mechanical. He was making sense, but it was all mechanical. I interrupted him and tried to get him to answer my questions rather than listening to what he had to say. And then the really astounding thought dawned on me. I realized that he was really unconcerned. I was looking into his eyes, but they were blank, like Orphan Annie's, and he knew, I guess from the amazement on my face, that I saw that. He knew what was happening, because as I searched his eyes he said to me, "Brother, you won't find anything there." '

Marina, meantime, was rapidly losing patience with her mother-in-law. The children were the sole bond between the two Mrs Oswalds. Apart from attending to their needs and getting rid of one of the snapshots showing Lee holding the assassination rifle (according to the recollections of the two women, Marina burned it in an ashtray and Marguerite flushed the ashes down a toilet) their relationship was abrasive and unfruitful. Marina, tired, lay down.

Really nothing they did could matter now. Undoubtedly the destroyed photograph had been damaging. But policemen searching the Paine garage had found an almost identical picture from the same roll in a brown cardboard box among Oswald's possessions. His tight-lipped arrogance in Fritz's office was similarly pointless. Of course, much of the public remained, and would continue to remain, sceptical of the documentation. The case against him looked too pat. Within a few hours of his arrest Dallas had received telephone calls from all over the world—a half-dozen from Australia alone—suggesting that the prisoner was a scapegoat. He wasn't. The chain of circumstantial evidence was binding him ever tighter. By early Saturday morning the witness had identified him, his flimsy curtain rod alibi had been demolished, the FBI was checking Bill Whaley's taxi manifest, and Justice Department laboratories in Washington were confirming every suspicion about the killer's fingerprints, palmprints, and the tuft of cotton shirt fibres he had left in the crevice between the metal butt plate of C2766 and the wooden stock. By daybreak the morning after the crime conviction was an absolute certainty. The possibility of a reasonable doubt simply did not exist. It was an embarrassment of riches; the assassin of the leader of the most powerful nation on earth, everyone felt, must have displayed *some* guile. It was as though a hydrogen bomb had been accidentally launched from its silo by a bumbling technician. The more one learned about the criminal, the more the mind balked. The relationship between cause and effect was preposterous. They couldn't be balanced.

Oswald's stupidity wasn't his captors' fault, nor were they entirely to blame for his lack of counsel. Certainly the Civil Liberties attorneys ought to have been received more cordially Friday evening, but there could be no court-appointed lawyer until there was a court, and the case had not yet reached that stage. The unforgivable errors in the treatment of the prisoner continued to lie in his unparalleled exposure to the press. The Lee Oswald Show was continuing without letup. In spite of the chorus of warnings, not a single klieg light had been dimmed, not a single microphone had been waved away. In a live interview with NBC's Tom Pettit, Fritz declared on Saturday, 'This man killed the President—we have a cinch case against him,' and when the FBI informed Chief Curry that its handwriting experts had identified the calligraphy on Klein's *American Rifleman* coupon as Oswald's, Curry revealed the details at a televised press conference. J. Edgar Hoover was furious. The Director called Dallas and warned that there must be no further discussion of FBI evidence in public. Curry admired Hoover and proudly displayed a signed photograph of him on his office wall. Nevertheless the disclosures went on, carried along, it almost seemed, by some self-generating momentum. No morsel was too shocking, no participant immune. District Attorney Wade hinted broadly that Jacqueline Kennedy and Lyndon Johnson might be summoned to Dallas to testify, and David Brinkley, the most circumspect of commentators, was flatly announcing that the President had been killed by a 'punk with a mail-order rifle'. By now virtually every distinguished member of the legal profession was frantic. Chief Justice Earl Warren, watching his own home screen, remembered a case in the previous term: a Southern sheriff had broadcast a confession over television, the lower court had found the man guilty, and the Supreme Court had been obliged to reverse the verdict.[4] This outrage, Warren realized, was far worse than that.

With the Attorney General out of action Nick Katzenbach was, in effect, Acting Attorney General, and he was proposing the investigative commission which the Chief Justice later headed. To his horror, Katzenbach learned that the new President had tentatively decided upon a Texas commission, with all non-Texans, including federal officials, excluded. Katzenbach went straight to Abe Fortas, the Washington attorney closest to Lyndon Johnson. He bluntly labelled Johnson's idea a ghastly mistake. From Fortas he heard for the first time that the President intended to release the forthcoming FBI report on the assassination the moment it was ready. That, too, would be improper, Nick argued, and he insisted that the report be channelled through the Attorney General and himself.[5]

It was not necessary to be Chief Justice or Deputy Attorney General to discern the ugly shape of events, or to be alarmed by possible consequences. In the Dallas Police Department itself there was concern about Oswald's safety. One captain telephoned Fritz about threats against the prisoner; he was told that the problem was Curry's. And Wade's implication that the widowed First Lady might be asked to take the stand in a Texas courtroom was greeted with general dismay. A widespread Dallas attitude was that 'with all the strife she had gone through . . . she shouldn't be expected to come back and face trial of this heinous crime'. The words are Jack Ruby's. Ruby, however, went one step farther. He was convinced that 'someone owed it to our beloved President' to make certain that the trip was needless. Obviously the debt could only be paid by a volunteer. All his life Jack had regarded himself as an avenger—an

[4] *Rideau* vs. *Louisiana*, 373 U.S. 723.

[5] Katzenbach took an exceptionally strong line on this issue, and like Fortas he played an unknown but vital role in the Commission's investigation.

anti-Semitic remark was enough to set him off—and his vengeance had always expressed itself through violence. He was a direct, simple, stunted man, with a childlike inability to foresee the consequences of strenuous physical protest.

Driving back to the mansion after an hour's cat nap at Timberlawn, the estate he leased in Maryland, Sargent Shriver reviewed Saturday's 'Repose Schedule', as Colonel Miller had christened the East Room timetable:

1000–1100	Family
1100–1400	Executive Branch; Presidential Appointees; White House Staff
1400–1430	Supreme Court
1430–1700	Senate; House; Governors
1700–1900	Chiefs of Diplomatic Missions at Washington

It was not flawless. No one had included President Johnson, and as Shriver and Dungan had tactfully explained to Miller, the Kennedy team disregarded all rule books; responding to drill now would be uncharacteristic of them and, in a way, disrespectful of the man for whom they sorrowed. Undeterred, the Colonel had ploughed ahead. Some of his details were fantastic. 'At 230930 Nov. 63' a joint service cordon was to be 'positioned on north portico drive . . . to guide visiting government and diplomatic officials through the Repose Room (East Room)'; the detail would be 'dismissed at 231900 Nov. 63'. A merchandise mart executive responsible for such turgid prose would have found himself in the novelty department. Still, Shriver conceded that the thing was workable: 'The family would have Jack first, then the government, and finally there would be the homage of the people on Capitol Hill Sunday and during Monday's funeral.'

The Chief familial occasion on Saturday was the Mass being held at what Miller called 1000 hours. The final telegrams of invitation had been dispatched at 8 a.m. (ironically, Bill Walton, the Repose Room's decorator, had been the last recipient), and they had been followed by a few last-minute telephoned requests to come; Bob Kennedy called Ted Sorensen during Ted's farewell staff meeting. The religious ceremony was conspicuously unofficial. Only relatives and close acquaintances had been asked. Several eminent men were coming, but only because a nation's First Magistrate forms personal ties among the great; the Ormsby-Gores were included as David and Cissy, not as the British Ambassador and his lady. She happened to be a Roman Catholic. It was not a condition. Mrs Kennedy's mother, after all, was an Episcopalian. So were the Dillons, who, despite his Jewish background, were about as close to the core of the White Anglo-Saxon Protestant establishment as you could get, and Republicans to boot; nevertheless they were at the top of the list.

It was impossible for a Cabinet member to divorce himself completely from his duties—twenty minutes before the service the Secretary of the Treasury was in his office, demanding a full explanation from the Secret Service—but through the long weekend, whenever men like Ormsby-Gore and Dillon were asked which hat they preferred to wear, the invariable reply was: 'I'm a friend.' Having known John Kennedy well was the highest possible accolade. David stressed his prized relationship with Kennedy even when other members of the diplomatic corps were present, and while the Secretary of the Treasury was having it out with the Secret Service, Phyllis Dillon was sending a little gold basket of flowers up to Jacqueline Kennedy, a private token of a private affection beyond pomp.

Assistant Secretary Jim Reed followed the Dillons through the White House East Gate—Reed entered the very door he had used Wednesday, when he had brought President Kennedy the Squaw Island lease for next July—at 9.50.[6] Passing the sentry box he noticed that Lafayette Park was grey with fog. The downpour was steady, and increasing in intensity. Obviously it was going to be a day of high precipitation. The first man Reed saw in the mansion was Walton, his cheeks streaming, and on the floor above, America's first Catholic First Lady had temporarily lost her spartan control in the presence of a priest. Father John Cavanaugh, an old friend, had come to her room to hear her confession. He was about to celebrate the Mass downstairs. Confession was a familiar ritual. Under these circumstances it seemed inappropriate however, and Jacqueline Kennedy told him so. Father Cavanaugh was at a loss. Had the 263 Popes since Peter been in that bedroom, they would have been equally tongue-tied, and presently the widow realized that there was nothing the priest could say. Feeling sorry for the man, she regained her poise. They stumbled through the rite—it was really not an orderly doctrinal confession—and then she walked into the hall in her weeds, took Caroline in one hand and John in the other, and headed downstairs staring straight ahead.

A portable altar had been erected in the family dining-room, directly across the hall from the State Dining Room. It was not an auspicious setting. The place was jammed with collapsible chairs.

[6] Reed recalls the time as 10.50. Beginning Saturday morning, shock and fatigue produced wild distortions in the impressions of many of the principals. A considerable number believe that the ten o'clock religious service was held at eleven, and for some all the days till Tuesday were to blur together. Agents' shift reports and military after-action reports are useful here.

The East Room would have been far more appropriate, but everyone responsible agreed that expecting Mrs Kennedy to celebrate Mass beside the coffin would be too much. Consequently they were all wedged in here, the President's sisters, the Auchincloss', and the Fitzgerald cousins in front; Shriver and Ethel and Joan Kennedy in the second row; and the others ranged behind. Robert Kennedy was dodging about, attending to last-minute details, and so, to the amazement and faint beguilement of the mafia, was Frank Morrissey. Morrissey had breveted himself house acolyte. Holding a gold ciborium in both hands like a snuff-box, he was strutting importantly from aisle to aisle, lugubriously inquiring who would be taking Communion. Ben Bradlee was furious. He wasn't a Catholic; he knew that Frank knew that, and when he was asked he glared malevolently. Ben observed that Frank was shaking the sacred vessel nervously. He felt certain that wasn't done, and he was right; Ken O'Donnell whispered wryly to O'Brien, 'I didn't know Morrissey was ordained.' Larry smiled fleetingly. He whispered back, 'We'll just have to assume that the wafers are in an unblessed state.' Then, to the secret delight of both men, they saw that Frank was miscounting the number of communicants. He was taking charge and confusing everything. O'Brien thought how John Kennedy would have thrown back his head and laughed lustily at the spectacle.

Jacqueline Kennedy entered in a daze. The only person she recognized was her uncle, Wilmarth 'Lefty' Lewis, and she wondered what he was doing here. She knew he lived in Farmington and was working on the Walpole papers for Yale; vaguely it struck her that this had been a long trip for an important man. This was a manifestation of the eye-in-the-storm syndrome: the principal mourners, pre-occupied with their own grief, were scarcely aware that hundreds of millions of others were grieving with them, or even that a relative might leave his study and drive three hundred miles to pay his respects to the President.

Lewis' presence, because unexpected, was somewhat startling. Conducting the Mass in this room was another matter. The executive mansion had been Mrs Kennedy's home for nearly three years. She had definite feelings about every hall and closet, and sweeping her eyes over the crouched, pallid mob in the family dining-room she knew that there had been a mistake. It was unseemly, it was uncomfortable, it would not do. She asked, 'Why is this here?' Muffled voices asked back, 'Do you want it in the East Room?' She nodded, and Robert Kennedy directed Father Cavanaugh to move the portable altar.

In the muted din—wooden chairs cannot be folded quietly—there were various murmurs, gestures, unspoken tokens of compassion.

Angie Duke pressed the widowed First Lady's hand and assured her that he was on the job. She touched Ted Sorensen's fingers and looked directly at him, her eyes telling him that she understood his own misery. Cissy Ormsby-Gore spoke to Maude Shaw as one compatriot to another. That was perceptive of her. Kennedy friends tended to take Miss Shaw for granted. She seemed so sturdy and self-reliant, so capable of looking after herself. But today she deserved a little special attention, for her burdens were special. Crossing the threshold of the East Room, young John stepped boldly forward from the nurse's side—so boldly that, until Mrs Kennedy restrained him, Lieutenant Sawtelle of the Death Watch was afraid the boy would upset one of the standing candles and set fire to the catafalque's black velvet pall. Caroline momentarily hung back. Dressed in her simplest white frock, she stood beside Miss Shaw, who was maintaining a nannie's respectful distance. The girl studied the flag-shrouded coffin and looked puzzled. 'Daddy's too big for that,' she said. 'How is he lying? Are his knees under his chin?' The nurse whispered that it was bigger than it looked. Then Caroline inquired, 'Why can't I see him?' 'Only grownups can see him,' Miss Shaw whispered.

In many ways the Mass resembled the blessing of five hours earlier. Not all the chairs were brought in. There was a large group of standees at the southern end of the hall, most of them non-Catholics wondering what to do. Cissy Ormsby-Gore mechanically knelt and crossed herself at the proper times, but there was much fidgeting on either side of her. Evelyn Lincoln kept glancing around. Every other woman there, she saw, was wearing black, and she bitterly regretted her choice of colour and lack of a hat. Bill Walton, the urbane sophisticate, looked like a Merriwell hero; barrel-chested and jut-jawed, he clasped his arms around Pam Turnure. Pam was making choking sounds; so, despite his liturgical incantations, was Ormsby-Gore; so was Ben Bradlee. Ben finally fled. Although the service was meaningless to him, the crepe-bordered setting was intolerable. His racking sobs were coming in spasms, and rather than disgrace himself he fled into the Green Room—leaving Toni hurt that he should desert her at this of all times. Then, halfway through the Mass, the weepers controlled themselves. An unnatural stillness fell over that end of the huge room, and the standees drew closer to one another, many holding hands. One man commented under his breath: 'We have to accept it; it's God's way.' In a flash a guttural voice replied, '*I* can't accept it.' The quiet returned. Jim Reed, beside Red Ray, became conscious of the room's darkness. It was mid-morning, but the only illumination came from the four candles around the bier, and the sinking barometer was producing a dramatic effect. To Reed everything appeared to be tinged with a sinister hue. He could hear the drumming of the rain outside. The eight-hour downpour was continuing with a hammering frenzy of raindrops. The voice of the priest became inaudible. No one minded; Pam rested her head against Walton's shoulder and thought, as Taz Shepard had, how right this was, and how wrong sunshine would have been.

These were the spectators. The participants—the family—were to have a quite different memory. *En famille* recollections of the Mass are dominated by the priest. This was especially true of the women. Robert Kennedy and Sargent Shriver felt the celebrant was able and gifted. They did not think him exceptional. For Jacqueline Kennedy, however, his intonation was eloquent. She was deeply moved by his expression—she thought he looked 'so destroyed'—and his every phrase had profound meaning for Joan Kennedy, Ethel Kennedy, and Candy McMurrey.

During Holy Communion there was another episode which President Kennedy would have relished. Jamie Auchincloss, Jackie's half-brother, had idolized the President. Like many bright sons of Republican businessmen, he had become an ardent Democrat. During his childhood he and his father had argued heatedly about Franklin Roosevelt's place in history, and to him his half-sister's husband had become a second FDR. Jamie had just turned sixteen and had been confirmed in the Episcopal Church. Nevertheless, when the moment of the Eucharist arrived, the boy participated, for ever endearing him to both the President's family and his own. It was the one bright moment in what was otherwise a ceremony of utter solemnity. Caroline was affected by the air of gravity, and with what Maude Shaw called the Bouvier intuition she moved to her mother's support. Early in the Mass the little girl had glanced around at Evelyn Lincoln, her brow arched high in perplexity. Towards the end, however, she seemed to grasp her mother's need for solace. Shriver was immediately behind them. He saw 'Jackie and Caroline kneeling side by side, and when they had finished prayer Jackie rose and turned, her face was a mask of agony. Caroline took Jackie's left hand in her right hand and squeezed it and then reached over with her other hand and patted her mother's hand and looked up with an expression of intelligence and compassion and love, trying to comfort her mother.'

Abruptly it was over, and Mrs Kennedy found herself at the head of an impromptu receiving line, standing in the main doorway debouching from the East Room into the marble hall, thanking the parting guests. It was the first of several similar scenes during those days; an individual would slip into a remote mansion alcove or anteroom and discover that he was formally shaking hands with a respectful, dolorous parade—often a parade of total strangers, like a grotesque scene in a Duerrenmatt play. Since the service had been set up in the family dining-room, the denouement of Saturday's Mass had not been anticipated. The standees could have left just as easily through the Green and Red rooms, but this was the customary exit, and consequently there was a series of what could have been awkward confrontations. They were not awkward here because Jacqueline Kennedy was appreciative of the loyalty of her husband's friends. For each she had a personal, affectionate phrase. Not everyone was strong enough to take them—rather than face her, Red Fay darted to a corner and buried his face in folds of drapery—and towards the end her own strength lagged. David and Cissy were among the last in the line. When their turn came she was near collapse. Her whisper was so low, of so fine a silk, that it was difficult to understand her. She told them something that neither the President nor she had divulged before: that they had planned to ask Cissy to be Patrick's godmother. Then she turned to J. Bernard West, the final guest (Fay had succeeded in enveloping his legs in yards of drapes), and gave him the wannest of smiles. '*Poor* Mr West,' she whispered. He attempted a reply. It was impossible. 'Will you take a walk with me?' she asked. He nodded once, like a dull-witted beast. She asked, 'Will you walk with me over to his office?' He nodded once again, and together they set off, Clint Hill gliding in their wake.

With her departure at 10.40 the others drifted off. Special assistants returned to their offices (Sorensen found the patient Buchwald waiting for him) and the family's closest friends gathered around Robert Kennedy in the State Dining Room. The two children went for a ride with their nurse, the kiddie detail, and Sydney Lawford. In Georgetown Mrs Auchincloss' Jaguar briefly joined them. Parking in an Esso station, they fetched cones from a Wisconsin Avenue ice cream parlour and drove off again through the Virginia countryside in what was now a torrential storm. Foster, Wells, and Maude Shaw were trying very hard to be discreet. It was a gallant attempt, and it was doomed. Miss Shaw in particular kept biting her lip, wishing she could recall slips of her tongue; out of habit, she repeatedly started to say, 'Your daddy wants you to do this,' or 'Your daddy likes that.' Caroline didn't correct her tenses. The girl had overheard a few fragments of adult conversation. They had been enough. Unlike most first-graders in the East, she knew precisely where Dallas was. Her father's travels had provided her with an extensive knowledge of geography. She didn't need a map of Texas. There was a map in her mind.

There was none in John's; the basic dimensions of the tragedy had not yet swum into focus for him. He sensed that something enormous had happened, but interpreting for him proved to be an insoluble problem. To the dismay of the agents, he would announce in one breath, 'A bad man shot my daddy,' and, in the next, 'I want to go to the office to see my dad.' Hoping to divert him, they altered course and headed for Andrews Field, holing up in MATS' VIP lounge. For a while the choice seemed wise. Though Caroline remained unapproachable and Sydney was plainly bored, the boy beamed excitedly at the powerful T-39's. Foster and Wells had known that Aircraft 26000 would be in its hangar, under guard, out of sight, and they had thought John would have forgotten it. They were expecting too much. His right hand described a dramatic arc, and he cried, 'Whoosh! Here comes my daddy, and he's landing!' Miss Shaw quietly explained that was impossible, that his father had gone to heaven. John asked curiously, 'Did he take his big plane?' She said, 'Yes, John, he probably did.' He appeared satisfied. Then, moments later, he said, 'I wonder when he's coming back?' The President's son was still incapable of grasping the concept of heaven.

His mother, meanwhile, was examining the West Wing rooms which had been refurbished during her absence from the capital. Clint Hill was unprepared for the scarlet carpeting, and he averted his eyes, as from a blasphemy. Jacqueline Kennedy, however, had been largely responsible for the renovation. Until today she had considered the Presidential office cosy and Victorian. Now, she thought, it was rather grand. She lingered there only a moment. Packing was in process all around her, and both there and in Evelyn Lincoln's office she felt that she was in the way. Besides, she could inspect the new rugs just as well in the third of the decorated rooms, the Cabinet Room.

For ten minutes she sat at the long polished table there with Mr West, reminiscing and plucking at the rugged fragments of her disordered present. The chief usher, tidy, spruce, and ordinarily phlegmatic, was still unable to respond. At one point she asked him, 'Mr West, will you be my friend for life?' and although he desperately wanted to tell her all that was in his heart, the best he could do was bow his head. She talked about her son and daughter: 'They're good children, aren't they? They haven't been spoiled?' Like the rest of the mansion staff, West felt a proprietary interest in Caroline and John. Foster and Wells, for example, had spent twice as much time with them as with their own children, and West would have defended them as zealously as any agent. Assuring their mother that they were unspoiled seemed grossly inadequate, but he couldn't talk, couldn't cope, couldn't think. Mrs Kennedy shared the President's talent for putting people at their ease. This was one of her rare failures. The chief usher felt monstrous.

Walking back past the Rose Garden, she reflected that this had been 'the cut'—the divider between the two administrations. Because of her highly developed visual sense, she was keenly aware of colour and form. A vivid tableau meant far more to her than the intricacies of the Tyler precedent, and she had deliberately made the trip from the mansion to see, really *see*, the transition. Now she grasped it. The snug old office was gone for ever. The elegant new appointments, which she had designed for her husband, were to become the splendid headquarters of President Lyndon Johnson.

The national audience did not know of her visit to the oval office, had not been told of the new rugs, and was scarcely conscious of the existence of the thirty-sixth Chief Executive. Though the iron gates of the White House had been closed as a security precaution, public interest was riveted upon the catafalque. In its century and a half the ballroom had witnessed homage to the coffins of five Presidents who had died in office—Harrison, Taylor, Lincoln, Harding, and Roosevelt—but to contemporaries those had been events which happened elsewhere, and which were read about in newspapers. On November 23, 1963, that lag was gone. The massive joint effort of mass communications brought the nation to 1600 Pennsylvania Avenue, and through the use of Zoomar varifocal lenses, across the barbered lawn to the rain-lashed steps of the mansion. When a seaman stamped his heels together to salute an arriving dignitary, tens of millions watched the resultant splash and the soggy leggings. Nina Warren's tears were visible as she left the portico, Shriver and Angie Duke could be seen extending their wet hands in greeting, and in the intervals between calls the shrouded north entrance was shown while Van Heflin, off-camera, read the lines Whitman had written after Lincoln's murder:

. . . I with mournful tread
Walk the deck my Captain lies,
Fallen cold and dead.

For over seven hours the stately pantomime went on. Occasionally the networks would switch to film clips, memorial concerts, or Dallas, and sometimes commentators spoke. They could not always be heard, however—producers, alert to the wavering pitch which signalled an imminent collapse, would switch them off—and the overriding impression was of the Death Watch's rigid dignity and the heartbreakingly slow salute as shifts were changed. It was majestic, it was awesome, and like everything else it didn't quite register. The cut had been too sharp. Associating funereal pomp with Kennedy vitality was asking too much. Afterwards Lady Bird was to remember 'the solemnity of Saturday in the East Room—the service men standing at each corner. At the foot there was a large crucifix. Or was it a candle? All the chandeliers were swathed in black. Or did they have time to do that so soon?' She couldn't be sure. The new First Lady, ordinarily a keen observer, wasn't at all certain that she had seen what she had seen.

Yet there was a minimum of confusion. Indeed, there was virtually no movement by the catafalque. The scene was static, the rubrics stylized. Visitors were ushered into the Blue Room, where members of the slain President's family took turns as hosts and hostesses; then they filed through the Green and East Rooms, paused at the foot of the bier, and proceeded downstairs and out to the south grounds. Because of the weather many guests arrived thoroughly drenched, so black rubber matting was placed in the entrance hall, and beginning at 1 p.m. the green-bereted Special Forces replaced the enlisted soldiers in the joint honour guard. These were among the very few digressions from form, and the only ones the audience saw. The rest was offstage. Jean Smith and Pat Lawford had changed dresses after Mass and were discussing the painting the family had planned to give to the White House when Bob Kennedy put his head in the Queen's Room and asked them to come down and welcome people in the Blue Room. Downstairs the sisters examined one another and flinched. Jean was wearing a grey suit, Pat was in brown. The small lapse went unnoticed; cameras missed them, and this was one broadcast which could hardly be in colour anyhow.

During Mass protocol had been revised in deference to the new President. Lyndon Johnson clearly had to be the first man to pass the coffin after the family had retired, and early arrivals were asked to wait for him. There were a lot of them. General and Mrs Taylor drove in as the service was ending. Two cars were already parked ahead of them, and a young aide, looking half drowned, hurried over and suggested they stay where they were. Dwight Eisenhower and his son John were inside the mansion, seated in the Blue Room. After Mrs Kennedy left, Mr West, the usher, was told that the former President had asked for him, and they chatted a while, recalling the days when Eisenhower had been master of this house. Earl and Nina Warren were also there, damp and haggard, speaking in husky whispers.

After Jacqueline Kennedy vacated the Cabinet Room the Cabinet had assembled there, thinking to follow Johnson. Then he appeared and thwarted the plan. He crossed West Executive with the Congressional leadership in tow and brushed past them, and the result was a second unforeseen receiving line. The President and his entourage circled the catafalque; then the Cabinet, having followed them, shook hands with them. Warren's prompt arrival meant that the Supreme Court later showed up without its Chief Justice. Individual mourners—Ormsby-Gore, Fred Holborn, Dick Goodwin's wife—were unconsoled by a single tribute and insisted upon returning. Moreover, although John Kennedy had been interested in the families of the men he led, there had been no provision for children. Some were brought anyhow. The Secretary of Defence and Mrs McNamara approached the coffin with thirteen-year-old Craig McNamara between them. Stephen and Andrew Bundy knelt with their parents, and Schlesinger brought his sons and daughters. Mac Bundy wrote: 'By some accident we had him to ourselves for the few moments that we had the strength to linger.' At noon the Galbraiths also found themselves alone with the bier, the candles, and the Death Watch. Both men felt that the absence of others was remarkable, and it was. Usually a crush was waiting for the enormous number of friends and officials who had received calls and wires—over a thousand holders of Presidential appointments, both houses of the Congress, all members of the federal judiciary, the governors of the fifty states, and the diplomatic corps—only one conspicuous absentee was noted; Herbert Hoover lay ill in Manhattan. Harry Truman went through. So did the dying Senator Clair Engle of California, in a wheelchair, his arm cradled in a sling; so did Ralph Yarborough and Albert Thomas, their eyes still wild from yesterday's harrowing hour at Parkland. All day jets were landing at Andrews, Dulles, and Washington National, skidding in through the grey porridge to bring the governors. Ross Barnett brought Mrs Barnett and Ross Barnett, Jr. An entire delegation of Mississippians arrived. Ethel Kennedy was on duty in the Blue Room when they entered, dripping rain water and mellifluous Southern compliments. She remembered the violent confrontation between state and national power in Oxford and thought the appearance of so large a retinue was distinctly odd. Ben Bradlee had reached the same opinion. 'The people who weren't good enough to hold his shoes were crawling in,' he bitterly recalled later, 'and when Harry Byrd came, I went.'

Kennedy's enemies came because they had no alternative. A flagrant snub of the White House that Saturday would have been unthinkable for anyone in public life. The haters had been too vocal in the past, and the question of whether the sniper had been part of a larger apparatus was still mysterious. Undoubtedly some of the callers were hypocrites. But a great many who had vehemently differed with the President had been attracted by the warmth of his personality. Politically he and Harry Byrd had been two centuries apart, but the Virginia Senator cherished the memory of the Chief Executive's helicopter landing in his orchard at the climax of a birthday party honouring him, and Barry Goldwater had been openly proud of his affection for the man with whom he had contested every issue of significance.

The East Room's crepe struck two groups with almost physical force: the Court, led by Justice Black, and the Assistant Attorneys General. Each had been a guest at Wednesday night's reception. The contrast was too sharp to be overlooked. Less than seventy-two hours ago this floor had been waxed, the ballroom had been vibrant with the lilt of music, and dancers had moved back and forth across the very place where the great sombre catafalque now stood. Joanie Douglas was wearing the same black velvet dress she had worn then, and irrationally she wondered whether it had been a harbinger, a sign of the coming terror.

The silent processions, the set faces, and the ceaseless drumbeat of the rain outside finally broke through Ken O'Donnell's mask. After praying by the coffin with George Smathers, Hubert Humphrey went over to the West Wing to console Larry O'Brien ('Poor Larry seems so lost,' he confided to his journal. 'He has no idea what the future holds, what his role will be in this government'), and in the hall just behind the lobby he met O'Donnell. A few hours later Humphrey wrote, 'We put our arms around each other—and I saw a strong, ordinarily taciturn and cool and calm man break down into tears, as did I. . . . We sat together for quite a few minutes. Kenny was shocked and shaken. He told me how brave Mrs Kennedy had been through all of this. That she wouldn't leave the casket for a single moment, that she stayed with it at Bethesda Naval Hospital and, of course, over at the Mansion. He was amazed, as he put it, at her calm fortitude and courage.' Later in the day, when the White House correspondents were permitted to file past the bier, O'Donnell embraced Mary McGrory and wept again. Of Ken she had written in the *Evening Star* that 'he would have died for him'. He thanked her. She said, 'Everybody knows that, Kenny.'

The working press was one of the last two delegations to pass the catafalque; the other was the White House servants. By then all the famous names had gone. The ambassadors were back on Massachusetts Avenue, the governors in their hotel suites, the Senators on the Hill. Newscasters were not interested in the homage of colleagues, or in the prayers of Master Sergeant Giordano, Maître Fincklin, or George Thomas, and the national audience was not told that they had called. Nevertheless they had and unlike the officials they had not been inspired by any sense of obligation. The homage of wire service reporters and special correspondents—indeed, that of butlers, carpenters, and upstairs maids—was extraordinary. It was not part of the state funeral plan. Like last night's crowds at Andrews and Bethesda and the reverent filling station attendants along Wisconsin Avenue at dawn, it was a measure of the extent to which the entire country had been drawn into the vortex of anguish. George Thomas had polished every shoe and pressed every pair of trousers upstairs; he felt he had to be here, too, and on his knees. The newspapermen, never regarded as slavish admirers of any President, walked across the naked floor in absolute silence, and afterwards they asked, and were granted, permission to follow the caisson on foot when the coffin would be borne up Pennsylvania Avenue to the Hill tomorrow.

Mary McGrory halted by the two *prie-dieux* at the foot of the catafalque and knelt. She tried to pray, yet all she could remember were four words, Horatio's farewell to Hamlet. Like a rondeau they ran through her mind over and over again: *Good night, sweet prince.*

The East Room was hushed and the oval office naked, but the Vice Presidential suite had never been busier. There was a physical, visible frontier between the two administrations that morning. It was West Executive Avenue, that one-way, one-block street, which actually served as the White House parking lot. On one side of the twin row of cars stood the elegant old executive mansion, haunted by the ghost of the youngest man ever elected to the Presidency; on the other side pre-occupied men darted in and out of the Executive Office Building or, as Dwight Eisenhower still called it, 'the old State, Army, and Navy Building'—an astonishing reminder that until World War II its French neo-classic façade had been large enough for the offices of both American diplomacy and the national military establishment.

Certain individuals crossed the frontier, Johnson himself among them. All were aware of its existence, however, and the leadership of the Executive Department was split into two camps, those who wished to hurry the day when West Executive was once again a paved strip used for VIP angle parking, and those for whom the very thought of transition was agony. In his office Arthur Schlesinger was once more writing a note to Mrs Kennedy: 'I feel in such a state of total and terrible emptiness—and I know that what any of us feel here can only be a fraction of the vacancy and horror which you feel.' He told her that he expected to devote himself to work on the President's papers; he had already submitted his resignation to Lyndon Johnson.

That summed up the loyalist position: the President was dead; the work of the Presidency must be carried forward by others. At one end of Saturday's spectrum were Schlesinger, Sorensen, O'Donnell, and their leader, Robert Kennedy, who despite the gloomy sky had donned dark glasses after the Mass to conceal his swollen eyes. At the other end stood men like Mac Bundy, who repeatedly reminded other members of the Kennedy team that 'the show must go on' and who declared that he, for his part, intended to remain as long as he was wanted and needed by the President of the United States. Ted Sorensen saw the issue rather differently. At 7.30 p.m. he went over to the EOB at the invitation of the President, who solicited his advice about personnel. Sorensen said quietly, 'You have two kinds of problems: those who will not make themselves available to you and those who will be too available.'

The last point was subtle, but some felt it keenly. As the day grew older, individual resentments deepened. To some, the conduct of those who could think of the Presidency as an impersonal institution was considered callous. Dodging across rain-swept West Executive, Kenneth Galbraith saw a member of the Cabinet, seized his arm, and said urgently, 'We've got to take care of some of these liberals now, so they don't go shooting off their mouths'—a curious choice of words from the author of *The Liberal Hour*. There were those in the administration who felt that such demeanour was correct, but it was undoubtedly controversial.

Some of those whose alacrity was regarded with disapproval were not conscious of the reproachful glances around them. One confided to his diary that he heard 'no bitter word, and only encouragement from both sides, in my double loyalty'. He was misinformed. The words were spoken. He just didn't hear them. Of this same man a colleague was writing in *his* diary: 'I have never seen his instinct for power more naked and ruthless.' The validity of such acrimony is disputable. 'To be charitable,' Arthur Schlesinger observed the following spring, 'the government would have been paralysed if everyone had behaved like me and Ken O'Donnell.' And at the time he wrote that 'for some people, personal emotion is very difficult. . . . Bundy has everything under iron control. I do not think that this means that they feel things less than the rest of us.' It didn't. Schlesinger was a man of generous spirit. Yet even he did not know that McGeorge Bundy, the efficiency expert, the human computer, the robot of tempered steel—that Mac had cried in the night for John Kennedy.

An individual's attitude towards the shift in power was, in short, almost entirely a matter of temperament. Background was entirely irrelevant. Schlesinger, Galbraith, and Bundy had all been recruited from the Harvard faculty. Ken O'Donnell was not seen in the Vice Presidential suite all day, yet Larry O'Brien went over to discuss a Congressional manoeuvre which would boost the Russian wheat sale, and Sargent Shriver, President Kennedy's brother-in-law, was a realist by any standard. Anxious to see an orderly change of government, Shriver walked across West Executive and volunteered his services. When he attempted to bring the two groups together and ran into what he called 'a lot of flak', he was baffled. In retrospect the flak may seem puzzling now. In the context of that Saturday, however, events were very different. The loyalists, swept up in the mightiest current of emotion in their lives, were determined to show proper respect towards the murdered President. The realists played a valuable and difficult role—and history may award them the higher grade, for their service to the national interest was great.

The country, hypnotized by the catafalque, was unaware of any conflict within the government. It was virtually impossible to think beyond yesterday's death and the coming funeral. Hugh Sidey argued (in vain) that *Time* should hold its cover portrait of the new Chief Executive for another week's issue because 'Nobody is interested in Johnson yet'. Not many were. Nevertheless, depicting his mood during his first full day in office is a matter of intrinsic interest. A precise delineation is elusive. The man's chameleon nature had never been more evident. There had never been so many Lyndon Johnsons. It was almost as though a score of identical Texans were holed up backstage in Room 274, each with the same physiognomy and drawl, yet each with his own disposition, ideology, sense of timing, and objectives. George Reedy stepped in, and Lyndon the clairvoyant appeared. 'Everything was chaotic,' Reedy said afterwards. 'Only the President knew what he was doing.' Galbraith was announced and greeted by the left-of-centre champion. 'I want to come down very hard on civil rights,' Johnson told him, 'not because Kennedy was for it but because *I* am for it. Keep in mind that I want a liberal policy because I'm a Roosevelt Democrat.' Averell Harriman arrived with his Edwardian gait, and Lyndon said: 'You know I've always thought of you as one of my oldest and best friends in Washington.'

The President was exploiting his great gift for exposing this or that facet of his character so that each visitor would leave with a feeling of warmth and reassurance. Since the visitors entered one at a time, his success was almost universal. The out-and-out loyalists, while remaining distrustful of colleagues who had raced to 274, saw a Lyndon so humble, so shattered by his own anguish, that even Sorensen and Schlesinger were impressed; to David Ormsby-Gore this Lyndon said brokenly, 'If my family took a vote on whether or not I'd stay, there'd be three votes for quitting right away—and maybe four.' That Lyndon vanished, and another appeared, shrewdly advising O'Brien on a technical point of parliamentary procedure. There is no way to reconcile the various members of the flexible Presidential cast. The fact is that each played his part superbly and richly deserved applause. Only the naïve would be offended by the variety; John Kennedy would have been engrossed by it. Despite the accuracy of Sidey's judgment, Johnson was a fascinating man that Saturday. One must merely recognize that the man was many men.

Which was the real Johnson is a question best left to his biographers. This much is certain: he was putting in his most active day in three full years. Last evening he had only been warming up, honing skills grown rusty from disuse. Now he was alive again. Overnight he had acquired fresh momentum, and those who were sceptical of his wisdom couldn't doubt his stamina. At each briefing or conference he seemed to be tapping fresh reservoirs of energy. Repeated calls were placed to the Connallys at Parkland;[7] he fenced sharply with the soft-spoken but immovable Nick Katzenbach over whether the assassination should be investigated by a federal or state board of inquiry; he applied the Johnsonian prod to J. Edgar Hoover, who by now was dispatching fleets of agents to Love Field; he proclaimed Monday a day of official mourning; he received Arthur Goldberg; and he took time to pose for still photographs with Rusk, Bundy, McNamara, and Eisenhower, which were released to the networks at 5.13 p.m. ('First Pictures of LBJ at Work as President').

In lesser jobs there is a direct correlation between effort and results, but as Kennedy could have told Johnson, and as Johnson painfully learned that first day, the ratio is meaningless in the Presidency. Historic achievements may be credited to a Chief Executive while he is fast asleep; awake he may sweat like a slave and accomplish nothing. Johnson's Saturday was a curve which alternately plunged and zoomed and ended nowhere. After his encounter with Robert Kennedy he had enjoyed an easier interim; the Congressional leadership had come to the EOB to pledge its support. Today, as yesterday, the Senators and Congressmen offered him nonpartisan backing. The GOP's Charlie and Ev Show had been unsuccessfully attempting to bait Kennedy since his inaugural; this morning Charlie Halleck was the first man to encourage Johnson,

[7] The President was not permitted to speak to the Governor, who lay all day in a convalescent's semi-coma. Instead he talked to Nellie, who in reply to her husband's groggy inquiries finally conceded to him that his suspicions were correct, that the President was dead.

and after he had spoken Everett Dirksen said, 'We'll work together for our country. God bless you, Mr President.' The rest of the delegation echoed, 'God bless you, sir.'

It was after this heartening pledge that the President, joined by Lady Bird, led the leadership past the waiting Cabinet, into the East Room. Leaving the catafalque, he sighted Dwight Eisenhower and invited him to cross the street for a twenty-minute talk. Actually, the appointment turned out to be the longest of Johnson's day. It lasted two hours, and to the thirty-fourth President the thirty-sixth seemed anxious:

> The President asked General Eisenhower's advice on a number of current problems ranging from internal matters such as the tax cut, to foreign policy, specifically Laos and Cuba. At this early stage Lyndon Johnson was chiefly concerned with informing and preparing himself so that he could continue his predecessor's policies. General Eisenhower saw that President Johnson was determined to come to grips with his new responsibilities.

During the long session Mac Bundy—Mac's own description of his function was of a 'maid of all work' who 'fussed around'—tiptoed in and placed Schlesinger's letter of resignation on the desk. Johnson glowered. 'Tell him to take it back,' he said. 'I don't want any such letters. And tell everyone I mean that.' Moyers, who was in the background, slipped out and phoned Schlesinger that the President wanted him to stay. General Eisenhower suggested to Johnson that the new President should choose his own team. Johnson regarded him moodily. After the funeral he was to become adept at shaping his staff, easing out even those advisers who would have preferred to stay; on November 23, however, he treated any suggestion of change with a negative, highly emotional response, and he seemed to regard retirement from the government as tantamount to desertion. At that afternoon's Cabinet meeting Dean Rusk reminded him that it was traditional for all Cabinet members to submit resignations when a new President took office. Johnson shook his head doggedly; he said that he wanted every man there as a Johnsonian adviser. Rusk pointed out that this was a matter of form, a tradition, the thing to do. Precedent was involved, he observed; some future Chief Executive might not want all his ministers to stay. Still Johnson balked. The Cabinet resignations, which went in anyhow, weren't even acknowledged. And when he met Sorensen that evening, and Sorensen mentioned his own note, the President replied brusquely, 'I know, I got your letter,' and quickly changed the subject.

The new President and the new First Lady attended a memorial service for Kennedy at St John's on the north side of Lafayette

Square. Twenty-four hours had now passed since the assassination. It was past noon once more, and Schlesinger had arranged what came to be known as 'the Harvard lunch' in a private upstairs room of the Occidental Restaurant, on the opposite side of the Treasury Building from the White House. The meal was characteristic of the transition. The diners—the host, Ken and Kitty Galbraith, Bill Walton and his son Matt, Sam Beer and his wife, Paul Samuelson, and Walter Heller—were all enervated and adrift in what everyone considered a national crisis. In attempting to peer into the future, they were failing miserably. They couldn't even agree among themselves upon a course of action. Afterwards Galbraith wrote in his journal that 'Arthur was in a rather poor mood. . . . He was reacting far too quickly to the chemistry of the moment and was dwelling on the possibility of a ticket in 1964 headed by Bob Kennedy and Hubert Humphrey. This of course is fantasy, unless of course Johnson stumbles unbelievably or even then.' (Schlesinger's own estimate of his guest is instructive: 'Like Mac, Ken is a realist. He would infinitely have preferred Kennedy, but he is ready to face facts and make the best of them. Like Kenny and Bobby, I am a sentimentalist. My heart is not in it.')

The aftermath of the luncheon was equally typical. Schlesinger attended a staff meeting, where Bundy implored everyone to stick to his post, and Galbraith collided with the new President on West Executive. 'I've been looking for you,' Johnson said—Galbraith doubted that this was true—'I want to see you. Come on up.' Towards the end of their chat Johnson asked him to write a speech for delivery before a joint session of Congress. Galbraith, having finished his *Post* eulogy to Kennedy that morning, craved another excuse to finger a typewriter keyboard, and was immensely flattered. He needn't have been. The President was making the same request of a half-dozen men. If you were literate, informed, and emphatic, you were being drafted.

In his subsequent notes on this conversation with Johnson, Galbraith referred to 'the speech he was to give to the joint session that Wednesday'. This was hindsight. At the time of their conversation the date had not been set. Johnson yearned to speak to Congress, and understandably so. The people had been badly shaken. The sooner they heard the voice of their new leader in an address of substance, the better. In the State Department that morning Harriman, George Ball, and U. Alexis Johnson had begun work on a seven- or eight-minute speech to be broadcast over all networks during the evening; the President was to deplore 'hysteria' and urge support for the United Nations, peace, and continuity. He had vetoed the Under Secretarys' plan on the ground that he didn't want 'to push myself forward'. He was still holding back, feeling his way. At 2.30 p.m., however, he would have a matchless opportunity to take a real sounding. That was the time set for the Cabinet meeting. Thick yellow pads and sharpened pencils had been laid out at each place along the perimeter of the long table in the Cabinet Room, the Vice President's chair had been moved around to the President's spot, and one of the men present would be the new head of the Kennedy family, Attorney General Robert F. Kennedy.

'Gentlemen, the President of the United States!' Rusk said at the outset, and they all rose. The meeting was not a triumph. Its prospects were dim from the beginning; the ministers, like the barometer, were in a state of abnormal depression. Johnson had a few things going for him: Bundy had prepared a discreet memorandum on what he 'might want to say', and everyone present was anxious to pull the country together. But the catastrophe had been too recent. They couldn't forget that the corpse of the man who had appointed them all rested in a wooden coffin on the other side of this same building. The new President was further hampered by his own bearing. A total stranger might have imposed his personality upon them. But Lyndon, as they still thought of him, was a familiar figure who had attended their previous sessions as a subordinate, and who now presided in his meekest manner. Recalling the President's treatment of his memo, Bunday wrote ten days later that it was 'typical of him that he made it his own in action'. Johnson opened with a silent prayer, begged their guidance in the perilous times ahead, and added a short appeal which several of them by now could have recited from memory: he told them that he needed them more than President Kennedy had.

The Attorney General's participation in the twenty-five-minute meeting must be treated scrupulously, for the friction between the two men may easily be distorted by partisans. Each was under unprecedented pressure. If Johnson's discomfort seems ungenerous, it should be remembered that to the new Chief Executive Bob Kennedy represented a problem which was unique in the history of Presidential succession. Here was a Cabinet member who looked like, sounded like, and thought like the slain leader; who had been his second self; who was one of his two chief mourners; and who, at times, had—as everyone around this table knew—exercised executive power in his brother's name. It was as though Edwin Stanton had been Abraham Lincoln's twin. Historians would be obliged to sympathize with Andrew Johnson, for his contemporaries would have made few allowances, and it is unlikely that Stanton would have been as forbearing as Kennedy.

The Attorney General, for his part, had been pre-occupied with the coming funeral. His very presence in the Cabinet Room was something of an accident. After the Mass he had walked over from the mansion with McNamara, Walton, Reed, Spalding, and Lem Billings to see whether all his brother's belongings had been removed. He had noticed that Giordano had neglected to take President Kennedy's Cabinet chair, and early in the afternoon he decided to check again. The Cabinet had already convened. Bundy, glimpsing him, persuaded him to enter and sit in his own chair. In Mac's words of eleven days later, 'Bobby was late and perhaps would not have attended if I had not told him he must; his condition was that there should be no pictures—which I now know was as hard for the President as a ban against smoking for a thirty-year addict—though he accepted it readily in the interest of harmony.' Mac's version that afternoon was more tart. To a colleague he said that he was 'worried about Bobby', that 'Bobby was reluctant to face the new reality', and that he had 'had virtually to drag Bobby into the Cabinet meeting'. Kennedy's own recollection was merely that 'I went by and Mac Bundy said it was very important that I come in. So I went.'

His appearance evoked a dramatic response. Several members leaped to their feet, and one clasped his hand and clapped him on the back. Others, including Johnson, did not move. The Attorney General sat back brooding, his heavy eyes hooded. Yet for a man in his position silence itself can be significant. A half-hour earlier one television network had openly speculated that he might resign. His immediate future was being debated in millions of offices and homes, and his laconicism was noted and remembered by everyone around the long table—by President Johnson, perhaps, most of all.

After the President had finished, two men spoke: Adlai Stevenson, because of his seniority in the party, and Dean Rusk, as leader of the Cabinet. Their motives were identical; they wanted the record to show that they intended to keep faith with the new administration. Stevenson was surprisingly awkward. The most experienced and eloquent orator there, he had written a five-paragraph testimonial, which he proceeded to read word for word. He reminded them that he had pledged his support at President Kennedy's first Cabinet meeting, repeated that pledge now, said that 'there can only be a moment's pause in the nation's business', and declared to Johnson, 'Your unique qualities of character, wisdom and experience are a blessing to our country in this critical hour, and our confidence in your leadership is total.' Rusk was equally generous in his praise of Johnson.

After the Johnson–Rusk colloquy over letters of resignation, the President asked that they all submit departmental recommendations by Monday. They then dispersed. Nothing had been accomplished, and it was impossible for any of them to leave with a feeling of achievement. Even Johnson who had been delighted by Rusk and Stevenson, appeared to be disappointed; his subsequent remarks that afternoon indicate that he had hoped for more. To Bundy it had been a 'drab little meeting'. Willard Wirtz thought it was 'awful' and 'almost mechanical'; another secretary, who had expected the President to be 'strong and affirmative', concluded that it was 'highly unsatisfactory'; and one member of the Cabinet decided to speak to him about it. Cliff Carter led him into the EOB office, where the Secretary emphatically recommended to the President that he speak first to the people and then to the Congress. To the astonishment of his caller, Johnson's style had been completely altered in the few minutes since they had adjourned. It was another of those quick-change miracles; sitting in the Cabinet Room he had been hesitant, but now, as the Secretary noted in his journal, 'the frustration seemed gone, he seemed relaxed . . . the power, the confidence, the assurance of Majority Leader Lyndon Johnson seemed to be there'.

To this distinguished diarist the new President spoke frankly of the tension between himself and the Attorney General. He said, 'Jackie has been just great. She said she'd move out as soon as she could, and I said, "Honey, you stay as long as you want. I have a nice, comfortable home, and I'm in no hurry. You have a tragedy and many problems." ' His 'real problems', he indicated, were with Bob. He was convinced that Kennedy's late arrival at the meeting had been intentional, and he insisted that Kennedy, bent upon humiliating him, had confided to 'an aide' that 'we won't go in until he has already sat down'.[8]

The charge was unjust, but it was perhaps an inevitable consequence of the LBJ–RFK relationship, or, to be more precise, of the relationship between certain of their advisers. Since the Los Angeles convention the association of the two principals had been repeatedly damaged by misunderstandings which could usually be traced to this or that 'aide'. Thus the Vice President had been convinced that the Attorney General had never forgiven him for Los Angeles remarks critical of Joseph P. Kennedy. Ironically, Robert Kennedy had neither heard the criticism nor read of it. Johnson men were convinced that Bob disliked their leader. Kennedy men repeatedly reassured them, without success, and the Johnson administration had scarcely begun to gather momentum before the press speculated at length on 'the feud' between the two men. To be sure, in temperament and in manner they were very unlike. That had also

[8] Kennedy denies this. When the President's interpretation was described to him, he expressed first amazement, then amusement.

been true of John Kennedy and Lyndon Johnson. It had not led to a vendetta then, nor did it now.

Yet whatever the source of the strain, its existence was unquestionable. The consequences of Robert Kennedy's tardiness, Johnson told his caller, had been deeply embarrassing; by entering in the middle of the President's remarks the Attorney General had destroyed their effect. The Secretary, who was sympathetic—and who immediately afterwards conveyed his sympathy to another Cabinet member who had regarded the meeting as a disaster—wrote that 'There was real bitterness in Lyndon's voice on this one.' Clearly he regarded the late President's brother as a formidable obstacle. He agreed with his visitor that he ought to speak to the Congress as soon as possible. Wednesday, he was afraid, might be too late. Congress was thinking of recessing. Yet Johnson was apprehensive that an earlier address 'might be resented by the family'.

Having made what he described as his 'pitch' for a quick address, the caller left. In the suite's anteroom, Sargent Shriver was waiting. Shriver's visit had been inspired by a sense of duty. He was one member of the family who had felt close to Johnson, and he wanted to wish him well. At the same time, he thought that he ought to touch base with Moyers. Apparently Moyers' status was about to change, but technically he remained Deputy Director of the Peace Corps, and he was one of Shriver's closest friends. The two men chatted in subdued tones until Johnson's visitor had left; then they entered the Vice Presidential office. Shriver thought Johnson 'very hospitable'. The new President said, 'Well, Sarge, it's a terrible thing. I'm completely overwhelmed, but I do want to say that I've always had a very high regard for you. It hasn't been possible for me to do anything about it until now, but I intend to.'

'Is there anything I can do?' Shriver inquired.

There were, he was told, two unsolved questions: the occupancy of the oval office and the timing of the address to the joint session. (Interestingly, Johnson displayed little interest in a nationwide speech during these days; he was concerned first with the Congress. A televised address on the Hill would, of course, reach just as many Americans as a White House fireside chat.) Johnson observed that Rusk and Bundy, among others, strongly believed that he should be meeting his appointments in the West Wing, pointing to the symbolic importance of Presidential residence in the mansion. Furthermore, he observed, he would be much closer to vital communications equipment there. Lastly, both Johnson and Moyers emphasized the urgency of a joint session on Tuesday.

The State Department was pressing him especially hard. Yet if Senators and Representatives were in fact preparing to quit the capital, there was no sign of it. The need for moving across the street is obscure, though here a distinction must be made. The President was in no hurry to evict Mrs Kennedy. On the contrary; he was content to sleep at the Elms indefinitely. It was the Chief Executive's office in the West Wing that he wanted, not the pomp of the executive mansion.

A century earlier, Abraham Lincoln's successor, like John Kennedy's, had been eager to avoid the impression that he was anxious to take up residence in the President's house. The resemblances between the seventeenth and thirty-sixth Presidents are uncanny in other respects. 'What President has ever had a wider training for the office?' asked Lloyd Paul Stryker, Andrew Johnson's biographer. Lyndon Johnson's biographers would quickly vow that the training of the second Johnson was wider. Like Lyndon, Andrew was tactless with men, gallant towards women, and eager to eclipse the record of his predecessor. Andrew had also called a Cabinet meeting the day after the assassination of Lincoln, at which he declared that he merely intended to carry out established policies. It was even raining outside. On the matter of office occupancy, however, the two Johnsons differ sharply. Andrew met his Cabinet in the Treasury Building, where he set up temporary headquarters, and it was not until June 9, 1865, eight weeks after Lincoln's death, that he took over the White House. As Senator Humphrey explained in his notes, the new Chief Executive was 'an action President. He wants to get things done. He is in a sense restless and demanding. . . .'

Shriver's position was awkward. He was foggy about precedents, and although he had been related to Kennedy by marriage his devotion to the Peace Corps had left little time to explore other governmental labyrinths. 'I remembered that the west basement had been chewed up when Jack was President,' he said later, 'and while I hadn't known what was going on, I had a hunch it had something to do with the hot line.' Shriver, normally quick to make up his mind, couldn't decide about the oval office. In his words, Bundy, whom the President was quoting to him, 'felt that it was first of all the President's office, while the family naturally felt that it was Jack's office. I'd been in the Navy, and I was inclined to agree with Bundy; you don't leave a command post empty because the commander has fallen.' On the other hand, 'It seemed unseemly speed to move into that office before Jack was out of the White House. Jack's body, after all, was still lying in the East Room.' This reluctance from the most sympathetic member of the late Chief Executive's family appears to have resolved the issue for Johnson; he did not mention the issue again that day.

That left the timing of the address. Once again Johnson cited pressures from 'the leadership of the government'. For those who were accustomed to Kennedy's frontal approach such obliqueness was perplexing. Kennedy had characteristically prefaced an order with the phrase, 'In my judgment.' If you disagreed, you debated with him. Johnson presented himself as an entrepreneur of other men's ideas. In the event that they proved to be bad ideas, the promoter wasn't at fault; he had merely offered them for consideration. His cautious introductions ('Bundy says,' 'Rusk says,' or 'McNamara says') absolved him from responsibility. On this issue, he told Shriver, the voices were unanimous. All agreed that the President should go to the Hill 'as soon as possible', that 'it was important to show that the Johnson administration was taking over'. Shriver agreed, though his reasons were his own. Extrapolating from his Peace Corps travels, he had realized that Asia, Africa, and South America would assume that 'whoever had killed President Kennedy would now be President'. Dispelling that notion was important. The sooner the world was told that Johnson was not an employer of bravoes, the better off the United States would be, and when both Johnson and Moyers said they preferred a Tuesday talk, Shriver replied, 'I'll speak to Bobby.'

The flak followed. Unknown to Shriver, Bundy had been assigned the same mission, and he had failed. Robert Kennedy had replied crisply, 'I don't like that. I think you should wait at least one day after the funeral.' Bundy had told Kennedy that 'they'—he was adjusting rapidly to the Johnsonian ambiguity—'want it on Tuesday'. The Attorney General snapped back, 'Well, the hell with it. Why do you ask me about it? Don't ask me what you want done. You'll tell me what it's going to be anyway. Just go ahead and *do* it.' If Johnson thought a Kennedy relative would make a more effective emissary, he was wrong. He was merely sending Shriver into a trap. Kennedy, exasperated by the new President's failure to communicate with him directly, listened to the proposal and then said sharply to Sarge, 'Why does he tell you to ask me? Now he's hacking at you. He knows I want him to wait until Wednesday.'

Shriver darted back between the parked cars, was ushered in by Moyers, and discreetly reported that 'Bob prefers you wait a day, unless there are overriding reasons for having the address earlier'. Johnson immediately picked up his telephone and began pressing plastic buttons. To his listeners he said tersely, 'It will be on Wednesday.' Each of them needed no briefing; every member of his staff was familiar with the background and was awaiting word from him. Shriver swiftly relayed the decision to his brother-in-law, and all that remained was a formal release from Salinger's office. Shortly before 6.30 the networks broadcast that President Johnson would speak to Congress at 12.30 p.m. on Wednesday, November 27, the day before Thanksgiving; CBS, NBC, and ABC would carry it live. No commentator hinted that the President was being either hasty or a laggard, and only a handful knew of the dissension behind the announcement. Shriver, however, was left with 'an inkling of the feeling that was involved. . . . It was clear that there was a condition which was exacerbating'.

Gauging the degree of exacerbation is difficult. Most of the insiders remained tight-lipped about their Saturday talks in the Vice Presidential suite. Bundy has withheld the larger part of his early assessment of President Johnson; with his uncommon detachment and good sense, he observed on December 4 that 'the important thing is to distinguish between what he is trying to accomplish and the specific means he may at first prefer, and to try to serve the real end while arguing against the means, if need be'. McNamara conferred with Johnson in the middle of the afternoon, but his comment—'It was not routine, but I do not feel at liberty to report a conversation of a President of the United States'—is both taut and unsatisfactory, since he has reported other such conversations in detail. It does seem obvious that Johnson felt balked, and that he blamed much of his frustration on Robert Kennedy. That was understandable. The Attorney General was symbolic of the past he had to overcome. It was also unfair. A study of Bob Kennedy's movements that day reveals that virtually all his time was preempted by funeral preparations. A satisfactory solution of the situation was clearly impossible; the need for the government to proceed was at odds with the Kennedys' grief. The President was being thwarted by something larger than any individual. He was attempting to start a new government, and everyone who could help him, including his own Texans and Washingtonians who had been close to him for a third of a century, was floundering in the greatest surge of emotion ever known.

His talk with Ted Sorensen came just before his departure for the Elms. It was a long session, and representative; the invisible obstacles between them would have existed had Robert F. Kennedy never existed. Although determined to quit quietly, Sorensen took his responsibilities keenly, and he was anxious to be helpful. Before crossing the lot he had prepared a list of exigent Presidential business. With Moyers taking notes, they checked off each item carefully. Ted recalls his own manner as 'blunt and tough'. Yet it was not hostile. He recommended a prompt address on the Hill. After brushing off his resignation, the President listened impassively to his evaluation of the White House staff. (Unknown to him, Johnson had been inquiring of others, 'Is Sorensen an easy man to work with?'

The answers had been mixed.) Early in the session the President asked, 'What do you think of the possibility of a foreign government being involved in this?' Ted said instantly, 'Do you have any evidence?' The answer was that there were no hard facts. Johnson showed him an FBI memo advising him that the rulers of an unfriendly power had been hoping for Kennedy's death. The report was too hazy for serious consideration. There were no names or facts, and the name of the FBI's informant was in code. 'Meaningless,' said Sorensen, handing it back. The President said nothing. He asked whether Sorensen thought unusual safeguards would be necessary to protect him during the funeral. Ted shook his head; he didn't.

Sooner or later—it was to be sooner—the relationship between the new President and the former President's Special Counsel was bound to deteriorate. As Sorensen had told a Cabinet member shortly after three o'clock, he had invested over ten years in John Kennedy's career, and now the investment was gone—gone as surely as though he himself had been the victim in Dallas. Kennedy had chosen him because their personalities had meshed perfectly. Both were young, literate, understated men of integrity; Sorensen had been the ideal abrasive for the intellectual facet of the Kennedy prism, just as O'Donnell had been a foil for the President's political talents, and Llewellyn Thompson a tutor for his Russian studies. But Ted Sorensen could never be an adequate companion for Lyndon Johnson. They were entirely different men. Their styles were a world apart.

Throughout that weekend the President gave every sign of believing that he could preserve the Kennedy team intact. He couldn't, and when he had grown surer of himself he realized that he had to create his own team. His delusion was a symptom of the Kennedy passion; of the need, as he himself had put it, to retain 'the aura of Kennedy'. On November 23, 1963, the nation's mourning was so intense that no other emotional climate seemed feasible. Afterwards, and especially after he himself had become an elected President in his own right, Johnson would forget that he had ever pleaded for the support of Kennedy's aides. The very mention of their names would annoy him. Within a year he would even resent the aura itself, and become so sensitive to it that any Secret Service man or White House chauffeur who wore a PT 109 tie clip would run the risk of incurring Presidential wrath.

Jacqueline Kennedy was a doodler, and seated at her second-floor Louis Quinze desk, by the casement windows overlooking the Rose Garden and the Presidential office, she filled sheets of White House stationery with lists of people she must call or write and reminders to herself. It is startling to realize that a bereaved First Lady should be obliged to cope with trivia. But like any other widow she had to determine particulars. Even Mary Todd Lincoln, who went to pieces after the murder in Ford's Theatre and deputized Robert Lincoln as chief mourner, had been obliged to select the place of burial. Mrs Kennedy could, of course, have retired into seclusion. No one would have criticized her or expressed surprise; that would have been consistent with her innate reticence. But she wanted to share in the planning.

It was good for her. She couldn't sleep, and she must do something; doodling was better than brooding. Thus she concentrated on tomorrow and the day after tomorrow, devoting herself to the majestic ceremonies which, with her special cachet, were to leave an everlasting impression on the national audience. She was rarely alone. In this sense a First Lady is set apart from other widows. Relatives, social secretaries, her staff, her friends, and her husband's friends slipped in and out of the West Sitting Hall's double sliding doors carrying more scribbled paper—more to think about, new barriers between her and sorrow.

Examined now, many of the notes seem either needless or inaccurate. One page is headed in block letters DALLAS POLICEMAN. Beneath is written: 'Mrs Marie Tippitt' (for Tippit), 'three children' (correct), and the address '238 Glencairn Street Oak Cliff Texas—Suburb of Dallas' (it was Glencairn Drive, another place entirely). But that is irrelevant. What counted was that Mrs Kennedy intended to send her condolences to the wife of the slain patrolman; the envelope could be addressed by someone else.

General Wehle afterwards declared that 'she held all the strings, and we marvelled at her clear thinking and sense of command'. There was, and still is, an understandable tendency to idealize the comportment of the President's widow. She didn't hold *all* the strings. No one could. The minutiae of a state funeral are incredible; they require almost as much staff work as an amphibious invasion. Nevertheless, Jacqueline and Robert Kennedy made all the major decisions. Between them they delegated authority to reliable subordinates, and, as her notes attest, spliced together, a lot of frayed ends. She was tentatively planning Monday's services, worrying about the executive mansion's inundation of house guests ('3rd floor 5 Single 2 Double'), and jotting down telephone numbers and names ('Jane DU 7-2480'; 'Alsop, David, Pam, Cushing, Nancy, Margie, Mary'; 'SCHLES—DILLON—MEDAL—JACK'; 'Salinger, Mr West, Clifton, Queen, de Gaulle, Bishop Hannan, Taylor, Tish').

The eminent ('Queen, de Gaulle') would receive appreciative

billets in her own handwriting. For others a handshake, a brief word would do. But in the mansion there was no such thing as informality. Every caller must be scheduled: 'Mon 730 McNamara; Tues 530 Katz; 630 Dillon; Wed 530 Grimes.' Reading her scribbles, with their deletions, marginal jottings, cryptic symbols, and underscorings, one senses her determination to drive away recollections of yesterday. Certain entries—'Mass Cards'—could be decided by her alone. But 'Menus', 'Xmas', 'WH Scrapbook', and 'Dave Powers pants Teddy' could have been put off. She was thinking about everything except the unthinkable, filling her hours with tasks.

Anticipating Christmas, household duties, and her brother-in-law's funeral attire would have been remarkable had she lacked other duties. In fact, she had never had so many, not even before her own wedding. There was, for example, the problem of her attire. Bridal gowns are easily acquired. During the next two days, she decided, she must wear black stockings and, during Monday's funeral services, a full mourning veil enveloping her entire head. Mary Gallagher acquired the stockings from Garfinkel's, but no store had carried mantillas for years, so the White House seamstress had to make one. Ralph Dungan was pressing for a decision about the horses which would accompany the caisson. Fort Myer's stables had two teams, matched greys and matched blacks. Which would it be? Eventually the word came down from Shriver that the family had settled on the greys. The Kennedy team could protect her from intolerable intrusions—every fraternal association, veterans' organization, and quasi-religious group was anxious to participate in the ceremony—but if she wanted it to bear the Kennedy imprint, she had to be active, and she even had to develop political finesse; the Church hierarchy had its own notions of ritual, and interservice rivalry was irrepressible. Telephoning Taz Shepard and asking him to provide an escort of seamen for the horse-drawn gun carriage which would bear the coffin wasn't enough. Colonel Miller had to be satisfied that the Navy really was her choice; otherwise the Army might feel slighted.

She didn't win every point. From her research on the White House guidebook she had learned that long before band leaders had adopted the custom of greeting prominent politicians with a sprightly chorus of 'Hail to the Chief', the air had been a Scottish ballad. The Scots played it largo. She remembered the President's fondness for the melody and thought Scottish bagpipers might pipe it as a dirge. Ted Clifton persuaded her to withdraw the request. Though no one knew just when John Tyler had confiscated the tune as Presidential property, and though the circumstances had been hardly solemn—at Tyler's direction, the Marine Band had used it to serenade his second wife-to-be—the inalterable fact was that 'Hail to the Chief' had acquired a semi-official status. An unorthodox performance by foreigners would be regarded as improper.

She lost another musical skirmish to the more formidable Church. She had asked to have a Navy chorus sing during the funeral Mass, and once again the Navy was eager to oblige. At first the possibility of an obstacle seemed remote here. In Annapolis three Academy choirs—Catholics, Protestants, and antiphonal—began rehearsing. None was destined to perform at the service, however, for in Ralph Dungan's office a priest, overhearing Shepard's phoned orders, took him aside and said, 'You can't do it. We have our own choir.' Taz protested that the first of the three consisted entirely of Catholic youth, but he was missing the nub; the Church was bent upon its own people. In the end Mrs Kennedy yielded and directed that the midshipmen sing on the mansion's North Lawn Monday.

The hierarchy was victorious there. It was defeated in the greater debates over the Mass. Cardinal Cushing was acceptable to everyone, of course, and His Eminence stipulated no preferences of his own. The conflict arose over the designation of the second prelate at the altar. If seniority were observed, the Cardinal would be joined at the altar by Archbishop Patrick A. O'Boyle of Washington. Mrs Kennedy had no objection to O'Boyle. But if any clergyman except Cushing were to speak, she wanted to see Auxiliary Bishop Philip N. Hannan at the lectern. He was young, gifted, and highly idealistic; she thought of him as 'sort of a Jack in the Church'. Shriver braced himself for a bolt of clerical disapproval. Surprisingly there wasn't even a spark, and Hannan was so assigned.

The real clash came over the selection of the cathedral. To the hierarchy the Shrine of the Immaculate Conception in north-eastern Washington was the obvious choice. The bishops and monseigneurs couldn't imagine a finer tabernacle. The Romanesque Shrine was the largest and most impressive Catholic edifice in the United States; it seated 2,500, was equipped with vast parking areas, and had become something of a tourist attraction—during the spring and summer glut of sight-seers there were scheduled tours, and an efficient basement cafeteria had been installed for them. Jacqueline Kennedy was unimpressed. She had never been inside the Shrine. She disliked the name. To her St Matthew's was far more appealing; she particularly treasured the memory of attending a Red Mass with her husband there. If any cathedral were to be identified with the President, this would be it. The hierarchy was dumbfounded. Compared to its magnificent Shrine, St Matthew's was shabby, ageing, unsplendid, unadorned by artistic treasures. The widow and the clerics deadlocked. In Robert Kennedy's words, 'The priests insisted on Immaculate Conception, but she was very insistent about St Matthew's.' He told her, 'I think it's too small. It only seats eleven hundred.' She replied, 'I don't care. They can all stand in the streets. I just know that's the right place to have it.'

Mrs Kennedy had another, unanswerable reason for her choice, and eventually she disclosed it. She refused to ride to her husband's funeral Mass 'in a fat black Cadillac'; she had resolved to walk behind the caisson, and since the gleaming Shrine was too far away it was automatically eliminated. That settled that. At the same time it raised other, secular dilemmas, some of the first magnitude. Nobody, including Bob Kennedy, had anticipated a phalanx of famous pedestrians. Everyone responsible for security was appalled. Angie Duke envisioned a protocol nightmare, and wasn't even sure that such homage wasn't un-American. At his suggestion the Library of Congress ferrets were once more unleashed in the stacks, and they returned staggering under volumes of yellowed newsprint and cartons of microfilm which disclosed that similar processions had followed the coffins of Washington, Lincoln, Grant, and the first Roosevelt. Between 32,000 and 33,000 veterans of the American Revolution had followed George Washington's body to its Mount Vernon grave. That was the best possible precedent, and Duke threw in his hand.

At first the widow wanted to walk every step—from the executive mansion to the Hill, from there to St Matthew's, and from the Mass to the burial site. Independently of her, the Joint Chiefs of Staff were taking the same line. To soldiers and sailors it seemed a fitting tribute to a fallen Commander in Chief. Ted Clifton gently pointed out that the consequences could be catastrophic. Gentlemen would refuse to be seated while a widowed First Lady was on foot, and few of these gentlemen were fit for such a hike. Clifton reminded Mrs Kennedy that doddering behind her would be the oldest members of the Congress, Supreme Court Justices who were septuagenarians and octogenarians, and the President of Turkey, who had been a major when Dwight Eisenhower—himself seventy-three—had been a cadet at West Point. Conceivably half the nations in the UN could be left leaderless. She meditated and then modified her order. They would walk from the White House to St Matthew's, eight blocks away; infirm Chiefs of State could be driven there in advance. Even then the funeral planners murmured dissent, but she declined to budge further. 'Nobody has to walk but me,' she said, when she was told they would insist upon joining her she shrugged. That was their affair, she said; 'That doesn't matter.' A diehard inquired, 'What will we do if it rains?' 'I don't care,' she said firmly. 'I'll walk anyway.' Her tone discouraged further argument. It dawned on them that not even a howling hurricane would prevent her from striding up Seventeenth Street and Connecticut to the cathedral at 1725 Rhode Island. Like staying with the body in Dallas, like her refusal to shed her stained clothing until she had been returned home, this was something she had to do.

By now Clifton, Duke, Shepard, Miller, and Shriver had almost become part of Dungan's office furniture. Each man had left word with a score of colleagues that he could be reached at these extensions. Thus the marathon meeting was really larger than it seemed; the two White House switchboards kept plugging in invisible participants. Dungan felt a strange longing for last night's simplicity. Today there were innumerable points of control, and they were not nearly so reliable. Bob Kennedy couldn't always be reached, Jackie frequently changed her mind, and the Church and the military were being mulish. Twenty-four hours hadn't decreased the sense of shock; if anything the men were more aware of their loss, and broke down more often. At the outset they had at least been rested. The accumulation of fatigue had begun to tell, both in emotional displays and sudden eruptions of temper. The one iron man there, Dungan thought, was Shriver. Except for occasional brief absences he sat hour after hour in front of the desk with a yellow pad in his lap, making meticulous notes and firing off orders.

But Shriver wasn't the only efficient conferee. Dungan himself was performing ably, and Saturday's accomplishments suggest that the general standard was very high. Dr Joseph English, no expert in transportation, arranged a transatlantic dash for Mary Ann Ryan, a distant cousin of the President's. A terse debate on mourning clothes ended, as Dick Goodwin put it, with the judgment that 'If there was any occasion which demanded the highest formality it was the death of a President; therefore we would wear tails.' The preparation of guest lists continued, and had become more orderly—two men worked on the diplomatic corps, two handled the Congress, one chose family friends, one clergymen, one the press—and here, too, the follow-ups were painstaking. Once the selection of St Matthew's had become definite, groups of planners travelled there and made preliminary charts of pews and standing room while Sandy Fox dispatched telegrams and spread the word that invited Washingtonians were to pick up the invitations—which Sandy was inscribing with his exquisite calligraphy—in the East Lobby, where Da Hackett and Dean Markham awaited them. Deciding upon musical titles was another initial step, and it was surprisingly complex. A state funeral is an intricate medley; not counting the national anthem, ruffles, and flourishes, there were to be thirty hymns. The bands had to be marshalled (Army seniority was disregarded; Mrs Kennedy had requested priority for the Marine Band), and the proper scores had to be distributed to the musicians. There may be a dozen versions of a familiar refrain. For the Kennedy funeral the Kennedy team was exacting, and Irving Lowens of the Library of Congress' music division was yanking volumes and folders from his own stacks, establishing the history of each composition.

In the case of 'Hail to the Chief' he even appointed an *ad hoc* committee, whose report was filed in the Marine Band library. This may seem like cavilling. But the President's campaigns had taught his campaigners that every line of fine print would be read by some-one, and as it happened Lowens' findings were to be cited more than once. The sheer mass of the television audience meant that the tiniest movement would be witnessed by experts. America has experts in everything. There are people who devote lifetimes to a study of Longstreet's movements on the morning of July 3, 1863; there are people who can recite the complete works of Robert W. Service; and there are people who make a hobby of 'Hail to the Chief'. The strains which Tyler had thought romantic were to be played four times that week-end, twice on the Hill and twice at the church. Renditions were rotated among the service bands, and later letters arrived from vigilant critics who had recorded each beat with stopwatches and wondered why the tempo had varied.

Now and then the planners boggled. At 1930 hours Fort McNair held a full-dress briefing for regular officers, the National Guard, the reserves, the Secret Service, the Metropolitan police, and the park police. General Wehle presided, coloured chalk in hand. He drew elaborate diagrams and even indulged in whimsey, dryly remarking to Captain William Smith, 'This is going to be a golden moment for you; you are going to be the first junior officer in history to issue the order, "Joint Chiefs of Staff! Forward March!"' Wehle thought nothing had been left to chance. He had told Shriver, 'I want every-thing in writing.' Nevertheless the meeting broke up with no men-tion of the Presidential flag. Late that evening Seaman Ed Nemuth was watching television at Anacostia when a petty officer informed him that he would carry the huge standard behind the coffin to-morrow and on Monday. It was to be one of the most conspicuous military assignments in the ceremonies; television watchers who never saw Wehle or the Joint Chiefs were to be left with a vivid impression of Nemuth. Yet he had never seen a President's ensign, had never carried a banner that large, and never dreamed that the pole would be too tall for the Capitol's bronze doors. He would have to deal with that vicissitude when it arose; the order had come to him too late for rehearsal. Similarly, the President's family should have reached a definite decision about the Mass card. Mass cards aren't like newspapers. Printers must devote meticulous care to them. Running one off on a crash schedule is extremely difficult. But after preliminary examination of those which had been used at the requiem Masses for Joe Kennedy, Jr. and Ethel's parents, the matter was set aside until Sunday.

Of course, there is such a thing as too much efficiency. The White House operators are so good, and their connections so swift, that often neither the caller nor the called knows where the other is. In Chicago Tish Baldridge, who had preceded Nancy Tuckerman as social secretary, had lain awake until 2 a.m. Giving up sleep, she had packed a bag and taken the first plane to Washington. Saturday noon she entered the East Gate, passed by the catafalque, and phoned Shriver on a mansion extension. Sarge didn't know it was an extension. He assumed she was in Illinois, and when she asked whether there was anything she could do, he suggested she think about the cemetery. This was consistent with the organizational approach Larry O'Brien had perfected for John Kennedy—give every volunteer a job; even if he blunders, he will be left with a feeling of participation. Had Tish been at her Merchandize Mart office her thoughts would have been ineffective. Since she was in Washington (and since she was a strong-minded woman) her presence was quickly felt. She approved the purchase of Joe Gawler's $700 copper-lined asphalt-concrete vault, and with Angie Duke's wife Robin she sketched an arbour of flowers for the grave. Tish and Robin were old friends of Mrs Kennedy, but neither understood her concept of taste. To her a floral arbour was like engraving RIP on a gravestone, and when they set out to buy up every rose in the capital they were embarking on a collision course. Jacqueline Kennedy had her own ideas about flowers.

Seaman Nemuth, the Mass card, and Tish were exceptional. With few exceptions the widow had but to express a desire and the achievement materialized like Aladdin's jinni. Because she had been expecting Patrick's birth in two months, she had been unable to accompany her husband to Ireland. Nevertheless he had told her of his affection for the people, had held her spellbound with dramatic tales of the April 1916 uprising in Dublin, and had described President Eamonn de Valera's youthful struggles in Brooklyn. She mentioned how moved he had been by Ireland's drill of mourning for departed heroes, and that was enough; Clifton, who had been with him there, had previously assigned a picked detail from Fort Myer to study a film showing the solemn salute, but now he knew that would not do. He phoned the Irish Ambassador, who, grateful for the opportunity to do something, declared that he would fly in a team of cadets from Shannon. Dungan's office made reservations for them at the Mayflower Hotel.

She remembered another, more recent incident; on November 13, during her convalescence, the bagpipers of the Black Watch Regiment had skirled on the south grounds to the delight of John and Caroline. After wittily glossing over Black Watch encounters with American colonists during the Revolutionary War, the President had spoken of his own affection for Scotland. He loved it, he had said, because it was a lost cause which, in the end, had triumphed. Mrs Kennedy felt that her husband had always had an affinity for lost causes. Now his own life was one. She thought it appropriate for the Black Watch to march behind the gun carriage in groups of three, between the Joint Chiefs and the U.S. Marines. Clifton called Ormsby-Gore's military aide. The Black Watch was still touring America, and the pipe major and eight pipers were flown up from Knoxville and billeted at Fort Myer. The American funeral pace was a hundred paces a minute, slightly faster than the heartbeat of a man. There was no equivalent in the British Army. The Scotsmen would have to maintain it for a mile, and they began round-the-clock drill.

Fort Myer's two drill fields were becoming rather crowded. Lieutenant Sam Bird was rehearsing his body bearers. Sergeant Keith Clark was practising taps. While Clifton had flinched at the idea of a mournful rendition 'Hail to the Chief', Jacqueline Kennedy's preference for the melancholy sound of bagpipe music was endorsed. The Black Watch men weren't the only skirlers; four Air Force pipers had been assigned to the graveside ceremony, and the old red-brick fort was made even more tristful by their plaintive wailing. The stables clattered with the sounds of hoisted harness. Old Guard archivists were familiar with the legends of Genghis Khan and Tamerlane, whose chargers were sacrificed after the burial of a lost conqueror in the Mongol faith that they passed through 'the gate of the sky' to serve their master in afterlife. Since then the riderless horse had become traditional in all state funerals. Fort Myer veterans knew that a caparisoned steed would follow the gun carriage, with boots turned backwards as a sign that the fallen leader would ride no more. At first the widow thought of using Sarder, a bay gelding which President Ayub Khan had given her; then, at 4 p.m., the fort's twenty-six-horse stable was ordered to pick one of its own.

Two chargers were available. 'Shorty' was the more phlegmatic and would be easier to handle, but to the stablemen he looked rather like a fat cow. 'Black Jack', his stablemate, was a magnificent seventeen-year-old. He had the vigour of a young stallion, and picking him was a risk; nevertheless the commanding officer of the Old Guard's 3rd Battle Group was confident that Pfc Arthur A. Carlson could handle him. Carlson himself was less sure. Black Jack's temperament was notorious; the crowds, the white traffic lines on Pennsylvania Avenue, and especially the slow progress of the caisson were disturbing prospects. Furthermore, he was even stronger than he looked. Carlson was a sinewy young Alabaman, but if the gelding shied and broke loose, the cavalryman would be left. Both Carlson and the sergeant who would lead the matched greys picked tight cinches, spur straps, and Pelhams (check reins). There was some feeling among old cavalrymen that the horses drawing the gun carriage should be mounted by senior non-coms. They were overruled. The hazards of skittishness were too great. The thought that runaways might gallop across Washington with the Commander in Chief's coffin was intimidating. Riders were picked for their brawn, horsemanship, and experience, and as things turned out the apprehension of the worriers was to be justified.

The vast majority of the infantrymen who were to march had been trained in quickstep cadence. Like the Black Watch pipers, they had to be redrilled. Mrs Kennedy was unaware of this at the time. Most of the participants were strangers to her. She hadn't met the marchers, the riders, the musicians, the Irishmen, the Scotsmen, or the generals at Myer and McNair. She didn't even know the name of the riderless horse. (Had she been told, she would have been startled; her childhood nickname for her father had been Black Jack.) From her eminence in the executive mansion she could only shape broad outlines and leave details to others. Her lieutenants were her husband's staff; in planning his state funeral she was, in effect, Acting President. She couldn't have done it alone. The entire Kennedy family, and particularly Robert Kennedy and Sargent Shriver, were indispensable; nevertheless she was the widow, the symbol. She kept a taut check rein on herself. When the pressures on her were at their height, an acquaintance who had been waiting in the second-floor hall outside the oval study noted that 'Jackie came out, looking very pale but most composed. She said that an acquaintance had "called me to say how wonderful I have been. How did she expect me to behave?" ' The fact was that her own friends had never fully understood her. Her husband had. Seven years earlier, sitting on the edge of a table in his Boston headquarters, he had remarked to a group of them, 'My wife is a shy, quiet girl, but when things get rough, she can handle herself pretty well.' Until now they hadn't realized that he had been displaying his flair for understatement.

Saturday's hardest decision had been the choice of a grave site. The dispute was so intense, the feeling so strong on both sides, that lasting bruises appeared to be inevitable. Until the issue was resolved the President's friends—indeed, the family itself—was divided into two clear-cut factions, with the Bostonians a heavy majority. In fact, several of the funeral planners didn't even know that an alternative existed. Except for Taft and Wilson, all previous Chief Executives had been buried near their homes. In Dungan's office Angie Duke glanced up from his FDR precedent book and inquired, 'What's the Hyde Park of the Kennedy family?' 'Brookline,' he was told. He instructed his protocol experts to prepare invitation for a funeral train and be ready with alternatives in the event of orders to move the body from St Matthew's by destroyer or aircraft. President Johnson's staff expected him to attend a Mass in Hyannis and graveside services in Brookline. Following the Cabinet meeting Johnson had told a visitor that he couldn't schedule any appointments early next week because 'I don't know about after the funeral; I may be in Massachusetts.' At 11.37 a.m. a State Department telecom had definitely informed Ambassador Bohlen in Paris, 'The burial will be in Brookline.'

O'Donnell, O'Brien, and Powers were unshakeable to the end. For them the thought of lowering the President's coffin anywhere else was unthinkable. They were professional persuaders, they were sure they were right, and they had converted both Salinger and Sorensen. Even Jim Reed, who was from western Massachusetts, couldn't imagine another cemetery. The President's sisters were definite; Eunice telephoned from Hyannis Port, 'We're all going to be buried around Daddy in Boston.' Robert Kennedy agreed. The arguments, he thought, were overwhelming: the family had come from Massachusetts, their father had made such a difference in their lives, and 'the President obviously felt it because he buried Patrick there'. If Brookline proved unsatisfactory, there was always Boston Common. The mafia had a half-dozen plans, and they were ready to discuss anything except a grave outside New England. To them that was outrageous. Consequently the emergence of a strong Arlington faction 'made it', as Bob Kennedy dryly put it afterwards, 'rather difficult for me'.

The truth was that none of them was familiar with Arlington. It lay just across the Potomac, and they had seen its markers shining in the sunlight as they drove past, but because of their youth Kennedy men and women were largely ignorant of all cemeteries, national and private. Sorensen pictured Arlington as 'a funeral factory'. The sisters felt that it sounded cold and remote. Even the Secretary of Defence, Arlington's most vehement advocate, was vague about it.

His department's real estate in the continental United States, it must be remembered, was approximately the size of Tennessee. He had reigned over the Pentagon for nearly three years, yet he had scarcely been within the cemetery's gates. His conviction that the President's coffin should lie in federal soil would have been quickly dismissed without Jacqueline Kennedy's support, and her persistence was chiefly instinct. She remembered her intuitive flash of nearly three years ago; she reflected upon how lovely Lee Mansion could be when you drove across Memorial Bridge and saw it all lit up, and recalled that the illuminated pillars had been one of the first Washington sights Caroline had learned to recognize.

The brooding house, with its eight white Athenian columns, belonged to American history. Erected in 1802, it had first belonged to an adopted son of George Washington. There Mary Custis married Lieutenant Robert E. Lee in 1831; there, thirty years later, Lee wrote out his resignation from the U.S. Army, dispatched the letter to the Secretary of War, and assumed command of the Army of Northern Virginia. In 1864 Secretary Stanton confiscated the rolling, 420-acre estate—Stanton simply called it 'Lee's Farm'—as a cemetery for the Union dead. Despite all this Arlington had somehow escaped partisan bitterness. The first man to be buried there was a Confederate soldier who had died in a Union hospital, and in 1883 the Supreme Court set aside Stanton's confiscation. The federal government then bought the land outright from Lee's heir for $150,000

After the Kennedy funeral everyone, including the diehards, agreed that the choice was ideal. Yet the Bostonians were acquiring so much momentum Saturday morning that its chances would have been extremely slight without a freak of human nature, the matutinal habits of Robert S. McNamara. The Secretary had been known to schedule appointments at 6 a.m., which in Washington, a city of late risers, was almost an act of insanity. McNamara was always in his office by eight o'clock, and on Saturdays he came in earlier, because with the brass in the sack he could get more done. November 23, 1963, was a Saturday. He was at his enormous old desk in the E Ring before the mafia proselytized Sorensen, and his first order of business was a self-briefing on the American Battle Monuments Commission and what Defence called 'Cemeteries, National'. The man he wanted, he found, was Arlington's superintendent, John C. Metzler. Jack Metzler was also up, and as ready as he would ever be. That was less than letter-perfect. It wasn't his fault. The cemetery was a managerial Gorgon. Pyramided atop the complexities of the funeral industry was the rigid caste system of the military: a dead soldier was entitled to taps and a firing party, officers up to lieutenant colonel were given caissons, the caskets of full colonels and generals—and naval captains and admirals—were followed by either Shorty or Black Jack. Men were even buried by rank. That was standard operating procedure in all national cemeteries, but Metzler had special problems. His knowledge of Arlington's boundaries, for example, was rather hazy. At one time the National Park Service, which maintained the mansion, had been responsible for the hill in front of it. Since then the line had been redrawn, and Metzler didn't know precisely which blades of grass belonged to Defence and which to Parks—to Interior. There was the further problem of upkeep. Some twenty thousand trees stood on the old estate, and in places the late November leaves were now a foot thick. Raking them all away before Monday was a hopeless task. Untidy foliage would make a bad impression on television, and he had already anticipated the blinding glare of limelight; 'I was,' he wrote afterwards, 'like the proverbial hen on a hot griddle.'

But Metzler wasn't unprepared. Although he had received no definite word, Friday's call from the Shriver–Dungan meeting had alerted him to the fact that an Arlington funeral was a distinct possibility, and while most commentators had continued to assume that the coffin would go to Boston, early Saturday Metzler heard two radio announcers speculating about his cemetery. The superintendent 'started to get more apprehensive'. In the gloomy dawn he toured his ten miles of winding roads, and by the time McNamara's inquiring call reached down through the daedalian tiers of the Department of the Army, the Military District of Washington, and the Office of Support Services, and found him, he and Colonel Paul Miller were ready to recommend three plots: Dewey Circle, a section near the Maine Monument, and the hill below Lee Mansion.

Then Robert McNamara arrived, accompanied by General Taylor, Secretary of the Army Cyrus Vance, and the rapidly developing mist. McNamara wordlessly took Metzler's Arlington map, and they all trooped around the three locations. Colonel Miller said he favoured Dewey Circle. The superintendent disagreed; the access roads were tortuous, and besides, there were all those leaves. McNamara also shook his head. He liked the slope beneath the mansion. He asked whether he had authority over it and Metzler said no, that was Park Service land. The Secretary made a note to call the Secretary of the Interior, and as he was jotting down Udall's name Metzler volunteered, 'Of course, it is now standard procedure for everyone buried here to have a grave of the same size.' McNamara absently asked for the specifications and was told 'Six feet by ten'. The Secretary looked up, incredulous. 'The rules should be changed in this case,' he said sharply. 'An exception should be made for the President of the United States.'

That was the first of four visits. He had to leave for the East Room Mass, but the moment it was over he began rounding up Robert Kennedy, Jean Smith, Pat Lawford, and Bill Walton for a second trip. 'Let's go to Arlington,' he said, tugging at Walton's sleeve, and the two men shared a taxi, for McNamara, with his distaste for special privilege, never thought to order a limousine. Entering Hatfield Gate he was met by a delegation. Udall was waiting by Vance, Metzler, and Miller, and standing off to one side were three ranking officers and their aides. This was one Saturday the brass wasn't taking off. The Pentagon grapevine had alerted them to the Secretary's movements. They had drawn the obvious conclusion and were sympathetic. Nevertheless they did form a separate group, and it is a revealing sidelight on the military attitude towards men in mufti that the generals, buttoned up in foul-weather gear, never thought to share their protection with civilians. Two members of the President's Cabinet were present; the arrival of the Attorney General a few minutes later made three. The cloudburst had been in progress for over an hour. McNamara, lacking both raincoat and rubbers, was not only drenched to the skin; his straight hair was plastered across his face, and at Dewey Circle the soles of his shoes became sodden with mud. Once Metzler attempted to hold an umbrella over him, but the superintendent was another civilian. A poncho briefly sheltered Jean Smith. She was a lady, however, and the officers were being professionally chivalrous. Whatever their political preferences, they were clearly in mourning for a slain Commander in Chief, yet accepting the Secretary of Defence as the Commander's deputy was something else. They had never been able to bring themselves to cross that threshold. McNamara knew they hadn't, and he wasn't surprised that not one of his subordinates—for that is what they were—offered to doff his own oilskin and loan it to him. Bill Walton, an artless taxpayer, was dumbfounded. During the past two centuries the United States had established elaborate control of the military by civilian authorities. Everyone paid lip service to it, including West Pointers, but in practice the emotional responses of the soldier hadn't changed since the Hamites. The man in uniform deferred to only one civilian, his Chieftain.

In the Presidential apartment Mrs Kennedy was being handed a note from Bob on White House stationery, telling her of the brief trip he and others were making to Arlington.

Like Bob McNamara and Bill Walton, Bob Kennedy expressed an immediate preference for the slope, and like McNamara he inquired, 'Who owns the rest of it?' To him the bottom of the hill (the part Metzler knew he owned) was unsuitable. 'It would make a major difference if we could have it higher,' he said, and though he strode off to examine the other two sites, he came back unmoved. The plot by the Maine Memorial had seemed to him to be particularly poor. It was altogether too small and was 'right down on the road [Porter Drive]'. He still liked this incline, though not the base of it. It was then that Walton pointed out something which had eluded the others. The artist's eye had noticed that the place Kennedy favoured met a classic architectural definition; it lay squarely on the invisible axis between the mansion and the Lincoln Memorial across the river.

McNamara, delighted, told Udall he would need as much of the 'Interior enclave' as possible. He suggested they designate the area on his map and sign it right there. Udall agreed. Unhappily the streaming downpour ruled out any paperwork; signatures would have been washed away. McNamara said, 'Have your attorneys examine ownership, Stew, and see if they can make it part of the national cemetery. I'll have Defence attorneys going over the same problem. We can meet out here this afternoon with plot maps and tapes. I want as much as possible for the sake of safety, and we might as well turn the whole thing over to the lawyers.'

He had forgotten that a lawyer was present. The soggy Attorney General was taking a hard look at that grassy bank. Few men could stare as intently as Bob Kennedy, and none had access to so much legal talent. On his return to the capital the brightest men in the Justice Department's Lands Division began probing into ownership. Almost simultaneously they and the colleagues in Defence and Interior discovered that the superintendent had been wrong about his frontier; the National Parks line ended twenty feet from the mansion portico. Udall's consent was, therefore, unnecessary. But the Lands Division didn't stop there. The young attorneys opened up Arlington's county courthouse, studied the entire history of the property, pored over the actual deed of March 31, 1883, under which the federal government had acquired ownership of Arlington, consulted all pertinent statutes, carved out a two-and-a-half-acre tract for the President's grave, and then submitted an airtight brief concluding the 'title to the John F. Kennedy cemetery plot as vested in the United States of America in simple absolute fee, without any restrictions or encumbrances of any nature'. While McNamara was rightly considered an actionist, he had left Hatfield Gate, Arlington's main entrance, with the vague feeling that the cemetery should become a burial ground for national heroes, an American Westminster Abbey. It was Justice which tied and double-knotted every conceivable loose end. The legal craftsmanship was exquisite and fitting; this punctilious attention to particulars had been a JFK trademark.

Jean Smith and Pat Lawford re-entered the executive mansion dripping but converted. Both had abandoned the Boston camp. Jean's notes on the trip—'Went to Arlington with Bob McNamara, Bobby and Bill Walton to look at site'—carried no suggestion of endorsement. Her greeting to Jacqueline Kennedy did: 'Oh, Jackie, we've found the most wonderful place!' Jean had gone to Virginia with foreboding, envisioning dreary ranks of grim stones, and the gently sloping lawn had been an inversion of everything she had expected. Even in the rain, with the autumnal grass drab and bleak, it had seemed splendid. Mrs Kennedy, hearing this and other enthusiastic reports from those who had crossed the Potomac, realized that it was time to decide. The next step was to form a group, headed by her, and at 1.58 p.m., she bade Douglas and Phyllis Dillon good-bye upstairs and left the White House in a black Mercury, accompanied by Jean, Pat, and Bob. A motorcade followed: Walton, Lem Billings, Jim Reed, other house guests, the Secret Service. At the Pentagon they stopped to pick up the Secretary of Defence, who by now looked like the survivor of a shipwreck. His socks gurgled as he walked. He had brought a raincoat from his office, but he never wore it; he gallantly presented it to Jean, and once more his trousers became frigid about his knees and calves. Walton had hurried out to Georgetown and changed—unwisely, as it happened, because he was now wearing his last dark suit, and it was doomed; he would have to attend the rest of the ceremonies in tan gaberdine. (At one point Bob Kennedy was to regard him reproachfully and murmur, 'No mourning?' Walton spread his hands in a gesture of defeat.)

Jacqueline Kennedy's first visit to Arlington was like the opening of the final act of *Our Town*. The steady rain was glacial, numbing. The arrival of the Commander in Chief's widow raised martial chivalry to a new pitch, and she stood beneath massed umbrellas, contemplating the silent scene for fifteen minutes. Her entourage was quiet. There was little to say. The fact that they were gazing upon the future grave of the President was awesome, and she obviously needed no words of persuasion; her own recollection of that quarter-hour is simple and direct: 'We went out and walked to that hill, and of course you knew that was where it should be.' At a nod from her, Walton slogged up the saturated turf and pointed at a tuft. He said, 'This is perfect.' Metzler came up and drove a tent peg in the ground. The artist's eye was uncanny; next morning a team of surveyors found he had been less than six inches off the axis.

The Bostonians had been routed by a *fait accompli*. The destroyer was still standing by, and an hour and a half would pass before the national audience would hear—from a correspondent covering the State Department, of all places—a report that 'a grave site has been picked out in Arlington Cemetery'. Nevertheless it was all over. The Irishmen were dismayed, but this was clearly the widow's prerogative; they kept their disappointment to themselves. In Dungan's office the planning team proceeded on the assumption that Monday's cortege would ride from St Matthew's to Arlington's Hatfield Gate. This is what happened, but Jacqueline Kennedy's visit and the driving of the stake were not the end of Saturday's activity on the hillside. The Justice Department lawyers had yet to submit their findings. Angie Duke's elegant protocol officers had to chart graveside assignments; the military services conferred over who would stand where; Mrs Kennedy pondered her own wishes, and Shriver translated them into orders.

Lastly, someone had to outline the Presidential plot. The outliner was the Secretary of Defence. He had begun the day with thoughts of Arlington, he believed in thoroughness, and at dusk he was back on the slope—wet, filthy, and wretched, but working effectively. Stewart Udall joined him for a while. The two Cabinet ministers had not yet heard of the attorneys' discovery. They were under the impression that the tent peg lay on Interior property, and at McNamara's request Udall left to find out whether a President could be buried in Park land. McNamara further asked the Army Corps of Engineers to send him a team of men equipped with measuring instruments. Secretary Vance led them up the hill, and as the second night after Kennedy's death fell McNamara showed them precisely what he wanted. He, Vance, and Metzler watched the men place twelve granite markers on the perimeter he had chosen. The torrential rain had by now thinned to a fine drizzle. It was possible to affix a scrawl which would remain legible, and McNamara and Vance signed authorizations setting aside any part of the plot which might belong to them. Since Defence was responsible for all of it, these papers, drawn up in the dark darkness, were binding and final.

McNamara walked back down the slope with a young Park Service employee, a college student who worked part time in Lee Mansion. The Secretary thought that he had never been more miserable in his life. He was nearly fifty, he had spent most of the day under conditions which would have been harrowing for a young infantryman—'I had the impression that it had been raining buckets,' he said later, 'raining on me personally'—and he had concluded his fourth Arlington expedition by demarcating the grave of the leader he had loved. Then the student told him that he had been present during the President's visit to Lee Mansion and had overheard him say that this was the most beautiful sight in Washington. McNamara had been toiling over the hill site since dawn. For the first time he was learning that Kennedy himself shared his feeling for it. The boy added, 'My father works for your department, Mr Secretary.' At that time the Defence payroll was roughly equivalent to the population of Norway, but after the funeral the Secretary made it a point to find out who the student's father was and speak to him. For McNamara this was out of character. He was an administrator, not a politician. He did it because he knew that was exactly what John Kennedy would have done.

The groggy country would later remember Saturday as a gap between days, between the shock of yesterday's assassination and the murder of the assassin on Sunday. The live broadcasts of the dramatic ceremonies in Washington on both Sunday and Monday added to the effect, and so did the improving weather. That one day of dreadful gloom stood alone. The University of Chicago study indicated that the average adult spent ten hours in front of his television set then, the weekend's peak, but the watchers didn't learn much. Afterwards most of them could recall only a few disjointed fragments: the heartbreaking ballet in the East Room as the Death Watch changed guard each half-hour; the outrageous contrast of the scenes in the Dallas jail, where a sequence showing Oswald changing his shirt was treated as an event of major significance; and, above all, a sense of astonishment that the young President was being mourned, not only by his own countrymen, but by the entire world. Just as Americans were beginning to grasp the extent of their loss—after the funeral the Chicago survey found that a full half of the population rated Kennedy 'one of the two or three best Presidents the country ever had'—they discovered that hundreds of millions of people who had never seen the United States were mourning, too.

Many incidents of the global grief were relayed to the national audience Saturday and early Sunday morning. In Westminster Abbey the choir sang 'The Battle Hymn of the Republic', Westminster's archdeacon delivered a eulogy, and every pew was jammed with kneeling Englishmen. Other memorial services were being held simultaneously at Windsor Castle and St Paul's. Sir Laurence Olivier, interrupting a performance at the Old Vic, asked the audience to stand while the orchestra played 'The Star-Spangled Banner'. The headline of Rome's *Il Giorno* simply read: '*Addio, John, Addio*', and the taxi drivers of Rome parked an empty cab with a huge black wreath propped against it outside the American

Embassy. In Berlin sixty thousand people massed to express their sorrow; the square outside Schoenberg Rathaus was renamed John F. Kennedy Platz. These were understandable, for the President had held the shield of U.S. power over Britain, Italy, and West Berlin. What was harder to absorb was that a Chief Executive had won so much affection in countries hostile to the United States in general and to him in particular. The grief of the Russians was incomprehensible. Nina Khrushchev, whose husband Kennedy had confronted with missiles thirteen months ago, wired her condolences to Jacqueline Kennedy. Andrei Gromyko, one of the toughest of the hard-line Reds, was seen weeping as he left the U.S. legation in Moscow. The mourning of the American networks was fully matched by the Soviet radio, which played nothing but Slavic dirges, hour after hour. New York businessmen setting up textile plants in the U.S.S.R. were approached by peasants anxious to display their sympathy, and at a travelling U.S. graphics exhibit Russian children laid flowers in front of the President's photograph.

Nina Khrushchev's message was merely one in a growing file that included anguished condolences to the widowed First Lady from Queen Elizabeth, from the Queen Mother, Gamal Nasser, and a moving telegram bearing the plain signature of Josip Broz Tito. The State Department, presumably an authority on moods abroad, was overwhelmed. Its files for November 23 became choked with cables from U.S. ambassadors describing the profound sadness around them and trying—since each diplomat assumed that his country's reaction must be exceptional—to account for it. Typically, a consul reported that an African native had walked ten miles through the bush to say, 'I have lost a friend and I am so sorry.' The consul was bewildered. How could a nomadic bushman be a Kennedy friend? What had the President done for the Kalaharis? Why should this one grieve? 'Not even President Kennedy and his immediate associates,' Dean Rusk subsequently explained, 'had understood the extent to which ordinary people around the world had read his speeches and become involved with him. In three years he had established the kind of rapport that FDR had.' Rusk was right; the men who had been close to Kennedy were as taken aback as the Foreign Service officers. Stanislaus Radziwill boarded a transatlantic jet to attend the funeral; the captain came back to sit beside him, said he understood Radziwill had married Mrs Kennedy's sister, and then, to the amazement of his passenger, commenced to weep. Godfrey McHugh, whose name had rarely been published, received between five and six hundred letters. Byron White, who was also deluged by mail, later observed that 'None of us had dreamt on Friday that the President's death would cut this kind of swath abroad.' Politicians abroad felt that same way. Prime Minister Douglas-Home confided that he was 'amazed at the depth of the British response, especially among our youth'. President de Gaulle told a friend, 'I am stunned. They are crying all over France. It is as though he were a Frenchman, a member of their own family.'

Rapid communication undoubtedly heightened the international passion.[10] So did the absence of other news; had China invaded India, for example, the attention of Asia would have been quickly distracted. Since there were no diversions and no valid historical parallels, Kennedy's death was unique, and the most one can say of world repercussions is that they were so fantastic that they were to draw eight heads of state, ten prime ministers, and most of the world's remaining royalty to St Matthew's.

Given time and prompt encouragement from the State Department, the international delegation would have been still larger. Friday afternoon State's under secretaries had discussed the question and then cabled all American ambassadors to discourage dignitaries from attending the funeral, on the ground that the presence of some might embarrass others. Beginning that evening there were answering rumbles of discontent. Queen Elizabeth was expecting a child and couldn't come herself, but she wanted to send her husband and her prime minister. Other national leaders notified Washington that they wished to come as individuals; one cabled that if an official invitation was out of the question he intended to present himself 'on a personal friendship basis'. State began to have second thoughts. Early Saturday Rusk called a staff meeting and reaffirmed Friday's decision. The funeral was only forty-eight hours away. Invitations, he felt, would arrive too late. By now, however, world capitals were beginning to feel mounting pressure from their own citizens, and at noon the dam broke.

It was broken by de Gaulle. De Valera, Ludwig Erhard, and Prince Philip and Sir Alec Douglas-Home had already declared that they would fly over, but de Gaulle's career and forceful personality had established him as a great symbolic figure. His first inclination had been to remain in Paris. The Americans had said that they wanted it that way, and he was a proud man. Moreover, his differences with Kennedy had been no secret. An abrupt turnabout might be interpreted as hypocrisy. France changed his mind. If the President of the United States had meant that much to Frenchmen, he told those around him, the President of France should go to the funeral, and he personally telephoned Hervé Alphand in Washington

[10] In Greece a Gallup affiliate reported that by Saturday noon 99 per cent of all Athenians knew of the slaying. When de Gaulle visited Athens, 25 per cent weren't even able to identify him.

to say so. The Quai d'Orsay made the announcement at 12.30 p.m. Washington time. Ten minutes later Brussels disclosed that King Baudouin would come; State hastily cabled formal invitations, and 'the telegrams', in Harriman's words, 'were followed by an extraordinary flood of acceptances'—the Queen of Greece, the Emperor of Ethiopia, the Grand Duke of Luxembourg, the Crown Princess of the Netherlands, the Crown Princesses of Norway and Denmark; the Presidents of Germany, Israel, Korea, and the Philippines; the Premiers of Turkey, Canada, and Jamaica; Anastas I. Mikoyan, First Deputy Premier of Russia; and Prince Norodom Sihanouk of Cambodia. Altogether, ninety-two nations were sending delegations. Ayub Khan of Pakistan was staying home, together with the Presidents of most Latin-American republics, but that was because legally they could not leave home without legislative approval. Even so, their constituents were angry, and it says much for the emotional climate of the weekend that they felt obliged to explain publicly why they couldn't stand by the grave of a foreign ruler.

On Kalorama Road Nicole Alphand measured every bed in the embassy residency and found that none was long enough for the towering frame of Charles de Gaulle; she telephoned the manager of a Washington furniture store, who volunteered to loan her a long bed without charge. Hanging up, she toured the building a second time, inspecting windows. The French President would bring bodyguards, and his hosts could be counted upon to provide additional protection. Nevertheless she wasn't taking any chances. Though assassination was new to this generation of Americans—few were old enough to remember the murder of McKinley—de Gaulle had been repeatedly marked for death by agents of the right-wing OAS. Madame Alphand was making sure that each latch was secure. That, too, says something about the temper of the weekend.

The name of one retired diplomat was conspicuously absent from the glittering lists of dignitaries about to converge upon the capital. Joseph P. Kennedy, U.S. Ambassador to the Court of St James's from 1937 to 1940, was physically incapable of attending his son's funeral. Until his stroke two years ago the family patriarch had been the toughest and shrewdest of the Kennedys, and his public critics had been ruthless. Now that he was helpless, overcome by the cruellest blow imaginable, he was left alone. The small band of correspondents standing watch outside the Hyannis Port compound was subdued, apologetic, and reluctant to intrude. Although the television audience was constantly aware of Washington and Dallas on November 23, Cape Cod was rarely mentioned. Coverage there was confined to brief reports about the arrival and departure of relatives and a series of still pictures showing the President's mother attending the first Mass of the day in Hyannis.

That had been at 7 a.m. Rose Kennedy stayed for the second Mass, but Ann Gargan, who had accompanied her, returned to the compound to breakfast with her uncle. Reading the thoughts of a stricken man is difficult; nevertheless it was becoming increasingly clear to those around the Ambassador that he sensed trouble. Ted Kennedy had told him that he was here for a Senatorial speech, yet Ted had gone off to the eight o'clock Mass with Eunice. With repairmen minutes away, the television set remained inoperable. Joe Kennedy gestured impatiently at Ann, and she realized that he had noticed the absence of any morning newspaper. Feebly she explained that Frank, the family chauffeur, had been unable to pick them up because he had driven Aunt Rose to church. His eyes sharpened. That, too, was unusual. Usually she drove herself. Then he looked out through the dining-room's big picture window and saw his wife emerging from the foggy lawn, dressed all in black, her face obscured by a black veil. He made a queer, jerky movement, which, Ann later believed, was a sign that he had felt the first wave of impending disaster.

The truth couldn't be kept from him much longer. Ted knew it, and after breakfasting himself the Senator asked Eunice to join him in their father's bedroom. By now the tension in Joe was alarming. He had been impatient with Ann and the nurse throughout his regular exercise period in his indoor pool. Back in his bed he stirred restlessly and glared at the dark television screen while Ann, in the corridor outside, clenched her hands together. Conceivably the blow could prove fatal. As a precaution his physician, Dr Russell Boles, had been summoned from Boston and was lurking down the hall, within earshot.

Ted and Eunice entered and sat by the bed. Joe waved indignantly at the screen. The Senator turned towards it, explaining that they had all been at Mass, and his father gazed out at the sea. In aphasia a patient's mind often drifts that way. One moment you have his undivided attention; a moment later he is off in a private reverie.

Ted said, 'There's been a bad accident. The President has been hurt very badly.'

Joe Kennedy's head snapped back. He stared directly into his son's eyes. He was following every word.

'As a matter of fact,' Ted said, 'he died.'

Several contemporary accounts declared that the President's father did not cry—'Joe is a tough old bird,' said *Time*; 'he . . . took it without visibly flinching'. That was entirely untrue. The retired tycoon was deeply emotional, devoted to his children and fiercely committed to their ambitions. When his oldest son had been killed in action, he had been well. Nevertheless he had wept then, and he wept now. Ted and Eunice did their best to comfort him, but they too had been ravaged; it was a time of unrelieved desolation. After a while Joe recovered sufficiently to ask for details. There were more tears, and Dr Boles advised Ann that immediate relaxation was imperative.

Unfortunately, that was impractical. There was no way his patient could be diverted now. Ann brought the Boston *Globe* and the Boston *Record American* in to the bedroom; her uncle saw the pictures from Dallas and collapsed again. The doctor entered and gave him a sedative. Like the drug Dr Walsh had administered to Jacqueline Kennedy at Bethesda, it had no effect whatever, and the day, having begun with the solemn dignity of religious services, became progressively more unravelled. Ted conferred with his brother by telephone; Bob agreed that he should stay there until their parents had settled down. Eunice, meantime, went to her mother, who was too upset even to see her husband, and who strolled back and forth on the wet, misty lawn, trying to talk to her daughter and her nephew Joe. The news having been broken, Ann thought her uncle might as well watch television. In twenty-five minutes a Hyannis technician had repaired the wires Ted had violently yanked away last evening and the President's father propped up on pillows, was looking at his son's coffin in the East Room, watching the honour guard change shifts. He began to sob again, and for the next several hours—indeed, throughout most of the next two and a half days—he alternated between a yearning for information and a revulsion against it. At his direction Ann and Rita Dallas switched the knob on and off, on and off. It wasn't good for him, but there was no alternative; he couldn't be expected to go to the pool or the movie theatre downstairs.

The crisis came later in the afternoon. Hyannis Port had reached a strange, unpredictable stage in which nothing seemed bizarre. Rita Dallas went home and received an anonymous telephone call telling her she should be ashamed of her name. Word reached the compound of rumours that the President's father had died of a heart attack, and Senator Kennedy hastily conferred with his cousins, debated the wisdom of calling a press conference to scotch the report, and concluded it was best to say nothing. At the height of this frantic activity Joe Kennedy decided he must go to Washington immediately. Ann stepped into the bedroom and found him struggling with his clothes and fumbling for his wheelchair. There was no way to dissuade him. Another elderly uncle might have been gently pushed back among his bedclothes, but nobody had ever pushed this man around, and his slender young niece didn't try. Instead she helped him dress and wheeled him to the car. She suggested they just ride around; he vehemently refused and directed her straight to the airport. Had adequate transportation existed, there is little doubt that the President's father would have appeared in the White House within three hours. He was in an inflexible mood, and none of Ann's arguments impressed him; he brushed aside the fact that Father Cavanaugh was coming up tonight to be with him. Since his stroke, however, Joe Kennedy had confined his flying to the *Caroline*. The plane wasn't there, so the two of them just sat in the gloaming squinting at commercial aeroplanes until he signalled her to start the car. She drove slowly back to the compound and helped him back into bed. Adjusting covers, Ann had the feeling that in some undefinable way the trip had helped him. He wasn't resigned. He remained unconsolable, groping in a solitary, unfathomable agony. But he had done something. He had tried.

Air travel was possible all day, although it was not recommended. The foul weather was discouraging, and the foreign dignitaries postponed their flights to the capital until Sunday. Even Archbishop O'Boyle and Bishop Hannan lingered in Rome. Lee Radziwill, Jacqueline Kennedy's sister, made it from London and was met at Dulles airport by her mother and stepfather. Darting down the ramp towards them, she was wrapped in a sheet of drenching rain, which was a common experience; travellers had to expect at least one change of clothes. You didn't fly unless you had to. Lee felt she had to—at the executive mansion Lem Billings told her it was nice of her to come; she whirled on him and cried, 'How can you say that? Do you think that I wouldn't?'—and so did Mrs Paul Mellon, whose journey was something of an epic. The fragile patrician took off from Antigua in a tremendous storm; as they gained air speed the captain informed her the field was closed behind them. After circling over Manhattan for two hours he was permitted to land at Idlewild, and she was met by her husband, who said the White House was trying to reach her. Before going through customs she called Mr West from a phone booth; he asked her to come to the mansion as soon as possible. In her New York apartment she changed clothes rapidly and headed for Washington aboard a Mellon plane manned by her own pilots. They saw no other flights. Peering down she glimpsed 'flashing lightning and whipping rain and terrifying gusts —the storm was like the horribleness of the occasion'.

Skidding across the tarmac of Butler Aviation, that section of Washington National reserved for private aircraft, they parked beside the *Caroline*. Her chauffeur and limousine were waiting for her and drove her straight to the mansion's Northwest Gate. Andrew W. Mellon's daughter-in-law entered unchallenged, not because of her wealth but because every member of the staff knew her as the custodian of the Rose Garden. On the dripping portico West put his arms around her and led her to the Blue Room. 'It's too awful,' he began. He choked up and continued, 'Mrs Kennedy is the most remarkable woman. She has never lost her head and has directed everything. If you should see her and she should want to talk, let her talk.'

Bunny Mellon had only the vaguest notion of what he meant. Her odyssey had isolated her from ordinary channels of communication. In New York she had picked up an afternoon newspaper, but the ferocity of the weather had distracted her; she knew that the President had been killed, and little else. On the portico she had seen the lines of sodden soldiers and heard the clicking of their heels. There was no sound here, however, and she had the peculiar feeling that she and West were alone in the great house. From her purse she drew a calling card and wrote across it, 'With my deepest love Dearest Jackie/Sorry to take so long getting back—Bunny.' She handed it to him and said she would wait until Mrs Kennedy was ready to receive her—all night, if necessary.

'You can't,' he said. 'You have a job tomorrow. She wants you to arrange the flowers at the Capitol, at the church, and at Arlington.'

Bunny looked blank. She knew nothing about the programme, hadn't even heard when the President was to be buried or where. West explained briefly and said, 'Be on the Hill at nine in the morning to receive all the flowers that have come in.' At the time neither of them understood how vast a task this would be, nor that two other women were making floral plans. The mix-up was no one's fault. If a state funeral is scheduled three days after a Chief Executive's death, confusion, like toil beyond the limits of exhaustion, is inevitable. Bunny wearily nodded assent. West asked whether she would like to see the catafalque, and she nodded again. Alone she went to the foot of the coffin and knelt among the rigid soldiers. 'That moment gave me strength,' she said afterwards. 'There was an overpowering dignity to the East Room. But the strength came after I had left. At the time I felt utterly drained. The tears would not stop. It was like the fall of all the hopes of youth—as though youth had tried and been thwarted. It seemed to me that this country had symbolically killed something.'

By now a dense darkness had gathered over Washington. The doleful guns which had thundered each half-hour since daybreak at Myer, McNair, and Anacostia had fallen silent, though in time zones to the west they could still be heard. The sun, which once never set upon the Union Jack, never set on the Stars and Stripes in 1963; seven thousand U.S. military bases ringed the globe. The artillery salutes, the proclamations, the declarations of Monday as a day of mourning were bits and pieces in the intricate mosaic of formal observances. The bereaved population responded spontaneously, but the bereavement of governments must be stylized. Although the Black Watch pipers insisted on paying their own fare to the capital, Queen Elizabeth had to approve the trip personally, for they were to participate in ceremonies for a foreign chief of state, and precedents were involved. Although Kennedy had been the first Catholic President, and the Pope himself was praying for his soul, it was necessary for the Vatican's Apostolic Delegate to grant extraordinary permission for one requiem Mass tomorrow in each American Catholic Church. Here again the issue was precedent. As a rule requiem Masses are never permitted on Sundays or major feast days. Each movement of former Presidents Truman and Eisenhower was being weighed carefully. After his return to Gettysburg the weather had confined Eisenhower to the farm, but he became involved just the same. As he was to recall, 'There were so many people of different ranks in Washington that it was a real problem. They called me and said Harry Truman was there without a driver. I said, "Hell, I'll have my car. He can ride with me." ' Truman was staying in Blair House, the nation's official guest house. It had been his home during his second Presidential term, while the executive mansion was being renovated—the Puerto Ricans' attempt on his life had been made there—and earlier in the day he had told Averell Harriman that his thoughts were very much with Lyndon Johnson, because he remembered how 'uneducated' he had been when Roosevelt died.

Their age and position brought Eisenhower and Truman special consideration. They needed some. Even the eight-block walk to St Matthew's was inadvisable for them. The non-stop, round-the-clock vigour of the Kennedy men and women made the quick funeral possible. Yet they, too, had special problems. The problems of parenthood lay beyond the polished skills of Angie Duke's staff. Taking their sons aside, Nancy Salinger, Margie McNamara, and Orville Freeman did their best to explain what remained inexplicable to adults; understandably the results were frequently bewildering. Bill Pozen's approach was almost identical to Jacqueline Kennedy's. He told his daughter that the assassin had been sick, not evil. Agatha said wonderingly, 'That means Caroline doesn't have a daddy, doesn't it?'—which is precisely what it did mean to her—and then, to his dismay, she began to worry about her own father's safety. The children of those who had been closest to the President often saw neither parent until two days after the murder. Sargent Shriver's secretary kept watch over Timberlawn; Barney Ross took Robert Kennedy's family on little excursions until a strange woman recognized them at a hamburger stand and lurched over, distraught. Senator Kennedy's wife was the only Kennedy mother who spent Saturday at home, and she was unable to see anyone. Like Montaigne, Joan found the mere contemplation of violence crippling.

Her behaviour was normal. The Chicago survey later revealed that the assassination left only one American in nine physically unmoved. It may almost be said that *any* mode of conduct was normal Saturday. Aldous Huxley died in Los Angeles, and sixty-three patients perished in an Ohio hospital fire. At any other time these would have been major news events. Today editors barely mentioned them. The national grief was the only consistent factor, and it was almost universal; the NORC study reported that even among anti-Kennedy Southerners, the hard core of his opposition, 62 per cent 'felt the loss of someone very close and dear'.[11] The manifestations of sorrow continued to vary, of course. Among the general population Friday's most common concern had been anxiety for Jacqueline Kennedy and her children; a sense of shame and unfocused anger had been close behind. In the capital the wrath persisted through Saturday. The Dallas *News*'s Washington bureau was flooded with threatening telephone calls, and those who knew no Kennedy critics frequently spoke sharply to one another.

That evening Kenneth Galbraith and Arthur Schlesinger met again at the Harrimans'. Galbraith, still convinced that he would be the chief author of President Johnson's address to the joint session, described his first draft to Schlesinger. It was like putting his hand in a stove. Galbraith had taken the line that the issue was continuity. America must look ahead; the future 'was greater than the life of any one man'. That was what the new President had told him, and he had taken the cue. Schlesinger felt this was heartless. He thought the speech ought to come down hard on Kennedy's achievements. In his journal Galbraith observed that 'Arthur was in an appalling mood and spent a considerable part of the evening attacking me'. Uptown in Cleveland Park Pat Moynihan was in an equally aggressive mood.

[11] It should be noted that the manner of the President's death had permanently altered his countrymen's concept of him. In 1960 he had been elected by 49.7 per cent of the popular vote. Voters are constantly editing their memories, however. In June 1963 surveyors discovered that 59 per cent claimed Kennedy had been their 1960 preference. After the assassination this figure leaped to 65 per cent.

Throughout dinner in Mary McGrory's apartment Pat continued to brood about the Dallas Police Department. The sooner Oswald was removed from their custody, he argued, the greater the chances of finding the truth. Otherwise, he said, 'We may never know who did it. This could cloud our whole history for a century.' None of the others there disagreed. Among Washingtonians Dallas credit could scarcely have been lower. At one point their hostess said tearfully, 'We'll never laugh again.' Pat answered gently, 'Oh, we'll laugh again, Mary. But we'll never be young again.'

In spite of Bunny Mellon's impression of solitude, the executive mansion had not been so crowded since President Kennedy's inauguration. Upstairs every bedroom was occupied. Maude Shaw, leading Caroline and John away from the swarming traffic in the great east–west corridor, plucked at a curtain hem occasionally and peered down at the undiminished mob in Lafayette Park, and in other parts of the White House several men lingered because they wanted to be close to the catafalque. Godfrey McHugh, for example, made up a bed in his office, and while Lieutenant Sam Bird was off duty and should have been asleep in Fort Myer's BOQ, he stayed all night on the first floor of the mansion, wandering from hall to hall, munching sandwiches from the platters, noticing the little Kennedy touches and thinking in awe, *This is the President's house; this is where he actually lives*.

This was where he *had* lived. Yet hardly anyone switched tenses. His presence was too evident. Even as he lay in state the dinner guests in the White House were his relatives and close friends. Maître Fincklin had set the table in the family dining-room for twelve. Among the diners were Bob and Ethel Kennedy, Lee Radziwill, the Smiths, the Dillons, and the McNamaras—Bob McNamara with the blotched pink complexion of one who has lain too long in a bathtub. Dillon thought the younger Kennedy looked awful, and McNamara told Jean Smith, 'Bobby should take a rest and go away and forget everything for a while. I'm afraid he'll get into a fight with Johnson.' This was an aside; the run of the conversation was not grave. The diners had formed a tacit pact to avoid the tragedy, and they succeeded, perhaps because men and women in public life cultivate an iron self-discipline, partly because recoil is part of shock.[12] There was even some puckish horseplay. Everyone present knew that when Ethel didn't have time for a hairdresser she wore a wig; it was snatched off and passed from head to head, winding up,

[12] G. L. Engel, citing Freud and others, concluded that grief includes a phase 'in which the sufferer attempts to deny the loss and to insulate himself against . . . reality'. *Psychosomatic Medicine*, XXXIII, No. 18, 1961.

in a pinnacle John Kennedy would have relished, on the slick, wrinkled pate of the Secretary of Defence.

After coffee the false façade crumbled. Suddenly there was nothing to say. In this hush the group stepped into the marble hall and drifted towards the East Room. None needed to be reminded that this would be President Kennedy's last night in the White House, and they moved up to the catafalque, some individually, some in pairs. Douglas and Phyllis Dillon entered together. They knelt by the coffin, and the Secretary of the Treasury, attempting prayer, could only bow his head and whisper, 'Good-bye, Mr President.'

Jacqueline Kennedy did not attend the dinner. Fincklin kept approaching her with sandwiches, and she kept shaking her head and murmuring, 'No thank you, not right now.' The most she would take was a cup of broth. She knew the cortege would leave the executive mansion at noon tomorrow. The pause for final instructions was shortening to hours, and it was now, not Friday night at Bethesda, that those around her felt an incisiveness in her. In the tower suite she had deferred and reserved judgment, even biding her time with her brother-in-law and McNamara on the vital issue of the closed coffin. By Saturday evening, however, her self-confidence was at its height. A State Department functionary protested to Clifton that the invitation to the Black Watch had to be withdrawn; Argentina had requested permission to send musicians and had been turned away, and other nations might offer bands. Mrs Kennedy said crisply, 'Jack loved bagpipes,' and there was no more talk of the Argentine. Shriver again raised the question of Church seniority, pointing out that the laziest Catholic knew an archbishop outranked an auxiliary bishop. She replied tightly, 'Just say I'm hysterical. It *has* to be Hannan.'

Bob rode up from the first floor with Ethel, and they agreed to postpone any discussions of encomia. The one matter which could not be put off was tomorrow's ceremony. It had to be settled tonight, Shriver reminded them; he was coming down to the wire. Plans for Monday could be redrawn after they had returned from Capitol Hill, but the rotunda was imminent. Momentarily the widow hesitated. Congress was something of a mystery to her. Her husband had understood legislative manoeuvres; she had only seen Senators and Representatives on social occasions, and she wasn't sure what would be appropriate. Then she remembered a small White House party the month before. Ben Bradlee had been there, goading the President about the sluggish progress of the tax cut and the Civil Rights Bill. Kennedy had snapped back, predicting that both measures would pass and even specifying when.[13] He had gone on to say, 'Why don't you put Mike Mansfield on the cover of *Newsweek*? Mansfield's the greatest Majority Leader we've ever had. . . .' Then, in a display of Kennedy virtuosity, the Chief Executive had rattled off a series of statistics, citing the high percentage of legislation which had passed under Mansfield. Now Jacqueline Kennedy remembered her husband's affection for the Senate Majority Leader. She said, 'The only person I want to speak in the rotunda is Mike Mansfield.'

Shriver returned to Dungan's office and announced to the marathon meeting, 'Jackie's decided about tomorrow. She wants Mansfield to deliver the eulogy in the rotunda.' He heard someone cough. It was William M. 'Fishbait' Miller, doorkeeper of the House of Representatives, major-domo of the Hill, and legislative liaison man. After shuffling his shoes several times Fishbait flatly told Shriver that Mrs Kennedy would either have to withdraw her request or settle for a compromise: 'That part of the Capitol is under the jurisdiction of the House,' he explained. 'It belongs to the Speaker.' Sarge asked in astonishment, 'You mean he *owns* it?' Fishbait swallowed. 'He doesn't exactly own it,' he said, 'but if you have any request concerning the rotunda, it will have to be made to the Speaker. It's just the way things work up there. That's going to be the Congressional part of the funeral, and you can't just walk in and say Mike Mansfield's going to speak, whatever Jackie's wish. You might hurt the Speaker's feelings.'

Shriver had the feeling that he was dealing with a foreign potentate. Then someone observed that there was a third branch of the government—that a role must be found for the Chief Justice—and Sarge concluded that it was more like a political convention; each factional leader had to be given his turn at the rostrum. The White House operators put through a series of hurried calls, specialists in parliamentary etiquette were canvassed, and the consensus was that there should be three eulogists: John McCormack, Earl Warren, and Mike Mansfield. 'I'll accept that,' said Shriver. Actually, even this was violation of convention. With the elevation of Lyndon Johnson the ranking officer of the Senate was the President Pro Tempore, Carl Hayden. No legislative body is more sensitive to prerogative than the U.S. Senate. Selecting the Majority Leader could only be justified on the ground that he was the choice of the widowed First Lady, although no one, of course, was prepared to challenge that.

[13] Mrs Kennedy had noted the dates, and as it later turned out, President Kennedy's forecasts of October 1963 were correct to the month. He had anticipated a Tax Law in February, a Civil Rights Law in July. President Johnson signed the first on February 27, 1964; the second on July 2, 1964.

The word went out, and the three men set to work—McCormack and Warren in their hotel apartments, Mansfield in his office. All wrote in longhand; otherwise their evenings differed sharply. The Speaker finished quickly. He had a hazy impression of rain blurring the window by his desk, then he was done. Earl Warren didn't finish at all. The Chief Judge's thoughts were incoherent. He fought with a series of soft pencils, scrawled a few ragged passages, read them over, and realized that they were quite unsatisfactory. He abandoned the struggle and turned back to the hypnotic eye of television, making a mental note to rise early in the morning and make a fresh start.

Mansfield was the only one to hear from Mrs Kennedy herself. He instantly agreed and then, hanging up, strolled restlessly through the rooms of Senate suite S208, poking at the fireplace, peering up at the chandelier, and examining his tall gaunt image in the gilt-framed Victorian mirror. He wondered what on earth he could say. His mind remained vacant until he remembered a broadcast yesterday afternoon. During an interview a Parkland attendant had described how Mrs Kennedy had placed her wedding ring on the President's hand. Awaiting Air Force One's return at Andrews Field the scene had preyed on Mansfield's mind, and tonight he resolved to make that his theme. Chewing his pipe and fighting back tears, he wrote a first draft on a yellow pad, took it home, and worked it and reworked it. In the early hours of Sunday morning he was still dissatisfied, but it was nearly complete. Then he laid his blunted pencil aside and attempted to read it aloud. He tried several times and never got past the third paragraph. The Majority Leader had been a public speaker since his youth, yet this might as well have been his first speech. He gnawed at his pipe stem until a semblance of self-control returned, then fell into bed exhausted.

Between 1 a.m. and 2 a.m. television channels signed off with the national anthem. In Dungan's office the ceaseless flow of orders and assignments went on, and on the floor above Mrs Kennedy prepared to retire. Her sister having moved into the President's bedroom, the Auchinclosses had returned to Georgetown. As Lee, Jean, and Pat saw Jackie to bed, she thought fleetingly how good it was to have her family around her. She had but to step into the corridor and a familiar figure would spring up, eager to help. Because they knew one another so well their conversations today had not all been solemn and grim. There had been wry asides, tart exchanges, small ironies —echoes of a pleasanter past. *Wake?* she wondered. *Is this what wakes are like?* She had never been to one. They had always sounded rather brutal to her. The Kennedys, Bouviers, Auchinclosses, Lawfords, and Smiths had deepened her understanding of mourning; by being themselves they were both supporting one another and honouring the President's memory. There was no brutality here. She had left that in Texas.

Because her mind was still whirling Dr Walsh gave her another half-gram injection of Amytal. Once more her constitution fought the drug. She had to talk to her brother-in-law again. Last night the prospect of an open coffin had tormented her; tonight she had to make sure its lid could be raised in private before they left for the Capitol. She sent for him and said, 'I have to see Jack in the morning, I want to say good-bye to him—and I want to put something in the coffin.'

He understood. It was a secret of his strength, and a source of the special affection shared by those close to him, that he never asked them for reasons. If you were a relative or a friend, that was enough. He assumed you knew what you were doing, and the franker you were, the better he liked it. He jotted down their Sunday schedule for her and said, 'I'll come for you. We'll go down there together.'

After he had gone Jacqueline Kennedy wrote her husband a letter. Later she was uncertain about the precise time of composition. Medication and accumulated sleeplessness had blunted her perception, and the servants had drawn her drapes in the southwest corner of the Presidential apartment so tightly that it was impossible to distinguish daylight from night.

In her darkened room, she wrote her final impassioned letter, filling page after page. Then she folded the pages and sealed the envelope.

9

PASSION

Sunday, November 24, 1963, was, among other things, the day upon which President Kennedy's gun carriage was to be drawn up Pennsylvania Avenue to the great rotunda off the Capitol, where the first formal tributes were to be delivered. Except for her rapid descent from Aircraft 26000 on Andrews Field's truck lift at 6.06 p.m. Friday, it would be Mrs Kennedy's first public appearance since the assassination, and her two children would stand with her before the national audience. Sunday was to be the second full day of the thirty-sixth President's administration; it would mark the arrival at Dulles and Washington National airports of the eminent funeral guests; it would provide final opportunities for the Shriver–Dungan planners, who would finally be joined by Richard Cardinal Cushing and Auxiliary Bishop Philip M. Hannan; and it would be the first of two consecutive days in which a martyred President would be consecrated as a national hero. All this had been envisioned the evening before. It was not a predictable weekend, however, and the day's most memorable events were to be entirely impulsive: a gesture by the widow, a massive invasion of the U.S. capital by the bereft American people and television's first live killing.

The weather had cleared. Robert Kennedy, peering out from a second-floor mansion window, saw a mild, flawless sky; he glanced down and was surprised at the size of the crowd in Lafayette Park. The mute witnesses were maintaining their vigil. Their identity was as striking as their mass. Usually Pennsylvania Avenue's sightseers are faceless, camera-hung anonymities: tourists, curious travellers passing through, high school seniors in chartered buses. This morning the park's spectators included Washingtonians accustomed to hand-lettered White House invitations—Dean Acheson; and Mr and Mrs John W. Macy, Jr.; and Bill Walton and his son who, like so many other Harvard students, had driven non-stop to be here. At 9.06 a.m. Merrill Mueller became the first commentator to point out a phenomenon which became increasingly evident: a clear majority of the weekend immigrants appeared to be in their early twenties. John Kennedy had been forty-six years old, but the youths beneath the almost leafless trees regarded him as the leader of their generation.

During the night the state of the nation had remained unchanged. Sunday morning 10 per cent of America's local stations began slipping in spot commercials (the suspension, auditors had told the networks, would cost nearly forty million dollars), and the switchboards of the thrifty were jammed with indignant calls. In a wealthy Long Island suburb a twenty-four-year-old English teacher who had told her class Friday that 'the country will probably be better' was informed that she faced summary dismissal. The public was intolerant, apprehensive, anxious, and united in its yearning to carry some share of the national burden. Political partisanship had vanished. On his Gettysburg farm Dwight Eisenhower rose early to prepare a memorandum of recommendations which President Johnson had requested. At 6.30 a.m., a half-hour before daybreak, Earl Warren groped for a box of sharpened pencils which his wife always kept by his bed. Six hours later he had a version, and though like Mike Mansfield he was unhappy with it, Mrs Warren typed it up for him. For once the Chief Justice had had no time for Sunday newspapers; for once his countrymen had time for little else. Spent, haggard, and drawn, the stubble beginning to show on men's faces, Americans scanned the headlines with bloodshot eyes. After two unbelievable days the national audience was virtually shockproof. Friday and Saturday had left people jaded. Only an event of extraordinary magnitude would stir the dishevelled viewers slumped in front of television sets. They were too tired to do more than gape.

The bright-eyed exception, once more, was Lee Oswald. His undisturbed sleep went unmentioned at the time. (It was one of the few titbits about him which were *not* reported.) The policemen guarding the jail's three maximum-security cells didn't think it remarkable, and there is little reason to believe that those outside would have drawn a different conclusion. Yet in retrospect his phlegm is singular. According to the NORC study, over fifty million men and women were suffering from insomnia, but for the second night in a row the man responsible for it enjoyed an untroubled slumber. To be sure, his rest had been threatened by few disturbances. Accounts that he was subjected to police brutality (these were widely credited in France) are preposterous. The opposite is true. He was not only unmolested; he was frequently ignored. During the whole of Saturday he had actually been interrogated less than three hours. Under local law a suspect accused of a felony had to be moved to the county prison twelve blocks away on Dealey

Plaza, between the Book Depository warehouse and the bronze, businesslike father image of the Dallas *News's* publisher, but Oswald's repose wasn't interrupted for that either. Chief Curry had assured the television technicians that he planned to make a real production out of the transfer. They could count on setting up their intricate equipment at ten o'clock Sunday morning—eleven o'clock in Washington, when, by coincidence, the Kennedy family would celebrate its last private Mass for the President in the East Room.

Except for his abortive attempt to telephone Marina and his frenzied moments on camera, when he had resembled a frontrunner at a political convention, Oswald had been largely idle. The assassin was the one principal figure in the drama with time on his hands. He had been returned to his cot at 7.15 p.m. Saturday, and for the second night in a row he had given every evidence of being blessed with an untroubled conscience. On April 22, 1964, exactly five months after the assassination, Captain Will Fritz was to muse: 'You know, I didn't have any trouble with him.' The Captain's ward might have returned the compliment. He had been deprived of Civil Liberties counsel, but he didn't know that. It must have struck him as odd that for a captive who had been charged with the premeditated assassination of the President of the United States and the killing of a popular police officer—not to mention the wounding of the Governor of Texas, whose condition was still considered critical—he himself was having remarkably little trouble with cops.[1] A scrupulous review of the records shows that he was never adequately grilled. Anyone familiar with police mentality knows that law enforcement officers interpret the law freely, and that it is an article of faith among them that a suspect is guilty until proven innocent. The case against the warehouse stock boy had been airtight within three hours of the murders, he had been in custody for forty-six hours, and he was being handled with conspicuous gentleness. The reasons are now transparent. If Oswald wasn't concerned about his future, Big D's civil leadership was. Appalled at the thought that the city's reputation might be further marred, they were following their police chief's investigation with the absorption of Argus watching Io, never dreaming that their solicitude might encourage vigilantism, and thus provoked the very backlash they feared most.

[1] Technically, Lee Oswald had been charged with 'Inv. Murder'—investigation for murder, a common catch-all. There were no entries on the form beside the spaces provided for information about how the arrest was made, the location of the offence, the complainant, or witnesses. This is not odd. Policemen are not CPA's. The arresting officers were M. N. McDonald, K. E. Lyons, and Paul Bentley. Under 'other details' the essence of the report was scrawled: 'This man shot and killed President John F. Kennedy and Police Officer J. D. Tippit. He also shot and wounded Governor John Connally.'

That much is clear. What is less lucid, and what muddles all memories of those late autumn days, is the total incompatibility between the bravo's last hours and the ritualistic splendour in the nation's capital. As Robert Kennedy looked down on the quiet dignity of Lafayette Park's standees, Forrest Sorrels of the Secret Service squinted through a pane on the third floor of the Dallas Police Department. He beheld a gaudily painted Edsel with a plugged .50 calibre machine gun mounted on the top. This monstrosity was parked on Commerce Street, and behind the wheel was a Dallas extrovert who advertised himself as 'Honest Joe Goldstein, the Loan Ranger'. Sorrels' sutler's eyes lingered briefly on the mounted gun and swept on. He knew the exhibitionist as a rich, generous pawnbroker who fawned upon policemen and ingratiated himself to them by marking down price tags. Sorrels was unaware that one of Honest Joe's best friends was named Jack Ruby. Had he been told, he would have thought the relationship irrelevant, which it really was. The significance of the scene lies in the fact that the world of the tawdry Edsel and the world of the Presidential gun carriage co-existed. The pairing of Dallas and Washington, like that of John Kennedy and Lee Oswald, is an affront, yet all were irrevocably joined in American history that weekend.

Probably any attempt to refurbish the city's reputation was doomed. If the findings of poll takers are valid, over 27 million Americans had broadly indicted 'the people of Dallas' for the crime; in Hyannis Port Rita Dallas had by now received so many crank calls because of her name that she asked the telephone company for an unlisted number. It would be a mistake to exaggerate that aspect of the drama, however. The same pollsters declared that 85 per cent of the public wasn't thinking about Texas at all, and in Washington chief participants in the coming ceremonies were preoccupied with their immediate obligations. Mike Mansfield and John McCormack were preparing an agenda of eulogies. Because of his seniority McCormack would speak last; Mansfield would be first. In the park across from Union Station an artillery battery had been chocked up, and to ensure prompt transmission of the word to commence firing the twenty-one-gun mourning salute a portable PRS-10 radio had been placed at a captain's feet by the Capitol's east steps. The Joint Chiefs of Staff had been issuing orders to one another; they would march up Pennsylvania Avenue in ranks of two. Seaman Nemuth was gingerly fingering the towering Presidential standard at the executive mansion. Lieutenant Bird had acquired a church truck to wheel the coffin from the catafalque in the East Room to the North Portico, where the caisson and Black Jack would be waiting, and

Elmer Young, the White House florist, was working on wreaths for Jacqueline Kennedy and Lyndon Johnson.

They were to be the only garlands in the great rotunda. Bunny Mellon, stumbling over the thick cords of video cables which lay in the gutters like tropical growths, was greeted on the Hill by a delegation: the director of the U.S. Botanic Gardens, an Army officer who had been placed under her command, and the president of the Allied Florist Association of Greater Washington. The first two delighted her, the third cheerfully informed her that every flower shop in the United States was remaining open this Sunday to accommodate people who wished to send bouquets here. Since all networks had broadcasted the family's appeal to omit flowers thirty-six hours earlier, this is puzzling. To Bunny it was appalling; she foresaw a deluge of blossoms descending upon the Capitol, and that, she knew, was the last thing Jacqueline Kennedy wanted. Fortunately, most of the tributes could be disregarded. For once constituents would have to nurse their hurt feelings. All the wreaths couldn't be ignored, however. It would be a grave error to slight the diplomatic corps. Bunny's solution was to bank their tokens in one of the marble halls adjacent to the rotunda entrance and to arrange those from states, lodges, veterans' organizations, and women's clubs in a similar chamber on the opposite side. No one would feel snubbed, yet Mrs Kennedy needn't see a single petal. Inspecting the scene, Bunny felt torn. It was grand but rather stark, and she murmured that she missed 'something softening, something green flanking the doors as you come in'. Within minutes gardeners bearing bright palms arrived from the Botanic Gardens. Another of the weekend's patterns was holding: the technicians, taking refuge in the rote of vocational skills, were performing superbly.

The President's mother again attended seven and eight o'clock Masses at St Francis Xavier; Cardinal Cushing presided over a pontifical Mass in Boston; and the last Kennedy White House Mass was held for close friends and members of the immediate family in the East Room. That service ought to have been memorable. It wasn't. The ritual was almost exactly like yesterday's, and the communicants had too much on their minds. The procession up Pennsylvania Avenue was now imminent. The Joint Chiefs were hoping they could keep in step; they were old men, and hard of hearing. Provi Parades was furtively removing the stained red rose from Mrs Kennedy's purse and putting it away for a calmer time. Bob Kennedy phoned the British Embassy, inviting David and Cissy Ormsby-Gore to come over for the day because 'Jackie's had another bad night'. Muggsy O'Leary couldn't attend the Mass at all. The clothing President Kennedy had been wearing in Dallas had been stored in Bill Greer's locker in the White House garage. Another agent told Muggsy that 'Jackie wants a medal or something for the casket, and it's in there'. Unfortunately Greer had the only locker key, and he was in his home off Maryland Route 50. Muggsy raced out there, picked him up, and delivered the key to Dr Burkley at the mansion.

After the Mass Jacqueline Kennedy and her brother-in-law went straight to the Presidential apartment. Maude Shaw had just dressed the two children in their powder-blue coats and red lace-up shoes—the clothes they had worn Thursday, when their parents had left for Texas—and she was adding a black mourning band for Caroline's hair when their mother entered the nursery with blue stationery. She told her daughter, 'You must write a letter to Daddy and tell him how much you love him.' John was too little to write, so she asked him to mark his as carefully as he could. It was, she said, to be a message for his father.

Holding a blue ball-point pen, Caroline wrote that they would all miss him and told him that she loved him very much.

Then, holding John's hand, Caroline helped him scribble up and down as best he could. It was wholly illegible, of course, but their mother, sitting on one of the little nursery chairs while Miss Shaw hovered over the children, saw that they were doing their best. Mrs Kennedy had three envelopes now, theirs and her own; yet the letters weren't enough. The impulse which had begun at Parkland when she had fastened her wedding ring to his finger had grown stronger. She had become obsessed by a yearning to leave something he had treasured with him. There were, she now remembered, two gifts from her that he had really loved. Before their marriage he had never been interested in men's jewellery; if he had needed a pair of cufflinks for a formal shirt he would pick up a Swank set in a drugstore. As a young girl her own allowance had been rather small, and at the wedding she had given him a briefcase. A year later, however, she had seen a beautiful pair of inlaid gold links in a New York show window. The price was staggering—$800—but she had splurged. It had been her first really expensive present to him, and it was a great success; he had worn them on every possible occasion and displayed them with pride.

The second present had begun as a light gesture. During their second year in the White House she had read a newspaper story about a man who had carved a likeness of the President. The craftsman's real specialty, the account went on, was scrimshaws—decorative articles carved from whalebone. She told Clint Hill it might be rather nice to have a scrimshaw bearing the Presidential seal. Clint found the man, and the result was an unexpected triumph. The man found an ancient bull whale's tooth, set it in timbers from a New Bedford whaling ship, and spent 180 hours embellishing it with an ornate, early-nineteenth-century design of the seal. On Christmas 1962 Mrs Kennedy had given it to her husband. That morning she had thought of it as 'just a little present', but he had been enchanted. From that day forward he had always kept it on the right-hand corner of his desk, and remembering how much it had meant to him she had asked Evelyn Lincoln to send it up to her when they returned from Bethesda.

Bearing the letters, the links, and the scrimshaw, she descended to the first floor with the Attorney General, and at 12.34 the widow and Robert Kennedy entered the East Room.

Robert Kennedy had alerted Godfrey McHugh; the General met them at the threshold. Clint closed doors while Godfrey folded back the flag, unlatched the casket top, and glanced inside to be certain everything was all right. Closing it and replacing the field of stars, he ordered Lieutenant Sawtelle to march the Death Watch out. Jacqueline Kennedy heard him. She whispered to Bob, 'No, they don't have to leave the room. Even though we're here, Jack would be so'—she groped for a word—'lonely. Just tell them to go to a far corner and turn their backs.' The joint services team had already started to withdraw; McHugh had refolded the flag and was propping the lid open on its hinge. The Attorney General spoke to the retreating honour guard. 'I don't want that,' he said quietly, and the Lieutenant halted his four men, ordered a leftface, and executed one himself. Flanked by Godfrey and Clint Hill, they faced the wall at attention.

Together the President's widow and brother knelt by the open coffin. This was the first time Mrs Kennedy had seen her husband since Parkland. *It isn't Jack, it isn't Jack*, she kept thinking; and she was so glad Bobby had agreed to keep it shut. She put the three letters, the scrimshaw, and the cufflinks in the coffin. Bob Kennedy took off his PT tie pin. He said, 'He should have this, shouldn't he?'

'Yes,' she whispered. Then he drew from his pocket an engraved silver rosary Ethel had given him at their wedding. Bob placed this with the letters.

Then, with a lock of her husband's hair she went out with Bob. To all of those awaiting the motorcade's departure for the rotunda it was clear that the widow was in agony. Mary Gallagher, standing with Dr Walsh, thought that 'I had never seen her look worse. Bobby was leading her by the arm, holding her up; she was limp, with her head down, weeping. She looked as though she were ready to fall.' She was swaying visibly; Clint Hill was afraid she might faint.

She didn't. Beyond consolation, wrenched by a torsion of pain which was tightened by the knowledge that in less than twenty minutes her children, whom until now she had fiercely sheltered from publicity, would become the centre of an unprecedented spectacle under the worst circumstances conceivable, she nevertheless retained the sense of purpose which had kept her going for two days.

The schedule was now inflexible. Sam Bird and his casket team had wheeled the coffin into the entrance hall. The Lieutenant was watching the electric clock on the stairway to the basement—he had been told that the gun carriage must leave at exactly 1 p.m., and obviously they weren't going to make that. Already a band on the lawn outside had begun to play 'Abide With Me'. Glancing about nervously, Bird saw a stocky woman in a white nurse's uniform and a black-and-white check coat. On either side of her were children in blue coats and red shoes, and with a sense of shock he recognized them. In the next moment Jacqueline Kennedy appeared, and Miss Shaw stepped back. Young John, watching the body bearers, asked, 'Mommy, what are they doing?' His mother said, 'They're taking Daddy out.' John asked, 'But why do they do it so funny—so slow?' She said, 'Because they're so sad,' and the Lieutenant looked away, and forgot the clock.

Colonel William Jackson, the Air Force officer who had been Vice Presidential military aide, had been especially agitated by the delay. Before the reappearance of Mrs Kennedy, Dave Powers had drawn the boy aside and was diverting him with stories when Jackson came up and said briskly, 'Mr Powers, you tell Mrs Kennedy that the President and the First Lady are here and are in the Blue Room.' Dave's reply illustrates the irreconcilable conflict between the staunchest of loyalists and the most uncompromising of realists. Moving up until his eyes were inches from the Colonel's, he answered starchily, 'That's impossible. The First Lady is in her quarters, and the President is in the East Room.'

President Johnson entered, departed, and re-entered a deeply disturbed man. After attending services at St Mark's Episcopal church with his wife and Lucy he had arrived at the mansion, and had been told by an usher that Dean Rusk wished to speak to him immediately on the telephone. He had heard from the Secretary of State what the entire country was learning—that Oswald had just been shot 'on television'. In the Blue Room Jean Smith whispered to Lady Bird that she had overheard a servant say the assassin was dying. Johnson greeted the Attorney General, who knew nothing of this, with 'You've got to do something, we've got to do something. We've got to get involved. It's giving the United States a bad name around the world.'

Three television cameramen were in Dallas' underground garage that noon. A comparison of their video tape reels (NBC-66, WFAA-16, KRLD-13), of Vernon Oneal's dispatcher's log, of Parkland's records, and of Secret Service shift reports establishes a chronology which, although it makes events no more believable, does provide some perspective:

Washington Time	*The White House*	*Dallas*	*Dallas Time*
11.47 a.m.	Mass for JFK ends.	Oswald jail transfer begins amid extraordinary confusion.	10.47 a.m.
12.17 p.m.– 12.18 p.m.		Ruby leaves Western Union office for Dallas jail.	11.17– 11.18 a.m.
12.20 p.m.		Oswald reaches jail garage.	11.20 a.m.
12.21 p.m.		Ruby shoots Oswald—televised on NBC.	11.21 a.m.
12.24 p.m.		Oneal ambulance arrives at jail.	11.24 a.m.
12.32 p.m.		Oswald is wheeled into Parkland's Trauma Room No. 2.	11.32 a.m.
12.34 p.m.	Jacqueline and Robert Kennedy enter East Room to see the coffin opened.		11.34 a.m.
12.44 p.m.		Operation on Oswald begins.	11.44 a.m.
12.46 p.m.	Jacqueline and Robert Kennedy ascend to presidential apartment.		11.46 a.m.
12.55 p.m.	The Kennedys meet the Johnsons in the Blue Room.		11.55 a.m.
1.08 p.m.	The gun carriage leaves the North Portico for the Capitol.		12.08 p.m.
1.47 p.m.	Cortege reaches the Hill.		12.47 p.m.
1.52 p.m.	Band plays 'Hail to the Chief' and 'Navy Hymn'.		12.52 p.m.
2.07 p.m.		Oswald is pronounced dead.	1.07 p.m.
2.17 p.m.	Mrs Kennedy and Caroline kneel by catafalque in rotunda.		1.17 p.m.
2.19 p.m.	Kennedy party leaves Capitol.		1.19 p.m.
2.25 p.m.		NBC announces Oswald is dead.	1.25 p.m.
2.28 p.m.	Kennedy party returns to White House.		1.28 p.m.

Oswald almost died in the same chamber where the President's body had lain; the cart was headed that way when a doctor reminded Jack Price that that would be wrong; Price swiftly saw the point and directed the attendants to swerve leftwards into Trauma Room 2. The fact is that three of Parkland's trauma rooms had been readied over two hours before the shooting against precisely this calamity. In the words of Nurse Bertha L. Lozano, 'At 11.00 a.m. I was informed by Jill Pomeroy, the ward clerk, that we might prepare for an emergency because there was a large crowd at the city jail.' The attack was anticipated, everyone in authority had been alerted, and still it was successful. Nellie Connally, on the hospital's second floor, became aware of what she called 'a sudden tightening of the security around us'; she asked for the reason, and a Texas Ranger said, 'Lee Harvey Oswald was just killed'. From the bed Governor Connally stared about, bewildered. This was his first day of complete consciousness—for several hours he thought it was Saturday—and the name Oswald meant nothing whatever to him.

In both Friday's assassination and Sunday's murder two vivid threads are evident: warnings of disaster had come from responsible sources, and peace officers, in weighing them, had miscalculated gravely. Actually, the Dallas Police Department's original plan had been to move Oswald at ten o'clock Saturday evening, and J. Edgar Hoover, among others, had retired under the impression that it was being carried through. At 2.15 a.m. Sunday Hoover's Dallas office began receiving anonymous telephone calls threatening the prisoner's life. The Dallas FBI urged a 3 a.m. transfer—in vain. Sunday morning Forrest Sorrels suggested to Captain Fritz that Oswald be taken out at an unannounced time, when no one was around, but all federal advice, and some from within the department itself, was rejected in deference to the fourth estate. Chief Curry, in Captain Fritz's words, 'wanted to go along with the press and not try to put anything over on them'.

Curry and Fritz were apprehensive, however. Accordingly, they had taken elaborate measures to deflect danger. The difficulty was that they were attempting to second-guess vigilantism, and their error was almost exactly the opposite of Friday's. Those responsible for the protection of the President then had assumed that any attack on him would be made either at the airport or the Trade Mart. The motorcade route had been slighted. While Kennedy was in motion, it had been assumed, he would be relatively safe; in any event, little could be done to shield him from a sniper. From the very first discussions of the Oswald transfer the Dallas police were thinking in terms of what they were calling 'the Committee of One Hundred'—a hundred men, it was rumoured, were going to abduct the captive during the drive to Dealey Plaza. Curry and Fritz felt they were ready for this. Oswald was to be handcuffed to a detective and surrounded by officers with tear gas; the use of a very large armed force was contemplated. What was *not* contemplated was that a lone individual, with no credentials, might penetrate the security screen before the movement from the jail basement had begun. As they walked towards the fifth-floor elevator James Leavelle, the plainclothes man to whom Oswald had been manacled, said, 'If anybody shoots at you, I sure hope they are as good a shot as you are.' According to Leavelle, Oswald 'kind of laughed' and said, 'Nobody is going to shoot at me.'

Somebody was; Jack Ruby was. Ruby's presence in the basement is utterly confounding. To some it will remain for ever mystifying, to others it will always provide positive proof of police collusion in a complex conspiracy, and even those who have sifted all the evidence are left with a vague impression of a Houdini effect. A jail, after all, ought to be as secure from invasion as from escape. Curry's department had been put on stern notice, and beginning at 9 a.m. Sunday morning his leading subordinates had begun intricate precautions to avoid the very fiasco which was imminent. The basement had been completely cleared. Guards were stationed at the two automobile ramps leading into the garage from Main and Commerce Streets, and fourteen officers searched the entire area, including air-conditioning ducts and the trunks of automobiles already parked in the garage.

Nevertheless, Ruby was there when Oswald emerged from the elevator. How did he manage it? Part of the answer lies in the fact that he was not there during the search. Indeed, as late as 11.17 a.m., three minutes before Oswald stepped down into the garage, Ruby was in the Western Union office on Main Street, 350 feet from the top of the Main Street ramp. He was sending a $25 money order to Karin Carlin ('Little Lynn'), a twenty-year-old stripper; a time stamp on the order places him at the counter then. From the counter to the murder scene was a minute-and-a-half walk. Of course, had security been as thorough as in the earlier search, he would never have been permitted to enter the ramp. Even Sorrels, who had been Dallas' Secret Service agent for twenty-eight years, was asked to identify himself before being admitted to the building that morning. Ruby had acquired no credentials since Friday, and his achievement in slipping past the ramp guard—Patrolman Roy E. Vaughn—was largely a matter of chance. It must be added that that chance arose because of incompetent police trimmers.

Pleasing every member of the press and removing any possibility of vengeance were mutually exclusive, and the debate between law enforcement officers over how they might best be reconciled was still continuing when Oswald, upstairs, donned a sweater for the trip. The obvious solution was to provide some sort of decoy. In 1901 the Buffalo Police Department had moved McKinley's assassin, Leon F. Czolgosz, from jail to jail by a simple trick; they had dressed him in a patrolman's uniform. That sort of ingenuity was missing in Dallas on November 24. The best Jesse Curry could come up with was an armoured car or truck, a vehicle normally used by banks for the transport of large sums of cash. The choice was neither imaginative nor practical, for when the truck showed up (its appearance was immediately noted by all members of the press), it was found to be too big for the ramp. The driver was reluctant to back it down into the basement garage from Commerce Street, and so, lacking adequate clearance, he left it at the top of the ramp.

This, then, was the scene in the last moments of Oswald's life. His killer was in the Western Union office. He himself was in Captain Will Fritz's office, wriggling into a sweater. Chief Curry was preparing to take him down to the cellar on the jail elevator, through the jail office, and into the garage. At Oswald's left, as he stepped forward, would be the ramp leading towards Main; to his right, the ramp towards Commerce, with the tank-like armoured truck at the top, its blunt snout protruding on to the sidewalk. Between the truck and the jail office were two cruisers, unmarked four-door Ford Galaxie sedans. They were to accompany the truck, one of them leading it to the county jail.

Astonishingly, the chief had communicated none of this to Captain Fritz, in whose custody Oswald would remain until the sheriff took over. Fritz first learned of it when he, Sorrels, and FBI agents were concluding their final effort to break through the prisoner's arrogant façade—a façade which Sorrels, for one, thought had begun to crumble. Curry thrust his head in to inquire how long the questioning would continue. They were, he said, ready to move. When Fritz was told of the method of conveyance, he objected vehemently. Instead, he proposed that Oswald be carried in the second of the two unmarked Galaxies. The order of the parade would be: the truck; then the first cruiser, occupied by detectives; then the second cruiser, with Oswald. The parade would only last one block, however. At the first intersection the second Galaxie would veer away and drive directly to the county jail while the other two vehicles leisurely wound through downtown Dallas. This was deception; some members of the press might resent being misled. But Curry agreed.

Word of the change in plan was telephoned to the basement. With it went instructions to obtain a new lead car from the garage pool and station it on Commerce Street, in front of the truck; Fritz assigned this task to Lieutenant Rio S. Pierce. Lieutenant Pierce's way was blocked by the truck. He had to drive out the Main Street ramp—violating an ironclad departmental regulation, for the ramp was one-way—and circle the block. As Pierce approached Main from the depths of the garage, Patrolman Vaughn stepped off the kerb to hold back other traffic. Vaughn was absent from his post for approximately ten seconds. During those ten seconds there was no sentinel at that entrance to the basement, and it was then that heavy-set Jack Ruby, wearing a hat and a business suit, strolled in unchallenged.[2]

In Ruby's right hip pocket was a .38 calibre revolver. He habitually carried the weapon—this was Dallas, not New York; there was no Sullivan Act—and today he was also carrying over $2,000 in cash. He had left another $1,000 in the trunk of his car, parked directly across the street from the Western Union office. His behaviour was in character. He was Jack the big spender, Jack the tough; and he was about to become Jack the vindicator. According to his own account, his trip downtown had a 'double purpose'. The first was to wire the money to Karin. She was at home with her husband, who wasn't working steadily. Saturday should have been her payday, and she had been left in financial straits by his decision to close his clubs in mourning; Little Lynn was four months pregnant, owed rent, needed groceries, and had less than fifty cents in her purse. It was Ruby's second purpose of course, which was to assure him his footnote in history.

Its inspiration is obscure. Perhaps he would never have gone downtown if his pregnant stripper hadn't phoned him of her plight, although according to her subsequent recollection he had replied, 'Well, I have to go downtown anyway. . . .' Given his restless temperament, it is unlikely that he would have spent the morning brooding in his apartment, and 'I have to go downtown anyway' should not be interpreted as premeditation. Ruby was probably incapable of craftiness that Sunday. Everyone who saw him later remembered his evident distress. He had become a creature of events. On every side he saw the debris of mourning, and an internal pressure was rapidly building up within him. Afterwards he was to recall his acute response to Rabbi Seligman's televised elegy; to a mawkish, two-column 'Letter to Caroline' in Sunday's Dallas *News* ('the most heartbreaking letter', he called it); and, as he drove down Main

[2] On September 23, 1964, this writer stood where Oswald had stood at the moment he was shot while a Dallas police inspector explained what had happened. The inspector concluded, 'It was sheer luck.' He was asked, 'Couldn't there have been *two* sentries there?' He flashed, 'That's hindsight on your part.' Possibly, but under the circumstances doubling the guard would seem to have been a reasonable precaution.

Street, to wreaths which had been left on the grassy slope beside the assassination site by Dallas citizens ('I saw them and started to cry again'). Passing the jail he noticed the sidewalk crowd, but he 'took it for granted', he later insisted to Earl Warren, that Oswald 'had already been moved'. Ruby repeatedly declared that the killing was entirely impulsive. He may have been lying. Certainly he had every reason to lie, for by then his own life was at stake. Yet an intensive study of his Sunday movements fails to reveal a single flaw, or even the suspicion of a flaw, in his story. All signs point to murder by whim.

Of Oswald's fatal ride downstairs it can only be said that the trip, like everything in his life, proceeded against a background of tastelessness and vulgarity. Handcuffed to Leavelle, he left the sickly green walls of Ritz's Room 317, passed a row of shabby straight-backed chairs, and entered the dark brown jail elevator, whose operator was walled away in a cage of sturdy bars. In the basement Fritz and four detectives led their prisoner along a semi-circular route through the cluttered jail office and debouched into the gloomy garage, a tan-walled vault whose roof was supported by pillars which had once been painted yellow and which after years of gusting exhaust, had become tawny, drab, and flecked with particles of oil. Oswald paused by a sign warning, 'DO NOT SIT ON RAIL OR STAND IN DRIVEWAY'. He couldn't have seen it. Too much was happening; two score newsmen pushed forward, thrusting microphones in his face and shouting questions; flash bulbs were exploding; the entire scene was bathed in a klieg glare. Tugged forward by the handcuffs, the captive moved approximately ten feet forward towards the cruiser. Then Ruby approached him from his left front. Shouldering forward through the straining crowd, the burly gunman passed between a reporter and a plain-clothes man, his .38 in his right hand. As he shoved it forward he shouted, 'You killed the President, you rat!' Then he fired. The bullet passed through Oswald's liver, spleen, and aorta, and in the next instant the murderer of the murderer lay on the basement floor, being pummelled by officers. In dismay, almost in plaintive reproach, he wailed, 'I'm Jack Ruby, you all know me!'

Bleeding internally, the mortally wounded assassin was carried back into the jail office, and there, if the memories of Forrest Sorrels and Jesse Curry are to be credited, he was deprived of whatever chance he had to live by clumsy first aid. Sorrels and Curry had remained upstairs; the chief was on the telephone, reporting to the mayor that the transfer had begun. Curry's subordinates shouted up news of the shooting, and the two men raced down to the office, where Sorrels, to his amazement, saw a plainclothes man kneeling between Oswald's thighs, administering artificial respiration. Sorrels did not recognize the man; later Curry would merely identify him as 'a detective'.[3] Artificial respiration is the worst conceivable treatment for abdominal injuries. It is like applying a bellows to a fire. The chances of haemorrhage multiply in proportion to the pressure applied. Ten minutes after his arrival at Parkland Oswald was on the operating table, with three of the same doctors who had attended Kennedy—Mac Perry, McClelland, and Jenkins—beside him. Now, as then, they went through the correct surgical motions, but in Jenkins' words, 'The trauma which patient Oswald had sustained was too great for resuscitation.' Two days and seven minutes after the President had been pronounced dead the sheet was drawn over his killer's face.

In the weeks which lay ahead Oswald's death, and especially the manner of his dying, were to loom ever larger until they had assumed undeserved dimensions. At the time this was untrue. The attention of the national audience was focused on the North Portico of the White House. The murder of the assassin almost seemed to be an intrusion. Most of those who had been closest to Kennedy had tuned Dallas out forty-eight hours ago. They had been so occupied with the coming funeral that they hadn't had time for the swarming humanity in Curry's dingy warrens. Nancy Tuckerman was as withdrawn as the Governor of Texas. Since the disruption of the motorcade outside the Book Depository she had devoted every waking moment to Jacqueline Kennedy's wishes. The President was dead; that eclipsed everything else, and when an excited secretary thrust her head into Nancy's office and cried that Oswald had been shot, Nancy mumbled, 'Who's Oswald?' To Robert Kennedy, President Johnson's Blue Room protest that the United States was getting 'a bad name around the world' was untimely; the Attorney General afterwards remembered that 'I thought at the time that . . . it wasn't, it couldn't be, the thing foremost in my mind'. Steve Smith 'just heard it, that's all'. On Capitol Hill, where reports were being relayed by functionaries glued to portable radios, Larry O'Brien was 'no more interested than if someone had been telling me the score of a ball game'. Ken O'Donnell was the same—he had been equally disinterested when told of Oswald's arrest Friday—and beside Sargent Shriver's desk Dick Goodwin, a *summa cum laude* graduate of Harvard Law School, felt an unprofessional disinterest, a 'complete indifference. . . . I wouldn't have cared if I'd been told that Connally had been charged with the shooting.' Sarge picked up the receiver,

[3] Thomas J. Kelley, a Secret Service inspector who had been flown down from Washington, also saw 'a man leaning over Oswald', but Kelley thought he must be applying a stethoscope to the prisoner's chest.

put it down, and announced, 'Somebody just shot Oswald.' No one in the office said a word. 'We went on,' Goodwin put it, 'with our business.'

That was one reaction to the murder. The fact that Shriver felt obliged to make the announcement had been another. His console was flashing all the time, and he didn't pass along other news. In relaying this he was displaying a common response; inner urges required that men blazon it. Early Sunday afternoon the same men and women who had telephoned or bellowed word of the assassination two days earlier were again responding to an instinct older than the invention of language, babbling away as self-appointed heralds to relatives, friends, and passers-by. Ted Kennedy yelled up the Hyannis Port stairwell to Eunice. Eisenhower's wife phoned him. Word-of-mouth bulletins reached the executive mansion's entrance hall, inches from the President's coffin, and were murmured to Lieutenant Sam Bird's body bearers by him; on the third floor Peter Lawford and his agent, watching George Thomas' set, had seen NBC's live telecast of Ruby's assault on Channel 4, and they darted downstairs to tell everyone of it.

Convincing non-viewers wasn't so easy. On the red carpet outside the Diplomatic Reception Room Tazewell Shepard heard of the report, stopped dead, and narrowed his eyes sceptically. This was another echo of Friday—intuitively one suspected a hoax. Congressman Albert Thomas was telephoning the Philippine Ambassador, who had one eye cocked on a television screen as they talked. The embassy's set was tuned to Channel 4. Listening to the Congressman with one ear, the diplomat heard commentator Tom Pettit, standing five feet from Oswald, describe the jail transfer. Pettit, ordinarily mild-mannered, gasped, 'He's been shot—Lee Oswald has been shot! There is panic and pandemonium! We see little in the utter confusion!' The Ambassador said to Thomas, 'My God, you Texans are just *crazy*. They've shot that boy.[4] I saw it a few seconds ago.' The Congressman concluded that it was the diplomat, a volatile Spaniard, who was deranged.

George Reedy and the Filipino witnessed the killing under almost identical circumstances—never in the seven centuries of trial by jury had a crime been committed in the presence of so many spectators—and Reedy was as dumbfounded as he had been two days before. He was cradling an EOB phone and monitoring Channel 4 from the corner of his eye. He saw the shot, but it didn't register; he ordered a secretary to flip off the switch. 'What are they doing breaking into the President's funeral with an old Hollywood gang thriller?' he

[4] Note the repetition from the earlier crime. 'They' were responsible for the shooting.

demanded indignantly. Then it came to him that this gunman wasn't an Edward G. Robinson, and he hung up in such bewilderment that to this day he cannot remember to whom he had been speaking. (Apparently the other man had the same reaction; he never called back.) Byron White, preparing to leave his home for the rotunda, responded similarly; 'I wasn't sure this wasn't the late movie.' Dave Hackett witnessed the murder in Robert Kennedy's home, and his emotional temperature didn't fluctuate a jot: 'I didn't care. It was too grotesque for me to absorb.' Chief Justice Warren, scribbling his coda at his desk, was not a spectator himself, but his daughter Dorothy burst into his study crying, 'They just shot Oswald.' The Chief Judge laid aside his pencil and said waspishly, 'Honey, *don't* pay *any* attention to those wild rumours.'

When Justice Douglas arrived home he was accosted at the doorway with the news by his young wife, who seemed, if anything, more breathless than he. Douglas took a deep breath and said pensively, 'Well, it's just unbelievable.' To Joanie Douglas, who had been an onlooker moments before, it had not only been believable; it had actually been satisfying. As the assassin crumpled she had leaped up, shrieking jubilantly, 'Good! Give it to him again!' This was atypical. Inevitably a minority had been feeling the red pangs of blood lust since Friday, and before Oswald's death was officially pronounced Parkland's embattled switchboard operators were fielding calls from anonymities who advised them to 'kill him while you still have him there' or accused them of being 'nigger-lovers and murder-lovers'. For many the spirit of revenge was temporary. Joanie later flushed over what she described as her 'barbarism'. The Chicago survey disclosed that 89 per cent of the American people had hoped (and had trusted) that 'the man who killed' Kennedy would not be 'shot down or lynched'.

Among the dissenting 11 per cent, surprisingly, was Ruth Paine. Mrs Paine was frankly glad, and she didn't repent later either. But her reasons were personal. Her Quaker faith was unshaken; nevertheless she was convinced that 'this way would be so much easier for Marina'. Americans less solicitous of the assassin's widow were disapproving and dismayed. Later that afternoon, when he had had time to reflect upon the day's events, Robert Kennedy remarked to Nick Katzenbach, 'It's too bad about the shooting of that fellow in Dallas.'

At the time his Deputy Attorney General, who was among those who had seen the whole thing on television, had rendered an instantaneous, one-word, four-letter verdict. A choleric backlash was probably the most widespread repercussion among those who had been following the events in Texas. It assumed many forms: in the

Blue Room Lady Bird's chill was temporarily replaced by a silent, burning anger; Marie Fehmer crouched weeping over her television set—to Marie this was another indelible stain on the name of her home town—and in Parkland Bill Stinson, Connally's administrative assistant, whirled on the orderly who had told him, punched him in the stomach, and cried, 'Be quiet! Be quiet!' Galbraith reflected in the rotunda that 'in some ways' this was 'the most unforgivable thing of all'. Llewellyn Thompson saw the murder as a diplomatic catastrophe. It struck Thompson that the timing, coming 'just as the funeral was about to restore our foreign image', couldn't have been worse. Two of the Joint Chiefs felt the same way. Maxwell Taylor strolled into the Fish Room and saw Curtis E. LeMay gaping at the screen. The Air Force Chief of Staff blurted out, 'Look! They just shot Oswald!' and as the generals watched a video tape replay Taylor thought how 'lawlessness was damaging our world-wide reputation'. In her McComb Street apartment Mary McGrory thought to herself, *The Republic is finished. We'll never be the same. It's all over.* Pat Moynihan, the one Washingtonian who had distrusted the Dallas police force from the beginning, was in his Labour Department office on Pennsylvania Avenue. His phone rang, and his wife told him of the killing. Pat had a sudden, vivid impression of newspaper stories beginning, 'The alleged assassin was shot while escaping.' He reared back, kicked the wall as hard as he could, and started telephoning everyone he knew, bellowing incoherently into the instrument.[5]

In the Fish Room General Taylor had a second thought. 'I also felt sure,' he later said, 'that there would be suspicion that the killing of Oswald by Ruby had been done to suppress something'. That was a shattering understatement. For those who gave the matter any attention at all the suspicion, in the first hours after the basement murder, was a certainty. Jesse Curry's explanations seemed pitifully inadequate. Even after the facts were in, dregs of doubt remained. Early the following year the Anti-Defamation Committee of B'nai B'rith was to confirm the findings of the professional polls, reporting that a majority of Americans remained convinced that the two slayings 'were the result of organized plotting'. But on Sunday there was

[5] Minutes earlier Pat had concluded a brief WTOP-TV interview which, for millions in the national audience, became one of the weekend's most memorable moments. He had opened by observing that at the end of Camus' life Camus had decided the world was absurd, which, to a Christian, was unthinkable. Then he had mused of Kennedy, 'We all of us know down here that politics is a tough game. And I don't think there's any point in being Irish if you don't know that the world is going to break your heart eventually. I guess we thought we had a little more time.' His voice drifted off. Almost inaudibly he added, 'So did he.'

scarcely any minority to dissent. Conspiracy seemed to be the only reasonable deduction.

Indeed, the more a man knew about conspirators, the firmer his conviction was. In the West Wing lobby a Secret Service agent watched Ruby disappear and muttered tightly, 'That was the messenger.' Independently of one another the Service, the CIA, and J. Edgar Hoover all assumed a previous link between Ruby and Oswald. In the rotunda Douglas Dillon speculated about the identity of the people behind the double murder, and Ted Sorensen cried rhetorically, 'This makes it worse. My *god*, when will it *end*?' In Dallas U.S. Attorney Barefoot Sanders was driving his wife and Judge Sarah Hughes to Love Field en route to Washington for the funeral. Sanders had just left them when his car radio blared out the first bulletin, and he raced directly back to his office, officially bringing the FBI into the case on the jurisdictional grounds—incredible to a layman, but legally above reproach—that Oswald's civil rights had been violated. The Secret Service had already plunged into its own inquiry; Forrest Sorrels was on the telephone with Jerry Behn, discussing how the Ruby–Oswald connection could be quickly uncovered. Behn said, 'It's a plot.' Sorrels said, 'Of course.'

Ironically, neither Oswald's wife nor his mother witnessed his final appearance. The two women had been shunted from hotel to hotel by Secret Service agents. That morning they were first in the Executive Inn and then at the Six Flags, between Dallas and Fort Worth. According to Marguerite's later recollection, her daughter-in-law said, 'Mama, I want to see Lee.' The older woman explained that 'She was hoping Lee was coming on the picture, like he did.' Marguerite's reply was negative, however: 'I said, "Oh, honey, let's turn the television off. The same thing over and over." And I turned the television off. So Marina and I did not see what happened to my son.'

Robert Oswald did not see it either, but he was the first member of the assassin's family to hear what had happened; Mike Howard, a Secret Service agent, took him aside and told him the news had just come over the radio. The Oswalds are not an attractive group, and the more closely one examines their conduct that weekend, the less attractive they become. Nevertheless Robert somehow stands apart. He was not always successful in his attempts 'to arrange my thoughts and my fears', as he put it in his makeshift diary, a ringed notebook. He did, however, manage a certain sombre dignity. Driving straight to Parkland, where a guard frisked him for weapons ('This I did not mind since he did not know me at all,' he confided to the notebook; Robert was no Lee), he was led into one of the emergency area's cubicles. An orderly later remembered him as 'a slender man wearing grey unpressed pants, with a matching coat lying on the table. He was wearing a white shirt but no tie. He seemed like a nice enough fellow.' An agent entered and said, 'Robert, I am sorry, but Lee is dead.'

Robert sobbed into his hands. The world knew Lee as a killer, but to his older brother he would always be the weedy little boy who had enjoyed playing hide-and-seek with cap pistols, styling himself as 'Two-Gun Pete'. The fact that the little boy had grown up, acquired two real guns, and killed a President with one and a policeman with the other could not alter the recollection. While Robert waited there for a minister a stranger remarked, 'Violence breeds violence.' The assassin's brother replied shakily, 'Does that justify anything—or all of this?' In his diary he observed, 'I do not recall if he answered that or not.' It was, of course, unanswerable. Robert did not bear a popular name. Though blameless himself, for two days and two nights he had lived with the fact that he would carry the stigma of his brother's guilt to his own grave; already other Oswald families were petitioning courts to permit them to call themselves Smith or Jones. The best he could do was try to carry himself like a man. He did remarkably well. He lost his temper with only one person, his mother. When Marguerite heard of Lee's death, she reached the extraordinary conclusion that he had been acting as a U.S. agent. To Robert's undisguised disgust she announced that since Lee had given his life for his country, he should be buried with full honours 'in the Arlington Cemetery'. He said, 'Shut up, Mother.'

Jacqueline Kennedy had appeared on the North Portico, a child in either hand. The President's son and daughter did not have to come out this way. They could have been driven out the south grounds and up Constitution, and before her departure for Texas their mother would have insisted upon that; at Andrews Field three days earlier she had forbidden John to leave the helicopter because photographers were present. But today and tomorrow were to be a season apart in her life. The shock of that brief scene was immense. In that one instant she revealed to the great audience the full measure of its loss. Old Guard infantrymen in dress blues and snowy gloves flanked the fatherless First Family, straining at attention. Caroline, her eyes hazy in reflection, gently rested her black headband against her mother's slim waist. John squirmed, wriggled free, and clenched his tiny fist behind his back in a crimping gesture which brought a stab of pain to those who remembered his father's restless right hand. Few saw it, however, for nearly every eye was upon the widow. Transfigured beneath the North Portico's hanging lantern she awaited the procession, her swollen eyes fixed on the caisson and the six matched horses. Her expression of ineffable tragedy was, in that flicker of a moment, indelibly etched upon the national conscience; in a survey of New England college students conducted later that week the investigators found that 'attention to Mrs Kennedy's actions and deportment bordered on the obsessive'.

This was her first exposure to it. It was also the first sunlight she had seen since Dallas, but she did not blink. Steadfast and still, she awaited the signal to move, her lashes heavy and her lovely mouth drawn down in a classic curve of grief. Immediately behind her, vigilant as always, stood Robert Kennedy. The cameras were frozen on the motionless widow, and omitting those who were reading newspaper accounts or talking to friends, nearly everyone in the United States was watching Mrs Kennedy. By its own account, a minimum of 95 per cent of the adult population was peering at television or listening to radio accounts.[6] To the Americans must be added all of Europe and those parts of Asia which were periodically reached by relay satellite. Even Russia had announced that the Soviet Union would televise the funeral, including the Mass in St Matthew's. By Sunday noon the U.S.A. and most of the civilized world had become a kind of closed-circuit hookup. Nothing existed except this one blinding spotlight.

Not only had commercials been cancelled; such routine reports as weather, newscasts, and sports were unmentioned. The National Football League was playing its full schedule, but the country was unaware of it. The communication industry's coverage was unprecedented. It was also superb. Spending three million dollars on equipment—a figure that did not include the loss in advertising revenue—CBS, NBC, and ABC had supplemented the Chesapeake & Potomac's outlay with over eleven miles of video and audio cables. No single network could have done this alone; cameras had to be pooled at key locations. The rotunda, for example, was assigned to NBC and shared by ABC and CBS.

Largely because of the celebrity of Chet Huntley and David Brinkley, NBC's audience outnumbered those of the other two networks combined; consequently its decision to keep its rotunda crews on duty throughout the coming night, when ordinary Americans circled the catafalque, meant that for over half the viewers there was no letup from 6.59 Sunday morning till 1.18 a.m. Tuesday —a forty-two hour telethon. In irresponsible hands this could have

[6] Every professional opinion surveyor agrees that only under exceptional circumstances are more than 80 per cent ever aware of any event. For example, only 88 per cent of Americans listened to *any* broadcast during FDR's three-day funeral. Contrast this with the 99 per cent of Athens—not even an American city—in late November 1963.

been dangerous. The possibilities were Orwellian. Art Kane, a short, nervous, thirty-three-year-old CBS producer, was co-ordinating forty-one pool cameras in twenty-two locations from a 30-by-10 feet electronics control booth under the Capitol steps. (At the eye of the storm, Kane didn't hear about the killing of Oswald until it was stale news.) Brinkley later calculated that 'the shocked and stunned nation was listening to six people at most, us commentators. It would have been so easy to start a phony rumour that would never die, that would be alive fifty years later.' Fortunately, the half-dozen broadcasters took their responsibilities extremely seriously. There were few sermons about Oswald, and the remarks about extremism were carefully worded. Each man tried to avoid exciting, provoking, or irritating his listeners. Of course, personal control wasn't always possible. Veteran commentators knew that they wouldn't be able to trust their voices during the rotunda ceremonies or the funeral. Therefore they let events unfold of themselves. Sometimes as long as fifteen minutes would pass with no comment whatever.

There were, to be sure, some lapses. As if to make up for these silences, other details were later inserted, sometimes needlessly. At one point the new President was seen rubbing his fingers. In light of the fact that he had just been observed shaking a great many hands, it was natural; elaboration was unnecessary. Nevertheless a newscaster spoke up with detailed descriptions of minor medical treatments the new President had once received for his palm. And undoubtedly mass media inspired a number of eerie side effects. One writer watched broadcasts closely and then held a group of distinguished men rapt with sensational accounts of 'what Jackie told me about Dallas'. He hadn't seen her since her return from Texas, but they were months finding that out. Other spectators insisted that they had seen things which could not possibly have happened, and this phenomenon became a genuine problem during the investigation of the Warren Commission and the inquiry which led to this book. Texas witnesses were easily muddled; they had difficulty distinguishing between events they had actually witnessed and scenes they had watched on their sets.

Yet singling them out would be unfair, because the same thing happened in the capital. Repeatedly one encountered intelligent men and women who couldn't possibly have met between Thursday and Tuesday but who *had* observed each other on television—and were convinced that they had talked together. Barney Ross actually heard himself being interviewed over radio. *Monitor* had taped sessions with members of the old PT 109 crew, and Kennedy's executive officer naturally came first. As Barney wearily trudged into his front hall in Bethesda every set in the house was on, blaring out his husky

Illinois drawl in concert—his own version of JFK's heroism twenty years and three months ago. He leaned against the jamb. If this could happen, he reflected, anything could. And he was right. In another national emergency the implications could be frightening. The United States had become the victim of voluntary hypnosis. There seemed to be no way for Americans to avoid concentration on the centre of the national stage. Volume knobs were turned up full everywhere—on the Presidential aircraft, at the LBJ Ranch, in Hyannis Port, in living and drawing and bedrooms, in hotels and motels and bars, on every floor of the White House and the Elms.

Frequently those who had deliberately absented themselves from the ceremonies, suspecting that the emotional stress would be too much for them, were subjected to an even greater strain than those who went. Most of the participants were to be on the outskirts, but the Zoomar lens of the camera eye took viewers right there. That was the experience of Dick Goodwin, who had elected to stay behind in the mansion while his colleagues were on the Hill, and of a Kennedy friend who watched a set at Butler Aviation, across the Potomac. Joseph P. Kennedy, propped on pillows, saw his daughter-in-law and his grandchildren and then, at 4.21 p.m., stared as his wife, youngest son, and Eunice boarded a Jetstar at Otis for the capital. John and Joyce Macy had agreed that the services on the Hill would be too much for them. Leaving Lafayette Park, they drove home across Memorial Bridge. They thought they could bear to listen to their car radio, however, and they erred; with the first strains of the Navy Band on the east steps of the Capitol Chairman Macy drew over to the side of the road and buried his face on his steering wheel.

None of official Washington was able to dodge the impact of the drama, for that matter, because reruns of the day's highlights—and, next day, of the funeral's—were endless. Just as young Caroline Hallett had been the first member of her family to identify Oswald Friday, so were other children, or disabled relatives, or neighbours, or even total strangers vigilant and eager to relay descriptions of close-ups to those who had merely stood on tiptoe on the outer fringes of the throng beneath the soaring rotunda dome. Justices Goldberg and White didn't see much on the Hill November 24; their chief memories were to be drawn from subsequent video tapes. Ed Guthman, like Dick Goodwin, had stayed away, watching the passing caisson from a Justice Department balcony—and watching also, as the gun carriage rolled slowly past, the dismay on his son's face as the boy, for the first time in his life, saw his strong father cry. Ed thought that would be the end of it. The coffin had gone, the cortège had passed. But like everyone else who had been close, or had felt close, to the President, the Guthmans went home and, in Mrs Guthman's phrase, 'remained glued to television'. Moreover, you didn't have to be a member of the government to feel that tug. It wasn't necessary to stand on Pennsylvania Avenue and see the Stars and Stripes flutter over the coffin for a man to weep before his children. He could sob sprawled on a couch, or in a leatherette rumpus room chair. It was happening to heads of families in every part of the country, ranging from a third of the anti-Kennedy Southerners to nearly two-thirds of the pro-Kennedy Northerners, with the national average well over 50 per cent.

Therefore flight was impossible. Every hatch was battened down, every roadblock impassable. An entire nation was trapped in grief. 'What has happened,' a network commentator said a half-hour after the Oswald shooting, 'has been too much, too ugly, and too fast.' The velocity of transmission, moving at the speed of light; the surfeit of horror; and the sense of shared sorrow bound the American people together more closely than any other nation since the beginning of man. The number of absentees was phenomenally small. Abe Zapruder, the camera enthusiast, was one of them. In the 8.3 seconds required for his colour film to record 152 historic frames—from the moment Zapruder saw the President had been shot once to the disappearance of the car from his camera's view—Abe had absorbed all he could take. He had become a casualty, one of the weekend's walking wounded; he couldn't bear to watch anything on television. There were a few others like him, yet they were never more than 5 per cent of the adult population Sunday afternoon. The average American, whatever his race, religious convictions, or politics, was gaping, anaesthetized by what after two full days he still felt could not be happening.

It was happening; or rather, to be precise, it was about to happen. As the clock over Lyndon Johnson's vacant Vice Presidential chair read 1.08, Angie Duke's protocol officers finished designating a great circle in the unlit hall beneath the rotunda's 183-foot canopy, segregating roped-off areas for the Supreme Court, Cabinet, Congressional leadership, White House staff, friends of the family, and the family itself. John McCone was having a final word with the three eulogists. They were inattentive, and Mike Mansfield was particularly tense. He had a polished draft ready, but though he had tried again to read aloud to his office mirror he still broke down in the fourth paragraph: 'There was a father with a little boy and a little girl and the joy of each in the other and, in a moment, it was no more. And so, she took a ring from her finger and placed it in his hands.' As typed, Mike's encomium ended with a tribute to John

Kennedy's gifts and asked rhetorically, 'Will we have, now, the sense and the responsibility to take them? Will we take them before it is too late?' Dissatisfied, Mike struck out the second sentence and uncertainly substituted, shakily, 'I pray to God that we will shall and—Under God—we will shall—we will!' In a firmer hand he scrawled across the left ear of the first page, 'To Jacqueline Kennedy with affection, love, respect—Mike Mansfield, Majority Leader, U.S. Senate.'

Waiting for her in the Senate Press Gallery, Joe Alsop was for the moment transformed:

> I love you, as I loved him—I hope you won't mind my saying it—and I wish now that one might send an enormous box of love like a box of flowers. But one can't; there is only one thing I can send—a strange thing to send at such a time, and yet deserving to be sent—I mean my thanks and my congratulations. To play a high role of history perfectly in a great moment of history—to be always warm, always true, always yourself under the glare of history—is not an easy thing to do, to put it mildly indeed.

Alsop wondered 'whether or when I have *ever* felt anything at all before this; for nothing has been quite like this'.

Once there had been something close. When Abraham Lincoln had become the first President to lie in state beneath this frescoed dome, which he himself had ordered completed in the bleakest days of the Civil War as a symbol of the enduring Union, a chronicler had described the spectacle as 'half circus, half heartbreak'. The hearse had been 'large and horrible' with 'black tassels and flounces that twitched and rocked'. That coffin had been mahogany, too, and then, as now, the mass of mourners had been unsettling: 'To enter the creeping lines at sun-up meant reaching the coffin five hours later.' But Kennedy's anonymous mourners were to be more orderly—in 1865 'The crush trembled always at the edge of riot. Hundreds were injured'—and as a hero's charger Black Jack was more splendid by far than Old Bob, the ageing bay who was led riderless far behind Lincoln's coffin. Furthermore, the excess of Victorian crepe had been dispelled. Today it was draped with decorum. A century earlier everything 'seemed to have been wounded and . . . bandaged . . . in black'.

All the same, the elements of carnival were there today. Mac Kilduff turned away several 'real creeps', including a man who insisted that he had been 'the President's personal veterinarian'; and Colonel Miller quietly barred the door to a Congressman and twenty of his constituents. Taken as a group, Congressmen left an unfortunate impression on the Kennedy men inside the rotunda. Red

Fay noticed several 'pushing against the ropes to have their pictures taken, and I felt very critical towards them, particularly those who had been political enemies of the President'. Two representatives who didn't make it stood immediately behind Jerry Wiesner, Mike Feldman, and Fred Holborn. In loud voices they wondered to each other who these 'young whipper-snappers' could be; then they speculated over whether or not it would be good politics for Johnson to go through with Kennedy's speaking engagements. In another segment of the huge circle, according to Galbraith's journal, 'The congressmen who were immediately adjacent to us seemed principally concerned in their conversation with whether or not they were to be invited to the funeral next day.'

Doubtless the leaderless Presidential aides were hypersensitive and alert for slights; it didn't take much to offend them. Galbraith himself outraged everyone within earshot by announcing that he had written 'a very good draft overnight' for the new President's address to the joint session, and when Walter Heller reported a 'fantastic' conversation—'LBJ tapped me on the chest with his finger and said, "I want you and your liberal friends to know that I'm no conservative; I'm a New Deal Democrat" '—Heller's friends turned away. His eyes glistening, McNamara described the progress at Arlington —'It will be almost a shrine'—and added, 'Nothing will be quite the same with him gone. Among other things he reached the hearts of people around the world with a quality and a style and a sophistication which epitomized the age and the times. Lyndon Johnson won't be able to approximate it.' Orville Freeman said, 'We're fortunate to have a strong man like Lyndon in the driver's seat, though.' McNamara nodded. Those around them said nothing.

From outside they heard the vibrant voice of a young Army captain. 'Mr O'Donnell!' he called. 'Mr O'Brien! Mr Sorensen! . . .'

The traditional state funeral plan called for a military honour guard on the east side of the Capitol, a double line of uniformed men who stood on every other step, facing one another and saluting the coffin as it passed between them. Sargent Shriver had substituted the thirty-six aides who had been closest to the President, and the captain's roster was a muster of New Frontiersmen: 'Mr Bundy! Mr Salinger! Secretary Fay! Secretary Reed! Mr Dungan! Dr Wiesner! Mr O'Leary! Mr Hatcher! Mr Schlesinger! Mr Feldman! Mr Holborn! Dr Burkley! Mr Kilduff! Mr White! Mr Powers! Mr Reardon! Mr McNally . . .'

They assembled in a bunch. The captain withdrew and Jack McNally replaced him. As Special Assistant in charge of staff administration, Jack felt that he should take over here. He was all business. 'All right, now,' he said, briskly, 'we'll line up out here in the order of rank.' Sorensen stared at him; the others looked around in bewilderment. '*Rank?*' someone repeated uncertainly. Everyone knew there was no such thing as rank among the Special Assistants. Had there been, Jack himself would have been at the bottom. O'Donnell, who would have been among those at the top, said wryly, 'It took the assassination of the President to put McNally in charge of the White House.' As Jack began assigning positions, Sorensen dryly made a mental note: To have seniority, it appeared, one must first be an Irishman.

McNally finished and placed himself tenth. Unconsciously assuming the stance of attention, they looked out over one another's shoulders. Red Fay and Jim Reed, side by side near the bottom, were remembering Lieutenant Commander Tom Warfield, the martinet on the PT base on Rendova. Sorensen was examining the façade of the Senate Office Building; he glanced at his feet and realized that he had stood on this very spot during Kennedy's inaugural address. Ted Reardon, who had been with the President longer than anyone here, recalled bounding up these steps with twenty-nine-year-old Congressman John Kennedy in January 1947. That had been the first time for both of them, and they had been young and exuberant. In a few minutes, Reardon thought numbly, Kennedy would be entering the Capitol for the last time. And in Muggsy O'Leary's mind there was a picture of the slender Senator with the bad back painfully ascending the stairs five years ago.

Mac Bundy shivered. It was cold. 'And somehow,' he wrote afterwards, 'it was good to stand and wait.'

They listened intently. The cortège would have to wind around the Capitol's East Wing; they would hear it before they saw it, and presently they did hear something. From the far end of Pennsylvania Avenue came a faint, unfamiliar, haunting sound:

Boom Boom Boom, Drrr
Boom Boom Boom, Drrr
Boom Boom Boom, Drrr
Boom: Boom-boom-boom

It was repeated over and over, growing more distinct as it approached them, until even those who were unprepared for it and had only read of it in books knew they were listening to the broken roll, the dreadful stutter of muffled drums.

Drums are muffled by loosening the tension on each drumhead thus deadening the resonance. The two bass and sixteen snare drummers had completed this task before falling in outside the White House, and had been holding their sticks with practised ease when

Mrs Kennedy shepherded her children into the limousine outside the portico. Accompanying them were Attorney General Kennedy, the new President and Mrs Johnson on the jump seats, and, somewhere in the back seat, a small and astonishingly mobile pair of white gloves.

The gloves belonged to John F. Kennedy, Jr. Miss Shaw had put them on upstairs, and his mother had noticed them and approved. Next time she looked they were gone. 'Where are your gloves, John?' she asked, and he produced them. She helped with the snaps, glanced way, glanced back, and started. No gloves.

'John, put your gloves on,' she said.

'He doesn't have to wear gloves,' Robert Kennedy said.

She thought he did; again the cycle was repeated, and this time he couldn't find them. They had been confiscated by the Attorney General. Gloves, he thought, were for sissies; he had been quietly urging John to peel them off, and rather than upset her with an argument he had waited until no one was looking and slipped them in his own pocket. He assured her that 'Boys don't wear gloves'.

She turned away, convincd though with trepidation, for if he was right, every marching unit in the cortège, including the Joint Chiefs of Staff, was effete. 'Dress w/white gloves' had been specified, and Major General Wehle raised an immaculate white hand to signal the start of the procession. As military commander of the nation's capital, he led it. Behind him were the drummers; an eighty-nine-man naval company, their fixed bayonets flashing in the sunlight; various clergymen; the Chiefs; Ted Clifton, Godfrey McHugh, and Taz Shepard; the horse-drawn gun carriage bearing the coffin; John Kennedy's Presidential flag; the riderless horse; Lieutenant Bird's casket team; and the widow's limousine and nine other cars carrying Kennedys, Fitzgeralds, Auchinclosses, Shrivers, Smiths, Lawfords, and their children. Behind the last bumper the White House press corps straggled in disorderly formation. Marching police and three automobiles brought up the rear.

Down the long drive they moved beneath the naked trees, and the fifty colourful state flags, ranged on either side, dipped in homage to the simple caisson; Wehle pivoted east on Pennsylvania, south for the three-block jog around the Treasury Building, and then east once more on Pennsylvania, wheeling elaborately by the Hotel Washington and striking out towards the Capitol dome eighteen blocks away. Usually the sounds of marchers on that street are lost in choruses of gay shouts, and today the crowd was enormous, but between the long drum rolls you could hear the precise thump of sailors' boots, the irregular tattoo of the Joint Chiefs, hopelessly out of step, and the clatter of hoofs. Black Jack had never been so wild. He threatened to break away at any moment, and his spectacular prancing was ominous. Yet the matched greys drawing the gun carriage were almost as menacing. Sergeant Thomas Setterberg was leading them on an ordinarily placid gelding. Despite Setterberg's mouth-spreading curb rein, the horse was shying badly, and the Sergeant was terrified that he might trample the men ahead underfoot.

In the cars scarcely anyone spoke. In the second limousine Shriver and Ethel Kennedy did, because they were watching over Bobby Shriver and two of Ethel's boys—the Attorney General was determined that his children should never forget these days—and from the front seat Agent Wells marvelled at how gently Ethel spoke of their uncle's death and how deftly Shriver fielded other questions, explaining that the reversed boots were for a warrior killed in battle and, observing young Bobby Kennedy's anxiety, diverting him by describing the functions of the government buildings they were passing and the symbolism of the statuary in front of them. Wells had passed the statues a thousand times and had never thought about it. To his astonishment he found the ride educational.

Adults in other limousines brooded or stared out moodily at the spectators, who moodily stared back. To Lieutenant Bird the stillness was almost unbearable: 'As the guards along the kerbs saluted the colours over the casket you could see the long faces of the people on the sidewalk, trying not to break down and failing over and over. One old man put his hand over his heart, and then his face screwed up and he clapped his other hand over his eyes.' Block by block the hush deepened. Sergeant Setterberg thought it 'spooky'. General Clifton remembered one afternoon in 1944 when, driving ahead of combat troops in a jeep, he had alighted and found that he seemed to be the only man in Florence. For three hours he had walked clear across the abandoned city, yet it seemed to him that 'there was more noise in Florence then than there was in Washington on this march. All you could hear was the drums and the clump of the horses.' Up ahead General Wehle heard 'only the drums, the terrible drums':

Boom Boom Boom, Drrr
Boom Boom Boom, Drrr . . .

'Oh, Lyndon,' Mrs Kennedy said suddenly, breaking for the first and last time her vow never again to call him by his first name, 'what an awful way for you to come in'.

The new President said nothing. Throughout the ride both he and Lady Bird were speechless. Robert Kennedy was also silent, comforting Caroline and watching Black Jack's fearful writhing. After the incident of the gloves the President's children were subdued, and to the best of everyone's recollection, including Bill Greer behind the wheel and Jerry Behn beside him, Jacqueline Kennedy's consoling remark was the only comment in the lead limousine.

Because those in the procession were looking ahead to the Capitol, and because the networks' pool cameras were trained on the marchers, neither the principals nor the national audience saw the most dramatic moment in the forty-minute cavalcade. According to the Shriver–Dungan plan, the last two units behind the gun carriage were to be the policemen and '[13] Other Mourners'. For eleven blocks the only walking pedestrians had been the correspondents. At Ninth and Pennsylvania, beside the FBI entrance to the Justice Building, this abruptly changed. The crowd which had been left behind surged into the street and pressed forward. The marching District policemen dropped out and, locking arms, formed a barrier across the street. It was pointless to follow the cortège, they shouted. Capitol Plaza was already packed solid. That was true, but reason was pointless here. It was like arguing with an incoming tide, for the entire area from Justice to the Treasury had become black with straining people. The mob was the quietest ever to break a police line, and the break was so quick and effortless that none of the riders up ahead suspected anything unusual. The spectacle was, in fact, spectacular; climbing the equestrian statue opposite the National Archives, three of the routed policemen attempted to estimate the size of the multitude. The best guess was that John Kennedy was being followed by a hundred thousand 'Other Mourners'.

General Wehle led the caisson around the Senate side of the Capitol and halted it beneath the east steps. The chief mourners stood by the bottom step, awaiting the sounding of honours. To the north, in Union Station Park, an artillery battalion commander held one hand aloft and listened intently to his headset while a captain in Capitol Plaza told him to stand by. Nearby another officer shouted 'Pre-sent!' As a rising wind fingered the casket flag the captain, allowing for a three-second echo delay, ordered 'Fire!' In the next moment the other officer cried, '*Arms!*' the first shot of the twenty-one-gun salute thundered overhead, rifles were raised, stiff hands touched the bills of caps, and the first note of the Navy Band came through sweet and clear.

The Band sounded ruffles and flourishes, and then, with the battery firing each five seconds:

Hail to the Chief who in Triumph advances!
Honor'd and bless'd be the evergreen pine. . . .

For millions this was the breaking point. Even the tone-deaf knew there was something different about the Navy's rendition. The Presidential march is usually a jaunty tune, played 120 beats to the minute. Now the country heard it as a dirge adagio, 86 beats to the minute, slower than a man's heartbeat. Each soaring strain was drawn out tragically, and when the last measure had been played—as Lieutenant Bird's casket team unbuckled the coffin and the wind-whipped flag—the band played in the same anguished measure the hymn which, to anyone who had been in naval service, was even harder to bear:

Eternal Father, strong to save.
Whose arm doth bind the restless wave,
Who bidd'st the mighty ocean deep
Its own appointed limits keep:
O hear us when we cry to Thee
For those in peril on the sea.

And one man, a former seaman, heard another line:

O God, protect the men who fly
Through lonely ways beneath the sky.

He stood a little apart, shoulders hunched, his hand worrying his hair, looking off in the distance, then down at young John. With Caroline and the President's widow he moved slowly up the steps, just behind the struggling casket team. Robert Kennedy did not know they were struggling, and the watching nation had no inkling of it, but they were really going through excruciating torture. Each member of the reinforced, eight-man team was near panic, and their lieutenant, holding the rear, wasn't at all sure they would not founder before they reached the top of that great marble mountain. Afterwards the weight of President Kennedy's coffin became a matter of dispute. The undertaker said it couldn't possibly weigh more than five hundred pounds. The estimates of others ranged from nine hundred to twelve hundred, but even the highest figure seemed absurdly low to the men who carried it, and since each of them was a veteran of over a thousand Arlington funerals their ordeal is inexplicable unless one assumes, as one must, that the answer lay within themselves.

Behind them Seaman Ed Nemuth dipped the great Presidential standard forward and arched his back to counterbalance it; the tip just passed beneath the top of the portal. It was too heavy for the stand inside, so he held it, standing stiffly as the casket team eased the coffin on the deck of the original Lincoln catafalque. The honour guard filed in, and the circle of mourners was complete. Furtively they eyed one another for signs of approaching hysteria. The accumulation of sleeplessness, pills, and shock—culminating, for those who comprehended it, in the shooting of Oswald—was evident; Mac Kilduff had collapsed on the steps as the President's children passed him, and the music had taken its toll of everyone. Jean Smith thought nothing could be harder to endure than 'Hail to the Chief'. Both she and Eunice were anxious about their sister Pat, the most highstrung of the Kennedys. They stood nearby, ready to help her, while Pat herself watched her brother's widow. *If Jackie can do it,* she thought, *I can.*

Jacqueline Kennedy was preoccupied with her son. In church even Caroline had been a pew-banger at his age. John had survived one Mass earlier in the fall, but then she had been able to entertain him with illustrated books, and her husband had been there on the other side. She was afraid the child wasn't going to make it here. She was right; ceremonies had scarcely started before he began to squirm and ask questions. Miss Shaw whispered, 'This is no place for a little boy.' Clint Hill and the kiddie detail helped her whisk him away to the Speaker's offices, an austere, rather intimidating suite furnished with red plush and much Victorian furniture. That didn't seem to be a place for a little boy either, but at least he could shout all he liked, be bounced on Clint's knee, and watch Dr Martin Sweig, McCormack's assistant, crawl around on the floor with a toy tank furnished by the agents.

Sweig was a collector of tiny flags. From a wooden stand the ensigns of all UN nations were arranged in a fan, and he handed his young visitor the Stars and Stripes. John said he wanted another 'for my sister'. Uneasily the agents saw his finger hover over Cuba's colours; then he chose Pakistan's. He told Miss Shaw the Union Jack was hers, but none of the others interested him. Wandering into the next room, he studied a display of governmental flags and pointed to one. No one there knew what it was, which isn't strange, because it wasn't anyone's flag. Years ago Congress had debated giving each Senator and Representative his own ensign. The resolution had been shelved, but the little flag for Representatives was still here. With its blue field and circle of yellow stars it bore a strong resemblance to the Presidential flag, which is undoubtedly the reason it attracted John's attention.

'Can I have that one?' he asked. 'I want to take it home to my daddy.'

'You certainly can,' Sweig said unevenly, and handed it to him.

In the rotunda, meanwhile, his father was being eulogized. Mansfield spoke, Warren spoke, McCormack spoke. Inevitably the circle of listeners was captious. No one criticized McCormack, because he didn't say anything, but the Chief Justice's strong denunciation of hatemongering had a mixed reception. Robert Kennedy thought talk of hatred inappropriate here, and Mac Bundy felt that 'the dominant meaning of the tragedy is that it was senseless. . . .' But Galbraith saw the point: 'He said the one thing that needed to be said: namely, that while few will advocate assassination, many will contribute to the climate which causes men to contemplate it.'

Mike Mansfield, however, was by far the most controversial of the three. Like Warren he grasped the essence of the Dallas crime—'the bigotry, the hatred, prejudice, and the arrogance which converged in that moment of horror to strike him down'—but in its imagery and high diction his address was altogether different. It was, indeed, an authentic masterpiece which went unappreciated, like so many great speeches, at the time of its delivery. Because of the dreadful acoustics many did not even hear it. Most of those who did had been raised in the tradition of understatement, and his frankness and emotional overtones shocked them. Douglas Dillon cringed inwardly; David Ormsby-Gore thought it 'absolutely appalling'. Scarcely anyone there realized that it was a tribute to a President *and* the president's First Lady. Those who were watching her thought Mansfield was being needlessly cruel to her, but they hadn't been in that car, they hadn't seen the blood, they hadn't known the antiseptic nightmare of Trauma Room No. 1, they were strangers to violent death. Only Jacqueline Kennedy could judge Mike Mansfield, and she couldn't believe what she was hearing; she didn't know a eulogy could be this magnificent; looking up into his suffering eyes and his gaunt mountain man's face, she thought his profile was like a sixteenth-century El Greco. To her the speech itself was as eloquent as a Pericles oration, or Lincoln's letter to the mother who had lost five sons in battle. It didn't turn aside from the ghastly reality—'It was,' she thought, 'the one thing that said what had happened.' He finished, and with his vibrant voice still echoing in the dome above he came over and handed her the manuscript. She said, 'You anticipate me. How did you know I wanted it?' Mansfield bowed his head. 'I didn't. I just wanted you to have it.'

Her wreath already stood by the coffin. Now Lyndon Johnson stepped forward for the ritualistic wreath-placing by the President of the United States. His floral tribute was huge, brilliantly green with red and white carnations, mounted on a stand held from behind by a lanky Army sergeant 1st class. As Johnson faced it and glided forward, the soldier retreated, matching his steps with the President's. The odd two-man waltz ended; the sergeant swiftly departed. Johnson paused in momentary prayer and returned to his place. Except for the muted sobbing of the sergeant—two colonels were leading him to an ante-room—the great rotunda was silent.

The plans had ended here. The fourteen-minute ceremony was over, and suddenly Mrs Kennedy, who had felt faint and was swaying slightly, realized everyone was waiting for her to leave first.

She wasn't quite ready. Facing Robert Kennedy she asked softly, 'Can I say good-bye?' He nodded once, and she took Caroline by the hand. She felt rather awkward, but she didn't want it to end just yet. To Caroline she whispered, 'We're going to go say good-bye to Daddy, and we're going to kiss him good-bye, and tell Daddy how much we love him and how much we'll always miss him.' Mother and daughter moved forward, the widow gracefully, the child watching carefully to do as she did. Jacqueline Kennedy knelt. Caroline knelt. 'You know. You just kiss,' whispered Mrs Kennedy. Eyes closed, they leaned over to brush their lips against the flag. Caroline's small gloved hand crept underneath, to be nearer, and in that single instant an entire nation was brought to its knees. The audience in the rotunda, the national audience, those who until now had been immune, those who had endured everything else were stricken in a fraction of a second. A chord deep in the hearts of men had been touched, and Justice Douglas felt paralysed, and General Clifton, half blinded by his own tears, looked across the circle and saw the Joint Chiefs standing at attention, their faces set and their cheeks streaming. Still clutching Caroline, she rose and stepped towards the door with simple majesty. The others stumbled after her.

Outside in the pellucid sunlight they beheld for the first time the size and character of the waiting crowd. Clifton looked down on 'a sea of faces—I felt as though the whole land was alive with people'. Albert Thomas explored it less out of curiosity than a sheer need to do something. That final, unexpected scene in the rotunda had hit him with tremendous impact; his throat was so thick he thought he was strangling. He found the gigantic complex of the Capitol surrounded. The overflow spilled down the streets between the Congressional office buildings, the Supreme Court, the Library of Congress, and the Folger Library, and to the west it ran from the Botanic Gardens to the Taft Tower. Shortly before the ceremonies commentators had briefly announced that the rotunda would be open to the public. Since then the traffic had been growing progressively more heavy on every bridge and highway leading to the District. On New York Avenue cars were bumper to bumper; by dusk that line would stretch all the way to Baltimore, thirty miles away. Of those already there a newscaster reported that they were 'young, people mostly in their early twenties', and Byron White was impressed by the number of students in college sweaters, some of them carrying textbooks.

On the sidewalk, by the waiting limousines, Mrs Kennedy stepped over to Mrs Johnson. She said, 'Lady Bird, you must come to see me soon, and we'll talk about you moving in.' Taken aback, the new First Lady replied, 'Now there's one thing I want to say about that—I can go and wait till whenever you're ready.' As she recalled later, the widow smiled faintly and said to her, 'Any time after tomorrow. I won't have anything to do after that.'

At 2.19 p.m. she entered her car and left the Hill, and six minutes later Frank McGee of NBC, who had withheld the news until now, confirmed that Lee Oswald had died. Jacqueline Kennedy hadn't even known he had been shot. The murder of the assassin, she thought, was 'just one more awful thing'.

The State Department, watchdogs of proper form, wavered significantly in its plans for the eminent guests who would be arriving that evening. Clearly there would have to be some sort of reception for them after the funeral. Dean Rusk first thought he would act as their host. It was tactfully pointed out to him that he was not a head of state. Neither was the Attorney General, but Rusk and Under Secretary Alexis Johnson, still living in the immediate past, decided that Robert Kennedy ought to receive them. By Sunday State had accepted the new President as President; he would meet the visitors at the department. Then Jacqueline Kennedy, at Bundy's suggestion, sent word that she wanted them at the White House. It had never crossed Alexis Johnson's mind that she would do it—'It seemed so far above and beyond the call of duty.' But the diplomatic gains would be enormous, and so two occasions were scheduled, one for each administration.

Departing the Hill as the public advanced on it, the two resumed work in the White House and the Executive Office Building. There is a fine architectural justice in this. Mrs Kennedy sat upstairs in the beautiful white mansion while Johnson prowled the corridors of the awful but functional EOB. When he entered his office after the rotunda ceremony, his first act was to telephone Nick Katzenbach. He wanted a report on Oswald. Katzenbach assured him that Jack Miller, the head of Justice's Criminal Division, was flying to Dallas, and that the FBI had formally entered the case. At three o'clock Henry Cabot Lodge and John McCone opened the President's first extensive briefing on Vietnam. Later in the day there was some discussion over which foreign visitors the President should see tomorrow; really it was a jurisdictional dispute between George Ball and Mac Bundy over who should draw up the list. The President settled it (in Bundy's favour), and at 5.15 he was introduced to the wonders of the federal budget—while Kennedy's financial advisers were introduced to the wonders of Lyndon Johnson. At noon Kermit

Gordon, the Budget Director, had conferred briefly with him. Now Gordon returned with Secretary Dillon, Under Secretary Fowler, and Walter Heller. They wanted his support of Kennedy's $11.5 billion tax cut, and they wanted him to understand that the new budget was in the final stages of preparation. To reach Congress in time, it had to be in the hands of the Government Printing Office within the next two or three weeks. Johnson was for the tax bill. Moreover, he instantly invested the budget with political import.

'Johnson's budget' was to become his first Presidential triumph. Determined to capture the support of as many businessmen as possible, he felt that the quickest way was to show himself as a tiger fighting spendthrifts. By the new year everyone outside the Executive Department believed that President Kennedy had planned a $103 billion budget and that President Johnson had cut it so sharply that it was below the previous year's budget. This was sheer myth. Before going to Texas Kennedy had pared nearly two billions from the $103 billion estimate, and he had told Dillon that it had to be driven below $100 billion. Otherwise, he said, the tax bill was doomed. Johnson wound up with a budget slightly higher than last year's $97.7 billion. Kennedy's would have been approximately the same. The real difference between the two was showmanship. It bewitched the financial community, creating the image of the most economical President since Coolidge. Not a single Washington correspondent saw that it had all been done by sleight of hand.

A year later Dillon and company would have been on the lookout for trap doors and other crazy-house devices, for by then Johnsonian techniques had become capital lore. That afternoon he was such an unknown personality in the Executive Branch that Bundy hadn't realized how much pleasure he derived from being photographed. A larger measure of the general ignorance was an unfortunate blunder by Ken Galbraith and three domestic Cabinet officers, Freeman, Udall, and Wirtz. Before coming to the EOB Heller had been in Freeman's office at the Department of Agriculture, at a meeting called on the initiative of the indefatigable Galbraith. Galbraith felt that his version of the joint session speech should be reviewed by what he called 'the liberal wing' of the government. Charlie Murphy, who had written speeches for Truman, was present, and he too had been working on a draft. Galbraith read it and found it much like his own. The President wanted Sorensen and himself to do the actual writing, Ken reported; he was eager to hear their suggestions. Under Kennedy this would have been perfectly acceptable. It wasn't acceptable to Johnson, because he hadn't been informed of it. Heller tattled. Suspicious, the new President told Heller that the Galbraith meeting was obviously 'a liberal caucus', held *in camera,* to chivy him. It didn't help liberal causes, it put everyone who had been present under a cloud, and it spelled the end of Galbraith as a transitional figure. The President was against secret meetings, and any meeting he hadn't authorized was 'secret'. He intended to run everything, literally *everything*, with a firm hand.

If he was unfair to the liberals—and it is entirely possible that he wasn't—it was irrelevant. For the United States the sole imperative was that Johnson swiftly create an atmosphere of confidence, and in that role he was proving superb. It didn't much matter that he was conjuring confidence, or that he himself may have suffered pangs of self-doubt; wisely he kept any stage fright to himself. Undoubtedly he suffered from it, but only rarely did he permit anyone to peer behind his elaborate stage props and see hesitancy there. Dillon had a fleeting glimpse of it. After the budget meeting the President and the Secretary discussed the Secret Service and tomorrow's walk from the executive mansion to St Matthew's. Since Oswald's murder strongly suggested an elaborate plot, Chief Rowley didn't want Johnson to follow the gun carriage on foot. At first the President had agreed. 'But then Lady Bird told me I should do it,' he told Dillon, 'so I changed my mind.'

Across West Executive the Shriver–Dungan meeting had become the Walton meeting. Sargent Shriver was upstairs with the family, and Ralph Dungan had stalked out in exasperation. After two days and two nights, it seemed to him, a kind of lunacy was creeping into the funeral preparations. Some fifty people were again jammed into his office and anteroom, and more and more he felt that they were going to wind up staging a jamboree. Godfrey McHugh wanted Aircraft 26000 to fly over Memorial Bridge at five hundred feet during the ceremonies; General Wehle protested that the horses would bolt. Tish Baldridge ('General Baldridge', as she became known to the meeting) appeared and reported that she had ordered the Old Guard's scarlet-uniformed fife and drum corps to stand in the green circle on the Virginia side of the bridge; they would toot and rumble as the cortège wound around them. Tenor Luigi Vena, who had sung during the Kennedy wedding, was coming to sing in St Matthew's at the funeral Mass; among the selections being proposed for him were 'When Irish Eyes Are Smiling', 'The Boys from Killarney', and 'Anchors Aweigh'. And at the grave site itself the military wanted to construct a tiny waterfall. They thought it would be sort of decorative. Dungan flushed. It was becoming wild—he half-expected the Flying Wallendas to swoop in wearing black tights. His head swimming with phrases like 'the Black Watch feed-in' and 'laying on the Irish drill', he struggled to his feet. 'You take over. I'm not putting up with any more of this,' he muttered to Bill Walton, addding a short obscenity.

Later he returned. By then the brouhaha atmosphere had disappeared. The most preposterous proposals had been quashed and most of the crucial issues solved. The best of the selections had been adopted. McHugh was going to have his Air Force One fly-by, together with that of jet fighters, despite vigorous objections from the Federal Aviation Agency. FAA's Chairman Jeeb Halaby told Godfrey he wouldn't allow it 'unless I have word from the highest authority'. McHugh said, 'It comes from the highest *possible* authority.' Halaby asked, 'Who?' and Godfrey, the man least likely to succeed in the new administration, said, 'The President.' That was that; Jim Swindal was ordered to rendezvous with fighter aircraft over Maryland tomorrow and chart a flight course for Arlington. General Baldridge's troop of Redcoats was still advancing on Washington, but only because Walton, the arbiter of New Frontier taste, approved. At the same time the pack of well-meaning kibitzers had thinned, partly because those who were to walk behind the caisson had to rent full-dress suits. At Fred Holborn's request rental agencies on L Street and Seventh Street had agreed to remain open until 4 p.m., a poignant reminder of inaugural eve, when this afternoon's clients had last patronized them. Most important to the restoration of balance, in Dungan's view, was the fact that 'Jackie had got things in control again'.

Mrs Kennedy's headquarters were the West Sitting Room. She rarely left it. Once she stepped into the Oval Room to greet the mafia wives and Mrs Tazewell Shepard, and once she paused to receive Ted Reardon, clasping his bowed head in her hands and saying, 'Oh, dear Ted, the first one with Jack.' Reardon mumbled, 'He'd be very proud of you, Jackie.' As he left he felt this had been a 'foolish, corny reply.' It wasn't; it was entirely appropriate.

Turning, she ordered the sitting-room's doors closed, sealing herself and those around her off from the rest of the Presidential apartment.

Isolation was important because she had to concentrate, and the mansion was overrun with guests. Arriving from London while everyone was in the rotunda, Stas Radziwill had been reminded of 'Versailles after the King had died'. Now it was more like his own Poland in 1939. The corridors reverberated with turmoil and the footsteps of harried strangers. There was even some marching—in the long second-floor hall Dave Powers lined up Caroline, John, and Sydney Lawford, barked 'Salute! Left face!' and then hup-hup'ed them up and down the rug. In the Treaty Room Ethel Kennedy and Ken O'Donnell were watching a rerun of the Oswald shooting.

Ethel, deeply disturbed, seized Arthur Schlesinger in the passage outside and asked him what it meant, what possible justification there could be for such a murder. Arthur had no answer. As a historian he was naturally appalled, but for Ethel, with her piety, the horror was far greater, and she was distraught.[7]

Schlesinger had been passing by, looking for Bob Kennedy. At one point half the mansion's visitors appeared to be looking for one another while the other half followed servants with suitcases. Bob was being moved to the southeast room so his mother could sleep in the Lincoln Room next door, and elsewhere shifts were made to assure everyone a place. The mansion was near capacity. Young John's crib was even brought in next to his sister's bed. That turned out to be unnecessary, and his room was to be unoccupied, but it was the only one which was. The Smiths, the Spaldings, Lem Billings, and Peter Lawford and his agent were on the third floor, and the widowed First Lady would be sharing the second floor with her sister, her mother-in-law, two brothers-in-law, a sister-in-law, a niece, and her own children.

One objected to his quarters. Lee Radziwill led her husband into the Chief Executive's suite and told him they would sleep there. He demurred. It was Jackie's wish, she explained, but the more he looked at the familiar four-poster, the bedside table with its pill bottles, and rubber boats and ducks which the President had taken into the tub when bathing with John, the firmer he became. In the end they compromised. A cot was brought over from the White House dispensary and set up at the foot of the huge bed. ('Poor Stas!' said Mrs Kennedy when she saw it. 'Like some slave!') With his old-fashioned European dignity he stiffly insisted he would be quite comfortable there. He even refused to use the bathroom. No one knew where he shaved; razor and toothbrush in hand, he wandered through the mansion for ablutions elsewhere.

Behind the double doors, Shriver had taken up a station by the white princess telephone, relaying instructions to the meeting he had chaired. Jacqueline Kennedy made few calls herself. Immediately after returning from the Hill she had phoned the three eulogists to thank them (with the result that all three became incoherent), but

[7] Though not as upset as those for whom Oswald's death came to overshadow everything else. That evening Schlesinger received a long-distance call from one of the country's most distinguished women novelists. She proposed the formation of a national committee to prove that Oswald had been framed. He acidly observed that he hadn't heard from her on Friday, and that if she and others gave the impression that they were more concerned about Sunday's murder than Friday's it would be 'an incalculable disservice to the American Left.' (Actually, he later learned, she had wept when she first heard of Kennedy's assassination.)

most of the time she sat in the centre of the couch by the window overlooking the Rose Garden, flanked by various Kennedy aides. Robert Kennedy paced about; other members of the family came and went. There was no agenda and, apart from her doodles, no record of deliberations. Judgments had to be made rapidly, based on her own sense of the fitness of things, for with time so short everything was coming at her at once. She was shaping a state funeral, and, at the same time, making certain tentative decisions about her own immediate future. She had no home now. This house had become the legal residence of the Johnson family. Their move here couldn't be delayed indefinitely, despite Lady Bird's kind offer. The mansion was the headquarters of the Chief Executive. That meant that every vestige of the Kennedys, including Caroline's White House school, must go elsewhere. At the moment she couldn't think where that would be.

Yet with so many resourceful friends around temporary solutions were offered very quickly. In mid-afternoon the matter of moving was virtually settled within a few minutes by two callers—Ormsby-Gore, who volunteered to house the school in the British Embassy, and Ken Galbraith. Galbraith was continuing to express his desolation in his own peripatetic fashion. He described, with the pride of authorship, his revised version of President Johnson's address. Observing Mrs Kennedy's distress, Ormsby-Gore quickly put in, 'Make it as good as you can, obviously, but good as it will be it won't match Kennedy's speeches.' Galbraith replied, 'As you are a loyal Tory, I am a loyal Democrat.' The Ambassador answered edgily, 'On occasions of this sort I am prepared to be a very disloyal Tory.' Their laughter was brittle.

Galbraith then turned to the widow's housing problem and solved it brilliantly. When she told him that she didn't know how much money she would have or when she would have it, he pointed out that Averell Harriman 'has more real estate than he knows what to do with. He could buy a house in Georgetown and turn it over to you—it would be a sensible investment for him.' It wasn't quite that simple. There were problems of furniture and domestic staff. But Harriman volunteered to move his family to a hotel and turn his own Georgetown home over to Mrs Kennedy, and after three telephone calls Galbraith reported to Robert Kennedy that it had been settled that way.

He reported to Bob, not Jackie, for by then she was once more absorbed in ceremonial details. To suggest that she was complete mistress of herself would be inaccurate. She wavered, for example, over the design of the Mass card. Dr English had sent up prayers of St Ignatius and St Francis, and Ethel brought in a third from her parents' card. The widow said, 'I don't want any of these on the back. I'm not going to be pleading with God to take Jack's soul to heaven.' Sketching the card for Shriver, she said, 'Well—I guess you could put a cross on the top if you want.' Ethel protested that there had to be *some* mention of God, and then Jackie did precisely what she said she would not do. She wrote out the plea: 'Dear God—please take care of your servant John Fitzgerald Kennedy. Please take him straight to heaven.' She meant both sentences to be included, but Bob, under the impression that she intended him to make a choice between the two, struk out the second. Other of her instructions miscarried or proved impractical. She wanted Luigi Vena to sing Bizet's 'Agnus Dei', as he had at her wedding—instead, he was told to sing '*Pie Jesu*' and 'Ave Maria'—and she specified a black border for the Mass card and didn't get it. Ethel was against black because she felt it should be 'not sad, not reminding you of death'. For Jackie that was the very purpose of the card, but it was too late; no printer could include a border in the time left. As it was the only way Sandy Fox could get the job done before the Mass was to use the Central Intelligence Agency press. The CIA agreed to run it through the night. (When Fox reported this to the meeting in Dungan's office, everyone there was dumbfounded. None of them had known the spies *had* a press.)

The issue of tomorrow's eulogies became the subject of a more protracted debate. The cortège would pause twice, at St Matthew's and in Arlington, and as things stood Sunday afternoon tributes were to be delivered at both. Bishop Hannan was going to speak in the cathedral, of course, between the Mass and Communion. The consensus was that he should be joined by a layman. But which layman? Three names were advanced: McNamara, Bundy, and Sorensen. All were discarded. McNamara was out because they couldn't have him without Rusk, and Bundy hadn't joined Kennedy until after his election.

They lingered over Sorensen's name much longer. He himself felt he would be inappropriate because he had never been inside a Catholic church. Furthermore, he hadn't been quite as close to the President as the public assumed; his role had been largely confined to Kennedy's public life. Thus the idea of a lay speaker in the church—which Cardinal Cushing would have scuttled anyhow—was set aside. That left the cemetery. Jackie said to Bob, 'If anybody's going to talk it should be his brothers. You and Teddy will have to say something somewhere. So you will say it there at the grave.'

To help them determine what should be said, Bundy and Sorensen were summoned. Bundy wrote afterwards: 'At the end of Sunday afternoon Ted and I went over to the mansion to talk with

Jackie and Bobby about readings for the funeral. In talking with Jackie earlier . . . I had suggested that the best tribute would be to use some of his own words. She agreed, but also wanted Bible readings. Ted thought of doing some of JFK's quotations from Scripture, as well as some of his own quotations. Now with a variety of excellent suggestions at hand from Ted, we all set ourselves to choosing and judging.' Sorensen had a long list; from the moment he heard of the drift of discussion in the Presidential apartment he had been poring over the President's papers. (Galbraith had heard of it, too, and had deposited on Ted's desk a marked copy of the inaugural address showing the lines he felt should be read during the funeral.) At Mrs Kennedy's request, Sorensen drew up a 'ballot' of selections, and Sorensen and Bundy marked it, indicating their choices.

Four passages were picked for each brother, and they then turned to Bishop Hannan's manuscript. Here the judging and choosing took rather longer. Mrs Kennedy wanted something supremely appropriate. The Attorney General suggested the Beatitudes, the nine declarations in the Sermon on the Mount. He particularly liked Matthew V:9 ('Blessed are the peacemakers'), because he felt that the Test Ban Treaty had been his brother's greatest achievement. Jackie shook her head. She wanted a sombre note, and sitting on the couch between Bundy and Sorensen she said, 'What about Ecclesiastes? Because he loved that so. The third chapter . . .' She crossed to the bookshelves lining the south wall and handed Sorensen the Bible she had studied at Vassar. He riffled through it, reading silently while she studied the speech excerpts in Mac's lap. Suddenly Ted said, 'Well, this mightn't be wrong at all.' He began reading:

To every thing there is a season, and a time to every purpose under the heaven:
A time to be born, and a time to die. . . .

'Oh, *yes*,' she breathed. It was, she recalled afterwards, 'so right that it just made shivers through your flesh'. Like Sarah Hughes, Sorensen was under the impression that there was a 'Catholic Bible', and he asked the widow whether she wanted him to check the Scriptural passages with the other one. 'The *Catholic* Bible!' she said, and then told him about her youth in the Church and how much she liked the King James version.

Bundy wrote of the meeting that 'it came out right—as did just about everything that Jackie touched those days—and she touched nearly everything'. That was written after the funeral, however, when it could be seen in retrospect. At the time there were grave doubts about certain aspects of it, and her most controversial decision came shortly after her return from the rotunda. The men had been going through papers while she sat alone, lost in thought. Abruptly she said, 'And there's going to be an eternal flame.'

She remembered afterwards that 'the thing just came into my head'. She also recalled that everyone else in the room looked 'rather horrified'. Shriver was particularly uncomfortable. 'We'll have to find out if there's one at the Tomb of the Unknown Soldier,' he said hesitantly, 'because if there is, we can't have one.'

'I don't *care* if one is there,' she said. She assumed that there was. She had seen France's under the Arc de Triomphe. She thought there must be a flame at every Unknown Soldier's Tomb. Yet that didn't matter; she wanted to make certain the country never forgot her husband, and she told Shriver, 'We're going to have it anyway.'

Sarge had made the same assumption. 'I think the only places with eternal flames are Paris and the one already out at Arlington,' he said. 'I want to be sure you're not subjecting yourself to criticism. Some people might think it's a little ostentatious.'

'*Let* them.'

Shriver still felt a twinge of apprehension. Turning to the phone he asked the military for clarification. To his amazement he discovered that Arlington hadn't a flame after all. To the best of the Pentagon's knowledge, the only ones in the world were France's and Gettysburg's. He ordered an immediate installation on the hillside. 'And fix it,' he added, 'so she can light it.'

Like him, those in Dungan's office received the news with mixed feelings. Bill Walton objected that a beacon would be 'aesthetically unfortunate'—later he became converted to it—and Tish Baldridge was disappointed because it meant the end of her flower-laced latticework. But there was no time for debate now. They had to hurry. The exasperating delay in providing a uniformed escort for the coffin's return from Bethesda still rankled, so Dick Goodwin was designated flame expediter. Goodwin was as tough as he was smart; brass and braid didn't impress him, and the past three years had taught him that the most common word in Army bureaucracy was 'can't'.

'We can't do it,' MDW's staff duty officer told him.

'Why not?'

'We'd have to fly to Europe. That's the only place they know about them.'

'OK,' Goodwin snapped. 'It's six hours to Europe. Go get it.'

There was an uneasy silence. Then: 'Maybe we can fabricate it.'

'Good. Fabricate it.'

The officer traced Lieutenant Colonel Bernard G. Carroll, Fort

Myer's post engineer, to Jack Metzler's Arlington office. 'We have a request from Mrs Kennedy,' he said. 'She wants an eternal flame at the graveside.'

To Carroll this sounded somewhat vague. He asked, 'What's "eternal"?'

'Before, during, and after the ceremony,' the officer said promptly.

That sounded easy. Carroll could use almost any kerosene pot which would burn for an hour or so. On reflection, however, it sounded *too* easy. He suspected that the widow had something else in mind, and he raised so many questions that the officer said he'd have to call him back.

In the West Wing Goodwin was summoned to a phone. He listened a moment and then said icily, 'Eternal means *for ever*.'

The staff duty officer hemmed and hawed, but each time he raised an objection he was cut down with whipsaw orders to stop giving reasons why it couldn't be done and start doing it. Goodwin was frankly exercising civilian control of the military, a Kennedy hallmark since the Bay of Pigs; it was one reason why uniformed panjandrums had quietly detested the administration for nearly four years. Driven back to his last outpost, the officer raised a final obstacle.

'She can't light it.'

'*Why not?*'

'There's too much danger. It might go out.'

'Listen,' Goodwin said. 'If you can design an atomic bomb, you can put a little flame on the side of that hill, and you can make it so she *can* light it.'

The gist of this was relayed to Colonel Carroll. His response was curious; with all the resources of the American military establishment available to him, he turned to the yellow pages of the metropolitan telephone directory. Leafing through it to the listings under 'Gas Companies', he dialled half the numbers while Metzler, on another telephone, dialled the other half. They quickly exhausted Virginia—not a single office was open—and began on Maryland. Halfway down Carroll's list Rockville's Suburban Propane answered. The answerer was a repairman who had just stopped in on his way to an emergency, and he readily agreed to send another man there and stand by. Then the Colonel located a torch in a Washington Gas & Light Company substation. He sent two sergeants to drive it to Fort Belvoir's metal shop, called Rockville again, and asked the cooperative service man to bring tanks and copper tubing in through Arlington's Hatfield Gate.

At 9 p.m. the torch arrived from Bevoir, welded to a frame. The tubing was buried in a trench; the tanks were out of sight. Technicians began the final step: connecting torch, tubing, and tanks. Ted Clifton had changed from blues to greens and crossed the river for an inspection, and he and the Army's chief of the engineers were present when Carroll tested the device for the first time. It was exactly midnight. A thick bright tongue of fire flared up, roiling with liquid movements in a light breeze. The colonel tried it a second time, a third, a fourth. 'This is going to work,' the chief of engineers said. Clifton asked, 'Can she do it herself?' The chief was hesitant. Nothing would be more embarrassing than to have the light fail then, he pointed out, and Clifton, half convinced, wondered aloud whether the torch should be ignited in advance and concealed beneath a cover. Mrs Kennedy could remove the cover at the end of the graveside service, and there would be no risk. The specialists who had set it up assured him that was unnecessary. Their commanding officer, Major Stanley Converse, would hand her a lighted taper, and when the taper touched the gas the propane would blaze up. As an added precaution, both Converse and the sergeant assisting him would stuff their pockets with match books and cigarette lighters. They would lurk near her like a couple of walking incendiary bombs. If anything went wrong they could set it right in a jiffy.

The installation of the torch capped the most frenzied day in the memory of the cemetery staff. Throughout Sunday the slope beneath Lee Mansion had been swarming with men and women, most of them strangers to one another: grave-diggers, communications experts laying video cable, carpenters building a press stand, Carroll's engineers, an Irish liaison officer, advance security men, and Robert S. McNamara, who once more slowly paced the borders of the plot, map in hand, checking off items on a little list. There were lots of generals hanging around, and they looked rather confused. They had attended many other Arlington funerals, but until now a stranger's rank had been visible on his shoulder insignia. Today that was reversed. The only uniformed member of the White House staff was Clifton. Drab young men in mufti could be members of the Commander in Chief's staff, with clearances denied to most flag officers, and some of the most urgent matters were being handled by women. Indeed, the last person to report to the Kennedys that afternoon had been Bunny Mellon, who had spent an exhausting day in the rotunda, at St Matthew's, and, finally, in the cemetery.

Jackie and Bob received her in the sitting-room. Both Kennedys, it seemed to Bunny, had far more dignity than she herself did. Bob thanked her for the pleasure the Rose Garden had given the President, and after he withdrew the widow talked quietly of flowers. 'I don't want the church to look like a funeral,' she said. 'Jack loved flowers, and that's why he hated the way flowers are used in most funerals.' She remembered Tony Biddle's funeral, with 'awful purple wreaths and gold ribbons all around, looking like Harlem or Coney Island'. It had been wrong for Tony, and it would even be worse for the President. She knew there would be flowers in Arlington, she knew the senders couldn't be insulted. 'But do one thing for me, Bunny,' she said. 'Please see that they're put far, far from the grave.'

Bunny had already done it; she had anticipated this. In the little time she had she had given the cathedral a touch of springtime, rejecting bushels of sickly Easter lilies and a series of tasteless rented vases. Pam Turnure had brought two simple blue vases from the executive mansion, and Bunny and Elmer Young, the White House florist, had filled them with simple arrangements of daisies, white chysanthemums, and fragrant white stephanotis. The vases were placed on little pedestals before the altar rail; then she and Young crossed the bridge and studied the grave site with Arlington's landscape gardener. Bunny pointed to a spot high on one side of the slope. In the morning, after the rotunda had been closed, she wanted the flowers there loaded in trucks and banked on that spot like an enormous floral blanket. From that distance the ribbons and easels and all the funereal trumpery would be lost in the mass of lovely colours.

So it was all done. Mrs Kennedy sat back, silent for a moment. Then she said 'when Patrick died you sent such a nice, simple basket. So there's one other thing I want at the grave. A straw basket with just the flowers he had in the Rose Garden. Only those flowers, and nothing else at the grave.' She rose; they walked to the double doors together. As they parted she said, 'Write a note to Jack, Bunny. When you pick the flowers, somewhere scrunched down, in the moss and the wet, put your own note to him.'

From Elmer Young's basement nursery Bunny took a fifteen-inch-long wicker basket and a pair of scissors. Outside the night was very black. The only illumination came from the windows of the mansion. Yet that didn't matter. She knew every blossom and stem in the garden, though at this season she had not expected to find much here; she thought she would have to fill the basket with flowers from her own greenhouse, where duplicates of every Rose Garden plant grew under glass. Much that had been here in mid-autumn was indeed gone. Frost had taken the blue cornflowers, the red geraniums, the carnations and nicotinia. But to her vast surprise she did find blue salvia, chrysanthemums, and dozens of white roses blooming in this last week of November. She plucked them, and cut berries from the sheltering hawthorn and crab apple trees. Then, kneeling among the foliage midway between the President's dark silent office and the blazing mansion—the same shrubs that had bowed to President Kennedy's farewell rotors three and a half days ago—she placed the brimming basket on the thick carpet of grass, and in a shaft of light from the State Dining Room she prepared a little place in the moss and the wet.

As Bunny Mellon rose to leave, a caravan of black Mercurys glided in through the Southwest Gate and drew up outside the Diplomatic Reception Room. The President's mother and her party had arrived from Cape Cod. Upstairs she embraced Jacqueline Kennedy and was shown to her room by Shriver. Until then she had been composed, but standing by the towering Lincoln bedstead—'that bed like a cathedral', her daughter-in-law had once called it—she collapsed in Shriver's arms. 'It just seems so incredible,' she sobbed. 'Jack being struck down at the peak of his career and my husband Joe in a wheelchair.'

'Grandma, you've had the book thrown at you,' said Shriver. 'Rosemary, young Joe, Kick, Mr Kennedy—and now this.'

'But think of Jackie! I had my nine children. She's so young, and now she doesn't even have a home.'

He told her he thought it 'simply amazing how both of you are holding up so well'. And Rose, repeating Jackie's words almost verbatim said, 'What do people expect you to do? You can't just weep in a corner.'

Collecting herself, she sent for her daughters. She had brought black stockings for tomorrow; she wanted to be sure they had some, too. Suddenly trivial details of mourning dress seemed extremely important to the women and to the men, too. When Eisenhower anxiously phoned from the Statler to inquire whether black armbands should be worn—a custom which was still observed at Army funerals—the question was weighed carefully before sending him a negative reply. The demand for refitted swallowtail coats was so great that a Georgetown tailor worked all night, his hands and teeth bristling with the tools of his trade and the measurements of six Cabinet members strewn about. Afterwards the only payment he asked of the client whose coat had taken the most time was a Mass card; the work, he explained, had been therapeutic. So it was for all of them. 'I had never understood the function of a funeral before,' Schlesinger observed afterwards. 'Now I realized that it is to keep people from going to pieces.'

Rose Kennedy dined upstairs with Stas Radziwill; Jacqueline Kennedy, her sister, and Robert Kennedy were served in the sitting-room. The rest of the Kennedys ate in the family dining-room with their house guests, McNamara, Phyllis Dillon, Dave Powers, and Aristotle Socrates Onassis, the shipowner, who provided comic relief of sorts. They badgered him mercilessly about his yacht and his Man of Mystery aura. During coffee the Attorney General came down and drew up a formal document stipulating that Onassis give half his wealth to help the poor in Latin America. It was preposterous (and obviously unenforceable), and the Greek millionaire signed it in Greek.

After dinner pilgrimages to the Hill began. Jackie and Bob rode up again in mid-evening, and an hour later the President's mother went with the Shrivers, the Lawfords, Lem Billings, and Radziwill. Waiting for the others in the second-floor hall, Stas told Jackie that he was anxious to put something in the President's coffin; he wanted his most treasured possession, an old Parisian rosary, to be there with it. From a table vase she drew a red carnation. 'Wrap it around this,' she said, 'and give it to one of the agents there.' At midnight Ted went with Joe Gargan and two of Ted's assistants. Each visit was of a pattern: the Mercurys parked unobtrusively by the east steps; the visitors rode up in a Capitol elevator, entering the rotunda from the south side; the endless stream circling the coffin recognized them and quietly parted; a soldier unhooked the velvet rope. One by one the Kennedys passed through and knelt in prayer by the catafalque and the wreath with the card reading, 'From President Johnson and the Nation'.

They did not pass unphotographed; the nation's amateur cameramen were present in force. At the time their squinting eyes and snapping lenses seemed to be an insensitive intrusion, but it wasn't that simple. They were prompted by more than curiosity. As a country the United States had long been conscious of documentation, and nearly everyone on the Hill—the famous principals, their quiet witnesses, the listening nation which was vicariously present—was in the midst of history. Most of them knew it, and millions were converted into chroniclers of events. The number and variety of Americans who were keeping written accounts of their impressions is striking. In Washington they included Kennedy relatives and aides, the new First Lady, Cabinet members, the White House Detail, and the White House Communications Agency; in Dallas they were Robert Oswald, Ruth Paine, Dallas policemen, and the entire staff of Parkland Hospital. The professional pollsters were working round the clock on their questionnaires, while New York and California psychiatrists were noting their patients' responses. New England professors were interviewing their students, and Long Island

and Illinois grade school teachers were planning how to gauge pupil reactions.

These men and women were professionals; their reports were later published in professional journals. It is the amount of unpublished material, however, which is overwhelming. There were literally tons of it. Judging from the mail which reached 1600 Pennsylvania Avenue immediately after the funeral, at least fifty thousand adults and children were writing poems Sunday evening, and railroad men, taxi drivers, and airline hostesses were setting down their own thoughts and observations of their passengers' behaviour. Dismissing them all as Paul Prys would be belittling. They were more than just inquisitive; profoundly moved by the historical catastrophe, they wanted to participate in the country's homage, and if their doggerel was often trite and their gestures clumsy, they were expressing themselves with all the eloquence they had, and sometimes it was a lot.

At the time the dimensions of this emotional upheaval were unperceived. The average individual lived in a cocoon with his own reflections, the commiseration of those he loved, and his television screen, which, baffled by the absence of formal ceremony Sunday evening, picked up what it could at Idlewild and Dulles airports, where the funeral guests were arriving. Despite the unprecedented number of eminent names on the passenger lists these scenes were disappointing. The dignitaries declined to make statements, and neither their Washington ambassadors nor the State Department could presume to speak for them. Indeed, State couldn't even meet them all. Dean Rusk, George Ball, and Averell Harriman were spelling one another at Dulles, lurking in the airport's big mobile lounges and speeding out as ramps were wheeled into place, but with important delegations touching down every few minutes the ambassadors had to take care of their own. Rusk bounded around, pumping the hands of King Baudouin, Paul-Henri Spaak, Chancellor Erhard, Eamonn de Valera, and the entire British delegation, and Angie Duke, masterminding international etiquette by telephone, found the newcomers from abroad most understanding; without exception they agreed that on all formal occasions the order of rank for chiefs of state should be by country, in alphabetical order, in the English language. Nevertheless, Dulles was a protocol officer's incubus. The inevitable language difficulties were compounded by the size of the deluge. Bishop Hannan landed with the President of Turkey, the Foreign Minister of Italy, and a Moroccan prince who didn't speak a word of English; the prince had to manage with one of Hannan's French-speaking priests. And when Charles de Gaulle told Rusk, "*Je ne fais qu'exprimer en ma personne la profonde douleur de mon pays. En vérité, je représente le people français. C'est lui qui m'a envoyé ici,'* the Secretary of State was obliged to wait uneasily for a translator.

De Gaulle had spoken for all the potentates: their people had sent them. The British Prime Minister explained that 'the convulsion' in England was unique in the experience of his government; London teenagers, he said, were 'just distraught, openly crying in the streets although they had never seen President Kennedy'. In fact, the Americans were entitled to some sort of explanation from the British. State had had no idea that the United Kingdom was going to send so many people. For a giddy moment it appeared that both houses of Parliament were on their way. Although Ormsby-Gore had pleaded with London to 'hold it down', he was surrounded by Sir Alec and Lady Douglas-Home, the Duke of Edinburgh, the Duke and Duchess of Devonshire, Harold Wilson and Jo Grimond—whose Labour and Liberal parties had insisted that they come—and teams of Scotland Yard inspectors, private secretaries, and valets. Ormsby-Gore telephoned apologies to Shriver for 'hogging space' in St Matthew's and then set about making room for everyone in his embassy. He didn't succeed. Wilson had to find a bed elsewhere.

The future prime minister didn't complain; no one did. The guests and their American hosts were being especially polite to one another, for the murder of Oswald had created a supercharged atmosphere. For two days the United States had been in deep mourning. Now its pride was stung, too. Its diplomats were anxious to skirt any mention of the new shame, and the foreign dignitaries, realizing that a slur tonight would never be forgotten, were tactfully keeping their mouths shut. Had contacts been confined to the greetings in the mobile lounges, they would have seen no traces of the ugly strain of violence in U.S. society which had brought them here. Unfortunately for diplomacy, the embassies were equipped with television and radio, which reminded them that all Americans weren't as sane and civilized as Rusk and his under secretaries. Outside the White House they learned, a picket had paraded on Pennsylvania Avenue with a hand-lettered placard read 'GOD PUNISHED JFK'. In Birmingham an Alabaman declared over a WQXI 'open-mike' show that 'Any white man who did for niggers should be shot'; he was instantly cut off the air, but the thing had been said. And at 10.55 p.m. the visitors were told that Astronaut John Glenn, the symbol of Kennedy's space dreams, had belatedly reached the airport here after a bomb scare—in Texas.

In the turmoil at Washington National some thirty state governors, a score of Harvard professors, and three Roman Catholic prelates reached the capital unobserved. Bishop Hannan and Archbishop O'Boyle split up and drove to their homes while Cardinal Cushing dined with the Most Reverend Egidio Vagnozzi, Apostolic Delegate to the United States. It was not a harmonious meeting. The Delegate had very strong views about how tomorrow's services should be conducted. A Catholic head of state was entitled to five absolutions at the end of a funeral Mass, Vagnozzi pointed out, and that was what John Kennedy should receive. His Eminence disagreed. The discussion, as he later put it, became 'a hassle'. He terminated it by saying sharply, 'If there are going to be five absolutions, you'll have to say them yourself. I won't do it because they'll last twice as long as the Mass itself. In the popular parlance, this family has had it.'

That was the Cardinal's first hassle of the evening. The second, more protracted, began at 10 p.m. He was staying in Archbishop O'Boyle's home at 4110 Warren Street, and there—after an irking half-hour exploration of the neighbourhood, trying to find the house —Ted Sorensen and Sargent Shriver arrived for a conference with the Cardinal, the Archbishop, and, in Sorensen's dry phrase, 'a frustrated archbishop named Francis X Morrissey'. Sarge and Ted thought Frank Morrissey was with Cardinal Cushing, the Cardinal thought he was with them. Morrissey, in the popular parlance, had crashed the meeting.

'Your Eminence, this is how the family would like it done,' Shriver said, and turned to Sorensen.

Sorensen began his presentation, and His Eminence listened with growing dismay. His chieftain's face was set, Archbishop O'Boyle was frowning deeply; clearly something was wrong. In point of fact, several things were wrong. Ted and Sarge was over-fatigued, and despite the lengthy deliberations in the mansion, Sorensen didn't know precisely how the family did want it done. His mind was a chaos of suggestions heard there, some of which—Mrs Kennedy's determination to have Hannan, not Boyle, at the lectern, and to hear her husband's favourite Scriptural passages, not Cushing's—were extremely delicate. The key difficulty, however, was his total ignorance of Roman Catholic ritual. Since this haziness was partly shared by the Catholic laymen who had been instructing him, including Shriver, no one had oriented him properly, and he innocently plunged ahead with proposals which were wholly unacceptable to the Church: secular music in the cathedral, for example, and even Kennedy quotations and Biblical readings 'scattered through the service'. Shriver knew *that* was impossible, but he was too groggy to speak up; coming in the door he hadn't even been certain whether a Cardinal was addressed as 'Your Eminence' or 'Your Holiness'. He had simply guessed right.

Sorensen finished, and there was a heavy silence. His Eminence shook his mane of white hair. 'Ted, I'll do anything in the world for Jacqueline Kennedy,' he said, 'but I can't change the text of that Mass. I have to read it exactly as it is in that book on the altar.'

'Jackie wants a Low Mass,' said Sarge, finding his voice.

The white mane nodded vigorously. 'That's in order. Why stretch it out with a long pontifical High Mass?'

'She'd like it to be as simple as possible,' Sorensen said.

The Cardinal eyed him quizzically. 'Don't worry, Ted. We'll bury him like a Jesuit'—Jesuits are buried in a pine box, with a Low Mass; no one comes—'but we have to do it according to the book.'

The bargaining (that is the only word for it) continued until midnight, with various interruptions. There was a long colloquy between the two prelates over the robes they should wear, and another digression after Ethel telephoned that her husband wanted Communion offered. Cushing and O'Boyle were apprehensive. If a thousand people decided to go to the rail, the delay would be greater than five absolutions; they would never get out of the cathedral. Shriver agreed to spread the word that only the family would take Communion, the robes were chosen—with Morrissey kibitzing—and the prickly issues Sorensen had raised were resolved by compromise. The Cardinal would read an orthodox Low Mass, the Archbishop would handle the music. Bishop Hannan would speak, however, and he would use the material Sorensen had brought.

After Sorensen and Shriver left for the mansion O'Boyle called Hannan at St Matthew's to tell him. 'They prefer to have his own words and his favourite Scriptural quotations, as an expression of his ideals,' the Archbishop explained. 'There are three typed pages. The first two are mostly from Ecclesiastes and Isaiah, including one he was going to deliver in Dallas. The third is from his own inaugural address.'

Hannan replied that he was simply too tired to pick them up now; he would drive over in the morning. Hanging up he fell into bed—falling, as hundreds of others had fallen in the capital, into a sleep so deep that it was indistinguishable from a dead faint. For the third time Mrs Kennedy received a half-gram injection from Dr Walsh in the White House and rolled over to her husband's ironhard bed board for four hours of fitful slumber. Her sister lay on the President's four-poster, her brother-in-law on the cot. Out Massachusetts Avenue the crowded embassies were dark and still, and only the spectral figure of Madame Alphand, rechecking window locks, and the shadows of Sûreté guards on the lawn outside, hinted that the French had special reason for concern. Twice during dinner an anonymous caller had warned that the embassy would be bombed tonight. Madame was deeply troubled. Charles de Gaulle was not; he had been through this too many times; he slept soundly on his long borrowed bed.

'Sunday night was less terrible,' Mac Bundy wrote, and the explanation was this numbing, pervasive *Dämmerschlaf*. Mac couldn't cry tonight because he was completely enervated. The accumulation of fatigue had reduced all the chief participants in Washington's farewell to President Kennedy to a comatose condition. They were either sleepers or somnambulists. At Fort McNair General Wehle faced seventy-five red-eyed officers, pointer in hand, taking them through a final briefing with the jerky movements of an automaton. At 2.30 a.m. he asked for questions. A sepulchral voice inquired about a bugler. They had none; the most obvious detail had been overlooked. A Virginia telephone rang, and Sergeant Keith Clark groped for the trumpet that would play taps in Arlington.

There were a few other slips. In St Matthew's Angie Duke inspected the seating capacity of pews for the last time and calculated each would hold five people. Unfortunately, his men had shucked their topcoats before the test; the appearance of an overcoated congregation next morning would spark a frantic order for a hundred folding Army chairs. And in Ralph Dungan's office Dean Markham became involved in a comic misunderstanding with Governor George Wallace's aide. The aide phoned in the complaint: Wallace hadn't received his tickets to the funeral. Markham replied tiredly, 'King's got them. Tell the Governor to get them from King.' He meant Sam King of Duke's staff, and was puzzled by the evident consternation on the other end of the line. Hanging up, he recounted the conversation to two men working on lists. In chorus they cried, '*Martin Luther* King?' Instantly he realized that if they thought that, Wallace would, too. The next instant he shrugged. Let it stand. There was poetic justice in it.

But oversights and blunders were very rare. Markham toiled through the night with singular efficiency, deciding who would walk behind the gun carriage, supervising the administration of B-1 shots to the exhausted staff, personally inviting the White House servants and gardeners to the Mass—Jack NcNally had excluded them by insisting they must wear full dress suits, which they couldn't afford; Markham, knowing that Mrs Kennedy would want them there anyhow, told them to come in their Sunday best—and finally walking up to St Matthew's with Joe Gargan at 4.30 a.m. to mark off pews for fifty members of the family and two hundred Kennedy friends.

At that hour St Matthew's resembled a convention of Interpol.

Never in the history of the secret police had such a cosmopolitan group of bodyguards assembled in a house of God. Roy Kellerman, checking security arrangements for President Johnson and the Kennedy family, had the impression that he was in a new Tower of Babel. The United States had enough men to handle the job alone; in addition to Kellerman's detail there were squads of FBI agents and the pick of the CIA, some of whom had been flown home from abroad because of their special linguistic talents. But Dallas had understandably shaken foreign faith in American police skills, so the aisles, the balcony, and even the altar swarmed with specialists from Scotland Yard's Special Branch and the Sûreté, lithe bowlegged Japs, Puerto Ricans, and West Germans in belted raincoats and sinister bifocals. Kellerman checked them out, as they were checking him and one another—much of the time was spent flashing credentials—and he saw no Russians. They may have been there, though. Offered U.S. protection for Mikoyan, the Soviets had replied, with characteristic evasiveness, that they were making their own arrangements.

There was no catafalque in the cathedral. Instead, a low church truck stood by the entrance. The coffin would be wheeled, not borne, up the centre aisle. This was a concession to Lieutenant Bird's description of his body bearers' agonizing ascent into the rotunda. 'It appeared,' he reported, that 'very little consideration' had been given to 'the tremendous weight of the casket'; carrying it had 'required every ounce of strength that all nine of us could muster to move the casket in an appropriate and respectful manner'. Bird's plea for a low cart had been approved, though his battalion commander didn't tell him about it until next morning. It would have been some comfort that evening, though not much; his team still had to bring the coffin back down the Capitol steps. The prospect had them petrified. Ordinarily six men could lift a casket with ease. Today Bird had added a Marine and a sailor, yet they had barely made it, and the descent was bound to be more difficult than the ascent, for they wouldn't have him bracing them from the rear. One young Army specialist had worked himself into a state of semi-hysteria; he was convinced that they were going to drop their precious burden on the marble and split it open before the eyes of a hundred million Americans. Only the Lieutenant would argue with him, and his heart wasn't in it. He himself, he confessed later, was 'near panic'. Therefore he decided upon a drastic measure; they would spend the night rehearsing.

The ensuing scene was perhaps the most bizarre of all those played out in the small hours of November 24–25. Borrowing a regulation Army casket from Fort Myer's honour guard company, the team drove it to the Tomb of the Unknown Soldiers at midnight, filled it with sandbags, and slowly carried it up and down, up and down the tomb's steps. After sundown the Unknown Soldiers' guard doesn't have to walk back and forth, so Bird ordered him to sit atop the coffin. Up, down, up and down the team trudged with the man straddling the lid. Finally the Lieutenant stopped them, told the guard to make room, and *he* got on, too. Lugging a sand-filled casket and two bodies, the eight bearers made the trip again, again, again, again. It was cruel, but absolutely necessary; his men had been demoralized, and now, sweating in the dark, they felt a flicker of hope.

These, then, were the small sounds of the professionals preparing for America's greatest state funeral—the rustling cloth of a Georgetown tailor, the scuffling tread of the world's most famous policemen searching pews, the rattle of dispensary syringes on White House trays, and, across the Potomac, enlisted men grunting over the Unknown Soldiers' Tomb, Black Watch pipers learning the unfamiliar hundred-paces-a-minute cadence on Fort Myer's north drill field, and the hum of the CIA press in McLean. Earlier in the evening there had been harsher noises; carpenters had been throwing up new platforms for the network pool cameras and a press stand on the slope beneath Lee Mansion, and in Washington—as in twenty other cities, including Dallas—the billboard industry had stripped boardings of advertising that afternoon and replaced it with the black-against-white reminder, in Old English lettering, 'Friday November 22, 1963'. Now, as the thermometer dipped into the low thirties, freezing the last blossoms in the Rose Garden, the night was unnaturally still. Only by crossing to the Mall and looking eastward could one have seen how deceptive that stillness was. The weekend had reached another of its unexpected, overwhelming climaxes; the Capitol dome was aglow, and beneath its immense beacon a quarter-million Americans were waiting in line.

As early as 3.11 Sunday afternoon, less than an hour after the eulogies, the District police had reported that 'a serious problem is developing with people surging towards the Capitol building'. The original plan had specified that the bronze doors should remain open to the public until 9 p.m. 'if necessary'. That was obviously unrealistic; some of the first waiters had been there since midnight Saturday, wrapped in blankets. It was at nine that Jacqueline and Robert Kennedy returned to the Hill, and they shared the universal amazement. After kneeling by the bier and genuflecting Mrs Kennedy had followed Bob to the car, but at the door she abruptly shook her head and said, 'No—let me walk.' For ten minutes they strolled down the curving path to First and Constitution. She spoke briefly to a group of nuns, and then, to her astonishment, she recognized a nearby standee, Sherry Geyelin, the wife of a *Wall Street Journal* writer who had been critical of the administration. The woman began to cry, and the widow, who had never known that she, too, had loved the President, embraced her. A reporter asked the Attorney General what he thought of the multitude. Bob looked around—by now it had reached 200,000 and was growing rapidly—and murmured, 'Fantastic, fantastic.'

Martyrdom had transformed John Kennedy so swiftly that even those closest to him found adjustment difficult. Friday morning he had been a popular but controversial young President. Tonight he was controversial only to the alienated. Alive, he had known a Washington inhabited by friends and enemies. Death had swept away both affection and enmity; they had been replaced by idolatry. The endless mass which inched forward, five abreast, was less a crowd than a congregation. Afterwards its more sophisticated members retrieved their scepticism, and today it is hard to recapture, or even to credit, the reverence they felt then. But it was real enough at the time. Its essence may be found in the phrases men and women spoke and wrote that Sabbath and in the days afterwards. To Mary McGrory he had become 'a warrior-chieftain', to David Bell 'a warrior-king', to Natalie Hemingway 'a dear godfather', and John Steinbeck, in a letter to Jacqueline Kennedy, wrote of 'this man who was the best of his people' and who 'by his life, and his death, gave back the best of them for their own'.

Veneration is the only explanation for their endurance in that line. The bitter weather and the length of the wait discouraged all except those who felt an uncontrollable compulsion to stay. They knew how brief their time inside would be. They would be permitted a few moments to circle the coffin, to kneel quickly, and to leave flowers with two soldiers; that was all. Yet they would not turn back. By midnight a hundred thousand had passed through, and the line behind them was three miles long—three miles of shivering shoulders and frosting breaths. Still five abreast, it stretched seventeen blocks, then twenty-eight, then forty, and at quarter of six in the morning policemen passed the word to newcomers, 'We have to close the doors at 8.30. Go home—only 85,000 more can get in.'

They stood anyhow. A mother knelt on the sidewalk and said to her children, 'We can pray right here. God and the President will hear us just as well as inside,' and when a boy told his girl, 'Look, honey, this is crazy; we can't possibly make it,' she answered, 'I don't care, I want to stay in line anyway. It's the least we can do.' Among those with no chance of reaching the doors were two teenagers who had walked thirty-five miles from Baltimore and forty Yale students who arrived at dawn in a chartered bus. They didn't complain and they didn't leave. They were there, they had to be there, and just being there was enough. It was unaccountable, of course, but scarcely anyone even tried to account for it. Russell Baker of the *New York Times* arrived at his house in Washington and was disquieted to find no one there. He turned on his television set and there, on Channel 4, beheld his wife leading their children around the bier. 'It was our *duty*,' she said fiercely when she reached home. 'Everyone in Washington should go for all the people who can't get here.'

If you were on the Hill that night, you remember the throng as the nicest you had ever known. Virtually no one shoved, or cut in, or was rude. There were many parents with children—families as large as nine—but even toddlers, sensing the mood of the adults, were undemanding and subdued. It may have been the most democratic occasion in Washington's memory. Eamonn de Valera and a member of Kennedy's PT 109 crew were admitted to the rotunda without waiting. But de Valera was a head of state, blind and in his eighties, and two other members of the old crew refused to ask for special privilege. Thirty-six nuns from New Jersey arrived on a rented bus and took their place at the end of the line; so did a youth on crutches, a woman in a wheelchair, and another woman, convalescing from a foot operation, who had to be propped up against trees and lamp posts by solicitous strangers. Pierre Salinger's fifteen-year-old son Marc stood for fourteen hours, right through the night; Jersey Joe Walcott, the former heavyweight champion, waited eight hours. There were Virginia farmers in denim, New York women in mink, and—everywhere, it seemed—groups of students, of Negroes, and of seamen who would square their caps and practise the salute they would deliver when they reached the catafalque where, as one of them put it, there lay 'in honoured glory a sailor well known to God'.

It was that kind of a night: emotive and unashamedly demonstrative. One felt, as in war, a kinship with everyone else there; one wanted to help, to share. Fritz Hollings, former Governor of South Carolina, had driven to the capital with a friend and the friend's children, who wanted to see the Lincoln Memorial first. As Hollings awaited their return at the kerb a young Southern Negro approached him and asked whether this was the rotunda. 'No, but I'll take you there,' said Hollings. He drove him to the hill, decided the line was too long for a man in his forties, changed his mind, and returned to wait from 11 p.m. to 6 a.m.

Fred Holborn, restlessly circling the Capitol on foot in the middle of the night, was again 'struck by the generational thing. There seemed to be college students everywhere often from far away. Along East Capitol some were singing folk songs gently.' Indeed, there seemed to be at least one guitar in every block. Miss McGrory noticed 'the many, *many* young people', and seven blocks from the Hill she saw a youth with a guitar case surrounded by children. She asked, 'Do you know the President's favourite song?' He didn't, she told him, and together they sang:

'Won't you come home, Bill Bailey, won't you come home?'
She moans the whole day l-ong. . . .

Then they sang 'Swing Low, Sweet Chariot', and the spiritual:

Hush, little baby, don't you cry,
You know your Daddy was born to die.
All my trials, Lord, soon be over. . . .

A quartet of seamen harmonized the 'Navy Hymn', and, to the music of 'John Brown's Body', 'He's gone to be a sailor in the Navy of the Lord'. The Negroes sang 'We Shall not Be Moved'; the students joined them and then led them in the old folk, new collegiate repertoire—'Sinner Man', 'Aunt Rhody', 'Hard Travellin',' 'On Top of Old Smoky', 'Careless Love', 'Michael', and 'Reuben James'. A strapping Negro in a shiny black suit that looked far too thin for this weather gave them Ed McCurdy's 'Strangest Dream' in a vibrant baritone:

Last night I had the strangest dream I ever had before,
I dreamed the world had all agreed to put an end to war.
I dreamed there was a mighty room, and the room was filled with men,
And the paper they were signing said they'd never fight again.

One towheaded tenor softly crooned the poignant, 140-year-old '*Ich hatt' einen Kameraden*':

Eine Kugel kam geflogen:
Gilt es mir oder gilt es dir?
Ihn hat es weggerissen;
Er liegt mir vor den Füssen,
Als Wär's ein Stück von mir.[8]

[8] A bullet came awhining.
Was it meant for him or me?
Away from me it snatched him,
And at my feet it stretched him,
As though a part of me.

And nearly everyone with a guitar, and many without one, sang:

. . . Someday . . .
Deep in my heart
I do believe
We shall overcome
Someday.

Melville Bell Grosvenor, president of the National Geographical Society, passed round the catafalque and paused to watch those behind him. One Negro woman entered crying. A white woman in front of her 'looked back reprovingly', Grosvenor recalled later. 'But as they reached the casket the white woman, too, broke out in sobs. Then she turned, put her arm around the coloured woman, and the two walked out together.'

There were stifled tears, mute prayers, signs of the cross, and the stiff salutes of uniformed mourners; nothing more. Their presence spoke for itself. As they shuffled forward Melville Grosvenor heard someone whisper, '*The Silent Americans*'.

10

LIGHT

Monday morning:

At 7 a.m., in the first quarter-hour of daylight, a wiry figure emerged from the Southeast Gate of the White House and struck out on foot for Union Station, two miles away. 'The weather was superb,' Mary McGrory wrote, as 'crisp and clear' as a Kennedy order, and the walker was the man who, with his brother, had symbolized that briskness and clarity throughout the dazzling three-year reign which was about to pass into history. The Attorney General was restless. Striding back, he was recognized on Pennsylvania Avenue; a crowd began to gather around him, and hailing a taxi he re-entered the mansion grounds and telephoned Ted Sorensen. He had been thinking about the quotations he was to read at the grave, he said. Something was missing. He wanted to add one more, about civil rights. . . .

Ken Galbraith walked breathlessly into Sorensen's office. He had finished still another draft of the joint session speech in Kay Graham's library. Arthur Schlesinger's secretary had rattled off two copies, one for Walter Jenkins and one for Ted. 'If I do say so myself, it's perfect now,' Galbraith told Sorensen. 'You won't have to change a word of it. . . .'

Ted put it aside. He couldn't bring himself to think about the new President until his President had been buried. Instead, he fingered the stiff brim of a silk hat. After Richard Nixon's defeat Alex Rose, the leader of the hatters union, had presented Kennedy and each of his chief lieutenants with expensive toppers for the inauguration. Sorensen, like his leader, never wore a hat. He had carried this one on January 20, 1961, and he would carry it again this November 25 and then pack it away for ever. . . .

'The agony continues,' Schlesinger was writing on the far side of the White House,

and one can still only intermittently believe it. I keep supposing that tomorrow morning I will come down to the White House, Evelyn will be in her office and Kenny in his, and in a few minutes the President will be along with some jokes about the morning papers. The thought that we will never see him again is intolerable and unacceptable and unendurable. But we never will, and nothing will ever be the same again.

In Blair House Harry Vaughn, a figure from the past, telephoned Dwight Eisenhower's suite at the Statler and stated the obvious: protocol was a mess. What could be done about it? To twenty million Republicans Truman's Vaughn had been an unprincipled 'influence peddler', but among professional soldiers his reputation was unimpeachable. He was just the man to heal the breach between the two ex-Presidents, and he did. They agreed not only to ride together in Eisenhower's limousine, but share the same pew in St Matthew's and return to Blair House afterwards. . . .

On Wisconsin Avenue Gawler's Funeral Home, continuing the pretence that this was a private funeral, chalked appropriate entries on its control board. Under 'NAME' was written 'President Kennedy', under 'RM' (room) 'White House', under 'CEM' 'Arl', and under 'REMARKS' 'Wilbert Vault' . . .

Mrs Paul Mellon rose early, fetched the basket of Martinique willowwork from her greenhouse around the corner from the British Embassy, and wrote to Kennedy a touching note of gratitude.

Monday morning Republican Senator Margaret Chase Smith laid a single red rose on the back-row Senate desk which had once been Senator John Kennedy's. Monday morning a New York newsdealer tacked a sign to his kiosk reading, 'Closed because of a death in the American family', Monday morning 730,000 American Telephone & Telegraph Company employees reported for work, and one of the first long-distance calls logged was from the Rev. Billy Graham, in Washington, to the tightly guarded hospital room of Governor John B. Connally, Jr., in Parkland Memorial Hospital. Nellie took it and thanked the evangelist for his good wishes. As she hung up her husband stirred. He emerged from a confused skein of dreams. The blur cleared; he was really conscious for the first time since the Presidential Lincoln had yawed beneath the Book Depository. An orderly brought him a breakfast of mush and coffee. A television set was wheeled in, and Nellie told him that their seventeen-year-old son Johnny had flown to the capital to represent him. Connally blinked at the screen, wondering whether he would see him.

The wounded Governor was one of the few men in Texas public life who could surrender to the national narcosis and watch the solemn pageantry in Washington. Duty required some to attend services for Officer J. D. Tippit in Beckley Hills Baptist Church and the subsequent graveside ceremony at Laurel Land Memorial Park, where the patrolman's grey coffin would be lowered into a plot reserved for men who had given their lives while working for the city, and others were quietly working behind the scenes to tidy up the debris left by Friday's tragedy. The most embarrassing chaff, of course, was the body of Lee Oswald. Luckily for its civic leaders, Dallas didn't have to worry about that. The Secret Service had assumed responsibility for the burial, and Marguerite had chosen Rose Hill Cemetery in Fort Worth, thirty miles away. Two Rose Hill workmen were told Monday morning to dig a grave for one 'William Bobo'. The fiction didn't deceive them long; when Oswald's cheap, moleskin-covered pine box arrived, it was accompanied by a hundred Fort Worth policemen, who sealed off the area to protect Marguerite, Robert, Marina, and her two children. The lid was raised. Forty reporters peered over the officers' shoulders. Marina, who had been following TV and was learning about images, kissed her husband and put her ring on his finger.

But burying Oswald didn't really dispose of him. Ruby was left; so were hundreds of unanswered questions, some infuriating, some sinister, and some—although the fact couldn't be faced then—for ever beyond reach. The issue of who should search for answers was obviously the first task of the new administration. Two years after the funeral Texas Attorney General Waggoner Carr revealed that the President had telephoned him that Monday to suggest that the state conduct its own investigation. This would spare the new President's sending federal agents to Texas. Carr was urged to announce the inquiry to the press without disclosing its inspiration. 'It was,' he recalled, 'to look as if it were my own decision.' He followed Johnson's advice, reading a four-paragraph statement at Washington's Statler Hilton. But keeping federal investigators out of the state was quite impossible. They were already there in strength. Jack Miller, head of Justice's Criminal Division, had arrived to coordinate their inquiries, and after the Tippit funeral he and Barefoot Sanders persuaded District Attorney Wade, and then Carr, to mark time until Nick Katzenbach could change the President's mind.

Carr was easy to convince. At his press conference he had felt that 'all the venom against Texas was poured on me'. The state's conservatives, of whom he was one, were smarting bitterly under outside attacks and some from inside. The clergy of Dallas was especially vocal. The Methodist Mr Holmes was already under police protection for disclosing that news of the President's death had been greeted with classroom applause, and another Methodist pastor, William H. Dickinson, Jr., had told his congregation that malice was not confined to the irresponsible: 'At a nice, respectable dinner party only two nights before the President's visit to our city, a bright young couple with a fine education, with a promising professional future, said to their friends that they hated the President of the United States—and that they would not care one bit if somebody did take a potshot at him.' Walter Bennett, a Presbyterian pastor, said the city had harboured 'a force of hatred that has erupted like a flame', and a Dallas Baptist, Dr James R. Allen, was writing a sermon charging that an 'element in our city' had been responsible for the assassination—that the 'white heat of a hate-filled atmosphere allowed the necessary warmth for this element to crawl out from under the rocks to be seen'.

This was very hard on civic rectitude, and civic leaders circled their wagons. Mayor Cabell observed that Oswald had not been a permanent resident and added, 'It could have happened in Podunk as well as Dallas.'[1] Councilman Carie Welch insisted that 'This should not reflect on the image or the character of Dallas.' And the Dallas *News*, resuming its offensive role, editorially demanded that its readers 'banish any feelings of rancour and guilt' and settle down to 'normal living'. The editorial conceded that the weekend had been difficult for Dallas. But 'a city, like a tree', it said, 'must weather the winds of adversity to reach the heights of stature'. Clearly the winds of the *News* were not going to be stilled indefinitely. More significantly, the city was enlisting powerful sympathy elsewhere. A half-hour after the assassination a Voice of America broadcaster had described Dallas as 'the centre of the extreme Right Wing'. Now Arthur Krock of the *New York Times* denounced 'this gratuitous, and, as it proved, false, suggestion that such was the affiliation of the assassin'. The *News* was concerned with the reputation of the conservative establishment in one city; Krock with the entire country's. In each case the attitude seemed to be, 'My image: may she always be right, but my image, right or wrong.' The esteem of a nation, and especially of one element in it was at stake. It was expedient to dismiss the killer as a freak who had existed *in vacuo*.

'And the hell of it is,' Ralph Dungan had said, 'they'll blame it all on that twenty-four-year-old boy.'

After morning coffee Colonel Swindal assembled his entire Dallas crew outside Andrews Field's MATS terminal. The only man

[1] 'If it had happened in Podunk,' *Newsweek* asked, 'would any of the schoolchildren there have cheered?'

missing was Sergeant Ayres, who would represent Air Force One in St Matthew's after delivering the last of the President's Texas clothes to Godfrey McHugh's office. Swindal wanted the Presidential plane airborne two hours early, because he anticipated a unique problem. Until today all other aircraft had yielded to 26000. But when Colonel Charles Walton at Lee Mansion gave the green light to the fifty jet fighters, one for each state in the union, they would streak for the river. The blinding speed of their F-105 engines could leave him far behind, so he climbed to the flight's Initial Point before them and fingered his headset, listening intently to Walton's walkie-talkie and to traffic from an H-43 helicopter posted over the parade route. Around his cockpit the fighters whined, forming inverted V's: the apex of their final V was vacant—the symbol, since World War I, of a fallen flier.

Nine miles away the H-43 looked down on a transformed Washington. It was to be one of the rare Mondays in history on which the Supreme Court cancelled a scheduled session; instead, the justices convened in Earl Warren's apartment and rode to the White House. At 10 a.m. a buzzer summoned the Senate to postpone action on the wheat bill. Senators followed Congressmen around the bier; then the men with seniority drove to St Matthew's while their juniors crossed the Potomac to submit identification to Secret Service men in Arlington. There was to be no business in the capital. There was only a funeral. And virtually everyone was going to attend it. At 9 a.m., when the rotunda doors were closed, 250,000 people had filed past the catafalque. All seemed to be still here. The cutoff had excluded a line of twelve thousand (including a family from Cleveland which had been twenty feet from the threshold). They quietly drew back behind the forming ropes, joining those who had been waiting on kerbstones, some since long before dawn, for the procession.

Actually, there were to be three processions. First, the Kennedy family and marching troops would escort the caisson from the Hill to the White House. Second, the widow would leave her car and lead those who were to follow the coffin on foot to St Matthew's. Finally, all mourners, in limousines, would proceed behind the gun carriage south to Constitution Avenue and then westward around the Lincoln Memorial, over Memorial Bridge, and down the Avenue of Heroes to Arlington. Altogether the route covered over six miles. A million people had gathered to line either side of it—'an enormous multitude,' wrote Russell Baker, 'in this city that normally shuns the streets during state occasions for the comfort of home and television'. It was, Mac Bundy wrote, 'as if the whole route to the cathedral and the longer route to Arlington were merely aisles in a theatre of solemn grief'.

By 10 a.m. the Cabinet, the Congressional leadership, the White House staff, the President's personal friends, and the eminent visitors from abroad had assembled in the mansion's East, Green, Blue, Red, and State Dining rooms, each man bearing a small card reading:

THE WHITE HOUSE

---

is respectfully invited
to join the procession on foot
leaving The White House at 11.30 o'clock
for the
Pontifical Requiem Mass
at St Matthew's Cathedral
Monday, November 25, 1963

Inside St Matthew's the church truck waited, draped in purple velvet. Six massive candles in towering gold holders stood upon the white marble altar, flickering redly on the vases Mrs Mellon had arranged. Overhead Grant La Farge's ornate dome looked down upon the gathering mourners: relatives of the dead President, the wives of the men who would walk, the diplomatic corps, the sub-cabinet, the elite of the New Frontier. And in Arlington the grave was ready. The Irish cadets stood at parade rest. The efficiency of the eternal flame was demonstrated for two generals who had been afraid it would ignite the pine boughs banked around it. In McClellan Circle an artillery captain named Gay stood by a battery of 76-millimetre cannon; Air Force bagpipers were at their posts; the vault below was open to receive the coffin from a mechanical lowering device.

To the national audience the tragic sweep of the ceremony would seem a triumph of majesty. So it was; but a state funeral is essentially high theatre, and like any other performance this one was to have its backstage byplay and missed cues. John Kennedy would have enjoyed all of them. He disliked ineptness onstage, but fluffs in the wings appealed to his sense of the grotesque, and in their small way the slip-ups were as appropriate as, say, the yarns spun at a wake. Most of them went unnoticed. The only conspicuous blunder —Sergeant Clark's broken note in taps—would be widely regarded as a deliberate effect. It wasn't. The grave site stage managers, in their anxiety to please network cameramen, stationed the Sergeant five yards in front of the riflemen who were to fire three volleys before him, which meant that he would come on stone deaf. There was a visual slip in the cemetery too, though black-and-white television didn't record it. The area around the grave and the sides of the press box were draped with gaudy yards of what Arlington calls 'artificial grass'. Mrs Kennedy would have far preferred the autumnal solemnity of November foliage to this bright fakery, suggestive of gangster funerals in old George Raft movies. Bunny Mellon would never have permitted it, but the draping was done after she had left the cemetery. Indeed, Bunny had been lucky to get Mrs Kennedy's little basket of Rose Garden flowers to the grave. She was barred from the slope by a cordon of suspicious soldiers until a Secret Service agent recognized her and hurried over. He promised to watch over the basket, Jack Metzler assured her he would supervise the unloading of the four truckloads of rotunda flowers, and then she and Nancy Tuckerman raced back to St. Matthew's—the last women over the bridge before it was sealed off.

At the cathedral Bishop Hannan was overwrought. As a native Washingtonian he had known the importance of proper salutations since boyhood. Lists of the dignitaries who would be attending today's Mass had been prepared by State, but none had been given to Hannan, the one man who would be addressing them. He decided to station himself on the steps outside and tick the celebrities off as they entered. (Halfway through his eulogy he would look down on Presidents Truman and Eisenhower and realize, to his horror, that he had omitted them; they had already been in their pew.) The bishop wasn't alone in his frenzy. During the hours before the service the church was, in fact, a most unchurchly place. The Lord's name was repeatedly invoked, usually in vain, for the chief problem was lack of space, and no one could do a thing about that. 'My God, do you mean we won't have a seat for *Kenny O'Donnell*?' Jack McNally yelled down the centre aisle. Dean Markham found one, found another for Secret Service Chief Rowley (after moving him three times), and turned his last 'emergency pew' over to Chief Marshal Jim McShane, who arrived unexpectedly with seven of Robert Kennedy's eight children. But Markham was beginning to wonder whether there would be room for President Johnson. Though every worshipper had proper credentials, how some had got them was a mystery. Several *Last Hurrah* Bostonians were there, including an obscure entrepreneur who advertised himself as 'the Leading Tomato Grower in the World'.

The congregation had come to mourn a martyred President. In their distress it was too much to expect them to put aside all private animosity, however, and perhaps these conflicts provided a necessary diversion. Usher Bradlee avoided Usher Morrissey. Mary McGrory hung back when she saw India Edwards. The Kennedy liberals looked on critically as Harry Byrd and Richard Russell jockeyed for position. They watched with furtive delight as ticketless George Wallace hopped about trying to find a vacant space, and they observed, without compassion, a highly agitated Ross Barnett praying aloud. And all this, too, was somehow appropriate. Kennedy had been a politician; politics is contention. He had liked the battle lines sharply drawn. To efface them in the name of grief would have been hypocrisy.

At the White House the tone was rather different. The chiefs of state examined the Mass cards Shriver distributed among them and heard Emperor Haile Selassie declare that Ethiopia needed no new Kennedy monument because the President's memory was enshrined for ever in the work of the Peace Corps. Kennedy friends quietly reminisced. The closest thing to an abrasive encounter was a comic misunderstanding between Jim Reed, the most courtly of the President's acquaintances, and a small dark stranger. Jim thought he knew everyone who had been close to Kennedy, but he had never seen this man before. He whispered around an inquiry. The whisper came back, *'That's the architect for Atoka.'* To Reed he seemed unaccountably rude, even for an artist. The man was crowding him and was oddly unresponsive. Finally he leaned over and said politely, 'I understand you're the architect for Atoka.' The stranger glared and said *'Non!'* It struck Jim that he probably spoke no English, and then the man handed him his card. It read, 'Jean Monnet.'

In a way Monnet's presence was a global equivalent to the domestic tensions in St Matthew's. Mac Bundy thought it 'a good stroke' to mark him among the marching acquaintances, and David Ormsby-Gore—who had taken the extraordinary step of deserting the diplomatic corps to be among the friends himself—reflected that Charles de Gaulle would have flown 'into a passion of rage had he known that Jean was in there marching in the procession as a close friend of Jack's'. Monnet was a symbol of a united Europe; the French President was its great adversary. De Gaulle was regarded with a mixture of awe and distrust. Averell Harriman believed that his very motives in coming to the funeral were suspect—that he was acting 'shockingly, disgracefully, even treacherously'.[2] Few would have gone that far, but nobody would have mistaken him as a marching friend either. Later, during the Mass in St Matthew's, he followed the French pattern of ritualistic responses, which meant that he was often standing bolt upright while the rest of the con-

[2] The quotation is included here at Harriman's suggestion. De Gaulle had promised to meet Kennedy in the capital the following February or March. The funeral became his Washington 'visit'; he refused to follow through with Johnson. Harriman also believes that if Kennedy had lived France wouldn't have recognized Red China, though this, he adds, is not a criticism of Johnson.

gregation sat and sitting when they stood. That evening the Kennedy sisters summed it up in one word: 'typical'. And when Larry O'Brien first saw de Gaulle, the Frenchman was beside Haile Selassie. Both were in uniform. Larry, behind him, had never seen the Emperor and didn't recognize him. *If that isn't just like de Gaulle,* he thought, *bringing a midget as his aide.*

Now in the East Room *le grand Charles* was being his usual obstinate self. This time, though, he was in excellent company. The number of anonymous threats had increased alarmingly since daybreak, and the prey most frequently mentioned were de Gaulle, Mikoyan, President Johnson, Robert Kennedy, and Earl Warren. All refused to be intimidated. One of Johnson's Texans quoted him as saying, 'I'd rather give my life than be afraid to give it.' This wasn't quite accurate. What the President really said—to his military aide, Colonel William Jackson—was: 'You damned bastards are trying to take over. If I listen to you, I'll be led to stupid, indecent decisions. I'm going to walk.' Bob Kennedy was equally decisive, if less earthy; when Nick Katzenbach and Ed Guthman pleaded with him to avoid exposure, he changed the subject. 'Talk to someone else,' he said when John McCone called him. 'I'm too involved.' Earl Warren's answer to the forebodings of the District police was the simplest of all. It was no answer. The Chief Justice pretended he had heard nothing.

In retrospect this is not very impressive, because it was all over quickly and nothing happened. At 10 a.m. Monday that outcome was by no means clear. Friday's assassination had been preceded by warnings; so had yesterday's murder; and now warnings were coming through again. Furthermore, the gunman this time didn't have to be a marksman or a faker of credentials. If he missed one celebrity, his chances of hitting another were excellent. The eight blocks between the mansion and the cathedral were the most densely populated in the capital. Down that swarming canyon, in slow pace, would tread all the powerful men in the world except Nikita Khrushchev and Mao Tse-tung, and Khrushchev had sent his deputy. Security had done all it could. The Pentagon and the District police had over four thousand men under arms, including a detachment of New York policemen who were paying their own expenses: in the procession itself would be the White House Detail, 64 CIA men, 40 FBI agents, 250 State Department security men, and picked squads from each foreign secret police—12 French bodyguards and 10 State Department guards for de Gaulle alone.

Still the dissatisfaction persisted. In the Blue Room Dean Rusk confided to the Cabinet that he was 'deeply worried'. He cited the risks, beginning with de Gaulle, 'four times the object of an assassin', and Anastas Mikoyan, 'a prime target'. Douglas Dillon agreed; he was 'scared to death that Mikoyan might be shot at', and Orville Freeman confessed he was 'worried sick'. George Ball was so apprehensive that he had decided against participating in any of the ceremonies. He and U. Alexis Johnson were maintaining a vigil in the State Department building at Twenty-first and Virginia, preparing to cope with an emergency should shots ring out six blocks away.

Attempts to get individual marchers into cars continued up to the last moment. Llewellyn Thompson reminded Russian diplomats that Mikoyan had an excellent reason for riding. Quite apart from his age, he was convalescing from surgery and postoperative hepatitis. But the First Deputy Premier was as adamant as the others. Even Eamonn de Valera, whose physical condition was so precarious that young Eamonn, a physician, would have to walk beside him with a syringe in his pocket, could not be budged. As anticipated, the key to their resolution was Jacqueline Kennedy. If she led, they had to follow. No leader of men could seek cover unless she did, and she remained inflexible. Jerry Behn approached Clint Hill and asked him if he thought she would share a limousine with Johnson. Clint shook his head. 'You can try if you want to, but it'll be a waste of time,' he said. 'She really wants to walk all the way, and if it weren't for the old men she would.'

The last three warnings came from the Royal Canadian Mounted Police, the Federal Bureau of Investigation, and the Central Intelligence Agency. The RCMP had 'received information' that an unidentified grievance was heading south to shoot General de Gaulle. The FBI was even vaguer: 'The Director' was 'concerned' and 'advised against' the march. This was too much for Sargent Shriver. Once more the precise businessman was confronted by the grey custard of bureaucracy, and once more he recoiled, emitting sparks. 'That's just ridiculous,' he snapped. 'We're *all* concerned. You don't have to be the Director of the FBI to know it's going to be dangerous—even the White House doorman knows that. It's a ploy, so that if anybody gets shot the Director can say, "I told you so." It'd be a different story if he'd turned up hard proof that some famous gangster had taken an apartment on Connecticut Avenue, or if the best agent in the OGPU had checked in at Washington National. Then I'd have to do a double-take. But this is just a self-serving device.'

The CIA was more specific. At 10.30 a courier with a direct line to CIA headquarters across the river handed John McCone a hot report. McCone became visibly excited. It was an 'A-1-A', agency jargon meaning 'absolutely reliable'. Relayed through Central Intelligence's nerve centre in New York, it was from agents in Geneva who had positively verified an elaborate plot to murder General de Gaulle on the stretch of pavement outside the cathedral. McCone was convinced it was 'ominous'. The General must be told at once. He sought out Angie Duke, whose French was better than his own, and Duke recruited Mac Bundy, whose command of the language was flawless. Thus, in Bundy's words, 'it fell to Angie Duke and me to approach the great man'. They explained the rumour and urged him to accept a limousine, explaining that 'it would be a courtesy to Mrs Kennedy if General de Gaulle would not endanger his life'. The response was inevitable, though those who were present have different recollections of it. Duke thought the General said that his 'courtesy to Mrs Kennedy' would be 'to show disregard for his life'. Bundy merely heard him reply ' "*Non*" in his most distant and nasal tone.' At that, the CIA came off better than the FBI. There can be no doubt about his reaction there. To backstop McCone he was shown the earlier report. Shriver saw his lips pucker in disdain. Charles de Gaulle's answer to J. Edgar Hoover was '*Pfft*'.

On the floor above, Monday had begun with a small birthday celebration in the dining-room. Miss Shaw had forgotten that young John would be three years old this Monday, but the realization came to her upon awakening, and she decided to make breakfast a little occasion. The boy had known that he had an anniversary coming soon. At his age dates meant very little, however. He didn't know what to expect, or exactly when it would come. And Caroline had been told that since their birthdays were so close they would be celebrated at a joint party later in the week. So there was no sense of disappointment, no outward sadness. There was only the crowing exultation of a three-year-old listening to his big sister and Miss Shaw sing 'Happy Birthday to You' and then opening two of his presents—a toy helicopter from Caroline and, from their nurse, a copy of Beatrix Potter's *Peter Rabbit*.

After breakfast Miss Shaw dressed them in their blue coats and red shoes. She put the black mourning band on Caroline's hair, slipped her own black-and-white check coat over her white uniform, and, leaving John with Dave Powers, took the girl down to the Red Room. Agent Foster walked over. There was a sudden hush among the adults sipping coffee. That was the thing about the children: every time people forgot the stark reality of the murder and began translating it into the niceties of protocol or national posture they were confronted by these terribly vulnerable little figures. Robin Duke stepped up and said, 'I'll take your hand, Caroline.' But Caroline had her mother's will. 'No, I'll hold Mr Foster's hand,' she whispered, and took it, making Foster feel, he said, 'like Jello.'

Her mother had remembered what today was to have been. One of her scrawled notes to herself began 'John's party—card.... Fos. to get pres here——.' At the bottom of one page she had written in large letters: 'LEAVE 10——' That was the deadline, and the whole family was racing to meet it. She herself was pinning her sister's black beret over the long veil—it fell below her waist—that Lucinda Moran had fashioned. Lee was calling that Dr Walsh had given her some blue 'anti-crying' pills, 'just in case'. Eunice had donned her best black maternity gown. All the sisters were wearing black stockings and gloves and worrying about their mother, who looked and felt extremely unwell. Joe Gargan had rented a full-dress suit for Ted, but it had arrived incomplete. He was missing a hat, gloves, and pants. Dressing with Bob, phoning furiously to retrieve the rest of his costume, and watching the creeping hands of the clock, the Senator had finally been forced to compromise. He would have to wear the President's gloves and go without a hat. Bob agreed to go hatless, too (with the consequence that all the other men—heads of state, Cabinet, diplomatic corps—went through the funeral bareheaded; it seemed so right that no one even noticed it). That left trousers, an essential. The only available pair had belonged to their brother. He had worn them on inauguration day. But he had been slender. Ted's waistline was a family joke. He turned around and they were gone. The next he knew they were in Stas's hands. Ted reclaimed them and tried them on—and they fitted perfectly. It was, he later told Jackie, 'a loaves and fishes miracle'. In a way it was. George Thomas, whose languor was another family joke, had snatched up the pants and let them out in minutes.

Abruptly it was time to go; time, and past time. Outside, the family entered a caravan of limousines and drove to Capitol Hill, where the long parade had formed and was waiting. General Wehle again stood at the head of it; behind him ranged a spectrum of colours as familiar to Americans as the Stars and Stripes: the scarlet tunics of the Marine Band, the grey of West Point cadets, the Navy blue of midshipmen, the lighter blue of the Air Force. Behind the bands, behind the braided Joint Chiefs, riderless Black Jack reared his superb head, the varnished boots and sheathed silver sword glittering in the cold sunlight.

In a well between the rotunda and the old Senate chamber Lieutenant Sam Bird had drawn the casket team around him in a tight circle. 'Bow your heads,' he said. He closed his eyes. 'Dear God,' he prayed, 'please give us strength to do this last thing for the President.' They straightened, he glanced at his watch. 'Let's move,' he said. His orders were to approach the catafalque at 10.27 after receiving a signal, a curt nod, from a captain on the far side of the great hall. But though 10.27 became 10.30 and then 10.40, the captain remained immobile. The family was eleven minutes late arriving, and on debarking Robert Kennedy improvised a change in plans. He wanted a final moment of privacy with the coffin. 'Let's go in,' he suggested to Jackie and Ted. Therefore Lieutenant Bird saw, not the expected signal, but the President's widow, flanked by her husband's brothers, advancing upon the bier.

The Kennedys knelt together, three heads against the flag, praying for ten minutes. Arising, they descended the marble stairs, and now the captain jerked his head. 'Secure casket,' Lieutenant Bird ordered. In the plaza the Coast Guard Academy Band played 'Hail to the Chief' in the slow measure which no longer seemed strange as Bird's pallbearers moved into the sun and paused on the portico, between the columns; then, to the hymn 'O God of Loveliness', casket team and casket came down the thirty-six steps. But today there was no strain. The fantastic weight of yesterday was gone. The coffin seemed incredibly light, and since it seemed that way to each of the eight bearers, who could neither speak to one another nor even exchange glances until it had been lashed to the gun carriage, the power of suggestion must be ruled out. Last night's lockstep torture at the Tomb of the Unknown Soldiers had been a success. It had broken their dreadful spell of fear, and they withdrew in wonder.

The Joint Chiefs had stood at attention, facing Clifton, McHugh, and Shepard, while the sliding casket grated across the metal bed of the caisson and was buckled into place. Now they wheeled behind it. Far ahead a huge baton flashed. The President had once banteringly referred to the Marine Band as 'the only troops I command—the rest belong to McNamara'. Jacqueline Kennedy had not forgotten, nor had they; they thought of themselves as his. The drum major brought the baton down and the cortège moved off to the crashing strains of 'Our Fallen Heroes'. In brilliant splendour, with that dash and flair which had marked his six years as Congressman and eight as Senator, John Kennedy left Capitol Hill for the last time.

The marching was almost too good to be true. One was accustomed to precision from the Military Academy and the Marine Corps, but even the company of women from the various armed services and the representatives of thirty-two veterans organizations were keeping proper intervals and maintaining the unfamiliar hundred-pace step. They appeared inspired. Really their matchless formation, like the career of the man they were burying, was an act of gracefulness achieved through meticulous planning. General Wehle had established an elaborate command net along the avenue to correct errors. Colonel Miller was racing up and down back streets in a radio car, radioing coded instructions for 'feed-ins' and 'feed-outs'—Lieutenant Bird's body bearers, for example, were being transferred by bus from 'Depot' (the Capitol) to 'Victor' (St Matthew's).

The one rebel against this machine was Black Jack. After the first five hundred yards the gelding broke into a sweat. Pfc Carlson had never known him to do that before. In the 30-degree weather his steaming flanks were unnatural, alarming. His steel hoofs clattered in jarring tattoo, an unnerving contrast to the crack cadence in front; his eyes rolled whitely. He was nearly impossible to control. Yet today his convulsions were scarcely noticed. The limousine passengers sat in utter stillness, for to them the way back was heart-rending. West on Constitution, northwest on Pennsylvania, north on Fifteenth, west on Pennsylvania—this was the very route Kennedy had followed after his inaugural address, on his first trip to the White House as President. Then the kerbs had been banked with slabs of snow. There had been no gun carriage and no detachment of Vietnam veterans among the troops; bleachers packed with spectators had cheered. Nevertheless the streets and buildings were the same. The stately federal triangle on the left and the souvenir shops and hamburger shops on the right hadn't changed. Every pillar, every silhouette against the sky—now, as then, a stainless blue—was unchanged, and at times only the haunting silence of the dense crowds reminded them that this wasn't yesterday, that yesterday was gone for ever.

The hushed crowds and the music. The melodies were very different. The Marines struck up 'Holy, Holy, Holy' and 'The Vanished Army', and the other service bands played 'Onward Christian soldiers', '*Vigor in Arduis*', the funeral marches of Beethoven, R. B. Hall, and Chopin—the most famous of them all and the most dolorous—and, at the end, the redeeming 'America the Beautiful':

. . . O beautiful for heroes proved in liberating strife,
Who more than self their country loved, and mercy more than life! . . .
O beautiful for patriot dream that sees, beyond the years,
Thine alabaster cities gleam, undimmed by human tears!

America! America! God shed His grace on thee. . . .

In the Oval Room O'Donnell, O'Brien, and Red Fay watched the procession on television. In the background Dave Powers was marching John up and down, halting him, commanding him to salute, and then tramping off again. Once, while the casket team was carrying the coffin down the east steps, the boy had run over and pressed his face against the glass screen. Now John was gone. An agent had taken him to join his sister, and Powers suggested they drink a champagne toast to their fallen leader. Maître Fincklin always kept a bottle on ice; he quickly filled goblets, and the four men in mourning clothes raised them to the caisson on the screen.

Putting his glass down, Dave said softly, 'I can just see the President in heaven. He's looking down and saying, "Look at that son-of-a-bitch Powers. He can always find an excuse for a toast when it's my liquor he's drinking." '

Across Lafayette Square the bells began to toll.

The bells tolled, the Annapolis choir on the lawn sang 'The Londonderry Air' and 'Eternal Father', the paraders shifted to left shoulder arms and halted on Seventeenth Street, beyond the mansion; the gun carriage peeled off and rolled up the driveway between the state flags, under the tortured shadows of the leafless trees overhead; and Agent Tom Wells became involved in a quiet struggle with the toughest bodyguards of the Sûreté Nationale. Jacqueline Kennedy had told Wells that during the walk to St Matthew's she wanted her children as close to her as possible, in a limousine. The car was parked by the portico, pointing towards the Northwest Gate. Caroline, John, and Miss Shaw were in the back seat, and the doors were locked from the inside. Agents Foster, Lynn Meredith, and Muggsy O'Leary were posted around it. 'Start easing up,' Wells told the White House sergeant behind the wheel. 'Just follow me.'

He stood in front of the front bumper and stepped into the diplomatic corps, doing a breast stroke with his arms. 'Pardon me, excuse me,' he said, pawing his way through ambassadors and prime ministers. Suddenly he was in the second rank. Only Charles de Gaulle and Haile Selassie were in front of him, and it was there that the trouble started. Burley Frenchmen rushed him from both sides. '*Non, non, non!*' they cried, clawing at him. Wells reached behind him to be sure the car radiator was still there and then resumed his breast stroke. 'Excuse me,' he said politely. '*Excusez-moi.*' The French guards were enraged, and Angie Duke, who had just finished lining up his heads of state—and was relieved to see that they would go through the gate in one rank, shoulder to shoulder—hopped over shouting, 'Stop! You can't do that!' 'Pardon me,' said Wells, beaming at him. '*C'est impossible!*' howled a Sûreté man. De Gaulle looked around, startled, and stepped back. That was the opening Wells had been waiting for. He strode forward between the General and the Lion of Judah, the car followed, and Wells flagged it down in exactly the right spot to enter the procession in front of de

Gaulle. Ahead of him the Vice Presidential limousine streaked out of West Executive and tore off towards the cathedral. It was not, as many assumed, a decoy—Lynda and Lucy were in it—but the new President and First Lady hadn't changed their minds either. Led by Jerry Behn, they were hurrying over from the EOB to join the Kennedys.

Alighting in the drive, the widowed First Lady stumbled a little, and as she righted herself she heard the last chorus of the 'Navy Hymn' fading away. The choir was preparing to sing a third hymn, but she was too quick for that. Pausing by the Grand Duchess of Luxembourg and Haile Selassie, she looked at General de Gaulle a moment. She appeared to be decisive. Actually, she was bewildered. This part of the funeral had been handled by other people. She hadn't given much thought to who the distinguished visitors would be, and really hadn't believed that they would walk. Now here they were, all lined up. From under her veil she peered up at de Gaulle. She nodded once, slightly, and saw him 'sort of nodding and bowing his head, his face just stricken'.

She turned on her heel and started to walk. The choir, which had filled its lungs for the canon '*Dona Nobis Pacem*', was cut off. The church bells continued to boom, however, and as Bob moved up on her right and Ted on her left their deep knell was joined by a shrill skirl. The nine pipers of the Black Watch were being fed into the column by Colonel Miller. In their shaggy black bearskins, tartan kilts, and snowy leggings they were as surprising as their music, but the bagpipes' plaintive wail, unlike Chopin's dirge, seemed fitting. Moreover, anyone could walk to it. Keeping in step didn't matter, though the three Kennedys (each unaware of it) *were* in step. At the first distant note of the pipes the widow wavered, close to tears. Then the American drummers began rolling their muffled drums, and she straightened. Turning off Pennsylvania and up Seventeenth, Ted said in a low voice, 'We'd better pick it up a little bit, to keep up with the band.' She had been holding Bob's hand. Now she dropped it and stepped forward briskly, head high, the wind fingering the long folds of her veil. She herself was conscious only of Bob and Ted saying 'This is too fast' or 'A little faster.' The great throngs, on the other hand, saw no one but her. Her impact on them was tremendous; in her bearing they saw a confirmation of her gallantry in the rotunda, a symbol of the national catharsis. Melville Bell Grosvenor, watching from a fourth-floor window, wrote: 'Jacqueline Kennedy walked with a poise and grace that words cannot convey—as regal as any emperor, queen, or prince who followed her.' Lady Jean Campbell cabled the London *Evening Standard* that the widow had 'given the American people from this day on the one thing they always lacked—majesty'. She wore her grief, another spectator thought, 'like a brave flag'.

She never looked back. Right behind her, equally intent, were Jamie Auchincloss, Sargent Shriver, and Steve Smith; then, after a five-yard interval, the Johnsons, followed by Caroline and John's unmarked car. The new President was nearly lost in a human convoy led by Behn and Youngblood, but his protection was dwarfed by that of the dignitaries behind the children's limousine. Twelve abreast, the foreign delegation strode and shuffled in sixteen ragged ranks. De Gaulle, Haile Selassie, King Baudouin, Queen Frederika, Ludwig Erhard, Chung Hee Park of South Korea and Diosdado Macapagal of the Philippines were conspicuous in front, and impressed onlookers assumed that the two hundred men around them were also sovereigns or chief mourners. In fact, over half were armed escorts, squinting up at windows. They surrounded Lee Radziwill and the Kennedy sisters, and so many had closed in on Mikoyan that he was completely obscured.

The formlessness of the pack undoubtedly helped security, but it wasn't planned. It simply couldn't be helped. Language barriers prevented whispered instructions, and age was a crippling handicap for men like de Valera, Lübke of West Germany, and Inönü of Turkey, all of whom had started in the first rank and who, by the time the procession turned half-left into Connecticut Avenue, were rapidly drifting astern. The jumble offended no one. It was quite enough to see the exotic figures in vivid purple, green, and red sashes trudging bareheaded past the Mayflower and the Peoples Drug Store and the Potomac Federal Savings & Loan, to know that an American President had meant this much to the world. Yet after they had passed, spectators felt a flicker of chauvinism to see the U.S. Supreme Court march up in one straight line, in perfect order; to watch the Cabinet in two even ranks, heads high; and to admire the almost martial air of the Presidential assistants, of Kennedy's personal friends, and of the White House servants. They looked so proud. And so they were. 'What friends he had, and how much they cared,' Mac Bundy wrote afterwards. 'Even in our grief we were . . . proud of his confidence and proud of each other.'

Passing the Metropolitan Club Bundy remembered that it was 'the President's persistent and not always gentle needling' that had led him to resign in protest against the club's segregation, though he had never got round to telling Kennedy. Now he never would. But he could do this. For him, and for all of them, marching, in Byron White's phrase, was 'a great surge of relief'. Ralph Dungan had asked Evelyn Lincoln whether she thought she could make it. She had answered, 'I'm ready to walk to Rockville.' Retired Justice

Stanley Reed was striding with the rest of the Court, and though Maxwell Taylor had been on his feet since leaving the Capitol and was beginning to limp, he still wished he could march all the way to Arlington.

On the steps of St Matthew's, a half-block off Connecticut, Cardinal Cushing waited in his black and red vestments and tall white mitre. To Jacqueline Kennedy, when she first glimpsed him, he appeared 'so . . . *enormous*'. He himself had just seen his President's coffin turn up Rhode Island Avenue; he was gently inclining his head and weeping briefly, wiping away the tears with a trembling hand. For seven years the Cardinal had known that he himself was a dying man. Malignant tumours had already taken his prostate and a kidney, and his asthma and emphysema were so severe that his voice box was practically a creation of throat surgeons. Yet he was always strong in an emergency. He *looked* like a high priest. And if in his long public prayers his rasping tones seemed to scold God, in private he was infinitely tender. The moment the Army Band finished 'Hail to the Chief' and began the hymn 'Pray for the Dead' he opened his arms to Mrs Kennedy and her children. He kissed her and let her kneel and kiss his ring—a gesture which he, with his strong convictions about the separation of church and state, would ordinarily never have allowed. Then, in her words, he 'sort of shepherded me in'.

He returned, followed by an acolyte holding a crucifix for the traditional antiphon and psalm sung for the dead at the church entrance. Lieutenant Bird hadn't counted on this. The casket team had unbuckled the caisson straps and was bearing the coffin to the top of the steps when the Cardinal reappeared with holy water, blocking the way. The eight body bearers were in the worst possible stance. The weight was unevenly distributed, and Bird desperately braced himself against the rear while the grating voice went on and on. The Lieutenant had never heard so long a prayer; totally ignorant of Catholic liturgy, he wondered wildly whether this was what was called a Mass. Just as he was about to whisper, 'Cardinal, you better move,' His Eminence reached the final '*Et lux perpetua luceat ei*'—'And let perpetual light shine upon him'—and, kissing the flag, stepped aside. The spent team lowered their burden to the waiting church truck. The Cardinal went in; Bishop Hannan remained, searching faces feverishly and composing his long salutation.

In the centre aisle the Cardinal, looking around for an usher, saw Mrs Joseph Kennedy standing to one side. 'Rose, my dear,' he said, and embraced her. 'Come with me.' She shook her head. The President's mother had been too upset to walk in the procession; she had made her way here with Ann Gargan and Bobby Fitzgerald, a cousin. Physically she was near collapse. She had refused to tell anyone but Ann and Bobby, however. She was determined to stay out of sight and enter the front pew at the last moment, and she waved the Cardinal on. Behind him came Lyndon Johnson. He, too, did not look himself. In the dim cathedral light the veined pouches beneath his lashes darkened, exaggerating his vulpine look. Slowly he paced behind the rolling coffin until in the transept, where the main aisle is bisected by the cross corridor, it was halted by clerical traffic up ahead. The President stopped by Ben Bradlee. Suddenly Ben felt compassion for him. 'I knew he would live in Kennedy's shadow for the rest of his life, and that he needed help.' Ben whispered, 'God bless you,' and the President responded with his eyes.

Overhead, St Matthew's choir sang the Gregorian *'Subvenite'* while Ben and the eight other ushers struggled to seat the marchers quickly. The family was easy enough. Jacqueline Kennedy's only special request had been to have Clint Hill directly behind her. Joe Gargan held a space between her and her children for the President's mother until Rose arrived. Bob and Ted were at the end of that row, and their wives, sisters, and children were in the second and third pews. The snag was over the dignitaries. This was Angie Duke's worry, and it was a stupendous one. The slight, sensitive chief of protocol had been working without rest for three days and three nights. Ahead of him, after the funeral, lay two crucial receptions—Mrs Kennedy's, in the executive mansion, and President Johnson's, at State. Nevertheless it was his hour in church that was to be his hour of trial. First he found that the pews he had earmarked last night had been confiscated by Jack McNally for President Kennedy's staff. He was obliged to lead his chiefs of state off to the right, to St Joseph Chapel—from which, he discovered in horror, the main altar was invisible.

Angie improvised. He seized a church functionary and demanded a television set. There was one in the cathedral, he was told, but using it in church during Mass was unthinkable. It *had* to be thinkable, said Angie, arguing furiously; diplomatic relations with ninety-one countries were at stake. The set appeared and was plugged in. It would be the only one in the cathedral, he told his charges, and they looked immensely pleased. Their pleasure diminished, however, when he started seating them. It was then he realized that in failing to allow for overcoats he had miscalculated badly. He had forgotten something else; the Emperor of Ethiopia, the King of the Belgians, and the husband of the Queen of England were all carrying bulky swords, more space-takers. Putting four bodies in a pew instead of five made a difference of twenty people—twenty world leaders who would have to stand. It wouldn't do. He would have to start cramming. Like a conductor on a crowded bus he kept urging them to move over. They complied, grunting. Some situations were especially awkward. When Princess Beatrix of the Netherlands came up, the only patch of bench left was between Mikoyan and Mikoyan's bodyguard. He put her there, where, as she later informed him, she had 'a silent service'. The last standee was Sir Alexander Bustamante, Prime Minister of Jamaica. The chapel had reached capacity, so Angie took him to the governors' section. Nelson Rockefeller jumped up, Sir Alexander sat, and Rockefeller started shoving. The governors crunched together. 'They were jammed in like sardines,' Angie said of the foreigners later. 'I stood throughout the Mass and suffered. Somehow we had got them all seated, but I hate to think how it was done.'

From the front pew in the main well of the church young John saw Haile Selassie. The Lion of Judah, who looked like a midget to Larry O'Brien, was a giant to John. Last summer he had come to the mansion bearing gifts; a leopard-skin coat for Mrs Kennedy (which she, as a token of respect, had worn at the time despite the sweltering heat) and two toys carved of pure ivory, a doll for Caroline and a warrior for John. Since then the children hadn't stopped talking about Haile Selassie, and John pointed towards the side chapel and gazed across at him admiringly. Then the formalities became boring to the boy. He fidgeted. St Matthew's bronze doors had clanged shut behind the last four persons to enter—Judge Sarah Hughes, Bunny Mellon, Martin Luther King, and Mary Ryan from Ireland. Luigi Vena was singing Leybach's '*Pie Jesu*' as the crucifer slowly returned the cross to the altar, accompanied by two other acolytes carrying candles. The Cardinal followed them, chanting in Latin. Behind him the casket team, moving stiffly like drugged automatons, wheeled the coffin into position in front of the first pew, a few feet from the widow.

'*In nomine Patris, et Filii, et Spiritus Sancti. Amen.*' His Eminence prayed. '*Introibo and altare dei . . .*'

'I am come to the altar of God . . .'

None of this had any meaning for the President's little son. From across the aisle Nina Warren and Joanie Douglas, in the Supreme Court section, heard him say, 'Where's my daddy?' The boy lifted his arms. 'Somebody pick me up.' Agent Foster, lurking near, carried him to the back of the church.

Ad Deum qui laetificat iuventutem meam . . .
To God, who makes me young and joyful . . .

It had been expected that the President's body would enter St Matthew's at 12.13 p.m. Attorney General Kennedy's decision to enter the rotunda had disturbed the officers riding around in command cars with stopwatches, but the widow, in rapidly walking away from Charles de Gaulle, had cut the time set aside for that phase of the parade, so that the coffin passed through the cathedral doors at 12.14. The martinets were relieved, which was irrelevant; what did matter was that millions of individuals, reading the funeral timetable in the morning papers, had spontaneously chosen that moment to express their own bereavement. Officially the entire day had been set aside for mourning, but the tide of public sorrow reached its crest while Cardinal Cushing finished sprinkling holy water under the anxious eye of Lieutenant Sam Bird, walked past Captain Cecil Stoughton (who, after three days of brilliant photography, suddenly toppled to the stone steps, weeping into his camera), and led the procession inside. For the next five minutes the continental United States was virtually isolated: telephone and cable communication with the outside world was suspended until 12.19. Yet the world beyond had read the timetable, too. The Panama Canal was closed. Around the globe the flags of the ninety-odd nations represented in the church dipped to half-mast. Ships at sea cast wreaths overboard. Seven thousand artillery pieces were firing twenty-one-gun salutes on seven thousand U.S. military posts, including those in Vietnam, where it was fourteen minutes past midnight. Warriors held a tribal feast of mourning in the darkness of Nairobi, and in Athens, which was at the height of its evening rush hour, Greek policemen stepped into the middle of intersections and stopped all cars.

For Americans in cities the halting of traffic was the most conspicuous observance of the moment. Chicago's Loop was deserted. 'NEW YORK LIKE A VAST CHURCH' read the front-page headline in next day's *Times*. And so it was: Times Square was utterly quiet, and taxi drivers standing by their cabs with bowed heads heard the sweet notes of taps coming from the Astor Hotel marquee, where two sixteen-year-old Eagle Scouts, bugles facing outward, played together. Yet the pause was not confined to urban America. The mob watching the Mass on the gigantic television screen in Grand Central Station was surprisingly large because travellers could not, for the time being, go anywhere. No trains were leaving, and those which had been in transit had stopped by farms, in woods, on mountain trestles; as the Eagle Scouts raised their trumpets in Manhattan, a conductor swung down from a braked car in Narberth, Pennsylvania, and blew taps there. The nation's entire transportation grid was frozen. Greyhound buses drew over. Planes cut their engines on tarmac take-off strips. The roar in subway tubes and the hum of elevator shafts were stilled, and the New Jersey Turnpike, which had been solid last evening with cars of mourners headed for the rotunda, was a barren wasteland.

This was the time for gatherings in the fifty state capitals, tributes made more touching by their very homeliness. National Guardsmen in tight uniforms formed uneven ranks, irregular volleys were fired, and local politicians stumbled through eulogies whose very heavy-handedness gave them a rough eloquence. It was also the juncture when the professional observers of the national audience noted a sharp drop in attendance. Between noon and 1.30 p.m. the number of watchers and listeners reached the lowest point in the long week-end. One obvious reason is that most Americans weren't Catholics; they didn't understand the rubrics in the cathedral. But an incalculable number were in churches and synagogues which had scheduled memorial services of their own to coincide with St Matthew's. Monday was the real Sabbath of that week. Almost every place of worship was open, including Buddhist temples in San Francisco's Chinatown. Twelve ministers presided over the congregation in Los Angeles' All Saints Episcopal Church. In the darkness of wind-swept outposts on Korea's western front the 1st Cavalry Division was holding special services. In New York over a thousand members of the Salvation Army gathered on Fourteenth Street to hear their famous band play the 'Navy Hymn'; on Fifth Avenue over five thousand Jews filled Temple Emanu-el, and another thousand were turned away. It was the one moment in those shredded days when Americans seemed genuinely responsive to religion. In the back of St Matthew's Bob Foster described the antics of 'Jasper the Jet' to young John. The boy was inattentive. It was very warm in their anteroom. He squirmed. A Marine colonel came in. The agent tried to interest John in his medals, without luck. Then Foster took a church leaflet from a rack. He began telling stories of Jesus, and John, engrossed, sat quietly.

From the altar the Cardinal's voice rose, harsh as a file.

Kyrie eleison.
Christe eleison.

Lord, have mercy.
Christ, have mercy.

His Eminence had recited the 129th Psalm, verses from Paul's letter to the Thessalonians, the thirteenth-century *Dies Irae*, and the Gospel reading; he had made his own confession of sin, and was preparing to consecrate the Eucharist.

Sursum corda.
Habemus ad Dominum.

Turn your hearts heavenward.
We are facing the Lord.

In the cathedral, as in the country, individual reactions to the rites depended almost entirely upon one's Catholicism or lack of it. To Arthur Schlesinger the changing of vestments, the kissing of the altar, and the singsong chants were 'incomprehensible'. Lady Bird, shivering, felt the ceremony was 'just ceremonial'. Bundy reflected that he was listening to 'the most grating priestly voice in Christendom', and Bunny Mellon was musing over how much more striking the urns would be had she had a few more hours and some magnolia. But Hubert Humphrey thought the rites had 'a purity of simplicity'. And the Cardinal, clearly moved, was comforting most of those who understood him. With the exception of Eunice and one other—Eunice thought that 'the service was sad instead of hopeful, and Jack was never sad in his life'—the family and friends felt strengthened. For O'Donnell the ritual was 'crisp, clean, and dignified'. O'Brien and Radziwill were proud of being Catholics, and to Ted Reardon the Mass was 'beautiful, typically Cushing. He was so great, and I knew how the Boss loved him so, that I was half in and half out of the world.'

Agnus Dei, qui tollis peccata
mundi, dona eis requiem . . .

Lamb of God, who takest away
the sins of the world, grant
them rest eternal . . .

The second exception in the family was Jacqueline Kennedy. She was unstrengthened and uncomforted, not because the liturgy was meaningless, but because it was altogether too rich in meaning. Everything was unbearably evocative—the 'Ave Maria' in the balcony, the prayers she had shared with her husband for ten years of Sundays, the celebrant who had married her and christened her daughter. And there was the coffin right next to her: 'There was everything going.' She filled up and commenced to cry uncontrollably. She couldn't stop shaking. Clint Hill reached over and gave her his handkerchief. It didn't help. She was racked by sobs. Then Mrs Kennedy felt a hand tighten. Caroline couldn't see her mother's face, but she had felt her spasms; she was comforting her. Presently the violent trembling subsided, and the widow prepared for Communion, praying three times with the others:

Domine, non sum dignus ut intres sub tectum meum; sed tantum dic verbo et sanabitur anima mea.

Lord, I am not worthy that Thou shouldst come under my roof; but only say the word and my soul will be healed.

The wafers had been blessed·

This is My Body.

And the wine:

This is the chalice of My Blood.

And now Jacqueline, Robert, and Edward Kennedy led the family to the rail while the Cardinal prayed over each, 'May the Body of our Lord Jesus Christ preserve thy soul unto life everlasting. Amen.' To the infinite relief of Archbishop O'Doyle, the number of communicants was small. More than family came—some Irish, who, understandably, considered this was the most important Eucharist in their lives—but not many more; the choir finished the '*Sanctus*' and '*Benedictus*', and Bishop Hannan mounted the triangular ambo midway between St Joseph Chapel and the family pews just fourteen minutes after Mrs Kennedy had received the Host.

'Your Eminence, Cardinal Cushing; Your Excellency, the Most Reverend Representative of the Holy Father; Your Excellency, the Archbishop, and Bishops; Mrs Kennedy and children-members of the family, the President of the United States and distinguished Heads of State, and Representatives of the Heads of State; distinguished friends of President Kennedy all——'

The Bishop read the five Scriptural passages Mrs Kennedy had approved last evening, from Proverbs, the Prophecy of Joel, Joshua, Isaiah, and Ecclesiastes. 'And now,' he said, 'as the final expression of his ideals and aspirations, his inaugural address:

> We observe today not a victory of party but a celebration of freedom, symbolizing an end as well as a beginning, signifying renewal as well as change. Let the word go forth from this time and place, to friend and foe alike, that the torch has been passed to a new generation of Americans....

As he spoke, Hannan's mind was travelling backwards to the days when the young Congressman from Boston and the young ex-paratroop chaplain had talked about the art of public speaking. He remembered the morning of January 21, 1961, when the new President had called him at his office and asked, 'Well, how did it go?'

And he remembered his reply: 'It's a masterpiece, the best inaugural address in one hundred years. But you should have spoken more slowly, to wait for the crowd reaction.' And here he himself was, delivering an abridged version of it in measured tones:

> Now the trumpet summons us again—not as a call to bear arms, though arms we need; not as a call to battle, though embattled we are; but a call to bear the burden of a long twilight struggle. . . .

His voice was bland, almost without inflection. And the cadences were so familiar, the message so relevant still, that there were those who yearned with an almost physical longing to hear once more the vibrant, exhorting, impassionate, inciting, ringing accents of the leader who would not wait, who was impatient with the biders of time, who was eager to get on with the job. If anything, the national audience felt this loss more keenly than those inside the church, for as the Bishop reached Kennedy's peroration and the most famous sentence the President had ever spoken, the pool camera focused on the lonely coffin:

> And so, my fellow Americans, ask not what your country can do for you; ask what you can do for your country.
>
> With a good conscience our only sure reward, with history the final judge of our deeds, let us go forth to lead the land we love, asking His blessing and His help, but knowing that here on earth God's work must truly be our own.

The Bishop left the lectern, and the Cardinal, at the altar, removed incense from hot coals—the rising smoke symbolizing rising prayers of supplication. The people recited the Lord's Prayer in unison as he slowly circled the bier three times, sprinkling each side with incense and holy water. He prayed:

> *Libera me, Domine, de morte aeterna, in die illa tremenda: Quando caeli movendi sunt et terra: Dum veneris iudicare saeculum per ignem. . . .*
>
> Deliver me, O Lord, from everlasting death on that day of terror when the heavens and the earth will be shaken, when You come to judge the world by fire. . . .
>
> *Requiem aeternam dona eis, Domine, et lux perpetua luceat eis.*
>
> Eternal rest grant unto them, O Lord, and let perpetual light shine upon them.

Libera me, Domine, de morte aeterna, in die illa tremenda: Quando caeli movendi sunt et terra: Dum veneris iudicare saeculum per ignem.

At this point the Cardinal, to his own surprise as much as to everyone else's, broke into English. It was, he said afterwards, 'an inspiration, like Pope John calling the Ecumenical Council. I hadn't thought of it at all before. But suddenly I wanted the human touch.' He cried:

'May the angels, dear Jack, lead you into Paradise. May the martyrs receive you at your coming. May the spirit of God embrace you, and mayest thou, with all those who made the supreme sacrifice of dying for others, receive eternal rest and peace. Amen.'

One didn't have to be a Catholic to understand that. The new First Lady thought it 'a plea, almost a wail; it didn't betray the dignity of the scene, and yet there was a human note at last. The Cardinal's personal anguish was showing through. It wasn't just a ceremony any more. He was saying good-bye to a man.' Across the aisle the widowed First Lady noticed that Cushing was crying. He was, she thought, one person who had a right to call her husband 'dear Jack', and the poignancy of it was too much; she began to shake again. She looked away, and Caroline saw her tear-streaked face. The small hand again reached up to clutch hers. Mrs Kennedy heard her daughter say, 'You'll be all right, Mummy. Don't cry. I'll take care of you.'

The Mass was over. The casket team shouldered the coffin and bore it out. Outside, Jacqueline Kennedy watched them lash it to the gun carriage for the third time. The Cardinal had quickly changed vestments by the altar; he had seen the little girl consoling her mother, and swooping out in a scarlet metre and scarlet robes he leaned over and embraced the child. 'I'll never forget you calling him "dear Jack",' Mrs Kennedy said. Her eyes were still damp. She was controlling herself with obvious effort, and it was a relief to see Foster come up with John, trying to wrestle the church leaflet away from him; handling the boy was something to do, a distraction when she needed one.

It lasted but an instant. The momentum of the pageant had caught them up again, and even as she firmly put John to her left, in front of the Attorney General, the band struck up 'Hail to the Chief'. This was the last time it would be played for President Kennedy. Soldiers snapped from parade rest to present arms. Officers, policemen, and the lead rider of the matched greys saluted. The clergy folded hands; laymen straightened. Jacqueline Kennedy, remembering how the boy had loved to play soldiers with his father, leaned over and took the booklet from him. She said, 'John, you can salute daddy now and say good-bye to him.'

The small right hand rose stiffly. Behind him Robert Kennedy's face crinkled in pain, and Bishop Hannan, glancing across the street, saw the spectators there crumple as though struck. Of all Monday's images, nothing approached the force of John's salute. Mrs Kennedy, standing erect, missed it, and when she was shown the photographs afterwards she was astounded. She had expected an unimpressive gesture; in the past his saluting had been both comic and, in her words, 'sort of droopy'.

But not now. Somehow the mood and meaning of the day had reached the President's son. His elbow was cocked at precisely the right angle, his hand was touching his shock of hair, his left arm was rigidly at his side, his shoulders were squared and his chin in. His bearing was militant, and to see it in a three-year-old, with his bare legs stiff below his short coat, his knees dimpled and his blunt red shoes side by side—to hear the slow swell of the music, and recall how the President had idolized him—was almost insupportable. Cardinal Cushing looked down on the small face. He saw the shadow of sadness crossing it and felt a burning sensation in his chest. Eight months later he could scarcely speak of it. '*Oh God,*' he whispered hoarsely, '*I almost died.*'

The band began 'Holy God, We Praise Thy Name', which luckily, is a long hymn; fifteen minutes were to pass before the cortège got under way, and even then it left scenes of wild disorder behind. The first car, with the prelates, and the second, with Jacqueline Kennedy and her brothers-in-law, were quickly loaded. Robert Kennedy took her arm and deftly guided her in. They then sat—and sat. To her the wait seemed endless. She wondered what could possibly be the matter.

The thousand men and women who had emerged from St Matthew's after her were also wondering. At the end of that quarter-hour most of them weren't even seated. Everything had gone awry. Chief Justice Warren's escort officer told him to wait on the sidewalk; he'd return in a jiffy with a limousine. The officer was never seen again, and Warren blundered around until he found a place at the tail of the line. The Joint Chiefs lacked transport because Agent Wells, in desperation, had evicted their Defence Department driver and confiscated the car for Caroline and John. Throughout the procession the distribution of seats was highly irregular. The limousines were like lifeboats after a badly managed 'abandon ship'. One had twelve passengers—Bill Walton remembers it as 'solid flesh'—while Sergeant Joe Ayres had another all to himself. Rank meant nothing. There were nine cars in front of President Johnson. For a long time the Prime Minister of Great Britain's car wasn't even allowed in the line. Eisenhower and Truman were way back, but Eveyln Lincoln, George Thomas, and Provi Parades were seated in No. 4.

Angier Biddle Duke had once more been flung into the fires of a protocol officer's hell. Emerging from the church he had been asked by Ken O'Donnell, 'Who should go first?' He had replied, 'There's no basis for discussion, there's nothing to argue about'; after the family and President Johnson, the men next in line 'should obviously be the chiefs of state'. This had been agreed upon in Ralph Dungan's office. Yet it wasn't working out that way. Angie suspected where the trouble lay. O'Donnell's very presence on the steps meant that people were coming out of the cathedral in the wrong order. The White House staff had bolted, and Angie had a strong hunch that the unruly Jack McNally was to blame.

He was dead right. To McNally the precedence was plainly unfair. The staff members had loved the President more than any foreigner, he reasoned. Putting them at the end was wrong: they might miss the graveside service. Therefore he had slipped away during Communion and reconnoitred Rhode Island Avenue's three lanes. Lane one was occupied by the Kennedy cars, lane two by the leading cars of the diplomatic corps. The third lane was vacant. Chief Stover of the White House police told him it was reserved for an emergency. This, Jack decided, *was* an emergency. He found the nineteen White House limousines parked a block away and ordered them into the emergency lane. Then he posted a White House sergeant in front of lane two and told him to block the foreign presidents and royalty until the staff had been threaded into the cavalcade.

That would have been bad enough. But once established form had been broken it became every man for himself. Mike Mansfield saw McNally and his wife entering the first White House car; despite Angie's anguished pleas Mike took off with the Congressional leadership. All semblance of order collapsed. Supreme Court Justices and governors were running around like emerging theatregoers hailing cabs in a downpour. Most of them wound up hitchhiking rides from resourceful colleagues who had commandeered empty limousines.

Charles de Gaulle declined to use his thumb. He looked down upon the mêlée and arched his brow at the American chief of protocol. Angie improvised brilliantly. Watching White House secretaries and servants occupying prime positions, he explained to de Gaulle and Haile Selassie that the President's family should, of course, go first. Naturally, they agreed. Doubtless they had heard, he went on, that the Kennedy family was very large. They nodded. Well, he said, extending his arm in a sweeping gesture, now they knew how big it *really* was. This seemed to satisfy them. They may have wondered how on earth George Thomas—who was as black as Haile Selassie—could possibly be a Kennedy, but their sense of tact kept them mute. And by now Angie's assistants had entered the free-for-all. The most eminent of the visiting dignitaries had lost their rightful positions, but they weren't going to trail everyone else.

Thus John Kennedy's last motorcade began, as so many chapters in his life had begun, in disarray. It had been a career of achievement, not of tidiness; nothing had ever been done according to the rules. The national audience, to whom the solemnity of the pageant meant so much, was unaware of the disorder. Throughout the drive to Arlington the networks focused on the progress of the gun carriage and on the waiting grave site three miles away. The watching country scarcely noticed the creeping limousines behind the horses. They were seen only as a hazy black blur. The identity of the occupants seemed inconsequential.

Sidewalk spectators were more curious. Once the caisson had passed them they ogled car windows, wondering, without much success, who was who. The Cardinal's bright robes and the Joint Chiefs' braid identified them, and the new First Family and de Gaulle could be spotted by the agents on either side of their cars, but most of the riders looked alike. There was a flurry of kerbside interest as the third limousine dropped out of the procession at Seventeenth and State Place—the kiddie detail was taking Caroline and John directly to the executive mansion—and another murmur when, as the end of the cavalcade passed the Red Cross building, a little blue Ford shot out of E Street and tooled along after the last Cadillac—Barney Ross and two PT 109 crewmen were bringing up the rear. Otherwise there wasn't much for bystanders to see. Even if they had monitored the conversations inside each limousine they wouldn't have learned much. The trip to the cemetery took an hour and a quarter, which is too long to sustain a high pitch of emotion. The chatter was low-key, often deliberately so, because taut nerves cried for release. The Kennedy brothers and Jacqueline Kennedy had begun the ride by debating the wisdom of going ahead with the graveside readings. The eulogies were on, then off, and finally they reversed themselves once more and decided to go ahead. Abruptly the subject was changed. Bob and Ted realized that if Jackie were to keep going she had to have some relief, and so they deliberately distracted her, telling her of the miracle of Ted's pants and speculating whimsically over whether General David Shoup, Commandant of the Marine Corps and one of President Kennedy's greatest admirers, could bring off a *coup d'état*. The conversation elsewhere was as trivial. Leaving the cathedral Maxwell Taylor had distributed sandwiches to Shoup and the other Chiefs; crouching low to avoid the crowds' gaze they surreptitiously nibbled chow. Eisenhower and Truman speculated briefly over whether the assassination had been the work of a cabal, decided it hadn't, and then reminisced about the past (delicately avoiding their public rows). In the front seat of the car behind them Joe Gargan peered through the windshield and thought how fine it was that the two ex-Presidents should be on speaking terms once more.

Outside the church Lieutenant Sam Bird had watched them approach Mrs Kennedy's car window to offer their condolences, and he too had been warmed. To the Lieutenant all Presidents were Commanders in Chief, and he would rather his gods not quarrel. Since the return of Kennedy's body from Dallas Bird had been near it during each stage of the journey—at Andrews Field and in Bethesda, the East Room, the rotunda, and the cathedral. His awe was undiminished. Back down Connecticut and Seventeenth, out Constitution, around the Lincoln Memorial and across the river he marched a few feet behind the caisson, calling out a soft cadence to the body bearers on either side. From the first car Bishop Hannan looked out over Black Jack and marvelled at the casket team's precision; though the gun carriage divided them into two groups, all the men marched as one. The explanation was Bird's quiet coaching. He was bent upon making this march faultless. An elevated brick ridge separated the lanes of Memorial Circle; it was only eight inches wide, but rather than mar the formation he marched straight down it on his slick steel heel plates.

The President, Sam Bird knew, had loved American history. As a participant in this moment of history he resolved to dictate his memories of it into his tape recorder before retiring tonight. All along the way he made mental notes: of the teenagers who had scrambled up edifices to watch; of the Negro woman who cried out, 'That's all right, you done your best, it's all over now'; of the 3rd Infantry's red-coated colonial fife and drum corps waiting on the green at Arlington's gate, and, inside the cemetery, of the wildly twittering birds overhead. All these he glimpsed from the corners of his eyes. He kept his gaze fixed on the coffin's flag, and as the cortège moved up towards the slope McNamara had chosen in the rain on Saturday the Lieutenant noticed something he had missed before. On the bunting over the coffin, by the field of stars, was a small label: 'Valley Forge Flag Company, Spring City, Pennsylvania.' He thought how proud the makers of the flag would be to know that it had lain over a President, and he decided to write them a letter.

Awaiting the procession beneath Custis-Lee Mansion were the riflemen, the bugler, Air Force bagpipers, Irish cadets, a platoon from each of the American armed services, and a spectator perched in a dogwood tree. Of the thousands surrounding the hillside, only this one had had the audacity and agility to shinny up to a superb observation point. He didn't stay there long. As the caisson wheeled past the fifers and drummers he was spotted, and after he had ignored four requests to descend, he was summarily plucked down. The pluckers, significantly, were MP's. Except for a group of nuns fingering their rosaries on the mansion steps the funeral participants waiting by the grave were all military. General Wehle was guiding the procession in, Lieutenant Bird's men would carry the coffin the last few feet, and the honorary pallbearers were to be the Joint Chiefs and the three Presidential military aides. The martial tone of the ceremonies was continuing to the last. It was ironic that John Kennedy, whom the world knew as a man of peace, and whose proudest achievements had been the Test Ban Treaty and the successful conclusion of the Cuban confrontation without bloodshed, should be buried as a warrior, but there really was no other way; if he must go in glory, and clearly he must, the troops were indispensable. There were no splendid traditions, no magnificent farewells, for a hero of peace.

At Hatfield Gate, Superintendent Metzler escorted Wehle up Roosevelt Drive. In spite of the sharp chill Metzler was perspiring. He had been assigned responsibility for the trickiest of the military tributes, the fly-by, and his anxiety had been increased by misinformation; he was under the impression that the jets were rendezvousing over Richmond, ninety miles away. The reason for the error is obscure. Very likely the Air Force didn't want to trouble him with technicalities. In any event, the superintendent had been warned that if the fifty fighters and the Presidential aircraft were to appear overhead on schedule, the colonel on the hill would need ten minutes' lead time, which was true. Metzler had broken the time down. He would hold the mourners in their cars for four minutes, allow two for the national anthem, three for the coffin to reach the grave, and one to get the family in position. He had a stopwatch in his pocket, and he was praying.

On Sheridan Drive, the curving road at the bottom of the hill, the procession halted. The gun carriage drew up by a cocomat runner leading to the grave. Two cars bearing the Chiefs and aides passed it and parked ahead; the first Kennedy car stopped behind Black Jack and the Presidential flag, still held aloft by Seaman Nemuth.

Metzler scrambled up the slope. Behind Mrs Kennedy the immense caravan wound darkly down to the gate and across the Potomac, vanishing below the shimmering columns of the Lincoln Memorial. Already the vanguard of the formation was breaking up in the cemetery, fanning out along Sherman, Grant, and McClellan drives. Suddenly President Johnson's limousine pulled out of line and braked beside Mrs Kennedy's, hubcap to hubcap. Metzler decided it was time to alert the jets. He punched the stem of his stopwatch and, simultaneously, nodded to Colonel Charles Walton.

Southeast of Andrews, at the flight's Initial Point, Jim Swindal was still eavesdropping. The H-43 helicopter pilot had been keeping all the fliers posted on the progress of the cortège. They knew it was nearly time to lunge. Now Walton checked the control tower at Washington National, over which the flight must pass. Everything was clear there; all commercial flights had been grounded or sidetracked. Walton gave the flight the countdown, then the go signal, and the fighters screamed away. Aircraft 26000 ripped after them. Prince Georges County fled beneath them; they heeled hard right over the river and darted up its glittering, narrowing band. The F-105's were losing Swindal; he could see the vacant point of the last V receding. Not much else was visible ahead, because they were flying westward into the sinking sun, and the light was dazzling. It made no difference, Swindal knew the river well. He spun the black trim-tab wheel counterclockwise, taking the plane down to five hundred feet. He had pushed his air speed past 600 mph, and he calculated that two hundred yards before reaching the grave he should start swinging his U-shaped wheel, canting the great wings in a graceful good-bye. Swindal's eyes were full, he wished he could cry. He stared into the sun and blinked his eyes, but the tears wouldn't come. He threw all his fuel controls on full and leaned into the wind.

Jack Metzler had asked the Secret Service agents to keep the Kennedys and Johnsons seated until he gave them the sign. He had no contact with the visiting heads of state, however, and Angie Duke had performed a marvellous feat; he had overcome the McNally handicap by extricating his wards from their limousines on a side road. The man least likely to congratulate him was Metzler. The superintendent was sweating out his first four minutes when he saw Prince Philip loping up the hill, using his sword as a cane. Beside and behind him were Charles de Gaulle, King Baudouin, Haile Selassie—all the pomp and circumstance from abroad. They paused in a phalanx twenty feet away and stared at him. He grinned weakly.

With his ovoid figure, pink face, and anxious expression he looked like a hopeful floor-walker. He peeped furtively at his stopwatch and saw, to his horror, that less than two minutes had passed.

There was nothing to say—the visitors wouldn't have understood him anyhow—so he decided to look pleasant. He beamed winningly at the semicircle formed by the Kennedy car, the Johnson car, and the august dignitaries. Nobody beamed back, though General de Gaulle appeared fascinated, as though he was examining some new and particularly bizarre specimen of insect life. Metzler's smile faded. Charm having failed, he resorted to sheer fakery. He thrust his head forward, looked intently over the heads of the heads of state, and slowly revolved his hand in a mysterious gesture. It was a grotesque dumb show, but he could think of no other way to buy time. Most of the illustrious group were transfixed, though 'one or two', Metzler later said, 'looked back to see to whom I was signalling. As they could see no one—for no one was there—they looked at me in a most perplexed manner.' Again he peered covertly at his watch. Three minutes and forty seconds had passed. He couldn't stand the ordeal any more, so he gave a genuine signal, for the Marine Band. Opening the doors of Mrs Kennedy's car, he motioned Jerry Behn to get the President out for four ruffles and flourishes which were already introducing 'The Star-Spangled Banner'.

The national anthem had the virtue of immobilizing everyone. It had the defect of unleashing them the moment it was over. In that instant, as Bill Walton put it, the slope became 'a mob scene, with people struggling uphill'. Walton ran into Mary McGrory. 'Bill, what are we doing at Jack Kennedy's funeral?' she asked dazedly, and he gallantly gave her his arm. Where men wound up largely depended upon how athletic their wives were. Phyllis Dillon was spry, so the Secretary of the Treasury reached the edge of the bogus grass. Mamie Eisenhower's foot was bothering her, and both the former Presidents ended, in Eisenhower's words, 'out in left field'. Stewart Udall tried manfully to fetch the Chief Justice and his wife, without luck. The Warrens, deep in the crowd, were to see nothing of the coming services; all they would hear were snatches of the Cardinal's commitment. Yet priority didn't depend entirely on physique. Angie Duke's advance man had reserved one side of the grave for the foreign guests. That was appropriate though Evelyn Lincoln, Muggsy O'Leary, and Dr Burkley were also given red-carpet treatment, which was senseless. The most serious slight—and the one which was bound to be bitterly resented—was the treatment of the new President. Metzler had forgotten about him. The only graveside request the superintendent had received was to place 'the family and staff' with the widow. He had assumed the President would be with the Kennedys too, and so, apparently, had Johnson. But the Secret Service remained concerned about his safety; they had moved him in with the Supreme Court. Metzler saw him raging at an agent, and General Wehle heard him fume, 'What the hell am I doing here?'[3]

Meanwhile the ceremonies were moving forward. The last double note of the anthem was the cue to a cue: the Air Force bagpipes began the dirge 'Mist-Covered Mountain', swinging in slow march towards the lip of the hill, and with the first cry of their pipes Lieutenant Bird ordered the coffin raised from the caisson. Up the fibre runner the body bearers moved haltingly, the Presidential standard and the honorary pallbearers behind them and an honour cordon of green-bereted guerrilla fighters on either side; then, on command, they deliberately overshot the grave and looped back in a wide arc so that the head of the coffin would be pointing towards the crest of the grave and facing east. Black Jack was led to one side. The horse's spirit seemed broken. His proud head was lowered; he stood docilely beside his exhausted guardian. All troops were presenting arms, all officers saluting until the coffin had been lowered to the metal device over the grave. Then:

'Pa-rade *Rest*!'

The casket team held the flag from Spring City in a smooth, waist-high plane while the lieutenant, at one end, and a cemetery employee, at the other, crouched to jockey the coffin into position. They were still stooping when the fifty jets shrieked above them. The fighters were a trifle early, but for Colonel Swindal the timing was near perfect. The startled crowd glanced up, and in the interval after the last echo of the F-105's the Presidential aircraft, racing ahead of its own thunder, loomed soundlessly overhead. For an astonishing instant the beautiful plane appeared to hang suspended, so low that one felt one could almost reach up and touch its blue flashes. Then Swindal rocked the swept-back wings 20 degrees to the left, came level directly above the taut flag, rocked right in another deep, three-second dip, and streaked off towards the Key Bridge. Godfrey McHugh thought it the most exquisite manoeuvre he had ever seen. For those who made the terrible trip back from Love Field over the hump of Friday's storm Swindal's fly-by was especially affecting, but all who knew of the President's love for Air Force One were moved, and as the mighty tail with the bold blue numerals '26000'

[3] All funeral plans had specified that after the Arlington services Mrs Kennedy would be escorted to her car by President Johnson, and some had assumed that he would also ride to the rotunda with her Monday morning. Several broadcasters reported this as fact, but there was no contact between the two on Monday.

vanished over the naked trees, into the vapour trails left by the fighters, Lee Radziwill wept.

Her sister had missed it. The hill had been so transformed since Mrs Kennedy's visit on Saturday that it was scarcely recognizable, and the hideous grass-type matting was befuddling. Walking up she saw only the coffin. She didn't know what was expected of her, or even where she was supposed to go. Thinking to kneel beside it she started towards the grave. Bob checked her; he steered her along, literally holding her up by the elbow. In his other hand he was holding the four selections he was to recite during the ceremony—Steve Smith had just darted up to him with Sorensen's final version—so he didn't see Jim Swindal's tribute either. Ted Kennedy did, though. He squinted up at the plane, looked down at the Irish cadets, and remembering how much both would have meant to his brother, he realized that they were far from being through the most moving moments of the funeral. In the car they had agreed that he would read first. He still doubted that the recitations were wise. Joan Kennedy, looking over at him, wondered whether her husband would be able to go ahead. The huskiest of the Kennedy men was obviously shaky.

Metzler was beckoning and gesturing, going through what in cemetery jargon is known as 'positioning'. Although the placing of individuals was largely being determined by factors over which the superintendent had no control, he strove to follow the chart Shriver had approved, and achieved a partial success. Most of the front-row positions, at least, were properly occupied. The Cardinal, Archbishop, and Bishop faced the head of the coffin, with the unlit flame between them and the field of stars. Behind the prelates were the Joint Chiefs and behind them, on the steepest part of the incline, the military aides. Counterclockwise from the flame were the family; staff and friends; governors; heads of state, with General de Gaulle at the very foot of the grave, facing Cushing; the Irish team; the Supreme Court; and the Marine Band. Beyond the band Bunny Mellon's blanket of flowers lay banked on its little rise; behind the family, in the space which had been set aside for Johnson, Truman, and Eisenhower, were the Congressional leadership and the Cabinet.

Nearly everyone here was seeing the President's grave for the first time. They found the setting unexpectedly lovely. Eunice Shriver, who had been at the Cape when it had been chosen, looked over the bandsmen's heads and thought how, if her brother could stand up, he would point past the sparkling instruments and shout '*Look* at those *flowers!*' Hubert Humphrey was behind Jacqueline Kennedy. 'We went to the burial ground area of the President,' the Senator observed afterwards. 'And how beautiful the site that was selected! I fail to find the words to adequately express it. But it seems to me as if he stands as a constant sentinel over the nation's capital. The president's grave is like an outpost for observation of the capital city.' Humphrey had seen the fly-by, and envisioned it as a crew 'paying its last respects to the captain of the ship'. He 'couldn't help but think again and again—why did this happen? Why, oh why in America did we have to experience such evil, such hate, such lawlessness, such violence?' Yet the peaceful, sunlit tableau before him was a reminder of how far away Dallas was. He marvelled that the scene could be so beautiful, so tranquil—'and yet so final. Then,' he added, 'we saw our President laid to rest.'

The cadets went through their silent drill, their rifle butts reversed in mourning for Ireland's martyrs, and marched off past the floral blanket to the muted lilt of a cadence counted in Gaelic; Cardinal Cushing stepped to the edge of the pine boughs around the torch and began the commitment. It turned out to be another Cushing surprise. The clergy was expecting the traditional 'Blessing of the Body and Burial'. Father Thomas McGraw, Arlington's Catholic chaplain, had buried more members of the Church than any of the august prelates here, and could chant the opening '*Non intres in iudicium cum servo tuo, Domine*'—'O Lord, do not bring your servant to trial'—without benefit of the missal. He awaited it, and heard instead the rasping voice pray, 'O God, through whose mercy the souls of the faithful find rest, be pleased to bless this grave and . . . the body we bury herein, that of our beloved Jack Kennedy, the thirty-fifth President of the United States, that his soul may rejoice in Thee with all the saints, through Christ the Lord. Amen.' Once more His Eminence had impulsively abandoned Latin and was delivering the blessing in English, with the agreeable consequence that much of it was familiar to Protestants on the slope and in the listening nation. Only the translation varied slightly as he intoned, 'I am the resurrection and the life. He who believeth in Me, although he be dead, shall live, and everyone who liveth and believeth in Me, shall not die for ever.' For the last time the Cardinal asked that the President be granted eternal rest and perpetual light. He led all who could hear him in the Lord's Prayer; then he broke off and stepped back.

'Pre-sent *Arms*!'

In McClellan Circle Captain Grey's battery fired its twenty-one-gun salute. The troops were brought to order arms for the benediction, the casket team tilted up the field of stars while the Cardinal sprinkled holy water on the coffin. Once more he stepped back, and the order to present arms was repeated. Lieutenant Bird, standing opposite the casket from the family, had been staring right into the

Attorney General's eyes. Now he saw Robert Kennedy's head turn. Bob, Jackie, and Ted were holding a whispered consultation. Metzler murmured anxiously to Bob, 'Honours are still being sounded.' 'Honours' means little to laymen, but in a military funeral they are the entire sequence of artillery, riflery, and music which pays homage to the departed. Presidential honours are complex anyhow, but these, for the first Catholic President, were further complicated by the need to consecrate this specific plot of ground in the name of the Church. The benediction, in short, had become part of the sequence. And the one inviolable rule about honours, is that once they have begun they cannot be interrupted. They had to run their course, from the first shot in McClellan Circle to the last trumpet note here. An interruption was precisely what the three Kennedys had had in mind. They wanted to interpolate their reading before taps. It was impossible. Ted whispered to Jackie, 'I don't think I should do it now, do you?' She whispered back, 'No, no, you should, too.'

'Firing party—fire three volleys!'

At the rim of the hill Sergeant William Malcolm barked: 'Ready!' A squad from the Old Guard executed a half-right face, whacked the ground with the butts of their M-1's, and came to port arms. Malcolm ordered: 'Aim!' The rifles came up together at a 45-degree angle. Then: '*Fire!*' The neat crack resounded across the copses and dells of Arlington as it had, for this squad, in four thousand funerals before. This time there was a difference, however. Twice more the sergeant snapped, 'Aim . . . *fire!*' and after the third volley, as the squad stiffened at present arms, an infant in the crowd began to cry like a banshee. Everyone on the crest heard the wail except Sergeant Keith Clark, whose eardrums felt ruptured. Clark's lips were numb, too; he had been standing in the same cold spot for nearly three hours. Nevertheless he was on now. In funerals, he believed, the trumpeter should play only for the widow, and pointing the bell of his bugle at Mrs Kennedy he began the sombre melody which had been proverbial on American military posts since General Daniel Butterfield composed it for the Army of the Potomac a century before: '*Day is done. Gone the sun. . . .*' And there Clark, after four years of playing taps daily, lost the first note of his career. It cracked; it was like a catch in your voice, or a swiftly stifled sob.

He finished sweetly, the troops thumped to parade rest, and Jack Metzler nodded at the Marine Band. Nothing happened. Agitated, he nodded again, and then again, violently, before the drum major's baton arched up for the slowest—eighty beats—of all the 'Navy Hymn' renditions. Now Lieutenant Bird's turn had come. His team had disregarded all the shouted commands. The eight men stood, four facing four, their white-gloved fingers tight on the VA flag they had placed over the coffin in the corridor outside Bethesda's morgue. Fingers provided the cue to what they did with bunting over graves; signals between them were transmitted by tension on the banner's hem. The Lieutenant gave a sign to Sergeant James Felder. Felder tugged hard and they were off, their arms moving like whips, folding the colours in a triangle as the cloth sped across the casket top, away from General de Gaulle and towards Cardinal Cushing. At the head of the coffin the last man clutched the triangle to his chest; it was passed from breast to breast, and then Sp/4 Douglas Mayfield executed a sharp right face, handed it to Metzler and saluted. As his forefinger touched the bill of his cap a pool camera in the press stand caught the young Californian full-face; 105 million Americans saw his lips tremble and his eyes brim.

The Marines were supposed to play one chorus of 'Eternal Father'. They played three while the superintendent waited with the flag and Cardinal Cushing pondered the torch before him. He was one of the few people around the grave who had known of its existence beforehand; during his final briefing that morning an Army officer had told him that as 'chaplain' he would be expected to bless it. The Cardinal had been somewhat nonplussed. He knew nothing about eternal flames and doubted there was a special prayer for them. After hasty ecclesiastical research the archbishop's office had reported that His Eminence was absolutely right. Very well, Cushing replied; he would make one up. Actually, improvisation didn't go that far. He settled for the Church's blessing '*Ad Omnia*'—that is, a blessing for everything which doesn't already have a blessing of its own—and when the band finally said Amen to the hymn, he chanted it over the torch, the pine boughs, and the copper tubing.

Major Converse, the engineer officer whose pockets were bulging with matches and cigarette lighters, ignited his taper. The major was understandably jumpy. He fully appreciated what would happen if the makeshift light failed. To his dismay he saw that he and his flaming stick would have to wait; Jack Metzler and the Cardinal were approaching Jacqueline Kennedy. The superintendent reached her first. Sidling up he said brokenly, 'Mrs Kennedy, this flag is presented to you in the name of a most mournful nation.' He didn't want to give it to her. He could see the puffiness of her lids under the veil, and he knew that for wives this was the most difficult part of the burial service. But that was only because it was the climax. He had to go on. Holding out the colours he finished in a whisper, 'Please accept it.' He faded back and left her alone with that dreadful, quite unique loneliness of widows at the grave—the bright triangle of blue, white, and red startling against the solid black of the suit she had first worn when her husband announced his Presidential candidacy, the five-pointed stars huge in her small hands, and on her veiled face a wide, puzzled look, the brow half arched and the lips parted as though about to ask, *Is this all I have of him?* 'With her eyes filling with tears,' Metzler wrote afterwards, 'she quietly clutched the flag and momentarily held it close to her. She did not speak. I do not believe she could at that moment.'

Her resilience was still there, however, and she displayed it when the Cardinal came up. Last evening Shriver had told him that the President's brothers would quote from his speeches in the cemetery. Cushing hadn't liked the idea—'It'll sound like politics,' he had said; 'you'll be tying a rope around his coffin'—but that wasn't his affair. Both the religious and military services were over. If the Attorney General and the Senator were to speak, it would have to be now, and he was here to lead Ted to the head of the grave and introduce him. But the Kennedys had finally resolved the issue of recitations among themselves. According to Jacqueline Kennedy, 'I think it was during taps or just after that Teddy, Bobby, and I looked at each other and the same thought was in all our eyes—and Teddy shook his head as if to say "No," and Bobby and I nodded—and as I was the one nearest the Cardinal, when he turned to me I said, "No, Your Eminence." ' Cushing, bewildered, again moved to take Ted by the arm, and Mrs Kennedy repeated firmly, 'I said *no*, Your Eminence.'

His Eminence understood now. He withdrew and embraced Mrs Joseph Kennedy. 'Good-bye, my dear,' he whispered. 'God be with you.' Meantime Major Converse had stepped into his place. 'This is the saddest moment of my life,' he said to Jacqueline Kennedy, and she looked up into his long, tense face and believed it. He handed her the taper and led her to the branches of evergreen. Leaning over them, she touched the blazing tip against the nub of the torch, and it sprang to life. She handed the rod to Bob. He repeated the gesture and turned towards his mother, holding it out. Rose Kennedy didn't see him. She hadn't known about the eternal flame. Her head was bowed in silent prayer, so he swung the other way and gave it to Ted. Ted hadn't expected to join them, but he too grazed the rod against the shimmering yellow-blue gout of fire. The engineers waited to see whether the new President would come forward. He couldn't. He was on the wrong side of the coffin, boxed in by bodyguards, and the Major took the taper from Ted and extinguished it. The little ceremony was over.

Indeed, everything was over—the burial service, the state funeral, the strangely congruous blend of Old World mysticism and American tradition, the parade of uniforms and vestments, of judges and secret agents, of princes and prelates and anonymous, nondescript citizens who had surged across the bridge in the wake of the marching columns because they couldn't bear to be left behind. The presence of the mob had been anticipated; in the past twenty-four hours the military District of Washington had learned a great deal about the appeal of President Kennedy, and to prevent disorder General Wehle had issued an order: 'No condolences will be received by next of kin at graveside.' Of course, it was unenforceable. The Cardinal had already consoled the President's mother, Bishop Hannan was moving towards his widow, the new First Lady was waiting by Jacqueline Kennedy's car, and turning from the pine boughs Robert Kennedy murmured to his sister-in-law, 'Say goodbye to General Taylor. He did so much for Jack.'

Cradling the flag under her left arm, she strained up to press her cheek against the General's, and there is a vivid photograph of the scene, in which America's first soldier is inclining his bare head towards her. The white gloves of the other Chiefs and aides are flying towards their own caps, to doff them. They are at attention, yet the most erect and militant figure there, despite his anomalous tails, is Robert Kennedy. At the time Taylor thought her incoherent, but that was because her voice was low and his hearing defective. 'Jack loved you so much,' she told him. Both Bishop Hannan and Mrs Johnson was astonished that she could be articulate with them. The bishop leaned over and said, 'God bless you, you are doing wonderfully well.' Having participated in many funerals, he expected no response, but she said, 'Thank you very much for the eulogy. It was splendid.' She walked down the hill holding Bob Kenndy's hand, and they were about to enter their car when she saw Lady Bird, with seventeen-year-old Johnny Connally at her elbow. The boy had a letter for the widow from his mother; she took it and gently inquired about his father's condition.

In the car Mrs Kennedy and the two brothers talked of the funeral—of how splendid it had been—and as the procession of returning cars came off the Washington side of the bridge and turned left, Robert Kennedy ordered the chauffeur of their car to leave the line and circle the Lincoln Memorial from the right. That way they could see the statue. He told the driver to draw over in front of it, and they did, as thousands of tourists do each day. From the back seat President Kennedy's widow and the two heirs of his political legacy inclined their heads leftwards to look up between the columns at Daniel Chester French's nineteen-foot-high figure of the sad, strong, brooding President Lincoln, the marble chin tilted in thought.

After a while Bob tapped the chauffeur. They drove on without having spoken.

'The end of the service at Arlington,' Mac Bundy wrote, 'was like the fall of a curtain, or the snapping of taut strings.' Undeniably the break seemed abrupt to those who left at once, and they included most of the principals. Bundy hurried to the executive mansion to intercept Charles de Gaulle. Buses carted off the honour platoons; Sergeant Keith Clark plodded gloomily back to Fort Myer, where he tried to turn in his bugle, and where Black Jack, submissive, was led to his stable. Harry Truman and his daughter gave the Eisenhowers a drink for the road at Blair House. Speaker McCormack, feeling it 'terribly important' that he 'be available at such a time', spent the remainder of the afternoon in his office and was given his first insight into that cold purgatory which is the lot of the man next in line of succession to the Presidency; no one even telephoned him. Cardinal Cushing had to catch a plane right after the service. The instant the new President had left the cemetery—it would have been an inexcusable breach of decorum for a prince of the Church to precede the leader of the state—Archbishop O'Boyle and Bishop Hannan hustled the Cardinal to Washington National. His red robes flapping, he bounded out of the car and into the terminal. His way was briefly blocked by a man who flung his arms around his neck and said, 'I was proud of you today, Cardinal Spellman.' His Eminence replied gravely, 'Glad to be of service any time.'

For those who lingered on the hillside, the graveside tableau dissolved more slowly. Just as the Marine Band hadn't wanted to stop playing the 'Navy Hymn', so, afterwards, were thousands loath to concede that they had said farewell to John Kennedy. Even Bundy, before he departed the cemetery, had noticed how Dean Rusk, leading the Cabinet past the grave, seemed 'held by the tie of his affection and loyalty, the one so well understood, the other so foggily hidden.... He stood for what seemed a long time and may have been even a half a minute—alone with the man he was leaving.' Jack Metzler observed that 'practically all of the dignitaries were either filing by or just standing and looking at the casket as though in a trance. Ever so slowly they began to move off as though they were reluctant to leave.'

The same unwillingness was discernible in the military. After the foreigners left, Lieutenant Bird marched his casket team down the slope and ordered an about-face and a last salute of the coffin. That was not part of the ceremony, he explained afterwards, but 'we had been with him so long and loved him so much that we just wanted to do it'. Metzler escorted the last of the eminent guests to Hatfield

Gate and returned to find that the Special Forces, on their own, had posted a guard of four men at the corners of the plot. When they had to leave, the Engineers pleaded for permission to relieve them. Some time between 4.15 and 4.45 p.m. one of the guerrilla fighters, Sergeant Major Frank Ruddy, returned alone. Two years earlier the President had revoked an order banning their green berets. Now Ruddy saluted, took off his own and laid it on the pine boughs. 'He gave us the beret,' Ruddy said later, 'and we thought it fitting to give one back to him.'

Beneath the slope the indomitable public knelt, hats in hand. They were waiting here patiently as they had waited last night on that other hill outside the rotunda, and later, when Metzler permitted it, they shuffled up from Sheridan Drive, cirling the plot and moving back down as newcomers lengthened the line below. Standard procedure required Arlington guards to start closing the cemetery's eight gates at quarter of five. It was tried today, but the crush of grieving figures was too great; for another hour and a half they plodded round and round in the thickening gloom.

By then Metzler had disposed of the invisible public. He hadn't foreseen that problem at all; after the Kennedys' departure, he had thought, the networks would turn elsewhere. Not so; they, too, were reluctant to leave, and in the press stand the pool cameras ground on, swinging from the torch to Lee Mansion to the shafts of sunlight filtering through the trees and lengthening shadows behind the other graves of Arlington. The networks were renitent to going, too. And they were holding their national audience, most of which was still watching its screens at 3.31 p.m., nearly a quarter-hour after the Kennedy's had left, when the lowering device began to bear the coffin down. (As it disappeared David Brinkley was saying, 'The act which killed the President was spawned out of bigotry and extremism, but it has had the opposite effect of drawing people together. . . .') At this point Metzler became concerned. He wanted to seal the vault, fill the grave, erect a picket fence around the plot, and dress the ground around the evergreen boughs with flowers. Expecting him to do it in front of a hundred million rubbernecks was too much, he heatedly told Colonel Miller. Miller agreed. He went to the Army's information chief and the NBC and CBS technicians, arguing that 'these things aren't for public view'. NBC's director agreed. He had been telling his New York office exactly that, without luck. 'You try,' he said, offering the Colonel his earphones. Miller had just started to when Metzler decided talk was pointless. He saw the red lights still shining on the cameras and summoned his post engineer. 'Pull the juice,' he said grimly. 'Yank the plug.' And that is precisely what was done. One moment the great audience was watching the liquid undulations of the eternal flame; a moment later all electrical power in the cemetery was cut off, and the screens went blank.

That was at 3.34 p.m. The networks quickly switched to the south grounds of the White House, where U Thant, Dr Ralph Bunche, Anastas Mikoyan, Haile Selassie, Sir Alexander Bustamante, Hayato Ikeda, Zalman Shazar, Diosdado Macapagal, and diplomats from Korea, San Salvador, Nigeria, Ghana, South Vietnam, Finland, Tunisia, Somalia, Spain, Peru, and Czechoslovakia were seen streaming towards the Diplomatic Reception Room.

On her return from Arlington Jacqueline Kennedy had set a two-week moving deadline. In the gift room, next to the Presidential swimming pool, Joe Giordano and Bootsy Miller had begun putting pictures, phonograph records, and four file cabinets of mementoes into cardboard cartons; upstairs Mr West was packing books, and George Thomas clothes. In the staff mess some forty Presidential advisers were sorting out their personal futures. The mafia was conferring in Larry O'Brien's office, Dr Burkley was repeating his offer to resign to Walter Jenkins, Pierre Salinger was serving as press secretary to two administrations, and Ted Clifton was explaining the nation's most intimate military secrets to Texans who didn't have security clearance and whom he didn't even know; Colonel Jackson stood beside him, identifying them as bona fide Johnson men. In the West Wing, Ted Sorensen settled into his tall leather chair and read Galbraith's joint session speech for the first time. He put it aside and read other drafts which had been sent to him, from Charlie Murphy and Horace Busby. He decided to start afresh.

He wrote:

> Mr Speaker, Mr President, Members of the House and Senate, my fellow Americans:
>
> All I have ever possessed I would have gladly given *not* to be here today.
>
> For the greatest leader of our time has been struck down by the foulest deed of our time—and I who cannot fill his shoes must occupy his desk.

Sorensen struck out the last eleven words. A President must not sound obsequious. He continued,

> No words are sad enough to express our sense of loss. No words are strong enough to express our determination to continue his work. Today John Fitzgerald Kennedy lives on in the immortal words and works he left behind. He lives on in the mind and

memories of mankind. He lives on in the hearts of his countrymen....

Sorensen wrote seven pages, setting down in rough form the address that the new President would actually deliver to the Congress two days later, including Johnson's plea for the early passage of Kennedy's civil rights and tax cut legislation ('No memorial oration or eulogy could more eloquently ennoble his memory than the earliest possible passage of the Civil Rights bill for which he fought. We have talked long enough in this country about equal rights. We have talked for 100 years or more. It is time now to write the next chapter'); the denunciation of fanatical absolutists ('Let us put an end to the teaching and preaching of hate and evil and violence. Let us turn away ... from the apostles of bitterness and bigotry, from those defiant of law and liberty and those who pour venom and vituperation into our nation's bloodstream'); and the concluding

And on this Thanksgiving eve, as we gather together to ask the Lord's blessing, let us unite in the simple, familiar:

'*America, America,*
God shed His grace on thee,
And crown thy good
With brotherhood
From sea to shining sea.'[4]

The Kennedys' duty lay downstairs, where Angie Duke was leading their exotic guests to two buffets in the state and family dining rooms. One of the President's traits had been to watch television reruns of himself with a critical eye—he had never missed his own press conferences that way—and several members of the family were standing upstairs in the west hall, studying a local channel's rerun of funeral highlights, when Jacqueline Kennedy appeared. She took them aside individually, comforting them and thanking them. Then she suggested they take turns greeting visitors; she would join them later. Ted Kennedy led them down and set up the first reception line in the Red Room with Eunice, Pat, and Jean. Meanwhile Mrs

[4] Tuesday evening in the Oval Office Johnson told Sorensen, 'That's great. I wouldn't change a word of it.' Immediately afterwards Rusk and McNamara reviewed the speech in Mac Bundy's office. Johnson entered with Jenkins and Abe Fortas in time to hear Bundy object that it sounded 'too much like JFK', and despite Sorensen's protests changes were made. Riding to the Hill next day to deliver it, the President sat with him and Salinger. Pierre remarked, 'That's a hell of a speech, Mr President.' Johnson replied, 'It's Sorensen's.' Ted said, 'No.' 'Well, 90 per cent,' said Johnson. '50 per cent,' said Ted. The President ventured, 'The *best* 50 per cent,' and found his consensus; Sorensen answered, 'I agree.'

Kennedy phoned Evelyn Lincoln in the staff mess and asked her to come to keep the President's mother company. She explained, 'I have to comb my hair for all these dignitaries.' Evelyn thought, *How* do *you do it?*

It is doubtful that any woman has ever prepared herself for a state function in less time. Before Peter Lawford entered the West Sitting Room to sit with Evelyn and his mother-in-law, Jacqueline Kennedy had removed her veil and black beret, raked her simple coiffure into shape, and was in the Oval Room, ready to meet people. She was not going downstairs just yet, though. Here as everywhere she had her own way of doing things. For a little while she was going to be nearly as great a trial to Angie Duke as Jack McNally. A protocol officer must think in terms of nations, not people; he must pretend that every country is like every other country, distinguishable only by the alphabet. Sovereigns understood that. At the buffet Angie proposed that Queen Frederika precede President Lübke, on the ground that she was a woman; she recoiled, pointing out that GErmany comes before GReece. Jacqueline Kennedy didn't like those rules. She only wanted to see four men in private, and she named them: Haile Selassie, Charles de Gaulle, Eamonn de Valera, and Prince Philip, Duke of Edinburgh.

The first stage of the Kennedy reception therefore had three foci: her salon in the oval study, Rose Kennedy's group in the sitting-room, and the others downstairs. Various intermediaries shuttled in and out of the study—the Attorney General usually, assisted by Mac Bundy, by Angie, who had reluctantly agreed to 'slip them up', and, unexpectedly, by the President's son and daughter. Caroline and John had been assigned no role. They were supposed to be playing with Miss Shaw. Their impromptu appearances were welcomed, however, because famous men are just as susceptible to the magic spell of the very young as their constituents, and brother and sister scored their own triumphs, notably with the Lion of Judah. Bundy noted how he saw their mother 'charm the old black Emperor and let him charm her children—which he did most sweetly'. Really they were the charmers. The language barrier was formidable—Jacqueline Kennedy and Selassie spoke French, for his English was extremely limited—but the children had their own ways of communicating. 'He was,' Mrs Kennedy remembered, 'their hero'; she fetched them from across the hall, and as they entered, timidly at first, she pointed to his glittering chest and said, 'Look, John. He's such a brave soldier. That's why he has all those medals.' The boy crept up into his lap and touched one. Then Caroline ran out to get the doll he had given her last summer. Her brother darted after her, and suddenly they were both in the Emperor's lap, showing him the ivory carvings they had treasured. Haile Selassie examined John's toy. 'You will be a brave warrior,' he said haltingly. 'Like your father.' They sat there for about twenty minutes, and to their mother the bond between them and the bearded old man in the gorgeous uniform was almost mystical. 'He had this thing of love, and they showed him their little presents,' she recalled later. 'And they were so happy, just staring at him and worshipping.'

The meeting with the President of France was very different. Mac Bundy had the impression that she was using the reception as 'an easy screen for what she really wanted, which was a chance for a private word' with selected individuals—'above all, de Gaulle'. The children were whisked out, for this occasion was to be more formal. Indeed, it is not too much to call it an episode in personal diplomacy. She received the General 'like a queen', to use Bundy's phrase. The French President merely wanted to repeat what he had told Rusk last evening, and Steve Smith a few minutes ago: that he was here as an emissary of his people. She had something else in mind. Leading him to facing couches beneath the mantel clock, she talked to him about 'this France, England, America thing', and reminded him that virtually everyone, including Herve Alphand, had become bitter over it. 'But Jack was never bitter,' she said. Then she led him out to Bundy and the waiting elevator, and crossing the wide hall she took the General's hand and said, 'Come, let me show you where your beautiful commode is.' On the chest he had sent them there was a vase of fresh oxeye daisies. She plucked one out and handed it to him. 'I want you to take this as a last remembrance of the President,' she said, and de Gaulle rode down holding the American flower.

The talks in the sitting-room and downstairs were less substantive. Their real value lay in the consolation they gave the family; as their visitors sought them out the Kennedys realized just how widespread the President's influence had been. While Haile Selassie was in the study de Gaulle had stepped into the sitting-room to tell Rose Kennedy of it, and Selassie, at Jacqueline Kennedy's suggestion, had followed him there. Here again the Emperor was especially effective. The President's mother recited his childhood diseases in French; 'He was never a strong boy,' she said, 'but he was so determined.' Selassie nodded and described how he had lost his own son, his crown prince. He and Rose discovered that they were the same age. 'It's wrong for parents to bury their children. It should be the other way round,' she said. He agreed: 'It's a violation of nature.' On the first floor the same feeling of shared sorrow was bringing political antagonists together in brief amity. De Gaulle and Prince Philip chatted over tea, with Shriver as *amicus curiae*; Eunice liked Alec

Douglas-Home so much that she hopped upstairs to tell Jackie she must meet him, with the subsequent result that Angie, taking Sir Alec up, met the President of Ireland on the way and introduced the two men. The President bore the scars of British misrule on his own body. He wasn't likely to become an Anglophile in his eighties. But he agreed with Eunice's appraisal of the Prime Minister, and later he participated in agreeable tête-à-têtes with both Douglas-Home and Prince Philip.

The Attorney General brought de Valera into the study and stayed. Inevitably this meeting was emotional for him and both Kennedys. He had with him a letter from his wife, whom the President had liked so much, and they talked of her, of the visit to Ireland, of Galway and Ballkelly Church, of Irish legend and Irish poetry, particularly the poem by Gerald Griffin (1803–1840) which Mrs de Valera had learned as a child in school, which she had recited to the President last June, and which he had then memorized:

'Tis, it is the Shannon's stream,
Brightly glancing, brightly glancing!
See, oh, see the ruddy beam
Upon its waters dancing!
Thus returned from travel vain,
Years of exile, years of pain
To see old Shannon's face again,
O! The bliss entrancing!
Hail, our own majestic stream
Flowing ever, flowing ever
Silent in the morning beam
Our own majestic river!
Fling thy rocky portals wide
Western ocean, western ocean!
Bend ye hills on either side
In solemn, deep devotion
While before the rising gales
On his heaving surface sails
Half the wealth of Erin vales
With undulating motion.
Hail our own beloved stream
Flowing ever, flowing ever
Silent in the morning beam
Our own majestic river.

Mrs Kennedy saw her brother-in-law's dauntless façade crack for the first time. The old man was also in tears, and when Bob took him away through the President's adjoining bedroom she went to the hall door sobbing—and opened it on an embarrassed Prince Philip. The Duke of Edinburgh had been squatting on the floor, chuckling with young John; in the background Angie was bringing Sir Alec up. Philip saw Mrs Kennedy's face and coloured. Straightening, he explained that John had reminded him so much of his own son at that age that he couldn't resist unbending. 'John, did you make your bow to the Prince?' she asked. 'I did!' he crowed, and discomfort vanished in laughter. Inside she sent for her sister. They were sipping Bloody Marys when Angie entered. The chief of protocol was perturbed. He thought it vital that she give equal time to the dignitaries at the foot of the stairs. Did she want to mingle with them, or have a receiving line, or what? She looked at Philip appealingly. He said, 'I'd advise you, you know, to have the line. It's really quick and it gets it done.'

Actually, most of the people around the buffets, including her own relatives, were surprised to hear that the widow had come down. It seemed far more than they had any right to expect. Their gratitude was obvious in their expressions and their anxiety to spare her as much as possible. Philip had been correct: the thing did go speedily. The only delays came when she herself paused for a special word for this or that guest. Standing under the bronze chandelier in the lovely red parlour, with Teddy on her right, Angie on her left, and Godfrey McHugh hovering in the background, she greeted them wanly, shook hands, responded with a few phrases when there was a common language or through an interpreter when there was none. Those for whom she had private messages emerged shaken; in this splendid setting of American Empire furnishings her wistful manner marked the cruelty of the hour. Ludwig Erhard was hardly likely to have forgotten that he was to have been John Kennedy's state guest today, yet he slumped perceptibly when she whispered, 'You know, you and I were to have had dinner this very evening. I had ordered German wine and German music, and just now you and I would be getting dressed.' The Queen of the Hellenes passed in a blur, extending both hands in commiseration, but farther down Mrs Kennedy could clearly see the Deputy Premier of the Soviet Union approaching. His distress was apparent. The tough old Bolshevik was trembling all over. She reached for his hand, and as he gave it he looked terrified. She said, 'Please tell Mr Chairman President that I know he and my husband worked together for a peaceful world, and now he and you must carry on my husband's work.' The interpreter translated. Mikoyan blinked and covered his face with both hands.

He was one of two men who broke. The other was last in line, and it was well he was, for it is doubtful she could have faced another after him. He had a particular significance for her. Once she had told the President, 'I just hope once before we get out of the White House I have an interview, because someone's going to ask me who's the greatest statesman that I've ever met. And it isn't going to be de Gaulle or Nehru or Macmillan or anyone; it's going to be Lleras Camargo of Colombia.' In 1961 Lleras had greeted the Kennedys in Bogotá; he had shown her through the presidential palace, which serves as a museum of national history, and that had been the inspiration for her own renovation of the executive mansion, including this very room. Now the gaunt, almost calvinistic ex-President stood before her, and he too was distraught. Falteringly she told him that of all the tours she and her husband had taken abroad the trip to Colombia had been the best. He began to cry, and Angie, who had been with them there, reached for his own handkerchief. Embracing Lleras she said, 'Please—don't let them forget Jack.'

Angie rode up with her on the agonizingly slow Otis elevator. They were both incapable of speech. He was past due at the new President's reception; in the hall he kissed her on both cheeks and left her there, standing by herself and weeping. And descending in the wrought-iron cage he himself lost all control, though not because of Lleras; there had been an earlier incident, when she greeted Prince Philip outside the Oval Room, and for an hour the grief had been building up inside him. Its origin went back to the President's first European trip. After the confrontation with Khrushchev in Vienna they had flown to London, and she had called Angie back to the rear of the Presidential aircraft to inquire whether she should bend her knee to Queen Elizabeth at that evening's dinner in Buckingham Palace. He had told her then that the wife of a chief of state never curtsies for anyone. Today, as she asked her son whether he had made his bow, she had curtsied to Prince Philip. Then, turning with a smile like a dim lost leaf, she had said gently, 'Angie, I'm no longer the wife of a chief of state.'

On Kalorama Road Charles de Gaulle was dining with the Alphands. President Johnson had been shaking hands in the State Department's candlelit reception room since 5 p.m., but 220 people were waiting to see him, and since this was his first opportunity to display as Chief Executive his demonstrative nature, the warm person-to-person persuasiveness that had made him master of the Senate, the process was obviously going to take some time. De Gaulle knew Johnson. They had met in Paris thirty months ago. Then the General had cut the Vice President short with the icy question, 'What have you come to learn?' Now he sent word that the President of France did not wait in line. He would eat, bathe, and change his clothes, and then he and his bodyguards would be over.

Yet it was part of the conundrum of de Gaulle that he could respond on several levels simultaneously; he was impervious to personal diplomacy but highly vulnerable to gracious gestures. Midway through his meal he stirred from an Olympian trance. Unbuttoning the side pocket of his khaki tunic, he turned to Nicole Alphand, on his right. 'Madame, this is the last souvenir I shall have of President Kennedy,' he said thickly, producing the daisy. 'She asked me to keep it, and I shall keep it always.' Carefully replacing it in his pocket, he added, 'She gave an example to the whole world of how to behave.'

On the seventh floor of the State Department Mikoyan was seeking out diplomats, repeating Jacqueline Kennedy's appeal to him. He was so obviously affected that next day his conduct became the subject of a memorandum to the White House:

> At the President's reception last night Mr Mikoyan ... showed convincingly by the way he discussed the matter that he had been unusually impressed by Mrs Kennedy. This was due not only to her courage and demeanour throughout the funeral ceremonies, but to some remarks which she had made to him when she received the visiting delegations.... He referred to this incident several times.

He did not mention it to the new President. There wasn't time. Johnson received the Deputy Premier unsmilingly, jerked his hand once, exchanged greetings through an interpreter, and posed for photographs. The confrontation lasted exactly thirty-five seconds, which made it one of the shortest of the 220. Since Mikoyan was the second most powerful man in the world's other superpower, this seems remarkable, but the Russian probably wouldn't have wanted it any longer. He didn't smile either. He was going to see the President privately tomorrow anyhow, and he had to be wary; as an exasperated member of the Soviet delegation conceded to an American, their dossier on Johnson was 'very thin'. All foreign dossiers were. Capitals abroad had few clues to the Johnsonian temperament, personality, grasp of international affairs, and influence in his own government. Satisfying that curiosity was the reason for the reception. The leaders were already here, and so, in the singularly unfortunate metaphor of one of the hosts, the State Department 'might as well kill two birds with one stone'. (No one then dreamed that de Gaulle would turn the occasion into a boomerang, using it to kill his promise to Kennedy.) Even so, the reception would be inadequate for the most prominent of them. The French President excepted, they had requested audiences *in camera*, and meetings had been scheduled over the next two days with Mikoyan, Selassie, Inönü,

Douglas-Home, de Valera, Erhard, and the Latin-American chiefs of delegations.

Lyndon Johnson was now beginning to feel the full tonnage of Presidential pressure. Thirty-five governors were waiting in the EOB to see him when he left here; a second full-scale budget meeting was scheduled for 8.45 p.m.; beside his twenty-button telephone console were messages to call almost every major labour and management leader in the country; and Marie Fehmer, whose greatest problem a week ago had been choosing terry-cloth hand towels for Jacqueline Kennedy at the LBJ Ranch, was coping with sixty LBJ cables to foreign heads of state who had been unable to reach Washington in time for the funeral. Of course, Marie didn't write the cables. Neither did Johnson. The full Kennedy team had placed itself at his disposal. Mac Bundy, hurrying over from the Red Room, was put straight to work on tomorrow's agenda for the South Americans, and Dick Goodwin was writing the message the President would read there. Similarly, Llewellyn Thompson was drafting the statement which Johnson would recite to Mikoyan next day. U. Alexis Johnson had prepared 3×5 briefing cards on every individual in the reception line, and before introducing a man to the new Chief Executive Dean Rusk would hold him up just long enough for an Assistant Secretary or protocol officer to mutter the gist of his card in the President's ear.

Coming here directly from the second floor of the mansion, Angie Duke was struck by the change in mood: 'The environment was pulsating; we were moving into the future.' Angie's heart was still in the past, and he left most details to his staff. The President, however, was enjoying himself hugely. The knowledge that work was accumulating in the EOB didn't depress him. Like John Kennedy he had an appetite for it. Furthermore, he relished physical contact. Men from banana republics and emerging nations were given a steely grip and a piercing glance; those he knew or wanted to know received what fellow Texans had long known as 'the laying on of hands' or 'the treatment'—while his right hand was pumping, his left would shoot out to waggle the shakee's elbow in a warm clasp. Willy Brandt, U. Thant, Jean Monnet, and Paul-Henri Spaak received the treatment, and had Presidential hands laid upon them. As a Southern politician he was strong on chivalry; when Angie roused himself to suggest that Mrs Johnson's presence would be appreciated by Queen Frederika and Princess Beatrix—Beatrix had just been twitting Angie about her seat in St Matthew's—the President boomed 'Fine!' and Robin Duke drove out to the Elms to pick up Lady Bird.

By six o'clock the tall trouper was massaging his right hand. The last of the line passed by and advanced on a buffet in the John Quincy Adams Room. In reply to a telephoned inquiry from Alphand, Angie replied that no, President de Gaulle wouldn't have to wait now, and President Johnson began the first of sixteen sofa conferences with selected guests in the Thomas Jefferson Room. Alexis Johnson cautioned him to limit each to three or four minutes; otherwise, he warned, a log jam would develop—as it did. 'The bodies,' in the words of one man, 'began to pile up.' Mac Bundy tried to press the pace. The results were disappointing, so State's senior men improvised what seemed a brilliant solution. The President would see all the Scandinavians together. In came Crown Prince George and Premier Jens Krag of Denmark, Crown Prince Harald and Premier Einar Gerhardsen of Norway, and Prince Bertil and Premier Tage Erlander of Sweden. Lyndon Johnson was, in effect, presiding over a conference of the Nordic Council, and it was all going smoothly when the one body which had no intention of languishing outside appeared in the doorway. At Dulles Charles de Gaulle's pilot was standing by. The plane was due to take off at nine o'clock. Eight hours later—5 a.m. in Washington—he expected to be in his Paris office, and striding forward he wrecked the conference. The Swedes, Danes, and Norwegians sprang apart with little cries of confusion; Dean Rusk hustled up and invited the two presidents into his private office.

According to the Secretary's memorandum of the subsequent discussion, Rusk opened it by thanking de Gaulle for coming to the funeral. 'With deliberation and perceptible emotion' de Gaulle answered that he had always had 'the greatest admiration and respect for President Kennedy', that his death was 'a great loss to the whole world', and that the people of his country had 'a sense of deep personal loss, as of a member of the family'. He spoke of the close ties between France and the United States. 'That is the reality,' he said. 'That is the only thing that counts.' Rusk didn't let that one get by him. How the ties were spliced also counted, and he emphasized that the new administration would 'pursue the same goals as President Kennedy', that 'the broad lines of our foreign policy' and 'our political and military commitments to Europe' would remain the same. President Johnson, as 'a very close associate of President Kennedy', could be counted upon to see to it that there was no 'slowing down or hesitation in the pace and the direction of the foreign policy of the United States'. The France, England, America thing, in short, would continue to be a thing.

Johnson kept quiet. He didn't know the language, he had more confidence in Rusk than Kennedy had had, and so he let his Secretary speak for him in this one conversation when, more than in any other, his vigorous personality might have left at least a dent. Otherwise the reception went well for him. It wasn't as easy as it looked on television. His fellow countrymen were accustomed to him. He had been a national figure since his rise as Majority Leader in the 1950's, when Eisenhower had been monarch and Johnson had performed superbly as his prime minister. The success of that relationship had been inevitable. Although they represented different parties and differed sharply in political philosophies and ability, both were cut from the same bolt of homespun. It was a cloth Americans knew well. To foreigners, especially in Europe, Johnson's folksiness was alien, and hence suspect. The fact that most of their representatives left Washington reassured on the evening of November 25 was a feat. The accomplishment, moreover, magnified when seen through the special pall under which the new Chief Executive laboured. Ben Bradlee may have exaggerated in assuming that Johnson would live out his White House years in Kennedy's shade, but that afternoon, with the unexplained events in Dallas looking more and more sinister, the shadow was certainly very long.

To those around him, General de Gaulle kept talking of Kennedy's youth and the tragedy that one so young should die. Presently there was a stirring among the guests near the reception room entrance; Galbraith and Harriman, whom so many of them knew well, were arriving together. Galbraith had come to tell the President that Jenkins and Sorensen had copies of his speech draft. Johnson thanked him shortly, and Ambassador Anatoly Dobrynin introduced Galbraith to Mikoyan as 'the prophet of affluence'. While the Deputy Premier was trying to sort out what this meant, Hervé Alphand asked the prophet whether he would like to meet de Gaulle. The two beanpoles began on a light note. Frowning across the room at Mikoyan, the General asked, 'Why have you been conversing with such a short man?' Galbraith smiled and said, 'Obviously you agree with me that the world belongs to the tall. They are more visible and therefore their behaviour is better.' De Gaulle nodded. Still lowering at Mikoyan, he said, 'We must be merciless with little men.'

Abruptly he turned to Galbraith. 'What does the death of President Kennedy mean?' he asked. 'It is the death of John Kennedy,' said Galbraith, 'not the U.S.A. The country goes on.' The General listened intently as Alphand translated. He brooded for a moment, peering off across the bobbing heads with that messianic stare which bewitched his admirers and had nearly driven Winston Churchill out of his mind. 'As I grow older I think we are too casual about death,' he said. 'Why is it that only in your country and mine do we have the fringe of violent men?' The French Ambassador translated the rhetorical question and chimed in to agree in both languages. Galbraith started to reply, 'But the Americans are better shots'; then he thought better of it.

After Angie Duke had left, Mrs Kennedy had recovered her composure and noticed a shy, strange girl sitting off to one side of the corridor. She looked lonely and frightened, which was only natural. Yesterday Mary Ann Ryan had been a nurse in the Irish hamlet of Dunganstown, County Wexford, grieving for the handsome cousin who had put his arm around her last summer and said, 'You know, you look like a Kennedy. You have the Irish smile.' Now Lee Radziwill came out of the sitting-room to introduce her to Jacqueline Kennedy, who wondered how on earth she had got here. Mrs Kennedy was too polite to ask, which was a good thing, for it is doubtful that the girl could have explained. Acting on Dean Markham's request, a task force of Irish police cruisers had plucked Mary from her home and raced to the nearest large airport. A Pan American transatlantic flight had made an unscheduled stop to pick her up, New York customs inspectors had waved her through, and Pan Am had chartered a twin-engine plane to ferry her to Washington in time for the Mass. She knew no one in the executive mansion. She had never been in such a grand house; she could easily get lost in it, and couldn't possibly find her way out of it and back to Dunganstown without a great deal of assistance. The situation was altogether new to her. Jacqueline Kennedy sensed her anxiety. Excusing herself, she went into the President's bedroom and returned with the rosary from his bureau drawer for Mary and another gift for her mother.

Then doors began opening; within minutes the hall was swarming with Shrivers, Smiths, Lawfords, Auchinclosses, Radziwills, and Kennedys of all ages. Once more Mrs Kennedy felt they were 'a family close', and the girl from Ireland was accepted as one of them. So were honorary members named Schlesinger and Powers, and one Bouvier relative who, like Mary Ryan, had just crossed the ocean. A Secret Service agent interrupted a chat between Janet Auchincloss and Rose Kennedy to say that a young man downstairs claimed to be the widow's first cousin. The White House Detail was edgy; after the reception in the Red Room there had been a serious bomb scare there. Would Mrs Auchincloss identify him? She did: he was Jack Davis, a schoolteacher who had hurried home from Italy too late for the funeral. Davis was exactly his cousin's age, and he was welcomed. As evening approached the mob was dwindling—the Shrivers had stumbled out, ready to drop, and the President's mother was leaving to fly back to her husband—and there was a kind of consolation in numbers. It was as though each of them, knowing that he had to maintain a semblance of poise with the others, was afraid seclusion would trigger private disintegration. In fact, this was the case. Those who broke were those who strayed from the tribe.

A TV set had been rolled into the sitting-room. There was only one programme, the Johnson reception, and from time to time the young woman who had been television's chief protagonist for three days joined the national audience. On Channel 4 Merrill Mueller, Edwin Newman, and Nancy Dickerson were identifying the figures passing NBC's dolly. The Apostolic Delegate had just received the treatment, and Nancy was speculating on the punishment Johnson's hand had been taking, when, at 5.45 p.m., Willy Brandt appeared on camera. 'I didn't know he'd come,' Mrs Kennedy said wonderingly to her sister. Lee had been in Berlin with the President; she remarked upon how much Brandt had impressed her. Jacqueline Kennedy remembered how warmly her husband had praised the Mayor, and recalled something else: yesterday she had been told that he had renamed the square where her husband had aroused 150,000 Germans with his pledge to defend West Berlin. The Attorney General entered the sitting-room. 'Why wasn't Willy Brandt in the line downstairs?' she asked him. The answer was that he wasn't important enough. He represented a city, not a nation. 'Well, I want to see him,' she said. They couldn't reach him through Angie Duke—Angie was there on the screen in front of them—so Mr West was asked to use his expertise. A White House car was dispatched to the State Department, the chief usher phoned word ahead to veteran attendants on the seventh floor, and ten minutes later the Mayor was shown into the Oval Room. Jacqueline and Robert Kennedy went in to receive him together.

She was struck by his height. He hadn't seemed nearly so tall in photographs. Nothing published about him had suggested that he was unusually demonstrative either, but like a great many public men who had remained steady under extraordinary pressures in the past, he had reached the end of his tether in Arlington. The moment the Kennedys entered the study he burst into tears. She inquired about the rechristening of the square in honour of her husband; wiping his eyes he acknowledged it and said he wanted to do more: a school should be named for Kennedy too. Did he have their permission? She looked at Bob. 'Fine,' he said. He couldn't say more. This was turning out to be more difficult for him than de Valera. Jacqueline Kennedy walked to the windows and looked out. Darkness had come down upon the city. Beyond the Truman balcony lay the south grounds, the Ellipse, the white needle of the Washington Monument, its winking red lights warning off aircraft; and, across the Tidal Basin, the lovely colonnaded shrine of the Jefferson

Memorial, which the President had ordered illuminated at night. 'He can't have this view any more,' she said, 'but he can have John F. Kennedy Platz. Thank you for that'. Though her eyes were full, she was composed, and pivoting she saw she was the only one there who was.

The Mayor was the last of the distinguished guests. Maître Fincklin set up a buffet in the study. There was a great deal of maundering about between there, the hall and the sitting-room as the family munched the chicken and ham sandwiches which had been the mansion's staple since Friday. Everywhere, it seemed, one could hear the reedy, hearty voice of Dave Powers. Dave might have been created for this evening. His career was over. Even the Kennedy team had found him trying at times; when he came humming down the curving corridor in the West Wing, men with work to do had closed their doors. He had been invaluable at ball games or in the pool, when the President wanted to relax, but Lyndon Johnson's sense of humour ran along different lines, and he would not suffer him gladly or for long. Tonight, however, Dave made the family gathering the apotheosis of an Irish wake. He performed as though it were the climax of his life, which it probably was, telling charming anecdotes of the President's early years in politics—how he had first met him under a dim 15-watt bulb on the landing of a Boston three-decker tenement and heard him say in his cultivated accent, 'My name is Jack Kennedy. I am a candidate for Congress. Will you help me?'; or stories of the Presidential trip to Paris, when Dave had his name translated into French and persuaded the doorman at the grand ball to announce him that way ('Kenny's right behind me, see, and he starts laughing so hard he falls right down the marble staircase. You should've seen the look on de Gaulle's face. Some doorman in silk knickers asks me, "What is zee matter with M'sieur O'Donnell?" and I say haughtily, "I'm sure I don't know, my mahn" '); or how he himself had announced guests to the President ('Our type Shah is in the Cabinet Room'; 'I hope this Russian is the real Mikoyan'). Dave entertained without intruding, gently reminding them that Kennedy, too, had known how to laugh when there had seemed to be no laughter left in the world.

He was still young John's indefatigable drill instructor, and the children couldn't get enough of his 'One, two, three, four: Cadence count!' Looking like a defeated alderman yet performing like a Pied Piper, he led them to the end of the South Hall, cried merrily, 'To the rear *March*!' and headed back to the dining-room. It was seven o'clock. John's birthday was to be observed again. A small table had been set for two. Caroline and John sat, and around them gathered their mother, Dave, Sydney Lawford, Bob Kennedy's children, Bob and Ethel, Steve and Jean, Lee and Stas, Pat, Jamie and young Janet Auchincloss, and Maude Shaw. There were presents from all of them—each time John exultantly ripped the wrappings off a box there was a little chorus of approval—and a cake with three candles. Ice cream was brought in for all the children, and Mrs Kennedy suggested they sing some of the songs the President had loved. Someone pointed out that the piano was in the hall, but Dave scoffed at pianos. 'We Irish don't need music to sing,' he said. 'The music's inside us.' The party became what Miss Shaw called 'a singsong affair'; Dave led them in 'That Old Gang of Mine', and then said, 'What about "Heart of My Heart"? It's a sort of comrady song.'

We're singing,
'Heart of My Heart,' I love that melody,
'Heart of My Heart' brings back a memory,
When we were kids
On the corner of the street,
We were rough and ready guys,
But oh! How we could harmonize. . . .

Bob Kennedy fled out of the door. It was, Stas thought, 'a terrible moment'. This was not a blithe yarn with a comic twist at the end; it brought back too much—summer evenings in the compound, singing on the beach after the sails had been furled, and that last night in the '58 campaign, when Senator John Kennedy, too played out to speak in Dorchester, had sung these very words with his two brothers to an enthusiastic crowd. But the children, not old enough for nostalgia, were delighted. And Red, who had murdered harmony in Dorchester, joined his strong baritone to Dave's tenor for the last lines:

. . . friends were dearer then,
Too bad we had to part.
Now I know a tear would glisten
If once more I could listen
To the gang that sang 'Heart of My Heart.'

The children were led to bed. The Auchinclosses left, the Smiths retired, Ethel took her brood to Hickory Hill, Ted and Joan returned to their home. Stas was stifling yawns. The rest didn't want the occasion to end, though—there was, after all, nothing to look forward to tomorrow—and Mrs Kennedy asked the Bradlees to come in from Georgetown. They arrived apprehensive. In Toni Bradlee's words, 'It was not something to walk into.' Their hosts tried valiantly to be cheerful, but their fatigue was evident. Even Kennedy energy had its limits. Mrs Kennedy's red eyes were painful to see. Both Ben and Toni thought Bob was displaying the best self-discipline, yet in a way he was the hardest to take. His voice was so much like the President's that they found themselves whirling about each time he spoke. Dave Powers, carrying on, had Lee captivated. The others weren't quite real. Stas tottered off to bed like a man already in a dream. Pat Lawford's face was a mask of agony, and Peter wandered in and out with his peculiar marionette gait; it was as though a gigantic invisible hand were clutching the cloth between his shoulder blades and hoisting him up—his legs actually seemed to dangle. The television set was on, endlessly recapitulating the long weekend. Toni asked if she might take one last look at the President's bedroom. She regretted it. So many private parties had ended in that room, with the last guests bidding one another witty farewells, that Toni's final glimpse of it should, she had thought, become a treasured keepsake. But it had changed. The personal bric-à-brac had already disappeared. Even the pyramid of pill bottles had vanished from the bedside table, and Stas, slumbering on the little cot, appeared to be an outrageous incongruity.

The Bradlees left quickly. All but Bob and Jackie drifted away, though Lee, before joining her husband, pinned a note to her sister's pillow. As children the Bouvier girls had had secret nicknames for one another. Lee had been 'Pekes', Jackie 'Jacks'. The note of love and admiration which she left for 'Jacks', only a sister could have written.

And so, at the last, the two chief mourners were left alone on the second floor of the mansion. Five evenings ago, before riding across Memorial Bridge to attend his own birthday party, the Attorney General had talked to the First Lady here for nearly forty-five minutes, inquiring whether she was sure she had recovered sufficiently from Patrick's death to endure the strain of the Texas trip and the campaigning ahead. Now, preparing to cross the river again, he needed no assurance; like him, he knew, she could survive anything except the thought that the yesterdays binding them together might be forgotten. Therefore, with that understated manner which, as much as his voice, stirred sudden memories of the President, he said quietly, 'Should we go visit our friend?'

She always kept lilies of the valley in a little gold cup on a hall table, and she stopped to gather a spray. Clint Hill phoned ahead to Arlington. Jack Metzler's house was inside the cemetery grounds; he dressed quickly and met their black Mercury by Hatfield Gate. Parking on Sheridan Drive, they walked up between cedar and oak to the new fence. Once more the scene was sharply altered. The vast throngs had disappeared. Standing by the white pickets were only the Kennedys, two military policemen, and the superintendent. The fake turf had been carted away. Inside the fence the wicker basket Bunny Mellon had placed by the grave had been obscured by ostentatious chaplets tied with gaudy ribbons. The night mercifully hid them. It was, Clint noted, 'very damp and dark and quiet'.

One of the military policemen unlatched the gate. Jacqueline and Robert Kennedy stepped inside, and under the flickering torch he saw the green beret. Sergeant Major Ruddy's gesture had been noticed by two other soldiers. An MP in the afternoon shift had left his black and white brassard on the evergreens; beside it a soldier of the 3rd Infantry had propped his buff strap and Old Guard cockade, the symbols of a military tradition which went back to the Revolutionary War. Bob silently pointed to them, and she nodded. Together they dropped to their knees. The tongue of flame, quite blue at night, flickered in the night wind; its ghost-candle flare danced unevenly on their bowed heads and averted faces, on Clint and the two guards, on the chauffeur waiting below. As widow and brother offered their prayers the clocks of the capital struck midnight, and rising she carefully laid her bouquet on the branches, a last gallant plighting of her troth. Then they turned from the scarred earth, leaving the beacon, and walked down into darkness.

Epilogue
LEGEND

In early April of 1960, during the lull that followed the Wisconsin Presidential primary, Senator John F. Kennedy read Mary Renault's *The King Must Die* in his Georgetown home. Although fictive, this novel is based on a custom which Sir James Frazier found in every early society: the ritualistic murder of the folk hero. The noble victim went by various names. In Britain he was Arthur, in Germany Siegfried, in France Roland, in Scandinavia Balder the Beautiful; Mediterranean tribes knew him as Apollo, Attis, Moses, Adonis, and Osiris, and ancient India had loved and lost Vitramaditya. These epics were more than fables. Undoubtedly all their protagonists existed under one name or another, and one heroine whose identity has survived was burned at a Rouen stake in the fifteenth century.

It is worth noting that Jeanne d'Arc was betrayed by the French on November 21, 1430. For what Miss Renault did not mention is that the martyrdom of heroic figures nearly always occurred in the waning days of autumn. The end of summer terrified men. Winter lay ahead, and the fear of starvation. Watching the corn die and the bitter days grow short, they believed that they were being punished. Unwittingly, they felt, they must have offended the omnipotent God who brooded over the land. What was needed was a powerful emissary, an ally in the skies. And so, over the ages, a solution evolved. They would sacrifice their most cherished possession, their prince. It would be agony, but it would also be a sign of contrition, and after the execution their mighty friend would ascend into heaven, to temper the wrath of the Almighty and assure a green and abundant spring.

In the twentieth century that legend is vestigial. Yet no one familiar with world religions can doubt its viability, and the nature of its atavistic power must be understood if one is to grasp what happened to the memory of John Kennedy after his burial. Folk heroes, for example, have no more to do with democracy than riderless horses and funeral pageantry. The origins of their appeal lie deep in the past, before written history or the emergence of the nation-state. But this much seems clear: no society had achieved cohesion without them. The yearning they satisfy is that basic. The United States of America, as the newest societal entity in the world (emerging nations are discounted here; they were established communities centuries before their colonizers recognized them as such), long felt this need. The spectacular murder of Abraham Lincoln was the first sacrifice to fill it—Lloyd Lewis suggested as much a generation ago in his brilliant *Myths After Lincoln*—and the martyrdom of John Kennedy was the second.

Once a leader becomes a martyr, myth naturally follows. The hero must be clothed in raiments which he would have found strange, but which please the public eye. As Edmund Wilson has pointed out, the Lincoln to whom Americans are introduced as children, and whom Carl Sandburg has done so much to perpetuate, has little in common with the cool, aloof genius who ruled this nation unflinchingly as the sixteenth President of the United States. That man was destroyed on the evening of April 14, 1865. The urbane scholar who became his nineteenth successor shared his fate. The Kennedy we knew in life vanished for ever on November 22, 1963. That Lincoln and Kennedy shared an abiding faith in a government of laws thus becomes an irrelevant detail; legends, because they are essentially tribal, override such details. What the folk hero was and what he believed are submerged by the demands of those who follow him. In myth he becomes what they want him to have been, and anyone who belittles this transformation has an imperfect understanding of truth. A romantic concept of what may have been can be far more compelling than what was. 'Love is very penetrating,' Santayana observed, 'but it penetrates to possibilities, rather than to facts.' All the people ask of a national hero is that he should have been truly heroic, a great man who was greatly loved and cruelly lost. Glorification and embellishment follow. In love nations are no less imaginative than individuals.

Those who had traduced John Kennedy and many who had admired him were puzzled by the surge of emotion which followed the state funeral and which was to grow year after year. The derisive dismissed it as 'the Kennedy cult', as though the death of every extraordinary man were not followed by a consolidation of devotion. The nub of the matter was that Kennedy had met the emotional needs of his people. His achievements had been genuine. His dreams and his oratory had electrified a country grown stale and listless and a world drifting helplessly towards Armageddon. Lincoln—'Father Abraham', his troops called him—had been paternal. Kennedy had been young, princely, dashing, handsome, charming, and the woman he had loved, and in whose arms he had died, had contributed enormously to the spectacle. 'I feel suddenly old without Mr and Mrs Kennedy in the White House,' a correspondent wrote James Reston after the funeral. 'Not only by ability but by sheer verve and joy, the Kennedys imparted their youth to everyone, and put a sheen on our life that made it more youthful than it is. Mr Johnson now seems Gary Cooper as President—*High Noon*, the poker game, the easy walk and masculine smile. But even Gary Cooper was growing older, and the companions around the poker table reflect a less fresh, if no doubt practical and effective mood. All will be well, I feel sure, but it is August, not June. . . .' The magic, in other words, was gone.

In the third year of the Johnson administration an exasperated aide was to complain that the public had come to think of the Kennedy administration as a Golden Age of Pericles. 'He wasn't Pericles,' he said, 'and the age wasn't golden.' No, it wasn't. (Pericles' wasn't either.) Yet as the same aide conceded, 'That doesn't matter—it's caught hold.' In point of fact, it had begun to take hold that midnight when Jacqueline and Robert Kennedy arose from the fresh grave and walked down the hill hand in hand. By the following day the green beret had been joined by caps of all the armed services. John C. Warnecke was commissioned to design a permanent memorial, with the passages the Attorney General was to have read during the graveside services engraved on tablets, but the pilgrims did not wait. The plain picket fence was enough for them. On Christmas Day 1963 a steady procession passed it all day, five abreast; a six-inch snow lay on the ground, yet the waiting line stretched the equivalent of several city blocks. Reston observed that 'the Kennedy legend grows and deepens. It is clear now that he captured the imagination of a whole generation of young people in many parts of the world, particularly in the university communities. Even those who vilified him now canonize him, and many of his political opponents who condemned him are now seeking a candidate who looks and sounds like him.'

Officially the period of mourning was to last thirty days, and that merely meant flags at half-staff and no social functions. Outside the government business opened as usual the morning after the funeral. Television commercials resumed, the stock market rebounded sharply, theatre marquees lit up. Those who had felt the impact of the tragedy more deeply quietly set about straightening out their lives. Mr West readied the White House for tourists. Henry Gonzalez packed John Connally's clothes and sent them back to Nellie. Jack Valenti took up temporary residence at the Elms until his family could join him. Colonel McNally kept trying to put in permanent telephone lines for the new President—it was to be six months, to the day, before Johnson was off the phone long enough—and Angie Novello carefully retaped to the walls of the Attorney General's office all the children's drawings she had removed on the day of the assassination while cleaning the office, in the forlorn hope that the room would seem normal to him when he returned. He flew off for a Thanksgiving rest with the Dillons; Mrs Kennedy took her children to the Cape.

The thirty days ended, the flags went up, the piano was moved back into the East Room, Washington hostesses began entertaining again—and then one realized that the mourning hadn't ended at all. To be sure, the fever of November 22–25 was over. That condition had been unnatural; between Wednesday and Saturday of the week after the assassination, the NORC survey found, three out of four adults had returned to normal behaviour patterns. A kind of nation-wide scar tissue had begun to form, and it thickened so quickly that anyone attempting to reopen the wounds encountered evasiveness or downright hostility. Still, the residue of sadness remained. In New York a thousand people walked slowly up Fifth Avenue, each holding a candle in memory of President Kennedy. Christmas shoppers were struck by the melancholy in city shops. Magazines began issuing JFK memorial editions, and every book store in the capital had its corner of memorial albums. Auctioneers of Americana found that handwritten Kennedy letters were as valuable as Lincoln letters. An autographed copy of *Profiles in Courage* was worth $375. Fragments of the platform from which he had delivered his San Antonio speech the day before the assassination became collector's items, and the 'Suite 850' plaque outside his last bedroom in the Hotel Texas disappeared.

To emphasize the transition the White House staff began distributing photographs of both Presidents during Johnson's trips outside Washington, but the practice was quickly discontinued; for every picture of the new Chief Executive, the public would take ten of Kennedy. The Secret Service seethed when Johnson rebuked an agent for wearing a PT tie clip, sharply reminding him that administrations had changed, yet Johnson's pique was entirely understandable. He was plagued by a ghost. Even the 1964 Presidential convention, which had been carefully planned as a Johnsonian feast, was stolen from under his very eyes. A month earlier he had scratched Robert Kennedy from his list of Vice Presidential possibilities. Nevertheless the most moving moment in Convention Hall was not his; it came when the Attorney General stepped to the podium to introduce a film about his brother's thousand days in the White House. For fifteen minutes the delegates gave Robert Kennedy a roaring, standing ovation, and then, in tears, they heard him softly quote Shakespeare in that inimitable voice:

... When he shall die,
Take him and cut him out in little stars,
And he will make the face of heaven so fine
That all the world will be in love with night
And pay no worship to the garish sun.

The more men pondered the legend, the less they understood it. The young Kennedy had done nothing to encourage the demonstration; he tried repeatedly to interrupt it, then smiled slightly and, biting his lip, lowered his head as against a storm. David Brinkley concluded that the assassination and its aftermath were unfathomable: 'The events of those days don't fit, you can't place them anywhere, they don't go in the intellectual luggage of our time. It was too big, too sudden, too overwhelming, and it meant too much. It has to be separate and apart.' All the same, people couldn't stop attempting to incorporate it in their lives. The most obvious approach was to name something after the President. Mrs Kennedy asked Johnson to rechristen Cape Canaveral Cape Kennedy. He immediately complied, and presently she wondered whether she would be driving 'down a Kennedy parkway to a Kennedy airport to visit a Kennedy school'. New York's Mayor Wagner renamed Idlewild, Congress changed the National Cultural Centre to the John F. Kennedy Centre for the Performing Arts, the Treasury began minting fifty million Kennedy half-dollars—and couldn't keep them in circulation because they were being hoarded as souvenirs. In every part of the country committees and councils were voting to honour the President by altering local maps. The Tobay Wildlife Sanctuary in Oyster Bay became the John Fitzgerald Kennedy Memorial Wildlife Sanctuary; the Padre Island Causeway, the John F. Kennedy Causeway. A bridge across the Ohio River, a New Hampshire recreation centre, the town square in Easton, Pennsylvania, a waterfront project in Yonkers, and an Arkansas highway were rebaptized. Canada had its Mount Kennedy—the first man to climb it was Robert Kennedy, by then U.S. Senator from New York—and the climax was reached when England set aside three acres of the historic meadow at Runnymede, where the Magna Carta was signed, as a Kennedy shrine. It was Queen Elizabeth's idea. On May 14, 1965, she presided at the ceremony, dedicating the tract to the President 'whom in death my people still mourn and whom in life they loved'. Mrs Kennedy replied that it was 'the deepest comfort to me to know that you share with me thoughts that lie too deep for tears'.

By then her own situation had reacquired some semblance of order, and she had begun studying plans for the tomb and the design of the library at Harvard which would house her husband's papers and memorabilia. In the days which followed the funeral, however, life had been a chaos. She had to cope with all the heavy tasks of the bereaved widow: cleaning out his bureau drawers, sorting through his belongings, which, because of the manner of his death, repeatedly brought stabbing reminders of Dallas—a week after the funeral the Secret Service delivered the wristwatch she had last seen in Trauma Room No. 1—and dealing with the bewildering, often callous mail which confronts wives whose husbands have always handled their joint affairs (e.g., the letter from the U.S. Finance Centre regarding the pay of 'your husband, the late John F. Kennedy, Lieutenant, United States Naval Reserve, Retired, from the period of 9 December 1953 through 22 November 1963'). In addition she faced urgent demands as a mother, as a symbol of the transition, and as her husband's representative. Meanwhile she was moving.

She felt, she told Nicole Alphand, 'like a wounded animal. What I really want to do is crawl into a corner and hide.' What she really had to do was keep turning from one task to the next. The family helped as much as possible. Her sister and Pat Lawford stayed with her through the winter, and her mother and Ted Kennedy brought the bodies of her two dead babies back for reburial with their father. But she dealt with most matters herself. She had refused to delegate her responsibilities during the funeral preparations, and in the aftermath, too, she wanted to make each touch her own. Frequently she had no choice. If she was determined to support the new President, her physical presence was absolutely necessary; no one could act for her there. And she was determined. Whatever her personal feelings, the office Lyndon Johnson now held exerted its own demands. Until he had acquired the country's confidence and felt confident himself there could be no substitute for a display of unity. The day after the burial she came down to the East Room to stand among the Latin Americans while he read the speech Goodwin had written, promising continued support of the *Alianza*. During that first week she telephoned him and wrote him encouraging letters, and while he could not grasp why she persisted in addressing him 'Mr President', he understood and appreciated her show of the flag. The Sunday after the funeral he wrote her:

DEAR JACKIE:

How could you possibly find that extra moment—that extra ounce of strength to call me Thanksgiving evening. You have been magnificent and have won a warm place in the heart of history. I only wish things could be different—that I didn't have to be here. But the Almighty has willed differently, and now Lady Bird and I need your help. You have for now and for always our warm, warm *love.*

Affectionately,
LYNDON.

She was evacuating the mansion for him as quickly as she could. Here again, this could have been left to servants and secretaries, but the White House had special significance for Jacqueline Kennedy. She had left her mark on nearly every room in it, and before walking out for the last time she wished to leave more tokens for her husband. In retrospect her anxiety that he might be forgotten seems odd. ('She wrote me not to forget him!' said one of her correspondents of those days. 'As though I could pass a single hour without remembering!') The scope of his legacy was not apparent then, though. He had been cut down after less than a full term, with his mightiest ambitions unrealized; in newspapers she read that he had not been in office long enough to achieve greatness. There was no way of knowing that the very brevity of his Presidency would add poignancy to his story. Therefore she made certain it would be pondered by future Presidents. First the family chose the picture which would be donated to the mansion in his name. Jim Fosburgh, the chairman of her committee on art, appeared from New York with a truck of priceless cargo—the treasures of six galleries—and lined up the paintings in the second-floor hall and along the walls of the Oval Room. The selection was narrowed down to a Courbet and a Monet of water lilies. Both were taken down to the Green Room, where the gift was to hang, and the choice settled when Eunice, ordinarily so matter-of-fact, said of the Monet, 'That pictures makes you want to dream, doesn't it?'

The widow's most striking farewell gesture was entirely her own. Among the sheaf of reminders to herself which survive from those days ('Good-bye operators') ('Good-bye staff') are several with the various headings 'Our Room', 'J's Room' and 'On side of mantel in JFK Room'. After several false starts she wrote in her spidery handwriting, 'In this room lived John Fitzgerald Kennedy with his wife Jacqueline during the two years, ten months and two days he was President of the United States.' It was carved directly beneath the old inscription, 'In this room Abraham Lincoln slept during his occupancy of the White House March 4, 1861–April 13, 1865.'

She met her self-imposed deadline. Eleven days after the funeral she was in the Harriman house. The following morning the new First Lady wrote her:

THE WHITE HOUSE
WASHINGTON

DEAR JACKIE—

We have just spent our first night here. I'm still lost—but will find my way!

How dear of you to leave for us the lovely lilies of the valley—Nancy put your note in my hand, and its reassurance I treasure.

Thank you and
love

LADY BIRD

President Johnson pinned the Treasury's highest award on Rufe Youngblood, hailing him as 'one of the most noble and able public servants I have ever known'. At Mrs Kennedy's insistence Secretary Dillon also decorated Clint Hill. Though both agents had performed admirably—Clint's dramatic leap in particular could not be ignored; everyone in the country had seen photographs of it—the ceremonies left an undercurrent of dissatisfaction in much of official Washington. The central fact was that the Secret Service had failed, and there was feeling that the first reaction ought to have been one of collective shame and not of pride in exceptional men—that the medals should have followed investigation of the failure. Investigations had begun, of course, but here, too, the first steps were disquieting. The FBI assigned fifty agents to a crash study, wrote a skimpy report which dismissed thorny questions with the recurring phrase 'There is no evidence'—and then leaked the report to a news magazine. The episode was a dismaying example of how threatened bureaucracies, turning a blind eye to the national interest, rise in defence of themselves.

The new President having been persuaded that a Texas inquiry would be doomed in advance as a whitewash, Nick Katzenbach and Solicitor General Cox called upon the Chief Justice four days after the funeral and urged him to head a federal commission. Warren refused. He had, he pointed out, repeatedly spoken out against extracurricular activity by judges; he suggested they ask one of the Court's two retired justices instead. His visitors left and advised the White House of their failure. This was the kind of circumstance in which Lyndon Johnson was at his most effective. The Chief Judge hardly had time to relay his decision to two of his colleagues before his phone rang. The President wanted to see him at once. In Warren's words,

> I saw McGeorge Bundy first. He took me in, and the President told me how serious the situation was. He said there had been wild

rumours, and that there was the international situation to think of. He said he had just talked to Dean Rusk, who was concerned, and he also mentioned the head of the Atomic Energy Commission, who had told him how many millions of people would be killed in an atomic war. The only way to dispel these rumours, he said, was to have an independent and responsible commission, and that there was no one to head it except the highest judicial officer in the country. I told him how I felt. He said that if the public became aroused against Castro and Khrushchev there might be war.

'You've been in uniform before,' he said, 'and if I asked you, you would put on the uniform again for your country.'

I said, 'Of course.'

'This is more important than that,' he said.

'If you're putting it like that,' I said, 'I can't say no.'

That same afternoon Johnson signed Executive Order 11130, appointing the six other members and charging them all to evaluate FBI material, make further investigations of their own, and to appraise 'all the facts and circumstances surrounding' Kennedy's murder, 'including the subsequent violent death of the man charged with the assassination'. As is customary with such *ad hoc* panels, the lustrous names of the seven appointees were for public consumption. The real work was done by the general counsel and his fourteen assistants, and especially by the younger lawyers. Over a six-month period ninety-four witnesses appeared at sessions attended by one or more members of the Commission itself. Individual staff men, on the other hand, questioned 395. Sworn affidavits were accepted from sixty-one people, and two—the President and Mrs Johnson—sent statements. On September 24, 1964, the full report was submitted to the Chief Executive and made public.

In the United States it was received with general approval. There were fewer endorsements abroad, where it was frequently dismissed as the 'official version' of the two crimes—a sly inference that another, true version was being suppressed. That was unjust. The Commission had met its mandate. Oswald was correctly identified as the assassin; the absence of a cabal was established. The treatment of related questions was less satisfactory. This was especially true of the findings on Presidential protection. Although the conduct of the Secret Service, the FBI, and the Dallas police was found to have been less than admirable, they were handled gingerly, and corrective suggestions lacked clarity and force. Their subsequent fate was disheartening. J. Edgar Hoover, furious that his bureau should be criticized at all, protested so vehemently that the public overlooked the report's harsher censure of the Secret Service (which wisely laid low); by the time the Director had finished disciplining his Dallas agents, including the unfortunate Hosty, a great many newspaper readers had forgotten which agency had really been accountable for John Kennedy's safety. As for the Commission's specific recommendations, the most important were filed and forgotten. Cabinet-level supervision of the Service was proposed; nothing was done about it. The Commission felt that the Head of the White House Detail ought to be an administrative officer with no personal ties to the President. Johnson replaced Behn with Youngblood. Few agents envied Youngblood; the new Chief Executive turned out to be far more difficult to protect than his predecessor. He plunged into crowds, invited swarms of passing tourists into the White House, and reprimanded bodyguards who came too close to him. The Service rebuilt the Presidential Lincoln in which Kennedy had died, adding a souped-up motor, two and a half tons of new steel plating, three-inch glass, and bulletproof tyres, but Johnson rarely used it.

On the issue of small-arms control the report was silent; the commissioners debated among themselves and decided this question lay outside their province. In the wake of the assassination the pressure for such legislation seemed irresistible; a Gallup poll revealed that eight out of ten Americans favoured new laws requiring police permits of weapons buyers. Robert Kennedy asked Congress to outlaw the mail-order traffic, supportive mail engulfed the Hill, and in the weeks after the funeral Senator Thomas Dodd of Connecticut introduced a sensible bill to ban mail-order sales, bar weapons from abroad unsuitable for sporting use, forbid sales to people under twenty-one, and require all purchasers to identify themselves so police could later trace them. The American Bar Association endorsed it and was ignored. The Director of the U.S. Bureau of Prisons pointed out that 'After all, cars have to be registered and drivers licensed' and was unheard. Indeed, though eighteen such measures were introduced on the Hill, none of the gun laws went off. The United States remained the only modern nation in the world without firm regulation of the sale and use of firearms—Oswald couldn't have assassinated Khrushchev in Russia—and in 1964 some 600,000 cheap firearms were brought into the country.

A great many men seemed to regard all proposals for tighter controls as a challenge to their virility. The powerful National Rifle Association urged its half-million members to write Washington, and its lobbyists went to work on Congressmen with the specious reasoning that 'It's the man that kills, not the rifle.' They demanded passage of another (Hickenlooper) bill, which would merely prevent the importing of guns not made by American firms. Katzenbach pointed out in vain that the association was protecting, not sportsmen's rights, but the profits of commercial gun dealers. 'Anti-Gun Extremists Are at It Again,' *Field and Stream* warned its readers, and *Outdoor Life* declared that 'Gun Owners Should Switch to the Offence.'[1] They did. In Texas they were especially militant. Elsewhere in the country courts took a benign view of some twenty thousand gun-control laws enacted on municipal and state levels. In Dallas an ordinance restricting the possession of weapons had been struck down by a local judge in 1962 on the ground that it would have been an 'unauthorized invasion of a natural right the citizens of this state have never relinquished to their rulers'. Presumably 'their rulers' meant the government of the United States, and the assassination didn't change that feeling. Once his arm had healed Governor Connally called upon Texas' Congressional delegation to oppose the Dodd bill, and Texas Republicans, meeting in Dallas, passed a resolution opposing any limitation whatever on the right of private individuals to buy and use guns.

Big D continued to be a peculiar community. During the last week in November there had been those in the liberal underground who had hoped the city's agonizing reappraisal might arouse its mass conscience. The watchman had wakened but in vain. The more Dallas changed, the more it remained the same. As the 'So Long, Pal' wreaths withered in Dealey Plaza the self-consciousness hardened into defensiveness, an uneasy What-will-New-York-think-of-us? attitude summed up by a local psychoanalyst: 'Dallas is very, very proud of Dallas. In an individual it is almost a narcissistic thing. Instead of worrying about the grief of others, he worries about the image of the city.' In the eyes of such people a long step towards rehabilitation was taken in the first month of the new administration. At the end of the 1963 college football season sportswriters had picked the University of Texas and the U.S. Naval Academy as the country's No. 1 and No. 2 teams. They met in the Cotton Bowl. The midshipmen were thoroughly trounced. Dallas was elated.

The mood of civic penitence evaporated quickly. Jesse Curry's policemen became resentful, not of their local leadership, but of the U.S. Supreme Court, whose insistence that the rights of prisoners be safeguarded had, they argued, hamstrung them in their interrogation

[1] In the February 1966 issue of *Outdoor Life* a mail-order firm advertised a scope-mounted cheap foreign rifle—'the Kennedy gun', as it had become known to riflemen. Next to it was an advertisement for a Kennedy memorial stamp. To see how far mail-order houses would go, an enterprising reporter in Paterson, New Jersey, sent away for one and signed his cheque 'L. H. Oswald'. He got the gun.

of Oswald. In the first shock of November 22 Superintendent W. T. White had vowed that he would dismiss the teacher who had told her pupils she wanted to spit in the President's face. Over the weekend he changed his mind. Two weeks later, however, he suspended another teacher for writing *Time* magazine that she has seen 'the seed of hate being planted by our newspapers and many of the leaders of Dallas' and believed this had paved the way for the assassination. The vice president of a Dallas oil company and a department store executive published sharp criticisms of the city's Radical Right. Both resigned under pressure. Of course, the majority of Dallas citizens deeply regretted it, and while public officials declined to contribute towards any Kennedy statue or marker (using public funds for such a purpose would be illegal, they explained), a committee of private citizens did plan to convert one of the rundown blocks near the courthouse into a memorial plaza. Somehow the work lagged. Eventually a monument was unveiled in the Trade Mart. There was nothing near the assassination scene, though, and the lack was most conspicuous the week before the release of the Warren Report, when the American Legion held its annual convention in Dallas. For six hours drum majorettes and uniformed formations marched past the Texas School Book Depository. No one stopped; there was nothing to indicate that anything out of the ordinary had happened there.

Then, in the spring of 1966, a year after the dedication of the Runnymede shrine, official Dallas re-examined its position and reversed itself; $20,000 was set aside from the park fund for a marker in the plaza. As originally worded, the inscription was ten paragraphs long. It began by noting that the square was dedicated to G. B. Dealey (no mention of the WPA) and went on to describe the first Dallas log cabin, built nearby in 1841; an act of the Texas legislature creating Dallas County in 1846; the erection of a toll bridge over the Trinty River in 1855; the incorporation of Dallas in 1856; early navigation of the river in 1868; the completion of a railroad from Dallas to the Gulf in 1972; and, in 1973, the building of the Dallas train terminal. 'With this background of constructive growth,' the inscription then declared, 'this site unfortunately became the scene of a tragedy which plunged the world into a state of shock.' Upon reading it *Times-Herald* editorial writers were plunged into a state of shock. Glossing over the assassination in this fashion, they noted acidly, would merely confirm outsiders who regarded the city as a defensive community preoccupied with its own navel. The Park Board then approved a simple text, omitting the recital of 'constructive growth'. At the same time, however, Dallas leaders were quietly discussing the possibility of razing the Book

Depository on the pretext that it was a traffic obstacle. The warehouse was a disquieting reminder. They looked at it as seldom as possible.

Overlooking Jack Ruby was clearly impossible. His trial disconcerted everyone, with the possible exceptions of the defendant, who was in a daze, and his chief counsel, a pyrotechnic lawyer with an insatiable lust for publicity. At times the proceedings became a circus. To the discomfiture of Judge Joe B. Brown it was revealed that he himself had sponsored Jack's admittance to the Dallas Chamber of Commerce in 1959. Brown declined to disqualify himself, explaining that he hadn't really known him. He further ruled that people who had watched the killing of Oswald on television weren't witnesses—the Texas Supreme Court upheld him—and an all-white, all-Protestant jury was seated. Once a recess was required because of a jail break elsewhere in the building. Twice spectators at the trial itself had to be disarmed. (One of them had been a stripper for Jack.) The judge decided to admit TV cameras to the courtroom for the verdict, and on March 14, 1964, Ruby was found guilty of murder. Since the jury had not recommended mercy he was sentenced to death. Ruby tried to kill himself three times. Thereafter he languished in the country courthouse, until, in October 1966, the Texas Court of Criminal Appeals reversed his conviction on the basis of judicial errors and ordered a new trial. The victory turned to ashes: in the first week of 1967 Ruby, stricken with incurable cancer, died at Parkland. The autopsy was performed by Dr Earl Rose.

To the continuing embarrassment of civic leaders, who wanted outsiders to pay some attention to Big D's urbanity, other grotesque sideshows kept cropping up. Klein's Sporting Goods revealed that 150 Mannlicher-Carcanos had been shipped to souvenir-conscious Dallasites. A local entrepreneur set up 'Historical Enterprises, Inc.' and marketed a novel desk set—a $3.75 bronze-coloured replica of the assassination site, with a slot for a ballpoint pen—and insensitive executives bought them. Vernon Oneal, the undertaker, was even more enterprising. After the President's funeral he invested in a duplicating machine, borrowed Judge Ward's death certificate, and mailed copies to fellow Texas morticians as souvenirs. On January 7, 1964, Oneal submitted his bill to the Kennedy family: 'Solid double-wall bronze casket and all services rendered at Dallas, Texas—$3,995.' A CPA representing Robert Kennedy requested a breakdown. On February 13 Oneal offered to deduct $500 on the ground that he had not provided certain items which were ordinarily thrown in, e.g., embalming and 'use of chapel'. The new total was $3,495. Actually, as he conceded to this writer, he was hoping for a return of the coffin. He made two trips to Washington in the hope of retrieving it. Word of this reached the right quarters, and to avoid an exhibition he was paid. The wholesale prices of coffins are a closely guarded trade secret, but at the request of the author a licensed funeral director and a cemetery manager made discreet inquiries at the Elgin Casket Company about its Britannia model. Both were quoted an identical figure: $1,150. Thus Oneal's fee represents a markup of $2,345.

The plight of Marie Tippit and Marina Oswald appealed to American generosity; mailbags of cheques and cash descended upon them. Mrs Tippit handled herself admirably. She thanked contributors for the $643,863 she had received, put half in trust for her children, and spent almost none on herself. In her living-room she kept a photograph of the Kennedy family inscribed by the President's widow: 'There is another bond we share. We must remind our children all the time what brave men their fathers were.' Marina, who could hardly do that, led a more colourful career. With $70,000 in donations she engaged a series of business agents. Her husband's Russian diary brought $20,000 and a picture of him holding the Mannlicher-Carcano carbine $5,000. Then she went after the gun itself, arguing that since Oswald was dead it could not be held as evidence. A Denver oil man who wanted it as a souvenir sent her a $10,000 down payment—about 49,900 per cent profit on Lee's original investment—and then sued Katzenbach for possession. Early in 1966 a federal court threw the case out. Late that autumn the Justice Department took title to C2766.

Marina had spent the money long ago. With affluence she had acquired mobility. At first she had told the press that the strongest force in her life was her love for the father of her children; she only wanted to live near his grave. This quickly changed. First she became a co-ed at the University of Michigan. Returning to Dallas, she bought an air-conditioned house, a wardrobe of Neiman-Marcus clothes, and membership in the Music Box, a private club. She became a chain-smoker and a drinker of straight vodka. In the Music Box she spun through a series of romances. Then, in 1965, in a Texas town called Fate, she became a June bride. The groom was a six-foot, twice-divorced drag racer. Eleven weeks later he was in jail. His bride had a string of complaints. In an affidavit she charged that 'He slapped me in the face and tried to get me to put the children outside so he could be alone with the gun he carried. I'm afraid he might try to do me bodily harm.' He replied, 'It's just time for her to have some more publicity.' A JP reunited them. 'Love triumphed,' the JP said. Marina said, 'I don't want these things to happen. I had too much of this with Lee.'

Neither Ruth Paine nor Marguerite Oswald saw Marina after November 1963. Marguerite grew increasingly critical of her former daughter-in-law. She read that the girl was dyeing her hair, using lipstick, and smoking, all of which, she felt, were bad examples for her dead son's children. Marguerite's chief grievances, however, lay elsewhere. She resented the Warren Report's treatment of Lee and the fact that she, unlike Marina, Mrs Tippit, and Mrs Kennedy—her information about the Kennedy wealth was astonishing—remained comparatively poor. Of the first she said, 'Publicwise we have not had the truth'; of the second, 'Moneywise I got took.' By failing to pay her for her testimony, she reasoned, the Commission had taken 'the bread and butter out of my mouth'. Actually, she sold letters Lee had written her to *Esquire* and refused to talk to magazine writers until she had been paid. With the money she bought a new two-tone Buick, an enormous reproduction of Whistler's *Mother* framed in brass, which she hung in her living-room, and a gold statuette of the Virgin Mary, which she wore around her neck. She kept her number in the Fort Worth telephone directory and was always ready to talk to journalists, though the phone rang less and less.

During the 1964 Presidential campaign the assassin's mother read a lot of right-wing literature, which doesn't mean much; the Goldwater forces had monopolized the state's paperback outlets, and shrill propaganda was everywhere—in news-stands, drugstores, hotels. The election results showed how ineffective it all was. In Texas as elsewhere the Republican candidate was thoroughly routed. The Senatorial race, however, was more complicated. In February the Connally–Yarborough feud had flared up again—even as national leader of the party Lyndon Johnson was unable to arrange a lasting truce—and the Governor quietly threw his weight behind the Senator's Republican opponent. Ironically, the assassination had severely damaged the prospects of Yarborough, the one avowed Kennedy man in the state's Democratic leadership. His handicap was that he hadn't been shot in Dealey Plaza. Before that Friday the Senator had been running ahead of Connally in Texas polls, but in the election the Governor ran away from all opposition.

The $350,000 which had been collected from ticket sales for the November 22 banquet in Austin was kept (though one man did ask for his $100 back on the ground that he had not been fed) and divided equally between the national and state parties. The Senator had trouble getting funds. On September 14 a preposterous situation arose: at seven o'clock that evening there were two testimonial dinners in Dallas, one at the Sheraton-Dallas for Yarborough and the other, for Connally, at the Trade Mart. Every Democrat was asked to choose sides. Byron Skelton threw up his hands and stayed home; later a Connally man replaced him as National Committeeman. Against all advice, Yarborough refused to ride on President Johnson's coat tails. Instead, his literature stressed his identification with President Kennedy, and on November 3 he squeaked through.

But not in Dallas. He lost the county by nearly 27,000 votes, the worst local drubbing he had ever taken in any election. Even Goldwater in defeat won more Dallas votes than the Senator. Earle Cabell unseated Bruce Alger, and Connally led the ticket, outrunning the opposition two to one. Here the influence of the Dallas *News* was evident; the Governor was the only candidate Dealey backed strongly. One might have expected that the ardour of the right-wing Texans would be dampened by Goldwater's eclipse, but they were undiscouraged. Locally their prestige had survived the assassination, they had a new Public Enemy No. 1 in Earl Warren (their literature now referred to the U.S. Supreme Court in lower case, viz., 'the warren court'), and whatever the image-makers of the Citizens Council said they saw no reason to revise their opinion of John Kennedy. Each season brought fresh testimony of the animosity they still bore towards the President who had been murdered on Elm Street. The week the Warren Report was published a book store on Commerce Street displayed *Legacy of an Assassination*, a 479-page tract which pictured Kennedy as a traitor who had led a sordid private life. The morning of the first anniversary of his death copies of *Thunderbolt*, the organ of the National States' Rights party, were hawked downtown with a front-page headline libelling the late President. The following May 29, which would have been his forty-eighth birthday, Texas radicals in the state legislature defeated a bill which would have renamed the state school for the mentally retarded in Kennedy's honour. The Governor's brother voted against it, and the *Texas Observer* quoted some of the reasons given by others who had voted in the majority: 'It's the politics of the man—the dead man'; 'Not well thought of'; 'Don't want to get hurt politically'; 'Just wouldn't be popular back home'; and 'I didn't like him'. That autumn, on the second anniversary of the assassination, a Lou Harris survey showed that the percentage of people who mourned President Kennedy in Dallas was dramatically below the national average. The following autumn William M. Henry reported in the Los Angeles *Times* that the USIA's deeply moving film tribute to JFK, *Years of Lightning, Day of Dreams*— which was drawing enormous audiences elsewhere in the country—'has been a complete flop in Dallas'.

During the winter of 1963–64 several people who had played

peripheral roles in the events of the previous November died unexpectedly or fell victims to strange violence. Warren Reynolds, a used-car lot employee who had witnessed Lee Oswald's flight after the shooting of Tippit, was himself shot in the same Dallas lot on the evening of January 23. The rifleman was seen but never found; one man was picked up but released on the testimony of a woman who, after her subsequent arrest on a charge of disorderly conduct, hanged herself in a Dallas cell. The general who had welcomed Kennedy to San Antonio on behalf of the Air Force, the waiter who had served him his last breakfast in Fort Worth, and the advertising director of the Dallas *News* all dropped dead. The advertising director, forty-five years old, had been in excellent health. So had the twenty-seven-year-old captain who had been Lieutenant Sam Bird's superior officer throughout the capital's ceremonial farewells to the President. The previous September he had passed his regular Army physical; his cardiogram had been normal. Ten days after the burial in Arlington he took a day off and toppled over at his dinner table, the victim of a heart attack. Two years later the odd toll took another jump: Earlene Roberts, Oswald's landlady, died of a stroke and Bill Whaley, his taxi driver, was killed in a traffic accident.

In the wake of the funeral every principal figure except Marguerite Oswald was troubled by physical discomfort of some sort. The complaints ranged from Lady Bird's persistent chills to Dave Powers' headaches—violent pains which were confined to the back of his skull, where he had seen the last bullet strike the President. For six months Ken O'Donnell suffered from violent nausea. Several people required extensive medical help. The doctor's bills of Howard Brennan, who had watched Oswald fire that final shot, reached $2,700, and Roy Truly, Oswald's boss, was ill nearly a year. Nearly everyone suffered from insomnia. Forrest Sorrels would start up from a bad dream. It was always the same one, and it always took him a while to realize it hadn't been a dream at all. Jesse Curry awoke each night between 2 and 3 a.m. and reached for his Bible; troubled also by hypertension, rising dissatisfaction among his subordinates, and the city council's decision to have outside experts investigate the police department, he resigned in February 1966 for 'medical reasons'.

In the innermost circles of official Washington emotional stress was heightened by the prolonged extension, from week to week, of the air of unreality which had begun on the afternoon of November 22. Each morning's newspapers brought news of some fresh Johnsonian triumph. As the Kennedy legend flourished, the profile of the new President emerged and took shape. It was, Reston wrote, 'almost a Texas "tall story"—Johnson conquering George Meany and Henry Ford, Martin Luther King and Harry Byrd, the savers and the spenders, Wall Street and Main Street'. Most of Washington wanted to be conquered; that is the only explanation for the near unanimity with which the press corps agreed that Johnson's joint session speech differed significantly from the addresses Kennedy had written with Sorensen. After the long weekend of grief the capital desperately wanted continuity to be an unqualified success, and so men who ought to have been known better persuaded themselves that the government could move ahead with no significant changes of personnel—that the galaxy of talent which Kennedy had brought to the city could remain and serve effectively under Johnson.

The day after his predecessor's burial in Arlington Johnson summoned Arthur Schlesinger to the oval office. 'I just want to say that I need you far more than John Kennedy ever needed you,' he began. 'He had the knowledge, the skills, the understanding himself. I need you to provide those things for me.... You have a knowledge of the programme, the measures, the purposes, of the history of the country and of progressive policies, you know writers and all sorts of people.... I have your letter of resignation, and that is fine as a gesture, but I reject it as a fact.' Arthur interrupted to remark that he felt every President ought to have his own people around him. Johnson replied that he considered Arthur one of his people. 'The men who have been working with me are good men,' he said, 'but they aren't in a class with you men here in the White House. I shall blend three or four of them into the staff, but I am counting on all the present members of the staff to stay.' He wanted them to remain for at least a year; by then, he said, he was confident that he would have convinced them he was worthy of their loyalty.

Back in the East Wing Schlesinger wrote this down and added: 'He said all this with simplicity, dignity, and apparent conviction. I am a little perplexed as to what to do. I am sure that I must leave, but I can see the problem of disengagement is going to be considerable.' His intuition was correct: no marriage between Johnson and Kennedy's men could have lasted long. He had to become his own President. Yet the new President's instincts were right, too. Despite the glowing praise from a sympathetic press, the inescapable fact was that he could not really become a national leader until he had been elected to the office. Meanwhile he must shore up Kennedy's selection of him three years earlier as Vice Presidential nominee by creating the impression that the entire Kennedy team had believed him to be the second-best man in the country.

In his second week in office the President summoned the Attorney

General to the West Wing. He mentioned misunderstandings over his presence in this office Saturday morning and the departure of the Presidential aircraft from Dallas Friday. Of the first he repeated that Rusk and McNamara had urged him to move in swiftly, which was true; of the second he insisted that 'We took off as soon as Jackie got there,' which was not. 'People around you are saying things about me,' he went on. 'I won't let people around me say anything about your people, and don't let any of your people say anything about me.' Robert Kennedy didn't want to argue with the President, and he couldn't bargain with him either. It was an impasse. The meeting lasted about five minutes, and apart from formal occasions and an exchange of telegrams at Christmas it was virtually the only contact between the two men that winter.

Early in December Pierre Salinger announced that he, Ted Sorensen, Ken O'Donnell, and Larry O'Brien would remain as long as they were needed. It was an empty gesture. No one working in the West Wing expected that the line could be held for long, nor was it. On January 16 Sorensen became the first man out. Jerry Wiesner returned to academic life two days later, Schlesinger made his resignation stick January 29, and Ted Reardon quit February 5. Next month Salinger himself left Johnson to seek a seat in the Senate. Andy Hatcher followed him to California. Godfrey McHugh resigned from the Air Force, Taz Shepard went to sea, Ralph Dungan was appointed Ambassador to Chile. In the East Wing the drawls of Liz Carpenter and Bess Abell replaced the finishing-school accents of Nancy Tuckerman and Pam Turnure, who ran Mrs Kennedy's temporary office on the first floor of the Executive Office Building. Evelyn Lincoln was given another EOB suite to catalogue Kennedy's Presidential papers; Mary Gallagher was next door. During Christmas week the White House school had been moved behind the black wrought-iron gate of the British Embassy on Massachusetts Avenue. Clint Hill, Muggsy O'Leary, and Provi Parades joined the President's widow in the Harriman house.

Lyndon Johnson held on to most of the big names through the campaign: Shriver, Bundy, and leaders of the mafia. Shriver and the Irishmen were priceless assets in preserving the illusion of harmony. Kennedy's brother-in-law reigned over his kingdom, of course; he wasn't a member of the White House staff. O'Donnell and O'Brien were, though, and Ken's attitude during the flight back from Love Field had scarcely encouraged hope that he might stick it out more than a few days. His decision to stay surprised nearly everyone, including, in private, Johnson himself. Like the President, Robert Kennedy was moving towards independence. He resigned from the Cabinet, went into New York, and, in November 1964, he ran on the ticket with Lyndon Johnson. On June 19 Ted had been gravely injured in a plane crash. Joan campaigned for him and was charming, which was all that was necessary; St Patrick couldn't have defeated a Kennedy in Massachusetts that year. The Republicans offered only token opposition, and Ted was swept back into office by over 909,000 votes. Salinger lost, but on Capitol Hill the two brothers inevitably came to be regarded as the nucleus of a government-in-exile.

The President, running against the most inept Republican of all, won the greatest victory of all: the highest percentage (61.3 per cent) of the popular vote in American history. The Radical Right's dreams of national power were annihilated on the night of November 3. Johnson interpreted the results as a personal mandate; running the government, in the words of one of his aides, had become 'a new ball game'. The first innings was to be the inauguration. The inaugural chairman was the Washington representative for the Dallas Chamber of Commerce. The celebrations of January 20, 1964, were advertised in advance as 'a Texas-style gala'. Texas bands led the parade down Pennsylvania Avenue, the slogan was 'Y'all come and see us', and so many did show up at the inaugural balls that there was little room for anyone except the jubilant President, who looked as though he could have danced all night and nearly did.

The change in Washington's mood was startling. The Ivy League army which had occupied the city four years earlier was rapidly disintegrating. One by one its fields marshals and enlisted men deserted or were picked off. Ken O'Donnell, Douglas Dillon, Ted Clifton, Mike Feldman, Dick Goodwin, Jack McNally, Colonel McNally, Dave Powers, Pat Moynihan, Cecil Stoughton—once they had all been familiar figures in the west lobby, and now they belonged to history. Larry O'Brien was appointed Postmaster General. O'Donnell ran for public office in Massachusetts and was defeated. Mac Bundy became president of the Ford Foundation. He was the last of Kennedy's special assistants to go. Only one Cabinet member who had been close to Kennedy was left. As Vietnam loomed larger and redder, the Secretary of Defence became Washington's No. 2 man, or, in Texasese, *Número Dos*. Both *Uno* and *Dos* surged with vitality. Nevertheless, they presided over a city which couldn't seem to stop looking over its shoulder. For two centuries the capital had been blasé towards changes in administrations, but this one was different. The shot from the sixth floor of Roy Truly's warehouse had turned back the clock. The new men had first come to Washington in the heyday of the New Deal. Towards the end of a farewell dinner for two New Frontiersmen at Hickory Hill, a guest said thoughtfully, 'You know, we're too young to be holding reunions.'

Jacqueline Kennedy attended no reunions in Washington. The autumn after the assassination she took up temporary residence in New York's Carlyle Hotel and then bought a $200,000 apartment at 1050 Fifth Avenue, near others owned by her sister and her husband's relatives. Her life came to revolve around Manhattan, Hyannis Port, Palm Beach, and her mother's summer home in Newport—a world of elegance and a culture which, in the eyes of most of her countrymen, was more European than American. Perhaps the move was inevitable. She had been a child of the East. Had she not met the young Massachusetts Senator with his eyes on the stars, the Brahmin establishment would probably have been the background of her middle years. It was familiar to her, sparkled with wit, was inhabited by celebrated members of the Democratic patriciate, and it was an environment in which she was accepted as a human being, not a museum piece.

Yet it was not what she had had in mind when she buried her husband in Arlington. The early years of her marriage had been spent in Georgetown and there, she then thought, she would raise Caroline and John. Their future was her new focus. She had no illusion: growing up without a father could not be the same for them. But her husband's brothers and friends would provide a vigorous masculine influence, and the capital, with all its historical associations, appeared to be the natural setting in which to raise the President's daughter and son.

Despite their two moves in Washington—first to the Harriman home and then, five weeks later, to a fawn-coloured, three-storey brick house she bought diagonally across N Street, at No. 3017—the rituals of their young lives were scrupulously observed. The joint birthday party was held the day before they left the White House. The men guests were Dave Powers, Godfrey McHugh, and Taz Shepard; Godfrey brought John a model of Air Force One, and from Nancy Tuckerman Taz acquired a huge soft bear for Caroline. Caroline had returned to first grade the morning after the state funeral. Miss Grimes kept the class occupied with rehearsals for a simple nativity play; they learned Christmas carols and recited Biblical verses. The season, so sad in other ways, was useful here. Caught up in its excitement, the small girl laboriously printed an envelope 'To Santa from Caroline' and dictated to her mother a plea for a Nancy Nurse set and a puppy.

She had, Maude Shaw thought, inherited Jacqueline Kennedy's flair for the fitting touch. Miss Shaw escorted her out for the selection of the presents she herself would give. Caroline went straight to a display of Van Gogh prints and studied them at length, picking an appropriate gift for each person—a woman and child for her mother, sailboats for her brother, and, for her nurse, a painting of a room much like the one that had been Miss Shaw's in the executive mansion. The girl's air of reserve had become core apparent. She had something of that remote look which was so pronounced in Robert Kennedy during those months. John was easier to reach. All he needed was Dave Powers. Each morning Dave left the White House and rode to 3017 N Street for two hours of romping. John would be Davy Crockett, his playmate a bear. During the most solemn conference on the first floor one could hear the hapless bear frantically fleeing among the zoo of stuffed toys, begging in his Boston accent, 'Have a haaht, Davy, a *haaht*!'

Mrs Kennedy drove Caroline to the hill in Arlington first. 'We're going to visit Daddy's grave,' she told her, 'and we won't take John.' Because of the vast crowds the visit had to be at night, after the gates were closed. As Clint Hill arrived in the back of the station wagon the girl asked, 'Couldn't we take the dogs? Because Daddy loved them so much.' Taking all five would be impractical, but her mother and Clint loaded three in the back of a station wagon: Clipper and Wolf and little Shannon, their Irish cocker spaniel. On Sheridan Drive Mrs Kennedy paused to leash the two big dogs while Shannon scampered ahead. It was cold and wet; they trudged up through slush. Suddenly they heard a menacing growl ahead, and a furious yelping. Clipper and Wolf strained on their rein. There was some sort of row in front of the picket fence.

It was almost a dogfight—given a few more seconds, it would have been one. A soldier had been posted by the gate with a massive police dog. Shannon was barking away, and the soldier was hard put to keep them apart. Clint took the leash from Mrs Kennedy while she scooped up the Irish cocker and put him back into the car. Caroline said, 'Well, Daddy always loved Shannon the best because he was so brave.' It was true. Her father had been allergic to dogs; they made him sneeze. But the cocker had arrived from Ireland at the right time. Patrick had just died, and the sight of the scrappy little puppy challenging all the mastiffs and boxers in Hyannis Port had diverted the President. Shannon would fight in the fields, he would fight on the beaches, he would never surrender; even when driven into the ocean he would yip defiance from the waves, and the President would cheer him on. So the near clash in the cemetery wasn't as upsetting as a stranger might have thought. The soldier, being a stranger, assumed it was a catastrophe. Here was the President's daughter visiting the grave for the first time, and his dog had spoiled it. He withdrew to one side, crying.

Mrs Kennedy had brought another bunch of lilies of the valley; Caroline had a mixed nosegay plucked from various vases at home. Mother and daughter knelt in the cold mud. They prayed, they crossed themselves, they laid their flowers beneath the eternal flame. Then they saw the soldier. If young John's salute outside St Matthew's had left an indelible picture on the memories of millions, his sister's compassion here would never be forgotten by one man. It was really a little thing. Seeing him weeping and understanding why, she walked over and patted his dog. Looking up she asked, 'What's his name?' He said, 'I call him Baron, Caroline.' 'Baron,' she repeated, stroking the smooth fur. Back in the station wagon she sat close to her mother. All the way home they held hands, gripping tight and saying nothing until they were nearly there. Then Caroline remembered that at the birthday party she had been given a cardboard dollhouse with punch-out figures. One was of a big dog—a police dog, she recalled excitedly. She said, 'Oh, Mummy, I'm going to name him Baron, after the dog who's watching daddy.'

In her six-year-old way she had found a simple peace that adults struggled towards in vain. Men and women often suffered when with the President's children, but the suffering lay within themselves. The son and the daughter had accepted their loss with the enviable resignation of small boys and girls. They never meant to cause pain in grownups. Nevertheless certain moments could be shattering. 'Davy Crockett had a rifle,' Dave Powers casually told John. 'A bad man shot my daddy in the head with a rifle,' John replied, and Dave didn't sleep that night. In Montrose Park a newspaper photographer recognized the boy, stepped around Agent Wells, and raised his camera. Hearing the click, John glanced up from a water fountain. 'What are you doing?' he asked. 'I'm taking your picture, John,' the man said. The boy stared. 'What are you taking my picture for? My daddy's dead,' he said, and Wells saw the man's shoulders heave as he ran off. On O Street, young Janet Auchincloss offered to split a wishbone with Caroline. 'Can I have any wish I want?' asked Caroline. '*Any one,*' said Janet, not seeing the trap. The little girl said, 'I want to see my daddy.'

That could have happened anywhere. What made Washington different for them and, in the end, impossible for their mother was the character of the Kennedy legend. During the funeral none of the people directly involved in it had thought much about the national audience. They had been too weary and too busy. The fact that a million people had been standing vigil on the kerbs had been startling enough once it had registered. It was weeks before they realized that for every spectator in the District that Monday a hundred others had been watching in the fifty states, and it was months before the implications of this sunk in. The pilgrims to Arlington were appreciated. The tourists were another matter. It happened to be a big tourist year; there was a world's fair in New York. Families from other parts of the country detoured south to include the N Street house on their itineraries. In dismaying numbers they stood across the street and gawked. They accosted friends of the widow who came calling. They took snapshots of one another on her steps, and rode by in buses which now included N Street in the capital's Points of Interest. The mansion became unlivable. Mrs Kennedy apologized to her neighbours and fled across the river with the children to Ethel's back yard.

She had asked Fort Myer for Black Jack's boots and saddle. Indeed, any sign that the President's sacrifice would not be forgotten was cherished. That was why she had held herself together for three days after Dallas. She had not counted on the fact that she herself, by her performance then, had become unforgettable. At the age of thirty-four she was a national institution. Archibald MacLeish epitomized her new position. Asked to write a dedication for the new cultural centre he forwarded, instead, a paean to 'Jacqueline Kennedy, wife of the thirty-fifth President of the United States, who shared the ardour of his life and the moment of his death and made the darkest days the American people have known in a hundred years the deepest revelation of their inward strength.' Everyone wanted to honour her. She was proposed as ambassador to France, designated a life member of the National Geographic Society, and was swamped with flags; John McCormack alone presented six which had flown over the capital that weekend. At Runnymede the common people of Britain referred to their guest as 'her American majesty'. The Senate passed a resolution of admiration and sent it, framed. She became the first widow of a President to receive Secret Service protection and a secretarial staff—which she needed, because bales of letters addressed to her were arriving in Washington. Nancy Tuckerman and Pam Turnure struggled to see that each was acknowledged. The file marked 'Especially Touching' grew to encyclopedic thickness, and only a few were beyond the pale. One was from Dallas. A committee of businessmen, concerned about their sagging out-of-state trade, wanted her to sign a testimonial to Dallas hospitality. She passed it along to Robert Kennedy, who managed to forget what he did with it.

Each step she took, it seemed, was being preserved for history. On St Patrick's day she left shamrocks on her husband's grave. The cemetery planted them there and was immediately deluged with requests for transplants. On what would have been her husband's forty-seventh birthday she took the children to St Matthew's. It was November 25 all over again: the Choir sang the 'Navy Hymn', and outside a horde of tourists made Rhode Island Avenue impassable. She couldn't even take her daughter into a drugstore, because every issue of every movie magazine carried her photograph outside. The captions were inexcusable: 'THE MAN IN JACKIE'S LIFE' (the story inside identified him as John F. Kennedy), 'THE MAN JACKIE CHOSE' (he was, it developed, the author of this book), 'IS JACKIE SEEING TOO MUCH OF BOBBY?', 'HOW LADY BIRD HURT JACKIE AND DIDN'T MEAN IT', 'THE SECRET IN JACKIE'S LIFE'—so it went, month after month. Salinger begged the pulps to stop, but they kept rolling, knowing she would never sue because that would merely bring more detested publicity. Even slick periodicals behaved questionably. Anything about her was news. A Hyannis Port stringer reported that she was considering attending the Democratic National Convention to stampede the delegates into nominating Robert Kennedy for Vice President. It was absurd. She had been reluctant enough to attend conventions when her husband was alive. All the same, it went out on the wire—and was taken seriously in the White House.

On N Street Mrs Kennedy reached the depths of grief. By spring she could no longer take refuge in work; Nancy and Pam were handling that efficiently. She was tormented by *ifs*: if only she had insisted on a bubbletop that morning, if she had just turned to her right sooner, if the Secret Service had put two men on the back of the car ... *if, if, if.* Brooding was pointless now. Nevertheless she couldn't cut it off. She would nap afternoons and lie awake throughout the night, turning things over and over in her mind. She considered Oswald, and hoped he had been part of a conspiracy, for then there would be an air of inevitability about the tragedy; then she could persuade herself that if the plotters had missed on Elm Street they would have eventually succeeded elsewhere. What was so terrible was the thought that it had been an accident, a freak, that an inch or two here, a moment or two there would have reversed history. 'I should have known that it was asking too much to dream that I might have grown old with him and see our children grow up together ... so now he is a legend when he would have preferred to be a man,' she wrote later in the year. 'I must believe that he does not share our suffering now. I think for him—at least he will never know whatever sadness might have lain ahead. He knew such a share of it in his life that it always made you so happy whenever you saw him enjoying himself. But now he will never know more—not age, nor stagnation, nor despair, nor crippling illness, nor loss of any more people he loved. His high noon kept all the freshness of the morning—and he died then, never knowing disillusionment.'

Her own disillusion with the life she had tried to piece together on N Street was complete. She would receive her husband's political friends and wish his brothers every success, but she took no interest in the Presidential campaign that should have been John Kennedy's. Although she was too recent a resident of Manhattan to vote there, she was still registered in Boston, and she could have flown there on November 3 or mailed an absentee ballot. She did neither, nor did she send President Johnson a congratulatory telegram. She had said good-bye to all that. Her adventure in national politics had begun with young Senator Kennedy. Now it was for ever finished; the burden had fallen on the two Senators Kennedy. Now it was for ever finished; the public would read of her at the Cape, on the Adriatic, in Rome, or—her preference—not at all. Only in obscurity could she heal. She, too, had known high noon. She wanted to forget that sun.

Unknown to her, the clothes Mrs Kennedy wore into the bright midday glare of Dallas lie in an attic not far from 3017 N Street. In Bethesda that night those closest to her had vowed that from the moment she shed them she should never see them again. She hasn't. Yet they are still there, in one of two long brown paper cartons thrust between roof rafters. The first is marked 'September 12, 1953', the date of her marriage; it contains her wedding gown. The block-printed label on the other is 'Worn by Jackie, November 22, 1963'. Inside, neatly arranged, are the pink wool suit, the black shift, the low-heeled shoes, and, wrapped in a white towel, the stockings. Were the box to be opened by an intruder from some land so remote that the name, the date, and photographs of the ensemble had not been published and republished until they had been graven upon the memory, he might conclude that these were merely stylish garments which had passed out of fashion and which, because they were associated with some pleasant occasion, had not been discarded.

If the trespasser looked closer, however, he would be momentarily baffled. The memento of a happy time would be cleaned before storing. Obviously this costume has not been. There are ugly splotches along the front and hem of the skirt. The handbag's leather and the inside of each shoe are caked dark red. And the stockings are quite odd. Once the same substance streaked them in mad scribbly patterns, but time and the sheerness of the fabric have altered it. The rusty clots have flaked off; they lie in tiny brittle grains on the nap of the towel. Examining them closely, the intruder would see his error. This clothing, he would perceive, had not been kept out of sentiment. He would realize that it had been worn by a slender young woman who had met with some dreadful accident. He might ponder whether she had survived. He might even wonder who had been to blame.

APPENDIXES

APPENDIX I

Words of President Kennedy which were to have been read at his graveside by Senator Edward M. Kennedy

'Accepting the nomination for President he said:

"The New Frontier of which I speak is not a set of promises—it is a set of challenges. It sums up not what I intend to offer the American people, but what I intend to ask of them."

'To the United Nations he said:

"However close we sometimes seem to that dark and final abyss, let no man of peace and freedom despair. For he does not stand alone. If we all can persevere, if we can in every land and office look beyond our own shores and ambitions, then surely the age will dawn in which the strong are just and the weak secure and the peace preserved. . . .

"Never have the nations of the world had so much to lose or so much to gain. Together we shall save our planet or together we shall perish in its flames. Save it we can, and save it we must, and then shall we earn the eternal thanks of mankind and, as peacemakers, the eternal blessing of God."

'To the Congress he said:

"Our Nation is commissioned by history to be either an observer of freedom's failure or the cause of its success. Our overriding obligation in the months ahead is to fulfil the world's hopes by fulfilling our own faith.

"It is the fate of this generation to live with a struggle we did not start, in a world we did not make. But the pressures of life are not always distributed by choice. And while no nation has ever faced such a challenge, no nation has ever been so ready to seize the burden and the glory of freedom." '

APPENDIX II

Words of President Kennedy which were to have been read at his graveside by Attorney General Robert F. Kennedy

'To Americans of another colour he said:

"This nation ... was founded on the principle that all men are created equal, and that the rights of every man are diminished when the rights of one man are threatened.... It ought to be possible for every American to enjoy the privileges of being an American without regard to his race or colour ... to have the right to be treated as he would wish to be treated, as one would wish his children to be treated.... This nation, for all its hopes and all its boasts, will not be fully free until all its citizens are free."

'To those who have been our adversaries he said, at American University:

"... If we cannot end now our differences, at least we can help make the world safe for diversity. For, in the final analysis, our most basic common link is that we all inhabit this planet. We all breathe the same air. We all cherish our children's future. And we are all mortal.

"This generation of Americans has already had enough—more than enough—of war and hate and oppression.... We shall do our part to build a world of peace where the weak are safe and the strong are just. We are not helpless before that task or hopeless of its success. Confident and unafraid, we labour on—not toward a strategy of annihilation but toward a strategy of peace."

'To the American people he said, upon conclusion of the Test Ban Treaty:

"Let us, if we can, step back from the shadows of war and seek out the way of peace. And if that journey is one thousand miles, or even more, let history record that we, in this land, took the first step."

'And finally, to all the world, his message on the recent Cuban crisis contained this simple prophetic sentence:

"The cost of freedom is always high—but Americans have always paid it ..." '

APPENDIX III

Jacqueline Kennedy to Nikita Khrushchev, December 1, 1963

THE WHITE HOUSE
WASHINGTON*

December 1, 1963

DEAR MR. CHAIRMAN PRESIDENT

I would like to thank you for sending Mr Mikoyan as your representative to my husband's funeral.

He looked so upset when he came through the line, and I was very moved.

I tried to give him a message for you that day—but as it was such a terrible day for me, I do not know if my words came out as I meant them to.

So now, in one of the last nights I will spend in the White House, in one of the last letters I will write on this paper at the White House, I would like to write you my message.

I send it only because I know how much my husband cared about peace, and how the relation between you and him was central to this care in his mind. He used to quote your words in some of his speeches —'In the next war the survivors will envy the dead.'

You and he were adversaries, but you were allied in a determination that the world should not be blown up. You respected each other and could deal with each other. I know that President Johnson will make every effort to establish the same relationship with you.

The danger which troubled my husband was that war might be started not so much by the big men as by the little ones.

While big men know the needs for self-control and restraint—little men are sometimes moved more by fear and pride. If only in the future the big men can continue to make the little ones sit down and talk, before they start to fight.——

I know that President Johnson will continue the policy in which my husband so deeply believed—a policy of control and restraint—and he will need your help.

* This handwritten letter was forwarded to Nikita Khrushchev by McGeorge Bundy after clearance at the State Department by U. Alexis Johnson. No reply was received through channels.

I send this letter because I know so deeply of the importance of the relationship which existed between you and my husband, and also because of your kindness, and that of Mrs Khrushchev in Vienna.

I read that she had tears in her eyes when she left the American Embassy in Moscow, after signing the book of mourning. Please thank her for that.

Sincerely
JACQUELINE KENNEDY

SOURCES

The sheer volume of material available to writers of contemporary history makes the preparation of a formal bibliography an exasperating task. This is a phenomenon of the communications revolution. All the old sources of information still exist: letters, diaries, memorandums, State Department cables, official schedules; and, among secondary sources, books and periodical articles. In addition, however, one is confronted with heaps of round pegs which won't fit the traditional square holes—video tapes, audio tapes, aerial photographs of ceremonies, teletype messages, microfilms, Xeroxed copies of untranscribed shorthand—there really is no end to the variety of forms data may assume. Where, for example, does one put notes gleaned from the author's own observations? Once the answer would have been that they were journalism, not history. In contemporary history, however, the two merge.

Behind this book are two chief sources of fact: the notes of participants, written or taped at the time of these events or soon thereafter, and the author's own interviews. A third vein, which I explored carefully but seldom mined, was the President's Commission on the Assassination of President Kennedy's twenty-six volume conglomeration of testimony, depositions, and exhibits. The quotation from Lee Oswald's diary which appears on page 52 of this book is from Commission Exhibit 24 (Volume XVI, pages 94–105). The Ruth Paine and Marina Oswald correspondence quoted on pages 123–4 may be found in Commission Exhibits 404–425 (Volume XVII, pages 81–153). The passages from Robert Oswald's diary on page 604 are in Commission Exhibit 323 (Volume XVI, pages 889–915). Other episodes or comments whose sources lie in the Commission's material include Marina's remark on page 324 that her mother-in-law had a 'mania' for 'money, money, money' (Volume I, page 79); August Eberhardt's account on page 376 of visiting the Carousel and Vegas clubs with Mrs Eberhardt (Volume III, page 183); Eberhardt's recollection, also on page 388, of Jack Ruby's appearance in the Dallas jail on the evening of November 22, 1963 (Volume XIII, pages 187–188); Karin Carlin's memory (page 579) of her phone conversation with Ruby before he shot Oswald (Volume XIII, pages 211–212); Marina's account (page 508) of burning one of the photographs showing Lee holding the assassination weapon (Volume I, page 79); and Marguerite's description of flushing the ashes of this picture down a toilet (Volume I, page 152).

My interviewing sessions were held as soon as possible, for memory does fade. There is, for example, a distinct difference in the quality of statements taken in the spring of 1964 and those of a year later. On the other hand, perspective does have its uses. The author's interview with Mrs Lyndon Johnson on June 15, 1964, is superior in many ways to the recollections which she set down immediately after her return from Dallas. The plausibility of witnesses has been weighed at each stage. Fortunately, the mass of circumstantial evidence makes corroboration or disproof possible on most points.

Of course, no one can ever root out the truth, the whole truth, and nothing but the truth. That is a game lawyers play. There is something touching about their naïve assumption that one gets the full story by putting a man under oath. In practice you get very little of it. Anxious not to perjure himself, the witness volunteers as little as possible. The President's Commission on the Assassination was dominated by attorneys. The record shows it. Their depositions of minor witnesses were remarkably brief. The author, with his tape recorder or shorthand notebook, gets a great deal more chaff; but in the long run he harvests more wheat, too.

I. AUTHOR'S INTERVIEWS

Name	*Position at 12 Noon, Nov. 22, 1963*	*Date of Interview*
Bess Abell	Personal secretary to Mrs Johnson	10.6.64
Nicole Alphand	Wife of French Ambassador to USA	17.4.64
H. H. 'Andy' Anderson	Managing Director, Hotel Adolphus, Dallas	24.9.64
Dave Andres	Dallas executive	26.9.64
Marvin Arrowsmith	Associated Press editor, Washington	11.8.64
Hugh Auchincloss	Stepfather of Mrs Kennedy	21.5.64
Mrs Janet Auchincloss	Mother of Mrs Kennedy	21.5.64
Sergeant Joseph Ayres	Air Force One Steward	9.6.64
John Bailey	Chairman, Democratic National Committee	7.6.65
Russell Baker	Correspondent, *New York Times*	15.4.64
Letitia Baldridge	Former social secretary, the White House	25.5.64
George Ball	Under Secretary of State	10.4.64
Charles Bartlett	Washington correspondent	3.5.64
Martha Bartlett	Friend of the Kennedy family	3.5.64
Robert Baskin	Washington Bureau Chief, Dallas *Morning News*	15.5.64
Deputy Chief Charles Batchelor	Dallas police officer (Assistant Chief)	23.9.64
Gerald A. Behn	Head of White House Secret Service Detail	18.12.64
Carmine Bellino, CPA	Washington attorney to the Kennedy family	5.6.64
1st Lt. Samuel R. Bird	Officer, Company E, the Old Guard, 3rd Infantry	30.4.64
Capt. Walter R. Bishop	Artillery officer, 3rd Infantry	30.4.64
Gerald S. Blaine	Secret Service agent	12.5.65
Hale Boggs	U.S. Congressman from Louisiana	14.5.64

Name	*Position at 12 Noon, Nov. 22, 1963*	*Date of Interview*
Benjamin Bradlee	Washington Bureau Chief, *Newsweek* Magazine	17.4.64
Toni Bradlee	Friend of the Kennedy family	1.6.64
Henry Brandon	Washington correspondent, London *Sunday Times*	12.4.65
Howard L. Brennan	Pipefitter	23.9.64
David Brinkley	NBC Television correspondent	28.5.64
Sir Denis W. Brogan	British scholar	31.12.64
Jack S. Brooks	U.S. Congressman from Texas	17.6.64
Mrs Charlotte Brooks	Congressman's wife	17.6.64
Jerry Bruno	Advance man, Democratic National Committee	1.12.64 4.12.64
Jack Bryant	Rice Hotel catering manager	18.9.64
Art Buchwald	Washington columnist	5.10.64
J. R. Bullion	Dallas attorney	19.9.64
McGeorge Bundy	Special Assistant to the President	9.4.64 2.6.64
George G. Burkley, M.D.	Rear Admiral, USN; personal physician to the President	10.4.64 14.4.64 23.4.64 3.3.65 11.7.66
Earle Cabell	Mayor of Dallas	1.6.65
Father Thomas Cain	Superior of the Dominican Fathers, Roman Catholic University of Dallas	21.9.64
Christine Camp	Secretary to Pierre Salinger	20.8.64
Capt. R. O. Canada, Jr., USN	Director, Bethesda Naval Hospital	14.4.64
Pfc Arthur A. Carlson	Leader of riderless horses, Fort Myer	30.4.64
Mrs Elizabeth Carpenter	Executive Assistant to the Vice President	10.6.64 28.5.65
Frank Carpenter	United Nations press officer	21.8.64
Lt. Col. Bernard G. Carroll	U.S. Army Post Engineer, Fort Myer	11.8.64
Cliff Carter	Political adviser to the Vice President	23.7.64
Douglass Cater	Washington Editor, *The Reporter*	29.5.64
George Christian	Aide to the Governor of Texas	15.9.64
Sergeant Keith Clark	Bugler, U.S. Army Band	20.5.64
Maj. Gen. Chester V. Clifton	Military Aide to the President	21.4.64 21.8.64 22.1.65 28.5.65
John B. Connally, Jr.	Governor of Texas	16.9.64
Mrs John B. Connally, Jr.	Wife of the Governor of Texas	30.9.64
Maj. Michael Cook, USAF	Assistant Air Force Aide to the President	8.6.64 21.6.64
Paul Cretian	Aide to the Director, CIA	8.10.64
Jesse E. Curry	Chief of Dallas Police Department	25.9.64
Richard Cardinal Cushing	Archbishop of Boston	13.7.64
Marilyn Dailey	Dallas Junior High School student	3.8.65
Mrs Rita Dallas	Nurse to Joseph P. Kennedy	20.7.64
E. M. 'Ted' Dealey	Publisher of Dallas *Morning News*	25.9.64
Joe Dealey	Editor of Dallas *Morning News*	25.9.64
C. DeLoach	Assistant to the Director, FBI	8.10.64
C. Douglas Dillon	Secretary to the Treasury	14.8.64

Name	*Position at 12 Noon, Nov. 22, 1963*	*Date of Interview*
William O. Douglas	Associate Justice, U.S. Supreme Court	2.4.64
Joan Douglas	Wife of Justice Douglas	3.4.64
Otto Druhe	Chief chef, Hotel Texas	19.9.64
Sergent Robert Drugger, Jr.	Patrol officer, Dallas Police Force	22.9.64
Angier Biddle Duke	Chief of Protocol, State Department	8.4.64
		3.6.64
Robin Duke	Wife of Angier Duke; friend of Mrs Kennedy's	11.6.64
Ralph Dungan	Special Assistant to the President	15.4.64
Dwight D. Eisenhower	34th President of the United States	27.8.64
Sgt. 1st Class Allen J. Eldredge	Wreath bearer, 3rd Infantry	30.4.64
Dr Joseph T. English	Chief Psychiatrist, Medical Programme, Peace Corps	18.8.64
Paul B. Fay, Jr.	Acting Secretary of the Navy	5.5.64
Marie Fehmer	Secretary of the Vice President	11.6.64
Charles E. Fincklin	Maître d'Hôtel, the White House	14.8.64
Ronald B. Fischer	Clerk, Auditor's Office, Dallas County Building	23.9.64
Bob Foster	Secret Service agent	18.11.64
Henry H. 'Joe' Fowler	Acting Secretary of the Treasury	26.6.64
Wesley Frazier	Fellow worker of Lee Oswald	21.9.64
J. W. 'Will' Fritz	Chief of Dallas Homicide Squad	25.9.64
J. William Fulbright	U.S. Senator from Arkansas	15.6.65
John Kenneth Galbraith	Former Ambassador to India	11.7.64
Mrs Mary Gallagher	Personal secretary to Mrs John F. Kennedy	2.4.64
		23.4.64
		2.5.64
		15.5.64
		10.6.64
		6.8.64
Ann Gargan	Cousin of President Kennedy	20.7.64
Joseph Gargan	Cousin of President Kennedy	20.7.64
Joseph H. Gawler	Washington undertaker	18.5.64
		1.6.64
		16.6.64
		19.5.65
Master Sergeant Joseph D. Giordano, USA	Baggage master to the President	2.6.64
		5.2.65
		25.5.65
Lt. Col. Thurman A. Glasgow	Information Officer, Brooks Air Force Base	17.9.64
Arthur J. Goldberg	Associate Justice, U.S. Supreme Court	24.6.64
Irving L. Goldberg	Dallas attorney	24.9.64
Henry Gonzalez	U.S. Congressman from Texas	25.6.64
Richard N. Goodwin	Secretary General of the International Peace Corps Secretariat	4.5.64
Dean Gorham	Director of the Texas Municipal Retirement System	15.9.64
A. C. Greene	Editor, Dallas *Times-Herald* editorial page	25.9.64
Jim Greenfield	Assistant Secretary of State	1.4.64
Bill Greer	Secret Service agent	19.11.64
Edwin O. Guthman	Special Assistant to the Attorney General	3.5.64
		10.6.64
		23.3.65

Name	*Position at 12 Noon, Nov. 22, 1963*	*Date of Interview*
Milton Gwirtzman	Assistant to Senator Edward M. Kennedy	8.6.64 15.5.64
David Hackett	Executive Director, the President's Committee on Juvenile Delinquency and Youth Crime	21.5.64
Joseph Hagan	Assistant to Joseph H. Gawler	18.5.64
Oliver S. Hallett, USN	Assistant Naval Aide, the White House	23.4.64
Mrs Joan Hallett	Wife of Commander Hallett	23.4.64
The Most Rev. Philip M. Hannan	Auxiliary Bishop of Washington	25.6.64 25.5.65
Lt. Col. Lewis Hanson	Presidential aircraft copilot	7.6.65
Warren G. Harding	Treasurer, Dallas County	8.10.64
Averell Harriman	Under Secretary of State	27.5.64
Mrs Marie Heintz	Staff member, Walter Reed Hospital	28.8.64
Clinton J. Hill	Secret Service agent	18.11.64 20.5.65
Jacqueline Hirsch	French teacher, White House School	23.4.64
Fred Holborn	Assistant to the President	9.4.64 8.9.64
The Rev. William A. Holmes	Pastor, Northaven Methodist Church, Dallas, Texas	8.10.64
Wesley Hooper	Rice Hotel executive	18.9.64
J. Edgar Hoover	Director, Federal Bureau of Investigation	4.6.64
James Patrick Hosty, Jr.	FBI agent	24.9.64
Father Oscar Huber	Dallas priest	26.8.64 20.9.64
Judge Sarah T. Hughes	Federal District Judge	19.9.64
Hubert H. Humphrey	U.S. Senator from Minnesota	16.3.65
H. L. Hunt	Dallas oilman	25.9.64
Hurchel Jacks	Texas State Highway Patrolman	20.9.64
Lem Johns	Secret Service agent	19.11.64
Mrs J. Lee Johnson III	Wife of Fort Worth civic leader	19.9.64
Lyndon Baines Johnson*	Vice President of the U.S.	24.6.65
Mrs Lyndon Baines Johnson	Wife of the Vice President	15.6.64
U. Alexis Johnson	Deputy Under Secretary of State	2.6.64 3.6.64
Nicolas de B. Katzenbach	Deputy Attorney General	5.6.64
Roy Kellerman	Secret Service agent	17.11.64 12.5.65
Thomas J. Kelley	Inspector, U.S. Secret Service	9.10.64
Bernard F. Kelly	Detective, D.C. Police Department Homicide Squad	9.6.65
Edward M. Kennedy	U.S. Senator	14.4.64
Ethel Kennedy	Wife of the Attorney General	17.4.64
Joan Kennedy	Wife of Senator Kennedy	23.4.64
Mrs J. F. Kennedy	The First Lady	7.4.64 4.5.64 7.5.64 8.5.64 20.7.64
Robert F. Kennedy	Attorney General of the U.S.	14.5.64 12.1.65

* At President Johnson's request, the author submitted his questions in writing; the President's answers were also in writing.

Name	Position at 12 Noon, Nov. 22, 1963	Date of Interview
Mrs Joseph P. Kennedy	Mother of President Kennedy	19.7.64
Malcolm Kilduff	Assistant Press Secretary to the President	2.5.64
Sam Kinney	Secret Service agent	19.2.65
Jack Krueger	Managing Editor, Dallas *Morning News*	23.9.64
Steve Landregan	Assistant Administrator, Parkland Memorial Hospital	21.9.64
Mrs Peter Lawford	Sister of President Kennedy	20.7.64 21.7.64
James Lehrer	Reporter, Dallas *Times-Herald*	23.9.64 8.10.64 3.6.65 7.6.65 8.6.65
Hal Lewis	Managing Editor, Dallas *Times-Herald*	24.9.64
Mrs Evelyn Lincoln	Personal secretary to President Kennedy	3.4.64 4.4.64 15.4.64 15.5.65
Walter Lippmann	Washington columnist	10.10.64
Billy Nolan Lovelady	Fellow worker of Lee Oswald	21.9.64
Irving Lowens	Chief, Music Division, Library of Congress	5.8.64
Robert MacNeil	Newscaster, NBC	15.6.65
John McCone	Director, Central Intelligence Agency	10.4.64
John W. McCormack	Speaker of the House of Representatives	14.5.64
Father Thomas McGraw	Catholic Chaplain, Arlington National Cemetery	1.9.64
Mary McGrory	Columnist, Washington *Star*	9.8.64
Brig. Gen. Godfrey McHugh	Air Force Aide to the President	6.5.64
Mrs M. K. McHugh	Secretary to the Chief Justice	22.4.64
Mrs Robert 'Candy' McMurrey	Sister of Joan Kennedy	10.6.64
Col. George J. McNally, U.S. Signal Corps	Commanding Officer, the White House Communications Agency	26.5.64 8.6.64 5.10.64 4.2.65
Jack McNally	Staff Assistant to the President	15.5.64
Robert S. McNamara	Secretary of Defence	25.5.64
John Macy	Chairman, U.S. Civil Service Commission	15.6.64
Sgt. William Malcolm	Firing Party Commander, 3rd Infantry	30.4.64
Senator Mike Mansfield	Majority Leader, U.S. Senate	27.5.64
Dean F. Markham	Executive Director, U.S. Narcotic Commission	24.6.64
Harry Martin	Houston caterer	18.9.64
Mrs Paul Mellon	Friend of Mrs Kennedy's	19.6.64
John Metzler	Superintendent, Arlington National Cemetery	30.4.64 10.8.64 21.6.65 7.7.65
George D. Miller, USA, Specialist 7th Grade	Assistant to Master Sergeant Giordano	2.6.64
Lt. Col. Paul C. Miller (Retired)	Ceremonies Officer, Military District of Washington	30.4.64
Robert Morgenthau	U.S. Attorney, New York	1.6.64
Bill D. Moyers	Deputy Director, Peace Corps	8.6.65

Name	*Position at 12 Noon, Nov. 22, 1963*	*Date of Interview*
Daniel P. Moynihan	Assistant Secretary of Labour	22.5.64 23.11.64 27.3.66
Seaman Apprentice Ed Nemuth	Flag bearer, Naval Ceremonial Company, Naval Air Station, Anacostia	18.5.64
Angela Novello	Personal secretary to the Attorney General	15.5.64
Lawrence F. O'Brien	Special Assistant to the President	4.5.64 4.6.64
P. Kenneth O'Donnell	Special Assistant to the President	4.5.64 4.6.64 6.8.64 23.11.64
John J. 'Muggsy' O'Leary	Secret Service agent	10.11.64
Vernon B. Oneal	Dallas undertaker	25.9.64
Mary Ann Orlando	Secretary to Sargent Shriver	12.8.64
Sir David Ormsby-Gore	British Ambassador to the U.S.	6.5.64
Marguerite Oswald	Mother of Lee Oswald	26.8.64 18.9.64
Robert Oswald	Brother of Lee Oswald	5.11.64
Michael Paine	Acquaintance of the Oswalds	20.9.64 13.1.65
Mrs Ruth Paine	Friend of Marina Oswald	20.9.64
Providentia Parades	Mrs Kennedy's maid	24.4.64
Max Peck	Manager of Rice Hotel, Houston	18.9.64
Henry Peters	Drum Major, U.S. Marine Band	21.8.64
Burrell Peterson	Inspector, U.S. Secret Service	9.10.64 17.11.64 18.11.64 5.2.65
Philip Potter	Correspondent, Baltimore *Sun*	26.3.64
David Powers	Assistant to President Kennedy	8.4.64 10.8.64 21.10.64 17.3.65 24.5.65
Walter I. 'Bill' Pozen	Assistant to the Secretary of the Interior	28.4.64
Elizabeth Pozen	Wife of Walter I. Pozen	28.4.65
Charles Jack Price	Administrator of Parkland Hospital	21.9.64 22.2.65
Prince Stanislaus Radziwill	Brother-in-law of Mrs Kennedy	11.6.64
Timothy J. Reardon, Jr.	Special Assistant to the President	4.6.64
James A. Reed	Assistant Secretary to the Navy	22.5.64
George Reedy	Assistant to the Vice President	23.6.64
Harold Reis	Attorney, Department of Justice	23.4.65
Richard L. Riedel	Press Liaison Officer, U.S. Senate	10.8.64
Charles Roberts	*Newsweek* correspondent	9.6.65
Earlene Roberts	Oswald's landlady	23.9.64
Emory P. Roberts	Secret Service agent	4.12.64 26.4.65
Mr Rodriguez	Aide to Congressman Gonzalez	16.9.64
Mrs Lillian Rogers	Secretary to Abraham Zapruder	21.9.64
Dr Earl Rose	Dallas County Medical Examiner	21.9.64
Barney Ross	Member, President's Commission on Juvenile Delinquency	9.6.64

Name	*Position at 12 Noon, Nov. 22, 1963*	*Date of Interview*
James J. Rowley	Chief, U.S. Secret Service	1.5.64
Dean Rusk	Secretary of State	6.4.64
Peter Saccu	Catering Manager, Hotel Texas, Fort Worth	18.9.64
Pierre Salinger	Press Secretary of the President	20.8.64
H. Barefoot Sanders, Jr.	U.S. Attorney, Dallas	22.9.64 26.9.64 27.5.65
James Sasser	Director, White House household budget	14.5.65
1st Lt. Donald W. Sawtelle	Honour Guard Commander, 3rd Infantry	30.4.64
Herbert Sawyer	Inspector, Dallas Police Department	23.9.64 24.9.64
Arthur Schlesinger, Jr.	Special Assistant to the President	29.5.64
John Schoellkopf	Reporter, Dallas *Times-Herald*	20.5.65 27.5.65
Brig. Gen. Robert L. Schulz, USA (Retired)	Executive Assistant to President Eisenhower	27.8.64
Sgt. Thomas M. Setterberg	Commander, Caisson Detail, Fort Myer	30.4.64
Maude Shaw	Nurse to the Kennedy children	24.4.64 18.5.64
Keith Shelton	Political writer, Dallas *Times-Herald*	27.5.64
Capt. Tazewell Shepard, USN	Naval Aide to the President	1.5.64 24.3.65
Mrs Tazewell Shepard	Wife of Captain Shepard	1.5.64
Eunice Shriver	Sister of President Kennedy	19.10.64 21.10.64
Sargent Shriver	Director, U.S. Peace Corps; brother-in-law of President Kennedy	12.8.64 19.8.64
Hugh Sidey	Washington Bureau Chief, *Time* Magazine	5.10.64
Byron Skelton	Democratic National Committeeman from Texas	14.9.64
Ruth Skelton	Wife of Byron Skelton	14.9.64
Jean Kennedy Smith	Sister of President Kennedy	18.6.64
Merriman Smith	White House correspondent, UPI	14.4.64
Stephen Smith	Brother-in-law of President Kennedy	27.7.64
Theodore C. Sorensen	Special Assistant to the President	20.7.64
Forrest V. Sorrels	Secret Service Agent in Charge, Dallas, Texas	26.8.64 24.9.64
Mrs Potter Stewart	Wife of Associate Justice Stewart	16.4.64
Capt. Cecil Stoughton	White House Photographer	27.4.64
Dr Martin Sweig	Administrative Assistant to the Speaker of the House	14.5.64
Col. James Swindal, USAF	Presidential aircraft commander	29.4.64 3.6.65
Arthur Sylvester	Assistant Secretary of Defence	5.11.64
Gen. Maxwell Taylor, USA	Chairman, the Joint Chiefs of Staff	5.5.64
Olin Teague	U.S. Congressman from Texas	29.9.64
Albert Thomas	U.S. Congressman from Texas	16.4.64 19.8.64
George Thomas	Valet to the President	7.5.64
Father James N. Thompson	Dallas priest	28.8.64
Llewellyn Thompson	Under Secretary of State	20.5.64

Name	*Position at 12 Noon, Nov. 22, 1963*	*Date of Interview*
Roy S. Truly	Superintendent, Texas School Book Depository, Dallas	21.9.64
Nancy Tuckerman	Social secretary, the White House	13.4.64 6.5.64
Pamela Turnure	Press secretary to Mrs Kennedy	21.4.64
Martin E. Underwood	Advance man, Democratic National Committee	21.6.65
Jack Valenti	Texas public relations man	5.6.64 26.4.64
Sue Vogelsinger	Secretary to Pierre Salinger	20.8.64
Maj. Gen. Edwin A. Walker, USA (Retired)	Retired Army officer	25.9.64
W. R. Walker	Assistant Manager, Hotel Texas, Fort Worth	18.9.64
John W. Walsh, M.D.	Physician to Mrs Kennedy	27.4.64
William Walton	Artist; friend of the Kennedys	27.4.64
Theran Ward, J.P.	Dallas County Justice of the Peace	21.9.64
Jack Warner	Inspector, U.S. Secret Service	2.6.64 18.11.64 5.2.65 12.5.65
Earl Warren	Chief Justice, U.S. Supreme Court	18.5.64 3.11.64
Capt. Robert Weare	Staff member, Bethesda Naval Hospital	14.4.64 1.6.64
Maj. Gen. Philip C. Wehle	Commanding Officer, Military District of Washington	29.4.64
B. E. Welch, M.D.	Brooks Air Force Base scientist	17.9.64
Thomas Howard Wells	Secret Service agent	18.12.64
J. Bernard West	Chief Usher, the White House	23.4.64 23.6.64 25.8.64
William W. Whaley	Dallas taxi driver	23.9.64
Byron White	Associate Justice, U.S. Supreme Court	22.4.64
Theodore H. White	Writer	21.6.65
Jerome B. Wiesner	Special Assistant to the President	13.6.65
Howard P. Willens	Attorney, Criminal Division, Department of Justice	8.7.66
Frank J. Wilson	Chief of the U.S. Secret Service—Jan. 1, 1936–Dec. 31, 1946	25.6.64
Willard Wirtz	Secretary of Labour	26.6.64
Ralph Yarborough	U.S. Senator from Texas	6.4.64 11.11.64 26.5.65
Rufus Youngblood	Secret Service agent	17.11.64
Abraham Zapruder	Dallas manufacturer of women's garments	21.9.64

II. UNPUBLISHED DOCUMENTS

Associated Press teletype files, November 22–25, 1963.

Auchincloss, Mrs Hugh. Letter to Jacqueline Kennedy, November 20, 1963.

Bales, Arthur W., Warrant Officer, U.S. Signal Corps. 'Sequence of Events—22 November 1963'; May 25, 1965.

Ball, George W., Under Secretary of State. State Department memorandum for the President, handed to Lyndon Johnson by U. Alexis Johnson at Andrews AFB, 6.15 p.m., November 22, 1963. Diagram showing where individuals sat in the Presidential helicopter from Andrews AFB to the White House, 6.15 p.m., November 22, 1963.

Ballantyne, Robert J., and Sullivan, William A. Memoranda on early State Department reactions to the assassination; dated June 1964.

Bartlett, Charles. Reflections on the death of President Kennedy, written on White House stationery; N.D.

Bartlett, Phyllis, switchboard operator, Parkland Hospital. Report of activities, November 22–24, 1963; N.D.

Basler, Roy P. 'Reference Department activity at the Library of Congress during the period November 22–25, 1963, covering the assassination and funeral of President Kennedy'; December 23, 1963.

Bass, J. W. Burial-Transit Permit No. 7992, Texas State Department of Health, Bureau of Vital Statistics, for 'removal of John F. Kennedy, deceased.'

Bird, 1st Lieut. Samuel R., U.S.A., Officer-in-charge, Joint Service Presidential Casket Team, funeral of President Kennedy. 'After-action report on events of 22 Nov. 63–25 Nov. 63.'

Bodensteiner, Sgt. Leon, U.S. Signal Corps. '22 Nov. 63 in Comm-cen.'; N.D.

Brazell, S/Sgt Robert D., U.S. Signal Corps. 'Physical Situation and Chronological Sequence of Events,' November 22, 1963; N.D.

Brinkley, David. Letter to the author on television network and pool cameras used to cover funeral events in Washington, May 28, 1964.

Bruce, David, Ambassador to the Court of St James's. Cable to the Secretary of State on British reaction to the death of President Kennedy, December 1, 1963.

Bruno, Jerry. Texas Trip Schedule, November 14, 1963.

Buchwald, Art. Letter to the author, September 14, 1964.

Bundy, McGeorge, Special Assistant to the President. Untitled memorandum of events, November 22–25, 1963; December 4, 1963. Memorandum to the President dated November 19, 1963, with handwritten notation by the President, November 21, 1963.

Burkley, George G., M.D. 'Report on my participation in the activities surrounding the assassination of President John Fitzgerald Kennedy,' November 27, 1963, 8.45 a.m.

Cain, Father Thomas. Handwritten notes on his participation in events at Parkland Memorial Hospital, Dallas, Texas, on November 22, 1963; September 21, 1964.

Carpenter, Elizabeth. Draft of remarks to be made by President Johnson at Andrews AFB; written in automobile from Parkland Hospital to Love Field and aboard Aircraft 26000, November 22, 1963.

Carpenter, Francis. Notes on the activities of Ambassador Adlai E. Stevenson, November 22–23, 1963; August 24, 1964.

Carriger, Harley, Sp/4, U.S. Signal Corps. 'Résumé of Events 22 November 1963'; N.D.

Chesapeake & Potomac Telephone Company. Records of toll and long-distance-direct calls, November 22–November 25, 1963.
Colt, Justice LeBaron Bradford. 'The Protection of the President of the United States,' an address delivered March 3, 1902, in Concord, New Hampshire, before the New Hampshire Bar Association.
Cuesta, Lourdes B. Letter to the author, May 6, 1965.
Dailey, Marilyn. Letter to the author, May 23, 1965.
Dailey, Mary Mathis. Letter to the author, May 23, 1965.
Ferguson, Anne, switchboard operator, Parkland Hospital. Report of activities, November 22, 1963; N.D.
Freeman, Orville, Secretary of Agriculture. Memoranda of events. The first section was dictated on November 23, 1963, at 5.15 p.m.; subsequent sections dictated from time to time through Monday, November 25, 1963.
Galbraith, Kenneth. Letter to Jacqueline Kennedy, November 22, 1963.
Notes on events of November 22–25, 1963; November 26, 1963.
Gawler, Joseph. Diagram showing where Jacqueline and Robert Kennedy sat in rear of ambulance during ride from Bethesda Naval Hospital to the White House, November 23, 1963; May 18, 1964.
Geilich, Peter N., administrative assistant, Parkland Hospital. Report of activities, November 22–24, 1963; November 26, 1963.
Goldberg, Arthur, Associate Justice, U.S. Supreme Court. Remarks delivered on evening of November 25, 1963, in memorial service for President Kennedy held by Washington Jewish Community.
Gonzalez, the Hon. Henry B. Letter to the author, May 7, 1965.
Greer, William R. Map of route followed by ambulance bearing President Kennedy's body, night of November 22–23, 1963.
'Information on Lincoln bubble top automobile since returning from Dallas'; memorandum to Gerald Behn, SAIC, White House Detail, November 22, 1963.
Gwirtzman, Milton. Handwritten notes of November 22, 1963.
Hannan, the Most Rev. Philip M., Auxiliary Bishop of Washington. Draft of remarks delivered from lectern during Mass in St Matthew's, November 25, 1963.
Harriman, W. Averell. Diary of November 22–26, 1963.
Heller, Walter W. 'Confidential Notes on a Quick Meeting with the President and other Leading Members of the Kennedy Family,' November 19, 1963. 'Chronology of events on board the aircraft carrying the Cabinet group to Japan on Friday, November 22, 1963, the day of President Kennedy's death'; November 23, 1963.
Hinchcliffe, Margaret, R.N., Parkland Hospital. Report of activities, November 22, 1963.
Hodges, Luther H. 'A (Sad) Trip Report, Nov. 21–22, 1963.'
Holborn, Frederick L. Letter to Hugh Sidey, November 21, 1963.
Holcomb, R. G., administrative assistant, Parkland Hospital. Report of activities, Parkland Hospital, November 22–24, 1963; N.D.
Hughes, Thomas A., Assistant Chief, Land Acquisition Section of the

Department of Justice. 'John F. Kennedy Plot in Arlington National Cemetery, Virginia,' November 27, 1963.

Humphrey, Hubert H. 'Memo for Record,' dictated November 23, 1963, and January 19, 1964.

Johnson, Mrs J. Lee, III. 'An Art Exhibition for The President and Mrs John F. Kennedy, The Presidential Suite, Hotel Texas, Fort Worth, 22 November 1963.'

Johnson, Ruth Carter (Mrs J. Lee, III). Letter to the author on John F. Kennedy's last telephone conversation of November 22, 1963.

Johnson, Lyndon, President of the United States. Letter to John Kennedy, Jr., 7.20 p.m., November 22, 1963.

Letter to Caroline Kennedy, 7.30 p.m., November 22, 1963.

Letter to Jacqueline Kennedy, November 29, 1963.

Letter to Jacqueline Kennedy, December 1, 1963.

Johnson, Mrs Lyndon. Letter to Jacqueline Kennedy, December 7, 1963.

Josephy, Alvin M., Jr. Handwritten notes taken aboard Cabinet plane, November 22, 1963.

Kennedy, Jacqueline. Letter to the President from L'Episcopio, Ravello, Prov di Salerno, Italy; N.D.

Letter to the President, March 13, 1963.

Notes on proposed activities at LBJ Ranch on Saturday, November 23, 1963; N.D.

Handwritten draft of speech delivered in Spanish at the Rice Hotel, Houston, November 21, 1963.

Draft of letter to President Johnson, December 1, 1963.

First and second drafts of letter to Nikita Khruschev, December 1, 1963.

Handwritten corrections on copy of 'After the Shots: The Ordeal of Lyndon Johnson,' an article by Fletcher Knebel in *Look*, March 10, 1964.

Letter to the author on graveside services in Arlington, November 25, 1963; postmarked July 8, 1964.

Notes and correspondence, 1963–64.

Kennedy, John F. Letter to Misses Patricia M. and Lynda A. Collins, Box 813, Kirbyville, Texas, signed November 21, 1963.

Tape of his last recorded remarks at breakfast in the Hotel Texas, Fort Worth, November 22, 1963.

Kennedy, Mrs Joseph P. Letter to Jacqueline Kennedy, November 20, 1963.

Kennedy, Robert F. Note to Jacqueline Kennedy on Arlington National Cemetery, November 23, 1963.

Kuhn, Father John G., St Matthew's Cathedral, Washington. Blessing delivered in the East Room, the White House, November 23, 1963.

Landregan, Steve, administrative assistant, Parkland Hospital. Report of activities, November 22–24, 1963; N.D.

Langbein, F. W. 'Chesapeake & Potomac Telephone Company Traffic Department Summary of Activity Following the Assassination of President Kennedy,' November 25, 1963.

Lehrer, James. Letters to the author, January 20, 1965, and April 30, 1966.
Lincoln, Evelyn. Phone log of President Kennedy, November 19–22, 1963.
Appointment Schedules of President Kennedy, November 19–22, 1963.
Lozano, Bertha L., R.N., Triage nurse, Parkland Hospital. Report of activities, November 22, 1963.
Lumpkin, Era, nurse's aide, Parkland Hospital. Report of activities, November 22–24, 1963; N.D.
McGrory, Mary. Letter to the author, July 25, 1964.
McHugh, Godfrey. Weather Report for Texas Trip, November 20, 1963.
McMurrey, Candace B. and Robert M. Statement of activities on November 22, 1963; July 24, 1964.
McNally, Colonel George, U.S. Signal Corps. 'Love (Commercial) Airport—Dallas, Texas, November 22, 1963,' handwritten notes made on the scene.
Majors, Rosa M., nurse's aide, Parkland Hospital. Report of activities, November 22, 1963; N.D.
Malraux, André. Cable to Jacqueline Kennedy from Paris, November 23, 1963.
Manchester, William. Floor plans and roof plan of the Texas School Book Depository, 411 Elm Street, Dallas, Texas.
Floor plan and description of the Paine house, 2515 West Fifth Street, Irving, Texas.
Plan of emergency room area of Parkland Memorial Hospital showing where principal figures stood, 12.38 p.m. to 2.08 p.m., November 22, 1963. (Prepared with co-operation of Sgt R. E. Dugger and hospital staff.)
Presidential motorcade route in Dallas, November 22, 1963. (Prepared with Secret Service Agent Forrest Sorrels.)
Floor Plans of the Presidential Apartment, the Executive Mansion, Washington.
Mansfield, Mike, Majority Leader, U.S. Senate. Original draft of remarks made in the great rotunda, November 24, 1963.
Markham, Dean. Notes, schedules, seating plans, and marching orders for state funeral, November 25, 1965.
Mellon, Mrs Paul. Note to Jacqueline Kennedy, November 23, 1963.
Metaxis, Colonel, aide to General Maxwell Taylor. 'Meeting of the Joint Chiefs of Staff with General Foertsch, Chief of the Armed Forces, Federal Republic of Germany, on Friday, 22 November 1963, at 1420 in Room 2E–924, The Pentagon'; May 5, 1964.
Metzler, John. Map of Arlington National Cemetery showing the three areas tentatively set aside for burial of President Kennedy; early morning, November 23, 1963.
Superintendent of Arlington National Cemetery's memorandum of events on the funeral of President Kennedy; N.D.

Meyer, Vincent. Letter to Jacqueline Kennedy from Paris, November 23, 1963.

Miller, Lt Col Paul C., U.S.A. (Ret.), Chief, Ceremonies and Special Events, Military District of Washington. After-action report on events of November 1963.
'Actual Time Sequence, State Funeral for President Kennedy, 25 November, 1963.'

Moynihan, Daniel Patrick, Assistant Secretary of Labour. Handwritten notes of November 22, 1963.

National Broadcasting Company Programme Log, November 22–25, 1963.

Nelson, Doris M., R.N., Parkland Hospital. Report of activities, November 22–24, 1963; N.D.

Newsweek magazine eyewitness memorandums from Robert B. Young, Charles Roberts, and James Burnham, November 22–23, 1963.

Nixon, Richard. Letter to Jacqueline Kennedy, November 23, 1963. Letter to the author on his activities in Dallas and New York, November 21–22, 1963; August 4, 1964.

O'Donnell, P. Kenneth. 'Texas Trip Folder', comprising President Kennedy's advance schedules for Texas, correspondence between Washington and Texas prior to the trip, and a confidential Department of Justice report on the political and social climate in Dallas; November 1963.

Orlady, Harry W., Chairman, Aeromedical Co-ordinating Committee. Letter to the author describing proficiency tests required of airline pilots, March 2, 1966.

Ormsby-Gore, Sir David, British Ambassador to Washington. Letter to Jacqueline Kennedy, November 26, 1963.

Parkland Hospital Patient Registration Sheet, 12.31–3.42 p.m. CST, November 22, 1963.

Peck, Max. Room assignments of the Presidential party in the Rice Hotel, November 1963.

Powers. David. Handwritten notes of November 22–23, 1963.

Price, C. J., Administrator, Parkland Hospital. Report of activities, November 22–24, 1963; November 27, 1963.
'Summary of My Activities from Friday Noon Until Sunday Night'; December 11, 1963.
Letter to the author, February 24, 1965.

Randall, Shirley, nurse's aide, Parkland Hospital. Report of activities, November 22, 1963; N.D.

Registration of Patients, Parkland Memorial Hospital, Dallas County Hospital District, Emergency Room, 12.31 p.m.–3.42 p.m., November 22, 1963.

Rusk, Dean, Secretary of State. Diary, November 23–25, 1963.

St Matthew's Cathedral. Mass Card and Missal, November 25, 1963.

Salinger, Pierre. Texas Schedule of the President, November 20, 1963. Memorandum of events of November 19–23, 1963; N.D.

Sanderson, James. 'March and Chorus in the Dramatic Romance of the

Lady of the Lake' ('Hail to the Chief'), published by G. E. Blake, Philadelphia; N.D.

Schlesinger, Arthur M., Jr. *White House Journal*, November 22–28, 1963.

Letter to the author, July 6, 1965.

Letter to Jacqueline Kennedy, evening of November 22, 1963.

Letter to Jacqueline Kennedy, November 23, 1963.

Schoellkopf, John. Pencilled notes and carbons made by all Dallas *Times-Herald* reporters in Dallas on November 22, 1963.

Shires, Tom, M.D., Chief of Surgery, Parkland Hospital. Report of Activities, November 24, 1963.

Sidey, Hugh. Letter to the author, October 9, 1966.

Sigel, Roberta S. 'Death of a President and School Children's Reaction to It—An Exploration into Political Socialization,' Wayne State University, Detroit, Mich.; N.D.

'Television in the Lives of Children During a National Crisis,' Wayne State University, Detroit, Mich.; N.D.

Skelton, Byron. Letter to Robert F. Kennedy dated November 6, 1963, with accompanying note from Robert F. Kennedy to P. Kenneth O'Donnell, November 8, 1963.

Letter to Walter Jenkins, November 6, 1963, with carbon copy to Mrs H. H. Weinert, Democratic National Committeewoman from Texas.

Telegram to Robert F. Kennedy, 10.10 a.m., November 23, 1963.

Smith, Jean Kennedy. Untitled notes on the events of November 22–28, 1963.

Sorensen, Theodore C., Special Assistant to the President. Original draft of joint session address delivered by President Johnson, written November 25, 1963.

Letter to the author regarding selection of Biblical and Presidential quotations to be read during President Kennedy's state funeral; March 7, 1966.

Spalding, Charles F. Letter to the author on his activities in New York and Washington, November 22–25, 1963; September 28, 1964.

Stevenson, Adlai, U.S. Ambassador to the United Nations. Statement read at the first Cabinet meeting of President Lyndon Johnson, Washington, November 23, 1963.

Swindal, Col. James B. Flight Chart for Aircraft 26000, USAF, November 22, 1963, Love Field, Dallas, to Andrews AFB, Md.

Letters to the author on his recollections of November 21–22, 1963; April 30, 1964, and July 1, 1964.

Mrs Eamonn de Valera. Letter to Evan Thomas, August 4, 1966.

Ward, Theran, J.P. Death certificate of John F. Kennedy, signed December 6, 1963, in Garland, Texas, and received by local registrar December 11, 1963.

White, Theodore H. Notes on November 29, 1963, interview with Jacqueline Bouvier Kennedy; December 19, 1963.

Witte, John C., Sp/4, U.S. Signal Corps. '22 Nov. 63 in Commcen.'; N.D.

Wolfenstein, Martha. 'Death of a Parent and Death of a President: Children's Reactions to Two Kinds of Loss,' a paper presented to the Conference on Children's Reactions to the Death of the President, Albert Einstein College of Medicine, April 3, 1964.

Wright, Elizabeth L., Director of Nursing Service, Parkland Hospital. Report of activities, November 22, 1963; N.D.

Yarborough, Senator Ralph. Sketch made on April 6, 1964, showing the position of vehicles parked outside Parkland Hospital's three emergency loading bays at 12.40 p.m. (approx.) CST, November 22, 1963.

Youngblood, Rufus. Map of route followed by President Johnson in Washington, D.C., evening of November 22, 1963.

Zapruder, Abraham. 18.24-second colour motion picture sequence (334 frames) taken in Dealey Plaza, 12.30 CST November 22, 1963, showing the Presidential car at the moment of the assassination. Observed by the author June 29, June 30, August 5, and October 9, 1964.

III. PUBLISHED MATERIAL

A. Books

Bell, Daniel, editor. *The Radical Right*, containing essays by Richard Hofstadter, David Riesman, Nathan Glazer, Peter Viereck, Talcott Parsons, Alan F. Westin, H. H. Hyman, S. M. Lipset. Anchor Books, Doubleday & Company, New York: 1964.

Four Days, compiled by United Press International and American Heritage Magazine. American Heritage Publishing Company: 1964.

Hearings Before the President's Commission on the Assassination of President Kennedy. Containing the transcripts of testimony and deposition (15 volumes) and exhibits (11 volumes). United States Government Printing Office, Washington: 1964.

Kennedy, John F. *Public Papers of the Presidents of the United States,* containing the Public Messages, Speeches, and Statements of the President, January 1 to November 22, 1963. United States Government Printing Office, Washington: 1964.

Leslie, Warren. *Dallas Public and Private: Aspects of an American City.* Grossman Publishers, New York: 1964.

Lewis, Lloyd. *Myths After Lincoln.* Harcourt, Brace, New York: 1929.

McGrory, Mary. *In Memoriam: John Fitzgerald Kennedy.* Washington Star Newspaper Company, Washington: 1963.

Memorial Addresses in the Congress of the United States and Tributes in Eulogy of John Fitzgerald Kennedy, Late a President of the United States. United States Government Printing Office, Washington: 1964.

Murray, Norbert. *Legacy of an Assassination.* The Pro-People Press, New York: 1964.

Report of the President's Commission on the Assassination of

President Kennedy. United States Government Printing Office, Washington: 1964.

Rossiter, Clinton. *The American Presidency*. Harcourt, Brace, New York: 1960.

The Torch Is Passed, compiled by the Associated Press: 1963.

The White House: An Historic Guide. The White House Historical Association, Washington: 1962.

B. ARTICLES

Austin *American*: files for November 1963.

Banta, Thomas J., 'The Kennedy Assassination: Early Thoughts and Emotions,' *The Public Opinion Quarterly*, Summer 1964.

'The Black Watch,' *The Red Hackle*, publication of the Black Watch Royal Highland Regiment, January 1964.

Breslin, Jimmy, 'A Death in Emergency Room No. One,' *Saturday Evening Post*, December 14, 1963.

Columbia Journalism Review, Winter 1964. An entire issue devoted to newspaper and television coverage of the assassination.

Dallas *Morning News*: files for 1963.

Dallas *Times-Herald*: files for 1963.

Dugger, Ronnie, 'The Last Voyage of Mr Kennedy,' *The Texas Observer*, November 29, 1963.
'Dallas, After All,' *The Texas Observer*, March 6, 1964.
'And Finally, as to John F. Kennedy,' *The Texas Observer*, June 11, 1965.

Fort Worth *Star-Telegram*: files for November 1963.

Greenberg, Bradley J., 'Diffusion of News of the Kennedy Assassination,' *The Public Opinion Quarterly*, Summer 1964.

Greenstein, Fred I., 'College Students' Reactions to the Assassination,' in *The Kennedy Assassination and the American Public School: Social Communication in Crisis*, edited by Benjamin S. Greenburg and Edwin B. Parker, Stanford University Press: 1965.
'Young Men and the Death of a Young President,' in *Children and the Death of a President: Multi-disciplinary Studies*, edited by Martha Wolfenstein and Gilbert Kliman, Doubleday: 1965.

Grosvenor, Melville Bell, 'The Last Full Measure,' *National Geographic*, March 1964.

Houston *Chronicle*: files for November 1963.

Huber, The Very Reverend Oscar L., C.M., 'President Kennedy's Final Hours,' *The Register*, Denver, Colorado, December 8, 1963.

Hughes, Sarah T., 'The President Is Sworn In,' *The Texas Observer*, November 29, 1963.

Humphrey, Hubert, 'Mental Health and World Peace,' Remarks to the National Association of Mental Health, Washington, D.C., November 21, 1963. *Congressional Record*, November 26, 1963.

Katz, Joseph, 'President Kennedy's Assassination,' *The Psychoanalytic Review*, Winter 1964–65.

Kennedy, Robert F., *Opinions of the Attorneys General*, XLII, 5, August 2, 1961.

Kirschner, David, 'The Death of a President: Reactions of Psychoanalytic Patients,' *Behavioral Science*, January 1965.

Lattimer, John K., 'The Wound That Killed Lincoln,' *Journal of the American Medical Association*, February 15, 1964.

Lowens, Irving, 'Accurate Listing of Funeral Music,' Washington *Star*, December 1, 1963.

New York Times: files for November–December 1963.

Rothstein, David A., 'Presidential Assassination Syndrome,' privately printed, Springfield, Mass., 1964.

San Antonio *Light*: files for November 1963.

San Antonio *News*: files for November 1963.

Sheatsley, Paul B., and Feldman, Jacob J., 'The Assassination of President Kennedy: A Preliminary Report on Public Reactions and Behaviour,' *The Public Opinion Quarterly*, Summer 1964.

'Three Patients at Parkland,' *Texas State Journal of Medicine*, January 1964.

U.S. Department of Commerce Weather Bureau, Local Climatological Data, Washington, National Airport, November 1963.

'Wanted for Treason', unsigned dodger attacking President Kennedy, distributed in Dallas, November 21, 1963.

West, Jessamyn, 'Prelude to Tragedy: The Woman Who Sheltered Lee Oswald's Family Tells Her Story,' *Redbook*, July 1964.

Wicker, Tom, 'Wicker Describes That Day in Dallas,' *Times Talk*, December 1963.

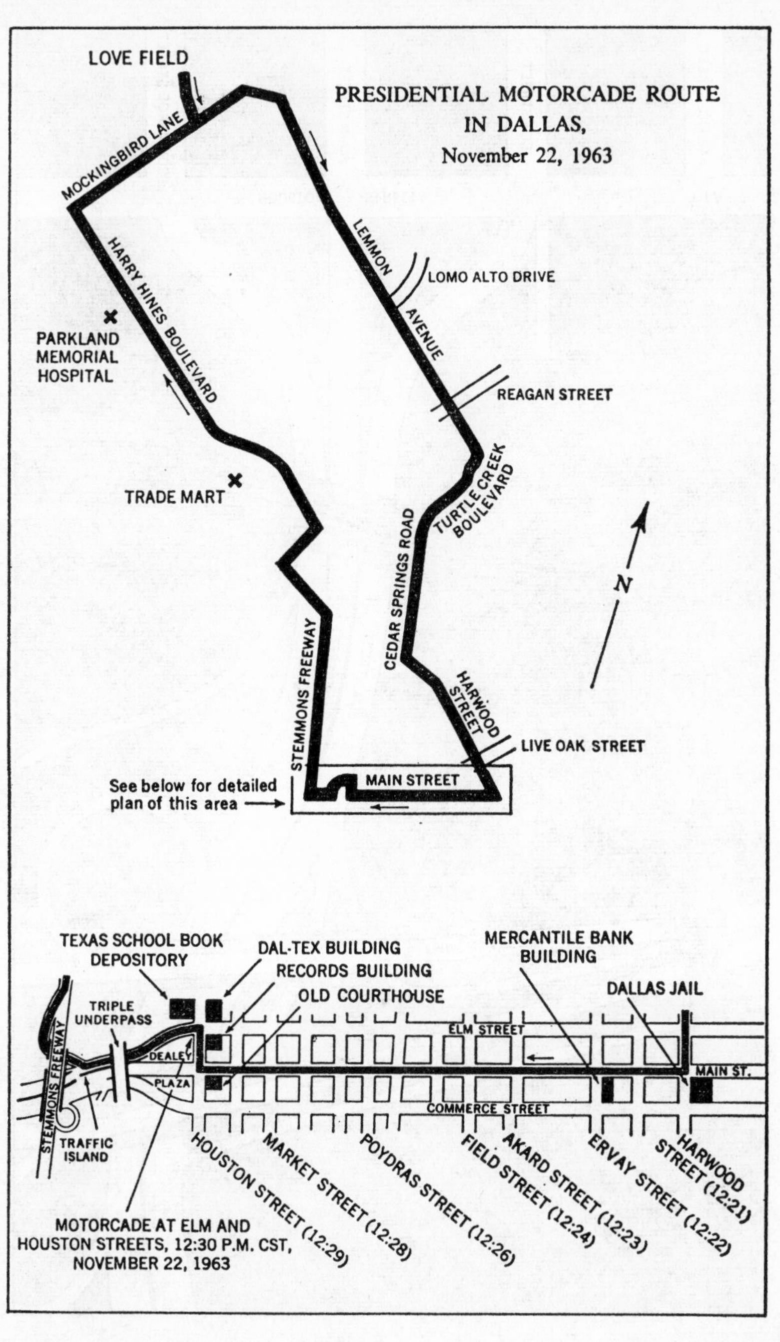
PRESIDENTIAL MOTORCADE ROUTE
IN DALLAS,
November 22, 1963
LOVE FIELD
MOCKINGBIRD LANE
HARRY HINES BOULEVARD
LEMMON AVENUE
LOMO ALTO DRIVE
PARKLAND MEMORIAL HOSPITAL
REAGAN STREET
TURTLE CREEK BOULEVARD
TRADE MART
CEDAR SPRINGS ROAD
N
STEMMONS FREEWAY
HARWOOD STREET
LIVE OAK STREET
MAIN STREET
See below for detailed plan of this area
TEXAS SCHOOL BOOK DEPOSITORY
DAL-TEX BUILDING
RECORDS BUILDING
OLD COURTHOUSE
MERCANTILE BANK BUILDING
DALLAS JAIL
TRIPLE UNDERPASS
ELM STREET
DEALEY
PLAZA
MAIN ST.
COMMERCE STREET
STEMMONS FREEWAY
TRAFFIC ISLAND
HOUSTON STREET (12:29)
MARKET STREET (12:28)
POYDRAS STREET (12:26)
FIELD STREET (12:24)
AKARD STREET (12:23)
ERVAY STREET (12:22)
HARWOOD STREET (12:21)
MOTORCADE AT ELM AND HOUSTON STREETS, 12:30 P.M. CST, NOVEMBER 22, 1963

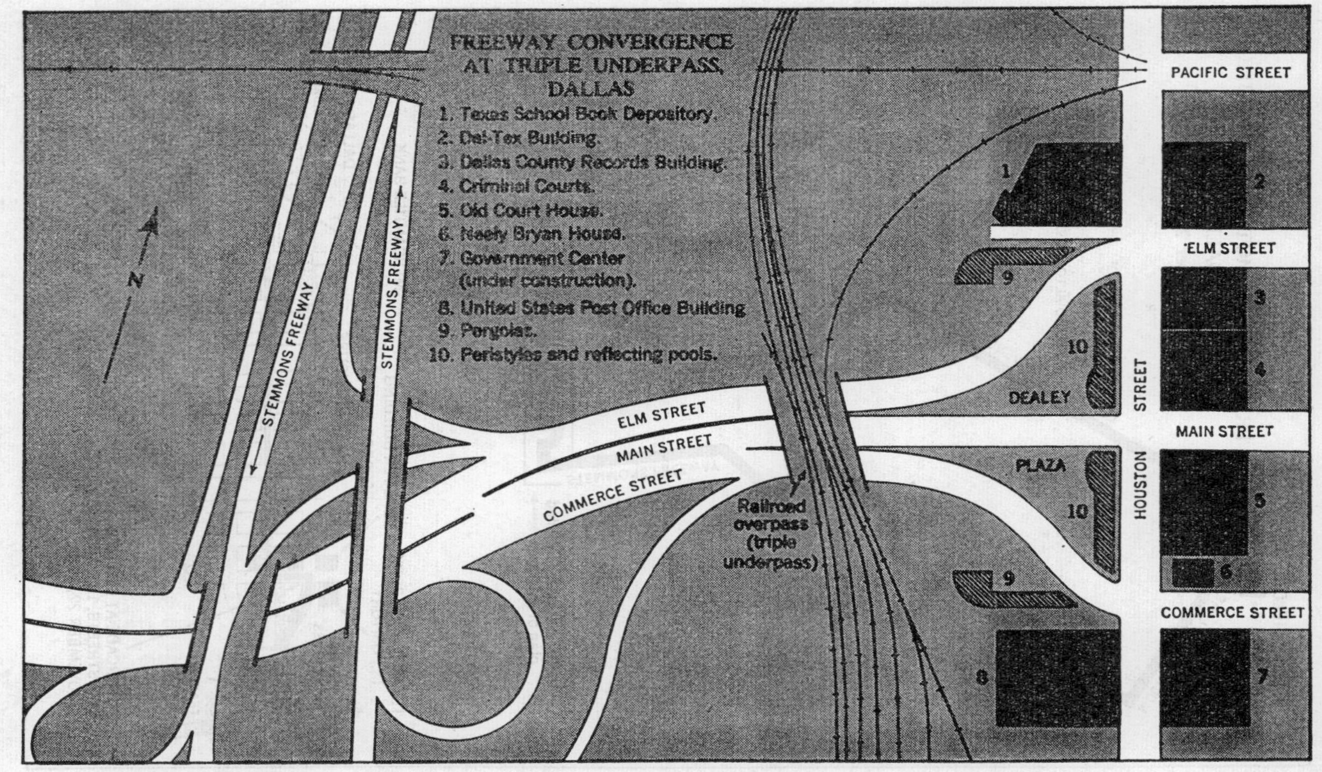
FREEWAY CONVERGENCE
AT TRIPLE UNDERPASS,
DALLAS
1. Texas School Book Depository.
2. Dal-Tex Building.
3. Dallas County Records Building.
4. Criminal Courts.
5. Old Court House.
6. Neely Bryan House.
7. Government Center (under construction).
8. United States Post Office Building
9. Pergolas.
10. Peristyles and reflecting pools.
PACIFIC STREET
ELM STREET
MAIN STREET
COMMERCE STREET
HOUSTON STREET
DEALEY PLAZA
STEMMONS FREEWAY
STEMMONS FREEWAY
ELM STREET
MAIN STREET
COMMERCE STREET
Railroad overpass (triple underpass)
N

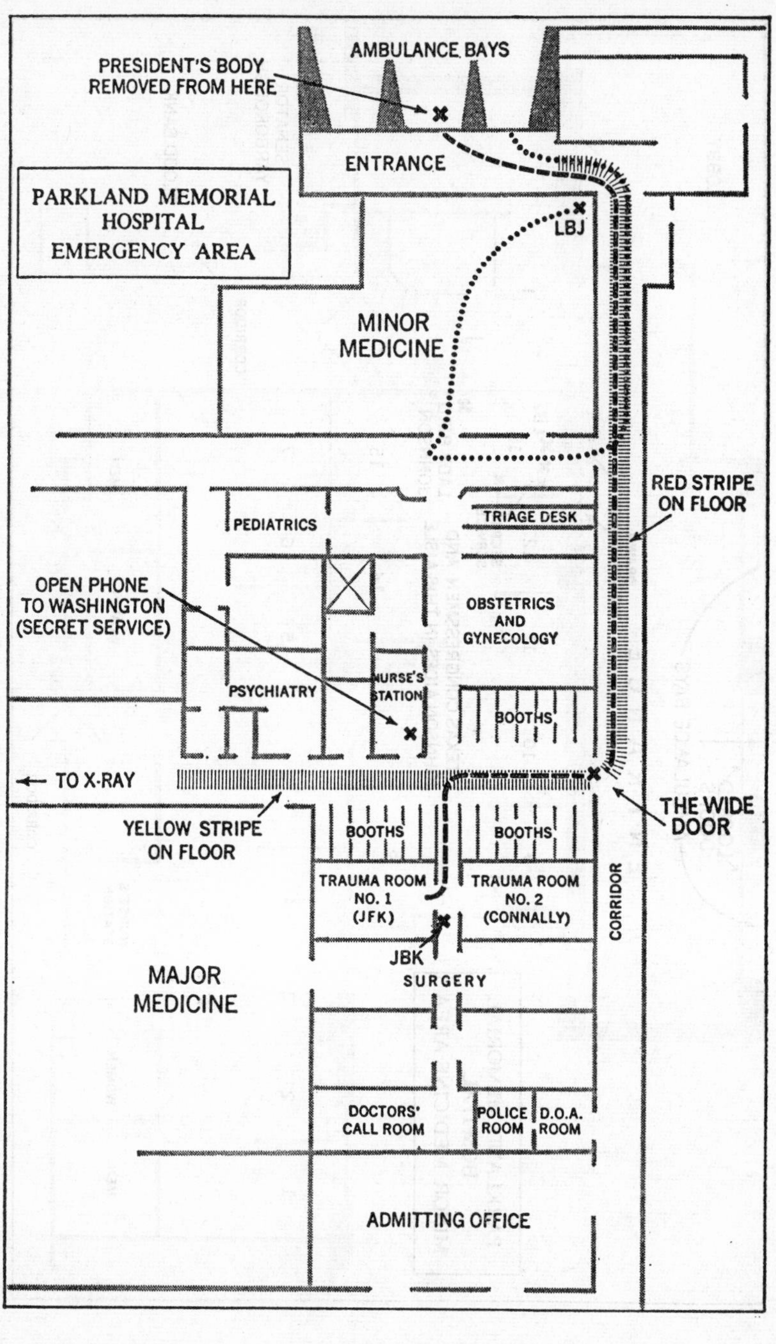

AMBULANCE BAYS
PRESIDENT'S BODY REMOVED FROM HERE
ENTRANCE
PARKLAND MEMORIAL HOSPITAL EMERGENCY AREA
LBJ
MINOR MEDICINE
RED STRIPE ON FLOOR
PEDIATRICS
TRIAGE DESK
OPEN PHONE TO WASHINGTON (SECRET SERVICE)
OBSTETRICS AND GYNECOLOGY
PSYCHIATRY
NURSE'S STATION
BOOTHS
TO X-RAY
THE WIDE DOOR
YELLOW STRIPE ON FLOOR
BOOTHS
BOOTHS
TRAUMA ROOM NO. 1 (JFK)
TRAUMA ROOM NO. 2 (CONNALLY)
CORRIDOR
JBK
SURGERY
MAJOR MEDICINE
DOCTORS' CALL ROOM
POLICE ROOM
D.O.A. ROOM
ADMITTING OFFICE

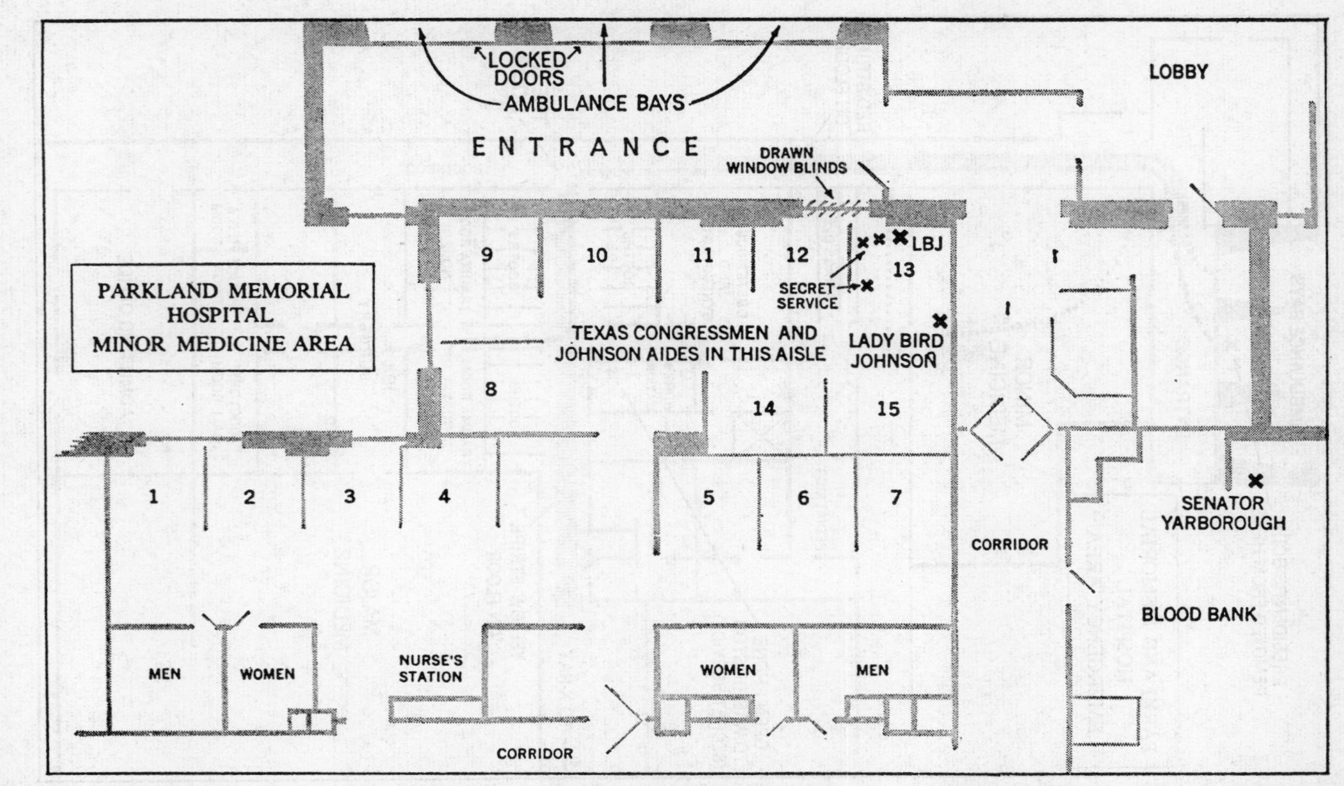
PARKLAND MEMORIAL HOSPITAL
MINOR MEDICINE AREA
LOCKED DOORS
AMBULANCE BAYS
ENTRANCE
LOBBY
DRAWN WINDOW BLINDS
9
10
11
12
13
LBJ
SECRET SERVICE
TEXAS CONGRESSMEN AND JOHNSON AIDES IN THIS AISLE
LADY BIRD JOHNSON
8
14
15
1
2
3
4
5
6
7
CORRIDOR
SENATOR YARBOROUGH
BLOOD BANK
MEN
WOMEN
NURSE'S STATION
WOMEN
MEN
CORRIDOR

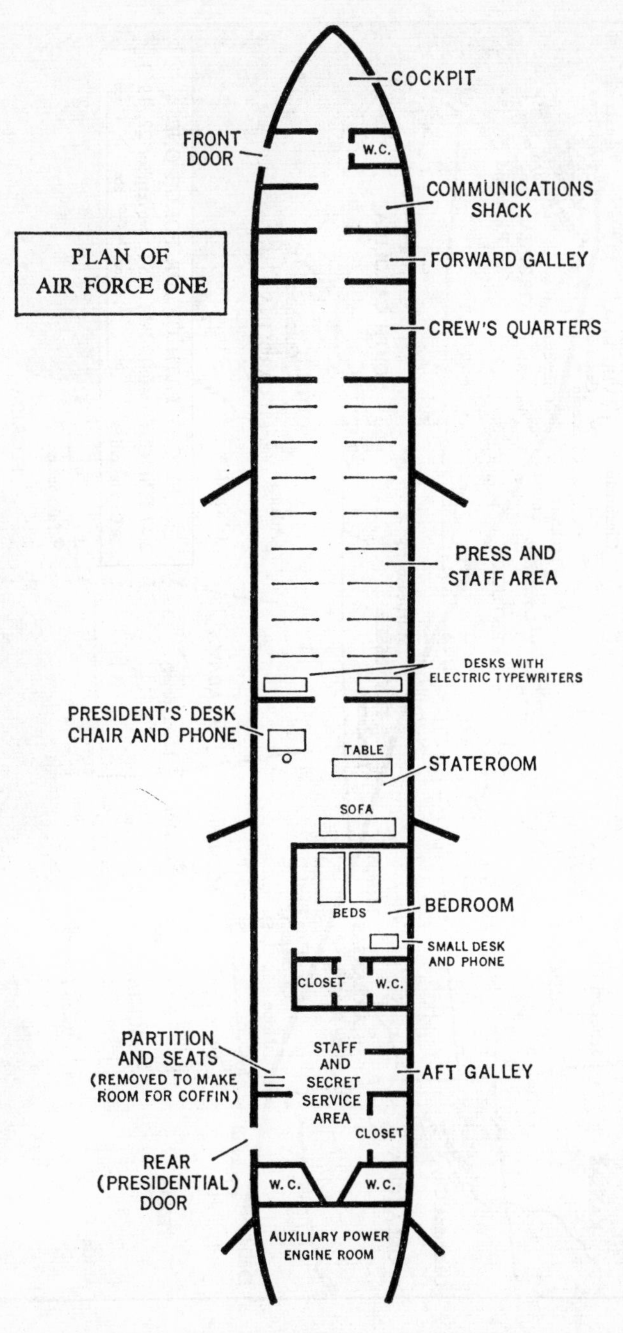

PLAN OF AIR FORCE ONE
COCKPIT
FRONT DOOR
W.C.
COMMUNICATIONS SHACK
FORWARD GALLEY
CREW'S QUARTERS
PRESS AND STAFF AREA
DESKS WITH ELECTRIC TYPEWRITERS
PRESIDENT'S DESK CHAIR AND PHONE
TABLE
STATEROOM
SOFA
BEDS
BEDROOM
SMALL DESK AND PHONE
CLOSET
W.C.
PARTITION AND SEATS (REMOVED TO MAKE ROOM FOR COFFIN)
STAFF AND SECRET SERVICE AREA
AFT GALLEY
CLOSET
REAR (PRESIDENTIAL) DOOR
W.C.
W.C.
AUXILIARY POWER ENGINE ROOM

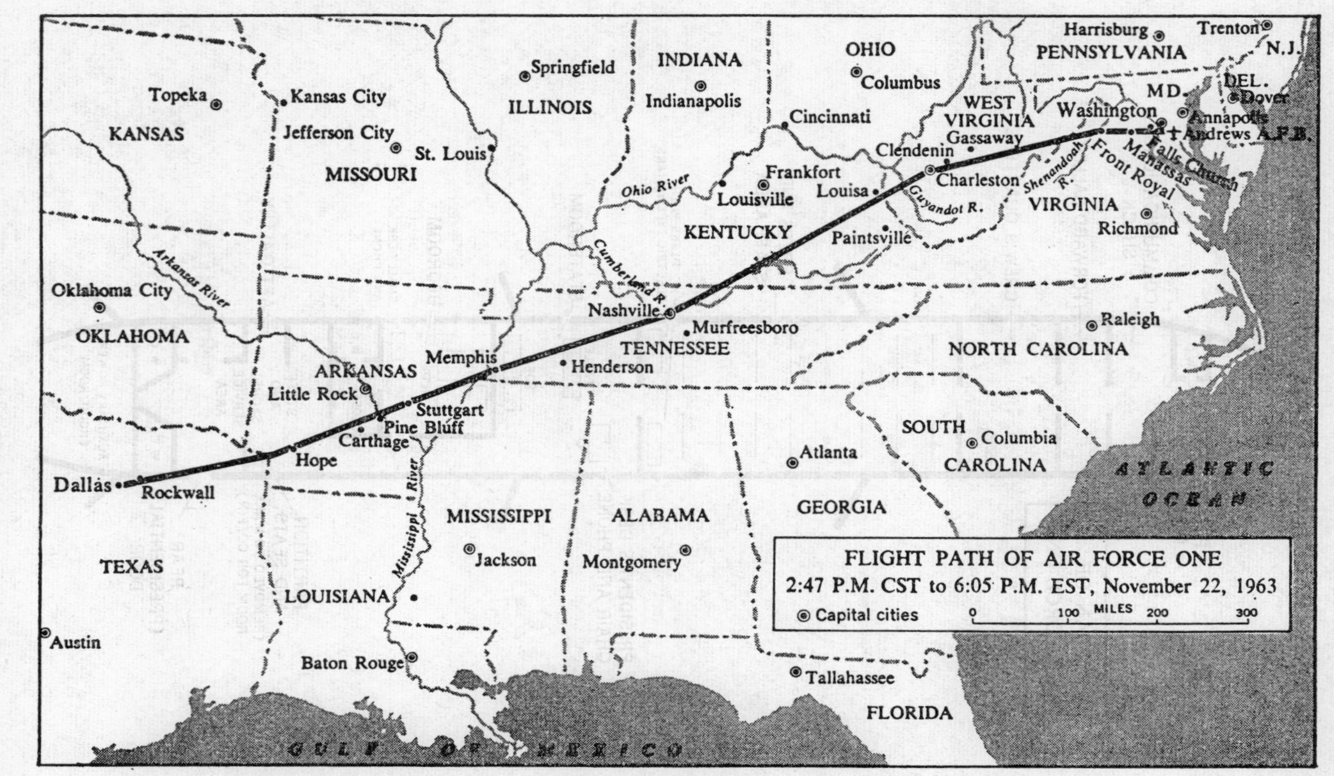
FLIGHT PATH OF AIR FORCE ONE
2:47 P.M. CST to 6:05 P.M. EST, November 22, 1963
Capital cities
0 100 MILES 200 300
KANSAS
Topeka
Kansas City
Jefferson City
MISSOURI
St. Louis
Springfield
ILLINOIS
INDIANA
Indianapolis
OHIO
Columbus
Cincinnati
PENNSYLVANIA
Harrisburg
Trenton
N.J.
DEL.
Dover
MD.
Annapolis
Andrews A.F.B.
Washington
Falls Church
Manassas
Front Royal
WEST VIRGINIA
Gassaway
Clendenin
Charleston
Shenandoah R.
Guyandot R.
VIRGINIA
Richmond
Frankfort
Louisville
Louisa
Ohio River
KENTUCKY
Paintsville
Cumberland R.
Nashville
Murfreesboro
TENNESSEE
Henderson
Raleigh
NORTH CAROLINA
SOUTH CAROLINA
Columbia
Oklahoma City
Arkansas River
OKLAHOMA
ARKANSAS
Memphis
Little Rock
Stuttgart
Pine Bluff
Carthage
Hope
Dallas
Rockwall
Atlanta
GEORGIA
ATLANTIC OCEAN
MISSISSIPPI
Mississippi River
ALABAMA
Jackson
Montgomery
TEXAS
LOUISIANA
Austin
Baton Rouge
Tallahassee
FLORIDA
GULF OF MEXICO

INDEX

INDEX